Clark's Publishing Agreements

A Book of Precedents

Clark's Publishing Agreements

A Book of Precedents

Eighth edition

General Editor
Lynette Owen

Bloomsbury Professional

Bloomsbury Professional Ltd, Maxwelton House, 41–43 Boltro Road, Haywards Heath, West Sussex, RH16 1BJ

Previously published by Tottel Publishing Limited

A CIP Catalogue record for this book is available from the British Library.

ISBN: 978 1 84766 544 7

Typeset by Phoenix Photosetting, Chatham, Kent
Printed and bound in Great Britain by CPI Antony Rowe, Chippenham, Wilts

Contents

Acknowledgements for the Eighth Edition

As always, the drafting of *Clark's Publishing Agreements* has been a team effort. The text of each previous edition is reviewed and revised by colleagues whose experience is based on their daily work in dealing with contractual agreements between author and publisher, between publisher and publisher in licence arrangements and between publishers and producers and distributors in media other than the printed word.

For this edition the Precedents and Appendices have been provided as follows:

Legal Developments:

An Introduction to the
Eighth Edition . . . . Hugh Jones

Precedent One . . . . Kevin Stewart

Precedent Two . . . . Brenda Gvozdanovic

Precedent Three . . . . Lynette Owen

Precedent Four . . . . Lynette Owen

Precedent Five . . . . Kevin Stewart and Mayer,
Brown, Rowe and Maw LLP

Precedent Six . . . . Leo Walford & Anjali Pratap

Precedent Seven . . . . Leo Walford & Anjali Pratap

Precedent Eight . . . . Leo Walford, Anjali Pratap & John Cox

Precedent Nine . . . . Diane Spivey

Precedent Ten . . . . The Translators Association/Lynette Owen

Precedent Eleven . . . . Lynette Owen

Precedent Twelve . . . . Lynette Owen

Precedent Thirteen . . . . Lynette Owen

Precedent Fourteen . . . . The Packagers Association/Lynette Owen

Precedent Fifteen . . . . Diane Spivey

Precedent Sixteen . . . . Michael Ridley & Alan Williams

Precedent Seventeen . . . . . . Nick Fitzpatrick & Alan Williams

Introduction to
Electronic Precedents . . . . . Duncan Calow

Precedent Eighteen . . . . Duncan Calow

Precedent Nineteen . . . . Duncan Calow

Precedent Twenty . . . . The Publishers Association/JISC/Leo Walford & Anjali Pratap

Precedent Twenty-One . . . . Duncan Calow

Precedent Twenty-Two . . . . Duncan Calow

Precedent Twenty-Three . . . Duncan Calow

Appendix A . . . . Andrea Shallcross

Appendix B . . . . Diane Spivey

Appendix C . . . . Diane Spivey

Appendix D . . . . Kevin Stewart

Appendix E . . . . Richard Balkwill & Alicia Wise

Appendix F . . . . Alicia Wise

Appendix G . . . . Lynette Owen

Appendix H . . . . Hugh Jones

Appendix I . . . . The Publishers Association

Appendix J . . . . Lynette Owen

Appendix K . . . . Lynette Owen

Editor's Preface to the Eighth Edition

The Seventh Edition of *Clark's Publishing Agreements* appeared in 2007. The intervening period of some four years has seen still further developments which impact on the publishing industry. On the legislative front, copyright and its relevance in the digital age has remained under the microscope at international, European Union and UK levels. The Gowers Report in December 2006 was generally supportive to the creative industries, but stressed the importance of reaching a fair balance between the interests of rightsholders and users. June 2009 saw the Digital Britain Report, whilst in October that same year came the Digital Economy Bill which received Royal Assent in amended form as the Digital Economy Act on 7 April 2010, one of the last pieces of legislation from the Labour government. Amongst other features, it places obligations on Internet service providers in connection with online copyright infringements, and increases the penalties for such infringements. The final Act did not however include provision for two key features of the Bill, a recommendation for extended collective licensing and the question of how to deal with orphan works. The Act has met with a mixed reception from interested parties.

There have also been significant legal developments involving technology companies and their moves to digitise content, including the as yet unresolved US Google Settlement. As for previous editions, Hugh Jones, Copyright Counsel for the UK Publishers Association, has provided an overview of recent and forthcoming legislation in his *Introduction to Legal Developments*; the impact of some of those developments can be seen in the updating of the Precedents, their accompanying Notes and the Appendices which follow.

The familiar overall structure of the book has been retained, with the first two precedents providing models for author-publisher agreements for the trade and educational/academic/professional sectors. These are followed by contracts with a publisher for a book editor, a book contributor and for a book series editor. Precedents Six to Eight relate to the academic journal sector, with a new Precedent Seven providing a model for publication of a journal on behalf of a learned society. We have continued to provide precedents to cover the sale of serial rights, a publisher-translator contract (updated in line with a recent review by the Translators Association) and a model licence for translation rights; this has an updated Appendix on licensing to less traditional markets including China and eastern Europe, where some oddities of licensing practice and contractual wording may still be required. We have also retained and updated the model for the licensing of low-price reprint rights, a contract between a publisher and an illustrator, a publisher-packager contract and an international coedition licence, as well as models for the exploitation of film and merchandising rights.

The four years since publication of the last edition have seen some radical and fast-moving developments in the field of technology, in particular a new wave of dedicated e-reading devices, 'apps' for ever more versatile smart phones and most recently the iconic Apple iPad, as well as the deep involvement of companies such as Google, Amazon and Apple in the provision of content in electronic form. The *Introduction to Electronic Precedents* highlights many of the developments to date and their impact on licensing practice, particularly in the area of e-books – a new Precedent Twenty-Two addresses the topical area of e-book distribution. We have deliberately not sought to include a model agreement for the provision of content to an electronic aggregator, since such companies normally use their own forms of contract which can vary considerably.

As usual, all precedents are accompanied by explanatory notes and the texts are provided on the accompanying disc.

The Appendices to this book aim to cover areas of licensing which for practical reasons cannot easily be covered by a single precedent, as well as information of practical use in the licensing area. We continue to cover the US market, with its ongoing questions of territoriality, and have updated the coverage of the now dwindling areas of paperback and book club rights. Appendix D covers the granting of permission to quote limited amounts of copyright material, although we remain constrained by the requirements of the Competition Act from providing any guidelines on rates for such usage. Appendix E covers collective licensing, undertaken in the UK via the Copyright Licensing Agency (CLA) and an area which has seen considerable developments in the extension of licences to cover copying by digital means and the copying of digital originals. Developments in providing access to content for the reading impaired (the visually impaired, but also sufferers from dyslexia and people physically unable to hold a book in the normal way) have been sufficiently significant to justify a new Appendix F. We have retained as Appendix G coverage of the reversionary provisions of the 1911 UK Copyright Act (a trap which can still catch the unwary for older titles), whilst Appendix H updates the situation on moral rights in the UK. The updated 2010 text of the UK Publishers Association Code of Practice is included as Appendix I. Appendices J and K (territories of the world and member states of the international copyright conventions) have been fully updated.

This volume is as always a team effort, with contributors – all specialists in the fields of contracts and licensing – devoting personal time to their input. My thanks are due to Richard Balkwill, John Cox, Brenda Gvozdanovic,

Hugh Jones, Anjali Pratap, Andrea Shallcross, Diane Spivey, Kevin Stewart, Alicia Wise and Leo Walford as well as to Duncan Calow, Nick Fitzpatrick, all of DLA Piper UK LLP and Alan Williams, a consultant at the same firm. The views of the contributors are however their own rather than those of their employers. Our thanks are due to Andy Hill and Jane Bradford of Bloomsbury Professional for their help in bringing the book to publication.

As for previous editions, all royalties from the Eighth Edition are donated to charity and are divided between the Book Trade Charity (formerly BTBS, the Book Trade Benevolent Society) and the Royal Literary Fund.

As for all editions, I must emphasise that a book of contractual precedents can only provide general guidance; contracts should always be tailored to deal with individual circumstances, and where necessary the parties should take professional legal advice.

The present edition remains dedicated to the memory of Charles Clark, whose name it bears, and also to the loyal and regular users of this book whose words of appreciation have continued to inspire our efforts.

LYNETTE OWEN
London
August 2010

Legal Developments: An Introduction To The Eighth Edition

Where it all begins: UK copyright

As in the seventh edition, it is worth quoting at the outset Charles Clark's own summary of the key principles of UK copyright law, on which all UK publishing agreements must be based:

> 'The Copyright, Designs and Patents Act of 1988 performs the four "bedrock" roles of modern copyright legislation – to establish the rights of authors of literary, dramatic, musical and artistic works; to establish the rights of those who invest, financially and creatively, in the works of authors; to balance the rights of such copyright owners with the needs of copyright users; and to protect the rights of copyright owners in both civil and criminal law.
>
> The rights of authors are expressed in the familiar language of various "acts restricted by copyright". The rights of the cultural industries that invest in what authors have created are established in the world of book publishing in two ways: first, through the status given to exclusive licences of rights acquired from authors, and secondly through an independent right of the publisher in the typographical arrangement of an edition which he/she has published (to which must now be added Database Right and Publication Right, on which see further below). The balance between copyright owner and copyright user interests is maintained through the familiar concepts of fair dealing and of library privilege. And there is, fourthly, a welcome strengthening of civil and criminal law provisions against infringement of copyright.'

UK developments since 2006

Key developments relevant to publishing contracts include the following:

Digital Economy Act 2010

The Digital Economy Act, passed in April 2010, contains important provisions relating to online copyright enforcement, particularly against websites persistently offering peer-to-peer filesharing via illegal downloads. The Act imposed new statutory obligations on Internet Service Providers to notify their subscribers of any claims of copyright infringement received from copyright owners, and to maintain a list of such complaints, with an ultimate threat of disconnection if nothing is done. At the time of writing, the government has not yet implemented the (controversial) disconnection power, but this will be introduced if letters fail to produce the desired effect. Ofcom, the independent regulator and competition authority for the UK communications industries, will also maintain a Code of Practice.

The Act also contained, at Bill stage, important provisions which would have authorised licences for orphan works, but these were lost (see now Forthcoming Attractions). Provisions extending Public Lending Right to audio and eBooks were, however, included.

Contracts for Third Parties

Although pre-2006, it is still worth bearing in mind the Contracts (Rights of Third Parties) Act 1999, which abolished the long-established rule of 'privity of contract', under which only the parties to a contract could enforce its terms. A third party may now acquire direct rights under a contract if that is clearly what the parties intend. So if an author specifies that royalties are to be paid to a friend, that friend may now be able to sue the publisher for breach of contract directly if the publisher fails to do so.

Proceeds of Crime

Under the Coroners and Justice Act, 2009, a civil scheme was introduced by which 'profits' such as fees or royalties may be recovered from authors convicted of serious crimes who have written about their crimes. The profits are recovered directly through an exploitation proceeds order, without necessarily involving the publisher, although publishers may be involved in due course, in any public interest defence.

Moral Rights

The two principal moral rights of authors, of paternity and integrity, were included in English law for the first time in the Copyright, Designs and Patents Act 1988, together with two others, but there have been surprisingly few moral rights cases in the UK since. There have been government consultations on some aspects of moral rights, such as the need to 'assert' the right of paternity, and it is possible that changes may lie ahead (see Forthcoming Attractions). Moral rights in general are surveyed in **Appendix H**.

Duration of Copyright

Although the Duration Directive – extending the term of copyright throughout the EU and the European Economic Area (EEA) to the life of the author plus 70 years – was implemented in the UK in 1996, the anticipated flood of disputes about extended and revived copyrights has failed to materialise, and publishers seem to be getting on with agreeing, among other things, reasonable royalties under Licences of Right, and what may constitute 'arrangements made' at the time the law changed.

However, many users and consumers have questioned whether a longer term of life plus 70 (which can mean protection for well over 100 years) can be justified for all works, especially computer programs and e-publications, and even some kinds of research articles. The US has now matched the EU term, so it is likely to remain in place for the immediate future. The term was unaffected by the 2001 Copyright Directive, but it was raised as a specific issue in 2006 by the Gowers Review. At the time of writing there have been no proposals for change.

Database Right

Apart from typographical copyright in published editions, which is always owned by the publisher, and the little-used Publication Right (below), the Database Right is the closest thing the UK has ever had to a true 'publisher's right'. It came about as something of a compromise, when it became clear that databases in the EU would not qualify for full copyright protection unless they displayed evidence of the authors' 'intellectual creation'. This intellectual standard of originality (common on the Continent) is a much higher standard than the previous UK standard, which required merely that copyright works should not have been copied from elsewhere, and which therefore included relatively mundane (but valuable) compilations of data, such as listings, timetables or alphabetical directories. There seemed a serious risk that such databases, important though they are to the UK publishing industry, would fail to qualify for copyright protection, and – in the absence of anything else – be left entirely without legal support. After much lobbying, a new *sui generis* (stand-alone) right was provided in the EU Database Directive. The Directive was implemented in the UK by the Copyright and Rights in Databases Regulations 1997, and came into effect on 1 January 1998.

The new Database Right, as it became known, lasts for a much shorter period of time than copyright at a mere 15 years (although this is renewable), but it gives those who make a 'substantial investment' in 'obtaining, verifying or presenting' the contents of a database the right to prevent extraction or re-utilisation of the material without consent. The *British Horse Racing Board v William Hill* case of 2005 decided (unhelpfully) that 'obtaining' had to be construed narrowly and excluded any elements of 'creation'. However, a more recent decision of the High Court of 2010 suggests that copyright in UK databases is more available than previously thought, provided the selection and arrangement of the data involves sufficient skill and judgment.

This now means that while Database Right is a considerably narrower right than previously thought, it is still potentially very valuable, particularly when copyright is also an option. Those seeking grants or assignments of rights in relevant publishing contracts would still be well advised to check whether any Database Right is included.

Publication Right

Publication Right protects those who first publish in the EEA previously unpublished works in which copyright has already expired. Many currently unpublished works will continue to be protected by what used to be perpetual copyright until 2039, but the right may, however, have considerable commercial significance in the future. It lasts for 25 years from the end of the year of first publication.

Rental Right

Rental or lending of copies of certain works (including literary works) to the public is a restricted act, over which the copyright owner has the exclusive right. The authors of literary, artistic and some other works are also given an 'unwaivable' right to equitable remuneration for rental of their works. Public Lending Right for public libraries was extended to audio and eBooks by the Digital Economy Act 2010, although at the time of writing this extension has not been brought into effect.

Human Rights

Thanks to the Human Rights Act 1998 the individual human rights protected by the European Convention on Human Rights are now directly protected under UK law too. These include the right to privacy and the right to freedom of expression. It is clear from recent court cases, involving celebrities such as David Beckham and Naomi Campbell, that these two human rights may conflict, with the media claiming that intrusive pictures merely represent freedom of expression on matters of public interest, while the celebrities photographed seek to protect their new privacy rights. However, it is clear that there is increasingly now a coherent law of privacy in the UK which courts will protect, even though it has to be balanced against other rights. This is bound to have implications for all publications which impinge on a person's private and family life.

Reading Impaired People

The Copyright (Visually Impaired Persons) Act 2002 gave blind and visually impaired people the right to make 'accessible' copies (such as Braille) for personal use, without infringing copyright. Organisations like the RNIB may also make multiple copies on their behalf, but only to the extent that no licensing scheme exists. Representatives of visually impaired and other reading impaired people, such as dyslexics, have been in discussion with publishers as well as UK, EU and international representatives about secure, monitored delivery of publishers' digital files, as close to publication date as possible, using Trusted Intermediaries. **Appendix F addresses the question of reading impaired people in more detail.**

Legal Deposit of E-publications

The Legal Deposit Libraries Act 2003 gave the government the right to introduce Regulations extending the current legal deposit regime to electronic publications. A voluntary scheme for offline publications (such as CD-ROMS) was established in 2000 and was renewed in 2009. To prepare the way for Regulations relating to online e-publications, a Legal Deposit Advisory Panel sat from 2004 until 2010, with representatives from publishing and the deposit libraries, as well as independent members and an independent Chair. Regulations have so far been proposed for deposit of e-journals and web harvesting, but these are subject to public consultation. At the time of writing it is unclear whether these will include fully commercial content, behind firewalls or technical protection measures, and what level of access will be allowed.

The Federation of European Publishers (FEP) and the Committee of European National Libraries (CENL) published a revised Statement on legal deposit of e-publications for the guidance of EU member states in 2006, to be monitored by a standing committee, including web harvesting.

The Gowers Review

The Gowers Review into Intellectual Property in the UK reported in December 2006, after lengthy consultation. It found that UK intellectual property was broadly fit for purpose in the 21st century, but (unsurprisingly) made 54 recommendations for change. Of those relating to copyright (many related to patents and trademarks), the changes most likely to be implemented soon, by Statutory Instrument, are (1) an extension of educational exceptions to cover distance learning via supervised intranets, and (2) extension of the library exceptions to include format shifting for archiving and preservation. Wider proposals to introduce a general personal copying exception, and a new exception for parody and pastiche, seem unlikely to be implemented.

Bribery

UK publishers need to be aware that the Bribery Act 2010 received Royal Assent on 8 April 2010, for implementation in late 2010. The Act provides definitions of offences in the areas of bribery and corruption, requirements for companies to put adequate procedures in place to ensure that they do not transgress, and for them to review any contracts with suppliers and other contractual partners to ensure that such contracts provide adequate protection against such offences. Whilst licence contracts are perhaps less relevant for this legislation, the provisions could affect contracts with suppliers and other contracted parties such as typesetters, printers, distributors and contracts for the provision of publishing services or books for government tenders.

Open Access

The OA movement, which aims to provide wider public access to research publications, continues to provoke debate. Funding bodies such as the Wellcome Trust and the US National Institutes of Health have made it a condition that research funded by their institutions should be made available on an OA basis. Academic publishers now produce a larger number of OA journals or journals published on a hybrid model including some OA content; in some cases they include material on an 'author pays' basis, with publication fees covered by individual authors, their academic institutes on their behalf or by their research funding organisations. However, at the time of writing, less than 10 per cent of global academic content is published online free of charge, and most publishers would maintain that the subscription-based model is more appropriate given the value they provide in bringing high-quality peer-reviewed research papers to market.

International and EU Developments

(a) International Developments

Australia: Parallel Importation

The Australian Copyright Amendment Act of 1991 permits importation of lawful editions not licensed for the Australian market:

- In the case of books published after 23 December 1991, if the book has not been published in Australia within 30 days of legitimate publication elsewhere.
- In the case of books published before or after that date, if the holder of Australian rights fails to confirm within seven days of receipt of an Australian order that such order will be fulfilled within 90 days, or if he fails to deliver such order within 90 days.
- In the case of books published before or after that date, if an Australian importer holds a single copy order for a book required by the end purchaser for private use (this would include single copy orders from libraries).

New Zealand: Parallel Importation

Despite taking powers to permit parallel imports under the Copyright (Removal of Prohibition on Parallel Importing) Amendment Act 1998, the New Zealand government has so far kept the question of parallel importation of books, recorded music and software under review.

TRIPs

The TRIPs (Trade Related Aspects of Intellectual Property Rights) Agreement of 1994 continues to provide member states with a powerful endorsement of Berne copyright standards, coupled with minimum requirements for domestic laws to facilitate 'effective action' against infringers, with expeditious and 'deterrent' remedies. An additional Anti-Counterfeiting Trade Agreement (ACTA) is being negotiated between developed countries at the time of writing.

WIPO

The World Intellectual Property Organisation (WIPO) – guardians of the Berne Convention – organised two copyright treaties in 1996 to update Berne standards and wording for the digital age – a Copyright Treaty, and a Performances and Phonograms Treaty. The 1996 Copyright Treaty (in force from 2002) not only provided a broader Reproduction and Distribution Right but a new Communication and Making Available Right, better attuned to a world of digital access. WIPO has also been kept busy over recent years with proposals for treaty extensions to copyright (e.g. educational) exceptions, largely in favour of developing countries, but these have so far been resisted (as over-broad) by the developed world. A proposed treaty on access for reading impaired people may, however, lead to voluntary agreement via a Stakeholder Platform, co-ordinating the many national initiatives already in place (see above).

Digital Millennium Copyright Act 1998 (DMCA)

The US was one of the first countries to ratify the WIPO Copyright Treaty, via the Digital Millennium Copyright Act 1998 (usually referred to for convenience as the DMCA). As well as providing for the newly-defined rights, it prohibited circumvention of copyright protection systems and set out in some detail Notice and Takedown requirements for service providers to deal with infringing material (now mirrored in the UK's Digital Economy Act – see above). It has already been challenged in the US courts, on the basis that it interferes with constitutional rights to freedom of speech, but so far US judges have been unsympathetic to the suggestion that hacking is a constitutional right.

Google

In 2005, US publishers and authors launched joint legal actions against Google for copyright infringement, following Google's implementation of their Google Library Programme, under which Google commenced scanning millions of copies of in-copyright works in participating US libraries without rightsholder consent. Google claimed that such scanning, and making available 'snippets' of the digitised text, fell under the 'Fair Use' provisions of US law. The resulting court case ran until a settlement was reached in 2008, under which Google would fund compensation for qualifying rightsholders, plus creation of a new Book Rights Registry. Substantial legal objections to the proposed settlement emerged, for example from the US Department of Justice (on competition grounds) and from non-US rightsholders, and at the time of writing an Amended Settlement is under consideration by the US court, which would among other things restrict the settlement to books registered with the US copyright office, or published in the UK, Canada or Australia. It is likely that, whatever the court decides, there will be further appeals, but meanwhile those negotiating contracts would be advised to check whether exploitation by search engines is covered appropriately.

(b) EU Developments

The Copyright Directive 2001

Following the 1996 WIPO Copyright Treaty (see above), the EU attempted a (not entirely successful) harmonisation of EU Copyright law, resulting in the Copyright Directive 2001. The UK implemented the required changes to its domestic copyright law via the Copyright and Related Rights Regulations 2003, and the Directive was finally implemented by all relevant member states in 2007.

The Directive requires EU-wide adoption of an updated scheme of digital rights and exceptions, including a Communication to the Public Right (including 'making available') (Art 3), up to 20 copyright exceptions (Art 5), a compulsory exception to permit temporary and transient copying (Art 5.1), balanced against stronger protection for technical protection measures (Art 6) and digital rights management information (Art 7). Enforcement, including provision for injunctions (but not – so far – automated Notice and Takedown) is provided for in Art 8.

The E-Commerce Directive

The EU's E-Commerce Directive 2000 provides generally for greater ease of electronic trade, including for example, specific provision for e-contracts and e-signatures (already partly covered in the UK's Electronic Communications Act 2000). The Directive was implemented in the UK in 2002. A particular feature is the detailed provision for limited liability of Internet service providers, who will normally escape legal liability for infringing material carried on sites hosted by them, provided that they act expeditiously to take down such material once they are put on notice that it is there.

The EU Enforcement Directive

The 2004 Directive on Anti-Counterfeiting and Enforcement of IP rights was restricted to civil enforcement via, for example, actions for damages, or applications for injunctions, and disappointingly omitted any reference to criminal sanctions (further proposals on criminal sanctions are still under discussion). The UK implemented the Directive on schedule by April 2006 but many member states are running late and the Directive is currently under review.

The European Digital Library (i2010 – now i2020) and EUROPEANA

As part of the Lisbon Agenda for EU digitisation initiatives (i2020), the European Digital Library is an EU Recommendation on digitisation and online accessibility of cultural material contained in Europe's extensive library collections. At the time of writing, the proposal covers only public domain (out of copyright) material, but there has unsurprisingly been regular pressure for inclusion of copyright works in due course, via the EU's new portal, EUROPEANA. The latest Communication on 'EUROPEANA – The Next Steps' in May 2010 highlighted the need for solutions for copying in-copyright works, out of print and orphan works (see Forthcoming Attractions), 'while complying with IP laws', although pressure to facilitate mass digitisation by libraries continues. Publishers are represented on a High Level Expert Group.

Coming Attractions

- *Orphan Works.* Users seeking permission to reproduce copyright works whose rightsholders cannot be found, despite due diligent search ('orphan works'), have been pressing for some time for a legal solution such as authorised licences, based on due diligence and reasonable remuneration, and it is likely that EU agreement will be reached before long, either in the form of a Directive, or possibly guidance via a Communication. An EU Impact Assessment is expected in 2010, which will set out relevant options, including not only mutual recognition but also possibly a fully-fledged copyright exception. At the time of writing, mutual recognition and guidance seems the more likely, probably utilising existing digital permissions initiatives such as the EU's ARROW programme; see **Appendix E, Item 12**.

- *Collective Licensing.* The EU Commission produced proposals some time ago for regulation and rationalisation of music licensing, and it is likely that before long there will be a framework Directive on Collective Rights Management generally. If it comes, it is likely to concentrate on rightsholder representation, copyright clearance and distribution across national boundaries, and efficiency and transparency of management. **Appendix E addresses collective licensing in detail.**

- *Guidance on Publishing Contracts.* After consultations on the relationship between publisher contracts and licences, and copyright exceptions (some stakeholders claiming that legitimate use of exceptions was being blocked), the IP Office and the Standing Advisory Board on IP (SABIP) have both suggested that best practice guidelines may be justified in due course. Assignments of copyright in contracts are also regularly criticised, although there are circumstances, such as collective works, where they may be clearly justified.

- *Moral Rights.* The UK's moral rights regime is often criticised as being narrow and subject to too many exceptions, and both SABIP and the IPO (above) have been consulting on a possible closer alignment of the UK regime with those in the rest of Europe, although at the time of writing no immediate initiatives are under discussion.

- *Libel law.* The UK has long been known as a haven for libel claimants, with higher damages awards and (in particular) penal costs risks. A number of government commissions have suggested improvements, for example limiting use of the notorious conditional fee arrangements, and it is likely that in due course legislation will balance the law more equitably between claimants and defendants (often publishers), to remove the current law's damaging 'chilling effect' on freedom to publish in the UK. Meanwhile current contract warranties and indemnities relating to libel remain as important as ever.

HUGH JONES
Copyright Counsel
The Publishers Association
London, July 2010

PRECEDENT ONE

General Book Author – Publisher Agreement

The agreement between author and publisher is the cornerstone of their relationship. Care taken by both parties together to ensure that the contract really reflects in detail the nature of the book they are discussing pays off time and time again, not only in focusing early attention on the points of real substance and in avoiding subsequent unsettling disputes, but in giving the author the confidence needed to let the publisher get on in equal confidence with its job to their mutual advantage.

The detail of Precedent One and the variety of rights and dealings in those rights set out in the other Precedents, many of which stem from Precedent One, may appear at first sight daunting and confusing, but behind the detail in Precedent One lies a very simple structure. The author owns the copyright in what he/she writes. In return for various payments, he/she licenses to the publisher, primarily exclusively at the publisher's own expense, the right to multiply principally in book form copies of what he/she has written and the right to license further to others exploitation in both book and non-book forms. The author writes, the publisher invests, and from sales of the book they create together and from exploitation of rights, the author earns royalties and fees, and the publisher earns its profit. It is as simple – and as complicated – as that.

The core of this Precedent has changed little since the last edition (the nature of rights acquisition having altered very little despite the explosion in e-book publishing). It remains essentially basic in its construction. However, the purpose of the chapter as a whole is to work on two levels: to provide a comparatively simple contract that will serve publishers of general (rather than educational) books as a suitable *starting* point whilst, within the extensive notes, to highlight the very many pitfalls that can follow using a basic document when the needs of the business and the concerns of the author are so different and potentially on a collision course.

Note: The views and opinions expressed in the Notes to this Precedent are those of the individual contributor and not those of his employer.

Preamble

(1) An agreement between author and publisher ideally sets out the rights and liabilities between them in the sequence of the events which lead up to and beyond the moment of publication. That principle is followed in this Precedent, and to help understanding headings have been given to each clause. Note, however, Clause 31.

(2) It is important, as takeovers and mergers continue, to distinguish between the assignment of a contract for an individual work held by a publisher and the selling by a publisher of his/her business to another company. In the latter situation, there is no change in the authors' contractual relationships: the authors continue to have rights against and liabilities towards the same publishing company, provided it continues trading under its new ownership. There may be considerable uncertainties where, for example, a publisher seeks to sell a part only of his/her business, possibly in the form of a publishing division or a subsidiary imprint, which is not itself a company at law, or where the acquiring publisher seeks not to continue the acquired business in its own name, but to transfer some of the works under contract with the acquired publisher to his/her own imprint/s. Legal advice should always be sought on this issue in advance by both acquiring and acquired publishers.

As to assignability of individual works, some authors may wish not to risk their work appearing under an imprint with which they do not want to be associated. A provision as a separate clause that 'the rights and licences hereby granted may not be assigned or transmitted by the Publishers without the prior written consent of the Author' is found in most contracts issued by literary agents. Such a clause should include a provision that such consent is not to be unreasonably withheld. Equally, the publisher who wishes to secure the benefit of assignability of the contract between him/herself and the author should probably have it specifically written into the contract. The following is an example of the wording that could be used:

> 'The Publishers may assign all or any of the Publishers' rights and transfer all or any of the Publishers' obligations under this Agreement to any person without any requirement to notify or obtain the further consent of the Author. Following any permitted assignment and/or transfer under this Clause, any reference in this Agreement to the Publishers shall, where the context allows, include the assignee and/or transferee.'

(3) Provision should always be made for the possible failure of the publishers' business: see Clause 24.

(4) In the case of a registered company it is important that signature of contracts should comply with the requirements of the articles of association. The person signing the contract is not entering into a personal contract, but is committing his/her firm.

(5) Publishers who trade through more than one imprint should be careful to allow for publication through all of those imprints and may find it sensible to include in the preamble wording like: 'The expression "the Publishers" as used throughout this Agreement shall be deemed to include any imprint of the [*name*] Publishing Group whether under its present or any future style and the benefit of this Agreement shall be transmissible accordingly' (but see also the caveat on behalf of authors made at Note (2) above).

(6) Where the author is shown on an agreement as a company, publishers should require the author him/herself to countersign a letter of inducement in which he/she undertakes to perform the author's obligations under the agreement. Such a letter is likely to be in the following terms:

Dear

Reference is made to the agreement ('the Agreement') which we are about to enter into with [*name of company*] ('the Company') a copy of which is attached hereto and made part hereof, concerning a work provisionally entitled '[*title*]'.

MEMORANDUM OF AGREEMENT made this [*number*] day of [*month*] 20 [*year*] between [*name*] of [*address*] (hereinafter termed 'the Author', which expression shall, where the context admits, include the Author's executors, administrators and assigns) of the one part and [*company name*] of [*address*] (hereinafter termed 'the Publishers', which expression shall where the context admits include any publishing imprint subsidiary to or associated with the Publishers, and the Publishers' assigns or successors in business as the case may be) of the other part

WHEREBY it is mutually agreed as follows concerning a work original to the Author and provisionally entitled: [*title*].

(hereinafter termed 'the Work')

In consideration of and as a further inducement to our entering into the Agreement you hereby warrant, guarantee and agree as follows:

1. That the Company has the full right and authority to enter into the Agreement, to furnish your services as therein provided and to grant the rights therein granted;

2. That you will be bound and will bind the Company by all the terms conditions and obligations of the Agreement and that you will look solely to the Company for any and all moneys, royalties or other consideration payable to you for your services under the Agreement;

3. That the Company will perform each and every provision of the Agreement and any changes and revisions in the Agreement as shall from time to time be agreed. This guarantee shall be construed as absolute continuing and unlimited and shall be enforceable against you, your heirs and assigns without the obligation to first proceed against the Company.

4. In the event that the Company shall for any reason fail or cease to perform or shall not have the rights to your services required by the Agreement or herein you agree to abide by and fulfil all said terms and conditions of the Agreement as if you had entered into the Agreement directly with [name of Publisher].

Yours sincerely

For and on behalf of [*name of publisher*]

Agreed and accepted

Signed [*name of Author*]

It should also be noted that the Agreement might require some redrafting of otherwise standard terms in order to differentiate between 'the Author' (i.e., the Company as the licensing party) and 'the author' (i.e., the person whose Company it is and whose name is put on the book). Additional care is necessary where the author is required to undertake personal duties (e.g., to promote the book: see Note (2) to Clause 10) where the Contract will need to bind the Company to procure the author's undertakings.

(7) Publishers' staff and authors should bear in mind that a binding agreement can be created by correspondence and even verbally if the essential terms of such an agreement are present; for example, length of typescript, delivery date, payment and a publication commitment. In this way, binding agreements could be unwittingly entered into. It is sensible to state all pre-Memorandum of Agreement negotiation is 'Subject to Contract'. Clause 32 (Entire Agreement) in this Precedent also serves to nullify any contractual effect that preliminary correspondence might have but does not, of course, take effect until the contract is signed. For more on a verbal contract specifically relevant to publishing see *Malcolm v OUP* (1990) Times (19 December, unreported).

1. Rights Granted

(1) This clause secures all volume rights, and the non-volume rights specifically included in the Agreement, in English or in any language (by contrast, **see Note 2 to Precedent 2** re the frequent practice of assignment of copyright for educational and academic works). As to the extent of 'volume rights' see Clauses 12, 13 and 14 and the introductory notes to Clause 14. One overall effect of a good publishing contract should be to place rights in the hands of those best able to exploit them (though to whose benefit is debatable). It follows that the publisher or literary agent who asks in his/her contract for control of certain rights, for example, film rights, has a responsibility towards the author to carry the professional skills needed to exploit the rights and to be active in doing so. This in turn leads to the questions of whether publishers are justified in requiring rights to be granted to them in order to protect their primary publishing interest and whether the author is acting reasonably by seeking to retain certain rights despite being in receipt of a substantial advance. It may be less than ideal, but a pragmatic solution is to grant the rights in dispute to the publisher providing they exploit them by a specific time (failing which the unexercised rights revert to the author). By the same test, the days of open-ended definitions of rights are clearly over **(e.g., see Note (2) below and Note re Clause 14 (xxii) relating to electronic versions)**. **See also Note (2) on Clause 4 regarding 'Derivative Works'**.

(2) All prudent publishers should include a grant of 'electronic book' rights and the Precedent includes specimen wording. This is probably the most significant issue in publishing contracts to have arisen since the last edition as the eBook revolution has truly taken hold in the UK.

There is no universal agreement as to whether eBook rights are 'volume rights'. However, it is generally accepted that electronic book rights should reside with the publisher, not least because the eBook (i) is in direct competition with the printed book and (ii) almost inevitably utilises the same publisher-edited script as the publisher's printed edition. The next hurdle is to define what an eBook actually is and what the publisher may (or may not) do with the underlying work in this format. Publishers maintain that 'enrichments' or 'enhancements' (the terms are often inter-changeable) such as author interviews, audio recordings, additional still or moving pictures etc are necessary to meet customer expectation. They therefore feel there is a need to broaden the definition given in the Precedent but should be aware of the possibility that these may encroach upon rights that would be granted to a film or television company. At the time of writing, this is unresolved but a pragmatic solution is to provide that nothing may be added (or taken away) from the printed book for the purpose of exploiting these rights without author agreement. If this is a complicated issue, it is at least controlled directly by the publisher. When the end-user technology takes over and there is a facility for text-to-voice, enabling the user to listen to the text being 'read' by an automated voice, this becomes even more problematic: are publishers required to ensure that the function is disabled unless they have acquired audio rights and the right to couple text and audio?

Whilst the author may seek early reversion of these rights if they are not exercised by a given time this is generally no longer accepted. For more on the exercise of rights and terms and conditions (including royalty) relating to 'electronic book' rights see Clauses 12 and 14. In addition, the grant/exercise of electronic rights raises questions concerning the 'in print' status of a work (see Note (4) to Clause 25).

(3) This Precedent includes specimen wording addressing the grant of straight (undramatised) audio recording rights. If the publisher has its own audio publishing list, it is usual practice for the publisher of the work in printed book form to retain the straight (undramatised) audio recording rights. With the shift from CD to download as the means of delivery, the granting of abridged to the publisher and the retention of unabridged rights by the author is no longer attractive to the publisher (especially if looking at coupling the eBook with the recording). Audio editions are largely exercised simultaneously with the hardback or paperback edition as a standalone product or, in the case of children's publishers, as an additional stand-alone audio or book and audio pack. For royalty and other relevant terms and conditions see Clause 12.9. Note that is not uncommon to be required to revert audio recording rights if not exercised by a given time but care should be taken to ensure that the failure to

1. Rights Granted

In consideration of the payments hereinafter mentioned and subject to the terms and conditions herein contained, the Author hereby grants to the Publishers the sole and exclusive right and licence to produce and publish and themselves further to license the production and publication of the Work or any adaptation or any abridgement of the Work or any substantial part of the Work:

- in volume form, which shall include the sole and exclusive right to publish the Work: as an electronic book, that is, using any means of manufacture, distribution or transmission of the Work, whether now known or hereafter known or developed (including but not limited to electronic and machine-readable media and online and satellite-based transmission) intended to make the Work or any part thereof available for reading ('Electronic Book Rights'); and in undramatised audio form (whether by means of a physical copy of an abridged or unabridged recording of the Work, by means of an audio digital download copy of an abridged or unabridged recording of the Work or by any other means of manufacture, distribution or transmission of an abridged or unabridged recording of the Work, whether now known or hereafter known or developed (including but not limited to electronic and machine-readable media and online and satellite-based transmission) intended to make the Work or any part thereof available for listening); and

- in the other forms specifically included under this Agreement

in the English language/in all languages for the legal term of copyright and any and all extensions, renewals and revivals thereof throughout the world/the territories listed on the attached schedule(s): the rest of the world excluding the US its territories and dependencies and the Philippine Islands [and Canada] shall be a non-exclusive market for the sale of the British and US editions of the Work.

The Author shall ensure that any licences granted or to be granted to third parties regarding publication of the Work in the English language shall expressly prohibit those third parties, their associated companies or overseas agents, from supplying the Work directly to any of the Publishers' exclusive territories as described in this Agreement (including by handling the Work for the purposes of such supply).

All rights not granted to the Publishers under this Agreement (as well as Public Lending Right) are reserved by the Author but the Author will not exercise or authorise any party to exploit any reserved right in a way that will impair the value of any of the rights granted to the Publishers under this Agreement.

exploit in every specific recording format does not lead to the loss of all unexercised formats. For example, it is not unreasonable to ensure that once audio rights are exercised in one format (e.g., unabridged download), then other formats (whether abridged or unabridged) are safeguarded. Perhaps there may still be room to differentiate between unabridged trade and library sales; although it is difficult to see how this would work for digital forms.

In the event that the author does not wish to licence the publisher audio recording rights it is not unreasonable for the publisher to insist upon the granting of an option on the rights. The terms of the option clause will largely follow those of Clause 27 (Option on Future Work).

(4) The territories within which the publishers are to exercise their exclusive licence to publish need to be carefully negotiated and set out, with an equally clear understanding of the territories from which their editions of the work may be excluded, and the territories within which both British and US editions may be sold non-exclusively. This is especially vital when using language like 'UK and British Commonwealth' and 'Europe' to define geographic areas. It is not unusual to find that each party understands these to mean different things – and this is exacerbated when there are UK and US deals for the same book. A list of territories attached to the individual contract (and preferably to the offer) is the most sensible way forward. **See Appendix J; this provides three schedules. Schedule 1 lists the nations of the world. Schedule 2 lists the territories outside the continent of Europe which are usually granted exclusively to a British publisher and Schedule 3 offers several approaches to dealing with the European Single Market.**

Special care should be taken to define (country by country) exactly what markets are being acquired as part of 'Europe'. The key issue is to remember that the contract being negotiated today has to address not only the world as of the date of expected publication but also throughout the work's backlist life. Therefore consider carefully whether your definition of 'Europe' should be limited only to those states that have acquired EEA/EU/EFTA membership to-date – or whether there is good reason to incorporate future members (those in accession talks as a minimum). **For more on 'What constitutes Europe?' see Appendix J.**

In response to free movement of goods legislation affecting the EU, UK publishers have for many years sought exclusivity in the EU in order to protect the UK and Irish ('home') market. Many now make this a matter of unbreakable policy where they are the primary English language publisher of the book. Alongside this resolution from publishers one must consider two other elements: (a) the willingness of UK publishers to pay higher royalties (sometimes on receipts, but sometimes on UK retail price) on sales in the EU, or to swap another major market such as Canada for exclusivity in the EU in order to render the remaining rights attractive to the US publisher; and (b) the ability of the author or their agent to licence rights to an American publisher without EU non-exclusivity – and whether it is in the author's best career interest. **See Appendix A.**

The efforts of US publishers to acquire non-exclusive rights to traditionally UK exclusive export markets continue to be resisted with India being a current 'flashpoint'. American insistence that local law will permit them into, for example, Malaysia or Singapore regardless of the contract wording is a difficult one to rebut when negotiations are pressured by the need to achieve signature. It seems that reliance has been placed upon relationships with local distributors and the availability of the UK edition ahead of the US copy; rather than challenging the legal issue. See also Note (5) below on further wording to protect exclusivity as well as Note (5) to Clause 12.1 and Note (4) to Clause 12.2 which ponder what could happen if exclusivity is lost in Europe or a specific market respectively.

Some US publishers seek, as a standard term of contract, to negotiate exclusivity for US bases throughout the world. There is no foundation in either territoriality, or in US purchasing requirements for this provision, which is strongly and successfully resisted by both publishers and literary agents in the UK.

(5) Australian copyright legislation requires that, to maintain exclusivity of copyright in Australia, any new work is available there within 30 days of first lawful English language publication anywhere in the world. It is important therefore to ensure that where the UK

publisher does not control world rights the author delivers the typescript and other material to the UK publisher simultaneously with its competitors. It is also prudent to seek assurance that approvals of, e.g., proofs and covers will not be unduly delayed and that the author will keep the publisher informed of US publication dates for each format. If the work has already been published in the US, Australia will potentially be a non-exclusive market. If this is the case, the UK publisher ought to expect to pay a lower advance.

New Zealand, on the other hand, has declared itself an open market to the importation of legitimately published copies of books from anywhere in the world regardless of the grant of exclusive rights to the UK publisher. The practical response to this matter is identical to that set out above concerning Australia.

In addition to the practical steps outlined above, some UK publishers are inserting a clause in the contract that provides them with further protection against the author's other licensees exploiting local copyright law which does not protect the UK publishers' exclusivity. This provision appears as the penultimate paragraph of this Clause of this Precedent.

For eBook and digital download/online delivery protection of exclusivity is not quite so simple an issue to address. Some publishers are agreeing the following with their US counterparts:

> 'It is understood and agreed that the US publisher and the UK publisher will not knowingly or systematically sell any [electronic product] into the other party's exclusive market, provided that the casual or inadvertent failure to comply with this restriction will not be deemed a breach of this Agreement and neither party will be held responsible for the actions of any separate third parties.'

Whilst this wording is not suitable for inclusion in an author contract, the principle is capable of being maintained by requiring the author to address the issue in his/her US contract.

(6) Publishers expect to acquire a licence for the duration of copyright (i.e., for the life of the author plus 70 years) although for property-based publishing a limited term licence is the norm. This means that care should be taken by authors to include strict termination provisions (see Clauses 24 and 25). With the explosion in eBook publishing (as well as the continuing trend to supply via print on demand technology), the issue of termination criteria has led to much discussion and the notes to Clause 25 address this aspect in detail.

Some publishers will include provision for a revision of terms in agreements that run for the full term of copyright, with wording such as the following: 'At any time after [ten/fifteen] years from the date of [signature of this Agreement/publication of the Work] either party shall give reasonable consideration to a request from the other to renegotiate such terms as are no longer in line with current publishing practice'. Authors should, however, note that this is a two-way street and entitles publishers to review terms that an author may not wish to return to. This general review is additional to any review of specific terms (such as over eBook royalties; see Note (3) on Clause 12.10).

(7) As to the relationship between duration of copyright and the limitation, under the Copyright Act 1911, on the author's power to assign or license an interest in his/her copyright beyond 25 years after his/her death, see **Appendix G**.

(8) Attention is drawn to the rights granted in 'any abridgement of the Work'. The opinion is sometimes held that, if the right to publish an abridgement or portion of the work is granted to the publishers, then that right should not be exercised without the author's consent. Consent for each such usage may become impractical as business models are developed for trade publishing (as they already are in the world of academic publishing) to enable digital access to extracts from a work online. It is not clear yet whether such models will be as pay-per-view or via subscription, but as many publishers are investing heavily to make commercial digital access possible, they will want the right to be able to sell a work or part of a work through these channels without onerous approval processes. For promotional use on-line see the notes to Clause 10. Any abridgement would naturally be subject to the same restrictions of language and territory as apply to the complete work. It would be sensible for the author to require that initial publication is of the work in unabridged form (see Clause 6).

The words 'any substantial part of the Work' reflect the position at law that the publication by a third party of an insubstantial part of an author's work is not an infringement of the copyright in the work. What amounts to substantiality depends on the facts in any given instance, and quality as well as wordage comes into account. In very broad terms 'substantial' may appear to the layman as fairly insubstantial – as low a wordage as 1 per cent of the total may amount to substantiality, especially if quality is an issue. This tendency to set the marker low reflects the judges' concern to protect the author's rights in copyright.

In November 2001 a ruling was given in *Sweeney and Camps v Macmillan Publishers Ltd and Rose* [2001] All ER (D) 332 (Nov) which confirmed that 'a substantial part' was as much a qualitative judgment as one related to the amount of copyright material used without licence. In this case only some 250 words were published in the Reader's Edition of James Joyce's *Ulysses*. Although they constituted less than one thousandth of the final text (the original book was first published in 1922), the inclusion of these words from the Rosenbach manuscript (published in 1974 and containing material additional to the 1922 edition) infringed copyright on the basis of their special and distinct importance.

(9) Note the caveat on the exercise of the reserved rights in the last paragraph of this Clause. Having invested heavily in the book, the publisher is unlikely to be impressed if an author exercises a reserved right in direct competition with the book. It is therefore prudent to caveat any 'reserved rights' to guard against this but authors and agents need to consider what effect this will have on other avenues to market, especially via electronic formats.

(10) The final paragraph mentions Public Lending Right. For more on this, visit ***www.plr.uk.com***

(11) For rights to publicise the Work see Note (1) to Clause 10. Some publishers retain the traditional view that they have an obligation to promote and advertise the Work and, therefore, the right to use parts of the book is implicit within that obligation. However, with (i) authors wishing to use extracts and often book covers on their websites, whilst (ii) the publisher also wants to use extracts on its site or as a taster at the end of a paperback, a clear grant both ways is preferable so as to avoid any misunderstandings. Commonly either party may use up to 10% without payment to the other and for no direct financial gain; but publishers should consider the wider rights needed if they are making books available through, e.g., Search Inside The Book.

2. Delivery of the Work

(1) A common source of disagreement between author and publisher is over exactly what was to have been delivered. The placing of important items such as length, delivery date and illustrations in an appendix is therefore a useful signal to both author and publisher to get these items clear in their minds before ambiguities can create confusion. If, for example, price ceilings for a particular market make a maximum length important, then that length should be agreed and incorporated in the appendix. Illustrations are a fertile source of misunderstanding: author and publisher should likewise grasp the nettle before they sign the contract. (See Clause 8 for further details on illustrations). Authors are owed proper care and clarity by their editors: neither author nor his/her new editor should have to rely on informal correspondence or memories of telephone or other conversations. (See Clause 32, Entire Agreement.)

A possible form of appendix is shown at the end of this Precedent. The appendix will clearly vary from book to book in detail and complexity. The common sense of setting out in an appendix just what is being commissioned from the author, and on what evidence (e.g., synopsis/specimen chapter), applies especially, but not only, to heavily illustrated works and to non-fiction. For example, the publisher may have expected a horror novel but is delivered a saga. If the description in the appendix simply says 'Fiction', there is a potential problem.

(2) Delivery of material electronically is now virtually universal and the formats for electronic delivery generally non-contentious. It would be prudent, however, for the parties to specify the format for delivery (e.g., a Word file). It should be noted that phrases like 'to the Publishers' requirements' may cause consternation to an author – they may require that the format is, at least, 'subject to agreement'.

2. Delivery of the Work

The Author *has delivered/shall deliver* material for the complete Work conforming to the specifications set out in the Appendix to this Agreement and by the date or dates specified therein.

The Author agrees to retain an additional copy of all material.

Should the Author fail to deliver material for the complete Work acceptable to the Publishers in accordance with Clause 3 by the due date or by such other date as may be agreed by the Publishers in writing, the Publishers shall be at liberty to decline to publish the Work. If the Publishers so decline in writing this Agreement shall terminate subject to the following alternative provisos the choice of which shall be at the sole discretion of the Publishers:

2 (i) that the Author shall not be at liberty to publish the Work elsewhere after its completion without having first offered it to the Publishers on the terms of this Agreement;

or

2 (ii) that the Author shall refund any part of the advance already paid by the Publishers [within thirty days of a request in writing from the Publishers to do so].

It is advisable that, in addition to the contract, any 'Author Guidelines' issued by a publisher address the format of delivery properly.

Publishers may also wish to include other specifications, such as the omission of formatting and may retain the right to charge to the author any costs incurred in converting to a compatible format (or in converting material – particularly artwork – so as to reduce it to the correct size).

One other technical issue to consider is whether the publisher wishes the contract to confirm that the author is responsible for the performance of the electronic version and therefore for any corruption of the publisher's or printer's systems.

(3) Since it is possible that authors may be late in delivering their typescripts, and since their publishers just as frequently simply make a note on the file and reschedule the work for a later season, it is the persistently overdue typescript at which the provisions are aimed. The alternatives follow the sense of **item 7, of the Publishers Association Code of Practice (see Appendix I)**. In short, the publisher cannot have it both ways, that is, both retain an option and reclaim any advance paid out. That said, if they do so, it does protect them against deliberate failure to deliver and termination, only to be followed by instant delivery to another publisher.

In view of the above comment, a publisher who really does mean what his/her contract states should make explicit provision that 'time is of the essence'. 'Event' publishing requires rigid time scheduling (e.g., for books tied to sports events or to historical anniversaries). If the 'event' is reasonably within the control of the author (retirement from their current position, opening of an exhibition relevant to the subject etc), to reinforce the significance of prompt delivery to the publication of the tie-in book the publisher would be well-advised to add to the contract a clause permitting at least renegotiation (if not termination) of the agreement if the extent or timing of the event is significantly brought forward, reduced or delayed (see also Note (7) to Clause 6). On the other hand, it should not, for instance, be invoked if delivery is delayed because the publisher has altered its requirements at a late stage.

(4) To give the UK publisher as little disadvantage as possible in matching US publication dates (to protect Australia and New Zealand for example) it is important to ensure that where the UK publisher does not control world rights the author delivers the typescript simultaneously to each publisher.

(5) With the advent of the celebrity autobiography, publishers are also well advised to ensure that the author is obliged to supply an update for the book covering their life between delivery of the initial edition and an agreed period before mass-market paperback publication. The terms and conditions outlined in the notes to Clauses 2 and 3 apply as much to delivery of that new matter as to the original script and illustrations (although the author may feel a little aggrieved if the agreement is drafted so that failure to deliver the updated material leads to the termination of the whole contract and repayment of the whole advance).

(6) Taking the issue of celebrity autobiography a step further, consideration may also need to be given to the mechanics of the subject (and publisher) working with a ghost writer, including such simple matters as 'Who is actually handing the script to the publisher?' and 'What happens if one or the other fails to perform as required and prevents delivery?'. For example, should the ghost be penalised if it is the celebrity who prevents delivery? Under those circumstances, if the publisher is due to pay the ghost, should the celebrity be required to bear that cost in addition to repaying their own signature advance? See also Note (8) to Clause 5 relating to the relationship between ghosts and celebrities.

(7) It is not uncommon for publishers to insist upon payment of interest on monies due to be repaid if the author clearly defaults on the delivery and acceptance criteria. It is certainly not unreasonable to add a clause to this effect if the author insists upon the inclusion of a clause requiring payment of interest on late payments (**see Note (7) to Clause 17**). It may not be unreasonable for a publisher also to seek reimbursement of out-of-pocket costs too (such as those relating to jacket design).

(8) The timing of repayment by the author is a matter that should be addressed in publishing contracts. However, publishers should be aware that authors may have spent the money on research and not be in a position to make the immediate repayment the publisher would like. A prudent author will ask the publisher to provide in the contract for the negotiation of repayment on a reasonable timescale. In particular, if the reason for termination is in respect of a subjective argument – acceptability, rather than non-delivery by the agreed date – the author may ask for the publisher to accept a 'first proceeds' clause. This is a clause that provides for the author to repay the publisher from the first proceeds of licensing the book (or one that is similar) to another publisher (thus showing the book was capable of publication). In the event that the publisher accepts this method of repayment a timescale for licensing the rights should be insisted upon by the publisher. After all, if the book is never licensed to another party, there will be no first proceeds to pass back to the publisher and the publisher will therefore remain out of pocket.

3. Acceptance and Conditions of Acceptance and Approval

(1) The publishers' commitment to publish depends on 'acceptance'. The publishers *shall* accept if the typescript fulfils reasonably the author's intentions **and** the publishers' expectation at the time of contract **and** the warranties given (**see Note (3) below**). If the typescript *does not meet all three*, then the publishers have a fallback position which is explicitly stated and known to the author from the start. This formula draws on several sources to try to resolve the most difficult issue in publishing contracts: the quality of the final typescript in which the publishers are to invest very considerable direct and indirect costs and resources. The prime responsibility for minimising the risk of disagreement must lie with the publishers: they must not only through the Appendix define as closely as possible and in writing *before*

3. Acceptance and Conditions of Acceptance and Approval

The Publishers shall accept the Work provided that the material as delivered by the Author shall be technically competent, shall conform to a reasonable extent to the specifications set out in the Appendix hereto and any amendments to that Appendix agreed by the parties in writing and shall conform to the warranties given to the Publishers under this Agreement; and they shall have the right as a condition of acceptance of the Work to require amendments to ensure that the Work does so conform. The Publishers shall inform the Author in writing within [*number*] days after receipt of the complete material for the Work as to whether amendments are required or whether the Work is to be accepted as delivered or to be rejected. If the Author is unable or unwilling to undertake amendments required by the Publishers or arrange for them to be made within such reasonable period of time as shall have been agreed by the Publishers, then the Publishers shall have the right to employ a competent person or persons to make the amendments and any fees payable shall be deducted from any sums due to the Author.

---

contract the book which they would like to publish, they must also satisfy themselves at that stage that the author both understands and is capable of meeting their requirements. It follows that if the brief is altered then each alteration must be clearly agreed to in writing and signed by both parties.

(2) When acquiring rights from outside the UK, the UK publisher should carefully consider what constitutes 'acceptability'. For example, (i) a book which is acceptable to American tastes may not be acceptable in the UK market and so provision may need to be built in for Anglicisation beyond the usual level of spelling and house style; (ii) if the work acquired is delivered in a foreign language it is advisable that acceptability is based upon receipt of the English translation (whilst taking care to ensure that it is not the translator who is actually at fault – the general principle of the comments at Note (6) to Clause 2 apply in this area).

(3) Care should be taken to ensure that acceptability is also subject to the work being publishable in the eyes of the publisher's legal advisers. If the typescript has to be approved within 30 days of delivery it is unlikely that a full legal review will be undertaken before this period has expired. In this case, it is advisable to ensure, either in this Clause or in Clause 5, that the publisher has the opportunity to turn a book down on legal grounds regardless of an earlier level of 'acceptance'. Authors need to be aware that agreeing an advance be paid 'on acceptance of the finally legally approved script' will often mean a substantial delay after initial delivery of the script to the publisher.

(4) It is advisable that the approval by the author of the final text of his/her work should be obtained before it goes to press in order to minimise any possible infringement of the author's moral right of integrity, described in the Copyright, Patents and Designs Act 1988 as the right to object to derogatory treatment of the author's work. For example:

> 'The Work, as finally amended and marked for press, shall be subject to the Author's approval and such approval shall not be unreasonably withheld or delayed'.

See Appendix H on moral rights in general.

(5) Provision is often also made for the publisher to acquire the work in progress and appoint another writer to complete the book should the author fail to do so. Careful consideration of the copyright and moral rights held by the original author and the subsequent writer should be taken (see Note (4) above and Notes to Clauses 19, 22 and 28). The publisher will most likely want to appoint a suitable person of their choice and to ensure that their

overall advance and royalty bill will not increase (usually by saying the author income will be reduced to cover the monies due the writer). Authors would be advised to have some say over who is to complete the work and what is to be deducted from their income (and which income precisely). When considering changes to the publisher's preferred position, it should be borne in mind that this Clause is most likely to be implemented in the event of illness or death (as opposed to the author making a choice not to deliver).

4. Competing Work

(1) An author may well be invited to provide a work precisely because of a reputation established by a previous book (**see also Precedent Fourteen**). This is only one example of a somewhat grey area. Authors must be able to maximise earnings, while publishers must be able to protect their investment in an author's work from unreasonable competition. Any objections by the publishers must therefore be reasonable, and some authors may wish the clause to operate only while the publishers keep the original work available.

Instead of restricting authors during the continuance of the agreement or while the work remains in print with the original publisher, time limits on the restrictions are sometimes included by some publishers so as to allow expert authors to continue to write about their specialist subjects, while at the same time protecting the publisher during the all important pre- and post- publication periods. Time limits can range from anything from one year before publication until two years after, down to three months before until six months after (although the author may be advised to ask for the calculation to run from delivery and acceptance). Additional considerations that may be built in so as to vary the clause include the recommended retail price, the target market (age group, in particular), and the exact subject matter of the book. For example:

> 'The Author will not without the Publishers' written approval (not to be unreasonably withheld or delayed) become involved in any competing work (i.e., a pictorial autobiography or biography of [*name*] or a work containing more than 10,000 words by [*name*] about his career at Liverpool Cement Works) within two years of first UK publication of the Work by the Publishers. Further, the Author will not without the Publishers' written approval (not to be unreasonably withheld or delayed) within two years of first UK publication of the Work by the Publishers authorise any biography of [*name*].'

(2) Some publishers also include an option to acquire rights to derivative works, on the following lines (see notes on Clause 27 re options in general):

> 'The Author hereby grants to the Publishers an option, exercisable on terms to be agreed, such terms to be fair and reasonable, to acquire the sole and exclusive right throughout [the world in all languages] to publish any work or works written partly or wholly by the Author which in subject matter or style may clearly be deemed derivative from the Work. A "derivative work" shall be understood to mean a work which clearly has been inspired by the Work and draws from its "essence" but which also has its own independent identity. If, however, the Author makes a proposal to the Publishers for a derivative work and the Publishers do not within 60 days of receipt of a full written proposal enter into negotiations with the Author with a view to agreeing fair and reasonable terms for publication of such work the Author may offer such proposal elsewhere but shall not accept from any third party terms less favourable than those offered by the Publishers; and furthermore the Author shall not publish or release or authorise publication or release of any such derivative work earlier than 12 months after the Publishers' first publication of the Work without the Publishers' prior written consent.'

(3) If the publishers turn down an option on a book, should the author be prevented from exploiting rights in that book by this Clause? It would seem less then equitable for an author to be stifled if the publisher felt the book was wrong for their list.

4. Competing Work

The Author shall not during the continuance of this Agreement without the previous written consent of the Publishers prepare or publish (or collaborate in the preparation or publication of) any work of a nature which may be reasonably considered by the Publishers to be likely to compete with or to affect prejudicially the sales of the Work or the exploitation of any rights in the Work granted to the Publishers under this Agreement.

5. Warranties and Indemnities

The Author hereby warrants to the Publishers and their assignees, licensees, printers, manufacturers and distributors that *he/she* has full power to make this Agreement, that *he/she* is the sole Author of the Work and is the owner of the rights herein granted, that the Work is original to *him/her*, and that it has not previously been published in any form in the territories covered by this Agreement and is in no way whatever a violation or infringement of any existing copyright or licence, or duty of confidentiality, or duty to respect privacy, or any other right of any person or party whatsoever, that it contains nothing libellous, that all statements contained therein purporting to be facts are true and that any recipe, formula or instruction contained therein will not, if followed accurately, cause any injury, illness or damage to the user.

---

5. Warranties and Indemnities

(1) Notes (3) and (4) to this clause in the First Edition of *Publishing Agreements* (1980) read as follows:

> *'(3) The most important warranty is that against publishing libels. The first and foremost responsibility must rest, in fiction and non-fiction alike, with the author. He/she alone commits to paper the words which the publishers pay to publish and there is no moral justification in moving the burden of care to the publishers, although, as the book goes through the press, the publishers will sometimes carry some of the financial burden of minimising the risk (e.g., through sharing the costs, which can be heavy, of libel readings and subsequent consultation with libel lawyers), and although, if a claim for libel is made after publication, the publishers will often help the author to meet his/her obligations.*
>
> *(4) Warranties and indemnities which include the phrase "to the best of his/her knowledge" and/or which limit the author's liability to "any breach of this warranty" only are of very little value. "Knowledge" is easily denied, and in most instances a speedy settlement takes place under which it is not definitely established whether an actual "breach" occurred or not.'*

Those notes are still valid 30 years on, but the situation is not satisfactory for either publisher or author. One significant discussion area is whether publishers should extend their insurance policies to cover their authors against claims of libel, negligent misstatement, etc, in order to provide protection jointly to author and publisher. This means that (i) the publisher is not put in the position of invoking remedies against his/her author which the author may be totally unable to bear (thus leaving the publisher with a pyrrhic victory), and (ii) the author is not necessarily faced with the whole cost of a claim. In effect, an extra premium brings the author's liability (which is still expressed through stringent warranties and indemnities which the insurer may require as a prerequisite for extending the cover) into the publisher's insurance cover, save for a residual liability of the author. The value of such a scheme to each party to the contract will depend on many factors: for example, the cost of the premium (and whether there is any sharing of that cost between the author and publisher), whether it covers only the publisher's own editions or whether it extends to any or all editions licensed by him/her; whether it covers publication outside the UK, especially in major markets such as the USA, Australia or Canada.

(2) Most major publishers have insurance policies, which have to be renegotiated annually. A policy is of limited reassurance if it does not include the author, the printer, the distributor and the publisher's licensees as 'additional insured'. Even so, the excess for which the author is liable can amount to a considerable sum, and is of small consolation to an author whose royalty account is in debit. The possibility of cover under the publishers' insurance policy aside, every author should take all available steps to avoid receiving a claim against them alleging they are in breach of one of the warranties given. The publisher certainly has every right to expect that the author, as creator of the work and expert in its content, should do so and thus to insist that its warranty and indemnity conditions are fully adhered to and met. Conversely, if the author is not (and perhaps even if they are) an additional insured party, the author may have grounds to insist on the control of any settlement which falls below the excess sum in the publisher's policy.

(3) Very much tied into the question of indemnity is the question of control of a claim. A publisher's insurance policy may be conditional upon the insurer having the right to take over the claim and settle as they deem fit. This has the effect of precluding the author having any right of approval. Many publishers will take the view that the author should be meaningfully consulted, but it is unlikely that most would be willing to give the author full control over a proposed settlement. Overall, the emphasis in negotiations needs to reconcile the ideal ('defend the claim to the hilt') approach with a pragmatic but justifiable ('this defence is risky … and will cost us XXX') approach.

(4) As a consequence of the potential for exposure of the publisher from claims and the anticipation that they may indeed need to rely (whether wholly or in part) upon the author's indemnity a prudent publisher may seek two additional assurances:

(i) on receipt of a claim: the explicit right to withhold monies otherwise due to the author pending resolution of the claim. Depending upon the nature of the claim and the sum still due the author under the contract, it is debatable whether there will be sufficient funds available under that single contract and so the publisher may seek to apply this to all contracts with the author. The author, on the other hand, could require that the monies withheld be put into an interest-bearing account in the expectation that the sum withheld will prove sufficient to cover the cost. The author may also want to put a time limit on when the monies withheld should be paid over to the author if the claim is not followed up by the claimant.

(ii) following settlement or adjudication: the explicit right to withhold monies otherwise due to the author. Again, the publisher may seek to apply this to all contracts with the author. In the absence of a suitable, verifiable guarantee to make payment, this may be difficult for the author to refute.

(5) An author could reasonably ask whether they should be responsible for somebody accurately following an instruction if it was clearly not reasonable to do so.

(6) In paragraph two of this Clause note the inclusion of 'nor is in any other way unlawful' which (not unreasonably) protects the publisher from a multitude of sins.

(7) Warranty and Indemnity clauses may also include provisions:

(i) that, where appropriate, the author has cleared or will clear copyright permissions and pay any fees as provided for in the agreement;

The Author further warrants that the Work contains no obscene or improper or blasphemous material nor is in breach of the Official Secrets Acts nor is in any other way unlawful.

The Author shall indemnify and keep the Publishers indemnified against all actions, suits, proceedings, claims, demands and costs (including any legal costs or expenses properly incurred and any compensation costs and disbursements paid by the Publishers on the advice of their legal advisers to compromise or settle any claim) occasioned to the Publishers in consequence of any breach of the warranties given in this Agreement, or arising out of any claim alleging that the Work constitutes in any way a breach of the warranties given in this Agreement.

The Publishers reserve the right having first notified the Author to alter, or to insist that the Author alter, the Work as may appear to them appropriate for the purpose of modifying or removing any material which in their absolute discretion or on the advice of their legal advisers may be considered objectionable or actionable at law, but any such alteration or removal shall be without prejudice to and shall not affect the Author's liability under this warranty and indemnity.

All warranties and indemnities herein contained shall survive the termination of this Agreement.

If either party receives any claim alleging breach of the warranties given to the Publishers in this Agreement, that party shall notify the other without delay.

If the Publishers reasonably consider it necessary to have the Work read for libel or other legal problems, half the cost of the reading shall be borne by the Publishers and half shall be invoiced to the Author. The Publishers shall endeavour to consult the Author about the reading and inform the Author of its likely cost.

(ii) that photographs commissioned for private or domestic purposes and containing likenesses of living persons were either taken before 1 August 1989 or, if taken on or after that date, the author has obtained and will deliver to the publishers a written waiver of the right to privacy by the person entitled to such right (the commissioner of the photograph). For more details of the right to privacy **see Appendix H**.

(8) Ghostwriter arrangements bear mentioning in this context, especially if the publisher is entering separate contracts with the ghostwriter and with a celebrity subject. In this case consideration has to be given to the respective responsibilities of the two 'writers'. Should the celebrity be responsible for the ghost's interpretation and gloss? However, why should the ghost be responsible if the claim arises from the 'facts' given to them by the celebrity? In an ideal world for the publisher, they should have collective *and* individual responsibility, but the publisher also needs to bear in mind the degree of control over the content wielded by the celebrity (if they have right of approval, does that place the burden of responsibility on the celebrity?) and the fact that it is the celebrity who receives the lion's share of the advance – and most likely has the wherewithal to back up their indemnity.

(9) Paragraph four of the Clause allows the publisher to alter (or require the author to alter) the text. Note that any revision does not affect the author's warranties and indemnity. There is some room to debate this as the author could argue that if the publisher requires a very specific alteration (e.g., change 'black' to 'brown'), then the publisher has to be responsible for any claim arising from that specific alteration. See also Note (3) on Clause 3 regarding acceptability.

(10) Paragraph five of the Clause allows for the warranties and indemnity to survive termination. This takes account of the fact that a claim may arise after termination of the contract under, for example, Clause 25. Any letter reverting rights should make it clear that this clause does survive termination.

6. Publishers' Responsibility to Publish

(1) Agreements should include a specified time by which the Publishers will publish the work, which can range from a few weeks for highly topical books up to two years, depending on the nature of the book and the amount of work needed after delivery. For that reason it is prudent to refer back to Clause 3, although publishers should not delay the copy-editing and other processes unduly if this formula is adopted (see Note (4) to Clause 3). Where other contributors (e.g., photographers) are to deliver key elements of the work, the publication date may be set at x months after delivery and approval of all major components; and the contract may also provide for termination and rights reversion if the publisher is unable to publish because of the failure of contributors of other elements to deliver. In that case it is not unusual for the publisher to seek to link any requirement to pay, for example, the author (who has fulfilled their obligations) to a right to claim back those monies from the party that has failed (see, e.g., Note (6) to Clause 2 regarding ghost writers).

(2) What are the responsibilities of the publisher who fails to publish in accordance with their obligation? If this is addressed by means of the termination clause (see Clause 24.1) as in this Precedent, it will mean that the publisher is obliged not only to pay the full advance but may also be liable to a claim against them for additional damages. It is therefore prudent for publishers to seek (a) a longer period to remedy any failure publish (six months from written notice to do so, for example) and (b) to limit their exposure. It is thus not uncommon for a publisher to state that, in the event of a failure to publish, the author's sole remedy is to claim for the full advance as a full and final settlement of any claim the author may have against the publisher. If a publisher wishes to limit the remedy to the author's right only to retaining monies then paid, care should be taken by the author to ensure that monies due on and after publication are tied to anniversaries of, e.g., the date of the Agreement or the date of acceptance.

(3) Whilst, typically, wording has been used in contracts to oblige publishers to publish within x months of delivery and acceptance, the inclusion of the 30-day approval provision in Clause 3 of this Precedent does cast doubt on whether a book that is subsequently read for libel and found to be actionable can be considered to be 'acceptable'.

(4) Trade publishing contracts often include a provision not only requiring the publisher 'first' to publish the book (typically as a hardback edition), but also to do so in paperback. This is usually expressed as being an obligation to publish in paperback within x months of first hardback publication. Publication in other specific formats is sometimes a requirement, but trade publishing contracts can address this obligation in the sense that failure to exploit rights in, for example, audio format by a given point in time will lead to reversion of those rights (see, e.g., Notes (1) and (3) to Clause 1).

(5) The position concerning an express commitment to publish is further complicated by the move to eBook. What guarantee has the author that the book will appear as 'a book' in the traditional sense? The author may therefore require publication first in print form but, with the market very fluid in this regard, the publisher may only agree with the proviso 'unless otherwise agreed (taking into account market conditions then prevailing)'.

(6) Allied to commitment to publish is the issue of review of new market terms (for example, eBook royalties – see Note (3) to Clause 12.10). Whilst the royalty Clause may offer

6. Publishers' Responsibility to Publish

The Publishers shall unless otherwise mutually agreed or unless prevented by circumstances beyond their control, at their own expense produce and publish the Work within [*number*] months of the Publishers accepting that the Work meets all the requirements of Clause 3, or within [*number*] months of the date of this Agreement, whichever shall be the later date.

---

a tempting undertaking to review once a certain period after publication of the format has passed, this is of little value if there is no obligation to publish in that format. That is likely to be more of an issue to the author if they feel the publisher is then currently paying below the 'norm'.

(7) The increase in event-related publication has led to the inclusion of less orthodox publication clauses such as the following: 'The Publishers will first publish the Work at their own expense to coincide with the exhibition provisionally entitled 'Bats and Balls' (the 'Exhibition') at the XXX Museum and currently scheduled to run for 12 months from January 2012. If the venue of the Exhibition is altered or the opening of the Exhibition is delayed beyond 31 March 2012 or if the Exhibition runs for less than six consecutive months the Publishers will be entitled to renegotiate the terms of this Agreement'. In certain instances, the Publishers may also wish to include a clause allowing for termination with full repayment of monies paid in certain extreme circumstances.

Similarly, if the publisher's deal is predicated on TV exposure of a given nature, the publisher is advised to address the matter of that exposure failing to eventuate. As with the example above, the clause may allow for a right to renegotiate or even terminate but, critical to the publisher's ability to action the clause, it must precisely define what level of exposure was 'guaranteed'. For example: (i) was it agreed that the TV programme would have a given title?; (ii) would it be of a given minimum duration (a series of four episodes of at least 50 minutes each)?; (iii) would it be shown at a given time (what is 'prime time'?)?; or (iv) would it only count as broadcast if shown on stated (normally terrestrial) channels? As with so much, the more detailed the 'guarantee' the easier it is to identify the rights and wrongs of any alleged breach.

(8) For highly illustrated books, the publication of the book may depend solely upon the acquisition of sufficient co-edition interest. If that is not forthcoming the inclusion of the following clause will be of comfort to the publisher:

> 'If the Publishers are unable to obtain sufficient co-edition interest in the Work the Publishers may decline to publish the Work and terminate this Agreement. If so, the sum or sums already paid under Clause 16 will, in full and final settlement, remain the property of the Author.'

Obviously, this clause is written from the perspective of the publisher so the author/illustrator will need to consider the effect of termination on their income. They may, for example, have declined work in anticipation of the expected publication advance and subsequent earnings.

(9) The co-ordination of publication between the UK and the US is important, not only to co-ordinate open market publication but also to protect the UK publishers' exclusivity in the UK (with respect to importation through the EEA) and for traditionally exclusive export markets like Australia, New Zealand or Singapore. US contracts for books which are sold first to the US publisher often include open market (and sometimes even exclusive market) publication restrictions which the author is required to pass on to the UK licensee. (**For more detail on the open market, see Appendix A.**) US paperback publication is virtually universally 12 months after the first hardback edition and the US publisher is keen to protect its open market against a UK edition selling in first. Solutions used by UK publishers facing this problem include the following:

(i) 'Neither party shall publish any paperback edition of the Work in their non-exclusive market within 12 months of their first hardback publication without giving the other party at least four months' prior written notice.'

(ii) 'The Publishers shall not publish any paperback edition of the Work in the open market prior to publication of a similar paperback edition of the Work by the American publisher. However, if the American publisher fails to publish such an edition within 12 months of first hardback publication of the Work by the Publishers then the Publishers may immediately publish in paperback'.

The key in these restricted Clauses is to provide for an end point and, in the personal world, to encourage the respective publisher's export sales people to communicate with each other as early as possible.

UK publishers should also take care to ensure that any restrictions take account of the prevalence of trade paperback editions in UK publishing plans. The above examples may need to be finessed so as to restrict only mass-market paperback editions.

Lastly it should be remembered that if the restriction is that *no* edition published by the UK publisher can be sold before the US equivalent, this will apply as much in the new digital world as in the old print on paper world: 'edition' is non-specific in nature and encompasses print, audio and digital editions.

7. Textual Copyright Material

(1) The need for an author to obtain clearance from rights holders of copyright works for inclusion of extracts from those works in the author's work is driven by whether the extract is 'substantial' *and* whether trade practice allows for fair dealing for purposes of criticism or review. Fair dealing for such a purpose is not an infringement of copyright at all. See Note (8) to Clause 1 for an important case on what constitutes 'a substantial part' and **Appendix D for a detailed note on the limits of fair dealing.**

(2) The need for care in clearing permissions of all kinds leads many editors to provide standard clearance letters for their authors to use and to insist that written evidence is produced showing that permission has been granted for the rights and territories acquired by the publishers (see Note (4) below).

(3) This clause provides for the author to clear and pay for any extraneous material included in the work. But this practice, while very common (particularly for, say, biographies) is not invariable. The publisher may agree to bear the first, e.g., £100 and the author everything thereafter (or vice versa), or all fees may be jointly shared. In the case of anthologies the publisher may bear the cost of the contributions (although sometimes up to a figure carefully defined in the agreement with the author) and reduce the rate of royalty payable, as appropriate.

(4) Although the wording provides for authors to clear permissions for all territories, forms and editions licensed to the publisher (whether as primary or subsidiary rights) before first publication, in practice this may be impossible (because rights holders will often wish to know print runs, prices etc for all requested forms and editions before granting permission) and certainly may be more expensive than obtaining clearance only for known or envisaged uses. Publishers may therefore wish to limit initial clearance only to use of materials in their own editions and those which can reasonably be expected to be licensed to others, but to require the author to obtain further clearances as and when further editions or rights sales make it necessary to do so. **Precedent Eleven (Translation Rights) and Precedent Fifteen (International Co-edition)** both seek to deal with the possible need for additional clearance of permission for reuse of third-party copyright material in sub-licensed editions; in each case the licensor will need to alert the licensee to this need and agreement should be reached between the parties on who should be responsible for re-clearance and payment of any attendant fees. See also Note (3) to the following Clause.

(5) What if the author has not cleared permission for everything? Whilst the publisher may rely upon a warranty to the effect that permission will be cleared by the author (or that the book

7. Textual Copyright Material

Should the text of the Work contain extracts from other copyright works, the Author shall at *his/her* own expense (unless otherwise agreed) obtain from the owners of the respective copyrights written permission (which shall be forwarded to the Publishers on delivery of the material) to reproduce such extracts in the Work in all territories and editions and in all forms which are the subject of this Agreement.

8. Illustrations

The Author shall, on delivery of the typescript of the Work, supply to the Publishers any photographs, pictures, maps, diagrams and other illustrative materials as set out in the Appendix.

In respect of any copyright illustrative materials the Author shall obtain from the owners of the respective copyrights written permission (which shall be forwarded to the Publishers on delivery of the material) to reproduce such materials in the Work in all territories and editions and in all forms which are the subject of this Agreement.

All illustrations supplied by the Author shall be in the form specified in the Appendix, but the Publishers shall have the right to reject such illustrations or to require of the Author such substitutions or amendments as may in the reasonable view of the Publishers be required on the grounds of poor quality, excessive cost or otherwise.

The cost of supplying illustrative material, including copyright fees, shall be borne *by the Author/by the Publishers*.

---

contains nothing which infringes copyright) it is more pragmatic to add language allowing the publisher to clear any permission and to charge the cost to the author. In some cases (e.g., anthologies) the publisher may also be justified in making failure to clear a termination event.

8. Illustrations

(1) This clause is suitable for a text with illustrations in a supporting role. Books which consist equally of text and illustration or mainly of illustration with accompanying text will often need two contracts unless the author is also the illustrator: one for the text and the other for the illustrations. As to ownership of original artwork, the licence to reproduce that artwork, etc, **see Precedent Thirteen**. Remember also that ownership of the physical property does not give ownership of the intellectual property and that payment alone will not create an assignment of copyright.

(2) Some authors may have strong views on the illustration of their texts and may therefore require a degree of consultation, or even approval over the proposed illustrator and illustration.

(3) It is important to clarify with the author the *extent*, in terms of geographical, chronological or other limitations, of the rights which are to be obtained by the author. Illustrations may be an important element in the book in the eyes of subsequent licensees of the publishers or of the author, for example, newspapers, foreign-language publishers and US publishers. Later expense in some instances, for example, with the picture agencies who have granted the rights to reproduce their illustrations in one edition only, may make such further exploitation of the work impracticable. See also Notes (2) and (4) to Clause 7.

(4) In the case of diagrams and maps, it is sensible to form some view as early as possible on their number and the form in which they are to be provided. These matters are often dealt with by professional technical illustrators and cartographers. The editor may need to bring in his/her production and design colleagues for an early meeting with the author. The publisher may also want to allow for the cost of redrawing author roughs to be passed to the author. **See also Precedent Thirteen**.

(5) When acquiring an image and licence from a picture library, ensure that the licence also grants the publisher the right to reproduce the content embodied within the image (i.e., the copyright material) as well as the right to reproduce the image supplied. It is not unknown for a licence from a picture library to state that the reproduction of copyright material within the image is not included within their licence and that it is the responsibility of the publisher to acquire the right to do so from the owner of the copyright.

(6) In works of trade non-fiction, it is not unusual for the publisher to agree a contribution to the cost of illustrating the work. Additionally, the author may be responsible for identifying a range of images the author would like to include in the book – but the clearance of the images (and permission to use them) is often taken on by the publisher due to practical considerations. In these cases, care may be necessary to ensure that the publisher does not incur unduly high costs and therefore the contribution by the publisher may be expressed as including not only copyright permission costs, but also picture research costs and image duplication costs (transferring to a usable medium). Thought may also be needed to address how the author's share of these costs is to be acquired by the publisher (e.g., by deduction from the advance or by invoicing?); see Notes to Clause 26.

(7) Where the author is clearing permission, it is sensible to clarify if they are doing so for use on the cover of the book and in promotional materials. The fees for such more obvious usage are much higher than those for inclusion within the book. Logically, if the publisher has control over the creation of the cover and the promotional material, it follows that it should be the publisher who bears the relevant fees for reproducing third-party material in that use.

9. Index

The importance of a good index cannot be overrated. Not only should publisher and author agree in principle on whether or not an index is to be included, but they should agree, ideally no later than final manuscript stage, on a clear briefing regarding its structure, density, etc; especially if the author is to create.

As the creation of an index is often the domain of the specialist indexer, it would seem fair that if the author requires an index he/she should bear at least half the cost of its creation if the author does not supply it. Naturally, if the publisher requires an index, the author may reasonably expect the publisher pay for it.

When buying rights from a third-party (e.g., American) publisher, consideration should be given to ensure that the acquisition also includes the right to use their index.

10. Production and Promotion Responsibility

The following two specimen clauses cover specific aspects of promotion. The first allows the publisher to use the author's likeness, name and biography etc; the second ties the author to promotional activity.

9. Index

If in the reasonable opinion of the Publishers an index is required it shall be supplied by the Author at *his/her* own expense in accordance with the specifications in the Appendix hereto ready for press within fourteen days of receipt by the Author of final page proofs. If the Author fails so to supply the index then the Publishers shall arrange for it to be supplied and the cost shall be debited to the Author's account unless such account shall contain insufficient funds, in which case the Author shall pay such cost within thirty days of receipt of the Publishers' invoice.

10. Production and Promotion Responsibility

All matters relating to the publication of the Work, including the paper, printing and manufacture, design, binding and jacket or cover, the manner and extent of promotion and advertising, the number and distribution of free copies for the press or otherwise, the number of copies to be manufactured and the price and terms of sale of the first or any subsequent edition or impression of the Work shall be under the entire control of the Publishers but the Author shall be shown the artist's roughs (or, if that is impracticable, proofs) of the *jacket/cover* design and shall be consulted thereon and on the *jacket/cover* copy in good time before they are passed for press; though the Publishers do reserve the right to take the final decision over these so as to take into account the known or likely views of customers.

The Author shall endeavour to be available, if so requested in advance by the Publishers, to assist the Publishers in the promotion of the Work.

---

(1) The Author will permit the Publishers, their licensees and other parties connected with the publication, promotion and sale of the Work to use the Author's name and [approved] likeness, the title of the Work and selections from the Work in advertising, promotion and publicity relating to the Work, including by means of the internet or broadcast or transmission or distribution in any medium, provided that the selections published, transmitted or displayed do not amount to more than 10% of the total length of the Work.

(2) The Author will be available for publicity in the United Kingdom for at least [*number*] working days (or the equivalent in partial days if the parties so agree) for promotion of the Work around the time of first UK hardback publication of the Work by the Publishers. This may include interviews in all forms of media (including print, radio and television), personal appearances and signing sessions and attendance at a book launch on the UK hardback publication date.

With regard to Note (2): (a) the advance at Clause 16 may be expressed as being conditional upon the author's completion of these specific obligations; (b) see also Note (6) to Preamble where the contracting party is the author's company, but the publisher really requires the author to promote in person; (c) it is generally accepted that the events are subject to agreement and the publisher bears all costs (including reasonable travel and subsistence).

A publisher may sometimes be asked to agree that the author's name be included on all advertising. Whilst this does not sound unreasonable, the publisher should consider how practicable this actually is before agreeing. There may be space constraints with some items the publisher wishes to issue.

11. Author's Corrections

(1) The period commonly allowed for the author's checking of proofs is 14 days, but a longer period may be required for a complex work, or if the author is not resident in the UK. Equally, care should be taken to shorten the turnaround time in the event of a fast-track publication.

(2) The author is generally expected to bear the amount by which the cost of his/her alterations exceeds 10% of the cost of origination. Some publishers include a higher percentage (e.g., 12.5% or 15%) in this clause. Care should be taken to address how this charge is to be recouped by the publisher (see Note (6) to Clause 8 and Notes to Clause 26).

(3) All alterations at proof stage are very expensive. Prevention is better than cure and editors should be especially meticulous over the approval by authors at draft stage of maps, charts etc.

(4) The author is entitled to know that unique materials (such as diaries or original photographs) will, at the very least, be insured by the publishers to a satisfactory value.

12. Royalties Payable on Own Editions

12.1 *Home Hardbound Sales*

(1) A rising scale of royalties is often agreed, generally rising by steps of 2.5% geared to the number of copies sold, which may take the royalty rate from, e.g., 7.5% to 12.5% or from 10% to 15%, depending on the nature of the work. Typically, the higher the unit cost of the book, the wider the gap between royalty change points.

(2) As publishers have to give high discounts to major booksellers in the home market so provision is made in the agreement for a reduced royalty to be paid on those high discount home sales. A royalty of four-fifths of the prevailing home royalty takes effect on discounts beginning at 50% (though 52.5% is common) for hardback editions, decreasing to three-fifths at discounts beginning as low as 57.5% (although others will go as high as 62.5%, with 60% probable common ground). It is also not uncommon for the three-fifths layer to be followed or even replaced by a royalty based on net receipts.

In order to protect revenue streams some agents seek to ensure that the three-fifths royalty applies only to extraordinary levels of business. They seek to restrict this royalty rule to sales to specific outlets like supermarkets or to sales for minimum level orders. In each case, it is one thing for the publisher's contract to agree such a provision, but the publisher should ensure that they are capable of monitoring sales to this level of detail to avoid mis-accounting (see Note (6) to Clause 17). This Precedent includes wording addressing the high discount royalty for both hardback and paperback editions.

(3) Reference to the UK recommended retail price remains appropriate in the trade sector (see definition in Clause 17.5). This is by contrast with current practice in the educational and academic sector (**see Note 3.1.2 to Precedent Two**).

(4) Prices continue to be printed on trade books. Most observers appear to accept that if this ceases then the price stated in the publisher's literature will establish the benchmark for the calculation of the royalty – whether based on the recommended retail price or on net receipts (i.e., the recommended retail price less discount).

The Publishers undertake to set the name of the Author in its customary form with due prominence on the title page and on the binding, jacket *and/or* cover of every copy of the Work published by them and shall endeavour to ensure that a similar undertaking is made in respect of any editions of the Work licensed by them for publication.

11. Author's Corrections

The Author undertakes to read, check and correct the proofs of the Work (and any finished artwork) and return them to the Publishers within fourteen days of their receipt, failing which the Publishers may consider the proofs and any artwork as passed for press by the Author. The cost of all alterations and corrections made by the Author in finished artwork and in the proofs (other than the correction of artist's, copy-editor's or typesetter's errors) in excess of 10 per cent of the cost of origination *and/or* origination of artwork shall be borne by the Author. Should any charge to the Author arise under this Clause the cost shall be paid on receipt of invoice by the Author or may be debited to the Author's account unless such account shall contain insufficient funds, in which case the Author shall pay such cost within thirty days of receipt of the Publishers' invoice.

All materials for the Work supplied by the Author shall be returned to the Author after publication if *he/she* so requests in writing. The Publishers shall take due care of such materials while they are in the Publishers' possession but they shall not be responsible for any loss thereof or damage thereto.

12. Royalties Payable on Own Editions

Subject to the terms and conditions set out in this Agreement the Publishers shall make the following payments to the Author in respect of sales of the Work, excluding such copies as may by subsequent provisions of this Agreement, or as otherwise mutually agreed in writing, be sold subject to a different royalty:

12.1 *Home Hardbound Sales*

On the UK recommended retail price of all copies sold in the United Kingdom of Great Britain and Northern Ireland and the Irish Republic (the 'home market') a royalty of [*number*] per cent

Except that (i) on sales at a discount of [*number*] per cent or more from the UK recommended retail price but at a discount of less than [*number*] per cent from the UK recommended retail price the royalty shall be four-fifths of the prevailing royalty on sales in the home market: and (ii) on sales at a discount of [*number*] per cent or more from the UK recommended retail price the royalty shall be three-fifths of the prevailing royalty on sales in the home market.

(5) In return for exclusive rights to the EU and other European territories, the publisher may be asked to pay a higher royalty; either a higher percentage of receipts but, more likely, the same UK recommended retail price royalty as applies to the home market. Care should be taken when drafting the contract to spell out exactly what is meant by the EU and/or exclusive European market (**see Appendix J**) and to ensure that any home high discount royalty breaks also apply to those sales where a UK recommended retail price rate is payable. If the publisher agrees to European exclusivity being altered to non-exclusivity (because, for example, US rights have become unsaleable) then export royalties on European sales should become payable from that point on.

12.2 *Export Hardbound Sales*

(1) Export sales are often conducted at high discounts of 60% or more off the UK recommended retail price. Royalty payments usually start at 10% of the net price received per copy sold but some publishers agree increased reward to authors as export sales build up. Sometimes agents will seek royalties at approximately one-half of the home royalty rate.

(2) Publishers pressed by authors or their agents to pay royalties on the retail price of the work in export markets like Australia or New Zealand should calculate carefully: (a) whether they can afford to do so at all; and (b) if they can, the effect on the retail price of such an arrangement in the market concerned. There is little point in securing for the author a royalty of 10% of the Australian retail price if the effect is to drive that price beyond the market ceiling and invite the importation to Australia of a competing American edition. Therefore it is not uncommon to see the local price royalty also subject to a high discount break point.

(3) For royalties on sales in Europe see Note (5) to Clause 12.1.

(4) If it is agreed that, e.g., India, Malaysia or Singapore are to be non-exclusive the publisher may wish to negotiate a lower royalty on sales in those markets.

12.3 *Small Reprints*

(1) In the Sixth Edition it was observed

> *'The growing tide of individual copy or small run print on demand technology makes this clause an interesting one to watch for future editions of this book. It is not the intention of the clause to reduce the royalty for these orders. For the future publishers may need to explain why they are insisting on such high quantities constituting a small reprint if there is the printing technology that allows runs of 500 copies or less to be undertaken at the same per copy rate as today – or lower.'*

The Clause is now less common but where it remains, authors and agents are entitled to question its inclusion. Is it really a legitimate clause, actioned *only* for the purpose of keeping the work in print (i.e., to avoid termination by going out of print)? Can the publisher differentiate between copies from earlier printings and those from the small reprint (and therefore account absolutely accurately for, e.g., returns)? From the publisher side the clause is perhaps bound up with finding answers to the criteria by which the publisher may retain rights (see Notes on Clause 25). Until a solution is found to the latter, although the absence of a small reprint clause does not preclude later agreement on a specific small reprint, publishers may continue to look to include this clause in the contract. The notes below reflect the hitherto standard provisions and issues.

(2) This sub-clause is seen by the publisher as a necessary provision to enable him/her to keep the author's work *in print*, when the continuing demand is small yet the past demand has earned the author one of the higher royalty rates, for example, 15%. To the author, the point may seem reasonable, but not one which should be a pre-condition of the contract. Where this sub-clause is accepted the rate usually reverts to the starting royalty rate, and the print number on which it operates needs consideration book for book. It is important that an author is protected from abuse of this provision through frequent small-run reprints, so the publisher may be asked to agree that they 'may not invoke this provision more than once in 12 months

12.2 *Export Hardbound Sales*

On all copies sold for export, except as otherwise specified in this Agreement, a royalty of [*number*] per cent of the net amounts received by the Publishers.

12.3 *Small Reprints*

On reprints of [*number*] copies or less the royalties under 12.1 and 12.2 above shall be reduced to [*number*] per cent of [*the UK recommended retail price*] and [*number*] per cent of the [*net amounts received by the Publishers*] respectively or to the lowest rates provided thereunder.

12.4 *Hardbound Cheap and Other Hardbound Editions*

On any hardbound cheap edition of the Work issued by the Publishers at two-thirds or less of the latest notified UK recommended retail price of the latest hardbound edition and on any other hardbound edition published by the Publishers, a royalty of [*number*] per cent of the UK recommended retail price on home sales and [*number*] per cent of the net amounts received by the Publishers from all copies sold for export.

---

without the prior agreement of the Author' (but see Note (5)). Literary agents often request that it should operate only after the first year following publication.

(3) A similar clause can apply to paperback editions too. In that case the quantity is usually a maximum of 5,000 copies for mass-market paperback editions and 3,000 for trade paperbacks. These quantities are often capable of reduction by negotiation to as low as 2,000 and 1,000 copies respectively. As with the hardback provision there could be a restriction against reducing the royalty within the first 12 months of publication and reducing the rate more than once in any 12-month period.

(4) It can be argued that a small reprint clause may be appropriate to each 'reprintable' edition/version (e.g., the economics around audio compact discs could be argued to be comparable to those for a printed book). If the principle is accepted then the issues outlined in these notes will apply.

(5) Important to the drafting of these clauses is to ensure that it is the reduction of the royalty that is prohibited – not the entitlement to reprint (where, of course, the original royalty will be payable).

(6) Finally, how do you ascertain what constitutes a 'small' reprint? Discussions as to costs aside, one measure is to compare the level of reprint to that of the first run. If the first run is only 5,000 paperbacks, is it reasonable to set the 'small' quantity as high as 3,000? Conversely, if 50,000 were first printed, is 10,000 'small' if this logic is applied?

12.4 *Hardbound Cheap and Other Hardbound Editions*

The royalty rates on a cheap edition are usually the base rates under Clauses 12.1 and 12.2 for home and export sales respectively. The wording of the clause allows for agreement should it be necessary to distinguish between home and export sales. Attention should also be paid to address home high discount sales. Authors may ask that these editions do not appear within 12 months for first hardback publication (due to the obvious reduced royalty implication).

In this edition the Clause has been extended to include 'other hardbound editions'. This can be used to catch items like board books and hardback novelty editions. Authors and publishers alike need to note the drawback to such a one-stop Clause in that it means a royalty has been agreed – without knowledge of the edition's price and costs. It may be a double-edged sword for both therefore.

12.5 *Publishers' Own Paperback Editions*

(1) Since the publishers benefit from sharing in the profits of any paperback imprint wholly or partly owned by them, it is generally accepted that they should pay over to the author 100% of the royalty earned from sales of the author's book published by such an imprint. Specific wording has been included to address the fact that there are often two separate paperback editions – a trade paperback (e.g., C format) and a mass-market paperback edition. (e.g., A or B format). The following notes also explore the differences between the two formats.

(2) The royalties paid are usually lower than hardback rates, e.g., 7.5% of the UK recommended retail price on home sales with the same or slightly higher rate (by 2.5%) payable on net receipts on export sales (but sometimes mass-market paperback export royalties are sought by agents at a level roughly equivalent to as high as four-fifths of the home royalty rate). As trade paperbacks tend to have far smaller runs any change point for a higher royalty ought reasonably to be far lower than for a mass-market paperback (e.g., 10,000 for trade paperback as opposed to 40,000 for mass-market paperbacks).

(3) Note (2) to Clause 12.1 confirms high discount sales attract reduced royalty rates for the home market: the percentage in respect of paperback editions is commonly 52.5% but often 55% for a reduction to four-fifths and normally in the 57.5% to 62.5% range for a reduction to three-fifths (65% rarely features as the change point and 60% seems common currency). It is worth noting that where a book is published as a trade paperback original, the discount breaks applied may be altered for that edition to mirror those suggested for hardback editions (see Note (2) to Clause 12.1).

(4) Very few paperback rights (except in backlist) now seem to be licensed by the hardback publisher. Rather there is a trend to publication of different paperback editions, each catering for a different readership. This multi-format approach is not solely related to a price/image conscious target audience, but can even cut across age groups with certain books having two jackets – one for the children's market, one for the adult readers. Meanwhile, it will hardly be surprising if the author, especially if represented by a literary agent, will want to be consulted before a final judgment is made by the publishers. **See Appendix B**.

(5) See also Clause 12.3 regarding small reprints.

12.6 *Non-Booktrade Sales*

Sales to supermarkets should be specifically excluded from the definition of 'Non-Booktrade Sales' as they are a mainstay of 'normal' retail sales – albeit at high discount. This clause is designed to address those outlets peripheral to the traditional book trade, but which represent a new audience for the publisher's products.

12.7 *Premium Sales*

Where copies of the book concerned are given away with other products or in exchange for tokens collected from other products (the latter sometimes being called 'redemption' sales) agents prefer that any deals should be agreed with authors before they are completed since authors may have particular objection to the products or companies with which their books are to be associated. Discounts to purchasers of books to be used for premium purposes will be very high as very large quantities are usually involved. An author's royalty of 5 to 10% of the amount received is not unreasonable.

12.5 *Publishers' Own Paperback Editions*

(a) In the event of the publication of the Work in a mass-market paperback edition (that is, A or B format paperback) by the Publishers or by their wholly or partly owned imprint a royalty of: [*number*] per cent of the UK recommended retail price of all copies sold in the home market

Except that (i) on sales at a discount of [*number*] per cent or more from the UK recommended retail price but at a discount of less than [*number*] per cent from the UK recommended retail price the royalty shall be four-fifths of the prevailing royalty on sales in the home market: and (ii) on sales at a discount of [*number*] per cent or more from the UK recommended retail price the royalty shall be three-fifths of the prevailing royalty on sales in the home market and [*number*] per cent of the net amounts received by the Publishers from all copies sold for export.

(b) In the event of the publication of the Work in a trade paperback edition (i.e., any paperback format other than A or B format paperback) by the Publishers or by their wholly or partly owned imprint a royalty of: [*number*] per cent of the UK recommended retail price of all copies sold in the home market

Except that (i) on sales at a discount of [*number*] per cent or more from the UK recommended retail price but at a discount of less than [*number*] per cent from the UK recommended retail price the royalty shall be four-fifths of the prevailing royalty on sales in the home market: and (ii) on sales at a discount of [*number*] per cent or more from the UK recommended retail price the royalty shall be three-fifths of the prevailing royalty on sales in the home market and [*number*] per cent of the net amounts received by the Publishers from all copies sold for export.

12.6 *Non-Booktrade Sales*

On sales in the home market of a special edition bearing the imprint of a third party for promotional purposes or for sale outside the traditional booktrade (including but not limited to mail order or coupon advertising but excluding sales to supermarkets) a royalty of [*number*] per cent of the net amounts received by the Publishers.

12.7 *Premium Sales*

Should the Publishers with the consent of the Author, which shall not be unreasonably withheld or delayed, sell copies of the Work to be given away in connection with services or goods other than books, a royalty of [*number*] per cent of the net amounts received by the Publishers.

12.8 *Omnibus Editions*

When looking at omnibus rates it is important to recall that the stated percentage is usually the overall royalty for the omnibus edition. Thus, the 'real' royalty may be expressed as 2.5% where the omnibus edition comprises three books, 3.75% if it comprises two books, etc. Authors and agents will be as interested to establish the content of the omnibus and positioning of this work in it as they will be on agreeing a suitable royalty. The publisher may be asked to justify an equal split of royalty if this is: (a) clearly the author with the highest public profile; or (b) is the longest book in terms of word count; or (c) the title is referred to specifically in the omnibus' title; and all this is before the author questions why their book is being associated with author X! Whilst an area that should be covered in a royalty clause, the publisher may find that the actual rate cannot reasonably be agreed until the content of the omnibus is settled.

Authors and agents will also look to differentiate between omnibus editions sold through non-traditional outlets and what are often called 'bind-ups' which usually appear in 'normal' trade outlets. This is often a practice of series publishers who bind up early books in the series to rejuvenate sales as the series gets longer in the tooth. When sold at normal trade terms it is difficult to see why normal trade royalties should not apply.

Whilst this Clause is aimed at book form omnibus editions, some of the issues raised can apply to any other compilation in any format which features the whole or part of the Work (see Note (2) to Clause 12.9).

12.9 *Audio Sales*

(1) These rights are exploited primarily in two formats: audio compact disc and audio digital download, with the latter being far more significant than at the time of the last edition. The recorded version may exist in various forms – e.g., in abridged or unabridged form and as a straight (undramatised) version or in a dramatised form.

(2) The existence of a master recording (usually the copyright of the publisher) also allows for secondary usage – in collections of the author's work in one product or the use of part of the recorded book in a product that comprises, for example, a collection of anecdotes on twentieth century British theatre. For other considerations see notes on Omnibus Editions above.

(3) Whilst the copyright in the underlying text usually rests with the author and the recording copyright with the publisher, if the product is a reading of an abridged text, there is copyright in the abridgement to consider – and, consequently, an assignment or licence needed for that part of the product too.

(4) The royalty payable on a single title stand-alone audio product is rarely calculated on the recommended retail price, but is most commonly paid on net receipts. In both cases, it is important to remember that the price to the customer includes Value Added Tax. The royalty should be stated as being calculated from the VAT exclusive price. Receipts based on royalties of 7.5% rising by increment through 10% to 12.5% are not uncommon for physical format copies. Remember that, in addition to paying the author, the publisher incurs the cost of paying the reader (sometimes a flat fee, sometimes a royalty of, e.g., 2.5% receipts) and, in some cases, an abridger too. Where the audio is sold as part of a book/audio pack, the publisher should make it clear that the pack rate is in lieu of the book edition royalty stated elsewhere in the contract.

(5) At the time of writing, royalties fluctuate wildly from as low as 10% of net receipts up to 25%; with 15% being fairly common. However, this is often accompanied by a right for either party to review the royalty rate after a certain time (see Note (3) to Clause 12.10 on issues pertaining to review language).

(6) Consultation or even approval (not to be unreasonably withheld or delayed) can be sought over the choice of reader (but, see Note (7) below if the author is the reader) and over the abridged text.

12.8 *Omnibus Editions*

On sales of omnibus editions in hardcover or paperback bindings:

A royalty based on the net amounts received by the Publishers of [*number*] per cent shall be payable in respect of the whole of each such edition, of which a proportion shall be payable to the Author. That proportion shall be calculated by establishing the fraction of such edition represented by the Work and then applying the same fraction to the royalty above unless otherwise agreed.

12.9 *Audio Sales*

(a) On sales of abridged recordings of the Work:

Royalties, based on the net amounts received by the Publishers, of [*number*] per cent

(b) On sales of unabridged recordings of the Work:

Royalties, based on the net amounts received by the Publishers, of [*number*] per cent

(c) Sales of abridged recordings in each format shall be accounted for individually.

(d) Sales of unabridged recordings in each format shall be accounted for individually.

---

(7) If the author is to read the audio version for the publisher, provision should be made in the contract for their remuneration for doing so. This can be in consideration of: (a) the general advance, (b) an additional fee, or (c) an additional royalty of approximately 2.5% of receipts. In addition, care needs to be taken to address such issues as the right to equitable remuneration from exploitation of the performance embodied in the reading.

(8) As these rights have moved into the vertical publishing model and away from that of a licence from the book publisher to a specialist audio publisher, agents have sought assurance that the rights will be exploited on a timely basis. A 'clawback' for these specific rights is not unusual. If a publisher has not released an audio version within an agreed period (two years after book publication is towards the end of the scale) the author may be entitled to serve notice on the publisher to exploit the rights within a further given period (six months from receipt of notice is common). If the publisher fails to do so, then the audio rights licensed to the publisher revert to the author who will be free to exploit them through another party of his or her choice. When acquiring the right to exploit in abridged and unabridged form and in multiple formats care should be taken to ensure that any reversion is clearly phrased so as not to allow the reversion of directly competitive rights – for example, whilst if only abridged CD rights have been exploited it is not unreasonable to see the unabridged rights revert, the same may not be the case if the author wanted the unexploited abridged download rights to revert (which would compete with the CD). With the increase in download sales, the divide between trade publishers handling abridged rights only and library publishers handling the unabridged rights is increasingly blurred. This is likely to become more so if trade publishers wish to enrich/enhance their eBooks with a reading of the book.

(9) Where the parties are unable to agree terms under which the publisher agrees to exploit the audio rights they may agree that the publisher has first option on the audio rights for a given time. A period expiring 12 months after first publication is not unusual though some agents will push strongly for a decision within a certain time after delivery and acceptance.

(10) Whilst some agents are willing to agree inclusion of the audio product in the general grant of rights, they may prefer the contractual issues to be addressed in an Amendment attached to the head contract. In this way they emphasise that the audio element of the deal is capable of separate termination. All other provisions specific to the audio product (like positioning the author's name on the inlay and crediting the book title and author's name in speech) logically should be found in this Amendment.

(11) For heavily illustrated books which also have an audio life (e.g., children's picture books) thought should be given to how the illustrator is rewarded for this form of exploitation. Is it right that the logic pertaining to the earnings from the printed book apply so that they receive one-half of the audio income if their only contribution (in copyright terms) is the art for the inlay and advertising? See also Note (4) to General Provisos to Clause 14.

12.10 *Electronic Book Sales*

This is the area where most has changed in the market place since the last edition of this book. Contractually, though, the issues facing licensors and licensees remain largely unaltered since they were addressed in Agreed Minutes of a meeting between the Publishers Association and the Association of Authors' Agents in July 2000. How they are being resolved is another matter...

In summary:

(1) Minutes: The publisher should guarantee to exploit the rights by an agreed date. This date could be relatively distant for less well-established authors.

Today: There is great reluctance to include any obligation to release an eBook that could render the publisher liable to either termination of the whole Contract (perhaps unlikely in reality) or to the loss of eBook rights (a more interesting resolution for an author). Against this is the common placing of a review of royalty and other terms at a date that is driven by eBook publication. It is clearly inequitable to agree a review based on an event that may never happen; but should the publisher be exposed to termination? Generally, the resolution is to agree an alternative date for the review (from Contract date or a simple calendar date) and for any obligation to exploit eBook rights to appear in the general publication Clause. Whilst the obligation may place the publisher at risk of losing the whole Contract if they do not exploit, it is the least worst option to adopt. If publishers seek an increasing array of electronic rights (e.g., so-called electronic versions where a product may be based on a book and include moving pictures, for example), it would perhaps not be unreasonable to see some form of reversion or clawback applied following a failure to exploit (see Note (8) to Clause 12.9). Generally, a limited licence term for the eBook rights only in a book Contract is not acceptable to a publisher but the balance may be in the author's favour where backlist contracts do not specifically grant eBook rights to the publisher.

(2) Minutes: Publishers indicated that they would be looking for royalties 'that were similar to book royalties', believing there would be a degree of substitution in sales of printed books to customers preferring eBooks and online versions. Agents 'felt that the royalty should be paid on the recommended download price exclusive of VAT and that publishers might be asked to agree to escalators'.

Today: A practice of 20% to 25% of net receipts for unembellished eBooks seems to have developed. For more complex product, the publisher will be sourcing and paying for additional content over and above the author's text and

12.10 *Electronic Book Sales*

On sales of an electronic book: royalties, based on the net amounts received by the Publishers, of [*number*] per cent.

---

will look for a reduced rate. Care should continue to be taken to establish exactly what is meant by 'net receipts'. Additionally, no recognition has been taken of advertising linked to specific products in this precedent: what share should author and publisher take from advertising revenue linked to a specific online book? That perhaps depends upon whom brought the advertiser to the product.

(3) Minutes: The royalty rates should be subject to renegotiation after a reasonably short period. Publishers sought three years, but agents preferred to leave the period to negotiation.

Today: A review is a common feature but it has its pitfalls: (a) the review should be expressed with a view to achieving something: to bring it into line with current industry practice for books of this type, for example; (b) thought should be given to the possibility that the parties may not agree: perhaps a temporary cessation of sales is the answer as the publisher will not want to be held to ransom over possible termination of the rights (and in this context there should be consideration given to the author's ability to invoke termination under an out of print Clause whose effect may be skewed by the absence of the eBook sales); (c) when will the review occur: on a practical note, is either party geared up to reviewing one book at a time? Or is it more likely that the publisher (or agent) will review its eBook royalty against the market as whole?

(4) Minutes: Publishers confirmed that electronic and print on demand would not be used to undermine reversion clauses – whether the reversion clause related to minimum sales or minimum/available stock criteria.

Today: Generally understood but this is explored in detail in Note (4) to Clause 25.

(5) Minutes: Both sides would make every attempt 'to uphold normal territorial protections'.

Today: See Note (5) to Clause 1.

(6) Minutes: The division of income from the licensing of rights 'would need to be individually negotiated on a contract-by-contract basis ... although publishers wanting actively to market these subsidiary rights would probably wish to negotiate splits in advance'.

Today: Whilst 50% is usually sought by publishers, agents argue that the potential end uses are so diverse that it is not possible to judge until there is a proposed licence on the table. Accordingly, the rate is all too often left to be agreed – unless the publisher capitulates to a split as high as 80/20 in the author's favour. In addition, and bolstering this position, agents are generally unwilling to allow licensing without approval (not to be unreasonably withheld or delayed), if at all. It should be noted that some modification of this position to allow these rights to be licensed as a part of a wider licence of e.g., American or translation publishing rights is not unreasonable.

Finally a note on security re eBooks: provisions requiring secure encryption to prevent copyright infringement and an undertaking to remedy a system that is systematically breached are not unusual as a condition of the licensing of the electronic rights.

General Provisos

The first proviso allows for the author to be paid on sales made to them.

The second proviso reflects the difficulties sometimes encountered by publishers in getting payment from certain countries where 'central bank' problems take priority over proper trading. The proviso is a safety net which should be used only in very serious cases of persistent non-payment and should never be used when the publisher has simply been guilty of overtrading.

13. Royalty-inclusive Sales

Clause 13.1 covers those transactions where copies are sold to the book club at a price inclusive of royalty. It is usual, where the book club manufactures, for a deal to be negotiated on an advance and royalty basis and this contingency is covered in Clause 14 (xii). In some cases, perhaps because the book is of minority or special interest or because it is being produced on a co-publication basis with editions in different languages being printed simultaneously by the originating publisher, sales will be made on a royalty-inclusive basis – that is, the publisher will print copies for the book club or overseas publisher and will sell those copies at a price which includes royalty.

From royalty-inclusive book club sales the author should normally expect to be paid 7.5% to 10% for hardback sales and 5% to 7.5% for paperbacks (sometimes with an escalator on either or both formats) of the total amount received by the publisher. Although the author will receive less money per copy than would be the case with a royalty sale, since the royalty is calculated on the price at which the copies are sold to the book club, the author does receive in one lump sum an amount which represents the royalties payable on *all* copies supplied – whether or not they are subsequently sold on by the book club. Such an arrangement facilitates sales of smaller quantities to book clubs and also often covers sales to small overseas publishers who would not otherwise be able to afford to take copies. For an overview of book club sales, **see Appendix C**.

Co-edition sales to American and other overseas publishers usually also work on this basis with varied royalties for copies or sheets produced for sale through different channels. For full price trade hardbound copies or sheets intended for such publication the author would usually be paid 7.5% to 10% of the publisher's receipts; for paperback or novelty edition copies or sheets supplied for such editions the author's royalty is usually about 5% to 7.5%. Again the sums received by the author are lower, but the royalties due on *all* copies or sets of sheets ordered are paid in full in advance of their actual sale by the licensee.

14. Subsidiary Rights

(1) This precedent sets out income due to the author under three heads. Clauses 12, 13 and 14 cover the different forms in which the work may be published by the publisher (Clause 12) or by other publishers licensed by him/her on a royalty-inclusive basis (Clause 13) or across the range of what many in the book trade term 'subsidiary rights' or 'ancillary rights' (Clause 14). This layout is convenient, but crosses the boundary from those subsidiary rights which are part of volume rights (e.g., paperback or book club rights, quotation and anthology rights, digest and digest book condensation rights, one-shot periodical rights and, some would have it, electronic text rights) to those subsidiary rights which are not part of volume rights (e.g., first serial rights, film and TV rights). Hence the careful wording of the introduction to Clause 14 which builds on the general grant of rights under Clause 1.

(2) In general, the point made in Note (1) to Clause 1 should be borne in mind especially by publishers' staff appointed to handle subsidiary rights. Once the publishers *have* the skills to handle various non-volume subsidiary rights effectively, they should negotiate forcefully, not least on their author's behalf, to secure those rights, retaining themselves only (but not less than) a fair percentage of the income from their exploitation. In many cases the publish-

General Provisos

Provided that no royalties shall be paid on copies of the Work given away to the Author or in the interests of the sale of the Work including review copies or on copies lost or damaged or destroyed.

Provided that the Publishers reserve the right not to pay royalties or sums otherwise due to the Author in respect of copies sold until payment for the sale of such copies is received by the Publishers.

13. Royalty-inclusive Sales

Subject to the terms and conditions set out in this Agreement the Publishers shall make the following payments in respect of the following editions:

13.1 *Royalty Inclusive Book Club Sales*

On all copies acquired at a price inclusive of royalty by book clubs or similar organisations for sale to their members [*number*] per cent of the net amounts received by the Publishers.

13.2 *Royalty Inclusive Overseas Sales*

Where a separate agreement is made for the publication in English or another language of the Work under which copies are to be supplied bound or in sheets on a royalty-inclusive basis

(i) On all copies of full price trade hardbound editions supplied bound or in sheet form: [*number*] per cent of the net amounts received by the Publishers.

(ii) On all copies of full price paperback or novelty edition copies supplied bound or in sheet form: [*number*] per cent of the net amounts received by the Publishers.

14. Subsidiary Rights

In consideration of payment by the Publishers to the Author of the following percentages of the Publishers' net royalty receipts in respect of the undermentioned rights the Author hereby grants to the Publishers such rights insofar as they are not granted by Clause 1 to the Publishers exclusively within the exclusive territories specified in Clause 1 and non-exclusively in the non-exclusive territories specified in Clause 1 during the subsistence of this Agreement. The negotiation of and final agreement to terms of exploitation of rights granted pursuant to this Clause shall be in the control of the Publishers who shall wherever practicable consult the Author concerning the sale of [*US, translation and first serial rights*].

ers, by the mere fact of contracting to publish a book, in turn accentuated by their services in its promotion and marketing, increase the value of these rights or may even bring them into existence. Furthermore, the original advance for rights often takes into consideration the value of volume and non-volume subsidiary rights, especially serial rights.

(3) Consultation with or the need to obtain the consent (not to be unreasonably withheld or delayed) of the author over proposed major volume rights deals is not unreasonable as a quid pro quo for acquiring the rights. Both parties should be aware that certain rights do require very swift responses in order to secure the deal so a 'deemed approved if no reply within x days' provision would not go amiss.

(4) It is not unreasonable for authors to expect copies of the contracts signed with the Publishers' licensees and copies of the licensees' statements of account to accompany the Publishers' own royalty statements; although the obligation could be to supply both on written request.

(5) Some publishers include a provision, applicable to the whole of the subsidiary rights clause, allowing them to exploit any of the rights listed themselves. If such a provision is included any such proposed exploitation could be subject to prior consultation with the author and confirmation either that the applicable royalty under Clause 12 will apply or that the royalty or other payment to the author is subject to mutual agreement (see General Proviso (2) to Clause 14).

(i) *and* **(ii)** *Quotation and Extract Rights, and Anthology Rights*

It is prudent to ensure that the definition includes confirmation that permission to reproduce extracts in electronic form is addressed. The Precedent does this with wording identical to that used in relation to serial rights. The publishers' interest does not usually exceed 50% although, in the case of a volume of verse, a greater share of the anthology fees may go to the publishers until costs of production have been covered. Where the author has expressed a wish in writing for or against inclusion in anthologies, the publisher should as far as practicable give effect to it. As to provisions relating to the exploitation of these rights, **see Appendix D**.

(iii) *Digest Journal/Magazine Rights*

A share of 50% to 75% to the author is normal.

(iv) *Digest Book Condensation Rights*

A share of 50% to the author is normal. See also General Proviso (1) to Clause 14 concerning the exploitation of these rights vis-à-vis the author's moral rights.

(v) *One-Shot Periodical Rights*

A share of 50% to 75% to the author is normal. That this right is part of volume rights was established in *Jonathan Cape Ltd v Consolidated Press Ltd* [1954] 1 WLR 1313; 3 All ER 253. There is no authority in the history of trade practice for regarding this right (exercised by a journal, periodical or newspaper which can, in each case, be properly so defined) as overlapping with or excluding the exercise of mass-market paperback rights, or vice versa. See also Note (3) at (vi) and (vii) below.

(vi) *and* **(vii)** *Serialisation Rights*

(1) If the definitions set out are accepted, any licence of serial rights for exploitation prior to publication of the book will rank as a sale of first serial rights and the author will be paid on that basis. The critical question is whether a serial right *is to be exercised* (i.e., whether the extracts are to be published) before or after the publication date of the work. Whether a contract for second serial rights *is signed* before or after the publication date of the work is irrelevant to that issue.

RIGHTS		PAYMENT DUE TO AUTHOR
(i)	*Quotation and Extract Rights (whether in print on paper or electronic form)*	[*number*] per cent
(ii)	*Anthology Rights (whether in print on paper or electronic form)*	[*number*] per cent
(iii)	*Digest Journal/Magazine Rights* (i.e., the right to publish an abridgement of the complete Work in a single issue of a journal, periodical or newspaper)	[*number*] per cent
(iv)	*Digest Book Condensation Rights* (i.e., the right to publish a shortened form of the Work in volume form)	[*number*] per cent
(v)	*One-Shot Periodical Rights* (i.e., the right to publish the complete Work in a single issue of a journal, periodical or newspaper)	[*number*] per cent
(vi)	*First Serial Rights* (i.e., the right to publish one or more extracts from the Work in successive issues of a periodical or newspaper including in any online version beginning before publication of the Publishers' first edition of the Work)	[*number*] per cent
(vii)	*Second and Subsequent Serial Rights* (i.e., the right to publish one or more extracts from the Work in successive issues of a periodical or newspaper including in any online version beginning at or following publication of the Publishers' first edition of the Work)	[*number*] per cent

(2) A share to the author of 90% of receipts from sale of first serial rights is normal. Practice varies greatly on the share to the author from sale of second serial rights, from 50% to as high as 75% and rarely 80%. For illustrated books featuring a large amount of photographs the share may be reduced to allow for payment to the photographer or recoupment of publisher costs.

(3) Despite the apparent meaning of the word 'serial', it has been trade practice to treat one extract only published before publication as an exercise of a first serial right and the author is paid accordingly. Hence the scope of (v) above becomes restricted to publication of a complete (probably very short) work.

(4) With major serial deals the licensee will often require that the author be available for an exclusive interview and photo session. Increasingly publishers are adding this as a condition of their agreement with the author.

(5) Prudence also dictates that the contract requires the author to confirm that they will remain mute over the (exclusive) content of the book so as to ensure the value of first serial rights. This is a major issue where those rights form a significant part of the publishers' promotion of the book (not to mention opportunity to recoup a substantial portion of the author's advance). Any failure by the author may have serious financial repercussions and, ideally, these will be set out in the Contract with the author. Thought should be given to 'gagging' any ghost too (whether appointed by the publisher or not).

(6) Where an author reserves first serial rights the publisher should consider what the effect will be on sales in terms of the timing of the serial and length of the extracts taken from the book. The publisher may be well advised to add a clause to the effect that the author shall fully consult the publisher over the timing and extent of the extracts to be issued prior to publication of the book, adding that in no event shall the author license the publication of more than 50% of the book in serial or extract form without their prior written approval.

(7) Note that the definition of serial rights also specifically includes the right to license the newspaper to publish in online form. This should not be confused with the right to license text (unconnected to a licence of rights to a print periodical) directly to a website which would be handled as part of Quotation and Extract rights (see (i) and (ii) above).

(8) Authors may request approval over the serial text and any interview (and headlines relating to either). This may be possible in some rare instances but, generally, the publisher may find that 'approval' is limited to checking factual accuracy in the text only.

For detailed information on Serial Rights, see Precedent Nine.

(viii) *Sub-Licensed Paperback Editions*

The percentage retained by the publisher is unlikely to be more than 50% and often only 40%. This may diminish (to 30% or even 25% with a well-established author) as sales increase. The increased return to the author may be 'triggered' either by the amount of money earned from the paperback licence or the number of copies sold.

Where the publisher has its own paperback list it can be expected that the author will wish to retain the right of approval over any proposed licensing of paperback rights to a third party.

For further commentary on Paperback Rights, see Appendix B.

(ix) *Hardcover Reprint Rights*

These may be 'library' reprints (typically of a book which has gone out of print in hardcover form, but for which there is a continuing library demand) or intended for a more general sale. In the latter category are included titles which have been published as paperback originals, but for which a hardcover reprint publisher sees a demand. The percentage payable varies quite considerably and may differentiate between: (a) the licensing of previously published hardback editions; and (b) the licensing of paperback originals. The percentage payable to the author may be as low as 50% or as high as 80%.

Where the initial publisher has its own hardback publishing list it is possible that the author will want an undertaking that the book will first appear on that list as opposed to under licence. Author approval may therefore be a condition of any proposed third party licence arrangement.

(x) *Educational Reprint and Simplified Reprint Rights*

An equal division of proceeds is common. Approval of any altered text may be requested.

(viii)	*Sub-Licensed Paperback Editions*	[*number*] per cent
(ix)	*Hardcover Reprint Rights* (i.e., the right to publish a straight reprint of the Work, without notes or annotations, in hard covers)	[*number*] per cent
(x)	*Educational and Simplified Reprint Rights* (i.e., the right to publish an educational edition of the Work, with notes and/or other educational apparatus, or in simplified language in hard or soft covers)	[*number*] per cent
(xi)	*Large Print Rights* (i.e., the right to publish a straight reprint of the complete Work in large type, primarily for readers with visual handicaps, in hard or soft covers)	[*number*] per cent
(xii)	*Reprint or royalty-exclusive Book Club Rights*	[*number*] per cent
(xiii)	*Reprint or royalty-exclusive publication rights in the United States of America*	[*number*] per cent

---

(xi) *Large Print Rights*

There seems to be a consensus that a *large print* edition will be one where the print size is not less than 14 point. The author's share of proceeds is likely to be 50% or 60%.

(xii) *Reprint or royalty-exclusive Book Club Rights*

This covers deals where the book club manufactures its own copies or buys copies from the licensor and pays an advance against a royalty. Sometimes the publisher will manufacture copies for the book club on this basis. It is usual to divide royalties and advances equally between the author and the publishers although some authors command a share rising to 60%. **See also Appendix C on book clubs.**

(xiii) *Reprint or royalty-exclusive publication rights in the United States of America*

Where the publishers have negotiated for world rights, they have a particular responsibility to make as good a deal as they can for their author in the US, since it comprises the world's largest single English language market. Consequently (and taking into account the possibility of licensing a sister company) a request for approval over any US deal is to be anticipated together with an assurance that all deals will be on an arms-length basis. Wherever possible the US publisher should pay a royalty on the US published price. The publishers' share depends on whether they negotiate themselves or employ a US agent. For commission see Note to (xv) below.

For many books of minority interest the much less satisfactory deal of a sale of sheets or of bound books at a royalty-inclusive price may be the only realistic possibility. For that reason, most publishers insert a fall-back clause of the kind set out at Clause 13.2.

(xiv) *Graphic Novel/Strip Cartoon/Picturisation Book Rights*

A share of up to 75% is often found. These rights, like translation rights, are specifically protected in copyright law as acts of adaptation of a literary or dramatic work.

Since the last edition the graphic novel market has increased noticeably. There is now more focus on the control of these rights than perhaps has been the case. Clauses covering competing works and reproduction of substantial parts need to be considered when addressing retention of these rights by an author. It would appear that a graphic novel can take various forms: some may be editions that do challenge the book publisher's rights (where the text is clearly followed and depicted by illustration) but others may not (where the book is adapted with wholly new text and illustrations which do not depict any substantial part of the book). Prudence dictates that publishers should look to retain these rights but it should be noted that some flexibility is necessary where film or TV rights are withheld.

(xv) *Royalty-exclusive Translation Rights*

This provision covers the division of royalty revenue either from foreign language co-edition copies manufactured by the original publisher and supplied on a royalty-exclusive basis, or from foreign language editions manufactured by the licensee. The author's share may vary from 70% to 85% according to the publishers' costs (by contrast, **see Note to Precedent Two, Clause 4** on the division of proceeds in the educational and academic sector). Any commission due to an agent acting on the instructions of the publishers is normally paid out of the publishers' share (though exceptions may be agreed for specific languages if the use of an agent is practically inevitable, e.g., in the Far East). If the publisher is paying an agent it should be remembered that the commission is often 10%, so it is inadvisable to pay the author as high as 90%! Translation rights are specifically protected in copyright law (see Note to (xiv) above). Alternatively, they could be dealt with under Clause 13.2 (and in the case of co-editions probably will be – though royalty - exclusive co-editions may be negotiable for larger quantities). **See Precedent Eleven on Translation Rights and Precedent Fifteen on Co-Editions.**

(xvi) *Dramatisation and Documentary Rights*

A share of 90% to the author is normal. **For Rental Right, see *Legal Developments: An Introduction* to this edition.**

(xvii) *Radio, Television and Public Performance Undramatised Readings*

This provision covers radio, television and public performances (usually, but not exclusively, using only one voice), but not audio recording rights (see (xviii) below). A share of between 50% and 75% to the author is normal.

With downloads of radio and TV shows now available publishers holding audio recording rights are advised to consider that these rights should be handled by them in order to prevent competition with a primary product.

No charge is usually made for pieces chosen by the competitor for competition recital unless the work (e.g., a poem) is included in any prize-winners' performance at the end of the competition (often a festival), when a very modest fee might be charged. **See Appendix D for more on performance fees and for the guidelines relating to broadcast use by the BBC current at the time of writing.**

By way of an aside, a radio broadcaster may need two licences if they wish to broadcast a publisher's recording of a book – one from the author who may have withheld broadcast rights, the other from the publisher who holds the rights in the recording they wish to broadcast.

(xiv) *Graphic Novel, Strip Cartoon Rights or Picturisation Book Rights* [*number*] per cent

(xv) *Royalty-exclusive Translation Rights* (i.e., where the translated edition is manufactured by the licensor on a royalty-exclusive basis or manufactured by the licensee) [*number*] per cent

(xvi) *Dramatisation and Documentary Rights* on stage, film, radio or television and videograms thereof, including transmission by cable, satellite or any other medium [*number*] per cent

(xvii) *Radio, Television and Public Performance Undramatised Readings* (i.e., the right to read from the text of the Work or to show still illustrations from the Work, whether as a public performance or on radio, television, by Internet streaming or other broadcast other than in the form of an audio only recording under (xviii) or as may be provided for under (xx)) [*number*] per cent

(xviii) *Recorded Undramatised Readings* (i.e., the right to read from the text of the Work in the form of an audio only recording (whether by means of a physical copy of a recording of the Work, by means of an audio digital download copy of a recording of the Work or by any other means of manufacture, distribution or transmission of a recording of the Work, whether now known or hereafter known or developed (including but not limited to electronic and machine-readable media and online and satellite-based transmission) intended to make the Work or any part thereof available for listening))

(a) In abridged form [*number*] per cent

(b) In unabridged form [*number*] per cent

(xviii) *Recorded Undramatised Readings*

This includes audio digital download rights. Note that the clause is divided into two parts so as to address abridged and unabridged rights individually. A share of 50% to 75% to the author is normal. It is common for fiction works with more than one narrator to be recorded by more than one voice, but there should be a clear distinction between straight readings and a dramatisation. See also Note (3) to Clause 1 and Notes on Clause 12.9.

(xix) *Merchandising Rights*

The share to the author may vary between 50% and 80%. **See Precedent Seventeen.** If the publishers use a merchandising agent (whose commission is likely to be high) the cost should be deducted from the gross receipts before division with the author – and the publisher should expect its percentage to be at the lower end of this scale.

(xx) *Other Mechanical Reproduction Rights*

It is difficult to envisage much life for these now but they are included as a catch-all. A share of between 50% and 75% to the author is normal. **For Rental Right, see *Legal Developments: An Introduction* to this edition.**

(xxi) *and* **(xxii)** *Electronic Book and Electronic Version Rights*

These clauses put the publisher 'in the driving seat' and clearly the publisher should be as vigilant in securing income from electronic publishers as it already is in pursuing, for example, translation rights income if it handles them as one of the rights granted under the contract. For authors the critical element will remain actual exploitation by the publisher as their own product.

If a publisher is by itself or as a joint venture capable of exploiting electronic rights (whether as electronic books or electronic versions or both) and intends to do so within the framework of a book publishing contract, provision should be made in Clause 1 for the necessary grant of rights and in Clause 12 for royalties to be paid to the author. See Note (2) to Clause 1 and Notes to Clause 12.10 for further discussion of the use of 'eBook', 'electronic version', 'enrichments' and 'enhancements'. It is important that both parties fully document what they agree is meant when granting specific electronic rights to publishers as these not only have an obvious impact on the publisher but also will press up against the range of rights a potential TV or film company will expect to acquire from the author. As noted before, the use of open-ended rights definitions seems likely to be coming to an end.

Electronic Book Rights – in which text in the form of print appears on the screen (and may be capable of being accessed or downloaded from a networked system, printed out etc) – clearly has the potential to compete with and, in some instances, replace the printed edition in book form. Publishers understandably require that they control electronic book rights. In general agents and authors accept this, provided that there is a clear distinction (as there is in the wording of Clause 1) between electronic book and electronic version rights. For further comments on electronic rights issues see Notes to Clause 12.10. The percentage of proceeds to be paid to the author should be a minimum of 50%.

For Rental Right, see *Legal Developments: An Introduction* to this edition.

Electronic Version Rights – in contrast with electronic book rights, the right to license electronic versions will often be withheld from the publisher where the author has an agent since in many cases there will be no or very little verbatim reproduction of the contents of the published work. The relationship between the published work and an electronic version is often akin to that between the book itself and a film. Where a publisher does control electronic version rights the percentage of proceeds to be paid to the author is often between 50% and 80%. Authors should look to state that these rights give the publishers no rights in relation to TV, film, merchandise or game rights.

For Rental Right, see *Legal Developments: An Introduction* to this edition.

(xix) *Merchandising Rights* (i.e., the right to exploit characters, movements, representations, names, logos, artwork and events in the Work through the manufacture, licensing and/or sale of goods and services, including but not limited to drawings, calendars, toys, games, novelties, figures, souvenirs, trinkets, fabrics, clothing, food and drinks) [*number*] per cent

(xx) *Other Mechanical Reproduction Rights* (i.e., the right to produce or reproduce the Work or to license the reproduction of the Work or any part thereof by film micrography, or by means of any other contrivance whether by sight or sound or a combination of both, whether now in existence or hereafter invented for purposes of mechanical reproduction except insofar as reproduction is for use as part of or in conjunction with a commercial cinematograph film or video reproduction of such a film or in conjunction with an electronic product or as an audio only recording) [*number*] per cent

(xxi) *Electronic Book Rights* (as defined under Clause 1) [*number*] per cent

(xxii) *Electronic Version Rights* (i.e., versions that include the Work, in complete or condensed or adapted or abridged versions and in compilations, for performance and display in any manner (whether sequentially or non-sequentially and together with accompanying sounds and images if any) by any electronic means, method or device. 'Electronic means, method or device' shall include but not be limited to digital optical and magnetic information storage and retrieval systems, online or satellite transmission and any other device or medium for electronic reproduction, publication or transmission whether now or hereafter known or developed but excluding Electronic Book Rights). [*number*] per cent

(xxiii) *Non-Commercial Rights for the Print-Handicapped*

The wording for this provision was approved jointly by the Society of Authors, the Association of Authors' Agents and the Publishers Association for the Fifth Edition. One common clarification is for agents to require that the publisher only licenses bona fide non-commercial organisations. See also **Appendix F**.

General Provisos

(1) The Copyright, Designs and Patents Act 1988 gives the author the right to object to derogatory treatment of his/her work. This could affect the exercise of, e.g., digest rights (where the publisher of a condensed version may not be willing to allow a right to approve the condensed version) or film or electronic version rights (where the producer may require a waiver of moral rights as a matter of course). To enable the publishers to exercise such rights, it is necessary for the author either to waive in writing his/her right of integrity or to give consent so as to cover specific rights. This Clause is largely author-friendly and many publishers require an outright waiver in respect of the specific rights granted, arguing that the retention of the moral right of integrity undermines the fact of the grant of rights that need waivers. If agreeing this, the author should consider the effect of the waiver and their right to protest at any treatment of their book; it may be that some degree of consultation over the proposed text is a fair accommodation. The right of integrity applies equally to authors and artists and photographers. (For a more detailed explanation, **see Appendix H on Moral Rights.**)

(2) The last General Proviso addresses the possibility of the Publisher exercising the subsidiary rights themselves and confirms the royalty procedure.

(3) See Note (9) to Clause 1 concerning rights reserved to the author.

(4) For picture and similar books certain rights (such as anthology and quotation rights) may be exercised only in part of the book and therefore the parties should address the question of dividing income between the author and the illustrator in those circumstances. A not uncommon (nor unreasonable) solution is to agree the following:

(a) where the text only is licensed – the author receives the full share;

(b) where the text and the illustrations are licensed – the author and illustrator are paid the stated share in the same proportion as the basic royalty (50/50, 60/40 etc);

(c) where the illustrations only are used – the illustrator receives the full share (note that some authors may feel that the illustrator has simply depicted their textual description and therefore they should still receive a share from the licensing of rights in the illustrations only).

15. Copyright Licensing Agency

The majority of British publishers and authors have mandated the Copyright Licensing Agency (CLA) to license the photocopying of extracts from their copyright works; some, but not all trade publishers and authors may also have granted CLA the right to grant digitisation licences **(see Note to Precedent Two, Clause 5).** Authors whose works are copied under a licence granted by CLA are entitled to receive a half share of the income collected by CLA in respect of such copying, payment to be made via the Authors' Licensing and Collecting Society (ALCS), the balance being paid to the publishers via the Publishers' Licensing Society (PLS). **Please refer to Appendix E** for details on the function and operation of CLA.

16. Advance Payments

(1) Payment of the advance, or more usually a part of the advance, on delivery of the typescript may amount to an acceptance that the typescript matches up to the publisher's expectation at the time he/she contracted the book. The wording set out under Clauses 2 and

(xxiii) *Non-Commercial Rights for the Print-Handicapped* (i.e., the right to convert the Work to Braille or to record it for the sole use of the blind and print-handicapped free of charge) — free of charge

General Provisos

(1) The Author on written request from the Publishers undertakes to give consent in writing or to waive *his/her* right to object to derogatory treatment of *his/her* work as provided for in Section 80 of the Copyright, Designs and Patents Act 1988 when such consent or waiver is an essential condition of the exercise of any of the subsidiary rights set out in this Clause.

(2) If the Publishers exercise any of the rights specified in Clause 14 themselves the royalty payable to the Author shall be as set out in Clause 12 unless otherwise agreed or, if no royalty is set out in Clause 12, shall be subject to agreement.

15. Copyright Licensing Agency

The Author and the Publishers shall license the Work non-exclusively to the Authors' Licensing and Collecting Society and to the Publishers Licensing Society respectively for the collective reprographic licences or licensing schemes operated by the Copyright Licensing Agency as agent for such Societies and the Author shall receive the Author's share of any proceeds from use of the Work under such licences or licensing schemes through the Authors' Licensing and Collecting Society in accordance with such Society's standard terms and conditions.

16. Advance Payments

The Publishers shall pay to the Author the sum of [*amount*] in advance and on account of all royalty and other earnings accruing to the Author under this Agreement payable as follows:

[*amount*] on signature of this Agreement by both parties

[*amount*] on full and acceptable delivery of the complete Work by the Author to the Publishers

3 grapples with this issue explicitly and encourages, especially in non-fiction works, author and publishers to agree most carefully at the time of contract exactly what kind of book the author is to write. This is also why the prudent publisher will only state that payment is due when the material has been 'delivered in acceptable form' and it is wording to this effect that is included in the Precedent. From the author's point of view, the author may wish to see it confirmed that 'acceptance' in this Clause means exactly the same as in Clause 3 (see also comment about 'legally acceptable' in Note (3) to Clause 3).

(2) It should be noted that the advance is against all earnings due under the agreement and is not merely on account of royalties derived from sales of the publisher's own editions and products. If a clause specifies that an advance shall be 'in respect of all the above sums', particular care needs to be exercised to insert the advance clause after all clauses capable of earning money for the author (most commonly the remainder Clause seems to come after where this does not happen).

(3) The prudent publisher will seek to ease the pressure on his/her cash flow and, especially in 'vertical' hardback/mass-market paperback deals, will try to spread advance payments forward to the date of paperback publication (see Note (4) below) and some may wish to do so beyond that event. He/she will in any event make sure that no earnings will be paid until their total exceeds the total advance (whether paid in full or in part still due under contract). An author may feel this is excessive and that any earnings dues, in excess of that portion of the advance already paid, should be paid but deducted from the following instalments.

(4) The main tension for vertical publishers is between paying in thirds (signature, acceptance and hardback publication) and in quarters (signature, acceptance, hardback publication and mass-market paperback publication). The principle that, whatever the staging, the publication advances are payable a set time after acceptable delivery (or, if the book is already delivered, contract date) is usually accepted providing the long-stop date mirrors the latest date by which there is a contractual obligation to publish the edition in question. Some publishers may also agree to pay the mass-market paperback advance an agreed period after the hardback edition publication date rather than from delivery or contract date. The author needs to consider the effect of the right to terminate for a failure to publish on their collection of the whole advance (they should not be penalised if the publisher has spread the payment schedule) – see Note (2) to Clause 6.

(5) Given that most publishers account to authors at intervals of not less than six months, authors' agents usually ask for the author's share of subsidiary rights monies, where that share is in excess of a certain sum, to be paid within 30 days of receipt (always provided that the original advance for the work has been earned) rather than wait to the next accounting. The sum in question will reflect the level at which it is economically viable for the publisher to draw a separate, often manual, statement and cheque (and may also relate to the viable economic level of the work in which the agent is involved in processing the payment); anything under £100 will probably not be economic for most publishers.

If the publishers agree to such a request, some other stipulations are prudent. First (and assuming the advance to be specified is on account of all earnings), such payments should not be made unless the total advance has been earned – or without deduction of any unearned balance of the advance before payment of the net amount. Secondly, although publishers should not appear to be hanging on to money arguably due to an author, there may be a problem in paying over the author's share of proceeds received prior to UK publication even if they exceed the UK publisher's advance. If, for example, the British publisher has contracted for world rights in an as yet unwritten work of non-fiction and has sold US rights on synopsis for a high advance, the British publisher may be wary of passing to the author his/her share of any such advance sums payable before delivery. Were they to pass the author share forward and then the author fails to deliver, the US publisher is almost certainly entitled to rescind the Agreement and to have his/her advance repaid. A similar set of considerations arises around paying over the author's share of first serial income where the rights were sold sight unseen or there is a significant danger of the newspaper's 'exclusive' being 'scooped'. The cautious publisher may take the view that publication of his/her own edition of the book is the earliest moment at which the author's share of subsidiary rights income should be paid.

[*amount*] on the day of first UK publication of the Work by the Publishers but in any event no later than [*latest date by which the publisher has to publish, see Clause 6)*, whichever is the earlier.

17. Statement of Sales

17.1 The Publishers shall prepare accounts for the Work twice yearly to 30 June and 31 December following publication and the said accounts shall be delivered to the Author and settled within three months thereafter, provided however that no payment need be made in respect of any period in which the sum due is less than £50 in which case the amounts shall be carried forward to the next accounting date.

---

(6) Bonus advances are comparatively common in trade publishing, though they can vary greatly in their means of calculation. Common criteria are: (a) sales of the author's last contracted book or the performance of the book under this contract at a certain time in its publishing history; or (b) on UK nation-wide release of a film or prime time TV broadcasting of a series based on the book, or (c) position in best-seller lists. In each case, the decision to include such a clause will depend on the acquiring publisher's judgement, but the contract should take care to ensure that payment is only due at the agreed point (e.g., after three consecutive appearances in the *Sunday Times* fiction best-seller list or release or broadcasting within the agreed definition of 'primetime' on one of the agreed channels).

(7) Celebrity publishing often depends upon the celebrity promoting the book in ways and at times agreed with the publisher. In certain cases failure to promote may break the book's profitability given the level of advance, but as the copies are already printed before the failure occurs the publisher has little room to terminate the agreement. It may be prudent, therefore, for the publisher to withhold a portion of the advance as a contingency should the author fail to promote to the agreed level. See also Note (2) to Clause 10.

(8) For multi-book contracts it should be made clear if the advance is to be accounted individually per book or whether earnings are to be jointly accounted against one advance. In the latter case, consideration should be given to what happens if the contract is terminated by either party in respect of one of the works. A clause stating that whilst the advance is to be jointly accounted, in the event of termination in respect of any book the notional value per work is £XXX, is prudent.

17. Statement of Sales

(1) *'It is perhaps time for a forthright view of the frequency of accounting to authors. The entire book trade depends on authorship. The writers of books are the publishers' most important "suppliers" by far, and it is hardly tolerable that they should be paid on an annual basis – no supplier of other goods or services to the book trade would contract for such an interval of time.'*

This was the view expressed in the Second Edition in 1984. Now most trade publishers account twice per year. Clause 17 therefore has 'twice yearly' wording.

(2) Hardback returns have reached at least the same level as paperback books (and for high risk celebrity/TV tie-in and anniversary titles will usually exceed them) and so publishers need to consider reserves carefully, almost on a genre-by-genre basis. Reserves for both formats are now rarely below 20%; and 30% seems to be the extreme 'norm'. Practice appears to lean towards allowing a traditional type of reserve at a rate of 10% to 20% where an audio or electronic product is a physical item (e.g., CD). No reserve should be taken where the product is sold firm or which exists only in downloadable or online form. It should be remembered that if the work is sold as a book and physical audio recording/electronic disc pack the contract should be clear as to what reserve may be withheld. See also Note (3) below.

(3) It is, of course, possible to apply reserve percentages selectively; children's books, for example, tend to suffer comparatively low returns so it is reasonable to reduce the reserve percentages for them. Crediting the reserve at the fourth account is, of course, only acceptable to authors if accounting is twice yearly but every publisher is likely to be looking to ensure that at least one Christmas period is included within the retention period.

Another approach, common in the US and sometimes encountered in the UK, is to make a deduction for reserves at the first account and credit the amount deducted at the second account, whilst making a new deduction from earnings at that account and crediting it at the third account, and so on. The US method often involves deducting a percentage from the sales figures (rather than the earnings); often the percentage is not quantified in the contract, but is merely stated as to be 'reasonable' and frequently the publisher is entitled to continue to deduct (and credit) throughout the life of the book. Whilst the last facet sometimes applies when such a system is used in the UK, the percentage is generally stipulated in the contract.

(4) Payments are not normally made where the sum accrued is less than £50; but an author should expect a statement regardless of the level of monies due.

(5) A detailed commentary on what information a good royalty account should contain is not really a subject for this book. Logically, it should be sufficient for the author to be able to verify on what basis payment has been made and should enable them to see whether they need to implement an audit or not (see Note (6) below).

(6) Most publishers, in allowing access to their accounts for the purpose of Clause 17.3, stipulate an acceptable margin of error. Setting that margin as a figure, for example, £100, may appeal as s simple solution but such a sum may, however, be trivial in relation to the cost of the audit, especially if the audit concerns a high-earning author. To express an acceptable margin as a percentage of error (here 2.5%) is clearly more prudent in that case and could sensibly be coupled with a set figure of e.g., £500. Additionally, some publishers may wish to include caveats prohibiting an audit after a certain period of time has elapsed.

(7) The timely payment of monies is usually seen as a central tenet of the agreement between author and publisher. If the publisher fails to ensure this, the author may take steps to terminate the agreement due to the publishers' breach (see Clause 24), though they may be able to institute a claim through Small Claims Court. It may, however, be an advantage for the author to add a second contractual right to his/her armoury and insist that late payment be penalised by the author's right to charge interest. From a publishers' point of view this is a Catch 22 situation – if they pay on a timely basis the clause will not be activated; but if they are not able to do so, why should the author be disadvantaged? Perhaps a fair compromise is for the interest only to come into effect after the author has given the publisher notice of late payment and offered the publisher a reasonable period in which to rectify the situation. Failure to do so within that period will mean that interest can be claimed from the date payment was due. Regardless of the inclusion of an interest rate clause, there is the Late Payment of Commercial Debts (Interest) Act 1998 to consider.

(8) At Clause 17.6, an author may be concerned to confirm whether or not the publisher is paying on local receipts or its UK receipts when selling to its sister companies, for example in Australia. Some publishers pay on local receipts (the price to the local retailer), whilst others calculate on the price paid by the sister company to the UK.

(9) In the Precedent wording at Clause 17.7, note that there is no entitlement to deduct any sub-agent's commission from the author's share. This dovetails with the Notes to Clause 14 (xv) concerning commission.

17.2 The Publishers shall at their discretion have the right to set aside as a reserve against returns a sum representing in the case of a hardback edition [*number*] per cent and in the case of a trade paperback edition [*number*] per cent and in the case of a mass-market paperback edition [*number*] per cent and in the case of a physical audio recording [*number*] per cent and in the case of a physical electronic version [*number*] per cent of the royalties earned under Clause 12 at the first accounting after publication or reissue of any such edition or version of the Work, and to withhold this sum for a period up to and including the third royalty statement following publication or reissue, after which all monies due shall be paid in full at the time of the next royalty statement.

17.3 Upon reasonable written notice and during the Publishers' normal business hours the Author or the Author's appointed representative shall have the right to examine the Publishers' records of account at the place at which they are normally kept, insofar as such records relate to sales and receipts in respect of the Work. Such examination shall be at the cost of the Author unless errors shall be found, to the disadvantage of the Author, in excess of 2.5 per cent of the amount due to the Author, in which case the reasonable cost of such examination shall be borne by the Publishers. Any amount thereby shown to be due to the Author shall be paid to the Author on receipt by the Publishers of the Author's account relating thereto. No more than one such inspection shall be made in any twelve-month period.

17.4 Any overpayment (which shall exclude any unearned balance of the advance paid to the Author in respect of the Work but without further limitation shall include any debit royalties caused by returns of copies of the Work for which the Author shall previously have received royalty payments from the Publishers) made by the Publishers to the Author in respect of the Work may be deducted from any sums due subsequently to the Author from the Publishers under this Agreement.

17.5 The term 'retail price' as used throughout this Agreement means the Publishers' UK recommended list price for the Work, excluding any Value Added Tax ('VAT') and other taxes to which it may be subject.

17.6 The term 'net amounts received by the Publishers' as used throughout this Agreement means the amounts actually received by the Publishers from sales of the Work, represented by the retail price less discounts given to the Publishers' customers.

17.7 The term 'net royalty receipts' as used throughout this Agreement means the amounts actually received by the Publishers from sales of licences in the Work and is represented by the gross sums due to the Publishers from these licences less any withholding or other local tax required by law and any bank transfer fees.

18. Value Added Tax

The second and subsequent sentences should, of course, be included if HM Customs and Excise *have* agreed a self-billing system for the publisher. Some publishers also require an indemnity from the author protecting them against the author supplying inaccurate or false information regarding the author's VAT status.

If the author is not a resident in the UK then sensible provision should be made for deduction of income tax. For example:

> 'If the Author is not resident in the United Kingdom for income tax purposes, the Author shall be responsible, where possible, for arranging for exemption from United Kingdom income tax on payments due to the Author under this Agreement; failing which the Publishers shall be obliged to withhold United Kingdom income tax at the standard rate then in force from any payments made to the Author under this Agreement and in such event the Publishers shall supply to the Author a certificate of any such income tax so withheld.'

19. Copyright

(1) Although the author under Clause 1 clearly grants only an exclusive licence to the publisher, it is desirable, not least in order to combat piracy (on the internet or overseas), to make crystal clear in the contract's wording that copyright is retained by the author (**see also, however, Note to Precedent Two**).

(2) The sign ©, printed on all copies of the work and accompanied by the name of the copyright owner and the first year of publication, is the only formality required to ensure protection for the work under the Universal Copyright Convention, irrespective of whether the work was published inside or outside the territory of a contracting state. The UK is a contracting state.

(3) International copyright is a minefield and professional advice should always be sought. Relationships between countries will vary according to membership (or otherwise) of the Berne Convention, UCC and/or WCT, according to ratification (or otherwise) by Berne member states of numerous amending conventions, and/or according to any direct bilateral agreements between individual states. For a list of countries belonging to the international conventions, **see Appendix K**.

20. Infringement of Copyright

Clause 20 places the initiative and the responsibility for fighting piracy in the hands of the publishers. The clause requires the total co-operation of the author (not least for reasons of copyright law) but does equally offer to the author a 50% share of any net profit or damages received as a result of enforcement action, which will have been funded at high cost by the publishers alone.

However, publishers may also want to give the author the opportunity to join with them as equal parties to an action for infringement, bearing half (or another agreed portion) of all costs and expenses. In that case, after the costs are deducted, the balance of monies received is likely to be divided in the same proportion as the costs were incurred. Finally, if the author wishes to act alone then the publisher will want to ensure that, after deduction of costs incurred by the author, the publisher is entitled to a share of any damages insofar as the publishers' exclusive rights have been infringed by the pirate.

21. Author's Copies

(1) The quantities suggested are examples only. A reduction in the number of free copies offered for very expensive or low print run editions is not unreasonable. Many agents will ask that the author copies be sent direct to the author and that the publisher supplies, for example, two additional copies of the publisher's editions to the agent.

18. Value Added Tax

All monies due under the terms of this Agreement are exclusive of any VAT due thereupon. The Publishers operate a self-billing system for the payment of royalties and to account for VAT. The Publishers therefore require details of the Author's VAT registration number where applicable which shall be supplied upon signature of this Agreement. Should the Author fail to supply a VAT registration number the Publishers shall not pay VAT on any sums due under the terms of this Agreement.

19. Copyright

The copyright in the Work shall remain the property of the Author and the copyright notice to be included in or on every copy of the Work published by the Publishers shall be in the Author's name, with the year of first publication. The Publishers shall use all reasonable endeavours to include in any contract with any licensee concerning any edition of the Work an undertaking that the same notice shall be included in or on every edition published or further licensed by the licensee.

20. Infringement of Copyright

If the Publishers consider that the copyright in the Work has been or is likely to be infringed they shall on giving notice to the Author of such infringement be at liberty to take such steps as they may consider necessary for dealing with the matter and if they desire to take proceedings they shall, on giving the Author an undertaking in writing to pay all costs and expenses and to indemnify the Author against all liability for costs, be entitled to use the Author's name as a party to such proceedings, but at the same time to control, settle or compromise as they see fit. The Publishers shall further be entitled to take urgent proceedings in their own sole name for interlocutory relief without prior notice to the Author. Any profits or damages which may be received in respect of any infringement of the copyright shall after deduction of all costs and expenses be divided equally between the Author and the Publishers. The provisions of this Clause are intended to apply only in the case of an infringement of the copyright in the Work affecting the interest in the same granted to the Publishers under this Agreement.

21. Author's Copies

The Author shall be entitled to receive on publication by the Publishers [ten] presentation copies of the hardback and [twenty] presentation copies of any paperback edition and [six] presentation copies of any physical audio recording and [two] presentation copies of any physical E-Book version. The Author shall be entitled to purchase further copies of the Publishers' editions

(2) If it is technically possible, there seems no reason for the author not to receive a free copy of audio downloads and eBooks.

(3) When ordering copies of their books some authors ask for the amount to be debited to their accounts. If the account is already in debit there is often little chance of the publisher recouping his/her money. Thus, as an inducement, some publishers will offer a greater discount (usually 50%) for cash with order or for advance payment. See also Clause 26, if credit is agreed to by the publisher.

22. Revision of the Work

The clause reflects the contention on behalf of authors in general trade publishing that until the author's death the author and publishers should jointly decide whether the work requires revision. The matter is, of course, of central importance in certain kinds of educational and academic publishing, as is the death of the author. The involvement of another party also leads to questions relating to credits, the adaptation (and reuse) of the original copyright material as well as potential moral rights issues. For these reasons any trade publisher likely to be involved in issuing revised editions of their own publications is advised to carefully consider **Clause 18 of Precedent Two** pertaining to revisions. However, by way of an introduction the following notes are supplied:

(1) Where rewriting constitutes a reasonable proportion (e.g., over 10%) of the total length of a work the publisher may be willing to pay a further advance – possibly based on a proportion of the original advance – if the original advance has been earned. An author, however, could point out that the advance was the publisher's risk and should not penalise them; they have a right to be paid for the creation of new copyright work.

(2) As to the meaning of 'substantially to reoriginate' production of the Work, **see Note 3.1.2 to Precedent Two** (*'when the book is substantially reset for the issue of a new edition'*). Some publishers, if substantial reorigination is required, prefer to negotiate with the author a new agreement altogether, and will therefore build this option into the wording of Clause 22.2. If the work is extensively revised or rewritten by someone other than the original author the royalties to the original author may need to be reduced below the lowest rate provided in the agreement: it may, for instance, be necessary to pay the reviser a royalty rather than an outright fee, in which case the percentage due to the original author will be shared between him/her and the reviser. The author would, of course, be well advised to look for some degree of consultation/approval over the person appointed, the sum to be deducted and from where that money will be deducted.

(3) In Note (5) to Clause 2 mention was made of the author being obliged to update for a paperback edition. Care should be taken in this clause to ensure that there is no conflict. This is easily done by stating in this clause that it does not apply to any update the subject of Clause 2.

23. Remainders/Disposal of Surplus Stock

(1) To define what is a remainder sale the simplest solution is to establish a discount from the edition's recommended retail price which both parties agree equates to the cost of production. This will always be a largely arbitrary decision, but once figures of 80–90% are reached, there is likely to be little disagreement. Once a definition is agreed, then it is important that it is observed as the labelling of a sale as a 'remainder' triggers for the publisher a number of obligations as opposed to a simple opportunity to dispose of the stock. An example of the potential consequences of the failure to do this is set out in Note (4) below.

(2) There is room for debate over whether the author should receive *something*, however small, in respect of proceeds from remainders sold off at cost price or below. Many publishers have stood firm on paying 10% of net receipts only if the remaindered copies are sold at above cost price. A few, though, have indicated some sympathy for the author's argument by agreeing to pay, for example, 5% of net receipts on copies sold at cost price or below. As a

at trade terms for personal use but not for resale and shall pay for such copies within thirty days of invoice. The Author shall receive two copies of any sub-licensed edition on receipt by the Publishers from the sub-licensed publishers.

22. Revision of the Work

22.1 Should the Author and the Publishers agree that a revision of the Work is necessary, the Author shall (without charge to the Publishers, unless the revision is substantial in which case any revision shall be subject to such terms as the parties may agree) edit and revise the Work during the currency of this Agreement and shall supply any new matter that may be needed to keep the Work up to date by such date as may be agreed. In the event of the Author neglecting or being unable for any reason to revise or edit the Work or supply new matter where needed within a reasonable period the Publishers may procure some other person to revise the Work, or supply new matter, and may deduct the expense thereof from royalties or other sums payable to the Author.

22.2 Should the revisions to the Work make it necessary in the opinion of the Publishers substantially to reoriginate production of the Work for the issue of a revised or new edition then the royalties payable on all copies sold of the revised edition shall revert to the lowest rates of royalty as provided under the terms of this Agreement.

23. Remainders/Disposal of Surplus Stock

If, after a period of one year from the date of first publication, the Work shall in the opinion of the Publishers have ceased to have a remunerative sale, the Publishers shall be at liberty to dispose of any copies remaining on hand as a remainder or overstock or to destroy them. The Publishers shall inform

---

backdrop, it should be noted that it is extremely rare for a remainder sale to proceed above cost price.

(3) In this Precedent: (a) no disposal should occur within 12 months from publication; and (b) authors must be notified of an impending remainder sale or destruction of remaining stocks and given the opportunity to acquire all or some of the remaining copies at the best remainder price. Beyond these constraints, neither a remainder sale nor disposal through destruction really should be left contingent on the author's approval.

(4) By way of example to the potential outcome of a failure to notify an author as required: in 1991, Truro Crown Court awarded an author compensation of just under £2,000 following the remaindering of 5,500 copies of two of the author's books after the publisher failed to offer the author the right to buy copies as required by the contract. The sum awarded included £250 for damage to the author's reputation. As with any other clause, inclusion of an obligation to an author must go hand in hand with the realisation that there must be a system in-house to ensure that it is adhered to. Some publishers thus add a sentence to the effect that 'inadvertent failure to notify' is not a breach. This is likely to upset authors who do not see

why an obligation central to their reputation and ability to buy books for their own sale can so readily be circumvented and the burden of proof passed back to them.

(5) Some, but by no means all, contracts drafted by literary agents include a provision to the effect that the exercise by the publishers of the right to remainder amounts to a repudiation of the contract, so that publishing rights revert to the author immediately. The issue is not made any easier by the practice of 'part-remaindering'. Publishers need to consider whether reversion of the publisher's rights should be permitted to take place if the book is in print in any other primary form edition published by the publisher – or, some will argue, under current licence from the publisher to a sub-licensee (at least in full-length book form through the ordinary book trade) – see Clause 25. Reversion should never be permitted to occur unless the book has actually been put out of print – serving notice of an intention to place the book out of print should not constitute grounds for termination as the intention may never be followed through.

24. Termination of Contract

Some publishers may find Clause 24.2 wider in scope than they would like. The appointment of a receiver is not the end of the road for a limited company. However, the receiver may well 'freeze' any earnings due to the company's authors as assets of the ailing company (as are, of course, the company's contracts with its authors). This precedent, on balance, puts the author's interests first.

On the other hand, authors may wish to consider whether Clause 24.3 should allow the publisher the right to participate in existing licences after termination under this Clause. They may also want to address any right to sell off stock following this type of termination.

the Author of their decision to remainder or to destroy the remaining copies and shall give *him/her* the opportunity of purchasing copies at the remainder price on offer or of taking copies intended for destruction free of charge except for carriage. The Author shall inform the Publishers whether *he/she* wishes to acquire part or all of the stock and, if *he/she* fails to so inform the Publishers within three weeks of the Publishers' posting of the notice, they may remainder or destroy the Work forthwith. If the price obtained is more than the cost of production the Publishers shall pay to the Author 10 per cent of the net amounts received by the Publishers. On disposal of stock at or below cost of production, no royalty shall be payable.

24. Termination of Contract

24.1 The Author may terminate this Agreement by summary notice in writing to the Publishers if the Publishers are in material breach of any of the provisions of this Agreement and either (i) have failed to remedy such breach within one month of notice to them from the Author of such breach if the breach notified to the Publishers is capable of remedy within one month of such notice or (ii) have not agreed with the Author (both parties acting reasonably and in good faith) within that month a programme to remedy the breach if the breach notified to the Publishers is capable of remedy but not within one month of notice to them from the Author of such breach; or (iii) if the Publishers fail to fulfil their obligations under any programme agreed under (ii).

24.2 This Agreement shall automatically terminate when a manager, receiver, or other encumbrancer takes possession of, or is appointed over the whole or any substantial part of, the Publishers' assets; or when the Publishers enter into any arrangement or composition with or for the benefit of their creditors (including any voluntary arrangement under the Insolvency Act, 1986); or when a petition is presented or a meeting is convened for the purpose of considering a resolution for the making of an administrative order, the winding up or dissolution of the Publishers (otherwise than a voluntary liquidation for the purpose of reconstruction).

24.3 Upon termination of this Agreement under 24.1 or 24.2 above, but subject to the terms of Clause 26, all rights granted herein shall revert to the Author without further notice, without prejudice to any rights of the Publishers or of third parties in respect of contracts or negotiations properly entered into by them with any such third party prior to the date of such reversion, and without prejudice to any moneys already paid or then due to the Author from the Publishers.

25. Out of print

(1) This provision makes it clear that if the original publisher does not have the work available in any edition then the author can give notice to reprint and, if the publisher fails to do so within the time stipulated, reclaim the rights. This does not seem unreasonable for a 'vertical' publisher which has the facilities to publish in hardcover and paperback form. For publishers which do not produce paperbacks themselves and indeed for publishers a substantial part of whose business may be overseas licensed editions it may be reasonable for rights to be retained on the basis of the existence of sub-licensed editions (though through unexpired licences where the licensee has no stock is more questionable), even though the work is out of print with the original publisher. Publishers will have to decide where they stand on this point: some publishers decline to revert rights where the book is available in English in an American or other full-length edition sub-leased by the publishers, whilst others consider that any translated edition should be capable of keeping the work in print. See Note (4) below on defining 'in print' and 'out of print'.

(2) Many agents require the publisher to agree to notify the author within four to six weeks of receipt of a reversion request as to whether they plan to reissue the book. In that case this clause should cover two scenarios: (a) failure within the agreed period to notify the author of the decision to reprint; and (b) having notified of the intention to reprint, failure to actually do so within the relevant period.

(3) The clause, if invoked, should not terminate any option clause which may be part of the same agreement. It is therefore advisable to make this explicit by the wording in parentheses in the drafted clause.

(4) The issue of when a book is 'in print' and 'out of print' is one of the significant by-products of the move into the digital/electronic era. The fact that 'available' is now being used in lieu of 'in print' is perhaps indicative of this.

Where movement has occurred from the definitions outlined in Note (1) above, the main trend since the last edition has been to a definition based on minimum sales over a given time (two to four accounting periods). That, in turn, means that the parties need to consider which sales should count towards the definition. For example, retaining rights through remainder sales would not seem overly reasonable; a premium sale deal may be more reasonable but most agents would be looking to trade sales. Publishers would then be looking to ensure that all editions they publish and sell in the agreed categories count (be it book, audio or eBook). If the work is available only through Print On Demand and/or eBook should the publisher keep the rights? That would largely depend on their success at selling in those forms: 10 copies a year may be insulting to many authors but what if they are selling 200? At present, if the author is unhappy with the definition and the publisher is unable to indicate how strong sales in similar books are in these channels (having only recently entered the field), perhaps an undertaking to review the definition against then current trade practice at a given point will square the circle.

And what happens if sales dip below the acceptable level? In the old world, notice was issued to reprint and if no reprint was issued, rights reverted. A reprint is probably the last thing on the publishers' mind if they are not selling significant numbers. That said, should they not be given the right to reinvigorate sales? If so, how is that to be gauged? On the face of it, ensuring sales reach the agreed minimum level already expressed in the Contract would look to be a fair benchmark; but the author will then have to wait probably another year. Perhaps, the Contract can do no more than say that good faith discussion will occur with a view to setting a target but that begs the question of what occurs if nothing can be agreed.

And what happens on termination under minimum sales criteria if the publisher has stock? A non-exclusive right to sell-off (subject to the general terms of the Agreement) would not be unfair but this should probably be for a limited period only. When negotiating this, the author should consider how long the publisher's performance was judged over and what period of time they had to reinvigorate sales. The longer those periods, perhaps the shorter the sell-off period should be.

25. Out of print

If the Work shall become out of print and unavailable in all editions issued by the Publishers then the Author may give notice in writing to the Publishers to reprint and reissue the Work within nine months. In the event of the Publishers' failure to do so, all the Publishers' rights in the Work (but not those deriving from the option in Clause 27 and subject to Clause 26) shall terminate upon the expiration of the said notice, without prejudice to all rights of the Publishers and any third party in respect of any agreement previously entered into by the Publishers hereunder with any such party and without prejudice to any moneys already paid or then due to the Author from the Publishers.

26. Monies Owing

Notwithstanding the foregoing provisions of this Agreement the rights hereby granted to the Publishers shall not revert unless any monies owing by the Author to the Publishers shall have been paid and always providing that any unearned balance of the advance shall not be deemed to constitute monies so owing.

---

26. Monies Owing

In many publishing agreements, invoices relating to the book are often expressed as being charged against the author's royalty account (for example, see Clauses 9 and 11). Often this proviso is refined so as to apply only to the account for that book. It follows that if the account is in debit, the amounts owing are unable to be recovered from the non-existent earnings.

The sums involved are often too small to make it worth the publishers' while to spend much time or money on collecting them by conventional means. This clause is, frankly, a blunt instrument: there is no direct relationship between such sums owing to publishers and the reversion of rights to authors – and in this Clause there is no limitation to monies being owed solely in relation to the book in question. But some publishers include it and report that it often results in payment of long-outstanding invoices when authors (or their agents) are anxious to revert rights. An alternative to doing so would be to include a clause stating any costs due to be borne by the Author will be invoiced (such as in Clause 21) or, more generally, as follows:

> 'Where this Agreement provides that the Author is to bear certain costs, the Publishers may invoice all or part of them to the Author and/or deduct all or part of those costs from amounts due to the Author. Except as otherwise provided in this Agreement where the Publishers invoice the Author, the Author shall pay those costs to the Publishers within 30 days of receipt of invoice.'

27. Option on Future Work

(1) This option clause can be adapted to cover the author's 'next full-length work', 'next full-length work of non-fiction', 'next work in the same series as the Work' etc. If the option is for more than one work it may be appropriate for the author to add: 'If, however, the Publishers decline the first of these works, the Author shall not be bound to offer them the second'. Should the option be for books in the same series then this refinement is even more advisable from the author's perspective.

(2) Some publishers require the author to offer the same rights and territories in the option work as those covered in the agreement. This is not popular with authors' organisations or agents as it could impinge on their ability to sell the book to their best commercial advantage (for example, to an American publisher who was willing to pay extra for Canada, a territory previously retained by the UK publisher).

(3) The publishers should not generally undertake to exercise their option in less than four weeks, but should not expect much longer than six weeks to do so. However, it is not uncommon for the publisher to wish to delay the decision until after publication of at least the author's next book, if not the last book under the contract being negotiated. In some cases, the publisher may also have a case for seeing the whole work rather than a chapter and synopsis (for example, a picture book text). Some option Clauses also add a limited period in which principal terms are to be agreed, failing which the author may offer elsewhere.

(4) It will, of course, be realised from Clause 25, Note (3), that the option secured by this clause is not lost upon the termination of the agreement for causes other than bankruptcy or failure to implement the agreement.

(5) It is advisable in negotiations over an author who is also published in the US to ensure that the option can be exercised at the same time as and not after the equivalent option clause is being exercised by the US publisher. Otherwise, the British publisher may be faced with a *fait accompli* over aspects of territory, release dates in open markets, etc which would seriously affect the prospects for the British edition of the work under option.

(6) Increasing investment in developing authors, especially through large marketing budgets, means that 'the gentleman's agreement' arrangement concerning options is under pressure. Publishers may therefore insist that they have matching rights on any preferred offer if initial negotiations break down and that no offer lower than the one they make can be accepted.

28. Moral Rights

For this very important provision of statutory law, **see Appendix H**.

See also General Proviso (1) in Clause 14.

29. Agency

If a contract is offered by or to an agent, this clause is usually in his/her standard form of words. If the publisher includes a Clause that states that the rights of third parties under the Contracts (Rights of Third Parties) Act 1999 are excluded from the Agreement an agent may wish to ensure that they have the right to pursue their commission if the author does not personally want to take action.

30. Arbitration

The Informal Disputes Arbitration offers fast, informal, inexpensive settlement of disputes between authors and publishers which even under arbitration rules may cost thousands of pounds to resolve where the amount of money in dispute may amount only to hundreds. For more information, visit ***www.publishers.org.uk***

27. Option on Future Work

The Publishers shall have the first opportunity to read and consider for publication the Author's next work suitable for publication in volume form. Such work shall be the subject of a fresh agreement between the Author and the Publishers, on terms which shall be fair and reasonable. If the Publishers and Author are unable to agree terms for its publication the Author shall be at liberty to enter into an agreement with another publisher provided that the Author shall not subsequently accept from anyone else terms less favourable than are offered by the Publishers. The Publishers shall exercise this option within six weeks of receipt of complete typescript or a synopsis and at least one substantial chapter of the next work, whichever is the sooner.

28. Moral Rights

The Author hereby asserts *his/her* right to be identified as the Author of the Work and the Publishers undertake:

(i) to include on every edition of the Work published by them the words: '[The Author] has asserted *his/her* right under the Copyright, Designs and Patents Act, 1988, to be identified as Author of this Work';

(ii) to use all reasonable endeavours to include in any contract for volume rights with any licensee concerning any edition of the Work to be published in the United Kingdom an undertaking that a notice of assertion in the same terms shall be included in every edition published or further licensed by such licensee.

29. Agency

The Author hereby authorises and empowers *his/her* Agents, [*name of Agent*], to collect and receive all sums of money payable to the Author under the terms of this Agreement and declares that receipt by [*name of Agent*] shall be a good and valid discharge to all persons paying such monies to them and that they shall be empowered to act in all matters arising out of this Agreement unless the Publishers are notified in writing otherwise by the Author.

30. Arbitration

If any difference shall arise between the Author and the Publishers touching the meaning of this Agreement or the rights and liabilities of the parties thereto, the same shall in the first instance be referred to the Informal Disputes Arbitration of the Publishers Association and, failing agreed submission by both parties to such scheme, shall be referred to the arbitration of two persons (one to be named by each party) or to a mutually agreed umpire in accordance with the provisions of the Arbitration Act 1996, or any amending or substitute statute for the time being in force.

32. Entire Agreement

This provision, if included, does of course require both publisher and author to commit agreed changes to the signed contract to writing – a discipline which some may feel to be unduly onerous. However, it may be highly unwise to rely on oral agreement to changes: see Note (7) to the Preamble.

33. Governing Law

Interpretation according to the laws of England with any actions being brought before the courts of England is preferred by most publishers in England. When dealing with, for example, American licensors this may not prove attainable. Then the UK publisher needs to consider very carefully the effect of agreeing that the contract be subject to the laws of any other jurisdiction, not least upon the value of the various warranties (such as that concerning libel) given under the agreement.

A common solution (pragmatic if nothing else) is to agree that the laws and courts of the place of domicile of the defending party apply. Whilst this gives no help with regard to the warranties, it does make the situation a little more even handed. It is often utilised when the two parties are engaged in reciprocal business so that, for example, an American publisher is required to agree that English law warranties apply when they buy from the UK publisher.

34. Force majeure

On occasion the licensor may seek to put a cap upon the amount of time that the publisher may delay fulfilment of its obligations under the Agreement in these circumstances. The problem is that each circumstance is likely to have very different effects and this means that a 'one size fits all' termination may not be in the publisher's best interest. A suitable period should always be insisted upon – for example, one that allows the publisher to publish the book to best effect if the problem occurs before publication – and, where possible, the publisher will wish to ensure that the consequences of the other party exercising the right to terminate should be as publisher-friendly as possible; although in reality this may only be capable of expression as 'good faith negotiation taking into account all the circumstances'.

35. Notices

A clause covering delivery of notices under this Agreement is included. The value of doing so should be self-evident and provides a clear template for each party to follow in order to address any alleged breach of the agreement.

31. Interpretation

The headings in this Agreement are for convenience only and shall not affect its interpretation. References to clauses are to clauses of this Agreement.

32. Entire Agreement

This Agreement is the entire and only agreement between the Author and the Publishers concerning its subject matter and supersedes any and all prior agreements, arrangements and understandings (whether written or oral) relating thereto. No addition to or modification of any provision of this Agreement shall be binding upon the parties unless it is in writing and signed on behalf of the Author and the Publishers.

33. Governing Law

This Agreement shall be deemed to be a contract made in England and shall be construed and applied in all respects in accordance with English law and the parties hereto submit and agree to the jurisdiction of the English courts.

34. Force majeure

The Publishers shall not be in breach of this Agreement if they are prevented from carrying out any of their obligations because of circumstances beyond their control in which case the time permitted for the Publishers to fulfil those obligations shall be extended by a period equal to the period of the effect of those circumstances or that delay.

35. Notices

Notices to be given by one party to the other under this Agreement must be in writing and sent by first-class post (by airmail, if available) or delivered personally to the address given in this Agreement for the addressee (or to any other address which the addressee may previously have notified to the other party in writing). Notices will be considered to have been received by the addressee at the time of delivery if delivered personally during the addressee's normal working hours. Otherwise, notices will be considered to have been received at 9am on the next working day following personal delivery or at 9am on the second working day following posting in the same territory as that in which the addressee resides or at 9am on the seventh working day following posting outside the territory in which the addressee resides.

AS WITNESS THE HANDS OF THE PARTIES

For and on behalf of the Publishers:

\- - - - - - - - - - - - - - - - - -

Director

For and on behalf of the Author:

\- - - - - - - - - - - - - - - - - - -

Author

APPENDIX (sample)

Author	James Bridges
Title (provisional)	A LITTLE FLUSHED
Nature of work	A history of the water waste preventer, for general readers

TEXT

Length	Between 80,000 and 100,000 words
Medium for delivery	Word file as email attachment and one hard copy printed from such file with no alterations
Date by which to be delivered to the Publishers	31 December 20 [*year*]

ILLUSTRATIVE MATERIAL

Type	Black and white photographs and line drawings
Extent	8 pages of photographs; up to 50 line drawings, to be integrated with text
Date by which to be delivered to the Publishers	Photographs: by 31 March 20 [*year*] Rough Diagrams: by 1 January 20 [*year*] Finished Diagrams: with text

Otherwise in accordance with Clause 8

INDEX

Extent	6 pages (approx)
Date by which to be delivered to the Publishers	within 14 days of receipt of final page proofs by Author

Otherwise in accordance with Clause 9

OTHER MATERIALS

Introduction by Sir George Jennings. 3 typescript pages. Already in Author's possession. To be delivered to Publishers with text. Otherwise in accordance with Clause 2.

UPDATE FOR PAPERBACK EDITION

The Author will procure that Sir George Jennings will deliver an additional chapter of approximately 3,000 words on the effect of the 'Hate Two O' legislation due before Parliament in 2011 governing water wastage to the Publishers by 31 March 20 [*year*].

PRECEDENT TWO

Educational, Academic, Scientific and Professional Book: Author – Publisher Agreements

An agreement between author and publisher for a school, university, college or professional book does not differ in essence from that for a general trade book. However, editors of books for schools and for the tertiary and professional markets will lay particular emphasis on some aspects of the agreement. Precedent Two and its Notes, therefore, deal with those matters where the emphasis differs and which may require special wording. In respect of those issues where the Notes on Precedent One apply equally to educational (i.e., in broad terms, schools, tertiary, scientific, technical, medical and professional) publishing agreements, the reader is referred to the appropriate section of those Notes.

Although the Publishers Association's Code of Practice **(see Appendix I)** tends to regard educational publishing as a special occupation, nevertheless editors in educational companies will increasingly recognise that some aspects of authors' rights have a proper place in their company's dealings with educational authors.

Preamble

For general commentary **please refer to the notes to Precedent One**.

(1) *Joint and multiple authorship* are common in educational and academic books. Joint authorship takes place where the authors act as one author; it is not possible to, and it is not intended that the reader, distinguish the contribution of each author to the final work. The authors carry joint responsibility and the publishers should emphasise this feature strongly to the authors in writing before contract.

Unfortunately, experience suggests that (possibly through a note signed by each joint author and to be read as part of the contract) provision should be made from the outset for any falling out among the joint authors. Young lecturers A and B jointly and enthusiastically write up their lectures on a new topic into a best-selling text. Fifteen years and three editions later, distinguished professors A and B have one of those violent academic disputes which so enliven the pages of academic journals. The publishers have on their hands a best-selling, internationally marketed textbook into which many publishing resources have been invested. Rival textbooks are on the scene: the publishers urgently need a new edition to keep competitive edge and are faced with two authors who are no longer on academic speaking terms with each other. What is to be done? The answer must depend on the infinite delicacies of each situation, but a contractual note on file of the kind suggested above may turn out to have been a very useful investment in the interest of all parties.

In some cases each author only takes responsibility for what he/she has written. Here, the question at issue is often the varying qualities of the contributions (works of 20 and more multiple authors are not uncommon in, e.g., medical publishing). **See Precedent Four, Clause 5 and Note 5.**

(2) *Institutional/corporate authorship.* Increasingly educational and academic publishers find themselves entering into agreements not with individuals, but with institutions (such as a local education authority or a college) or companies. In essence, the rules of authorship do not change, but the following points should be borne in mind:

(i) It is important to establish, before contract, whether the institution or company owns the copyright – either by virtue of the work having been written by its employees during the course of their employment or by virtue of separate contracts; if so, the contract should be entered into with the institution or company as the proprietors, rather than the author and Precedent Two amended accordingly. Where the copyright is claimed by the author, the publishers may wish to consider including a specific warranty to this effect such as that suggested in Clause 14.1(ii), even though the author is already required to warrant that he is the legal owner of the copyright and has the right and power to make the agreement.

(ii) In royalty payments, a distinction may need to be made between the copyright owner as in (i) above, and the author(s). The latter may be paid employees of the institution, or company and it must be made clear not only with whom the agreement is to be made, but whether or not the individual authors are entitled to separate payment (depending on the circumstances, the institution or company may regard the writing done as part of the author(s)' contractual commitment to that entity).

(iii) The terms on which an institution receives or purchases copies of the work may form part of the agreement, for example, bulk supply at no cost to the institution, but in lieu of royalty. Alternatively, the institution or company may prefer to purchase a specified number of copies of the work on publication at a substantial discount off the publishers' list price; such an arrangement should form part of the agreement, as should the terms of supply of any reorder.

(iv) It is obviously important that bulk copies supplied under (iii) above do not attract royalty earnings to the purchasing entity. Contract and Accounts departments need to be warned of any 'royalty-free' supplies such as these.

MEMORANDUM OF AGREEMENT made this [*number*] day of [*month*] 20 [*year*]

BETWEEN: [*name*]

of [*address*] ('the Author' which expression shall, where the context admits, include the Author's executors, administrators and assigns) of the one part, and [*company name*] of [*Address*] ('the Publishers' which expression shall, where the context admits, include the Publishers' successors in business and assigns) of the other part,

WHEREBY it is agreed as follows concerning a work by the Author at present entitled: [*title*] ('the Work')

1. Delivery and Acceptance of the Work

1.1 The Author undertakes to deliver to the Publishers by the [*number*] day of [*month*] 20 [*year*]

(i) the complete manuscript of the Work consisting of approximately [*number*] words as an email attachment in [*specify word processing package to be used*] format together with one identical hard copy printout in double line spacing;

(ii) artwork or roughs for a maximum of [*number*] line drawings (the finished artwork for which shall be prepared by the Publishers); a maximum of [*number*] transparencies; a maximum of

---

1. Delivery and Acceptance of the Work

1.1 The manuscript delivery date will clearly be of particular importance where the work is required to be available to coincide with the publishers' main selling season, or with a new syllabus, or course or examination requirements, and the production schedule is tight. However, it is often the case when syllabus changes occur that these changes will not have been published in final form when the author starts writing, and the work in progress will have to be amended to take account of such changes as they are finalised. The inevitable result is that deadlines may slip through no fault of the author or the publishers and it is sensible to provide in the agreement for an extension to the manuscript delivery date. See Clause 1.4 **and note to Precedent One, Clause 2**.

(i) Both parties should be clear from the outset as to the proposed extent of the work being commissioned as this may well reflect market expectations or requirements, and the publishers' production estimate and other costings will have been based on what has been agreed. If the author is to submit the manuscript electronically on disk or by e-mail, as is increasingly the norm, then it is important to agree the word processing package which is to be used and the style in which the text is to be laid out, more particularly if the disk is to be used in typesetting and other production processes, and time is of the essence. For further comment on submission of text on disk, **see the note to Precedent One, Clause 2**.

The publishers may require the author to submit one or more hard copy printouts together with the disk or other electronic files for mark-up and estimating purposes.

(ii) Care over illustrations is especially necessary in educational works and publishers of, for example, primary school reading books or medical texts or technical manuals may consider using or adapting Precedent Twelve.

However, the costs of originating and producing full-colour highly illustrated school textbooks without the benefit of trade prices may make the need to pay the fee without a recurring royalty a condition of publishing the book. Most illustrators understand this, but it is particularly important that the terms of the assignment of copyright, and of any waiver of moral rights (**see Appendix H**), are clearly understood and that any agreement to return artwork to the artist for personal reasons does not entitle him/her to reuse it in reproduced form.

Sometimes, the cost of originating the artwork will not be borne entirely by the publishers. Specialist artwork, for example, may be prepared under the auspices of the authors within their own university department in return for which the publishers will pay a reasonable fee.

Where artwork is submitted by the author in the form of roughs it is wise to stipulate in the agreement who is to redraw the artwork and at whose cost.

Where valuable or irreplaceable transparencies are submitted by the author, arrangements should be made for their safe-keeping and eventual return to the author, and the issue of insurance should also be discussed.

(iii) If the author is to prepare additional material such as exercises, answers or an index for inclusion in the work at no additional cost to the publishers, then this should be made clear at the outset. If the index (or any other additional material) is not to be supplied by the author, this should likewise be stated in the agreement, together with details of who is responsible for the preparation of such material and for bearing any associated costs.

(iv) Where material taken from third party sources has been included in the work, the publishers will need to be aware of precisely what material has been used and from where it has been taken. If the publishers are to obtain permission for the use of such material on the author's behalf, then their in-house editorial staff will need to set the wheels in motion when the manuscript is delivered, in order to ensure that all the relevant permissions are obtained, appropriate acknowledgement copy prepared and any necessary fees paid in advance of publication. This is particularly important in respect of 'fast-track' textbooks with a very short production lead time.

1.2 More detailed guidance to authors in the preparation of their manuscripts may be available in the form of the publishers' 'Guide for Authors', often a short booklet in print or online form, produced in-house and providing broad guidelines on manuscript formatting and presentation, together with other useful information. Where such a document exists and it is expected that authors will follow the guidance it offers, it is wise to make reference to the fact in the agreement.

1.3 Lest the unthinkable happen, it is prudent for the publishers to recommend that the author retain for safe-keeping a copy of all the material he/she has submitted to the publishers.

1.4 Whilst the majority of manuscripts appear (more or less) on time, inevitably some do not despite numerous extensions to deadlines and coaxing and cajoling on the part of editors. In such circumstances the publishers may exercise one of two options: either to require the author to repay any advance payments made to him/her; or, alternatively, to require the author to give the publishers first option on publishing the manuscript if the author does subsequently complete it. In the case of educational books where syllabus changes and topicality of subject matter are of great importance, the publishers may often elect to do the former and terminate the agreement. **For further comment on late delivery see the note to Precedent One, Clause 2.**

1.5, 1.6 and 1.7 **See the note to Precedent One, Clause 3 (Acceptance and Conditions of Acceptance and Approval).**

[*number*] charts/maps/diagrams ready for reproduction/to be redrawn by the Publishers;

(iii) any additional matter for inclusion in the Work such as notes/appendices/exercises/answers and an index, if so required by the Publishers;

(iv) a complete list of all material taken by the Author from other sources for inclusion in the Work.

1.2 The Work shall be prepared in accordance with the Publishers' 'Guide for Authors' and submitted in a form ready and fit for editorial processing or in any other form agreed with the Publishers.

1.3 The Author shall retain a duplicate copy of the complete manuscript of the Work and all other material supplied by the Author to the Publishers for inclusion in the Work.

1.4 Should the Author neglect to deliver the complete manuscript, together with any illustrative and/or additional matter by the prescribed date (or by any extension mutually agreed in writing) the Publishers may, if they so wish, decline in writing to publish the Work in which case this Agreement shall terminate with immediate effect, subject to one or other of the following as the Publishers in their sole discretion shall elect:

EITHER:

1.4.1 the Author shall not be at liberty to arrange for the publication of the Work elsewhere without first offering the complete manuscript to the Publishers on the terms of this Agreement;

OR:

1.4.2 the Author shall, upon the Publishers' written request, repay to the Publishers any monies which have been paid to the Author under this Agreement.

1.5 The Publishers shall accept the Work provided that the complete manuscript and any illustrative and/or additional matter as delivered by the Author conforms in nature, scope, length and style to the specifications agreed in writing between the parties.

1.6 Should the manuscript not so conform the Publishers shall have the right either to decline in writing to publish the Work in which case this Agreement shall terminate with immediate effect and any sums which have been paid to the Author under this Agreement shall be immediately repayable, or as a condition of acceptance of the Work require the Author to make amendments to the Work to ensure that it does so conform.

1.8 The publishers will wish to seek to minimise their risk in respect of claims for libel, negligent misstatement, breach of copyright and the like. **See the note to Precedent One, Clause 5** for further discussion of this issue.

1.9 **See the note to Precedent One, Clause 6.**

2. Rights Granted to the Publishers

Traditionally, educational and academic publishers have sought to obtain assignments of copyright from their authors. Where copyright is not assigned, the publishers may seek to acquire the exclusive right of publication of the work throughout the world in all forms and in all languages for the full legal term of copyright and all renewals, revivals and extensions thereof, together with the exclusive authority to dispose of all subsidiary rights. Where digital rights are to be acquired as part of such a licence this should be clearly stipulated in the agreement. **For further commentary on the acquisition of rights, see the note to Precedent One, Clause 1.**

The coming into force of the Law of Property (Miscellaneous Provisions) Act 1994 has necessitated the replacement of the once familiar concept of the author as 'beneficial owner' with the author as the owner with 'full title guarantee' in the grant of rights clause. The enactment into UK law of the Duration of Copyright and Rights in Performances Regulations 1995 extended the period of copyright protection in the UK to the life of the author plus 70 years from the end of the year in which the author died (as is now the case throughout the territories of the EU albeit with some notable exceptions) and created a number of 'revived copyrights'. Additionally, publishers of materials which together may be considered to constitute a 'database' (e.g., directories, dictionaries, books of readings) will wish to obtain an assignment of the database rights in the material for the duration of such rights, in those cases where the author rather than the publishers is responsible for the creation of the database. The database right is a *sui generis* right conferred upon the creators of databases by the Copyright and Rights in Databases Regulations 1997 to protect them against unfair extraction of material from the database, which in itself would not meet the necessary threshold for copyright protection as a literary work in the majority of European jurisdictions. The right lasts for a period of 15 years from the end of the year in which the database was first completed, renewable for further periods of 15 years each time a substantial revision is made to the contents of the database. **See also Legal Developments: An Introduction**.

3. Payments to the Author

3.1.1 Advance payments to the author are no longer the exception in educational or academic publishing; however, they remain, by trade publishing standards, modest and rarely are large amounts paid on signature of the agreement. Whilst a token amount or 'carrot' may be paid on signature, the more substantial balance is likely to be paid on receipt and approval by (not delivery to) the publishers of the complete manuscript or on publication of the work, or alternatively on evidence of progress, or delivery of a given portion, for example, half, of the manuscript. Payment of the entire advance on signature of the agreement with the author is most unwise unless the manuscript has been received and approved. **See the note to Precedent One, Clause 16 (Advance Payments)** for further comment.

1.7 If the Author is unable or unwilling to make the amendments, or to arrange for them to be made, within such reasonable period of time as shall have been agreed with the Publishers then the Publishers, after consultation with the Author, shall have the right to employ a competent person or persons to make such amendments and to deduct the cost of doing so from any sum which may become due to the Author under this Agreement. The Work, as finally amended and marked for press, shall be subject to the Author's approval, such approval not to be unreasonably withheld or delayed.

1.8 The Publishers reserve the right to alter or to insist that the Author alters the text of the Work in such a way as may appear to the Publishers appropriate for the purpose of removing or amending any passage which on the advice of the Publishers' legal advisers may be considered objectionable or likely to be actionable at law without affecting the Author's liability under Clause 14 of this Agreement in respect of any passage not so removed or amended.

1.9 Unless prevented by circumstances beyond their control, or unless otherwise mutually agreed, the Publishers shall publish the Work at their own expense by the [*number*] day of [*month*] 20 [*year*], provided that the Author delivers to the Publishers an acceptable manuscript by the date (or by any extension mutually agreed in writing) provided for in this Clause.

2. Rights Granted to the Publishers

In consideration of the sums payable to the Author hereunder, the Author with full title guarantee hereby assigns where relevant by way of present assignment of future copyright to the Publishers the entire copyright and all other rights of a like nature in and to the Work throughout the world (including for the avoidance of doubt all Digital Publishing Rights) for the full legal term of copyright and all renewals, revivals and extensions of such period.

3. Payments to the Author

The Publishers shall make the following payments to the Author:

3.1 *Publication of the Work by the Publishers in book form:*

3.1.1 The sum of [*amount*] in advance and on account of any sums which may become due to the Author under this Agreement, payable in the following manner, namely:

3.1.2 In recent years the trend in educational and academic publishing has been away from payment of royalties based on the recommended retail price, to payment of royalties on the net sums received by the publishers. As a result, home and export sales are usually paid at the same rate and no particular provision need be made in the agreement for high discount export sales, as was previously the case. Royalties may be paid on a 'flat rate' or on a 'stepped' basis depending on the prevailing market conditions for the book and whether the publishers can afford it. The base rate for school textbook royalties is usually lower than for general trade works and the breakpoint for royalty rate rises tends to be higher. This is because such classroom textbooks depend on high print runs and low prices. (The argument is analogous to that which justifies the low opening royalty rate for mass market paperbacks). Where a 'stepped' royalty is agreed, it is usual for the rate of royalty to revert to the lower 'step' when the book is substantially reset for the issue of a new edition, the reason being that the publishers' origination costs for such an edition are often on a par with those for a new book. To maintain royalty payments to the author at the higher rate could endanger the price competitiveness of the work. The publishers will cut their costs and margins and can reasonably expect the author to accept a cut in royalty rates in order, to their mutual advantage, to maintain the work's success. For this reason many publishers in this sector insert in the royalty clause of their contracts a proviso of the kind offered here following 3.1.2(ii). As to what the words 'substantially reset the Work for the issue of a new edition' in this formula mean, the publishers will come to a reasonable view in the circumstances of each work: a rough and ready view would be that 'substantially' means a cost for corrections to text and illustrations of not less than one-third of the original cost of composition and origination.

For further comment on royalties and fees to the author, including provision for 'small reprint' royalties, **see the note to Precedent One, Clause 12 (Royalties Payable on Own Editions)**.

Educational and academic publishers will also wish to consider the inclusion of royalty clauses relating to sales of custom publications, that is, 'bespoke' publications created for a specific university or other institution comprising selected material from, possibly, several works by different authors published by the publishers, together with lecturer material to meet the requirements of a particular course. Consideration may also need to be given to bundling and value packs, that is, the provision of the work together with another work or works published by the publishers to meet specific market requirements or in the interests of increasing sales.

3.2 Although the rate of royalty payable to the author is provided for in the case of publication by the publishers of the work in adapted or abridged form, **see Note 8 to Precedent One, Clause 1**.

3.3.1 The number of educational and academic publishers with experience of publishing their authors' works in digital form continues to increase and clear norms or standards for the payment of royalties on digital products continue to emerge. With regard to royalty payments a cautious 'guesstimate' may be preferable to an agreement to agree and avoids a situation where the publishers are prevented from exercising their digital publishing rights due to inability to agree an appropriate royalty to the author, as will wording such as that offered in Clause 3.3.4. Clause 3.3.3 suggests a mechanism for review if, with the benefit of hindsight, the percentage suggested in the agreement should prove to be particularly disadvantageous from the author's or the publishers' point of view.

(i) The *sum* of [*amount*] on signature of this Agreement.

(ii) The sum of [*amount*] on the receipt and approval by the Publishers of the complete manuscript of the Work as prescribed in Clause 1 of this Agreement.

(iii) The sum of [*amount*] on publication of the Work.

3.1.2 A royalty based on the Net Sum Received on all such copies sold by the Publishers, wherever sold:

(i) A royalty of [*number*] per cent on the first [*number*] thousand copies sold.

(ii) A royalty of [*number*] per cent on all copies sold beyond the first [*number*] thousand.

Provided that should the revisions to a printing of the Work make it necessary in the opinion of the Publishers to substantially reset the Work for the issue of a new edition then the royalties payable on the sales of each such new edition shall commence at the original rate of [*number*] per cent based on the Net Sum Received on the first [*number*] thousand copies sold rising to [*number*] per cent based on the Net Sum Received on all copies sold thereafter, subject to the general terms and conditions of this Agreement.

3.2 *Publication of the Work by the Publishers in adapted or abridged form (other than as provided for in Clause 3.3):*

A royalty of [*number*] per cent based on the Net Sum Received on all such copies sold by the Publishers, wherever sold.

PROVIDED THAT:

No royalties shall be payable on copies of the Work sold at cost or less than cost, destroyed in transit or otherwise, presented to the Author, or distributed as specimen or inspection copies, the number and destination of such copies so distributed being left to the judgment and sole discretion of the Publishers.

3.3 *Publication of the* Work *(or any part of the Work) or any adaptation or abridgement of the Work, by the Publishers in Digital Form*:

3.3.1 Should the Publishers publish the Work (or any part of the Work), or any adaptation or abridgement of the Work, by exercising their Digital Publishing Rights, the Publishers shall pay to the Author a royalty of [*number*] per cent based on the Net Sum Received in respect of sales of the Work in whole or in part in Digital Form, subject to Clause 3.3.2.

3.3.2 Where the author's work is to be combined with the works of other authors in digital form, a formula needs to be agreed for dividing up the total royalty payable on the combined work between the authors of its constituent parts. In such cases, a pro rata arrangement seems sensible, although inevitably issues such as the relative eminence of the authors and the importance of the individual contributions to the work, may come into play.

4. Subsidiary Rights

4.1 Unlike trade publications, educational books are not written primarily with a view to their subsidiary rights earning potential. By their very nature, they are closely tied to school or university courses, examination syllabuses and other statutory requirements of the education system in the UK. Nevertheless, medicine, the 'hard' sciences, mathematics, computer science and history at undergraduate level travel reasonably well: school textbooks, as a general rule, less so. Bearing this in mind, any additional income generated for the author through the efforts of the publishers' subsidiary rights team is a plus. The subsidiary rights listed are those which educational, academic and professional publishers are most likely to exploit on behalf of the author. A 50:50 share of the income from the exploitation of such rights between author and publisher is often the norm in this sector, except in the case of digital rights, where no widely accepted norms have yet emerged. In agreeing a share of the income from the exploitation of such rights with the author, the publishers may wish to take account of any costs they themselves may incur, such as the provision of data to the licensee in a particular file format; the provision of explanatory documentation to accompany the data; and/or other materials.

Initiatives by both Google™ (Google™ Book Search) and Amazon (Search Inside!™) which enable readers to browse a work online within pre-determined limits, offer a potential additional revenue stream for both publishers and authors. The income generated comes not from the right to view, which is free, but rather from the sale of contextual advertising on the content pages where the work is displayed. This revenue is shared with the publishers and through them with authors. In addition, traditional sales revenue is driven by a 'click through' or link to an online bookstore. What remains to be seen is if and how publishers will share the new revenue source with authors. OUP, which has entered into an agreement with Google, has written to authors proposing to treat the income as subsidiary rights income and share it accordingly. Others may take a different view.

For a more comprehensive list of subsidiary rights and further commentary, **please see the note to Precedent One, Clause 14 (Subsidiary Rights)**.

3.3.2 If the Work (or any part of the Work), or any adaptation or abridgement of the Work, is combined in Digital Form together with other works published by the Publishers the rate of royalty payable to the Author shall be the same proportion of [*number*] per cent as the Work (or any part of the Work) or any adaptation or abridgement of the Work constitutes of the total combined works in Digital Form.

3.3.3 On the date falling [*number*] years from the date of first publication of the Work in Digital Form and every [*number*] years thereafter either party may serve notice on the other for a review of the rates of royalty provided for in this Clause 3.3 in which case the rates of royalty shall be considered in the light of comparable terms then prevailing in the trade and shall be altered with effect from the date of the notice to an extent that shall be fair and reasonable.

3.3.4 The existence of a dispute over the royalties shall not prevent the Publishers continuing to exploit the rights granted under this Agreement and the current royalties shall apply.

4. Subsidiary Rights

4.1 In consideration of the payment to the Author of the applicable percentages of the Publishers' receipts listed below, the Author grants to the Publishers the sole and exclusive right during the period of this Agreement to exercise and/or to license others to exercise all subsidiary rights in the Work including but not limited to the following:

	RIGHTS	PAYMENTS DUE TO THE AUTHOR IN RELATION TO THE EXERCISE OF THE SUBSIDIARY RIGHTS BY THIRD PARTIES
(i)	*Adaptation Rights* (i.e., the exclusive right to adapt the Work).	(*number*) per cent
(ii)	*Anthology and Quotation Rights* (i.e., the exclusive right to publish extracts from the Work, including all original maps, plans or other illustrations supplied by the Author).	(*number*) per cent
(iii)	*Book Club Rights* (i.e., the exclusive right to license the Work to Book Clubs and similar organisations on a separate royalty basis).	(*number*) per cent

5. Copyright Licensing Agency

The majority of educational publishers will have mandated the Copyright Licensing Agency (CLA) in the first instance to license the photocopying of extracts from their copyright material, for example, books, journals and periodicals, together with the right to license, within clearly defined limits, the 'retrodigitisation' of the material, that is, to convert and store digitally short extracts of material not previously available in digital form. As increasing numbers of resources are being created in digital form the demand for photocopied printed pages is likely to decrease. Consequently, CLA is currently working with publishers and other rights holders to increase the scope of certain of its licences, e.g. those for Schools and FE Institutions, to include copying of digital originals. Authors whose works are copied or converted to digital form under a licence granted by CLA are entitled to receive a half share of the income (fees) collected by CLA in respect of such copying or retrodigitisation payable via the Authors' Licensing and Collecting Society (ALCS); the balance being paid to the publishers via the Publishers' Licensing Society (PLS). **Please refer to Appendix E for details on the functions and operation of CLA**.

(iv)	*Digital Publishing Rights* (i.e., the exclusive right to publish the Work in Digital Form).	(*number*) per cent
(v)	*Paperback Rights* (i.e., the exclusive right to publish the Work in paperback format).	(*number*) per cent
(vi)	*Reprint Rights* (i.e., the exclusive right to reprint the Work).	(*number*) per cent
(vii)	*Translation Rights* (i.e., the exclusive right to translate and publish the Work in languages other than English).	(*number*) per cent
(viii)	*Online Preview Rights* (i.e., the exclusive right to license the use of the Work in its entirety in online Digital Form (free of charge to users) in search engines providing users with search functionality and limited access and display rights.)	(*number*) per cent
(ix)	*Non-commercial rights for the Reading Impaired* (i.e., the right to transcribe the Work into Braille or to record the Work for the sole use of the blind and reading impaired free of charge).	No payments to the Author

4.2 Should the Publishers themselves exercise any of the Subsidiary Rights the payments to the Author shall be mutually agreed in writing.

4.3 In respect of the exploitation by a third party of any subsidiary rights not specified above the payments to the Author shall be mutually agreed in writing.

5. Copyright Licensing Agency

5.1 The Publishers have mandated the Copyright Licensing Agency (CLA) to grant non-exclusive licences to reproduce by photocopying, other reprographic means and in Digital Form literary works published by the Publishers.

5.2 The Work is accordingly deemed to be included with such literary works and CLA shall divide the proceeds from such reproduction of the Work authorised by CLA equally between the Author and the Publishers.

6. Accounts

The policy of most major educational and academic publishers is to account to authors on a six-monthly basis rather than annually as was previously the case. Pressure to remain competitive, the influence of the authors' organisations and trade publishing practice have undoubtedly been instrumental in bringing about this change. For further discussion of good accounting practice, author access to the publishers' accounts, and reserves against returns, **refer to the Notes to Precedent One, Clauses 16 (Note 5) and 17**.

7. Tax

Under certain circumstances publishers may be required to deduct withholding or other taxes from royalties and this clause makes provision for such eventuality.

9. Copyright Material from Other Sources

9.1 and 9.2 The publishers will require details of any material taken by the author from third party sources. The reasons for this are several. First, the publishers will want to ensure that what they are getting is an original work, which does not draw excessively on material written by others. Secondly, the publishers will wish to ensure that, wherever necessary either they, or the author, obtain permission for the use of any third party material for the required markets; any necessary fees are paid; and appropriate acknowledgment is made in the publishers' publication. Finally, the publishers will not wish to incur the cost of permissions fees unnecessarily, that is, if the author could write original material instead. If the onus for clearance of such permissions lies with the author, the publishers will need to provide a clear brief on the exact rights to be cleared in terms of language, territory and media and also whether permissions should be recleared for the re-use of the material in sub-licensed editions (**see Precedent One, Note 4 to Clause 7 on textual material, and Note 2 to Clause 8 on illustrations**).

5.3 The Author shall receive the Author's share of such proceeds through the Authors' Licensing and Collecting Society (ALCS) in accordance with ALCS standard terms and conditions.

5.4 The provisions of this Clause shall survive the termination of this Agreement.

6. Accounts

6.1 The Publishers shall make up accounts for the sale of the Work twice yearly to [*date, month*] and [*date, month*] and accounts shall be sent to the Author together with any payment due within [*number*] months of each accounting date.

6.2 No account need be submitted unless specifically demanded nor payment made in respect of any period in which the sum due is less than £50.00 (fifty pounds) in which case the sum will be carried forward to the next accounting date.

7. Tax

The Publishers may deduct from any amount due to the Author under this Agreement, any sum that the Publishers are or may be under statutory obligation to deduct in respect of any tax, duty, or other similar levy.

8. Value Added Tax

All sums due to the Author under this Agreement are exclusive of Value Added Tax (VAT), which shall, where applicable, be paid in addition at the rate in force at the time of payment, provided the Author has supplied the Publishers with a current and valid VAT registration number.

9. Copyright Material from Other Sources

9.1 The Work shall not contain any textual or illustrative or other material taken from third party sources, except with the prior written consent of the Publishers and the copyright holders of such material.

9.2 The Author shall advise the Publishers on submission of the manuscript of the quotation or inclusion in the Work of any textual or illustrative or other material from any third party source and the Publishers shall obtain, so far as is possible, any necessary written permission from the copyright holders for the inclusion of such material and shall ensure that appropriate acknowledgment is made in the Work.

9.3 Where heavy use of third party material is unavoidable, for example, in course readers or anthologies, the publishers may undertake to pay the cost of including such material in the work up to an agreed maximum amount but, in such circumstances, the publishers may also wish to consider reducing the rate of royalty payable to the author. The publishers may further wish to reserve the right to require the author to substitute alternative material that is available at a more acceptable cost. **See also the note to Precedent One, Clause 7** re authors obtaining their own permissions.

12. Moral Rights

See Appendix H for a comprehensive explanation of moral rights. Publishers of works in digital form, in particular, may wish to consider obtaining a waiver (or partial waiver) of the author's moral rights of paternity and integrity in respect of exploitation in digital form. Digital products by their very nature may require the work to be presented in an order other than that originally anticipated by the author; its combination with the work of other authors; and manipulation or amendment of the text; all of which may be considered to be 'derogatory treatment', that is, treatment of the work which is prejudicial to the honour and reputation of the author. In addition, there may be difficulty in identifying the author as the author of the work each time material written by him/her is accessed on screen by the user.

9.3 The Publishers shall bear the cost of any necessary fees for permission to include textual, illustrative and other material in the Work up to a maximum of [*amount*] Should the permissions fees payable exceed [*amount*] the Publishers after consultation with the Author shall either:

(i) require the Author to substitute alternative materials which are available at a cost acceptable to the Publishers;

(ii) after first informing the Author in writing of the amount of the excess, deduct the same from any sum which may become due to the Author under this Agreement.

10. Control of Publication

The Publishers shall have the entire control of the production, publication, promotion, pricing, reprinting and sale of the Work, including but not limited to the design, format, paper, print run, binding, cover, jacket (if any), advertising and distribution of free copies for the press or otherwise. The right to reproduce the typography and design of the Work is reserved by the Publishers.

11. Inclusion of Author's Name

The Publishers shall include the Author's name with due prominence on the cover, jacket (if any) and title page of every print on paper copy and in any Digital Form version of the Work published by the Publishers and in all appropriate publicity material for the Work and shall impose a similar obligation in respect of any editions of the Work licensed by them.

12. Moral Rights

12.1 The Author hereby asserts to the Publishers *his/her* moral right to be identified as the Author of the Work in accordance with sections 77 and 78 of the Copyright, Designs and Patents Act 1988.

12.2 The Publishers undertake:

(i) to print the following notice with due prominence on every copy of the Work published by them:

'The right of [*name of author*] to be identified as author of this Work has been asserted by him/her in accordance with sections 77 and 78 of the Copyright, Designs and Patents Act 1988';

(ii) to make it a condition of contract with any licensee concerning any edition of the Work to be published in the United Kingdom

13. Copyright Notice

See note to Precedent One, Clause 19.

14. Warranties and Indemnity

See note to Precedent One, Clause 5.

that a notice of assertion in the same terms as above shall be printed in every edition published by such licensee.

12.3 No accidental or inadvertent failure by the Publishers or by any third party to include such a notice shall constitute a breach of this Agreement or the Author's rights.

13. Copyright Notice

All copies of the Work published by the Publishers shall bear on the title verso a copyright notice comprising the copyright symbol, the name of the copyright holder and the year of first publication.

14. Warranties and Indemnity

14.1 The Author hereby warrants to the Publishers that:

(i) the Author is the legal owner with full title guarantee of the copyright in the Work, and has the right and power to make this Agreement;

(ii) the Work is an original work, except for material in the public domain and such excerpts from other works as may be included with the written permission of the copyright owner, and will in no way whatever give rise to a violation of any existing copyright or a breach of any existing agreement (including any contract of employment), or infringe any duty of confidence or duty to respect privacy or any other right (including any moral right) of any person; and

(iii) all and any software programs prepared by the Author for inclusion in the Work have been prepared with due care and attention, have been adequately tested and are free from harmful code of any description; and

(iv) the Work contains nothing obscene, indecent, defamatory or libellous and all statements contained in it purporting to be facts are true; and

(v) any recipe, formula or instruction contained in the Work will not, if followed accurately, cause injury or illness to or damage the user.

14.2 The Author will indemnify the Publishers against any loss, injury or damage (including any legal costs or expenses and any compensation costs and disbursements paid by the Publishers on the advice of the

15. Proof Correction

See note to Precedent One, Clause 11. All alterations to proof, particularly at a late stage in the production process, are very expensive: many texts for technical markets, for example, need not only careful but formal signed approval by the author at a very early stage of, for example, the accuracy of technical drawings, the cropping of photographs, or the positioning of colour illustrations. If this is not done, costs of alteration multiply and any formal contractual liability of the author may be quite without value.

More generally, printers in the final account for a book itemise all corrections simply as 'corrections' – as indeed from their point of view they are. In the making of a book, page for page, there are however many elements contributed by the author and the publishing staff and corrections to the production files of a complex textbook will often be a mixture of author's errors not previously noticed, of 'house' editorial second, and third, thoughts on some vital point, of design adjustment, etc. No contractual formula can really deal with this vexed point and editors must be on the watch in order to settle apportionment at the final stages of production. Otherwise, after the printer's bill has come in, and when the first royalty account goes out, the unfortunate author may find his/her opening royalties virtually wiped out by a massive 'corrections' charge which is only partly his/her liability. Clause 15.2 suggests a formula to pre-empt unanticipated costs.

16. Author's Copies

See Note 2 (iii) to the Preamble to this Precedent **and also note to Precedent One, Clause 21**.

Publishers' legal advisers to compromise or settle any claim) arising out of any breach or alleged breach of the warranties.

14.3 The warranties and indemnity shall survive the termination of this Agreement.

15. Proof Correction

15.1 The Author undertakes to read, check, and correct the proofs of the Work and return them to the Publishers within such period of time as shall have been mutually agreed, failing which the Publishers shall consider the proofs passed for press.

15.2 Costs of all corrections and alterations made by the Author in the finished artwork and the proofs (artists', copy-editors' and printers' errors and those alterations made necessary by changes in professional practice excepted) in excess of 10% (ten per cent) of the cost of origination of the Work shall be borne by the Author provided that:

(i) before passing proofs for press the Publishers shall advise the Author in writing of the amount of the excess;

(ii) the Author shall have the opportunity exercisable within 14 days of receipt of written notice from the Publishers to remove or reduce such corrections and alterations.

15.3 Should any charge arise under this Clause the amount may be deducted from any sums which may become due to the Author under this Agreement.

16. Author's Copies

The Author shall be entitled to receive on publication six free copies of the first and any new edition of the Work and to purchase on normal domestic trade terms additional copies for personal use but not for resale.

17. Remaindering

17.1 The Publishers shall be entitled not less than [*number*] years from the date of first publication of the Work to dispose of copies as a remainder at a reduced price and shall pay to the Author the rate of royalty based on the Net Sum Received provided for in Clause 3.1.2 on such sales, except that where copies are sold at cost or less than cost, no royalty shall be payable.

18. Revision of the Work

(i) Most successful educational and academic books need bringing up to date at regular intervals in order to retain market share, and control of the decision about the need for the author to start work on a revised or completely new edition should be the publishers' (**cf the view offered at Precedent One, Clause 22 and note**), since they are in most cases very much closer to the needs of the market than perhaps the author is, and also have to juggle with the practicalities of stock levels, small 'bridging' reprints, etc.

(ii) For professional works, for example, in law, accountancy and medicine where a work of authority may command the market for several generations with updates, some very vexed questions may arise unless the publisher grapples categorically with the consequences of the author's death. The precedent tries to balance the right of the author's estate to continue to draw income from his/her authorship with the need of the publishers to find a new contributor to the work without either overloading the royalty costs or damaging heavily the market power of the work through having to withdraw the original author's name.

(iii) Following the death of the author payments to the author's representative(s) will only be made subsequent to the publishers having sight of Probate or other evidence of entitlement.

17.2 The Publishers shall give the Author six free copies of the Work under this Clause and the first option for a period of six weeks to purchase copies at the said reduced price.

18. Revision of the Work

18.1 If in the opinion of the Publishers a new edition of the Work is desirable or necessary, they shall so notify the Author in writing.

18.2 The Author undertakes to revise and edit the Work and to supply to the Publishers by such time as shall be mutually agreed any new matter that may be needed to keep the Work up to date, such new matter to be supplied at no cost to the Publishers.

18.3 Should the Author neglect or be unable or unwilling to supply such new matter or to revise or edit the Work, the Publishers may after written notice to the Author arrange for a competent person or persons to do so and may deduct the expense from any sums which may become payable to the Author or the Author's representatives under this Agreement.

18.4 In the event of the death of the Author the following provisions shall apply:

(i) all sums payable under the terms of this Agreement shall be paid to the deceased Author's representatives on any edition in print at the time of his/her death and on any reprints of such an edition.

(ii) all sums payable under the terms of this Agreement shall be paid to the deceased Author's representatives on further editions (including any reprints) published subsequent to the Author's death, less any fees and/or royalties payable to an editor or reviser in the course of preparing such editions and reprints for press, provided that such editions and reprints contain material written by the Author.

18.5 The Publishers may display in the revised Work and in all appropriate publicity material for the revised Work, the name of the person or persons who revised the Work together with the name of the Author. Should the Author or the Author's representatives object to having the Author's name acknowledged in connection with the revised Work, the Author or the Author's representatives shall so notify the Publishers in writing upon receipt of the written notice from the Publishers provided for in Clause 18.3.

19. Infringement of Copyright

See note to Precedent One, Clause 20.

20. Out of Print

See note to Precedent One, Clause 25 (Out of Print). With the ability of educational and academic publishers to reprint books to order by means of 'print on demand' systems, whether in-house or out-sourced, the concept of a work going out of print must be reconsidered. Publishers may wish to consider defining the term 'out of print' by reference to the number of copies of the print on paper edition sold in the previous two accounting periods, or alternatively, by the number of copies sold by means of the publishers' print on demand service over the same period. However, the mere ability to produce and sell a single copy of an author's work, should the occasion arise, cannot in itself justify retaining publishing rights, which before the advent of 'print on demand' would in many instances have been reverted to the author. Authors whose contracts did not anticipate the availability of print on demand systems may, justifiably, object to the automatic inclusion of their work in a 'print on demand' programme and publishers will have to put systems in place to ensure that authors are duly informed about such programmes and the necessary consents obtained from them.

For new contracts Publishers may wish to address the issue of print on demand publishing from the outset. Alternatives to Clauses 20 and 21 are suggested below:

20. Out of Print

20.1 Should sales of the Work decline to the extent that in the Publishers' reasonable commercial judgement it is no longer economic to keep it in print, the Publishers shall automatically include the Work in the Publishers' Print On-demand Programme unless or until the Publishers receive written notice from the Author giving notice of termination of this Agreement in accordance with the provisions of Clause 21 hereof.

20.2 Should the Work be unsuitable for inclusion in the Publishers' Print On-demand Programme the Work shall be allowed to go out of print and the Author shall have the right on written notice to the Publishers to request that rights in the Work revert to the Author in accordance with the provisions of Clause 21 hereof.

21. Termination

21.1 This Agreement shall automatically terminate if the Publishers go into liquidation other than voluntary liquidation for the purpose of reconstruction, or have a receiver

19. Infringement of Copyright

19.1 It is agreed that if at any time during the continuance of this Agreement the Publishers consider that the copyright in the Work has been infringed they shall be at liberty to take such steps as they may consider necessary in their sole discretion to deal with the matter and if they wish to take legal proceedings they shall on giving the Author an undertaking to pay all costs and expenses and to indemnify the Author against all liability for costs, be entitled to use the Author's name as a party to such proceedings but at the same time to control, settle or compromise as they think fit.

19.2 The Author agrees to execute any documents and do any acts reasonably appropriate to give effect to the rights of the Publishers granted by this clause.

19.3 Any profits or damages which may be recovered in respect of any infringement of the copyright shall after deduction of all costs and expenses be divided equally between the parties hereto.

20. Out of Print

20.1 If the Work is allowed to go out of print and is not available in any English language edition published by the Publishers or licensed by them, the Author may give nine months' written notice to the Publishers to put in hand a reprint or a new edition. For the purpose of this Clause 20.1 'out of print' shall mean when fewer than [*number*] physical copies of the print on paper edition of the Work remain in the Publishers' warehouse and the Publishers have no plans for a reissue or a new edition.

20.2 The Author's requirements that the Work be reprinted shall be regarded as satisfied if at the time of the Author giving notice the Publishers have sub-licensed rights for an English language edition of the Work scheduled for publication within 12 months of such notice being given.

20.3 Should the Publishers fail to comply with such notice, other than through circumstances beyond their control, all rights in the Work granted to the Publishers under this Agreement shall upon expiration of the said notice revert to the Author in accordance with the provisions of Clause 21.

21. Termination

21.1 This Agreement shall automatically terminate if the Publishers go into liquidation other than voluntary liquidation for the purpose

or an administrative receiver appointed over the whole or any substantial part of the Publishers' assets.

21.2 The Author may terminate this Agreement by summary notice in writing to the Publishers if:

(i) the Work is allowed to go out of print and is not available in any edition (excluding any edition published under the Publishers' Print On-demand Programme) or format in the English language or in any medium, and the Publishers shall fail to put in hand a reissue or a new edition within nine months of having received a written request from the Author;

(ii) the Publishers are in material breach of any of their obligations under this Agreement and shall not have remedied such breach to the extent possible within three months after written notification from the Author giving details of such breach.

21.3 Upon termination of this Agreement under Clauses 20, 21.1 or 21.2 hereof, all rights in the Work granted to the Publishers herein shall revert to the Author without prejudice to:

(i) all rights of the Publishers and any third party in respect of any agreement properly entered into by the Publishers with such third party prior to the date of such termination;

(ii) any claim which the Author may have for monies due and/or damages and/or otherwise;

(iii) the right of the Publishers to continue to sell any copies of the Work in their possession, custody or control at the date of termination.

A definition of 'the Publishers' Print On-demand Programme' should be inserted in Clause 29.

See note to Precedent One, Clause 24.

22. Competing Works

Scientific, technical, medical and professional publishers may want a competing works clause which suits the specific needs of their authors; the precedent offers one such formula. Consideration should also be given to the duration of the restriction, that is, whether it is for the entire period during which the work remains in print, or for a given period of years from the date of first publication of the work and whether the educational level, subject matter and anticipated target market or geographical market for the competing work can be more tightly drawn, so that the author is not unfairly prevented from earning his living, but the publishers' investment in the work is adequately protected. Reasonableness is the key.

of reconstruction, or have a receiver or an administrative receiver appointed over the whole or any substantial part of the Publishers' assets.

21.2 The Author may terminate this Agreement by summary notice in writing to the Publishers if the Publishers are in material breach of any of their obligations under this Agreement and shall not have remedied such breach to the extent possible within three months after written notification from the Author giving details of such breach.

21.3 On termination of this Agreement under Clauses 20, 21.1 or 21.2, all rights in the Work granted to the Publishers under this Agreement shall revert to the Author without prejudice to:

(i) all rights of the Publishers and any third party in respect of any agreement properly entered into by the Publishers with such third party prior to the date of such termination;

(ii) any claim which the Author may have for monies due and/or damages and/or otherwise;

(iii) the right of the Publishers to continue to sell any copies of the Work in their possession, custody or control at the date of termination.

22. Competing Works

22.1 While the Work is in course of preparation or in current publication:

22.1.1 the Author shall be entitled to use material written or compiled by him/her for the purposes of the Work in articles submitted to learned or professional journals, in papers presented at professional conferences; in connection with training courses and for the Author's professional purposes generally, provided that the Author so advises the Publishers in advance and makes appropriate acknowledgment to the Work and the Publishers, but

22.1.2 the Author shall not without the prior written consent of the Publishers (which shall not be unreasonably withheld) write, edit or contribute, jointly or severally, to any work which may reasonably be considered by the Publishers to compete with or prejudice sales of the Work or the exploitation of any of the rights granted to the Publishers under this Agreement.

23. Arbitration

For details of the Publishers Association's Informal Disputes Settlement Scheme **see note to Precedent One, Clause 30**.

23. Arbitration

If any difference shall arise between the Author and the Publishers touching the meaning of this Agreement or the rights and liabilities of the parties hereto, the same shall be referred to the arbitration of two persons (one to be named by each party) or their umpire in accordance with the provisions of the Arbitration Act 1996 or any amending or substituted statute for the time being in force.

24. Entire Agreement

24.1 This Agreement sets forth the entire agreement between the parties at the date of this Agreement and supersedes any prior written or oral agreement between them with respect to the subject matter of this Agreement.

24.2 Any amendment of or variation to this Agreement must be in writing and signed by both parties.

25. Applicable Law

This Agreement shall be governed by and construed in accordance with the laws of England whose courts shall have exclusive jurisdiction.

26. Headings

Headings to the clauses of are for guidance only and are not to be taken into account in the construction of this Agreement which has been prepared in [*number*] copies.

27. Notices

Any notice, consent or the like required or permitted to be given under this Agreement shall be in writing and shall be deemed sufficiently given as of the date delivered or mailed, postage pre-paid by registered post or the equivalent to the address of the party set out above or at such other address as any party may designate in writing to the other.

28. Rights of Third Parties

The parties do not intend that any term of this Agreement shall be enforceable solely by virtue of the Contracts (Rights of Third Parties) Act 1999 by any person who is not a party to this Agreement save that a person who is a

permitted successor to or assignee of the rights of a party is deemed to be a party to this Agreement and the rights of such successor or assignee shall be regulated by the terms of this Agreement.

29. Definitions

In this Agreement the following words and expressions shall have the following meanings unless the context requires otherwise:

'Associated Company'	shall have the meaning attributed to that term in sections 416 (et seq) of the Income and Corporation Taxes Act 1988, as amended;
'Digital Form'	shall include but shall not be limited to offline electronic storage and information retrieval systems of a digital, optical or magnetic nature including (but not limited to) floppy disk, CD-ROM, DVD, ROM-card, compact disc, video, integrated circuit; mobile and hand-held devices; online transmission by satellite and other means of telecommunication; and any other Digital means of reproduction, publication, dissemination and transmission (including online broadcasts made available through streaming and downloads) whether now in existence or hereafter invented;
'Digital Publishing Rights'	means the right to produce, copy, store, publish and sell, to perform, display, stream, download, transfer, broadcast and transmit the Work whether in whole or in part, adapted or abridged, on its own or in combination with another work or works, together with any accompanying sounds and images, in any manner and in any Digital Form and to license the foregoing rights in digital versions of the Work;
'Net Sum Received'	means the amount received by the Publishers and any amounts receivable by the Publishers after deducting any discounts granted by the Publishers and any sales or other similar taxes or duties incurred by the Publishers in respect of sales of copies of the Work;
'Work'	means the Work (and any new editions of the Work) written by the Author under this

30. Assignment

See note to Precedent One, Preamble.

Agreement together with any abridgements, adaptations, or digital versions of the Work;

'[*insert name*] Group' means any Associated Company of [*name*] Limited.

30. Assignment

The Publishers may assign any benefit or transfer, delegate or subcontract any of their duties or obligations under this Agreement to any company within the [*name*] Group without the prior written consent of the Author.

AS WITNESS THE HANDS OF THE PARTIES

Signed by ....

[*author*]

Signed by ....

Director

For and on behalf of [*name of publishers*] Limited

PRECEDENT THREE

Agreement for General Editor of a Book

Many academic and professional books are works with multiple contributors, compiled under the direction of a general editor, a specialist in the subject concerned. The general editor is responsible for briefing and dealing with individual contributors, overseeing progress on the work and acting as a contact point between the contributors and the publishing house. The general editor will normally provide an introduction to the book and may in addition contribute one or more chapters or articles to the book.

The general editor will normally receive an advance payment and modest royalty percentage on sales, whilst individual contributions are normally paid for on a lump sum basis (**see Precedent Four**).

Many of the general provisions of this model parallel those in **Precedent Two**.

1. Responsibilities of the General Editor in Preparation of the Work

This clause sets out the responsibilities of the general editor during the preparation stages of the work.

The contributions written by the general editor personally will depend on what has been agreed with the publishers; this precedent covers provision of an overall introduction and for one or more sections of the work (1.5).

Because of the complexity of multi-author works, the general editor is responsible for ensuring that each contribution is submitted promptly and in suitable form (1.3).

In this precedent, responsibility for arrangements for assignment of copyright from individual contributors rests with the publishers, who would then draw up a separate letter of agreement with each contributor (**see Precedent Four**). An alternative would be for that responsibility to lie with the general editor, in which case alternative wording here might be:

> 'The General Editor shall be responsible for securing from the Contributors written confirmation of assignment of copyright in each contribution to the Publishers.'

THIS AGREEMENT is made this [*number*] day of [*month*] 20 [*year*] BETWEEN [*name*] of [*address*] (hereinafter termed 'the General Editor', which expression shall, where the context admits, include the General Editor's executors, administrators or assigns) of the one part and [*company name*] (registered number) of [*address*] (hereinafter termed 'the Publishers', which expression shall, where the context admits, include the Publishers' successors in business and assigns) of the other part,

WHEREBY it is agreed as follows concerning a work to be edited by the General Editor at present entitled: [*name of work*] (hereinafter termed 'the Work')

1. Responsibilities of the General Editor in Preparation of the Work

The responsibilities of the General Editor shall be as follows:

1.1 The General Editor shall be responsible for commissioning contributions to the Work from appropriately qualified third parties (hereinafter termed the Contributors) on terms to be agreed with the Publishers. The final choice of Contributors is subject to the written approval of the Publishers (such approval not to be unreasonably withheld).

1.2 The General Editor shall be responsible for briefing each Contributor on the nature and length of *his/her* contribution and for ensuring that the content of each contribution meets the designated requirements of the Publishers for the Work.

1.3 The General Editor shall be responsible for ensuring that each Contributor delivers *his/her* contribution in appropriate form and in due time to enable the General Editor to meet the Publishers' required schedule as specified in Clause 2.1 hereof.

1.4 The General Editor shall be responsible for the overall checking and editing of each contribution and (where appropriate) for arranging for reviews of individual contributions by appropriate external advisers.

1.5 The General Editor shall be responsible for writing an Introduction to the Work of no less than [*number*] and no more than [*number*] words and also for writing [*number*] contribution/s to the work (hereinafter termed the General Editor's part in the Work).

1.6 The General Editor shall, if so required by the Publishers, supply an index for inclusion in the Work. If the General Editor is unable for any reason to supply the said index, the Publishers may make appropriate arrangements for the supply of the said index and may deduct the

2. Delivery and Acceptance of the Work

This clause covers the general editor's responsibility for the delivery of the complete text of the work in a form acceptable to the publishers. The general editor's responsibilities for briefing and vetting contributions under the terms of Clause 1 should ideally mean that no radical amendments or replacement of contributors is required at this stage.

expense thereof from any sum which may become payable to the General Editor under the terms of this Agreement.

1.7 The Publishers undertake to be responsible for arranging separate letters of agreement to each Contributor to cover assignment of copyright in each contribution to the Publishers and also to cover separate payment to each Contributor.

2. Delivery and Acceptance of the Work

2.1 The General Editor agrees to deliver to the Publishers by the [*number*] day of [*month*] 20 [*year*]:

(i) the complete manuscript of the Work consisting of not more than [*number*] and not less than [*number*] words as an e-mail attachment in [*specify word processing package to be used*] format together with one identical hard copy printed out in double line spacing;

(ii) artwork or roughs for a maximum of [*number*] line drawings (the finished artwork for which shall be prepared by the Publishers); a maximum of [*number*] half-tones/colour transparencies; a maximum of [*number*] charts/maps/diagrams ready for reproduction/to be redrawn by the Publishers;

(iii) any additional matter for inclusion in the Work such as notes/ appendices/exercises/answers and an index, if so required by the Publishers;

(iv) a complete list of all copyright material taken by the General Editor and the Contributors from other sources for inclusion in the Work.

2.2 The Work shall be prepared in accordance with the Publishers' 'Guide for Authors' and submitted in a form ready and fit for editorial processing or in any other form agreed with the Publishers.

2.3 The General Editor shall retain a duplicate copy of the complete manuscript of the Work and all other material supplied by the General Editor to the Publishers for inclusion therein.

2.4 Should the General Editor neglect to deliver the complete manuscript, together with any illustrative and/or additional matter by the prescribed date (or by any extension thereto mutually agreed in writing) the Publishers may, if they so wish, decline to publish the Work in which case this Agreement shall terminate with immediate effect, subject to

one or other of the following as the Publishers in their sole discretion shall elect:

EITHER:

2.4.1 The General Editor shall not be at liberty to arrange for the publication of the Work elsewhere without first offering the complete manuscript to the Publishers on the terms of this Agreement;

OR:

2.4.2 The General Editor shall, upon the Publishers' written request, repay to the Publishers any monies which have been paid to the General Editor under this Agreement.

2.5 The Publishers shall accept the Work provided that the complete manuscript and any illustrative and/or additional matter as delivered by the General Editor conforms in nature, scope, length and style to the specifications agreed in writing between the parties hereto.

2.6 Should the manuscript not so conform the Publishers shall have the right either to decline in writing to publish the Work in which case this Agreement shall terminate with immediate effect and any sums which have been paid to the General Editor under this Agreement shall be immediately repayable, or as a condition of acceptance of the Work require the General Editor to make amendments to the Work to ensure that it does so conform.

2.7 If the General Editor is unable or unwilling to make the amendments, or to arrange for them to be made within such reasonable period of time as shall have been agreed with the Publishers, then the Publishers after consultation with the General Editor shall have the right to employ a competent person or persons to make such amendments and to deduct the cost of doing so from any sum which may become due to the General Editor under this Agreement. The Work, as finally amended and marked for press, shall be subject to the General Editor's approval, such approval not to be unreasonably withheld or delayed.

2.8 The Publishers reserve the right to alter or to insist that the General Editor alters the text of the Work in such a way as may appear to the Publishers appropriate for the purpose of removing or amending any passage which on the advice of the Publishers' legal advisers may be considered objectionable or likely to be actionable at law without affecting the General Editor's liability under Clause 15 hereof in respect of any passage not to be removed or amended.

2.9 Unless prevented by circumstances beyond their control, or unless otherwise mutually agreed, the Publishers shall publish the Work at

3. Rights Granted to the Publishers

Here the general editor assigns copyright in his or her own part in the work.

4. Payments to the General Editor

This clause outlines payments to the general editor; an advance payable in instalments and a modest royalty on sales (the percentage is likely to be less than 5%). Since the demise of the UK Net Book Agreement, payment for educational and academic titles will almost certainly be based on the publishers' net receipts (**see also Precedent Two**).

their own expense by the [*number*] day of [*month*] 20 [*year*], provided that the General Editor delivers an acceptable manuscript by the date (or by any extension thereto mutually agreed in writing) provided for in this Clause.

3. Rights Granted to the Publishers

In consideration of the sums payable to the General Editor hereunder, the General Editor hereby assigns where relevant by way of present assignment of future copyright to the Publishers the entire copyright and all other rights of a like nature in the General Editor's part in and to the Work inclusive of *his/her* contribution/s written for inclusion therein throughout the world (including for the avoidance of doubt all Digital Publishing Rights) for the full legal term of copyright and all renewals, revivals and extensions of such period.

4. Payments to the General Editor

The Publishers shall make the following payments to the General Editor, namely:

4.1 *Publication of the Work by the Publishers in book form*

4.1.1 The sum of [*amount*] in advance and on account of any sums which may become due to the General Editor under this Agreement, payable in the following manner, namely:

(i) The sum of [*amount*] on signature of this Agreement.

(ii) The sum of [*amount*] on the receipt and approval by the Publishers of the complete manuscript as prescribed in Clause 2 of this Agreement.

(iii) The sum of [*amount*] on publication of the Work.

4.1.2 A royalty based on the Net Sum Received by the Publishers on all such copies sold by the Publishers, wherever sold:

(i) A royalty of [*number*] per cent on the first [*number*] thousand copies sold.

(ii) A royalty of [*number*] per cent on all copies sold beyond the first [*number*] thousand.

Provided that should the revisions to a printing of the Work make it necessary in the opinion of the Publishers to substantially

reset the Work for the issue of a new edition then the royalties payable on the sales of each such new edition shall commence at the original rate of [*number*] per cent based on the Net Sum Received on the first [*number*] thousand copies sold rising to [*number*] per cent based on the Net Sum Received on all copies sold thereafter, subject to the general terms and conditions of this Agreement.

4.2 *Publication of the Work by the Publishers in adapted or abridged form (other than as provided for in Clause 4.3 hereof):*

A royalty of [*number*] per cent based on the Net Sum Received on all such copies of the Work sold by the Publishers, wherever sold

PROVIDED THAT:

No royalties shall be payable on copies of the Work sold at cost or less than cost, destroyed in transit or otherwise, presented to the General Editor and the Contributors, or distributed as specimen or inspection copies, the number and destination of such copies so distributed being left to the judgment and sole discretion of the Publishers.

4.3 *Publication of the Work (or any part thereof) or any adaptation or abridgement of the Work by the Publishers in Digital Form:*

4.3.1 Should the Publishers publish the Work (or any part of the Work) or any adaptation/or abridgement of the Work by exercising their Digital Publishing Rights, the Publishers shall pay to the General Editor a royalty of [*number*] per cent based on the Net Sum Received in respect of sales of the Work in whole or in part in Digital Form, subject to Clause 4.3.2 hereof.

4.3.2 If the Work (or any part thereof), or any adaptation or abridgement of the Work, is combined in Digital Form together with other works published by the Publishers the rate of royalty payable to the General Editor shall be the same proportion of [*number*] per cent as the Work (or any part of the Work) or any adaptation or abridgement of the Work constitutes of the total combined works in Digital Form.

4.3.3 On the date falling [*number*] years from the date of first publication of the Work in Digital Form and every [*number*] years thereafter either party may serve notice on the other for a review of the rates of royalty provided for in this Clause 4.3 in which case the rates of royalty shall be considered in the light of comparable terms then prevailing in the trade and shall be altered with effect from the date of the notice to an extent that shall be fair and reasonable.

5. Subsidiary Rights

This precedent provides for the sale of a range of subsidiary rights in the work, with a share of the proceeds to be divided between the general editor and individual contributors. If, however, the contributors were to be paid an outright fee for their work with no provision for any share of rights income, a smaller percentage of the proceeds would be payable to the general editor alone.

4.3.4 The existence of a dispute over the royalties shall not prevent the Publishers continuing to exploit the rights granted under this Agreement and the current royalties shall apply.

5. Subsidiary Rights

5.1 The General Editor grants to the Publishers the sole and exclusive right during the period of this Agreement to exercise and/or to license others to exercise all the subsidiary rights in the Work including but not limited to the following. The applicable percentages of the Publishers' receipts listed shall be divided equally between the General Editor of the one part and the Contributors (including the General Editor acting as a contributor) of the other part, except when any contribution is sold separately, quoted from exclusively or translated exclusively in whole or in part, in which case all monies due in respect thereof shall only be paid to the Contributor who wrote the contribution concerned.

	RIGHTS	PAYMENTS DUE TO THE GENERAL EDITOR/ CONTRIBUTORS
(i)	*Adaptation rights* (i.e., the exclusive right to Adapt the Work)	*(number) per cent*
(ii)	*Anthology and quotation rights* (i.e., the exclusive right to authorise the reproduction in other publications of extracts and quotations from the Work, including any maps, charts, diagrams, or other illustrations original to the General Editor or the Contributors)(*number*) per cent	
(iii)	*Book club rights* (i.e., the right to license the Work to book clubs and similar organisations on a separate royalty basis)	(*number*) per cent
(iv)	*Digital publishing rights* (i.e., the exclusive right to license the use of the Work in Digital Form*)*	*(number) per cent*
(v)	*Reprint rights* (i.e., the exclusive right to license a reprint of the Work to another Publisher)	(*number*) per cent
(vi)	*Paperback rights* (i.e., the exclusive right to license the use of the Work in *paperback* format)	(*number*) per cent
(vii)	*Translation rights* (i.e., the exclusive right to license the exploitation of the Work in languages other than English)	(*number*) per cent

(viii) *Online preview rights* (i.e., the exclusive right to license the use of the Work in its entirety in Online Digital Form (free of charge to users) in search engines providing users with search functionality and limited access and display rights) (*number*) per cent

(ix) *Non-commercial rights for the reading impaired* (i.e., the right to transcribe the Work into Braille or to record the Work for the sole use of the blind and reading impaired free of charge) No payment

5.2 Should the Publishers themselves exercise any of the Subsidiary Rights the payments to the General Editor and Contributors shall be mutually agreed in writing.

5.3 In respect of the exploitation by a third party of any Subsidiary Rights not specified above the payments to the General Editor and Contributors shall be mutually agreed in writing.

6. Copyright Licensing Agency

6.1 The Publishers have mandated the Copyright Licensing Agency (CLA) to grant non-exclusive licences to reproduce by photocopying, other reprographic means and in Digital Form literary works published by the Publishers.

6.2 The Work is accordingly deemed to be included with such literary works and CLA shall divide the proceeds from such reproduction of the Work authorised by CLA equally between the General Editor and the Publishers.

6.3 The General Editor shall receive the General Editor's share of such proceeds through the Authors' Licensing and Collecting Society (ALCS) in accordance with ALCS standard terms and conditions.

6.4 The provisions of this Clause shall survive the termination of this Agreement.

7. Accounts

7.1 The Publishers shall make up accounts for the sale of the Work twice yearly to [*date, month*] and [*date, month*] and accounts shall be sent to the General Editor together with any payment due within [*number*] months of each accounting date.

10. Copyright Material from Other Sources

As with a single author work, it is vital that the publishers are alerted to the use of external textual or illustrative material. The question of responsibility for clearance of such permissions and payment of any fees to the external copyright owners will depend on what has been agreed between the publishers, the general editor and the contributors themselves. This precedent assumes that the contributors will be responsible (**see Precedent Four, Clause 2**) and that the general editor will have overall responsibility for ensuring that clearance has been obtained.

In some cases, the publishers may be prepared to reimburse the cost of permissions clearance up to an agreed amount. In such cases a further sub-clause could be added as follows:

> '10.3 The Publishers agree to reimburse the cost of any necessary fees for permission to include such material in the Work up to a maximum of [*amount*]. Should the permissions fees payable exceed [*amount*] the Publishers shall after consultation with the General Editor exercise one of the following options:
>
> (i) require the General Editor to substitute alternative materials which are acceptable to the Publishers;
>
> (ii) after first informing the General Editor in writing of the amount of the excess, deduct the same from any sums which may become due to the General Editor and/or the individual Contributors under this Agreement as appropriate.'

7.2 No account need be submitted unless specifically demanded nor payment made in respect of any period in which the sum due is less than £50.00 (fifty pounds) in which case the sum will be carried forward to the next accounting date.

8. Tax

The Publishers may deduct from any amount due to the General Editor under this Agreement, any sum that the Publishers are or may be under statutory obligation to deduct in respect of any tax, duty, or other similar levy.

9. Value Added Tax

All sums due to the General Editor hereunder are exclusive of Value Added Tax, which shall, where applicable, be paid in addition at the rate in force at the time of payment, provided the General Editor has supplied the Publishers with a current and valid VAT registration number.

10. Copyright Material from Other Sources

10.1 The Work shall not contain any textual or illustrative material taken from third party sources, except with the prior written consent of the Publishers and copyright holders of such material.

10.2 The General Editor shall advise the Publishers of the quotation or inclusion in the Work of any textual or illustrative material from any third party source and shall ensure that written permission has been secured from and fees paid to the copyright holders for the inclusion of such material. The Publishers shall ensure that appropriate acknowledgment is made in the Work.

11. Control of Publication

The Publishers shall have the entire control of the production, publication, pricing, reprinting and sale of the Work, including but not limited to the design, format, paper, print run, binding, cover, jacket (if any), advertising and distribution of free copies for the press or otherwise. The right to reproduce the typography and design of the Work is reserved by the Publishers.

12. Inclusion of General Editor's Name

The Publishers shall include the name of the General Editor with due prominence on the cover, jacket (if any) and title page of every print on

13. Moral Rights

The general editor can assert moral rights only for his/her own contribution to the work.

15. Warranties and Indemnity

The general editor can only provide warranties and an indemnity relating to his/her own contribution to the work. It is important that this clause takes account of the general editor's relationship with his or her employer in terms of copyright in the material he or she produces.

paper copy and in any Digital Form version of the Work published by the Publishers and in all appropriate publicity material for the Work and shall impose a similar obligation in respect of any editions licensed by them.

13. Moral Rights

The General Editor hereby asserts to the Publishers *his/her* moral right to be identified as the Author of the General Editor's part in the Work in accordance with sections 77 and 78 of the Copyright, Designs and Patents Act 1988.

14. Copyright Notice

All copies of the Work published by the Publishers shall bear on the title verso a copyright notice comprising the copyright symbol, the name of the copyright holder and the year of first publication.

15. Warranties and Indemnity

15.1 The General Editor hereby warrants to the Publishers that:

(i) the General Editor has the right and power to make this Agreement;

(ii) the General Editor's part in the Work is an original work, except for material in the public domain and such excerpts from other works as may be included with the written permission of the copyright owner, and will in no way whatever give rise to a violation of any existing copyright or a breach of any existing agreement (including any contract of employment);

(iii) the General Editor's part in the Work contains nothing obscene, indecent, defamatory or libellous and all statements contained therein purporting to be facts are true;

(iv) any recipe, formula or instruction contained in the General Editor's part in the Work will not, if followed accurately, cause injury or illness or damage to the user.

15.2 The General Editor will indemnify the Publishers against any loss, injury or damage (including any legal costs or expenses and any compensation costs or disbursements paid by the Publishers on the advice of the Publishers' legal advisers to compromise or settle any claim) arising out of any breach or alleged breach of the warranties.

15.3 The warranties and indemnity shall survive the termination of this Agreement.

16. Proof Correction

This precedent provides for the general editor to have overall responsibility for the checking of proofs. If the individual contributors are required to check proofs of their own contributions (**see Precedent Four, Clauses 6 and 7**) there will need to be an adjustment to the correction limits permitted.

16. Proof Correction

16.1 The General Editor undertakes to read, check and correct the proofs of the Work and return them to the Publishers within such period of time as shall have been mutually agreed, failing which the Publishers shall consider the proofs passed for press.

16.2 Costs of all corrections and alterations made by the General Editor in the finished artwork and the proofs (artists', copy-editors' and printers' errors and those alterations made necessary by changes in professional practice excepted) in excess of ten per cent of the cost of origination of the Work shall be borne by the General Editor provided that:

(i) before passing proofs for press the Publishers shall advise the General Editor of the amount of the excess;

(ii) the General Editor shall have the opportunity exercisable within 14 days of receipt of written notice from the Publishers to remove or reduce such corrections and alterations.

16.3 Should any charge arise under this clause the amount may be deducted from any sums which may become due to the General Editor under this Agreement.

17. General Editor's Copies

The General Editor shall be entitled to receive on publication six free copies of the first and any new edition of the Work edited by the General Editor and to purchase on normal domestic trade terms further copies for personal use but not for resale.

18. Remaindering

18.1 The Publishers shall be entitled not less than [*number*] years from the date of first publication of the Work to dispose of copies thereof as a remainder at a reduced price and shall pay the General Editor the rate of royalty based on the Net Sum Received provided for in Clause 4.1.2 hereof on such sales, except that where copies are sold at cost or less than cost, no royalty shall be payable.

18.2 The Publishers shall give the General Editor [*number*] free copies of the Work under this clause and the first option for a period of six weeks to purchase copies at the said reduced price.

19. Revision of the Work

In the case of a revised edition, the publishers would be responsible for paying existing or replacement contributors for revised material included in the work (**see Precedent Four, Clause 5**).

20. Infringement of Copyright

Since this contract covers a multi-author work, any profits or damages resulting from a successful action against infringement of copyright will be divided in proportions to be agreed.

19. Revision of the Work

19.1 If in the opinion of the Publishers a new edition of the Work is desirable or necessary, they shall so notify the General Editor in writing.

19.2 The General Editor undertakes to make arrangements for the revision of and to edit the Work and to supply to the Publishers at no additional cost to the Publishers by such time as shall be mutually agreed any new matter that may be needed to keep the Work up to date.

19.3 Should the General Editor neglect or be unable or unwilling to supply such new matter or to arrange for the revision of or to edit the Work, the Publishers may after written notice to the General Editor arrange for a competent person or persons to do so and may deduct the expense from any sums which may become payable to the General Editor or the General Editor's representatives under this Agreement.

19.4 In the event of the death of the General Editor the following provisions shall apply:

19.4.1 all sums payable under the terms of this Agreement shall be paid to the representatives of the deceased General Editor on any edition in print at the time of his/her death and on any reprints of such an edition.

19.4.2 the representatives of the deceased General Editor shall then cease to participate financially in any new editions or substantially revised reprints of the Work.

20. Infringement of Copyright

20.1 It is agreed that if at any time during the continuance of this Agreement the Publishers consider that the copyright in the Work has been infringed they shall be at liberty to take such steps as they may consider necessary at their sole discretion to deal with the matter and if they wish to take legal proceedings they shall on giving the General Editor an undertaking to pay all costs and expenses and to indemnify the General Editor against all liability for costs, be entitled to use the General Editor's name as a party to such proceedings but at the same time to control, settle or compromise as they think fit.

20.2 The General Editor agrees to execute any documents and do any acts reasonably appropriate to give effect to the rights of the Publishers granted by this Clause.

20.3 Any profits or damages which may be recovered in respect of any infringement of the copyright shall after deduction of all costs and

21. Out of Print

See Precedent Two, Note to Clause 20 re the implications of print on demand publishing on the definition of when a work is out of print.

22. Termination

Allows for the continuation of any sub-licences properly granted during the term of the licence, for any claims the general editor may have against the Publishers, and for the Publishers to continue to sell any stock on hand at the point of termination.

expenses be divided between the parties hereto in proportions to be mutually agreed.

21. Out of Print

21.1 If the Work is allowed to go out of print and is not available in any English language edition published by the Publishers or licensed by them, the General Editor may give nine months' written notice in writing to the Publishers to put in hand a reprint or a new edition.

For the purposes of this Clause 21.1 'out of print' shall mean when fewer than [*number*] physical copies of the print on paper edition of the Work remain in the Publishers' warehouse and the Publishers have no plans for a reissue or a new edition.

21.2 The General Editor's requirements that the Work be reprinted shall be regarded as satisfied if at the time of the General Editor's giving notice the Publishers have sub-licensed rights for an English language edition of the Work scheduled for publication within 12 months of such notice being given.

21.3 Should the Publishers fail to comply with such notice, other than through circumstances beyond their control, all rights in the General Editor's part in the Work granted to the Publishers under this Agreement shall upon expiration of the said notice revert to the General Editor in accordance with the provisions of Clause 22.

22. Termination

22.1 This Agreement shall automatically terminate if the Publishers go into liquidation other than voluntary liquidation for the purpose of reconstruction, or have a receiver or an administrative receiver appointed over the whole or any substantial part of the Publishers' assets.

22.2 The Author may terminate this Agreement by summary notice in writing to the Publishers if the Publishers are in material breach of any of their obligations under this Agreement and shall not have remedied such breach to the extent possible within three months after written notification from the Author giving details of such breach.

22.3 On termination of this Agreement under Clause 22.1 or 22.2 hereof, all rights in the Work granted to the Publishers under this Agreement shall revert to the General Editor without prejudice to:

(i) all rights of the Publishers and any third party in respect of any agreement properly entered into by the Publishers with such party prior to the date of termination;

(ii) any claim which the General Editor may have for monies due and/or damages and/or otherwise;

(iii) the right of the Publishers to continue to sell any copies of the Work in their possession, custody or control at the date of termination.

23. Competing Works

23.1 While the Work is in course of preparation or in current publication:

23.1.1 the General Editor shall be entitled to use material written by *him/her* for the purposes of the Work in articles submitted to learned or professional journals, in papers presented at professional conferences and for the General Editor's professional purposes generally, provided that the General Editor shall make appropriate acknowledgment to the Work and the Publishers, but

23.1.2 the General Editor shall not without the prior written consent of the Publishers write, edit or contribute, jointly or severally, to any work which may reasonably be considered by the Publishers to compete with or prejudice sales of the Work or the exploitation of any of the rights granted to the Publishers under this Agreement.

24. Arbitration

If any difference shall arise between the General Editor and the Publishers touching the meaning of this Agreement or the rights and liabilities of the parties hereto, the same shall be referred to the arbitration of two persons (one to be named by each party) or their umpire in accordance with the provisions of the Arbitration Act 1996 or any amending or substituted statute for the time being in force.

25. Entire Agreement

25.1 This Agreement sets forth the entire agreement between the parties at the date of this Agreement and supersedes any prior written or oral agreement between them with respect to the subject matter of this Agreement.

25.2 Any amendment of or variation to this Agreement must be in writing and signed by both parties.

26. Applicable Law

This Agreement shall be governed by and construed in accordance with the laws of England whose courts shall have exclusive jurisdiction.

27. Headings

Headings to the clauses hereof are for guidance only and are not to be taken into account in the construction of this Agreement which has been prepared in [*number*] copies.

28. Rights of Third Parties

The parties do not intend that any term of this Agreement shall be enforceable solely by virtue of the Contracts (Rights of Third Parties) Act 1999 by any person who is not a party to this Agreement save that a person who is a permitted successor to or assignee of the rights of a party is deemed to be a party to this Agreement and the rights of such successor or assignee shall be regulated by the terms of this Agreement.

29. Definitions

29.1 In this Agreement the following words and expressions shall have the following meanings unless the context requires otherwise:

'Associated Company' shall have the meaning attributed to that term in sections 416 (et seq) of the Income and Corporation Taxes Act 1988, as amended;

'Digital Form' shall include but shall not be limited to off-line electronic storage and information retrieval systems of a digital, optical or magnetic nature including but not limited to floppy disk, CD-ROM, DVD, ROM-card, compact disc, video, integrated circuit; mobile and hand-held devices: online transmission by satellite and other means of telecommunication; and any other Digital means of reproduction, publication, dissemination and transmission (including online broadcasts made available through streaming and downloads) whether now in existence or hereafter invented;

'Digital Publishing Rights' means the right to produce, copy, publish and sell, to perform, display, stream, download,

	transfer, broadcast and transmit the Work whether in whole or in part, adapted or abridged on its own or in combination with another work or works, together with any accompanying sounds and images, in any manner and in any Digital Form and to license the foregoing rights in Digital versions of the Work;
'Net Sum Received by the Publishers'	means the amount received by the Publishers and any amounts receivable by the Publishers after deducting any discounts granted by the Publishers and any sales or other similar taxes or duties incurred by the Publishers in respect of sales of copies of the Work;
'Work'	means the Work (and any new editions of the Work) edited by the General Editor under this Agreement together with any abridgements, adaptations, or electronic versions of the Work;
'[*Insert name*] Group'	means any Associated Company of [*insert name*] Limited.

30. Assignment

The Publishers may assign any benefit or transfer, delegate or sub-contract any of their duties or obligations under this Agreement to any company within the [*insert name*] Group without the prior written consent of the General Editor.

AS WITNESS THE HANDS OF THE PARTIES

Signed by ....

(GENERAL EDITOR)

Signed by ....

For and on behalf of [*name of publishers*] LIMITED

PRECEDENT FOUR

Agreement for Contributor to a Book

As indicated in Precedent Two, multiple authorship is often necessary, especially for the publication of texts for specialist readers. It is not uncommon to find more than 20 specialist authorities each writing a chapter (each with its own copyright implications) to make up a definitive text or reference work for scientific or medical readership. In this Precedent, which is set out (as such agreements often are) in letter form, that is the context which is assumed.

1. In the case of a multi-author work, failure to deliver on time by one contributor may wreck publication plans, particularly in the case of academic textbooks with tight publication time limits. It may sometimes be preferable to cancel a commissioned chapter or article which is running late and to recommission, rather than to hang on indefinitely to the increasing irritation of those contributors who have delivered on time and who may threaten to withdraw from the project.

Delivery in electronic form as an e-mail attachment is now expected as the norm, but it is important to ensure that contributors have been properly briefed on the publishers' requirements from the very beginning.

2. As for single-author books, it is vital that the contributor alerts the publishers to any textual or illustrative material quoted from outside sources and provides evidence that permission has been properly sought and obtained. The publishers may wish to provide a sample clearance letter, particularly if they wish to ensure that clearance includes the right to reuse the quoted material in any sub-licensed editions of the collective work, for example, translations. As many contributors may be employees of universities or commercial companies, it is important that warranties and indemnities take account of the contributor's relationship with his or her employer in terms of copyright in the material he or she produces.

Dear

We are happy to learn that you have agreed to contribute to our publication: [*title of publication*] ('the Work')

Edited by: [*name of General Editor*] ('the General Editor') of [*address*]

Your contribution will be published on the following terms:

1. You will contribute the chapter on [*name of chapter*] ('the Contribution') which will consist of not more than [*number*] words and not less than [*number*] words as an e-mail attachment in [*specify word processing package to be used*] format together with one identical hard copy printed out in double line spacing, retaining a further hard copy for your own files. The Contribution will be delivered to the General Editor no later than [*date*] together with any illustrations, photographs, drawings, charts or graphs in a form suitable for reproduction as agreed with the Publishers.

Should you fail to deliver the Contribution by this date or by such other date as may have been agreed in writing by the Publishers, or should you fail to deliver the Contribution in the form specified, then the Publishers shall be at liberty to decline to publish the Contribution, in which case the sum specified in Clause 8 hereof shall not be payable to you.

2. You as the Author of the Contribution warrant to us (hereinafter called 'the Publishers') that the Contribution is original to yourself except for material in the public domain and such excerpts of other works as may be included with written permission of the copyright owner, that it has not hitherto been published in any form, that it will in no way whatever give rise to violation of any existing copyright or a breach of any existing agreement, including any contract of employment. You further warrant that the Contribution contains nothing obscene, indecent, defamatory or libellous, that all statements therein purporting to be facts are true and that any recipe, formula or instruction contained in the Contribution will not, if followed accurately, cause injury or illness or damage to the user. You undertake to indemnify the Publishers against any claims, any loss, damage or costs, including any legal costs properly incurred, occasioned to the Publishers in consequence of any breach of this warranty or arising out of any claim alleging that your Contribution constitutes a breach of this warranty. The warranties and indemnity shall survive the termination of this Agreement.

You accept responsibility for obtaining permission for publication in the Contribution at your expense of any textual and/or illustrative material in which copyright vests in any other person or party and will

3. As with many other publications, publication and reproduction of a specialist multi-author work may be in print-on-paper form, but will increasingly take place via electronic media; STM (scientific, technical and medical) works have increasingly taken advantage of online forms of publication. It is therefore vital that the publishers secure control of such rights, either to exploit them directly or via licensing. The question of whether publication in part and in electronic form (perhaps as part of a work containing other material and allowing for interactivity) constitutes a breach of the contributor's moral right of integrity is a vexed one and publishers may wish to seek a waiver of such rights for contributors (**see also Notes to Clauses 5 and 10 and Appendix H**).

5. The prudent publisher will, under the guidance of the general editor, commission contributions for the first edition only. If the book then succeeds, and a second edition is called for, any less satisfactory contributions can be quietly dropped with minimal embarrassment, and new/replacement contributors can be commissioned.

Whether heavy revisions by a general editor may or may not infringe the moral rights of integrity of a contributor has yet to be extensively tested under the provisions of the Copyright, Designs and Patents Act 1988.

deliver to the Publishers for safe keeping any documents relating to the granting of such permissions.

3. For the consideration mentioned in Clause 8, you, by way of assignment of present or future copyright, hereby assign to the Publishers the entire copyright and all other rights of a like nature in and to the Contribution throughout the world (including for the avoidance of doubt all digital publishing rights) for the full legal term of copyright and all renewals, revivals and extensions thereof, and the Publishers shall have the exclusive right during such period to publish, and to license for publication, the Contribution in whole and in part in all editions forms and media in the English language and in any translations without limitation.

4. You may republish the Contribution in whole or in part at no charge with the Publishers' prior written permission, such permission not to be unreasonably withheld, provided that proper acknowledgment is given to the Publishers in such republication.

5. The Contribution will be offered by you and subject to the decision of the General Editor (see below) and the terms of Clause 1 (above) will be accepted for publication in the first edition of the Work only and the Publishers shall have the right to include the Contribution in any subsequent revised edition or editions of the Work on the terms set out below.

The General Editor shall have the right to make any revision to the Contribution which he may deem desirable in the interests of uniformity and style of the Work. The General Editor shall have the final decision on the inclusion or omission of the Contribution in or from the first and any subsequent editions of the Work.

You will, if so required by the General Editor, revise the Contribution for any new edition of the Work and you agree that such revised Contribution shall be subject to the terms and conditions herein generally stated except that the payment for such revised Contribution shall be mutually agreed between yourself and the Publishers.

6. To reduce the length and expense of production time, the Publishers may agree with the General Editor to dispense with proof corrections by you in which event the Publishers and their printers will ensure the correction of any typographical errors, and you will see the artwork of all redrawn illustrations before their reproduction in the Work. Accordingly the Publishers request your co-operation in making all reasonable efforts to ensure that all required amendments and corrections are incorporated in the final completed text before it is submitted in the required form to the Publishers.

8. If it has been agreed that the individual contributors should receive a share of any subsidiary rights income resulting from exploitation of the whole work or in an individual contribution, this clause would need to be amended.

> 'You will receive a share of any income generated from the sale of any subsidiary right in the Work involving the use of your contribution, such share to be agreed with the Publishers.'

10. Those publishers who fear that exploitation of the work, particularly in electronic form, could be restricted by the adherence of every contributor to their moral right of integrity, could take advantage of the fact that (unusually in Europe) the UK Copyright, Designs and Patents Act 1988 permits for waiver of moral rights (**see Appendix H**). Wording to cover a full waiver might read as follows:

> 'You hereby irrevocably and unconditionally waive all moral rights under section 80 and pursuant to section 87 of the Copyright, Designs and Patents Act 1988.'

It should be remembered that the copyright laws of most other countries supporting the concept of moral rights do not permit waiver and hence any attempt to extend the waiver beyond the UK is unlikely to be valid.

It is likely that contributors will need to be carefully persuaded of the reasons for seeking such a waiver, particularly in subject areas where manipulation of content could be held to be dangerous (e.g., in medical publications).

Some publishers seek to obtain a partial waiver of the right of integrity for publication in electronic form only.

Should proofs of the Contribution (and finished artwork) be provided to you, you undertake to read, check and correct them and return them to the Publishers within 14 days of their receipt, failing which the Publishers may consider the proofs and artwork passed for press by you.

7. The Publishers will absorb the cost of your corrections up to but not exceeding an amount equal to 10 per cent of the cost of origination of the Contribution but any cost incurred in excess of that amount will be charged against payment to you referred to in Clause 8.

8. As full consideration for the copyright and all other rights in the Contribution assigned to the Publishers in Clause 3 and subject to the terms of Clause 5 as regards acceptance of the contribution and any revised Contribution the Publishers will pay you on publication the sum of [*amount*] and in the event that there is more than one author of the Contribution payment will be divided equally between each of you unless the Publishers are authorised to the contrary in writing signed by each of you.

9. The Publishers shall include your name with due prominence on the title page of the Contribution in any print on paper edition of the Work or elsewhere as determined by the Publishers and in any Digital Form version of the Work as the author (or co-author as the case may be) of the Contribution.

10. You hereby assert to the Publishers and to our licensees your moral right to be identified in the Work as the Author (or co-author as the case may be) of your Contribution, in accordance with the Copyright, Designs and Patents Act 1988.

11. All sums payable to you under this letter are exclusive of UK Value Added Tax which shall, where applicable, be paid in addition at the rate in force at the time of payment, provided you have supplied the Publishers with a current and valid UK VAT registration number.

12. The Publishers may deduct from any sum due to you under this letter of agreement any sum that we are or may be under an obligation to deduct or withhold in respect of any tax, duty or other similar levy.

13. You will receive one free copy of the Work on publication. In addition you are entitled to purchase further copies directly from the Publishers at normal trade discount off the UK recommended retail price. You are also entitled to purchase from the Publishers at a discount of [*number*] per cent other publications published by us.

14. Any dispute or difference of any kind whatsoever which arises between you and the Publishers in relation to any matter in connection

with this letter of agreement shall be referred to the arbitration of two persons (one to be named by each party) or their umpire in accordance with the provisions of the Arbitration Act 1996 or any amending or substituted statute for the time being in force.

15. This letter of agreement shall be governed by and construed in accordance with the laws of England whose courts shall have exclusive jurisdiction.

16. Also enclosed is a contributor card for your completion to be returned to the General Editor together with the material for your Contribution. It is most important that this document is completed as fully as possible. If your Contribution is being co-authored please photocopy the card, as appropriate, for completion by your co-author/authors.

Would you please sign and return to us, the Publishers, the enclosed duplicate copy of this letter to confirm your agreement to the terms of this letter. Where more than one author is involved, please all sign and return the duplicate copy.

I/We confirm our agreement to the above terms.

Yours sincerely

Signed

Date:

(for the Publishers)

PRECEDENT FIVE

Book Series Editor – Publisher Agreement

The purpose of this Precedent is to confirm the terms and conditions under which a series editor is appointed to the task of editing a series of books. The contract itself will sit alongside a set of contracts with individual authors (**see Precedents One and Two**). Care should be taken to ensure that both this contract and each author contract dovetail correctly and do not allow either contradiction or gaps in their fulfilment of their respective obligations to the publishers. One aspect of particular interest to the publishers is to ensure that the combination of the two contracts does not lead to the publishers acquiring an obligation to pay a higher total royalty than intended as a result of a failure to take into account in one contract the obligations under the other.

The contributor would like to thank Mayer Brown International LLP and Hodder Education for their permission to reproduce this Precedent.

1 The Series Editor as an Author

This precedent says that the contract will apply to any book of which the Series Editor is an author – but his/her authorship will often be subject to a separate author contract. In other words, the Series Editor will receive two contracts and will be paid a Series Editor royalty on his/her own book under this contract. See also comments on Clause 7.

THIS AGREEMENT is dated the *(number)* day of *(month)* 20 *(year)* and made between:

(1) [*Name of series editor*] of [*address: series editor's own address or c/o agent*] [trading as [*insert trading name, if series editor uses one*]] (the 'Series Editor'); and

(2) (THE PUBLISHERS) a company incorporated in England and Wales (registered number XXXXX) whose registered office is at (*address*), (the 'Publishers').

Background:

This Agreement sets out the terms on which the Series Editor is appointed to edit the Series.

IT IS AGREED that:

1. The Series

This Agreement concerns the series presently entitled [*name of series*] which has been or is to be edited by the Series Editor. This series and all the materials which this Agreement requires to be included in it are collectively referred to as the 'Series'.

Where this Agreement refers to more than one such series, the expression 'the Series' shall refer to each of them individually (unless only one of them is identified in the Clause concerned).

Clause 18 (*Interpretation*) explains how this Agreement is to be interpreted where there is more than one Series Editor.

The expression 'Editorial Material' means all material written, prepared or contributed by the Series Editor for use in the Series including any foreword, introduction, revisions, additions and deletions made by the Series Editor to text or illustrations prepared by others but excluding any material relating to a Work or the Series in respect of which the Series Editor has entered into a separate agreement with the Publishers which is not expressly terminated by this Agreement. Any Work of which the Series Editor is to be an author shall be subject to this Agreement but the terms and conditions applicable to the Series Editor's role as the author of that Work shall be the subject of a separate Agreement between the Series Editor and the Publishers.

The expression 'Work' means each work to be included in the Series and all materials included in that Work. Where this Agreement refers to more than one such work, the expression 'the Work' shall refer to each of them individually (unless only one of them is identified in the Clause concerned).

2 Series Editor's Appointment, Obligations and Copyright

2.1 *Duration of Series Editor's Appointment*

Whilst due consideration needs to be given to the exact role the Series Editor is to undertake, it is also important for the publisher to consider (i) how to terminate the appointment; (ii) the circumstances under which the publisher may wish to do so and (iii) the consequences for both parties of termination. In the event that notice is given under this clause, then the appointment will be terminated, but the Series Editor's surviving interest in respect of work completed is protected under Clause 9.2. See also Clauses 3.5 and 7.3 for other specific termination conditions.

2.2 *Series Editor's Obligations*

(1) This should clearly define what is expected of the Series Editor and to what extent she/he has control. For example, whilst the publisher may expect and require the Series Editor to source authors in the field in which the Series Editor is specialist, the publisher is very unlikely to want the Series Editor to have any latitude to actually appoint the authors or agree terms (beyond perhaps some specific limits). To this end, the more detail that is included in this clause (either directly or, more likely, by use of a Schedule), the better it will be in the event of a dispute.

(2) Care should be taken to define the timetable to which the Series Editor is working. For this reason a Schedule and/or Specification is a very useful tool. This can include details specific to individual books (including in relation to the review/editing to be undertaken by the Series Editor) as well as more general matters such as 'acquiring six authors of sufficient calibre by x date to write on y topic for a z level of reader'.

2.3 *Assignment of Copyright*

It is important to acquire the right to publish any material contributed by the Series Editor – be it stand-alone material like a Series Introduction to be included in each book in the series or the edits of another author's work on a single book. It thus follows (i) at Clause 3.2 that the Series Editor should clear third-party copyright material in their material only and (ii) at Clause 7 that the Series Editor gives warranties and indemnities for that material to the same level as any other author/contributor.

2 Series Editor's Appointment, Obligations and Copyright

2.1 *Duration of the Series Editor's Appointment*

The Publishers appoint the Series Editor (and the Series Editor accepts the appointment) as series editor for the Series with immediate effect. The appointment will subsist until the earlier of:

(a) [*date*];

(b) the Publishers giving the Series Editor not less than six months' notice in writing of termination (but no notice may take effect prior to [*date*]);

(c) the Publishers giving the Series Editor, at the Publishers' option, immediate notice of termination in writing, prior to commissioning a new edition of the Series or of any Work;

(d) the Publishers giving the Series Editor immediate notice in writing of termination following the Series Editor's failure to fulfil any of the terms of this Agreement;

(e) the Publishers giving the Series Editor immediate notice in writing of termination following an event concerning the Series Editor which the Publishers consider is likely to harm the reputation of the Series Editor or the Publishers or affect sales of the Series.

2.2 *Series Editor's Obligations*

The Series Editor shall select and secure authors to each Work in compliance with the guidelines set out in the Specification and with the Schedule (each as defined below). The Series Editor shall obtain the Publishers' prior written approval for each author. The Series Editor shall undertake any necessary editing of the authors' contributions to the Series at synopsis and final delivery stage to ensure that they conform to the Specification and are delivered in accordance with the Schedule. The Series Editor shall comply with the obligations which are allocated to the Series Editor in the Schedule and the Specification, within the time stated for their performance. Where so stated in and as described in the Specification or the Schedule, the Series Editor shall also contribute content for the Series.

2.3 *Assignment of Copyright*

By signing this Agreement, the Series Editor hereby assigns to the Publishers with full title guarantee, free of all third party rights of any kind, all right, title and interest in and to the Editorial Material including all copyright in the same, throughout the world, for the full term of such rights, including all extensions and renewals. In relation to Editorial Material which is not

yet in existence, this assignment shall be effective immediately on the Editorial Material coming into existence. The rights so assigned include the right to sue for, and to recover damages and other remedies in respect of, any infringement of the rights in the Editorial Material which took place before the date of this Agreement. The Series Editor will, at the Publishers' reasonable expense, promptly do all acts and execute all documents which the Publishers consider are necessary or desirable to give full effect to the above assignment.

3 Specification and Delivery of the Editorial Material

3.1 *Specification*

The 'Specification' and the 'Schedule' mean, respectively, the details set out in Appendix 1 (*Specification*) and Appendix 2 (*Schedule*) [or, if none are set out there, [*other specification/similar details which have been agreed between the Publishers and the Series Editor before contract signing*]]. The Series Editor agrees that the Editorial Material as delivered to the Publishers will:

(a) comply with the Specification and the Schedule; and

(b) be technically competent, fit for publication and in a condition ready for use by the Publishers,

and that the Editorial Material shall comply with the warranties, representations and undertakings set out in Clause 7.1 (*Warranties*).

3.2 *Obtaining Permission*

All contents of the Editorial Material should, wherever possible, be original to the Series Editor. Only in exceptional circumstances will the Publishers accept third party copyright material for inclusion in the Editorial Material. If this Agreement provides that the Editorial Material is to include material any rights in which are owned by others (including realia and others' illustrations and quotations) or the publication of which may in any way infringe others' rights (including privacy rights and rights relating to patient confidentiality), it is the Series Editor's responsibility to obtain all relevant permissions at the Series Editor's expense. The Series Editor shall therefore obtain, on a timely basis before first publication of the Editorial Material, written permission from each owner of any relevant rights and from each person whose rights might be infringed through publication, to use that material (and, if applicable, to adapt, translate or make changes to the material) within the Editorial Material in all forms and languages which are the subject of rights assigned under this Agreement. The Publishers will credit those who give permission in the acknowledgements page of each Work, subject to the Publishers being provided with the relevant details on a timely basis. The

Book Series Editor – Publisher Agreement – Notes

Series Editor shall not offer or agree to any other kind of credit. If requested by the Publishers, the Series Editor shall promptly provide the Publishers with copy correspondence proving that the Series Editor has obtained and paid any fees required for permissions.

3.3 *Delivery of Editorial Material*

Time shall be of the essence of this Agreement in relation to this Clause 3.3. The Series Editor shall deliver the following to the Publishers on or before [*insert date*] (subject to any extensions to that date which the Publishers may agree under Clause 3.5 (*Non-delivery*)), the ('Delivery Date'):

(a) an original and one copy of the complete final typescript of the text of the Editorial Material, in paper form;

(b) a copy of that complete final typescript as electronic files in an appropriate file format as set out in the Specification or otherwise required by the Publishers; and

(c) roughs for artwork and photographs, or final artwork and photographs, and realia associated with the Editorial Material,

which are together referred to as the 'Deliverables', and in each case as set out in the Specification or, if not set out there, as notified by the Publishers to the Series Editor, as well as:

(d) any source material as set out in the Specification or, if not set out there, as notified by the Publishers to the Series Editor (the 'Source Material').

3.4 *Care of Material*

The Publishers shall take all reasonable care of the Editorial Material and the Source Material but shall not be responsible for any loss of or damage to these while in the Publishers' possession or in the course of production or transit. The Series Editor shall keep a backup copy of all contents of each Work as edited and/or commented upon and/or reviewed by the Series Editor (together with copies of any comments and review notes of each Work made by the Series Editor) as hard copy and electronically as delivered to the Publishers, as well as backup copies of any illustrations, photographs and realia associated with the Editorial Material, the Source Material associated with the Editorial Material and correspondence relating to permissions associated with the Editorial Material. On request, the Series Editor shall provide these backup copies to the Publishers, without charge to the Publishers.

3 Specification and Delivery of the Editorial Material

3.5 *Non-delivery*

In contrast to an author contract, it is possible that non-delivery of, for example, a series introduction is unlikely to require termination of the series. As a result the publisher may elect to terminate the agreement in connection with the undelivered material, in which case the Contract provides that (i) the publisher is only entitled to seek redress for the part of the material not delivered in an acceptable state and (ii) therefore for repayment of only that part of any monies paid to the Series Editor in relation to that specific material. Likewise, in contrast to similar circumstances in an author contract, no provision is built in to require the Series Editor to repay out-of-pocket expenses.

3.5 *Non-delivery*

If the Series Editor has not delivered the Editorial Material and the Source Material in a form which complies with Clause 3 (*Specification and delivery of the Editorial Material*) on or before the Delivery Date or otherwise fails to comply with the Schedule and the Specification:

(a) the Publishers may extend the time for delivery or compliance if the Publishers wish, but will only be bound by such an extension if it is confirmed in writing by the Managing Director of the Publishers' Education Division, and time shall be of the essence of this Agreement in relation to any such extended date. In this case, 'Delivery Date' and any date specified in the Schedule or the Specification for fulfilment of an obligation shall from then on mean the extended date; or

(b) the Publishers may terminate this Agreement either in its entirety, or only in respect of the undelivered Editorial Material and the undelivered Source Material, immediately on giving the Series Editor notice in writing, in which case the Series Editor shall immediately repay to the Publishers all sums received from the Publishers or (where termination is not of the whole of this Agreement) all sums so received in respect of that undelivered Editorial Material and that undelivered Source Material only.

3.6 *Proofs and Alterations*

The Series Editor shall read the proofs of each Work and shall return them to the Publishers with any necessary corrections within 14 days of their receipt, or as is otherwise agreed [in writing] to maintain the publishing schedule for that Work. The Series Editor shall bear the cost of the Series Editor's alterations:

(a) to proofs, other than the correction of printer's errors, to the extent that the cost exceeds 10 per cent of the cost of typesetting, and

(b) to any illustrative material, other than costs relating to the correction of illustrator's errors.

3.7 *Costs*

Where this Agreement provides that the Series Editor is to bear certain costs, the Publishers may invoice all or part of them to the Series Editor and/ or deduct all or part of those costs from amounts due to the Series Editor. Except as otherwise provided in this Agreement where the Publishers invoice the Series Editor, the Series Editor shall pay those costs to the Publishers within 30 days of receipt of invoice.

Book Series Editor – Publisher Agreement – Notes

4. Production and Publication

4.1 *Production, Advertising and Selling*

The Publishers shall have entire control over the following matters in relation to the Series and each Work: publication date; production; materials; manufacture; design; binding; jacket; inlay and embellishments (if any); the manner and the extent of any advertising; the number and distribution of any free copies and the price, format and terms of sale. Except where this Agreement expressly states otherwise, the Publishers shall bear the entire cost of producing, advertising and selling the Series and each Work.

4.2 *Series Editor's Name*

The Series Editor irrevocably agrees that the Publishers shall have the right to use the Series Editor's name in connection with the Editorial Material, the Series and any editions, versions or publications of any Work and in connection with any subsequent editions of the Series and of any and all Works (whether or not under the same name as set out in this Agreement or as it was first published by the Publishers) and whether or not it contains material edited or written by the Series Editor. In relation to each edition of each Work of which the Series Editor is the only series editor or a principal series editor, the Publishers shall include the Series Editor's name as set out in the Specification and with due prominence on the title page of each copy of that Work issued by the Publishers.

4.3 *Changes*

Except as set out in Clause 7.3 (*Alterations*) or as may be reasonably necessary to exploit the rights assigned to the Publishers under Clause 2.3 (*Assignment of copyright*), the Publishers shall not make any significant alterations to the Editorial Material without the permission of the Series Editor, which shall not be unreasonably withheld or delayed.

4.4 *Publication*

The Publishers will first publish the Series over the [*name*] imprint.

4.5 *Series Editor's Right to Copies*

On the day of first publication of each Work, the Publishers shall send the Series Editor [one] free copy of that Work in [*insert details of relevant format(s)*]. The Series Editor may buy further copies for personal use, but not for resale, at 50 per cent of the Publishers' recommended UK list price, as long as the Series Editor pays for these by cheque or major credit card at the time of ordering. If the Series Editor first obtains the Publishers' written approval of the proposed resale, the Series Editor may also buy further copies for resale, at such discount from the Publishers' recommended UK list price

from time to time that the parties may agree, as long as the Series Editor pays for these by cheque or major credit card at the time of ordering. The Publishers will not charge postage costs for copies sold to the Series Editor for personal use and sent to UK addresses, but will charge postage costs on copies sold to the Series Editor for resale or sent outside the UK.

4.6 *Conflicting Publications*

The Series Editor agrees not to edit or publish or endorse or be otherwise associated with, and not to allow or assist any person to edit or publish, in any format (including on the Internet) any series

[*preferred option*:] which would directly interfere with, compete with or tend to lessen any sales of the Series,

[*second option, as explained in notes*:] [which is on the same subject] [and/or] [the target age range of which includes the same age group] [and/or] [which would be published in the same price range] [and/or] [which is aimed at the same examination board or boards] as those of the Series

without the Publishers' consent in writing

[*fallback wording follows:*] except that the Series Editor may use the Editorial Material, in articles which the Series Editor submits to learned or professional journals for publication after first publication of the first Work to be published in the Series, in papers which the Series Editor presents at professional conferences and in connection with training given by the Series Editor, as long as the Series Editor notifies the Publishers of this in advance and acknowledges the Series and the Publishers when doing so.

The Publishers shall not unreasonably withhold or delay the Publishers' consent.

5. Royalties

5.1 *Receipts and other Definitions*

The following terms which are used in calculating the Series Editor's royalties have the following meanings:

(a) 'Electronic Publications' means all electronic, digital, optical and magnetic forms of distribution, publication or transmission of all or part of the Work, or of adaptations of the Work, which are intended to make the Work available to the public for reading, or other access (whether or not sequentially and whether or not with any sound and/or any static or moving images), including by electronic, digital, optical or magnetic information storage and retrieval systems, online

or satellite transmission and further including CD-ROMs (including interactive CD-ROMs) but excluding all print-on-paper versions and audio-only versions; and

(b) 'Net Receipts' means the amounts actually received by the Publishers for sales of the relevant copies of the Work, namely the Publishers' recommended list price for that copy less discounts given to agents, wholesalers and/or booksellers, net of VAT and any other taxes or, where sales are of a work or material of which the Work (or an abridgement of it) is only part, the proportion of those amounts actually received which the length of the Work (or abridgement) bears to the length of the whole work or material in question.

5.2 *Royalty Rates*

Except where this Agreement expressly states otherwise, the Publishers shall pay the following royalties to the Series Editor in respect of sales of each Work:

(a) On hardcover editions of the Work published by the Publishers: (*number*) per cent of Net Receipts.

(b) On paperback editions of the Work published by the Publishers: (*number*) per cent of Net Receipts.

(c) On audio-only versions of the Work (or an abridgement of the Work) published by the Publishers (including sound recordings in any tangible medium, such as cassettes and compact discs, and in any non-tangible medium, such as digital downloads): (*number*) per cent of Net Receipts.

(d) On Electronic Publications published by the Publishers: (*number*) per cent of Net Receipts.

(e) On visual-only versions of the Work (or an abridgement of the Work) published by the Publishers other than those which are printed and other than those which are included within Electronic Publications: (*number*) per cent of Net Receipts.

(f) On audiovisual-only versions of the Work (or an abridgement of the Work) published by the Publishers other than those which are included within Electronic Publications: (*number*) per cent of Net Receipts.

(g) On all other versions and forms of the Work (or an abridgement of the Work) published by the Publishers which are not specifically referred to in this Clause 5.2: (*number*) per cent of Net Receipts.

(h) On single products published by the Publishers containing at least one copy of each of two or more versions of the Work (or an abridgement or abridgements of the Work) published by the Publishers: (*number*) per cent of Net Receipts.

(i) On copies of the Work (o r an abridgement of the Work) published by the Publishers and sold on the basis of a retail price which is lower than the then applicable UK retail price: (*number*) per cent of Net Receipts.

(j) On copies of the Work (or an abridgement of the Work) published by the Publishers and sold as special sales including sales to pharmaceutical companies: (*number*) per cent of Net Receipts.

(k) The Publishers may reduce the royalty rates specified in paragraphs (a) to (h) of this Clause 5.2 to (*number*) per cent of Net Receipts respectively, and those specified in paragraphs (i) and (j) to (*number*) per cent of Net Receipts respectively, if the Publishers propose to issue re-printings (or other tangible forms of publication) of XXX copies or fewer. This is because the increased cost of manufacture caused by the small quantities being manufactured would be uneconomic at the normal royalty rate.

(l) On print-on-demand editions of the Work published by the Publishers: (*number*) per cent of Net Receipts.

(m) On copies of the Work (or an abridgement of the Work) (whether or not printed or specially printed and if printed, whether bound or in sheets) sold by the Publishers to publishers in the United States of America at a price inclusive of royalty: (*number*) per cent of Net Receipts

(n) On copies of the Work (or an abridgement of the Work) (whether or not printed or specially printed and if printed, whether bound or in sheets) sold by the Publishers to book clubs and similar organisations at a price inclusive of royalty: (*number*) per cent of Net Receipts

(o) On copies of the Work (or an abridgement of the Work) published by the Publishers and sold by the Publishers at a discount of 80 per cent or more of the Publishers' recommended list price: (*number*) per cent of Net Receipts, unless the copies are sold below production cost, in which case no royalty shall be payable.

5.3 *Free Copies*

No royalty shall be payable on copies of any Work given away to the Series Editor or for the purpose of aiding sales or for review (including as inspection copies), nor on any copies of any Work lost, damaged or destroyed (even if damaged copies are sold).

5.4 *Promotional use by the Publishers*

The Publishers may reproduce all or part of the Editorial Material or any Work in any media (including websites and paid-for media) for the purposes of promoting the Series, that Work or the Publishers. No royalty shall be payable for this use.

5.5 *Photocopying*

The Publishers have allowed the Copyright Licensing Agency (CLA) to grant non-exclusive licences to copy works published by the Publishers by photocopying and other forms of reprography. Any Work published in printed form as a hardcover or paperback book is included in this arrangement. CLA divides the proceeds from reprographic reproduction of that Work authorised by it equally between the authors of that Work. If the Series Editor has contributed text to that Work, the Series Editor shall receive the Series Editor's share of such proceeds through the Authors' Licensing and Collecting Society (ALCS) in accordance with ALCS's standard terms and conditions. Therefore, the Publishers shall not have any obligations to the Series Editor in relation to any proceeds of licences granted by CLA.

5.6 *Publishers' Group*

For the avoidance of doubt, if the Publishers sell copies of any Work to other members of the same group of companies, those sales shall be treated in the same way for royalty purposes under this Agreement as if they were to unconnected third parties. Any such sale will be on an arm's-length basis.

6. Accounting

6.1 *Payment*

Once-yearly Version

The Publishers shall prepare accounts of sales of each Work, once a year, for the 12-month period ending on 31 December (an 'Accounting Date'). Except as stated below, the Publishers shall send these accounts to the Series Editor within three (3) months of each Accounting Date and shall at the same time pay any royalties due to the Series Editor. If a statement prepared under this Clause shows that the total due to the Series Editor (or, if more than one person is the Series Editor, until the total amount due to all of them together) under this Agreement is £50 or less, no account need be sent (unless the Series Editor requests one in writing) and no payment need be made to the Series Editor. The sum due shall instead be carried forward until the total amount due to the Series Editor (or, if more than one person is the Series Editor, until the total amount due to all of them together) under this Agreement exceeds £50 and shall then be paid on the next following normal payment date.

Book Series Editor – Publisher Agreement – Notes

Twice-yearly Version

The Publishers shall prepare accounts of sales of each Work, twice a year, for the six-month periods ending on 30 June and 31 December (each an 'Accounting Date'). Except as stated below, the Publishers shall send these accounts to the Series Editor within three (3) months of each Accounting Date and shall at the same time pay any royalties due to the Series Editor. If a statement prepared under this Clause shows that the total due to the Series Editor (or, if more than one person is the Series Editor, until the total amount due to all of them together) under this Agreement is £50 or less, no account need be sent (unless the Series Editor requests one in writing) and no payment need be made to the Series Editor. The sum due shall instead be carried forward until the total amount due to the Series Editor (or, if more than one person is the Series Editor, until the total amount due to all of them together) under this Agreement exceeds £50 and shall then be paid on the next following normal payment date.

6.2 *Payment Details*

Payments due under this Agreement shall be made in sterling, until the euro is adopted as the sole lawful currency of the United Kingdom, in which case they shall be made in euros. They shall be made by bank transfer to the bank account notified beforehand by the Series Editor to the Publishers or, if no account has been so notified, directly to the Series Editor by cheque.

6.3 *VAT*

All payments due to the Series Editor under this Agreement exclude VAT. VAT will be added, under the Publishers' self-billing system, after written notification of the Series Editor's UK VAT registration number. The Series Editor will notify the Publishers of any change to the Series Editor's UK VAT registration number. The Series Editor shall indemnify the Publishers from any Losses (as defined in Clause 7.2 (*Indemnity*) below) arising out of the Series Editor failing to provide to the Publishers the correct information about the Series Editor's UK VAT registration number.

6.4 *Foreign Payments*

Where the Publishers receive payments in a currency other than that in which the Publishers pay the Series Editor and this Agreement requires sums payable to the Series Editor to be calculated on the basis of those payments, the rate for conversion shall be the exchange rate at the time the Publishers receive those payments.

6.5 *Withholding Taxes*

(a) If laws or regulations require the Publishers to withhold any taxes imposed upon the Series Editor on account of any payments made

7 Series Editor's Warranties and Indemnity

7.1 *Warranties*

A full-blown set of warranties has been included here. Note that the warranties relating to content apply solely to the content of the editorial material and *not* to the balance of the book. The author should, of course, give full warranties in respect of their material under the author contract.

under this Agreement, such taxes shall be deducted as required by law from such remittable payment and shall be paid to the proper tax authorities. Official receipts of payment of any withholding tax shall be secured and sent to the Series Editor as evidence of such payment if requested.

(b) The Series Editor shall be responsible for obtaining all certificates and permissions for relief from withholding taxes as may be available to the Series Editor under the relevant double taxation agreement. The Publishers shall be entitled to withhold such taxes as are required by law unless and until the Series Editor (or, where relevant, the appropriate tax authority) has provided the Publishers with evidence that, in the Publishers' reasonable opinion, entitles the Series Editor to receive payments at a reduced rate, or free of withholding. The Series Editor shall indemnify the Publishers from any Losses (as defined in Clause 7.2 (*Indemnity*) below) arising from the Series Editor providing incorrect information to the Publishers or failing to notify the Publishers of any change in the Series Editor's status in relation to the Series Editor's entitlement to receive payments under this Agreement at a reduced rate, or free of, withholding.

6.6 *Calculation of Earnings*

(a) Sales of versions of the whole of any Work and of abridgements of any Work, and sales in each format, shall be accounted for individually for royalty calculation purposes.

(b) Sales of each Work comprised in included in the Series shall be accounted for individually for royalty calculation purposes.

7. Series Editor's Warranties and Indemnity

7.1 *Warranties*

The Series Editor warrants, represents and undertakes to the Publishers that:

(a) the Series Editor is the sole legal and beneficial owner of copyright and all other right, title and interest in and to the Editorial Material (or will be once the Editorial Material is in existence), except for rights in respect of which the Series Editor has obtained permissions in accordance with Clause 3.2 (*Obtaining permission*);

(b) the Series Editor is entitled to enter into and perform this Agreement and to enter into the assignment set out in Clause 2.3 (*Assignment of copyright*);

(c) the Editorial Material is the Series Editor's original work (or will be once the Editorial Material is in existence) and has not been published

7.2 *Indemnity*

As the indemnity relates solely to the warranties given – and those warranties primarily relate solely to the content of the Editorial Material – it is stated that the indemnity does not apply to the balance of the book. Similar to the position adopted in the Notes to Clause 7.1, the publisher should have a full indemnity from the author for their material under their author contract.

(and will not have been published before first publication of the Editorial Material by the Publishers) anywhere in the World in any form;

(d) the Series Editor has not entered into and will not enter into any arrangement which would or purports to assign or grant to any person any rights which conflict with those assigned to the Publishers;

(e) the creation of the Editorial Material and its publication and exploitation did not and will not infringe or breach any other person's intellectual property (including copyright and trade-marks), privacy and/or other rights;

(f) the Editorial Material does not and will not contain anything defamatory, libellous, obscene, indecent or blasphemous, and/or which, or the publication of which, would be a breach of the Official Secrets Act and/or which is in any other way unlawful;

(g) all statements in the Editorial Material which are presented as facts are true;

(h) the Editorial Material does not and will not contain any erroneous or negligently prepared or presented material, including any information which, if a person were to act on it, could cause physical injury or any kind of damage or loss to that person or anyone else; and

(i) the Editorial Material has not been and is not the subject of any complaint, claim or legal action (whether or not this might amount to a breach of any of the above warranties and whether or not well-founded or resolved).

For the avoidance of doubt the warranties above apply only to the Editorial Material and not to any other content of any Work.

7.2 *Indemnity*

The Series Editor shall indemnify the Publishers against all Losses suffered or incurred by the Publishers or any of the Indemnified Persons in respect of any breach of any of the warranties in Clause 7.1 (*Warranties*) and any claim which, if true, would amount to such a breach. This obligation to indemnify shall include the costs of all copies of any and all Works which are withdrawn from sale as a result of a claim and any costs of revisions to any and all Works. 'Losses' means, in respect of any matter, event or circumstance, all losses (whether direct or indirect), demands, claims, actions, proceedings, damages, payments, awards, fines, orders, costs, expenses (including reasonable legal fees and expenses) and other liabilities. 'Indemnified Persons' means all licensees, printers, typesetters, manufacturers, distributors and retailers who deal in the Work, or parts of it, or in rights in it, other than the Publishers,

7.3 *Alterations*

As with Clause 3.5, the Publishers may decide that termination of the agreement as a whole is necessary, but may prefer to continue with a part of the agreement. Significantly the issue is that the Series Editor is required to take responsibility for their material in these circumstances. The publisher should, of course, be protected under the author contract where an issue arises in respect of the author's material.

7.4 *Libel Readings etc.*

The obligations of the Series Editor are limited to their material.

together with any subsidiary or holding company of the Publishers or subsidiary of any such holding company.

For the avoidance of doubt the indemnity above applies only to the warranties given under Clause 7.1 (*Warranties*) in the Editorial Material and not to any other content of any Work.

7.3 *Alterations*

If at any time the Publishers consider or are advised that any of the proposed or actual contents of the Editorial Material may be unlawful, the Publishers may require the Series Editor to alter the Editorial Material. However, this shall not limit Clauses 7.1 (*Warranties*) and 7.2 (*Indemnity*). If the Series Editor is unable or unwilling to do so within the Publishers' stated timescale, or if the alterations would result in any of the Works or the Series no longer complying with the Specification and/or being materially different from that envisaged in the Specification, the Publishers may terminate this Agreement either in its entirety, or only in respect of the Editorial Material requiring alteration, immediately on giving the Series Editor notice in writing, in which case the Series Editor shall immediately repay to the Publishers all sums received from the Publishers or (where termination is not of the whole of this Agreement) all sums so received in respect of the Editorial Material requiring alteration only.

7.4 *Libel Readings etc.*

If the Publishers consider that any Work or Works should be read for libel and/or for other potentially unlawful material, the Publishers and the Series Editor (or, if more than one person is the Series Editor, those persons collectively) shall share the related legal costs [50/50] insofar as they relate to the Editorial Material only. This Clause 7.4 shall not limit Clauses 7.1 (*Warranties*) and 7.2 (*Indemnity*). For the avoidance of doubt, the Series Editor will not be asked to bear any costs incurred from a reading in so far as it relates to any other content of any Work, under this Agreement.

7.5 *Set off*

The Publishers may set off any sums owed to the Publishers, or to other members of the same group of companies from time to time, by the Series Editor (whether or not owed under this Agreement) against any sums which the Publishers or any other such member(s) owe to the Series Editor. The Publishers may also withhold payments due to the Series Editor pending resolution of any claims and matters giving rise to any obligation of the Series Editor to indemnify or make payments to the Publishers or any such other member(s), up to the total sum which the Publishers reasonably anticipate is due to the Publishers. The Publishers shall promptly notify the Series Editor of any payments withheld on the grounds of this Clause 7.5.

9 Termination

9.2 *Effects of Termination*

Note the requirement at (c) to hand over work in progress and all other material associated with the series.

8. Copyright Infringement

If the Series Editor or the Publishers become(s) aware that copyright in the Editorial Material has been, is being, or is likely to be infringed (an 'Infringement'), it shall promptly notify the other. The Publishers alone may take action against the Infringement. The Series Editor agrees either to join in any such action or to allow the Publishers to use the Series Editor's name as a party to litigation, and shall allow the Publishers to exercise sole control over the action taken. The Series Editor shall provide reasonable assistance to the Publishers in connection with action against Infringements, including by helping the Publishers to prove copyright subsistence and ownership, if requested by the Publishers. Recoveries (such as awards of damages and costs and settlement payments) shall belong to the Publishers alone.

9. Termination

9.1 *General*

Clause 2.1 (*Duration of the Series Editor's Appointment*), Clauses 3.5 (*Non-delivery*) and 7.3 (*Alterations*) set out situations in which the Publishers may terminate this Agreement and certain of the effects of termination. This Clause 9 sets out other effects.

9.2 *Effects of Termination*

Following termination of all or part of this Agreement for any reason:

(a) the Publishers shall have the right to continue to sell copies of the Works and shall pay royalties to the Series Editor as required under this Agreement on sales of any edition of any Work edited by the Series Editor which, at the time of the termination, is available in exchange for payment in any format published by the Publishers or has been delivered to and accepted by the Publishers, and on any subsequently manufactured copies of such an edition, where the name of the Series Editor is the only series editor's name used on that edition;

(b) where termination relates only to Editorial Material and Source Material, the remainder of this Agreement (including therefore the Series Editor's rights and obligations as editor of the Series) shall remain in force in accordance with their terms;

(c) the Series Editor shall promptly deliver to the Publishers without charge to the Publishers any and all copies and drafts of materials intended for inclusion in any Work or prepared in connection with the Series (including any Source Material);

(d) for the avoidance of doubt, copyright owned by the Publishers at the time of termination (including in the Editorial Material and in the

10 Death of Series Editor

See Notes on Precedent Two, Clause 18.4.

typographical arrangement of each Work and the Series) shall remain owned by the Publishers and the Publishers shall therefore continue to have the right to sell and to exploit and grant licences of the rights in the Editorial Material and each Work;

(e) Clause 7 (*Series Editor's warranties and indemnity*) shall survive termination as shall all provisions required to interpret or enforce this Agreement; and

(f) the parties' accrued rights and obligations which exist immediately before termination shall not be affected.

10. Death of the Series Editor

If the Series Editor dies while this Agreement is in force:

(a) this Agreement shall remain in effect, as varied by this Clause 10, and the Publishers shall remain owners of the rights assigned to them under Clause 2.3 (*Assignment of copyright*);

(b) the Publishers' obligations to make payments under this Agreement shall continue on any edition of any Work edited by the Series Editor which, at the time of the Series Editor's death, is available in exchange for payment in any format published by the Publishers or has been delivered to and accepted by the Publishers, and on any subsequently manufactured copies of such an edition;

(c) in relation to any other edition of any Work published after the Series Editor's death whether edited by the Series Editor or not, and any subsequently manufactured copies of such an edition, no payments shall be due to be made by the Publishers under this Agreement; and

(d) the Publishers shall continue to have the right to use and permit the Publishers' licensees to use the Series Editor's name on any editions, versions and publications of or including all or part of any Work or any part of the Series published after the Series Editor's death, whether or not they contain any material prepared by the Series Editor, and may give priority to the name(s) of any others who prepare them.

11. Notices

11.1 *Methods of Giving Notice*

All notices and other communications relating to this Agreement:

(a) shall be in writing and delivered by hand or sent by post or fax (but not e-mail);

Book Series Editor – Publisher Agreement – Notes

(b) shall be delivered or sent to the party concerned at the relevant address or number, as appropriate (subject to any amendments notified by the relevant party to the other in accordance with this Clause); and

(c) shall take effect only when actually received at the appropriate address. For these purposes, a fax is received when a complete and legible copy of the notice, whether the notice sent by fax or a copy sent by post or hand, has been received. However, if any communication would otherwise become effective on a non-Business Day or after 5pm on a Business Day, it shall instead become effective at 10am on the next Business Day.

'Business day' means a day when banks generally are open in the City of London for the transaction of general banking business, excluding in any event Saturday, Sunday and 25 December to 1 January inclusive.

11.2 *Initial Notice Details*

The initial details for the purposes of Clause 11.1 (*Methods of giving notice*) are:

Party: The Series Editor

Address: [*Insert address from beginning of agreement – if appropriate, c/o agent*]

[Fax No:]

Party: The Publishers

Address:

For the attention of: The Managing Director

Fax No:

11.3 *Notices Following the Series Editor's Death*

If the Series Editor dies then, until the Publishers have received a certified copy of the grant of representation to the Series Editor's estate, any notice or other communication addressed to the Series Editor or to the Series Editor's personal representatives which is sent or delivered in accordance with Clause 11.1 (*Methods of giving notice*) shall be deemed sufficient service of it on the Series Editor and on the Series Editor's personal representatives and shall be effectual as if the Series Editor were still alive.

12. Assignment

12.1 *No Assignment by the Series Editor*

The Series Editor may not assign any of the Series Editor's rights, nor sub-contract any of the Series Editor's obligations, under this Agreement.

12.2 *Assignment by the Publishers*

The Publishers may assign all or any of the Publishers' rights and transfer all or any of the Publishers' obligations under this Agreement to any person without any requirement to notify or obtain the further consent of the Series Editor. Following any permitted assignment and/or transfer under this Clause 12.2, any reference in this Agreement to the Publishers shall, where the context allows, include the assignee and/or transferee.

13. Third Party Rights

The parties do not intend any term of this Agreement to be enforceable by any person who is not a party to this Agreement.

14. Law and Dispute Resolution

14.1 *Governing Law*

This Agreement shall be governed by and construed in accordance with English law.

14.2 *Dispute Resolution*

Any dispute or question which may arise under or in connection with this Agreement, or the legal relationships established by it, shall be referred to the arbitration scheme operated by the UK Publishers' Association from time to time. However, if there is no such scheme in operation, or if its results would not be binding upon the parties, or if the dispute or question would not be eligible for resolution under it, or if the Publishers consider that the Publishers require urgent resolution of the dispute or question, each party irrevocably submits to the exclusive jurisdiction of the English courts to settle any such dispute or question.

15. Force Majeure

If the Publishers are delayed or hindered in or prevented from performing any of the Publishers' obligations under this Agreement by an event beyond the Publishers' reasonable control, the Publishers' obligations shall be

suspended for so long as and to the extent that the Publishers are so delayed, hindered or prevented. The Publishers shall not be deemed to be in breach of this Agreement, or otherwise be liable to the Series Editor, by reason of any delay or failure in performance of any of its obligations under this Agreement, to the extent caused by such an event and time for performance shall be extended accordingly.

16. Entire Agreement

This Agreement, any separate document which may be referred to in it (such as an option agreement), including in the definition of 'Specification', and any separate agreement already entered into between the parties (such as an author or contributor's agreement) which is not expressly terminated by this Agreement, together represent the entire agreement between the parties in relation to the Series and the Editorial Material and supersede any and all previous agreements, whether written or oral, between the parties in relation to that subject matter. All other terms, conditions, representations, warranties and other statements which would otherwise be implied (by law or otherwise) shall not therefore form part of this Agreement. Neither party shall have any liability or remedy in tort in respect of any representation, warranty or other statement (other than the warranties set out in Clause 7 (*Series Editor's warranties and indemnity*)) being false, inaccurate or incomplete unless it was made fraudulently. Each party acknowledges that in entering into this Agreement, it places no reliance on any representation, warranty or other statement relating to the Series, any Work or the Editorial Material (other than the warranties, representations and undertakings set out in Clause 7).

17. Amendments, Waivers and Rights

17.1 *Amendments*

No amendment or variation of the terms of this Agreement shall be effective unless it is made or confirmed in a written document signed by both the parties.

17.2 *Waivers*

No delay in exercising or non-exercise by either party of any right, power or remedy provided by law or under this Agreement shall impair, or otherwise operate as a waiver or release of, that right, power or remedy. Any waiver or release must be specifically granted in writing signed by the party granting it. Any single or partial exercise of any right, power or remedy provided by law or under this Agreement shall not preclude any other or further exercise of it or the exercise of any other right, power or remedy.

17.3 *Rights and Remedies not Exclusive*

The rights, powers and remedies of each party under this Agreement are cumulative and not exclusive of any rights or remedies of that party under the general law. Each party may exercise each of its rights, powers and remedies as often as it shall think necessary.

18. Interpretation

18.1 *Application to other Editions*

This Agreement shall apply to any new edition of the Series or any Work in the same way as it does to the existing edition of the Series or Work. The 'Work' shall include any new edition required by the Publishers and references to 'first publication' of the Work shall from then on mean first publication of that new edition.

18.2 *Where More than One Series Editor*

Where more than one person is defined as the Series Editor:

(a) those persons' obligations under this Agreement are joint and several;

(b) any reference to 'the Series Editor' is to any and all of them unless only one or some of them is or are specifically referred to and except as stated in sub-paragraph (e);

(c) payments due to the Series Editor under this Agreement shall be allocated to each person equally unless otherwise set out in this Agreement (and, if the Specification states that there is more than one editor of the Series, the payments due to the Series Editor under this Agreement shall instead be allocated to each of the editors equally, even if they are not each a party to this Agreement);

(d) free copies due to the Series Editor under this Agreement shall be divided equally and sent separately to each such person unless otherwise set out in this Agreement; and

(e) if any one such person should die, Clauses 10 (*Death of the Series Editor*) and 11.3 (*Notices following the Series Editor's death*) shall apply in relation to that person only, but not to the others.

18.3 *Contents Page and Headings*

In this Agreement, the contents page and headings are included for convenience only and shall not affect the interpretation or construction of this Agreement.

19 Advance/Grant/Expenses

Wording for three alternative methods of payment to a Series Editor is set out in the Precedent.

18.4 *Meaning of References*

In this Agreement, unless the context requires otherwise, any reference to:

(a) this Agreement includes the Appendices, which form part of this Agreement for all purposes;

(b) a Clause or to an Appendix is, as the case may be, to a clause of or appendix to this Agreement;

(c) Indemnify and indemnifying any person against any Losses by reference to a matter, event or circumstance includes indemnifying and keeping him indemnified immediately on demand against all Losses from time to time made, suffered or incurred by that person as a direct or indirect result of that matter, event or circumstance;

(d) a party is a party to this Agreement;

(e) a person includes any individual, firm, company, corporation, government, state or agency of state or any association, trust or partnership (whether or not having a separate legal personality);

(f) a statute or statutory provision includes any consolidation or re-enactment of the same and any subordinate legislation in force under the same from time to time; and

(g) writing shall include any modes of reproducing words in a legible and non-transitory form.

18.5 *Companies Act Definitions*

Unless the context requires otherwise, any words and expressions defined in the Companies Act and not defined in this Agreement shall have the meanings given to them in that Act.

18.6 *No Restrictive Interpretation*

In this Agreement, general words shall not be given a restrictive interpretation by reason of their being preceded or followed by words indicating a particular class of acts, matters or things.

19. Advance/Grant/Expenses

19.1 *Advance*

The Publishers shall pay the Series Editor a total of £[*amount*] per Work as an advance against, and on account of, all royalty and other earnings due to

the Series Editor under this Agreement in respect of that Work, divided up as follows:

(a) £[*amount*] within thirty (30) days of the agreement between the Publishers and the author/s of each Work having been signed by both parties; [and]

(b) £[*amount*] within thirty (30) days of the Publishers accepting each Work which is delivered to the Publishers; and

(c) £[*amount*] within thirty (30) days of the Publishers first publishing each Work in the UK.

OR

19.1 *Grant*

The Publishers shall pay the Series Editor a total of £[*amount*] as a grant towards the Series Editor's expenses of editing the Series. This shall be paid [*insert date or other timing of payment*].

OR

19.1 *Expenses*

The Publishers shall reimburse the Series Editor's pre-agreed expenses incurred in connection with the Series Editor's obligations under this Agreement up to a total of £[*amount*]. These expenses shall be met by the Publishers within 60 days of receipt of valid receipts and an itemised invoice from the Series Editor.

EXECUTION:

The parties have executed this Agreement after the Appendices.

Book Series Editor – Publisher Agreement – Notes

APPENDIX 1

Specification

Series Title:

Titles included:

General description of series: topic:

objectives:

readership:

Name(s) of series editor(s)

Number of words or number of pages (inclusive of illustrations):

Number, size and format of illustrations:
- artwork (roughs)
- artwork (final)
- black and white photographs
- colour photographs

Contribution of text and illustrations by Series Editor, if any, under this Agreement.

Guidelines for selecting contributors:

Format of disk for electronic delivery of typescript:

Form of Series Editor's name to be used:

Book Series Editor – Publisher Agreement – Notes

APPENDIX 2

Schedule

SIGNED by [name of series editor])

SIGNED by a duly authorised Director for))
and on behalf of (the Publishers))

PRECEDENT SIX

Academic Journal: Editor's Agreement

The provision of a neat precedent for a journal editor is not always straightforward since circumstances can vary considerably; the journal may be owned and published by a learned society; owned by a learned society but published by a publisher under contract with the society, or jointly owned by the society and the publisher. Whilst the normal duties of a journal editor can be generally defined, the methods of recompense to the editor can vary from a fee to cover an agreed timespan (or number of issues) to a royalty-based arrangement; the latter will be based on revenue received from subscriptions and other (related) income. In some cases there is provision of an agreed expenses budget to cover editorial expenses for an agreed time period. The following precedent is for an agreement directly between an editor and a publishing house and shows alternative wording for either an honorarium or a royalty. A publishing contract for a society-owned journal is provided as **Precedent Seven**.

It is worth noting that many editors will expect to negotiate on the terms of their contracts, certainly concerning remuneration but also on duties and the extent to which they are willing to warrant and/or indemnify. Given the importance of the relationship between the publisher and the editor, it is important to engage seriously with potential editors on these points and be willing to explain terms in the contract and the reasons behind them.

Preamble

This Precedent covers an agreement made between a journal editor and a publishing house rather than a learned society; the publication of a journal by a publisher on behalf of a learned society would be the subject of a separate contract (**see Precedent Seven**). In the case of an agreement between a learned society and a publisher, the agreement with the editor would be more complex since some responsibilities (e.g., appointment of the Editorial Board) might well reside with the society. The statement concerning copyright ownership in the journal should be adjusted to reflect the legal circumstances (**see Precedent Eight**). As the frequency of publication and the extent of each issue may alter in future, current details are attached in the Appendix which can then be amended as necessary. If the journal currently exists only in paper form, the wording could be amended to remove electronic publishing rights or left as it is on the basis that subsequent publication in electronic form would be likely at some point.

It is important to be clear about ownership of the journal. This may seem so obvious as to not be worth stating but it may prove necessary to avoid ambiguity in the future.

1. Appointment of Editor

The point at which the tenure of the Editor commences should be specified. This clause may need to be adjusted depending on whether the editor is appointed on signature or at the commencement of publication of a new journal. If there is a change of editorship for an established journal, the change of editor should ideally take place at the commencement of publication of a new volume of the journal.

2. Editor's Responsibilities

The tasks of the Editor may vary according to circumstance and the responsibilities listed in this section should be adjusted accordingly. Publishers may wish to make it explicit that the Editor has editorial control, though in practice this amounts to performance of the responsibilities set out.

(i) For a journal owned by a learned society, the society may be responsible *inter alia* for appointing the members of the editorial board. For a wholly owned journal, it may be preferable for the Editor to recommend, but for the Publishers to appoint the editorial board members, thus enabling the Publishers to ensure appropriate balance of expertise and geographical location and an orderly succession through staggered terms of office.

(ii) The majority of contributions to learned journals (primary research papers) are submitted voluntarily and are not paid for.

(iii) Fees for such material may be paid for by the Publishers, in particular for review articles.

(iv) The precise form of the peer review process to be followed (e.g., number of reviewers, whether or not the identity of the author and/or reviewer is to be disclosed) may be spelt out in separate guidelines. Most editors will have a view about how they wish to manage peer review, and it is good practice for the editor and publisher to be clear about this. Whatever method is used, it must be underpinned by good record-keeping. See Irene Hames, 'Peer Review and Manuscript Management in Scientific Journals: guidelines for good practice' (ALPSP/Blackwell, 2007).

MEMORANDUM OF AGREEMENT made this [*number*] day of [*month*] 20 [*year*] BETWEEN [*name*] (hereinafter termed 'the Editor') of [*address*] of the one part, and [*name of company*] (hereinafter termed 'the Publishers') of [*address*] on behalf of themselves, their successors in business and executors, administrators and assigns of the other part

WHEREAS the Publishers are the owners of the journal entitled [*title*] (hereinafter termed 'the Journal') including its legal goodwill, title and all rights including copyright and renewals and extensions of copyright, the exclusive right to publish, distribute, licence and sell the journal in any forms, media and languages throughout the world which appears with a current frequency of publication and average extent per issue as specified in the Appendix hereto

NOW IT IS HEREBY MUTUALLY AGREED AS FOLLOWS:

1. Appointment of Editor

The Editor is hereby appointed as editor of the Journal, commencing from Volume [*number*] Issue [*number*] with a publication date of *date*/from signature of this agreement. The duration of this appointment is as outlined in Clause 11 hereof.

2. Editor's Responsibilities

The Editor agrees to prepare for the Publishers and to the schedule agreed between the parties issues of the Journal commencing with Volume [*number*] Issue No [*number*] to be dated [*date*]. The Editor is responsible for [editorial control of the journal including] the following tasks:

(i) *Recommendation/appointment* of members of the Editorial Board of the Journal;

(ii) Soliciting suitable contributions to the Journal;

(iii) Commissioning authors to write editorials, review or other articles as agreed with the Publishers and the Editorial Board;

(iv) Arranging for peer review of contributions submitted to the Journal in accordance with guidelines laid down by the Publishers and the Editorial Board/the Journal's policy/best practice;

(v) Making arrangements with appropriate reviewers for book reviews for inclusion in the Journal [and ensuring that copies of book reviews are sent to the publishers of the books reviewed];

(vi) Publishers should normally secure either an assignment of copyright or an exclusive right of publication (or exclusive licence to publish) for each contribution (**see Precedent Eight**); in either case, the document must be signed. In exceptional cases, the rights granted may be non-exclusive.

(viii) The duties here may involve the Editor ensuring that contributors have obtained appropriate permissions where necessary. If so this should be explicitly stated.

(ix) An Editorial is not always required, or may be commissioned by the Editor from external contributors. A table of contents may not be required as it will be generated at the publishers.

(xii) The processing of articles varies between journals so it may be worth giving more detail on the editors' responsibilities here. In particular where there is an electronic submissions process articles may be passed to the publisher when received.

In some cases, the editorial structure is more complex, with a number of different people (e.g., Section Editors), all reporting to an Editor-in-Chief, responsible for different parts of the journal or of the process. Publishers may choose to reflect this in the contract with the editor, create separate contracts for the different roles or leave the more minor roles uncontracted (especially those where there is no remuneration).

3. Publishers' Responsibilities

The Publishers will normally have full control of all aspects of publication. It has become increasingly important that they should also have clear control of any licensing arrangements which may include electronic delivery of the whole journal (**see Precedent Twenty**) or the licensing of material in whole or in part to third parties – these could include licensees such as document delivery suppliers and aggregators; this clause should also cover translations of individual articles or the whole journal.

(vi) Securing written confirmation in the form specified by the Publishers of publication arrangements for each contribution to the Journal, to include *assignment of copyright/an exclusive publication licence* and the appropriate legal warranties and indemnities for each contribution;

(vii) Checking the content of all contributions to the Journal to ensure that there are no breaches of warranties provided by the contributors;

(viii) Communication with contributors concerning the acceptance, rejection or revision of contributions to the Journal;

(ix) Ensuring appropriate coverage and quality of contributions for publication in the Journal;

(x) Reading and undertaking overall supervisory editing of contributions accepted for publication in the Journal;

(xi) Preparing an Editorial, Table of Contents and other preliminary material for each issue of the Journal;

(xii) Submitting to the Publishers sufficient edited material for each issue in accordance with the required schedule as outlined in the Appendix hereto;

(xiii) Proofreading material for the Journal in accordance with the required schedule;

(xix) Where appropriate, providing original contributions to the Journal;

(xx) Providing advice and assistance in marketing of the Journal;

(xxi) Attendance at meetings with the Editorial Board and the Publishers as appropriate.

3. Publishers' Responsibilities

The Publishers shall be responsible for the entire control of the production, publication, pricing, promotion and sale of the Journal, including but not limited to the functions of copyediting, design (in consultation with the Editor), print buying and management, [*online mounting and delivery,*] sale of advertising space, pricing (including discounts), marketing and promotion, order processing and despatch. The Publishers shall also be responsible for all licensing arrangements for the Journal including the licensing of material from the Journal in whole or in part to third party licensees, in all media, whether in the original language or in translation.

4. Grant of Rights

The grant of rights applies to the Editor's own editorial work on the journal and any individual contributions written by the Editor for publication in the Journal. It should be remembered that although this work may be undertaken by the Editor, the copyright in his/her work may in fact lie with his/her employer (e.g., a university). This should be clarified and if necessary a separate document should be signed with the employer.

The Editor also has the responsibility of securing a satisfactory grant of rights from each contributor (see Clauses 2(vi) and 8). The same issue may apply with regard to ownership of copyright by the contributor's employer, and the Editor should be responsible for clarifying this.

5. Payments to the Editor

The payment models for journal editors can vary considerably.

Some will include an agreed sum to cover editorial office expenses over a specified number of issues or period of time. The agreed amount is then paid on publication of each issue or on the specified dates. Some journals published in electronic form are issued on an article by article basis, in which case the payment would need to be on specified dates.

In the case of a new journal it is common to pay an additional sum in advance of publication of the first issue, to cover the costs of setting up the editorial office (this may also apply on the appointment of a new editor for an existing journal). This contribution to expenses is sometimes treated as an advance on royalty in which case this advance would be unlikely to be recovered in the early years of a new journal, and the contract should state whether it is recoverable, whether any unearned advance accrues, or whether it is written off at the end of each accounting year.

An alternative approach is to set a maximum budgeted amount, and for the Publishers to cover expenses as they occur up to that amount; part of the total may be paid to the Editor to cover out-of-pocket expenses, although all such expenses would need to be accounted for.

An honorarium (or royalty) is treated separately from expenses as it is likely to be taxable.

Royalties are likely to be based on income received from subscriptions; other related revenue is often also included in the calculation. It is important to be clear both on what income streams are included in the calculation of royalties and what the basis of the income is (e.g. is it gross, net of subscription agents' discounts etc)

The payment date will depend on the Publishers' usual schedule.

4. Grant of Rights

Subject to the terms detailed in this Agreement, the Editor as owner of the copyright in the Editor's own editorial work on the journal and any individual contributions written by the Editor for publication in the Journal hereby assigns to the Publishers the entire copyright/a perpetual exclusive licence in such work and contributions and all other rights of a like nature which are or may be conferred in respect of such work and contributions throughout the world (including for the avoidance of doubt all electronic publishing rights) for the full legal term of copyright and all renewals, revivals and extensions thereof.

5. Payments to the Editor

The Publishers shall make the following payments to the Editor, namely:

5.1 An honorarium/stipend of [*amount*] per *issue/year*, payable annually/ on publication of each issue of the Journal. The honorarium shall be increased annually from [date] by the amount of the UK Retail Price Index (and any alteration in the number of papers published.)

[AND/OR]

5.1 A royalty of [*number*] per cent based on the sums received by the Publishers *on all subscription sales after deduction of any agent commission or bookseller discount of/all sums received by the Publishers related to* the Journal, payable in accordance with the terms of Clause 6 hereof.

[AND/OR]

5.2 A contribution to editorial expenses of [*amount*] per issue during [*year*]. The contribution to the editorial expenses budget will cover the general costs of the Editor communicating with potential contributors and referees including office accommodation, secretarial support, telephone, fax, stationery and postage costs and travel expenses for attendance at appropriate meetings in connection with the tasks of the Editor. The Publishers shall pay the Editor the sum of [*amount*] on signature of this Agreement followed by a payment of [*amount*] per issue of the Journal payable on publication of such issue. The contribution to editorial expenses shall be increased annually from [*date*] by the amount of the UK Retail Price Index (and any alteration in the number of papers published). The Editor shall supply to the Publishers by [*date*] in each year a detailed accounting of all expenses incurred in connection with the Journal.

6. Accounts

This clause will only be relevant if a royalty is payable.

8. Warranties and Indemnity

The Editor is only providing warranties and indemnities for his/her own input into each issue of the journal; if (s)he refuses to sign the clause in this form the Publishers may have to be content with a variant which states that to the best of the Editor's belief all is in order. Alternatively, the contract could provide that the Editor will sign a contributor agreement for every contribution they make to the journal. Again, it should be remembered that even if the Editor's work is original, the copyright may in fact belong to his/her employers (e.g., a university); this should be clarified and if necessary covered in a separate document signed on behalf of the university. There is an obligation on the Editor to secure adequate warranties and indemnities from each contributor as part of the Contributor Agreement (**see Precedent Eight** and Clause 2(vi) of this Precedent) and there may also be an obligation to make adequate checks that contributors' content does not breach these warranties (see Clause 2(vii)), although some editors will argue that this is beyond their remit or ability.

6. Accounts

Accounts shall be made up annually by the Publishers to December 31 and the account rendered and the balance due shall be despatched by the Publishers to the Editor not later than the following [*date*]. No account need be submitted unless specifically demanded nor payment made in respect of any period in which the sum due is less than £50.00 (fifty pounds) in which case the sum will be carried forward to the next accounting date.

7. Tax

The Publishers may deduct from any amount due to the Editor under this Agreement any sum that the Publishers are or may be under an obligation to deduct or withhold in respect of any tax, duty or other similar levy. The Editor shall keep the Publishers informed as to changes in the Editor's Value Added Tax status and if registered supply the Publishers with the registration number.

8. Warranties and Indemnity and Legal Reading

8.1 The Editor hereby warrants to the Publishers that the Editor has the right and power to make this Agreement and that the Editor's contributions to the Journal as set out in Clause 2 hereof are the Editor's own work, and will in no way whatever give rise to a violation of any existing copyright, or a breach of any existing agreement and that the Editor's contributions to the Journal as set out in Clause 2 hereof contain nothing defamatory or libellous and that all statements contained therein purporting to be facts are true and that nothing in the Editor's contributions to the Journal as set out in Clause 2 hereof is liable to give rise to a criminal prosecution or to a civil action for damages or any other remedy and the Editor will indemnify the publishers against any loss, injury or expense arising out of any breach of this warranty or arising out of any claim alleging that Editor's contributions constitute an infringement of copyright or contain libellous or defamatory matter. The Editor also undertakes to secure the necessary warranties and indemnities as specified in Clause 2(vi) hereof to cover each contribution accepted for publication in the Journal.

8.2 Should the Publishers require the Editor to alter any text of the Journal which may be construed as legally objectionable, infringing copyright, libellous, obscene or likely to be actionable by law, the Editor will be responsible for altering or removing the text as advised, but any such alteration or removal shall be without prejudice to and shall not affect the Editor's liability under this Agreement.

10. Changes to Frequency and Extent of Journal

Publishers may prefer a more informal approach of a simple confirmatory email/letter rather than an Addendum.

11. Period of Agreement and Termination

It is wise to have a clear agreement on the initial duration of the editor's appointment with provision for renewal if the editor's performance is deemed satisfactory. If provision for automatic renewal is included in the contract, then it is important to ensure that it also contains provision for either party to give reasonable notice of termination at other times than the end of a term. When inserting dates in this clause, it is wise to try and avoid a change of editorship during the course of a volume of the journal as this will necessitate changes to journal covers and promotional material.

Again it should be remembered that some electronic journals are issued article by article so the wording concerning 'issues' may have to be adjusted accordingly.

9. Failure to Deliver Material

The Publishers reserve the right to terminate this Agreement without notice should the Editor fail entirely to deliver material for any issue of the Journal or if sufficient material for more than one issue of the Journal in a twelve month period is not delivered by the due date.

10. Changes to Frequency and Extent of Journal

Any changes to the frequency and/or extent of the Journal shall be made by mutual agreement and covered by a further Addendum to this Agreement. Any such changes shall commence with the first issue of the next volume of the Journal to be issued.

11. Period of Agreement and Termination

Subject to Clause 9 hereof, this Agreement shall endure in the first instance until [*date*]. Thereafter this Agreement may be renewed for a further period of [*number*] years by mutual agreement between the parties, except that the Publishers have the right to terminate this Agreement:

(i) by giving the Editor no less than two months' notice in writing if the number of contributions falls to less than [*number*] per issue of the Journal over a six month period; or

(ii) by giving the Editor no less than three months' notice in writing if subscriptions fail to reach [*number*] within twelve months *of first publication of the Journal/of the Editor's appointment as Editor of the Journal.*

Should termination take effect under the terms of subclauses (i) and (ii) hereof the Editor's term of office shall cease following publication of the final issue of the then current volume of the Journal.

(iii) by giving the Editor twenty eight days' notice if, in the opinion of the Publishers, the Editor's performance under this Agreement is unsatisfactory. Unsatisfactory performance under this Clause shall include, but not be limited to a failure to perform to an adequate standard all or any of the tasks set out under Clause 2 of this Agreement.

Should the Editor wish to give notice of termination he/she shall do so by giving the Publishers no less than [*number*] months' notice in writing and his/her term of office shall cease following publication of the final issue of the current volume of the Journal/or at a different date by mutual agreement.

12. Editor's Copies

The Publisher may choose to provide the Editor with electronic access in addition to print copies and/or other benefits such as electronic access to other titles.

13. Force Majeure

Publishers should seek advice over whether this term might be more enforceable if reciprocal.

12. Editor's Copies

The Editor shall be entitled to [*number*] free print copies of each issue of the Journal on publication.

13. Force Majeure

The Publisher's performance of the Agreement is subject to governmental restrictions and controls on prices, materials and supplies, natural disasters, accidents, acts of war, civil disorder, strikes and other conditions beyond its control.

14. Applicable Law

This Agreement shall be governed by and construed in accordance with the laws of England regardless of its place of execution.

15. Arbitration

If any difference shall arise between the Editor and the Publishers touching the meaning of this Agreement or the rights and liabilities of the parties hereto, the same shall be referred to the arbitration of two persons (one to be named by each party) or their umpire in accordance with the provisions of the Arbitration Act 1996 or any amending or substituted statute for the time being in force.

15. Rights of Third Parties

A person who is not a party to this Agreement has no right under the Contracts (Rights of Third Parties) Act 1999 to enforce any term of this Agreement.

16. Entire Agreement

This Agreement sets forth the entire agreement between the parties at the date hereof and supersede any previous written or oral agreements, negotiations and understandings between them with respect to the subject matter hereof, and cannot be changed orally.

AS WITNESS THE HANDS OF THE PARTIES

Signed......................................

The Editor

Signed......................................

For the Publishers

Appendix

This sets out the current frequency of publication and average extent (pages or articles, as appropriate) of each issue of the journal. It also provides a schedule for submission of material for each issue and for the return of material proofread by the editor. In some cases the publisher may wish to include the journal's aims and scope in the Appendix, either in addition to or instead of the details above. This provides both parties with clarity as to the content expected in the journal.

APPENDIX

Current frequency of publication:

Current average extent of each issue:

Schedule:

VOLUME & ISSUE NUMBER	DELIVERY TO PUBLISHERS	RETURN OF PROOFREAD MATERIAL TO PUBLISHERS

(aims and scope of the journal)

PRECEDENT SEVEN

Society-Owned Journal Publishing Agreement

This new precedent covers publication of a journal by a publisher on behalf of a learned society. Society publishing agreements vary greatly because of a number of factors including the nature of the publishing arrangement, whether the contract covers the launch of a title or is a transfer from another publishing arrangement, the influence and views of any lawyers on either side involved in negotiating the contract (recognising that the lawyer that a society uses for advice on a publishing contract is frequently not a publishing specialist), and specific conditions or concessions which may have been negotiated during the 'wooing' stage of the society relationship. At a basic level, the contract should cover: who owns the journal; who is responsible for what; what money flows which ways (money may flow in both directions); protections offered by each party to the other (these may not be reciprocal); provisions for content published prior to the start of the agreement; post-termination provisions for content published during the term of the agreement; term and termination including renewal, and other standard contractual points such as jurisdiction.

Note: Transfer Guidelines

Some publishers are signatories to these guidelines, which address what happens when a journal moves between publishers. These situations are complex and are governed not only by the presence of the guidelines but also by any relevant surviving terms in predecessor contracts.

The guidelines are available at: http://www.uksg.org/Transfer/Code

Preamble

This precedent covers an agreement made between a learned society and a publisher. It assumes that the contract which deals with the appointment and duties of the editor will be a separate contract between the society and the editor, and that the society will be responsible to the publisher for the performance (or otherwise) of the editor. It assumes that the journal is owned by the society outright.

In some cases, societies will wish to limit the contract to the publisher, removing provision for subsidiary imprints, executors, administrators, assigns or successors to perform the contract in place of the publisher. Note that as the contract has a value to the publisher as an asset, the publisher may wish to push back on this point.

Rights and Responsibilities of the Proprietor

1. The Proprietor owns the journal. In some cases, it may be worth spelling out what this covers: e.g. goodwill, title, copyright, existing subscription list etc.

2. In some cases, society and publisher may jointly appoint the editor or the society may wish to have the publisher's input into editorial appointments.

Grant of Rights

5. It is usual for the society to grant all publishing rights to the publisher, including the right to sub-license. That is the cleanest approach, and is the one which gives the publisher the greatest opportunity to do its best for the society. Where the parties agree to a different split of rights it is important to define that clearly to avoid confusion later on.

MEMORANDUM OF AGREEMENT made this day of between [*name of Society*] of [*address*]

'the Proprietor' which expression shall, where the context admits, include the Proprietor's executors, administrators and assigns or successors in business as the case may be

AND

[*name of* Publisher] of [*address*] 'the Publisher', which expression shall, where the context admits, include any publishing imprint subsidiary to or associated with the Publisher, and the Publisher's executors, administrators and assigns or successors in business as the case may be.

It is mutually agreed as follows concerning a journal entitled

[name] 'the Journal'

Rights and Responsibilities of the Proprietor

1. The Proprietor owns the Journal including its legal goodwill, title and all rights including copyright and renewals and extensions of copyright.

2. The Proprietor has editorial control of the Journal, including appointment/*and remuneration* of the Journal's Editor(s) and Editorial Board.

3. The Aims and Scope of the Journal are set out in Schedule 1. The Proprietor shall be entitled to change the Aims and Scope of the Journal. The Proprietor shall consult with the Publisher prior to making any change to the Aims and Scope of the Journal which might reasonably be construed as significantly affecting the Journal's saleability to its existing subscribers.

4. The Proprietor will not publish a journal or other publication that competes substantially or wholly with the Journal, except with the Publisher. This does not apply to journals or other publications which were contracted or published at the time of signature of this Agreement.

Grant of Rights

5. The Proprietor grants to the Publisher the sole and exclusive right and licence to produce, print, digitise, publish, market and sell the Journal and all materials original to the Journal throughout the world

6. It is important that the agreement covers what happens to content (print and/or electronic) which is produced by the publisher during the term of the agreement, including who owns it and what rights each party has to use it. Given the increasing sale of products which have an ongoing access commitment built in (such as backfile) and systems which allow for automatic licensing of material (electronic permissions systems such as Rightslink) it is simpler, safer and more desirable if the publisher can retain at least a non-exclusive licence to use this content post-termination. Any financial arrangement relating to this material, such as the payment of royalties, should also survive termination.

Contributor Agreements

8. Arrangements for management of contributor agreements will vary, but it is important that the contract sets out clearly that who is responsible for collecting contributor agreements.

9. It is important that the Publisher is not required to publish a contribution without an acceptable contributor agreement.

10. Rights retained by a contributor will be set out in the contributor agreement, but the society and publisher may wish to agree the basic form of these. Depending on the parties' stance on author deposit and open access, they may wish to include provision for these.

Publication

11. In the event that stock of back issues is transferred to the Publisher, it may make sense for the Publisher to handle any claims on behalf of the society, but the principle that the Publisher is not responsible for anything before it starts publication should be maintained.

in all formats and all present or future media and to license further the Journal or any part or abridgement of the Journal or any part of the Journal in all present or future media and in all languages and formats, throughout the world for the term of this Agreement and all renewals thereof.

6. Any arrangement made under the terms of this Clause for material published, digitised and made electronically available by or for the Publisher shall remain valid after the termination of the Agreement. All printed copies, digital files and electronic media and products created by or for the Publisher at the Publisher's expense shall remain the exclusive property of the Publisher. The Publisher reserves the non-exclusive right to continue to generate, create/manufacture and sell such copies and any further copies, whether print copies, digital files or any other electronic media or products, as created or licensed for creation or manufacture by the Publisher or its licensee, contractor or agency, after termination of this Agreement. The Publisher shall pay the Proprietor royalties on such net sales receipts as required under Clause 32 below.

Contributor Agreements

7. The Contributor Agreement set out in Schedule 2 sets out the obligations and rights of authors of contributions to the Journal.

8. The Proprietor, or the Editor(s) appointed by and acting on behalf of the Proprietor, shall obtain for every contribution to the Journal a Contributor Agreement signed by the author(s) of that contribution which grants to the Proprietor and the Publisher all necessary rights to publish the material original to the contributor and all third party material contained in the Contribution.

9. In the absence of a signed Contributor Agreement acceptable to the Publisher, the Publisher reserves the right not to publish the work.

10. The Proprietor reserves the right to allow a contributor of an article in the Journal to use all or part of such an article in any printed book or article they may subsequently write or edit provided it is re-published after it appears in the Journal and that correct acknowledgement is given to the original publication and copyright holder.

Publication

11. The Publisher shall begin publication of the Journal starting with volume [*number*] Issue [*number*], [*month*], [*year*]. The Publisher shall have no responsibility for the issues published prior to this

12. Different publishers and societies prefer different levels of flexibility on numbers of pages and issues.

13. While this clause is unlikely ever to be invoked, it does provide both parties with some protection, for example where a contribution might prompt an accusation of libel.

Subscription Lists and Back Issues

14 and 15. The agreement between a society and a publisher often starts with an offer made by a publisher based on information provided by the society. These clauses provide a mechanism for ensuring that that information is accurate and for dealing with renegotiation where there are significant discrepancies (which might affect the financial viability of the arrangement). These clauses should be changed to reflect the income streams that the journal has. Note that while it may be uncomfortable for both parties to raise the issues that discrepancies may cause so early in the relationship, they do provide a vehicle for ensuring that the agreement gets off onto a good footing and that any misunderstandings or differences in view are quickly corrected.

16. This may not always be possible. It is important for the parties to be clear about what rights in back issues are licensed to the publisher, and also how any existing obligations to supply customers will be dealt with.

issue, including claims for issues arising from prior contractual arrangements with the Proprietor or their licensee(s) (for example the previous publisher of the Journal).

12. The Journal will be published [*number*] times per year, with each annual volume consisting of not more than [*number*] pages. The publication schedule shall be decided by mutual agreement between the Proprietor and the Publisher.

OR

12. The number of issues and pages of the Journal published each year and the schedule of publication shall be decided annually in advance by mutual agreement between the Proprietor and the Publisher.

13. Neither the Proprietor nor the Publisher shall be under any obligation to publish any contribution to the Journal. In the event that a contribution is not published within a period of 3 years from signature of the Contributor Agreement, all rights in that contribution shall revert to the contributor and the Contributor Agreement signed by the contributor shall be deemed to be cancelled.

Subscription Lists and Back Issues

14. The Proprietor shall supply the Publisher with a complete list of current and past subscribers (where available) up to the last issue published in volume [*number*]. In the event that the Publisher is unable to obtain said information from the Proprietor, or if the subscription details vary considerably from the information previously supplied by the Proprietor, then the Publisher reserves the right to request further due diligence and the right to renegotiate and revise the terms of this agreement. The Proprietor shall make every reasonable effort to assist the Publisher in obtaining this information.

15. The Proprietor warrants to the best of its knowledge that at the time of signature of this Agreement, there are no fewer than [*number*] paid-up individual subscribers and [*number]* paid-up institutional subscribers to the Journal. In the event that the subscription information transferred to the Publisher under Clause 14 above or the actual number of subscribers renewing to the Publisher does not support this warranty in terms of the actual total number of subscribers to the Journal, the Publisher reserves the right to request further due diligence and the right to renegotiate and revise the terms of this Agreement.

16. The Proprietor will make every reasonable effort to assist the Publisher in obtaining all back stock of the Journal including any electronic versions/digital files of the Journal and the necessary rights and

Responsibilities of the Editor

19–21. Editorial duties will be agreed between the society and the publisher. In many cases where the journal already has an editor is place, the society will seek to keep the editor's duties as close to the current ones as possible, and the publisher may need to be flexible on this, recognising that there may be cost implications.

permissions for the Publisher to make use of the electronic versions/ digital files of the Journal.

Member Copies

[*AS APPLICABLE:*]

17. The Proprietor undertakes to purchase [*number*] copies of each volume of the Journal at [*price*] per volume. The Proprietor may purchase additional volumes of the Journal at the same rate. Both the per volume and additional volume price [SELECT ONE: are subject to the movements of the UK Retail Price Index, the level on 1st January of the current financial year will apply OR will be renegotiated annually.] Such copies may not be offered for resale except to the Proprietor's members. Payment for copies supplied under the terms of this clause shall be [invoiced to the Proprietor for payment by 1st January of the year in which the volume appears] [set against the annual payment due to the Proprietor]. If the sum due for such copies is greater than the sum due to the Proprietor, the difference shall be paid by the Proprietor when requested by the Publisher. No royalties shall be payable on such copies.

Society Activities

[*OPTIONAL:*]

18. For the term of this Agreement the Proprietor agrees to provide the Publisher with an exhibition booth or table space, at no extra charge to the Publisher, for each conference organised by the Proprietor. It is understood that the purpose of providing exhibition space is to promote the Journal, the Publisher and any other related publications of the Publisher. The Proprietor agrees to waive the registration and exhibitor's registration fees for up to [*number, e.g. three*] representatives of the Publisher at each conference/meeting.

Responsibilities of the Editor

19. The Editor(s) shall be responsible for the compilation of each issue and shall provide the Publisher with all contributions electronically via email or if necessary, on disk or in print, together with all necessary illustrations in a form suitable for publication, acceptable to the Publisher and ready for production no less than [*number*] weeks prior to the publication date of each issue. The Editor(s) of the Journal shall be responsible for editing the articles of each issue of the Journal for technical content, form, conciseness, clarity, and accuracy. The

22. In some case this will be covered in the Society-editor agreement.

Warranties and Copyright Infringement

23–25. Given that the society appoints (and oversees) the editor, and the editor 'oversees' the contributors, there is chain of responsibility for the 'legal health' of the content which is largely outside the control of the publisher. However, it is the publisher that is likely to be in the front line of any legal difficulties or claims for damages. Although the risk of any problems is comparatively low, it is real. These clauses provide the publisher with protection and also emphasise to the society (and via the society the editor and authors) the importance of this issue. Publishers may choose to accept a watering down of this clause, but are advised to check whether such a watering down might have an impact on any insurance that they maintain.

Publisher shall be responsible for copy-editing, typesetting and proof-reading unless otherwise agreed in writing between the Proprietor and the Publisher.

20. The Editor(s) will read, check and correct the proofs and return them to the Publisher within [*number*] days of their receipt, or as otherwise agreed with the Publisher, failing which the Publisher may consider the proofs as passed for press. The Editor(s) may alter the text of any article in the proofs thereof, on condition that all charges for alterations made by him/her (exclusive of correcting printer's or the Publisher's errors) shall be charged to the Proprietor and paid for by the Proprietor, and the Publisher shall have the right to charge and collect such excess from the Proprietor from future earnings.

21. The Editor(s) shall be responsible for sending copies of any reviews of books published in the Journal to the publishers of the books.

22. The Editor(s) shall sign a Contributor Agreement for each contribution that they make to the Journal.

Warranties and Copyright Infringement

23. The Proprietor warrants to present for publication only material which is in no way whatever a violation or an infringement of any existing copyright or licence, which contains nothing libellous, in which all statements purporting to be facts are true, and in which any recipes or formulae or instructions are not injurious to the user and indemnifies the Publisher against all actions, suits, proceedings, claims, demands, damages and costs (including any legal cost or expenses properly incurred and any compensation costs and disbursements paid by the Publisher on the advice of their legal advisers to compromise or settle any claim) occasioned to the Publisher in consequence of any breach of this warranty or arising out of any claim alleging that the Journal constitutes an infringement of copyright or contains libellous or defamatory matter. By signing their Contributor Agreement as a condition of publication in the Journal, Contributors warrant and indemnify the Proprietor and the Publisher against any actions and claims.

[*APPLICABLE ONLY IF PUBLISHER IS HOSTING THE JOURNAL'S BACKFILE:*]

24. The Proprietor hereby warrants to the Publisher and their assigns and licensees that all backfile content in the Journal published prior to Volume [*number*] issue [*number*] does not violate or infringe any existing copyright or licence nor contain libellous or defamatory matter and the Proprietor indemnifies the Publisher against any legal actions, claims or costs arising out of any claim alleging an infringement.

Responsibilities of the Publisher

29. Prices may be determined by the publisher or in discussion with the Society. Note that because it is the publisher taking the financial risk in performance of the contract, it would be unusual for the publisher not to have some say in pricing.

31. Terms will vary.

25. Should the Publisher require the Proprietor to alter any content of the Journal which may be construed as legally objectionable, infringing copyright, libellous or likely to be actionable by law, the Proprietor will be responsible for altering or removing the content as advised, but any such alteration or removal shall be without prejudice to and shall not affect the Proprietor's liability under this Agreement.

26. If at any time during the continuance of this Agreement the copyright of the Journal in the reasonable opinion of the Publisher be infringed, and the Proprietor after receiving written notice of such infringement from the Publisher refuses or neglects to take proceedings in respect of the infringement, the Publisher shall be entitled to take proceedings in the joint names of the Publisher and the Proprietor upon giving the Proprietor a sufficient and reasonable security to indemnify the Proprietor against any liability for costs, and in this event any sum received by way of damages shall belong to the Publisher.

27. If the Proprietor is willing to take proceedings and the Publisher desires to be joined with them as a party to the proceedings and agrees to share the costs, then if any sum is recovered by way of damages and costs such sum shall be applied in payment of the costs incurred and the balance shall be divided equally between the Proprietor and the Publisher. The provisions of this clause are intended to apply only in the case of an infringement of the copyright in the Journal affecting the interest in the same granted to the Publisher under this Agreement.

Responsibilities of the Publisher

28. The Publisher shall be responsible for all matters relating to the production, manufacturing, design, promotion, marketing, and distribution of the Journal. The Publisher shall have the sole right to determine production, manufacturing procedures, processes and materials.

29. Following consultation with the Proprietor the Publisher shall have the sole and final right to determine all prices and discounts whether related to subscription sales, single copy, back issue or other sales, and the Publisher reserves the right to review such prices as future circumstances dictate.

30. The Publisher shall have the right to solicit advertising in the Journal using its best efforts and reasonable care in the sale of advertising space in a manner consistent with the purposes and policies of the Proprietor.

31. The Publisher shall make available to the Proprietor [*number*] complimentary print copies of each issue of the Journal, which

Payments

32–34. Exact terms should be set out clearly and unambiguously. It is likely that pre-contract negotiations will have determined whether any advances or guarantees are payable and on what basis.

includes any print copies due to the Editor, the editorial board and for exchange with other journals. The Publisher shall provide access to the published PDF of each article free of charge to the corresponding author of that article. In addition, the Publisher shall provide the corresponding author with one copy of the Journal issue in which the author's article appears. In the case of multi-authored articles the PDF access is available for onward distribution by the corresponding author. The Publisher shall also provide additional copies of the Journal issue to the corresponding author up to a maximum of [*number*] copies. Where the number of co-authors exceeds [*number*] the distribution of the five print copies of the Journal issue will be at the discretion of the corresponding author. In addition, the Publisher shall provide the corresponding author with one copy of the Journal issue in which the author's article appears.

Payments

32. The Publisher agrees to pay to the Proprietor royalties on net sales receipts from the Journal at the following rates:

Subscription sales: [*number*] per cent

Consortial sales: [*number*] per cent

Backfile sales; [*number*] per cent

Licensing: [*number*] per cent

Commercial sales (advertising, supplements, reprints, sponsored subscriptions); [*number*] per cent

Other sales: [*number*] per cent

Net receipts for the purposes of this Agreement shall be defined as all sales income received by the Publisher after deduction of normal agent commission or bookstore discount, local taxes and bank charges. The Publisher shall submit to the Proprietor an annual royalty statement by [*date*] of each year for the preceding 12 months ending the 31st of December. Within thirty days of the statement date the Publisher shall pay the Proprietor all royalties then due.

[*OPTIONAL ADVANCE WORDING – THIS IS BASIC WORDING ONLY AND MAY NEED REDRAFTING TO SUIT THE NEEDS OF THE CONTRACT:*]

EITHER

[33. The Publisher agrees to pay the Proprietor in advance and on account of all sums that may become due to the Proprietor under this Agreement the sum of [*amount*] per volume per year commencing with Volume [*number*], and payable by [*date*] each year.]

OR

[33. The Publisher agrees to pay the Proprietor each year in advance and on account of all sums that may become due to the Proprietor under this Agreement a guaranteed minimum sum equivalent to [*number*] per cent (*number%*) of the projected royalty due to the Proprietor for that year to be paid annually by [*date*] each year.

The Publisher shall inform the Proprietor of the projected royalty on or before [*date*] preceding the relevant year.]

[*OPTIONAL STIPEND WORDING:*]

[34. The Publisher shall provide an editorial stipend of [*amount*] to be paid annually by [*date*] each year.]

General

35. The Proprietor or their representative shall have the right upon written request to examine during normal business hours the records of account of the Publisher in so far as they relate to the sales and receipts in respect of the Journal, which examination shall be at the cost of the Proprietor unless errors exceeding £10.00 to their disadvantage shall be found, in which case the cost shall be paid by the Publisher.

36. Unless the context otherwise requires words in this Agreement denoting the singular shall include the plural and vice versa and words denoting any one gender shall include all genders and words denoting persons shall include corporations, partnerships, limited liability companies and other legal entities.

37. A person who is not a party to this Agreement has no right under the Contracts (Rights of Third Parties) Act 1999 to enforce any term of this Agreement.

38. This Agreement contains the full and complete understanding between the parties and supersedes all prior arrangements and understandings whether written or oral appertaining to the subject matter of this Agreement and may not be varied except by an instrument in writing signed by all the parties to this Agreement. Nothing in this Agreement excludes either party's liability for fraud or death or personal injury caused by a party's negligence.

Term, Termination and Notice

41. It is important that the term of the contract is long enough to give both parties time to settle in and for the publisher's investment in marketing etc. to begin to take effect. This clause should be clear about termination date and the basis of any renewal.

42. See 6 above.

43. While it is reasonable to ask that a society allow a publisher to rebid and to match another publisher's bid to take over publication, it is going too far to require a Society to accept a bid it does not wish to accept simply by virtue of it being better financially.

39. The headings in this Agreement are for convenience only and shall not affect its interpretation. References to Clauses are to clauses of this Agreement.

Breach and Notice

40. If either party breaches any of the material terms of this Agreement, the other party shall be permitted to terminate this Agreement upon giving one hundred and eighty (180) days' written notice to the breaching party; provided, however, that such notice shall be given no more than sixty (60) days after the discovery of any such breach; and provided, further, that such notice shall specify the exact nature of the breach and allow the breaching party sixty (60) days in which to correct such breach.

Term, Termination and Notice

41. This Agreement shall become effective on [*date*] and continue for a period of [*number*] years through the publication of the last issue due in the volume for [*year*]. Unless notified in writing one year before termination of this Agreement (by 31st December of the year preceding the final year of publication), this Agreement shall be renewed automatically for further successive periods of [*number*] years, with the same notice period as specified above.

42. In the event this Agreement terminates, all rights and obligations of the parties automatically terminate except for those specified in Clauses 6, 23, 24 and 25 above and all obligations in respect of material from the Journal to which access continues to be required by paid subscribers, licensees or purchasers. In this event, the Publisher reserves the non-exclusive right to continue providing in perpetuity online/electronic access to all content of the Journal, including all backfile, published and/or digitised and/or made electronically available by the Publisher to customers who have subscribed to, purchased or otherwise obtained the rights to that content prior to the date of termination or who subsequently purchase any products conceived, manufactured or licensed for manufacture by the Publisher or its licensees, which include content of the Journal published and/or digitised and/or made electronically available by the Publisher. Net revenues arising from such supply shall be treated as net sales receipts for the payment of royalties in Clause 32 above.

43. In the event the Proprietor does not wish to renew this Agreement and gives Notice to the Publisher, the Publisher has the right to re-bid to publish the Journal and hereby reserves the right to be informed by the Proprietor of another successful bid and to have the opportunity to

match this bid to publish the Journal. The Society shall not be obliged to accept such a bid.

44. This Agreement shall be construed in accordance with the laws of England regardless of its place of execution.

45. Any notice required or permitted by this Agreement to be given to a party shall be in writing, and shall be delivered in the case of the Proprietor to

[*address*]

and in the case of the Publisher to

The Editorial Director

[*name of Publisher*]

or to such other address as either party may specify.

For [*name of Publisher*] Date

For [*name of Society*] Date

Schedule 1

See clause 3. It can be useful to include the journal's aims and scope.

SCHEDULE 1

Aims and Scope

Schedule 2

It is useful to include the journal's standard contributor agreement. Note that it is likely that when a journal moves publisher, the journal will take on a contributor agreement that conforms (by and large) to the new publisher's standard agreement.

SCHEDULE 2

Journal Contributor's Publishing Agreement

PRECEDENT EIGHT

Journal Contributor Agreements

It is vital that journal publishers – be they learned societies, university presses or commercial publishers – secure clear written arrangements for publication of each contribution in each issue of the journal in question. Traditionally, journal contributors do not receive payment for their work – publication in a peer-reviewed academic journal has long been regarded as crucial to academic advancement.

Arrangements are normally covered by means of a short-form of agreement specifying the journal, the author, the title of the article and the extent of the rights granted to the publisher. The author is expected to provide warranties and indemnities as to the originality of the material, that it has not been previously published elsewhere and that it does not contain material likely to give rise to any legal action. There may be a statement on the moral rights of the author, although it can be argued that these are not applicable to journal contributions. It is wise for the publisher to include clear details of how and when the author may use the material elsewhere, for example, posting a version of the article online, use for teaching purposes or as the basis for further research in the author's field.

It is important that the journal contributor agreement is clear on the question of who owns copyright in the contribution. There are differences of opinion here; some publishers may insist that copyright is assigned to them, whilst others may be content provided they have secured a grant of rights which is sufficient to enable them to use the material in the way they require. This will often be an exclusive licence. Most publishers would now view the control of electronic rights as crucial as so many journals are now published either in both print and electronic format or in electronic format alone.

A number of research funders, as well as some universities and other institutions, now either request or require recipients of their grants to deposit a freely available copy of a version of their article in an institutional or other repository. Most such funders permit a short time delay (e.g., 6–12 months) after publication, if required by the publisher, before this copy is made freely available to all. The journal contributor agreement should be clear on the length of any delay ('embargo') and also which version of the article may be deposited. In specifying the version, it is best to avoid terms such as 'preprint' or 'postprint' without further clarification as their meaning can vary.

Some authors (or – particularly in the case of Open Access journals which are free to the reader – the publisher) may wish to use one of the Creative Commons licences (www.creativecommons.org). These allow the author to specify whether others may reuse the content freely, or only with attribution, or only for non-commercial purposes.

Some funders or individual institutions may suggest that their authors substitute a different agreement, or append an addendum to the publisher's agreement (often based on that created by SPARC (http://www.arl.org/SPARC/author/index.html)). These should be scrutinised carefully to ensure that they are compatible with the publisher's policy and interests.

In considering whether to accept Creative Commons licences or institutional addenda in place of the usual journal contributor agreement, the publisher should ensure that they will still have enough rights to publish the article in its normal way, including any sub-licensing or granting of permissions.

Authors and institutions are more aware than ever of their rights and interests and the different publishing models made available by the internet. When this is combined with the fact that a single journal could have hundreds of contributors, publishers may wish to cut down on individual negotiations by having a contributor agreement that strikes a balance between their commercial interests and the needs of the author and their institution.

Publishers should consider carefully the question of whether to require all authors of an article to sign an agreement. Doing so decreases the risk of an author being included who has not contributed to the work but may significantly increase workload. It is much more difficult to guard against authors being excluded and publishers may wish to set out how they will deal with such issues in the instructions they provide to authors, in order to encourage careful listing of all authors, as resolving authorship disputes is difficult and time-consuming.

This section contains three precedents. The first two are models recommended to members of the Association of Learned and Professional Society Publishers (ALPSP): a licence to publish, where ownership of copyright is retained by the author, and a copyright transfer and publication agreement; both of these include wording to address the requirements of research funders outlined above. The third precedent also covers an assignment of copyright arrangement with explanatory notes to the contributor; this was prepared by John Cox (www.johncoxassociates.com).

The ALPSP Model Grant of Licence (Precedent Eight A) provides recommended wording for an agreement between the publisher and journal author about copyright. It gives a clear explanation of the rights of both parties and includes rights for contributors to post an article on a website or a preprint server. The Model Copyright Transfer Agreement (Precedent Eight B) adapts the same wording for use where copyright is transferred to the publisher, but the author retains the same rights.

The journal contributor agreements below take account of the growing number of research funders which now either request or require their grant recipients to deposit a version of their article in an institutional or other repository. Publishers may wish to consider whether or not their subscriptions are likely to be impacted by widespread self-archiving; if they believe this is a serious risk, they may wish to impose a suitable time limit before which authors may not deposit. Journals in different disciplines, and with different frequency of publication, might require different approaches. When possible, publishers may also wish to consider taking on the responsibility of depositing on behalf of authors; this would not only save the authors trouble, but also ensure that the appropriate version is deposited at the appropriate time, and with a correct link to the definitive published version.

The second version of a Copyright Assignment for journal authors (Precedent Eight C) is similar, but uses more formal legal language.

PRECEDENT EIGHT A: Licence to Publish

This Precedent covers an exclusive grant of publishing rights to the publishers in any medium, throughout the world, and includes the right to publish the abstract – crucial to journal publishers. Copyright in the material is retained by the author.

Preamble

The author is usually the copyright owner; however, it is important for the publishers to be clear whether this is the case or whether copyright may be owned by the author's employer, for example, an academic institute, commercial company or indeed government. The situation will depend on the terms of the author's employment.

1. This spells out the publication rights granted to the publishers, including the right to license the material to third parties including reprographic rights organisations (**see Appendix E**).

2. This provides the publishers with the necessary warranties to cover the author's work. The author must also provide confirmation that permission has been secured for the inclusion of any copyright material (textual or illustrative) belonging to third parties which does not fall under one of the copyright exceptions and that such material is clearly acknowledged. The warranty covering libel and legality generally in this agreement is qualified to the 'best of the author's knowledge'. This is not the case in all contributor agreements. On the one hand, an author cannot be expected to have in-depth knowledge of the law. On the other, they should be expected to have in-depth knowledge of their content. Similarly, there are no indemnities in this agreement. Indemnities are not always popular with authors since they feel that the publisher has more resources to carry the risk of legal action. That said, without an indemnity publishers are vulnerable to situations over which they have no control because the author writes the work and is in the best position to know whether what they wrote contains infringing material and whether statements that are critical of people or institutions are true. An indemnity could be seen as a crucial backup to a warranty and some media perils insurers may require it. A typical indemnity might be: 'and you agree to indemnify us against any claims in respect of the above warranties [promises]'.

3. UK copyright law requires that the author asserts his or her moral rights for them to be effective (**see Appendix H**), although it is not entirely clear whether or not this is applicable to journal contributions. Here, in turn the publishers agree to give clear acknowledgment to the author and to consult him or her if they make any substantial changes to the material. Arrangements for peer review, if appropriate, and acceptance/rejection of the material are covered here. While most journals are peer-reviewed, it is not always the practice to include mention of this in the contributor agreement.

PRECEDENT EIGHT A

Licence to Publish

In order to publish your article we need your agreement in writing. Please take a moment to read the terms of this licence, sign the form and return it to us as quickly as possible.

Name of Journal...

Title of Article ....

Name(s) of Author(s)...

....

....

Name of Copyright Owner, if not Author(s) ....

- By signing this form, **you (the author(s)) agree** to grant to us (the publisher) the exclusive right both to reproduce and/or distribute your article (including the abstract) ourselves throughout the world in printed, electronic or any other medium, and in turn to authorise others (including Reproduction Rights Organisations such as the Copyright Licensing Agency and the Copyright Clearance Center) to do the same. You agree that we may publish your article in the journal named above, and that we may sell or distribute it within the journal, on its own, or with other related material.

- **You promise** that the article is your original work, has not previously been published, and is not currently under consideration by another journal. If it contains material which is someone else's copyright, you promise that you have obtained the unrestricted permission of the copyright owner (please attach evidence of this) and that the material is clearly identified and acknowledged within the text. You also promise that the article does not, to the best of your knowledge, contain anything which is libellous, illegal, or infringes anyone's copyright or other rights.

- [**You assert** your Moral Right to be identified as the author, and] **We promise** that we will respect your rights as the author(s). That is, we will make sure that your name(s) is/are always clearly associated with the article, and we will not make any substantial change to your article without consulting you. [We will have your article fairly reviewed by [at least two] impartial referees, and will let you know the outcome as quickly as possible.] When the article is accepted, we undertake to publish it as soon as we reasonably can. If it is rejected, this agreement

4. This clause confirms that ownership of copyright is retained by the author, but allows the publisher to take legal action in case of copyright infringement and provides for half damages after costs to be paid to the author. The publisher may want to consider whether this is necessary for an arrangement where the author does not receive royalties or a fee in the first place. It also specifies the ways in which the author may make use of the material provided that this does not conflict with the publishers' own commercial use of the material. There is provision for the publisher to specify a time delay before the author's self-archived copy may be made freely available. Optional wording is provided for use where the publisher prefers to take an active role in depositing articles on authors' behalf in specified repositories.

Where there are multiple authors, many publishers consider it desirable (though sometimes arduous) to obtain a signed agreement from each named contributor; this avoids erroneous inclusion of authors who have not made a real contribution, or who for any reason do not wish to be named, although it unfortunately cannot guard against erroneous omission of any author (see *Committee on Publication Ethics Guidelines on Good Publication Practice* (http://www.publicationethics.org.uk/guidelines) and Hames, *Peer Review and Manuscript Management in Scientific Journals: guidelines for good practice* (ALPSP/Blackwell, 2007)).

A pragmatic solution, when the number of contributors is large, is to ask the corresponding author to warrant that all the other named contributors have given him their consent in writing.

is automatically cancelled and all the rights come back to you. On publication, we will send you [*number* free offprints][a free copy]. We will take all reasonable steps to maximise the visibility of the journal, and of your article within it.

- **Copyright remains yours**, and we will acknowledge this in the copyright line which appears on your article. However, you authorise us to act on your behalf to defend your copyright if anyone should infringe it, and to retain half of any damages awarded, after deducting our costs. You also retain the right to use your own article (provided you give full acknowledgement of the published original) as follows, as long as this does not conflict with our business: for the internal educational or other purposes of your own institution or company; mounted on your personal web page;]; in whole or in part, as the basis for your own further publications or spoken presentations. [In addition, you may post/a copy of the originally submitted version of your article ('preprint')/*a copy of the version of your article incorporating changes made during peer review ('postprint')*/to a free public institutional or subject repository, no sooner than (*number*) months after publication in the journal; such copy must include the following notice:

  © [name of author, year]. The definitive, peer reviewed and edited version of this article is published in [name of journal, volume, issue, pages, year, DOI or URL].]

  [If the funder of your research so requires, we will on your behalf post/a copy of the originally submitted version of your article ('preprint')/a copy of the version of your article incorporating changes made during peer review ('postprint')/*a copy of the final published version of your article*/to the repository specified by your funder, (*number*) months after publication in the journal. Please notify us of your funder's requirements.]

- We will keep the **information** you have provided for record purposes; you permit your name and address to be reproduced in the journal and on indexing and abstracting and bibliographic services. Your details will not be used for any other purpose.

Signature(s) of Author(s) .... Date ....

.... Date ....

.... Date ....

.... Date ....

Note: every named author must sign this form, or a copy of it

Signature of Copyright Owner, if different .... Date ....

Note: if your employer, government or someone else owns the copyright, please ask them to sign here

Please return this form by post or fax to [*address details*]

PRECEDENT EIGHT B: Copyright Transfer and Publication Agreement

1. This precedent differs from the Licence to Publish version in that it provides for a full assignment of copyright from the author to the publisher. One alternative to offering separate forms for government employees is simply to have a separate tick boxes for authors to register their status.

PRECEDENT EIGHT B

Copyright Transfer and Publication Agreement

In order to publish your article we need your agreement in writing. Please take a moment to read the terms of this agreement, sign the form and return it to us as quickly as possible.

Name of Journal ....

Title of Article ....

Name(s) of Author(s)...

....

....

Name of Copyright Owner, if not Author(s) ....

Address of above (if applicable) ....

....

....

- By signing this form, **you (the author(s) or other copyright owner) hereby transfer** your copyright to us (the publisher). If you do not own the copyright yourself, the copyright owner (e.g., your employer) should sign the form. If you are a UK government employee, we will send you a special form to sign; if you are a US government employee, your work is not subject to copyright (although, if one or more of the authors are not government employees, they should still sign).

- In particular, this means that **you grant** us the exclusive right, for the full term of copyright and any renewals/extensions thereof, both to reproduce and/or distribute your article (including the abstract) ourselves throughout the world in printed, electronic or any other medium, and in turn to authorise others (including Reproduction Rights Organisations such as the Copyright Licensing Agency and the Copyright Clearance Center) to do the same. (If you receive any direct requests for permission to use your article, please pass them on to [*permissions contact*]; we will respond as speedily as possible.)

- **You agree** that we may publish your article in the journal named above, and that we may sell or distribute it within the journal, on its own, or with other related material. In return, we agree to publish your article at our expense.

4. This confirms that copyright is assigned but that the publishers grant back to the author the right to reuse the work in designated ways which do not conflict with the interests of the publishers.

This provides the publishers with the necessary warranties to cover the author's work. The author must also provide confirmation that permission has been secured for the inclusion of any copyright material (textual or illustrative) belonging to third parties which does not fall under one of the copyright exceptions and that such material is clearly acknowledged. The warranty covering libel and legality generally in this agreement is qualified to the 'best of the author's knowledge'. This is not the case in all contributor agreements. On the one hand, an author cannot be expected to have in-depth knowledge of the law. On the other, they should be expected to have in-depth knowledge of their content. Similarly, there are no indemnities in this agreement. Indemnities are not always popular with authors since they feel that the publisher has more resources to carry the risk of legal action. That said, without an indemnity publishers are vulnerable to situations over which they have no control because the author writes the work and is in the best position to know whether what they wrote contains infringing material and whether statements that are critical of people or institutions are true. An indemnity could be seen as a crucial backup to a warranty and some media perils insurers may require it. A typical indemnity might be: 'and you agree to indemnify us against any claims in respect of the above warranties[promises]'.

- **You warrant (i.e., promise)** that the article is your original work, has not previously been published, and is not currently under consideration by another journal. If it contains material which is someone else's copyright, you promise that you have obtained the unrestricted permission of the copyright owner (please attach evidence of this) and that the material is clearly identified and acknowledged within the text. You also promise that the article does not, to the best of your knowledge, contain anything which is libellous, illegal, or infringes anyone's copyright or other rights.

- **You assert** your Moral Right to be identified as the author, and **we promise** that we will respect your rights as the author(s). That is, we will make sure that your name(s) is/are always clearly associated with the article and, while you do allow us to make necessary editorial changes, we will not make any substantial alteration to your article without consulting you. [We will have your article fairly reviewed by [at least two] impartial referees, and will let you know the outcome as quickly as possible.] When the article is accepted, we undertake to publish it as soon as we reasonably can. If it is rejected, this agreement is automatically cancelled and all the rights come back to you. On publication, we will send you [XX free offprints][a free copy]. We will do everything we reasonably can to maximise the visibility of the journal, and of your article within it.

- **Copyright is transferred to us**, and we will indicate this in the copyright line which appears on your article. However, we grant back to you the right to use your own article (provided you acknowledge the published original in standard bibliographic citation form) in the following ways, as long as you do not sell it [or give it away] in ways which would conflict directly with our commercial business interests. You are free to use your article for the internal educational or other purposes of your own institution or company; mounted on your personal web page; or in whole or in part, as the basis for your own further publications or spoken presentations.

  [In addition, you may post *a copy of the originally submitted version of your article ('preprint')/a copy of the version of your article incorporating changes made during peer review* ('postprint')/to a free public institutional or subject repository, no sooner than (number) months after publication in the journal; such copy must include the following notice:

  > <u>© [name of publisher, year]. The definitive, peer reviewed and edited version of this article is published in [name of journal, volume, issue, pages, year, DOI or URL].]</u>

  [If the funder of your research so requires, we will on your behalf post/*a copy of the originally submitted version of your article*

('preprint')/a copy of the version of your article incorporating changes made during peer review ('postprint')/a copy of the final published version of your article to the repository specified by your funder, X months after publication in the journal. Please notify us of your funder's requirements.]

- We will keep the **information** you have provided for record purposes; you permit your name and address to be reproduced in the journal and on indexing and abstracting and bibliographic services. Your details will not be used for any other purpose.

Signature(s) of Author(s) .... Date ....

.... Date ....

.... Date ....

.... Date ....

Note: every named author must sign this form, or a copy of it

Signature of Copyright Owner, if different .... Date ....

Please return this form by post or fax to [address details]

PRECEDENT EIGHT C: ASSIGNMENT OF COPYRIGHT

This precedent covers a full assignment of copyright to the publishers and is accompanied by explanatory notes for the contributor, including details of how he or she may use the material.

1. This provides a clear assignment of copyright in the material to the publishers. If copyright is owned not by the author but by his or her employers, the form may have to be signed on behalf of the employers; details of how it might need to be adapted in such circumstances are provided in the notes to the contributor. In addition to the word 'beneficial' it may be advisable to also describe the author as legal owner of the copyright.

1 and 2. These make clear that it is the act of preparing the article for publication, and publishing it constitutes the 'Consideration' in return for which the author hands over his or her copyright.

1. Since copyright has been transferred in its entirety, there is no need to specify the particular rights which the publisher may exercise (for example, licensing of third parties to reissue the article in aggregations, translations etc), but this may be helpful. Here some such uses are specified in the notes.

3. This provides for consultation with the author in the case that substantial changes to the material are required but allows for flexibility, for example if the author is difficult to contact.

4. Although English law is unclear as to whether moral rights in fact apply to journal articles (articles published in 'a newspaper, magazine or similar periodical' are explicitly excluded), there is no harm in including this clause.

5. This provides the necessary warranties for publishers.

PRECEDENT EIGHT C

Assignment of Copyright

Please read the notes overleaf and fill in, sign and return this form with your corrected proofs.

So that we can ensure both the widest dissemination and protection of material published in [*publisher*]'s journal(s), we ask authors to assign world-wide copyright in both print and other media in their papers, including abstracts, to [*publisher*] (referred to here as '[*short form of publisher name, if applicable*]'). This enables us to ensure copyright protection against infringement, and to disseminate your article, and our journal(s), as widely as possible.

1. In consideration of the undertaking set out in paragraph 2, the Author as beneficial owner hereby assigns to [*short form of publisher name*] the copyright in the Article entitled:

....

by ....

to be published in .... ('the Journal')

for the full legal term of copyright. So that there is no doubt, this assignment includes the right to publish the material in the article in electronic form (subject to paragraphs 3 and 4); the Article may be published in printed, online, CD-ROM, DVD-ROM, microfiche, or other forms appropriate for its readership.

2. [*Short form of publisher name*] hereby undertakes to prepare and publish the Article named in paragraph 1 in the Journal.

3. The Editor of the Journal and [*short form of publisher name*] are empowered to make such editorial changes as may be necessary to make the Article suitable for publication. Every effort will be made to consult the Author if substantive changes are required.

4. The Author hereby asserts *his/her* moral rights under the Copyright, Designs and Patents Act 1988 to be identified as the Author of the Article.

5. The Author warrants that the Article is the Author's original work, has not been published before, and is not currently under consideration for publication elsewhere; and that the Article contains no libellous or unlawful statements and that it in no way infringes the rights of others, and that the Author, as the owner of the copyright, is entitled to make this assignment.

6. Some would argue that it is safer to obtain the signature of every author who is named on the article, to avoid 'gift' authorship (inclusion of someone who has not in fact contributed actively to the work).

7. The majority of publishers currently permit authors to self-archive a version of their article in a publicly accessible repository of some kind (see Cox & Cox, *Scholarly Publishing Practice; Academic Journal Publishers' Policies and Practices in Online Publishing (Second Survey)*, ALPSP, 2005). However, it is increasingly common to specify a time delay before the self-archived version may be made freely available.

6. If the Article was prepared jointly by more than one author, the Author warrants that *he/she* has been authorised by all co-authors to sign this agreement on their behalf.

7. Notwithstanding the assignment of copyright agreed herein, the Author shall retain the right to post *his/her* final post peer-review manuscript version of the Article to *his/her* institution's repository or subject-based repository or personal web page, and to use the content of the Article in *his/her* personal teaching or research, provided only that the full reference to the Journal is cited as the source, and a live link to the published version on [*short form of publisher name*]'s site is provided.

Signed by the Author... [*name of Author*]

Date.......................................

Assignment of Copyright: Explanatory Notes to Author

[*Short form of publisher name*]'s policy is to acquire copyright for all contributions, for the following reasons:

1. ownership of copyright by a central organisation helps to ensure maximum international protection against infringement;

2. requests for permission to reproduce articles in databases, books and other types of publication, course packs or for library loan can be handled efficiently and with sensitivity to changing library and reader needs. This relieves authors of a time-consuming and costly administrative burden;

3. the demand for research literature to be delivered in electronic form online, or on physical media such as CD-ROM or DVD-ROM, can be met efficiently, with proper safeguards for authors, editors and journal owners.

There are opportunities to reach institutions (e.g., companies, schools and public libraries) and individual readers that are unlikely to subscribe to the journal itself. [*Short form of publisher name*] works with other organisations to publish, where appropriate, in online databases or to deliver copies of individual articles. It has also registered the Journal with the Copyright Licensing Agency, which offers centralised licensing arrangements for photocopying. Income received from all of these sources is used to further the interests of the Journal.

Your Article will be published in the Journal both in printed form and online, and will be stored electronically to enable [*short form of publisher name*] to meet library and faculty demand for access to the Article individually, as part of the Journal, and as part of a larger collection of articles to meet the specific requirements of particular markets. Assignment of copyright signifies agreement to [*short form of publisher name*] making such arrangements.

It may be that the Author is not able to make the assignment solely by him- or herself:

1. If it is appropriate, the Author's employer may sign this agreement. The employer may reserve the right to use the Article for internal or promotional purposes (by indicating this on the agreement) and may also explicitly reserve all rights other than copyright.

2. If the Author is a UK government employee, the government will grant to [*short form of Publisher name*] a non-exclusive licence to publish the Article in the Journal in any medium or form provided that Crown Copyright and user rights (including patent rights) are reserved.

3. If the Author is a US government employee and the work was done in that capacity, the assignment applies only to the extent allowed by US law.

Under the UK's Copyright, Design and Patents Act 1988, the Author has the moral right to be identified as the author wherever the Article is published, and to object to its derogatory treatment or distortion. [*Short form of publisher name*] encourages assertion of this right, as it represents best publishing practice and is an important safeguard for all authors. Clause 4 asserts the Author's moral rights, as required by the Act.

The Journal will permit the Author to post a version of the Article online, and to use the Article elsewhere after publication, provided acknowledgment is given to the Journal as the original source of publication and a link to the original is included. This permission is set out in Clause 7.

Thank you for reading these notes. This assignment will enable [*short form of publisher name*] to ensure that the Article will reach the optimum readership.

PRECEDENT NINE

Agreements for Serial Rights

The sale of serial rights to newspapers and magazines provides excellent publicity for the book in question. Depending on the financial health of the newspaper industry at the time, it can also be a lucrative source of licence income for general trade publishers. Popular topics for serialisation include biography and autobiography with subjects ranging from sports and entertainment personalities to politicians and the royal family; books on political or business scandals and some lifestyle topics. Fiction tends to be less popular, though the review sections of some broadsheet newspapers will pay for extracts from new literary novels. The financial sections of some national newspapers may sometimes be prepared to acquire extracts from business books on topical subjects.

Two contract precedents are included in this section. The first is a simple agreement, adequate for the licensing of one or more extracts from a work to a periodical where the amount of money to be paid is relatively low and few conditions are likely to be laid down by either party. This would also be appropriate for the sale of second serial rights (i.e., for publication in a periodical after publication in book form) and for the sale of serial rights to a periodical outside the UK.

The second is a more complex agreement which is closer to the type of contract supplied by the legal department of any of the major newspaper publishing groups for the licence of first serial rights (i.e., for publication in a periodical before publication in book form). The relative complexity of this reflects two main issues: the need to protect the periodical's exclusive right to reveal any newsworthy material from the work in its proposed serialisation; and the need to protect the sum of money which a newspaper has agreed to pay for the right to publish such material ahead of book publication (this sum could in some cases be very substantial).

It is recommended that users of the second precedent also study the notes to the first.

A sample letter of confidentiality is also included in this section. Such letters are commonly exchanged before submitting newsworthy or confidential

material to newspapers or magazines for consideration. The aim is to prevent newspapers leaking information from the book, and to prevent a newspaper which has been unsuccessful in acquiring the serial rights preparing a 'spoiler'. A 'spoiler' is a news story or feature published before the agreed serialisation, which, even though it does not use extracts from the book, would still have a detrimental effect on the official serialisation.

1. Grant of Rights

The Licensor will need to agree with the Publisher whether this deal precludes further sales of different extracts from the Work to other periodicals. If two serialisations are not seen as competitive by the periodicals concerned, retaining this right could be valuable both in financial and in publicity terms to the Licensor.

The number of extracts to be published as well as the total word count should be specified in this clause.

The last italicised phrase should be omitted in the case of a sale of second (post-publication) serialisation.

2. Payment

Most periodicals will require a VAT invoice before raising any payment.

The first responsibility of a newspaper is to break news and their page-length is also affected by the levels of advertising booked for that issue, so proposed book serialisations are occasionally omitted when space in the paper is at a premium. It is therefore important to secure the payment of the agreed fee whether or not the periodical publishes the extracts. Some periodicals will agree to pay the entire sum on signature of the contract, some will agree the split suggested here, some will not agree to pay until they publish, in which latter case a finite deadline for total payment is necessary.

3. Publication Schedule

For the reasons indicated in the previous note, a periodical may be reluctant to commit to a firm date for the extracts, in which case a range of dates may need to be included, or a provision for the periodical to amend the proposed date with the Licensor's prior written approval.

4. Abridgement

If an author has not waived his/her moral rights in the author contract, an incompetently abridged or misrepresentative extract from the Work could be regarded as derogatory under the author's moral rights, so care needs to be taken by the Publisher to preserve the integrity of the original.

Approval of the extracts will be necessary if the author has requested it in the head contract. If it is to be achieved within the tight deadlines required by many periodicals the Licensor must be sure that the author is available to give immediate approval or comments.

5. Acknowledgments

As publication of extracts is useful advance publicity for the Work, the Licensor may need to stress the importance of including this wording, which otherwise can get cut by sub-editors short of space. Care is required with the wording if the author's name is not the same as that of the copyright holder (which may be, for example, a limited company set up by the author) to ensure that both names appear.

SERIAL RIGHTS AGREEMENT

made this [*number*] day of [*month*] 20 [*year*] between [*company name*] of [*address*] (hereinafter termed 'the Licensor') and [*company name*] of [*address*] (hereinafter termed 'the Publisher') regarding

[*title*] by [*Author*] (hereinafter termed 'the Work')

WHEREBY IT IS AGREED as follows:

1. Grant of Rights

The Licensor grants to the Publisher the *exclusive/non-exclusive* right to publish in the English language one extract from the Work not exceeding [*total number of words*] in [*name of periodical*] ('the Periodical') *before first publication of the Work in book form by the Licensor.*

2. Payment

The Publisher shall pay to the Licensor the sum of [*amount*] payable half on signature of this Agreement and half on publication of the final extract from the Work by the Publisher or by [*date*] whichever is the sooner.

3. Publication Schedule

The Publisher shall publish the extract(s) in the Periodical not sooner than [*date*] and not later than [*date*].

4. Abridgement

Any abridgement of the Work by the Publisher to create the extract(s) shall be undertaken competently and shall preserve the sense and intention of the Work. The abridgement shall not subject the Work to derogatory treatment. The text of the extract(s) shall be submitted to the Licensor before publication for prior written approval (such approval not to be unreasonably withheld or delayed).

5. Acknowledgments

The Publisher shall print prominently after each extract from the Work the following notice of copyright and acknowledgment: © [*copyright notice as printed in the book*]. From [*title*] by [*name of author*] (to be) published by [*Licensor's imprint*] on [*Licensor's publication date*] at [*Licensor's list price*].

6. Off-the-page Sales

Off-the-page sales of books are becoming an important part of a serialisation deal. Many newspapers have their own mail-order fulfilment house which will negotiate the purchase of books and may wish to offer a discounted price to readers; otherwise the Licensor may wish to include direct ordering details here.

7. Complimentary Copies

This is particularly important if the periodical is not readily available on the newsstands or is outside the UK or the Licensor does not use the services of a press cuttings agency.

8. Territory

For UK-based periodicals this will usually be the UK. Most UK periodicals are also widely available in the Republic of Ireland, which licensors will need to take into account if they plan to sell serial rights separately to an Irish periodical. For overseas periodical publishers the Licensor would adapt the territories accordingly, for example, sales into New Zealand may be important to an Australian periodical.

9. Reversion of Rights

If extracts do not appear when originally planned, the Licensor needs not only to protect the agreed fee, but also to ensure that rights revert to them to prevent this being an open-ended agreement.

10. Retained Rights

Many newspapers syndicate articles to other regional or international papers and it is important to make it clear that any other periodicals interested in the Work should be referred to the Licensor and take out a separate licence. However, if substantial amendment or abridgement has been undertaken by the Publisher, another periodical wishing to use the same 'cut' will also need to get permission from the Publisher.

6. Off-the-page Sales

The Publisher shall include wording to accompany the extract(s) offering the Work for sale to readers of the Periodical.

7. Complimentary Copies

The Publisher shall send to the Licensor free of charge two copies of the issue(s) of the Periodical in which the extract(s) is/are published.

8. Territory

The Publisher's rights under this agreement shall extend to the following territories only: [*add territories*].

9. Reversion of Rights

The rights granted to the Publisher in this Agreement shall revert to the Licensor immediately after publication of the final extract in the Periodical or by[*date*] whichever is the sooner.

10. Retained Rights

All other rights (including syndication rights) in the Work are reserved by the Licensor.

Signed:	Signed:
Name:	Name:
Position:	Position
For and on behalf of the Licensor	For and on behalf of the Publisher

2. Non-exclusive Rights

Most major newspapers export copies of the UK edition outside this country and need to protect their right to do so. However, care needs to be taken if a periodical has a wide global circulation, or publishes customised versions for different markets in which it wishes to include the serialisation, as this could damage serial rights sales in other English language markets.

3. Website Publication

Many periodicals also publish an online edition and the right to use this material on their website may be a condition of the deal. Licensors must ensure that they have the right to grant such usage, especially as regards photographs or other material from the Work which is not the copyright of the author. Many periodicals also archive their editions online with public access, hence the need for an extension of the licence to cover this use. The ability to request prompt removal of material from the website is important if libel or other legal issues arise, and it is also worth bearing in mind that an infelicitous abridgement or adaptation will remain accessible online long after the physical newspaper has gone out of circulation.

4. Photographs and Illustrations

It is important to ensure that the rights cleared by the Licensor or by the author for use in the book extend to such use in the serialisation. If rights for use in a periodical are retained by a picture library or other source this needs to be made clear to the Publishers who would then be responsible for clearing permission themselves.

FIRST UK SERIAL RIGHTS AGREEMENT

made this [*number*] day of [*month*] 20 [*year*] between [*company name*] of [*address*] (hereinafter termed 'the Licensor') and [*company name*] of [*address*] (hereinafter termed 'the Publishers')

regarding a work to be published by the Licensor presently entitled: [*title by Author*]

('the Work')

1. Grant of Exclusive Rights and Payment

The Publishers shall pay to the Licensor an outright sum of [*amount*] payable as set out in Clause 9 below for exclusive first serial rights in the English language throughout the United Kingdom [*and the Republic of Ireland*] ('the Territory'), for publication in [*name of Periodical*] ('the Periodical').

2. Non-exclusive Rights

The Publishers shall also have the non-exclusive right to distribute copies of the Periodical containing the Serialisation outside the Territory in the ordinary course of the Publishers' business.

3. Website Publication

The Publishers shall also have the right to publish each instalment of the Serialisation on its own website concurrently with (but not before) publication of each instalment in the printed issues of the Periodical on the understanding that each of the instalments published on the website shall comprise the identical text as the printed version and shall include the copyright acknowledgment and sales details specified in Clause 15. The instalments may remain on the website for archive purposes at the Publishers' discretion or until required by the Licensor in writing to remove one or more of the instalments from the website within 48 hours of receipt of such written request.

4. Photographs and Illustrations

The Publishers shall have the right to publish in their Serialisation all photographs or illustrations from the Work, in so far as the right to grant such right is with the Licensor.

5. Supply of Material

Availability of electronic files will be of value to the Publishers as it makes the process of preparing extracts much simpler. If the Licensor incurs costs in preparing the electronic files, they may wish to negotiate an additional fee for supplying them. It is important that the periodical works from the final, edited (and legally vetted) version of the text at this point.

8. Publication Schedule

If the topic of the Work is newsworthy and/or the Licensor's plans for publicity are time-sensitive, the publication dates of the Serialisation can be crucial. Few newspapers, however, will commit absolutely to publishing on a particular day and will not want their failure to publish on a specified date to be considered a breach of the agreement.

9. Payment Schedule

If this deal is concluded before the final manuscript of the Work has been received, then an intermediate payment stage on delivery of the complete text is useful, especially if the sums due are substantial.

5. Supply of Material

The Licensor will provide the Publishers with a complete copy of the text of the Work, together with any photographs or illustrations. Subject to availability, the text will be supplied as an electronic file in a form in which the text may be manipulated by the Publishers.

6. Length of Extracted Material

The total number of words which may be extracted from the Work and be printed in the Periodical shall not exceed [*number*] words and shall appear in not more than [*number of instalments*] instalments in the Periodical ('the Serialisation').

7. Once-only Publication

Subject to the provisions of Clause 3 above the rights granted in this Agreement are solely in respect of once-only publication of the Serialisation in the Periodical prior to publication in volume form of the Work by the Licensor scheduled for [*Licensor's book publication date*]. All rights granted in this Agreement shall revert to the Licensor immediately after publication of the final instalment of the Serialisation in the Periodical or by the Licensor's publication date whichever is the sooner.

8. Publication Schedule

The dates of publication in the Periodical of the Serialisation shall be mutually agreed between the Licensor and the Publishers. The Serialisation may not commence before [*date*] and shall be completed by [*date*].

9. Payment Schedule

Payment of the sum agreed in Clause 1 shall be made as follows:

one third on signature of this Agreement by both parties;

one third on delivery of the complete text of the Work to the Publishers;

and one third on publication of the final instalment of the Serialisation or by the Licensor's publication date whichever is the sooner.

10. Abridgement and Approval

10.2 It is unusual for a major newspaper to allow the Licensor or author unqualified approval over the extracts, though most will co-operate in the correction of errors. If it is agreed in the Licensor's head contract that the author has approval then this condition will need to be made clear to the Publishers at the time of negotiating the deal. In such an instance, the author will need to be available and willing to read and approve the text very quickly, probably within 12 to 24 hours, to meet the Publisher's print deadlines. See also the note to Clauses 13 and 14 regarding warranties and indemnity.

11. Protection of Exclusivity

(iii) The payment of substantial money for the serial rights by the Publishers may depend on the Licensor's ability to keep confidential the material contained in the Work. In some cases this may involve issuing special instructions to the printers and warehouse, arranging for third parties to sign confidentiality agreements, and getting written agreement from the author that he/she will not disclose material from the Work. A leak or 'spoiler' (a news story published by a rival newspaper) may lead to the Publishers cancelling the deal or renegotiating the amount of money they are due to pay. Licensors should be aware that they may not be able to guarantee this exclusivity if there is prior or simultaneous publication of the Work or a serialisation from it in the US or other territory over which they have no control and they may need to make the Publishers aware of this fact. Early publication of material on the internet may also jeopardise this exclusivity.

10. Abridgement and Approval

10.1 Any abridgement of the Work for the Serialisation shall be undertaken by the Publishers competently and accurately and the Work shall not be subjected to derogatory treatment. The Publishers shall be entitled to introduce, select and link extracts from the Work but shall not distort or misrepresent the meaning of the Work in any way, either in the Serialisation or in headlines, or other matter accompanying the Serialisation.

10.2 The Licensor shall have the right to inspect the text of each instalment of the Serialisation prior to its publication by the Publishers to check for any errors or misrepresentations. The Publishers shall submit the text of each instalment (including headlines, captions and any accompanying material) by fax or e-mail to the Licensor not later than [*date and time of day*]and approval of the text or comments on the text will be communicated by fax or email to the Publishers not later than [*date and time of day*].

11. Protection of Exclusivity

The Licensor will use all reasonable endeavours to protect the exclusivity of the rights granted to the Publishers in this Agreement by:

(i) ensuring that no advance copies of the Work are released for sale before the publication of the final instalment of the Serialisation or [*date*] whichever is the sooner;

(ii) ensuring that no advance copies of the Work are sent for review purposes or otherwise to other newspapers, magazines or broadcast media before the publication of the final instalment of the Serialisation or [*date*] whichever is the sooner;

(iii) ensuring that the author gives no interviews for radio or television, newspapers or magazines relating to the content of the Work for publication before the publication of the final instalment of the Serialisation or [*date*] whichever is the sooner.

12. Licensor's Warranty on Exclusivity of Licence

The Licensor warrants that it has not and that it will not license publication or broadcast of any extract or previously unpublished information from the Work to any other periodical or through any other media outlet including radio or television within the Territory for publication or broadcast before the publication of the final instalment of the Serialisation or [*date*] whichever is the sooner.

13. Warranties

It is recommended that Licensors do not offer the periodical a warranty broader than that which the author has granted to them. The high circulation figures of newspapers increases the risk of claims from parties who feel they have been libelled, and of potential damages awarded by a court. Newspapers are increasingly requesting warranties that the work does not breach any right of privacy, or breach the Data Protection Act by supply of private information on individuals, which may not be covered by a Licensor's author contract.

14. Indemnity

If appropriate, the text of the Work that the Licensor supplies to the Publishers should have been previously checked by the Licensor's lawyers. Approval of the final text of the extracts by the Licensor or the author prior to publication might imply that the warranties and indemnities extend to the changes made or additional material added by the Publishers unless it is made clear that they do not.

13. Warranties

The Licensor warrants that it has full power to enter into this Agreement and to comply with its terms, that the Work is an original work, and is in no way an infringement of any existing copyright and contains nothing defamatory, libellous or otherwise unlawful.

14. Indemnity

The Licensor agrees to indemnify and keep indemnified the Publishers against all costs, claims and actions, including legal expenditure, in consequence of any breach of this warranty. This indemnity shall not extend to any claims or actions arising out of the Publishers' manner of Serialisation or arising from additional material (including but not limited to headlines or other headings) added by the Publishers.

15. Acknowledgments

The Publishers shall print prominently in each instalment of the Serialisation a notice of copyright and acknowledgment as follows: '© [*copyright notice as printed in the book*]. From *title* by *Author* (to be) published by [*Licensor's imprint*] on [*Licensor's publication date*] at [*Licensor's list price*].

16. Off-the-page Sales

The Publishers shall include wording to accompany the extract(s) offering the Work for sale to readers of the Periodical.

17. Complimentary Copies

The Publishers shall send to the Licensor free of charge two copies of each issue of the Periodical in which the Serialisation appears.

18. Retained Rights

All rights including but not limited to syndication, sub-licensing and republication rights not specifically granted to the Publishers in this Agreement are retained by the Licensor.

19. Non-assignment

This Agreement may not be assigned by the Publishers to any third party.

22. Additional clauses

Other provisions commonly added to contracts for popular biographies, autobiographies and controversial current affairs books include the following:

(1) The Licensor may have agreed to grant to the Publishers, an exclusive interview with the author, to be published alongside the Serialisation. Newspapers would normally own the copyright in any such interview and might want to syndicate it after their first UK publication, which could jeopardise subsequent serial deals – for example an exclusive Australian serial deal arranged to follow the UK deal.

(2) The Publishers may want the author to advertise the Serialisation on television or radio in advance of its publication. In fact, an offer by a newspaper to invest in advertising for the Serialisation, which will also impact upon the book, can be an attractive part of the deal to the Licensor.

(3) The Publishers may want to send their own photographer to take photographs of the author to illustrate the Serialisation.

All of these provisions will require the co-operation of the author, and although the Licensor is unlikely to be able to negotiate an additional fee, they should ensure that the author is not unduly inconvenienced and any reasonable expenses are paid by the Publishers.

20. Arbitration

If any difference shall arise between the Licensor and the Publishers touching the meaning of this Agreement the matter shall be referred to arbitration in accordance with the provisions of the Arbitration Act 1996 or any subsisting statutory re-enactment or modification thereof.

21. Applicable Law

This agreement shall be governed by English law and be within the exclusive jurisdiction of the English courts.

22. Additional Clauses

Agreed for and on behalf of the Licensor	Agreed for and on behalf of the Publishers
Name:	Name:
Position:	Position:

1. Specify here the nature of the material to be provided: a manuscript, a set of proofs, an early finished copy of the book, etc.

2. It is important to ensure that the person reading the material is in a sufficiently senior position to make a decision, without having to share the information with a large number of superiors or colleagues.

3. If the material is an early unedited version of the book, the text may be subsequently amended or removed by editors, or on legal advice. It is important that the newspaper does not reveal any excised material at a later date.

SAMPLE CONFIDENTIALITY AGREEMENT FOR SALE OF SERIAL RIGHTS

Licensor's company letterhead

Addressee [*Name and Address of Newspaper Company*]

DATE

Dear [*Contact Name*]

[*Title by Author*]

We control the publication rights to the above book ('the Work'). We understand that [*name of Newspaper Company*] ('the Company') wishes to review *the typescript of* the Work ('the Material') to determine whether it wishes to acquire First UK Serial Rights ('First UK Serial Rights'). We will give the Company access to a copy of the Material subject to the following terms and conditions:

1. The Company acknowledges that all information (other than information already in the public domain) contained in the Material and the Work is highly confidential and is exclusively the property of [*insert Licensor's company name here*].

2. The Company will use the Material solely for the purpose of determining whether it wishes to acquire First UK Serial Rights to the Work.

3. The Company will not disclose, publish or otherwise reveal any confidential information concerning the Work or the Material to any other person, except to those employees who need to consider such information in order to make a decision about the acquisition of First UK Serial Rights.

4. The Company undertakes to keep the Material securely under lock and key when it is not in use, and to return the Material promptly to us on request.

5. The Company will not take notes of or in any way record any information contained in the Material or the Work, and will not copy or otherwise reproduce any part of the Material or the Work.

6. The Company will not contact any third party to confirm or otherwise enquire about any information contained in the Material and the Work.

7. The Company agrees that it will not use or publish any confidential information contained in the Material before the date of publication

of the Work by [*name of Publisher*] ('Publication Date'), except in connection with its exercise of First UK Serial Rights acquired from our Company and subject to a separate agreement signed by both parties. The Company further agrees that it will not commission and/or publish any article, feature or interview that is based on the Material or Work or any confidential information contained therein before Publication Date.

8. As to all confidential information in the Material which is contained in the Work as finally published, the Company's obligations under this agreement will end on Publication Date. As to all confidential information in the Material not contained in the Work as finally published, the Company's obligations under this agreement will continue indefinitely.

9. A breach of these terms and conditions by any of the Company's officers, employees or agents will constitute a breach by the Company.

Please indicate your acceptance of these terms and conditions by returning one signed copy of this letter. On receipt of the signed letter, we will provide you with access to the Material.

Yours sincerely,

Name

Title

For and on behalf of [*name of licensor*]

Accepted and agreed to:

Signature:

Title:

Date:

for and on behalf of [name of Newspaper Company]

PRECEDENT TEN

Translator's Agreement

At the General Conference of UNESCO in Nairobi in 1976, 20 years of campaigning by FIT (Fédération Internationale des Traducteurs) culminated in the adoption of a Recommendation, dated 28 October. This Recommendation sought to assimilate the status of translators to that of authors. The United Kingdom, together with 49 other states, has approved the Recommendation which, if not an international convention, must yet carry considerable force.

The problem of holding a fair balance of reward for the original author, the original foreign publisher and the translator as the creator of the translated text, while preserving the necessary margin of profit for the publisher of the translation, is not easy. The precedent and notes which follow here take careful account of the specimen publishing contract for in-copyright works drawn up by the Translators Association in its latest revised version of 2009. The Society of Authors flags the fact that in cases where the original work is in the public domain, the contract would need to be adjusted to remove references to an underlying licence from the original publisher of the work.

If the translator is to be assimilated to the author in some respects, then his/her status needs to be spelt out as in the comparable preamble to an author's contract. The statement of the publishers' rights in the work goes some way to meeting UNESCO Recommendation III 5(e).

The assumption of the words 'in which the Publishers hold the English-language volume rights together with the secondary rights mentioned hereinafter' is that the publishers do indeed hold those rights throughout the world for the designated territories for the term specified in their licence for the English language rights. It is the publishers' responsibility to check very carefully the extent of the translation rights they hold, and to draft accordingly. It may be advisable to specify here the duration of said rights as the translator is not a party to the contract under which these rights have been acquired from the Proprietors.

1. Grant of Rights

If we follow the 'Nairobi principles', it is not necessary to require from the translator a grant of copyright. The publishers have, as exclusive licensees of all rights in the translation, all the powers they need to make subsidiary deals on behalf of the work. However, scientific, technical and medical (STM) works are frequently translated into the English language, and some STM publishers request a grant of copyright so that they are in the strongest position to take fast action against pirate editions.

The Society of Authors notes that publishers may seek a broad grant of rights in the English language in all forms, but that the rights granted by the Translator should not exceed those acquired by the publishers from the original publishers of the work (the Proprietors).

2. Delivery of Work and of Translation

See also the comment on delivery in electronic form at Precedent One, Note (2) to Clause 2.

2. and 5. Delivery of Work and of Translation/Alterations/Adaptations to Translation

The fitness of the translation for the market envisaged by the publishers is often a delicate question. Early and thorough discussion should avoid later recriminations. Given the sad circumstances contemplated under Clause 5, an arbitration clause is included in this precedent. Clause 6.1 makes provision for payment of the second half of the advance payment to be subject to delivery and acceptance by the Publishers of the translated text. The Society of Authors notes that a translator should not be penalised for any delays to the schedule caused by a requirement for the translation to be approved by the original author or (for example) by a US copublisher.

MEMORANDUM OF AGREEMENT made this [*number*] day of [*month*] 20 [*year*] between [*name*] of [*address*] (hereinafter called 'the Translator', which expression shall, where the context admits, include the Translator's executors and assigns as the case may be) of the one part and [*company name*] of [*address*] (hereinafter called 'the Publishers', which expression shall, where the context admits, include any publishing imprint subsidiary to or associated with the Publishers, and the Publishers' assigns or successors in business as the case may be) of the other part

WHEREBY it is mutually agreed as follows concerning the translation from the [*name of language*] language into English (hereinafter called 'the Translation') of a work of about [*number*] words in the original [*name of language*] language at present entitled [*title*] by [*name of Author*] (hereinafter called 'the Work') in which the Publishers hold the exclusive English-language volume rights in print/*and e-book* form together with the additional rights mentioned hereinafter under licence from the Proprietors of the Work until *(date of expiry of Publishers' licence from the Proprietors) throughout the world/in the United Kingdom and British Commonwealth territories/in Europe and the British Commonwealth territories/as listed on the Schedule hereto.*

1. Grant of Rights

In consideration of the payments hereinafter mentioned the Translator grants to the Publishers the exclusive licence to print, publish and sell the Translation in volume form in print/*and e-book format/in all forms* together with the right to handle the additional rights mentioned in Clause 7 hereof during the period and in the territories granted under the Publishers' exclusive licence for the Work.

2. Delivery of Work and of Translation

The Publishers have delivered one copy of the Work to the Translator and the Translator shall deliver to the Publishers within [*number*] months from the date of this Agreement one copy of the Translation in electronic file form as an e-mail attachment together with two copies in paper form which shall be faithful to the Work and rendered into appropriate English.

3. Copyright Material from Other Sources

If the Work includes quotations or other material from in-copyright sources, the Publishers will obtain the relevant permissions and pay any fees incurred.

4. Warranties and Indemnity

This clause expresses the view of the Translators Association that translators should be held harmless against action in respect of anything not introduced into the translation by their own work. Some publishers may wish to secure from the translator full warranty and indemnity clauses of the kind set out in Precedent One at Clause 5.

6. Payment

In some cases the translator may be paid on the basis of a lump sum equivalent to a rate per thousand words of translated text; this may be payable half on signature of the contract and half on delivery and acceptance of the translated text. In the previous edition of this book, this precedent provided for a subsequent payment of royalties after an agreed number of copies had been sold. However, it is more common practice today to pay the translator an advance against a modest royalty rate on sales.

(a) From the publishers' viewpoint it is advisable to make the second instalment of the advance payment payable on delivery and acceptance of the translated text as satisfactory.

(b) The question of the basis on which royalties should be calculated is a vexed one and much may depend on the type of work in question. Academic publishers, who tend to export a substantial proportion of their sales at high discount, moved some time ago towards paying their authors royalties on the basis of the net sum received; trade publishers have generally continued to pay their authors on the basis of the domestic recommended retail price, although there have been recent discussions on a move to payment on net receipts, given the high level of discounting by the book trade and online retailers. These practices will inevitably affect the method of paying royalties to translators as well. Some publishers may be prepared to pay royalties on normal trade sales in the home market on the basis of the domestic recommended retail price, but will specify that royalties on high discount sales are payable on the sum received. In such cases the wording might read:

> 'On copies of the Translation sold by the Publishers at a discount of [*number*] per cent or more, wherever sold, royalties shall be calculated on the basis of the sum received by the Publishers for such sales. In the context of this Agreement, "sum received" means the amount received by the Publishers in respect of sales of the Translation wherever sold after deduction of any discounts granted by the Publishers and any sales or other similar taxes or duties incurred by the Publishers.'

If the publisher has acquired the right to publish in e-book form under the terms of Clause 1, this could be covered in a separate subclause 6.3:

> 'On sales of the Publishers' edition of the Translation in e-book form, wherever sold, the Publishers shall pay to the Translator a royalty of [*number*] per cent based on the sum received by the Publishers from all such sales.'

The current practice is for publishers to base such royalties on net receipts to allow for the discounts accorded to intermediaries such as Amazon or Apple.

4. Warranties and Indemnity

The Translator guarantees to the Publishers that he/she will not introduce into the Translation any matter of an objectionable or libellous character which was not present in the Work. In reliance on such guarantee the Publishers undertake to hold the Translator harmless from all suits against or incurred by them on the grounds that the Translation contains anything objectionable or libellous.

5. Alterations/Adaptations to Translation

The Publishers will not make any alterations to the Translation without the prior consent of the Translator, such consent not to be unreasonably withheld. (*If such consent is unreasonably withheld, the Publishers may make such changes as they think fit and the Translator may withdraw his/her name from the Translation with such amendments to the terms of this Agreement as shall be mutually agreed.*) If the Publishers hold the right to adapt the Work for publication in the English language they shall notify the Translator and any adapting to be carried out by the Translator and any remuneration for it shall be agreed separately between the parties.

6. Payment

The Publishers shall make the following payments to the Translator, namely:

6.1 In advance and on account of all sums which may become due to the Translator under this Agreement, the sum of [*amount*] which shall be payable half on signature of this Agreement and the balance on delivery [*and acceptance*] of the translated text.

6.2 On sales of the Publishers' edition of the Translation in print form at home and abroad the Publishers shall pay to the Translator the following royalties based on the *UK recommended retail price/the Publishers' net receipts* from sales of the Translation:

(i) [*number*] per cent on the first [*number*] thousand copies sold;

(ii) [*number*] per cent on copies sold between [*number*] thousand and [*number*] thousand;

(iii) [*number*] per cent on all copies sold beyond the first [*number*] thousand copies.

No royalties shall be paid to the Translator on copies of the Translation sold at or below cost, presented by the Publishers free of charge, lost through theft or damage or destroyed by fire, water, in transit or otherwise.

7. Payment on Sale of Other Rights

This clause is intended to gain the translator a modest share of revenue from the permitted sale of subsidiary rights in the Translation; a larger share will be payable to the Proprietors who will in turn pass on an agreed share to the original author. The exact wording here will depend on the range of rights granted to the Publishers by the Proprietors. It should be remembered that the sale of some rights such as book club rights involving the sale of physical copies at high discount operate on a very slim margin (**see Appendix C**) which may necessitate special royalty arrangements (**see also Precedent One, Clauses 13 and 14**). Co-edition sales (**see Precedent Fifteen**) also operate on narrow margins.

7. Payment on Sale of Other Rights

Under their licence of rights for the Work from the Proprietors, the Publishers also control the following rights (*include/delete as appropriate*) and the Translator hereby grants to the Publishers the exclusive licence to handle such rights during the term of this Agreement and subject to the Publishers paying to the Translator a share of the proceeds from the sale of such rights as specified hereunder:

(a)	*First serial rights:*	*[*number*] per cent*
(b)	*Second serial rights:*	*[*number*] per cent*
(c)	*US rights:*	*[*number*] per cent*
(d)	*Paperback rights licensed to another publisher:*	*[*number*] per cent*
(e)	*Book club rights:*	*[*number*] per cent*
(d)	*Anthology and quotation rights:*	*[*number*] per cent*
(e)	*Single voice readings on radio or television:*	*[*number*] per cent*
(f)	*Audio rights:*	*[*number*] per cent*
(g)	*E-book rights licensed to a third party:*	*[*number*] per cent*
(h)	*Large print rights:*	*[*number*] per cent*

* *Retranslation of the Work from the Translation rather than from the original Work: [*number*] per cent.*

* *Dramatisation rights for stage, film, television, radio and other media: [*number*] per cent.*

* *The licensing of such rights is subject to the Translator's approval/The Translator will be informed of the licensing of such rights and the Publishers will use their best endeavours to ensure that the Translator is prominently credited on the licensed version.*

Public Lending Right (PLR), rental and lending rights, and any other rights not specified above are reserved by the Translator.

The Translation shall be included in the scheme administered by the Copyright Licensing Agency, with the Translator's share of any income from the CLA to be paid to him/her by ALCS.

9. Moral Rights

Acknowledgment of the translator's contribution follows acceptance of his/her status as a secondary author. The good intentions concerning copyright follow UNESCO Recommendation III (5(i)).

The translator, under UK law, now has the moral rights of paternity and of integrity in his/her translation. **See in general Appendix H**. The first sentence of Clause 9 meets the requirement of UK law that the right of paternity must be asserted. The wording of the copyright notice relating to the translated text will depend on the rights granted to the Publishers in Clause 1; if copyright in the translated text has been assigned (e.g., as often happens in academic publishing), the copyright notice will be in the name of the Publishers.

10. Publication Schedule

The period to be inserted here is that specified in the publishers' agreement for the English-language translation rights. If no such period is specified in the agreement between the original language publisher and the publishers, then a 'reasonable time' clause should be inserted. The translator, who may have spent a great deal of time, energy and creativity in completing the translation is surely entitled to a time clause, and to proceed under Clause 16 against the publishers if they turn out to be in material breach of it.

12. Accounts

See also in Precedent One, notes to Clause 17.

8. Proof Correction

The Publishers shall send two sets of proofs of the Translation to the Translator and the Translator undertakes to read, check and correct the proofs and return one set to the Publishers within [*number*] days after their receipt by the Translator. The cost of alterations made by the Translator in the proofs (other than the correction of artists', copy editors' and printers' errors) above 10 per cent of the original cost of typesetting shall be paid by the Translator.

9. Moral Rights

The Translator asserts *his/her* moral right to be identified as the Translator of the Work in relation to all such rights as are granted by the Translator to the Publishers under the terms and conditions of this Agreement. The Publishers undertake that the Translator's name shall appear on the title page and *jacket/cover* of their edition of the Translation and in all appropriate publicity material (catalogues, advertisements, website etc) concerning it, and shall use their best endeavours to ensure that this undertaking is adhered to also in other editions of the Translation and that the name of the Translator is mentioned in connection with all reviews of and quotations from the Translation. The Publishers shall print the following copyright notice relating to the Translation on the reverse of the title page of the Translation: 'English language translation © [*name of copyright holder (year of publication)*]'.

10. Publication Schedule

The Publishers shall publish their first edition of the Translation within the period specified in their licence for the English language rights in the Work and in no event later than [*number*] months after delivery and acceptance of the translated text.

11. Complimentary Copies

The Publishers shall send to the Translator on publication [*number*] complimentary copies of the Translation and [*number*] copies of each subsequent reprint issued either by the Publishers or under licence from them. The Translator shall have the right to purchase further copies of the Publishers' edition of the Translation at normal trade terms for personal use but not for resale.

12. Accounts

The Publishers shall make up accounts for sales of the Translation to [*date*] and [*date*] in each year following the date of first publication of the Translation

15. Out of Print

The importance of rights in the translation of a work as well as rights in the work itself must always be kept in mind. If the publishers are unwilling or unable (possibly because they cannot renegotiate a contract with the original foreign-language publisher) to keep the work in print in the translation which they themselves arranged, then it is reasonable for the translator to be entitled to have rights in the translation returned to him/her, although there is provision here for what may happen if the Translation remains available in print-on-demand and/or e-book form. The clause may be irrelevant if the translator of an STM work has assigned the copyright itself to the publishers, or if the translator was paid on the basis of an outright fee for all rights.

The return of rights in the translation to the translator under this clause and Clause 15 or otherwise does not in itself, of course, allow him/her to authorise its publication by another publisher. Such a third party would have to acquire translation rights *de novo* from the original foreign-language publisher or by assignment from the original English-language publishers.

and the said accounts shall be delivered to the Translator and settled within three months of each accounting date. Any sum of £100 or more due to the Translator in respect of sub-licensed rights shall be paid to the Translator within one month of receipt if the advance specified in Clause 6.1 hereof has been covered. The Translator or his/her authorised representative shall have the right upon written request to examine the Publishers' books of account insofar as they relate to the Translation, which examination shall be at the cost of the Translator unless errors exceeding £50 shall be found to his/her disadvantage in which case the costs shall be paid by the Publishers.

13. Value Added Tax

The Publishers operate a self-billing system for the payment of royalties and to account for Value Added Tax. The Publishers therefore require details of the Translator's VAT registration number where applicable. Where the Translator fails to provide a VAT registration number the Publishers shall not pay VAT on any sums due under the terms of this Agreement.

14. Remainder

The Translation shall not be remaindered within one year from first publication without the Translator's agreement. If the Translation is remaindered, the Publishers will pay the Translator (*number*) per cent of receipts on copies sold at above cost and will give the Translator first refusal to purchase copies at the remainder price.

15. Out of Print

If at any time the Publishers allow the Translation to go out of print or off the market in all editions issued by the Publishers (*or the Publishers' stock falls below 50 hardback copies or 100 paperback copies*) and if within [*number*] months after receiving written notice from the Translator to do so they have not reprinted and placed on the market a new edition, then all rights granted under this Agreement shall forthwith and without further notice revert to the Translator.

Should the Translation be available from the Publishers only as print-on-demand *and/or in e-book form* and sales have been below [*number*] copies in the preceding twelve-month period, provided the advance specified in Clause 6.1 hereof has been earned out, or more than three years have passed since publication (whichever is the sooner) the Translator may terminate this Agreement on one month's notice to the Publishers.

17. Arbitration

The status of 'secondary author' may raise some unforeseen points. What is to happen if the publisher and the original language publisher fall out so that there is a breach of the agreement between them? What is to happen if the manuscript is acceptable to the UK publisher, but not to the original foreign publisher, who has a difficult author on his/her hands anxious to approve the translation of his/her work under a clause between him/herself and the original publisher only? What is to happen if the translator, following the publisher's instruction (agreed with the foreign publisher and author) in changing some names and the milieu, commits in such changes a libel on some real person? The guarantee contained in Clause 4 may look somewhat unclear in such circumstances. The status of an author carries rights *and* responsibilities, and it seems best to have a broadly drafted arbitration clause in reserve.

This clause provides for referral in the first instance to the Informal Disputes Settlement Scheme of the Publishers Association.

18. Applicable Law

This could be adjusted where appropriate to allow for the law of Scotland.

16. Termination

16.1 Should the Publishers fail to fulfil or comply with any of the provisions of this Agreement and not rectify such failure within one month after receipt of written notification from the Translator to do so or if the Publishers shall go into liquidation (other than voluntary liquidation for the purpose of reconstruction) or shall have a receiver appointed then in either event this Agreement shall terminate automatically and all rights hereby granted shall revert to the Translator forthwith without prejudice to all rights of the Publishers in respect of any contracts or negotiations properly entered into by them with any third party prior to the date of such reversion, without prejudice to any claim which the Translator may have for damages or otherwise and without prejudice to any monies already paid or then due to the Translator from the Publishers.

16.2 If the Publishers' rights in the Work revert to the Proprietors of the Work, this Agreement shall terminate automatically and all rights in the Translation shall revert to the Translator.

17. Arbitration

If any difference shall arise between the parties touching the meaning of this Agreement or the rights and liabilities of the parties thereto, the same shall be referred to the Informal Disputes Settlement Scheme of the Publishers Association.

18. Applicable Law

This Agreement shall be governed by and interpreted in all respects in accordance with the laws of England whose courts shall have exclusive jurisdiction.

AS WITNESS THE HANDS OF THE PARTIES

Signed...

(the Translator)

Signed..

(for the Publishers)

PRECEDENT ELEVEN

Agreement for Sale of Translation Rights

The negotiation of translation rights is the daily bread-and-butter work of rights and contracts departments in many publishing houses. Correspondence can sometimes be lengthy and it is, therefore, very much in publishers' interests to keep down the overhead expenses of this service to authors by having a good standard contract. Precedent Eleven provides a contract on an advance and royalty basis, probably the most common form of arrangement for translation licences. Alternative clauses are provided in the notes to cover arrangements on the basis of a lump sum for a designated print run, which can sometimes be a preferable arrangement for licences involving very modest sums, or for countries where remittance of payment abroad is problematic.

Although the majority of licences may be covered by standard agreements, special contracts may still need to be devised to reflect different publishing, payment or legislative practice in some markets. The Appendix to this Precedent has again been retained and updated to provide an overview of licensing conditions in central and eastern Europe and the countries which once formed part of the Soviet Union – markets still in the aftermath of transition from a command to a market economy – and the People's Republic of China, a market which has a history of less than 20 years of authorised licensing arrangements and where Western publishers must take into account the implications of the transfer of rule of Hong Kong and Macao to China from 1 July 1997 and 20 December 1999 respectively, and also China's troubled relationship with Taiwan.

Preamble

Automatic transfer of the contract to the successors and assigns of the licensee may not always be desirable in countries where the publishing industry is in a volatile state. In more stable licensing circumstances, some proprietors may be prepared to include wording to cover automatic transfer to the successors and assigns of the licensee.

If the work is not yet delivered to the proprietors in the original language in typescript or electronic form, it may be necessary to add a description of the material, delivery date etc.

See also note to Clause 16 re restricting licences to the current edition of non-fiction works.

1. Grant of Rights

This clause defines the rights granted to the licensee. This precedent covers an advance and royalty arrangement deal for a print edition with no specific limit on the number of copies of the translation which may be printed. In some cases, a lump sum payment to cover a designated print run may be preferable in which case the words '[*number*] copies only of' should be inserted after the words 'the exclusive licence to translate, produce and publish' in this clause.

In the case of languages confined to limited markets, it may be advisable to grant world rights in that language to cover the core market and some expatriate sales. However, for languages such as English, Portuguese, Spanish and French, which are the national languages in more than one market, it may be advisable to limit the licence territorially – for example, granting separate licences for Portugal and Brazil. It should be remembered that licences cannot be limited territorially within the European Union (**see also note to Precedent Fourteen, Clause 1**). Licensing Chinese rights requires special care, both in terms of distinguishing between simplified and traditional character versions and in terms of territory (**see Appendix to this Precedent**).

Some foreign language publishers are content to acquire only volume rights in print form or perhaps only volume rights in a designated binding; however, to license hardback and paperback translation rights separately to different publishers in the same market is problematic, and raises too the question of access to the translated text. If the book in question has potential for publication in both forms, it is best handled by a single licence which then permits the licensee to sub-license within his designated territory (see note to Clause 11).

Increasingly, foreign language publishers are seeking to acquire electronic rights as well as print rights in the translation. These should never be included as a matter of course; licensees should be asked what arrangements they already have in place for the pricing, distribution, and marketing of electronic editions, usually in e-book form: whether e-books will be supplied to customers direct from the Publishers' own website, via third party retailers or both, whether the files will be DRM-protected and how the pricing of the e-book version of the Translation will relate to that of the print version. If rights are to be granted, this might best be covered by a paragraph inserted at the end of Clause 1, with the range of usage permitted to depend on whether the Publishers have convincing existing arrangements or plans for delivery to such platforms:

> 'The Proprietors also hereby grant to the Publishers the exclusive licence to publish the said Translation in e-book form with DRM protection for delivery to customers via the Publishers' own website and/or via e-retail sites for use on personal computers, laptop computers, dedicated e-reading devices and mobile phones.'

If the proprietors do not wish to allow the licensee to reproduce the artwork, typography or design of the original jacket or cover of the work, the following words should be added to this clause:

> 'The right to reproduce the artwork, typography or design of the Proprietors' jacket/cover is not included in this Agreement.'

Translations are traditionally published under the sole imprint of the licensee. However, there may be occasions where publications under the joint imprint of the proprietors and the foreign language publisher may be desirable (e.g., to establish brand visibility in the case of business

MEMORANDUM OF AGREEMENT made this [*number*] day of [*month*] 20 [*year*] Between: [*company name*] of [*address*] (hereinafter termed 'the Proprietors') of the one part, and [*company name*] of [*address*] (hereinafter termed 'the Publishers') of the other part

WHEREAS the Proprietors are the proprietors of a work by [*name*] (hereinafter termed 'the Author'), entitled: [*title*] [*number of edition, original ISBN number*] (hereinafter termed 'the Work'),

NOW IT IS HEREBY MUTUALLY AGREED AS FOLLOWS:

1. Grant of Rights

Subject to the terms detailed in this Agreement, the Proprietors hereby grant to the Publishers the exclusive licence to translate, produce and publish the Work in *hardback/paperback* volume form at the Publishers' own expense in the [*name of language*] language under the Publishers' imprint (hereinafter termed the Translation) for sale *throughout the world/the following territories* [*list territories*] *only*:

2. Payment

The Publishers shall make the following payments to the Proprietors, in accordance with the terms of Clause 20 hereof, namely:

---

or computing books). The use of a joint imprint should be discussed in advance of signing the contract and clearly specified if such use is to be permitted; some proprietors may charge an additional fee for the use of their imprint or brand. Proprietors who are concerned that their imprints or logos may be used without their permission may wish to add to this clause:

> 'The Publishers shall not reproduce the Proprietors' imprints, logos or brands (*specify*) without their prior written consent.'

2. Payment

The advance payment and royalty rates are to be inserted. If the advance is to be paid in instalments rather than in full on signature of the contract, it is normally advisable to specify that each instalment shall be paid by a designated calendar date rather than by dates which may be unpredictable, for example, 'on publication of the Translation' or 'six months after publication of the Translation'. A compromise might be to specify that an instalment is payable 'on publication of the Translation or by [*date*], whichever is earlier'.

Royalty rates for translations normally take into account the fact that the licensee has additional costs for the translation work, either in the form of a royalty or an outright fee payable to the translator. It is customary for the royalty rates to escalate after an agreed level of sales has been reached. The royalty percentages and the level and number of the escalation points are, of course, open to negotiation between the parties. It is customary for different royalty rates to apply to hardback and paperback editions, and if e-book rights are to be included these should be covered in a separate sub-clause (best inserted as subclause 2.5) as the royalty rates and payment model may be different from that of the print edition/s; for example, the licensee may wish to base royalties on net receipts rather than a recommended price, and the royalty rate should be adjusted upwards accordingly.

The pricing basis on which the royalty will be calculated for print editions should be agreed between the parties. Some countries retain a fixed price system; others use a recommended retail price. Many former communist countries still favour the use of a 'publisher's price', the price which they themselves receive from their distributors and it is important that this is made clear to the licensor so that they can adjust royalty rates accordingly (**see Appendix to this Precedent**). For countries which apply Value Added Tax to the price of books, the price on which royalties are to be calculated should be specified as less such tax.

If the royalties are to be calculated on a basis other than on the retail or recommended retail price (e.g., on the wholesale price or sum received in countries where market circumstances make it impossible to set either a fixed or a recommended retail price) Clause 2.2 would have to be modified accordingly. In such cases it would be advisable to negotiate higher percentage royalty rates to allow for the lower price on which the calculation will be based.

If the contract is to be based on a lump sum for a designated printing rather than on an advance and royalty basis, Clause 2 should be amended to read:

> 'For the right to produce the aforesaid [*number*] copies of the Translation, the Publishers shall make the following payments to the Proprietors in accordance with the terms of Clause 20 hereof, namely:
>
> A lump sum of [*amount*] payable on signature of this Agreement and a lump sum [*amount*] on publication of the Translation or by [*date*] whichever is earlier.'

It is also highly advisable to add to this alternative clause some protection against inflation, since the lump sum will be calculated on the estimated price of the translation at the time of the negotiations and the final price could well be significantly higher. Wording to cover this might read:

> 'Should the Translation be issued at a price higher than the estimated *retail/wholesale* price of [*amount*] the total payment due to the Proprietors shall be increased on publication of the Translation by a percentage equivalent to the increase in the price of the Translation.'

The lump sum model can only realistically be applied to a designated quantity of copies produced in print form.

3. Validity of Agreement

The contract is only valid when the proprietors have received the sum due on signature of the contract.

4. Accuracy of Translation

Since any proposed changes to the work in translation will almost certainly require consultation with the author, this clause provides for details of any changes or additions to be supplied in English. There is also provision for full approval of the translated text prior to the licensee commencing production, although in practice only a small number of manuscripts are likely to be vetted in this way. In such cases, it may be desirable to add that approval should not be unreasonably withheld, and that a response should be given within a reasonable time of receipt of the text of the translation (e.g., 60 days). Some rights owners may wish to add a provision that the Publishers shall be legally liable for any problems resulting from inaccuracies introduced during the translation process.

2.1 The sum of [*amount*] payable on signature of this Agreement in advance and on account of any sums which may become due to the Proprietors under this Agreement from sales of the Translation.

The said payment in advance is not recoverable in the event of any default by the Publishers in carrying out the terms of this Agreement.

2.2 On the *recommended* retail/wholesale price of all copies of the Translation sold by the Publishers:

(i) A royalty of [*number*] per cent on the first [*number*] thousand copies sold.

(ii) A royalty of [*number*] per cent on all copies sold between [*number*] thousand and [*number*] thousand.

(iii) A royalty of [*number*] per cent on all copies sold beyond the first [*number*] thousand.

2.3 No royalty shall be payable on copies of the Translation presented in the interests of sale of the Translation, lost through theft or damaged or destroyed by fire, water, in transit or otherwise.

2.4 On remainder copies of the Translation sold by the Publishers at or below cost no royalty shall be payable to the Proprietors but no such remainder copies shall be sold within a period of two years from the date of first publication of the Translation.

3. Validity of Agreement

This Agreement shall not come into effect until the Proprietors have received the advance payment detailed in Clause 2.1 hereof.

4. Accuracy of Translation

The Publishers shall arrange for the translation of the Work to be made at their own expense faithfully and accurately by a qualified and competent translator, whose name and qualifications shall be sent to the Proprietors. Abbreviations, alterations and/or additions shall only be made with the prior written consent of the Proprietors. Where such changes are agreed, details thereof are to be supplied by the Publishers in English if so requested by the Proprietors. The Publishers agree to include if requested by the Proprietors any new manuscript and/or illustrations supplied during the preparation of the Translation, such new manuscript and/or illustrations remaining the copyright of the Proprietors/Author. The Proprietors reserve the right to request the Publishers to submit the text of the Translation to the Proprietors for their prior written approval before commencing production of the Translation.

5. Copyright Material from Other Sources

This clause is intended to alert both parties before they sign the contract to the need to agree which party will undertake any necessary re-clearance for the re-use of copyright material (illustrations and/or quoted text) controlled by external owners if the proprietors did not pre-clear rights for sub-licensed editions; also who will pay any attendant fees. The circumstances of each book vary so much that it may be best to finalise the exact details by separate correspondence. A sharing of costs may at times be appropriate.

If the onus for the reclearance work and the payment of any attendant fees is to be placed on the publishers as licensees, wording might read as follows:

> 'The Publishers shall be responsible for obtaining, wherever necessary, permission for the use in the Translation of copyright material from the Work controlled by third parties and shall also be responsible for paying any fees required for such permissions and for ensuring that appropriate acknowledgement is made in the Translation.'

If the proprietors are prepared to undertake such work on behalf of the Publishers for administrative reasons, an alternative might be:

> 'The Proprietors shall be responsible for obtaining on behalf of the Publishers, wherever necessary, permission for the use in the Translation of copyright material from the Work controlled by third parties and shall recharge the cost of any fees required for such permission to the Publishers with the addition of an administration charge of [*number*] per cent of such charges. The Publishers shall be responsible for ensuring that appropriate acknowledgement is made in the Translation.'

The proprietors reserve the right not to supply duplicate production material for the illustrations in the work to the licensee until full re-clearance has been obtained, as to do so earlier may place them in breach of their own contracts with the external copyright holders, such as picture agencies or museums.

6. Control of Publication/Production Quality

It is recognised that in some countries it may not be possible to produce the licensed edition to standards comparable with that of the original edition.

7. Acknowledgments

It is advisable to spell out in detail the obligations of the licensee to credit the author properly; in some countries there can be a danger that the translator is credited more prominently, particularly if the translator is better known as an academic or educator in the market concerned.

It is also wise to spell out in full detail the exact text of the copyright notice relating to the original edition, to the original title (and edition number if appropriate) and the form in which acknowledgment should be made to the proprietors as the original publishers. The licensee should also add a copyright notice relating to the translated text. It is a favourite tendency of some publishers who are tardy in publishing a translation of a scientific book to omit the year of first publication from the copyright notice relating to the original edition, thus making the book appear more recent.

The licensee should also add a copyright notice relating to the translated text of the work. This may be in the name of the translator or the name of the licensee, depending on what arrangements have been made between those parties. In recent years, there has been an increasing tendency by large multinational publishers to request an assignment of copyright in the translated text from their licensees either from signature of the licence agreement or when the licence terminates; neither scenario may be acceptable to the licensee, especially if the licensors have the facility to publish local translations themselves via subsidiary companies.

Since the introduction of moral rights in the UK by virtue of the Copyright, Designs and Patents Act 1988, some head contracts with British authors place a requirement on the British publisher to ensure that any editions published under licence reproduce the statement in the original work in which the author asserts his or her right of paternity. If this is the case, this obligation should be included in this clause, clearly specifying the required words of the statement.

5. Copyright Material from Other Sources

The Proprietors and the Publishers shall mutually agree responsibility for obtaining, wherever necessary, permission for the use in the Translation of copyright literary or artistic material incorporated in the Work and belonging to third parties, and shall also agree upon responsibility for paying any fees required for such permissions and for ensuring that appropriate acknowledgment is made in the Translation. The Proprietors reserve the right not to supply the Publishers with duplicate production material for any illustrations contained in the Work until such permission has been obtained.

6. Control of Publication/Production Quality

The paper, printing, binding, jackets or covers, the promotion, the manner and extent of advertisement, the number and distribution of free copies for the press or otherwise, the pricing and terms of sale of the Translation shall be in the sole discretion of the Publishers who undertake to ensure that, wherever possible, the printing, paper and binding of the Translation shall be of the highest quality.

7. Acknowledgments

The Publishers undertake that the name of the Author shall appear in its customary form in the English language with due prominence on the title page, spine and jacket/cover of every copy of the Translation issued and on the reverse side of the title page shall appear the following copyright notice: '© [*name of copyright owner* [*date*]]' together with the following acknowledgment: 'This translation of [*title*, *number of edition*] is published by arrangement with [*name of Publisher*]. The Publishers shall also include an appropriate copyright notice to cover the text of the Translation.

8. Complimentary Copies

The Publishers shall supply the Proprietors with [*number*] free copies of the Translation on publication, together with details of the actual date of publication and the recommended retail/wholesale price of the Translation.

---

8. Complimentary Copies

This clause allows for provision of the required number of finished copies of the translation to be sent to the proprietors; a larger number will be required if there are several authors involved. There is an additional requirement to confirm details of the publication date and final price; the latter may indicate a rise in the estimated price which may necessitate calculation of a pro-rata increase if a lump sum arrangement has been negotiated (see note to Clause 2).

If any subsidiary rights have been granted under the terms of Clause 10, provision should also be made here for the supply of an agreed quantity of any sub-licensed editions.

9. Failure to Publish/Out of Print

9.1 The publication time limit will depend on the length and complexity of the book, but may also be affected if the content of the book is time sensitive; this might mean a short time limit for a highly newsworthy topic, or for computer books which have a short lifespan and are often licensed to appear in translation virtually simultaneously with the original edition. If the licensee subsequently has a valid reason for delay (e.g., the death of a specialised translator) the time limit can be extended by an addendum to the contract. Educational and academic publishers will need to monitor the schedule for the next English edition in order to decide whether the licensee should switch over to the new edition, perhaps with some renegotiation of the terms.

9.2 The contract can be terminated if the translation goes out of print or off the market; it is important to have a clear understanding between the parties on what this means, particularly if the publishers have a print-on demand programme in place; it might then be preferable to specify that termination should only come into force if the translation is not available from the publishers in any form. Some publishers may choose to insert a definition, for example, 'if sales have fallen to less than x copies per year' or 'if royalty revenue has fallen to less than x per year'. It should, however, be remembered that if any subsidiary rights are permitted under the terms of Clause 10, it may be necessary to adjust this clause to permit any properly negotiated sub-licences to continue to run their term.

For licences negotiated on the basis of a lump sum for a designated print run, the following wording should be substituted:

> 'The Publishers shall inform the Proprietors when the Translation goes out of print, whereupon all rights shall revert to the Proprietors, but the Publishers shall have the first option of producing and publishing a further printing of the Translation on terms to be agreed between the parties hereto and shall not proceed with publication of such further printing until written permission has been obtained from the Proprietors and terms have been agreed.'

Some licences may provide for ownership of the translated text to be transferred to the proprietors on termination of the contract.

10. Subsidiary Rights

This precedent confines the rights granted to volume rights only in the designated language; many specialist works licensed for translation do not have potential for the exploitation of sub-licences.

For trade titles, the situation may well be different. If the licensee wishes to acquire a range of additional rights in the language and territories granted, these should be discussed at the negotiation stage and a division of the proceeds between the licensee and the proprietors should be agreed. In such cases, Clause 10 might be replaced by the following:

> 'In addition to the rights granted under Clause 1 hereof, the Proprietors hereby grant to the Publishers the following rights in the [*language*] language in the sales territory specified in Clause 1 hereof, subject to payment of the designated percentages of all monies received from the sale of such rights:

Reprint rights licensed to another publisher:	[*number*] per cent
Book club rights licensed on a royalty basis:	[*number*] per cent
First serial rights:	[*number*] per cent
Second serial rights:	[*number*] per cent
Digest and condensation rights:	[*number*] per cent
Anthology and quotation rights:	[*number*] per cent
Single voice reading rights for radio:	[*number*] per cent

> All such licences shall be subject to the prior written approval of the Proprietors, such approval not to be unreasonably withheld. All sums due to the Proprietors from such sales shall be paid to the Proprietors within Thirty days of receipt of such payments by the Publishers.'

9. Failure to Publish/Out of Print

9.1 Should the Publishers fail to issue the Translation by [*date*] all rights granted hereunder shall revert to the Proprietors without prejudice to any claim which the Proprietors may have for monies due, for damages or otherwise.

9.2 Should the Translation go out of print or become unavailable in any form the Proprietors shall be at liberty to terminate this Agreement on giving to the Publishers six months' notice in writing to reprint the Translation and on the expiration of such period of six months should such reprint not have been made all rights granted under this Agreement shall revert to the Proprietors without prejudice to any claim which the Proprietors may have for monies due.

10. Subsidiary Rights

The Publishers shall not dispose of any subsidiary rights in the Translation without obtaining the prior written consent of the Proprietors.

The inclusion of subsidiary rights in a translation licence assumes that the proprietors have themselves the authority to grant such rights (e.g., the literary agent representing the author may have held back first serial rights, film and television rights etc). Each contract must be carefully negotiated according to the specific bundle of rights held by the proprietors.

The notes to Clauses 1 and 2 above deal with the possibility of including electronic publishing rights for the translation in the main grant of rights to the publishers, i.e. to cover situations where the licensee will be selling e-books direct from their own website. It is normally unwise to include electronic rights in the subsidiary rights granted to a foreign publisher unless the type of sublicence is clearly specified, as financial models – and hence the required share to be paid to the proprietors – may vary considerably depending on onward arrangements with any sublicensees. These rights can always be granted at a later stage via an addendum if necessary.

In some Scandinavian countries, broadcasting organisations are allowed to use extracts without permission from the copyright holder. Fees are paid for such use to an equivalent to the Performing Right Society and can be recovered only by someone whose business is registered in the Scandinavian country concerned. For such countries, therefore, it is important to allow control of broadcasting rights to be in the hands of local publishers.

It should also be remembered that the legislation of many communist or ex-communist countries still permits very broad use of copyright material, often without permission or payment. This includes the right to quote from copyright works extensively 'provided the use is justified'; some countries also permit extracts from copyright works to be broadcast without permission or payment provided that the source is acknowledged.

The division of proceeds from sub-licences between the foreign publisher and the proprietors may vary from 50/50 for all rights (common in the case of many educational and academic works) to 75/25 for sub-licensed paperback rights and 80/20 in the case of first serial rights. Care should be taken that the proprietors receive a higher proportion of the receipts in the case of arrangements for paperback editions or book club editions produced by a publishing operation within the same publishing group as the licensee, that is, a form of 'vertical publishing'. In such a case it may be possible to negotiate for the proprietors to receive the full royalty on the sub-licensed edition and an additional advance.

11. Accounts

Accounting is commonly half-yearly in the Anglo-American tradition, and yearly in the Continental tradition; the clause offers alternative wording. Some countries (in particular in Scandinavia) ask for three months in which to render statements and a further six months in which to render any monies due. This practice should be resisted; a further three months may be acceptable.

If e-book rights are to be included under the terms of Clauses 1 and 2, accounting for e-book sales will need to be clearly distinguished from print sales in this clause; in addition, a number of the requirements for reporting information for print sales (e.g. copies in stock) are not applicable to e-book sales. This could be done by prefacing the present first paragraph of Clause 11 with the heading:

> '(a) For sales of the Translation by the Publishers in print form:'

A new subclause to cover e-book sales could be inserted after item (x) as follows:

> '(b) For sales of the Translation by the Publishers in e-book form:
>
> (i) The number of copies sold during the accounting period:
>
> (ii) The cumulative e-book sales of the Translation since publication;
>
> (iii) The sum received for each e-book sale of the Translation;
>
> (iv) The royalty rate payable;
>
> (v) The total payment due to (name of Proprietors)'

The clause would then continue: 'Accounts and royalties shall be paid in accordance with the provisions of Clause 20 hereof.' etc.

NB this clause covers accounting for royalties on the licensee's own edition or editions of the book; if subsidiary rights are granted under the terms of Clause 10, provision is made for the proprietors' share of such income to be remitted within 30 days of receipt from the sub-licensees.

If the licence has been granted on a lump-sum basis, it will be sufficient to retain for Clause 11 only the penultimate paragraph of the precedent, 'Should any of the payments detailed in this Agreement …'.

In the final paragraph of this clause concerning the right to inspect the licensee's accounts, some rights owners may wish to add more stringent wording on what should happen if under-reporting is discovered. This might read as follows:

> 'in the event that such examination reveals an understatement of 5 per cent or more, the Proprietors may at their sole discretion terminate this Agreement without prejudice to any claims the Proprietors may have for monies due.'

11. Accounts

Accounts for the sale of the Translation shall be made up *annually/twice annually* by the Publishers to [*date/dates*] and the account rendered together with any sums payable for such sales within three months of the/each accounting date. Accounts will show:

(i) the original English language title of the Work together with the original ISBN;

(ii) the number of copies in stock if any, at the beginning of the accounting period;

(iii) the number of copies printed if any, during the accounting period;

(iv) the number of copies sold during the accounting period;

(v) the number of copies presented free of charge during the accounting period;

(vi) the number of copies remaining in stock at the end of the accounting period;

(vii) the cumulative sales of the Translation since publication;

(viii) the retail/wholesale price of the Translation;

(ix) the royalty rate payable;

(x) the total payment due to (name of Proprietors)

and accounts and royalties shall be paid in accordance with the provisions of Clause 20 hereof.

Should any of the payments detailed in this Agreement be three months overdue the licence herein granted shall forthwith lapse and all rights conveyed by it shall, without further notice, revert to the Proprietors without prejudice to any claim the Proprietors may have for monies due, for damages or otherwise.

The Proprietors or their authorised representative shall have the right upon written request and reasonable notice to examine during normal business hours the records of accounts of the Publishers in so far as they relate to sales and receipts in respect of the Translation, which examination shall be at the cost of the Proprietors unless errors exceeding 5 per cent of such sales and receipts in the last two preceding accounting periods to their disadvantage shall be found, in which case the cost shall be paid by the Publishers.

12. Clearance for Further Printings

This clause appears in the advance and royalty agreement as a safeguard against the licensee continuing to print copies of an edition which may have been found to be unsatisfactory, either in terms of translation or production quality. Clearance for further printings can be obtained swiftly by fax or e-mail.

13. Warranties and Indemnity

The proprietors provide warranties and indemnities to the licensee under English law since they cannot be expected to be familiar with the exact details of legislation in the country of the licensee. Care should be taken to ensure that the warranties and indemnities match those given to the proprietors by the author. If the licensee requires further warranties (e.g., against libel or obscenity) these can be granted under English law provided that the author has provided such warranties to the proprietors.

NB Despite the inclusion of this clause, the People's Republic of China requires additional documentation from licensing publishers if the copyright notice in the work to be licensed is in the name of the author rather than that of the publisher (**see Appendix to this Precedent**).

14. Restrictions on Transfer

If subsidiary rights have been granted to the licensees under the terms of Clause 10, this clause should be amended to read:

> 'The licence hereby granted to the Publishers shall not be transferred to or extended to include any other party other than in connection with sub-licences properly granted under the terms of Clause 10 hereof; nor shall the Translation appear under any imprint other than that of the Publishers or their duly authorised sub-licensees, except with the prior written consent of the Proprietors.'

16. Duration of Licence

The duration of the licence may be for the full term of copyright or (more commonly) for an agreed number of years as specified here; in either case there should be provision for termination of the contract if the translation is allowed to go out of print and is not being exploited by any authorised sub-licensees (see Clause 9.2).

It is preferable that the term of the contract should run from a fixed date given at the commencement of the contract, rather than from a less precise date such as 'the date of signature of this Agreement' (as there could be a delay between the date of signature by both parties) or from the date of publication of the licensed edition, which could be delayed.

Publishers of non-fiction works, in particular textbooks which are likely to be regularly updated, may find it advisable to restrict the contract not by a period of years, but by the life of the edition which is being licensed. This can be covered by omitting Clause 16, inserting the number of the relevant edition after the title in the Preamble (e.g., Second Edition, add

12. Clearance for Further Printings

The Publishers undertake not to reprint the Translation without first informing the Proprietors and obtaining their consent in writing.

13. Warranties and Indemnity

The Proprietors hereby warrant to the Publishers that they have the right and power to make this Agreement and that according to English law the Work will in no way whatever give rise to a violation of any existing copyright, or a breach of any existing agreement and that nothing in the Work is liable to give rise to a criminal prosecution or to a civil action for damages or any other remedy and the Proprietors will indemnify the Publishers against any loss, injury or expense arising out of any breach of this warranty. If in the opinion of the Publishers and on the advice of their legal advisers the Work contains any passage that may reasonably be considered actionable at law in the territories granted to the Publishers under this Agreement, the Publishers shall have the right upon prior written notice to the Proprietors to modify or to remove such passage from the Translation.

14. Restrictions on Transfer

The licence hereby granted to the Publishers shall not be transferred to or extended to include any other party; nor shall the Translation appear under any imprint other than that of the Publishers, except with the prior written consent of the Proprietors.

15. Retained Rights

All rights in the Work, other than those specifically granted to the Publishers under this Agreement, are reserved by the Proprietors.

16. Duration of Licence

Subject to the terms of Clauses 9, 11, 17 and 23 hereof, the licence hereby granted shall last for a period of [*number*] years from the date of this Agreement and may thereafter be renewed by mutual agreement between the parties.

---

ing the original ISBN of that edition for added clarity) and adding to the end of Clause 1 the words: 'This Agreement does not grant any rights with respect to subsequent editions of the Work'. Although in practice it is usually preferable to continue to license subsequent editions to the same licensee, this limitation does enable alternative arrangements to be made for a new edition if the original licensee proves unsatisfactory or if licensing policy changes (e.g., if the proprietors develop their own local language publishing programme in the country concerned). For additional safety, the following clause could also be inserted:

> 'The Proprietors shall be free to license the rights in any subsequent revised edition of the Work elsewhere at their discretion but on the understanding that such publication shall not take place unless sales of the Translation have fallen below 50 copies per annum in which case the Proprietors shall not unreasonably recover the rights, subject to satisfactory arrangements being made for the remaining stock of the Translation.'

It should, however, be remembered that the acquisition of translation rights in a large and complex work (such as a major medical textbook) involves considerable investment and labour on the part of the licensee, who may be employing large teams of translators. In such cases the licensee may well be reluctant to accept such limitations and may instead seek an option to publish the next edition. The decision of the proprietors must then depend on the circumstances (see note on option clause at the end of these notes). The proprietors must also take into account the situation on ownership of copyright in the translated text as there may be substantial amounts of unchanged text carried over into the new edition (see Note to Clause 7).

19. Arbitration

Whilst arbitration under the terms of the country of the proprietors may be preferable, publishers in some communist or ex-communist countries may not accept this. A compromise might be to substitute the following wording:

> 'Unless otherwise agreed, any disputes arising out of or in connection with this Agreement shall be settled under the Rules of Arbitration of the International Chamber of Commerce by a single arbitrator appointed in accordance with such rules. The award of the arbitrator shall be final and binding on the parties and judgement upon the award rendered may be entered in any court having jurisdiction or application may be made to such court for judicial acceptance of the award and an order of enforcement as the case may be.'

NB The People's Republic of China requires contracts to specify arbitration in China (**see Appendix to this Precedent**).

20. Method of Payment

If the accounting department of the proprietors is located at a different address from the main address given at the commencement of the contract, details should be inserted into this clause.

Licensees in some countries (e.g., Latin America, central and eastern Europe, the former Soviet Union and mainland China) may find it easier to remit payment in US dollars and this point should therefore be discussed at the negotiation stage. It may then be preferable to specify all payments in Clause 2 in dollars.

In recent years there have been moves by some countries (in particular Russia) to impose VAT on royalties remitted to foreign countries. The wording in this clause seeks to clarify that any local VAT liability should be discharged by the licensee before remitting the contractual amounts due to the Proprietors, rather than the Publishers deducting such VAT from the amounts agreed and expected by the Proprietors. Some licensees may require the Proprietors to invoice them for the amounts due (advances or royalties) with the addition of the VAT amount, then showing this amount deducted to arrive at the net amount which will actually be remitted.

Documentation on any withholding tax deductions is required for those British publishers who are entitled to set such deductions against corporation tax.

17. Termination

In the event of the Publishers being declared bankrupt or should they fail to comply with any of the provisions of this Agreement and not rectify such failure within one month of having received written notice from the Proprietors to do so by a registered letter sent to the Publishers at their address given at the commencement of this Agreement, then in either event this Agreement automatically becomes null and void and the licence granted to the Publishers herein shall revert to the Proprietors without prejudice to any monies paid or due to the Proprietors.

18. Notices

Any and all notices given hereunder shall be in writing and sent by fax, e-mail, courier or registered mail to the parties at their respective addresses herein specified. The parties undertake to notify each other of any change of address within thirty days of such change.

19. Arbitration

If any difference shall arise between the Publishers and the Proprietors touching the meaning of this Agreement or the rights and liabilities of the parties hereto, the same shall be referred to the arbitration of two persons (one to be named by each party) or their umpire, in accordance with the provisions of the Arbitration Act 1996 or any subsisting statutory modification or re-enactment thereof.

20. Method of Payment

All sums which may become due to the Proprietors under this Agreement shall be paid by the Publishers in *sterling/US dollars/euros* without any deduction in respect of exchange or commission to:

[*address of Proprietors' appropriate accounts department*]

OR:

[*name and address of Proprietors' bank, account number, sort code, SWIFT code and IBAN number*]

The Publishers shall not have the right to withhold any part of sums due to the Proprietors as a reserve against returns and/or credits. The amounts due are net of any withholding VAT that may be applied in the Publishers' territory and represent the sum of money that the Proprietors will receive after any withholding VAT is deducted from a VAT-inclusive figure. Should

21. Applicable Law

In the Anglo-American tradition, it is the proprietors' jurisdiction that is usually stated as applicable (although American publishers increasingly insist on their own jurisdiction whether they are buying or selling rights). The issue must be faced and settled before signature of the contract, otherwise it may actually be unlawful from the start, especially if the law chosen is that of one of the Continental countries which limit the transfer of rights in publishing contracts, for example, Switzerland, Germany, France or Italy. An excellent note in the Contract Column of *Rights*, Vol 4, No 1, by Andre Bertrand on the subject concludes:

> 'The choice of applicable law is therefore the first question to be resolved in the transnational contract. Once this choice has been made by the parties they can proceed to write a publishing contract which is in conformity with this law. If the parties do not respect this rule, they risk drawing up a contract that will not be legal with regard to the stipulations of the law to which the contract will be submitted in the event of a dispute.'

It should be noted that some communist or ex-communist countries may not be prepared to accept a contract which is operable under the law of the proprietors. Compromise wording might be:

> 'Any dispute between the parties not resolved by arbitration or agreement shall be decided by the court of the summoned party.'

NB The People's Republic of China requires contracts to be operable under Chinese law (**see Appendix to this Precedent**).

22. Local Registration and Copyright Protection

Some countries have formal registration procedures in order to secure copyright protection. This clause places the obligation on the licensee to fulfil any such procedures and also to take action against any infringement within the market granted.

23. Assignment by Proprietors

This clause is likely to be required by British publishers to minimise the need to consult all licensees in the event of the sale of all or part of their list.

24. Entire Agreement

Any variations to the original agreement must be agreed in writing.

25. Signature of Agreement

It is recommended that the Proprietors predate the Agreement before sending it to the Publishers.

Additional Clauses

Agency arrangements: if the deal has been arranged via a sub-agent in the country concerned, it will be necessary to cover this in the contract:

> 'All payments due under this Agreement are to be made via [*name and address of agent*] and will be subject to [*number*] per cent agency commission.'

Option clause: some licensees may seek to acquire an option either on the next edition of the work (see note to Clause 1) or on the next book to be written by the author. If the proprietors agree to this, the following clause could be inserted:

> 'The Proprietors agree to grant to the Publishers the first option on the [*language*] translation rights for *the next edition of the Work/the next Work* by the Author providing rights in such work are controlled by the Proprietors. The Publishers shall reach a decision within 60 days of receipt of suitable material from the Proprietors and any licence arrangements will then be covered by a separate agreement on terms to be agreed between the parties.'

the Publishers be obliged by law to deduct any taxes other than VAT they shall send a declaration to this effect with the relevant statement of account showing the amount deducted.

21. Applicable Law

This Agreement shall be governed by and interpreted and construed in accordance with the laws of England whose courts shall have exclusive jurisdiction.

22. Local Registration and Copyright Protection

The Publishers agree to take any necessary steps to register the title of the Work in the name of the copyright owner under local copyright laws at the sole expense of the Publishers. The Publishers also agree to protect such copyright and to prosecute at their own expense any person who infringes such copyright in the territories granted to them under this Agreement.

23. Assignment by Proprietors

The Proprietors may assign this Agreement without the consent of the Publishers in the event of the sale of all or part of the Proprietors' businesses.

24. Entire Agreement

This Agreement contains the full and complete understanding between the Parties and supersedes all prior arrangements and undertakings, whether oral or written, concerning the subject matter of this Agreement and may not be varied except by agreement in writing between the Parties.

25. Signature of Agreement

This Agreement shall be deemed to be legally binding only if the Publishers sign this Agreement within 6 (Six) weeks from the date of this Agreement.

AS WITNESS THE HANDS OF THE PARTIES

Signed...

For the Publishers

Signed..

For the Proprietors

APPENDIX

Transitional and Post-transitional Markets: The People's Republic of China, Central and Eastern Europe and the Post-Soviet Union Republics

In previous editions of *Publishing Agreements*, the appendix to this Precedent has dealt with the sale of rights to the People's Republic of China, the Soviet Union and its successor and former satellite states. Although all have now moved to more 'normal' trading conditions, these markets still merit some special treatment in terms of historical and legislative background and contractual conditions, hence the retention of this Appendix.

The People's Republic of China

Introduction

For many years the People's Republic of China was the largest country in the world remaining outside membership of the Berne Convention and the Universal Copyright Convention; foreign books and journals were reprinted and translated in China on a vast scale, usually without permission from or payment to the original publisher and the author. It was sometimes possible to reach agreement on the basis of a payment in blocked currency to be used within China. Foreign recorded music, video tapes and DVDs, computer software and CD-ROMs have been and continue to be reproduced on a substantial scale with consequent losses to the industries concerned.

Domestic copyright legislation was finally introduced on 1 June 1991, at which point the authorities reiterated their intention to seek membership of both conventions. Although the domestic legislation contained a number of welcome features, including a term of copyright protection of 50 years *post mortem auctoris*, a number of other areas including very broad provisions for fair dealing, the blanket use of copyright works by the state, and lack of automatic protection for foreign works except through membership of an international convention, gave cause for concern. A revision of the domestic copyright law in effect from 27 October 2001 contains a number of welcome elements designed to bring China into line with the TRIPs requirements of the GATT and the WIPO Copyright Treaty, but does not extend the term of copyright protection from 50 to 70 years *post mortem auctoris*. It also contained a worrying provision for the compulsory licensing of short extracts or short works for inclusion in state textbooks; it was however unclear whether this provision could be extended to foreign works. Further revisions to domestic legislation are to be implemented in 2010.

Following strong trade pressure from the West (in particular from the US), China finally acceded to the Berne Convention on 15 October 1992, to the Universal Copyright Convention on 30 October 1992 and to the Geneva Phonogram Convention on 1 June 1993. In the case of Berne and UCC, China ratified the Paris texts of 1971, although there has still been no evidence of its seeking access to compulsory licences. China also agreed to provide retrospective protection to all US works created before the signing date of a bilateral accord between the two countries provided that those works were still protected by copyright under US domestic legislation. More recently, it ratified the World Intellectual Property Organisation (WIPO) Copyright Treaty on 9 June 2007.

Despite membership of the international copyright conventions and the World Trade Organisation, piracy continues in China although the music, video and software industries are now probably more seriously affected than the book industry. However, piracy of academic journals in print form continued on a huge scale until late 2001 when strong pressure from the UK and US publishing industries resulted in the Chinese government banning the purchase of pirated copies by academic institutions. Despite this, in the last two years there has been large-scale electronic piracy of foreign academic journals and the US and UK publishers' associations continue to lobby the Chinese copyright authorities.

A number of successful prosecutions for piracy have been brought on behalf of foreign copyright holders with the assistance of the National Copyright Administration of China, and there are special intellectual property divisions in the regional courts. China remains a key country on the 301 Watch List produced by the International Intellectual Property Alliance (IIPA) and is on the Special 301 Priority Watch List for 2010.

Method of payment

Until the mid-1990s, many Chinese publishers and academic institutions had difficulty in obtaining hard currency for the purchase of rights, but this is no longer a problem provided that the licence contracts have been registered by the Chinese licensee with the appropriate local copyright authorities.

Despite moves to 'privatise' and to consolidate many publishers and distributors into regional groups, the official Chinese publishing industry remains in effect state-controlled and this has implications in terms of the approval of licences for foreign works and potential censorship issues, in particular relating to content considered politically unacceptable to the Chinese authorities (references to the Tian'anmen incident, the status of Taiwan and China's treatment of minorities in Tibet and Xinjiang Province are obvious examples). There are now many unofficial Chinese publishing operations (referred to as the 'second channel' publishers or 'cultural studios'). However, such operations still have to resort to 'buying' ISBNs from official publishing houses in order to bring their publications to market and in recent years there have been moves by the Chinese publishing authorities to encourage 'alliances' with the state houses, presumably with the aim of harnessing the energy of and gaining more control over the activities of the private publishers.

Although most Chinese publishers now apply for rights in the normal way, some still have much to learn in terms of applying for rights from the West, and even the larger publishing houses can still behave in an unorthodox manner. There are still instances where a Western author is approached by an individual Chinese translator, who has either already translated a book by that author, or is intending to do so. Usually there is no mention of payment or even the name of the publishing house concerned. The author is often asked to confirm that he or she has no objection to the translation going ahead free of charge, and in some cases the author may also be asked to provide revisions or a special preface for the Chinese edition. It has, unfortunately, been the case that some authors – most of them unaware of the copyright history of China – have gladly endorsed such translations, even in cases where the copyright has been assigned to the British publishing house, or where rights are within the control of the publisher. Such endorsements make it extremely difficult for the publisher to enter into negotiations with the translator and the Chinese publisher at a later stage.

Where an approach is first received from an individual translator, it is usually advisable to respond by explaining that negotiations must be undertaken with the publishing house or academic institute concerned. Care can be taken to explain that whilst the British publisher is aware of factors such as the relatively new recognition of copyright, low book prices in China, and the shortage of hard currency available, a book represents a major investment of expertise, time and money by the author and the original publishing house, and these factors should be recognised if the book is to be used in China. Any commercial negotiation should be conducted with the Chinese publishing house or institute rather than with the individual translator; however, in the area of academic publishing it has become apparent that some individual translators are actually paying Chinese publishers to subsidise the cost of publication of the translation. It is important to stress that since 1992 there has been a legal obligation to pay for the rights but that this should not be the responsibility of the individual translator. There have been cases of individual translators offering several months of their salary for the rights or of Chinese publishers threatening to withdraw from publication (to the distress of the translator) if the foreign copyright holder or his representative requires payment. It is vital to continue to reinforce the principle of copyright recognition and avoid waiving copyright fees, whilst recognising the economic reality of the individual situation.

In the years following China's initial accession to two of the international copyright conventions in 1992, it was often preferable to negotiate royalties in the form of a lump-sum equivalent to an agreed royalty percentage of the local price for a designated print run, and to renew the licence for further printings if appropriate. This corresponded with the traditional Chinese system of payment for their own authors and still has the added advantage that licensing policy can be regularly reviewed. Some Chinese publishers may be prepared to pay the whole lump sum on signature of the contract; some may agree to half of the total payment on signature of the contract and the balance on publication, whilst others may wish to make the total payment within three months of completion of printing of the designated quantity.

As Chinese publishers have gained more experience in acquiring rights from the West, many have preferred to move towards the Western model of paying an advance on signature of the licence contract, set against annual or semi-annual royalties on sales. Some may be prepared to pay the total royalty on the first printing in the form of an advance, and indeed evidence of intermittent or non-existent accounting for sales and royalties by some Chinese licensees has led some foreign copyright holders to seek payment of the total royalty on the first printing on signature of the licence contract on the grounds that this may be the only payment they ever see. There is no reason why royalty percentages should be lower than those negotiated with Western licensees for similar titles; the royalties will be based on local prices far lower than those in the West, so to accept lower percentage rates would constitute a double concession by licensors.

Western publishers new to the market may question whether the print run or sales reported by a Chinese licensee are accurate. Technically, Chinese publishers are still required to print details of their print quantity in the book itself and this should always be checked on receipt of finished copies; however, it is inevitable that there may be some cases of under-reporting by the licensee or of printers running on excess copies in addition to the official print run.

Contracts

When contracting with publishers in China a number of special points are still worth bearing in mind.

It should, of course, be remembered that the PRC is not the only Chinese language market where rights can be licensed: Hong Kong, Singapore and

Taiwan all have strong local publishing industries and higher customer purchasing power than the mainland, despite their smaller populations. The markets differ linguistically, economically and politically; these differences may affect licensing strategy and should certainly be reflected in contractual arrangements with the different markets. Chinese editions published for the PRC or Singapore will utilise simplified characters, whilst Hong Kong, Macao and Taiwan use traditional (complex) characters. It must, however, be remembered that the PRC views Taiwan as a renegade province rather than as an independent country; trade between the two markets has increased in recent years despite the continuing ideological divide and periodic incidents of political tension and there is therefore a need to make a clear geographical as well as a linguistic distinction when defining licences to the two markets. The fact that many Western publishers and literary agents still choose to allow world Chinese rights to be handled via Taiwanese publishers or Taiwan-owned sub-agents such as the Big Apple-Tuttle-Mori Agency and the Bardon-Chinese Media Agency remains a source of considerable annoyance to mainland publishers, especially as there are now no real barriers to remitting hard currency abroad.

The position of Hong Kong when granting licences to mainland Chinese publishers is important. From 1 July 1997 political rule of Hong Kong was transferred to China and Hong Kong became a Special Administrative Region (SAR), but it has long had an established publishing industry of its own, using traditional rather than simplified characters and with a far higher purchasing power than the mainland. It is as yet unclear whether China may seek to introduce the use of simplified characters in Hong Kong, which would then remove another means of distinguishing between licences to what are currently separate markets. Until the situation on this is clearer, it would be advisable to define licences to PRC publishers as being for the Chinese language in simplified characters only, and to define the sales territory as being the mainland territory of the People's Republic of China only, excluding Hong Kong and Macao. Macao, an SAR from 20 December 1999 should also be excluded, although it is a far less significant book market. A clear market restriction should appear on the cover and title verso of licensed editions; a tactful way of also excluding Taiwan can be achieved by stating that a licensed edition is for sale in 'the mainland territory of the People's Republic of China only, excluding Hong Kong and Macao'.

An unwelcome requirement which has emerged as Chinese publishers acquire more licences from Western publishers and agents is substantiation of the right of the western publisher or agent to grant the licence if the copyright in the work to be licensed is in the name of the author rather than that of the publisher. Whilst this should not be necessary if the western licensor provides a warranty and indemnity clause in the licence contract, the Chinese authorities have proved persistent in this matter and on occasion have required notarised documents from the author or a copy of the original head contract between the author and the Western publisher as a condition for remitting licence payments. This is somewhat ironic in the light of China's history in copyright matters, but remains difficult to avoid; failure to provide such evidence can delay signature of licence contracts and the remittance of advances. Providing copies of the relevant pages of the head contract, including the page signed by both parties, has proved to be sufficient, but licensors may wish to make a point of principle to the Chinese publisher that the head contract is a private document covering the legal and financial arrangements with their author, and it should not be necessary to show it to a third party if adequate warranties and indemnities are in place.

Chinese publishers are obliged to register all licences they acquire with the local authorities. The following clause should be included as an obligation on the licensee:

> 'The Publishers have already reported the details of the Translation/Licensed Edition to the China National Copyright Administration and have received approval to use all endeavours to protect the copyright in the Translation/Licensed Edition within the People's Republic of China according to the appropriate regulations of that country. The Publishers further agree to prosecute at their own expense any person or organisation who infringes such copyright.'

It is unlikely that the Chinese authorities will agree that the contract should be operable under UK law. The following wording is considered acceptable:

> 'This Agreement is made subject to the laws of the People's Republic of China and any disputes or differences arising between the parties in respect of the construction or otherwise of this Agreement shall be referred to the Chinese International Economic and Trade Arbitration Committee and the decision of the Committee shall be final and binding upon both parties hereto.'

Literary agents

There are no private literary agencies of domestic origin operating in mainland China. The Copyright Agency of China in Beijing is a state-owned organisation operating from the same offices as the National Copyright Administration of China. There are also a number of small regional agencies in the individual provinces which can provide assistance to Chinese publishers seeking to make contact with Western copyright holders, subject to charging a 10% commission on revenues. The Taiwan-based Big Apple-Tuttle-Mori Agency was eventually able to establish a Beijing office after initial opposition from the Chinese authorities. In mid 2002, the British literary agent Andrew Nurnberg opened a representative office in Beijing.

Central and Eastern Europe

Introduction

Depending on the pace of political change in the individual countries, it was possible to establish private publishing houses in the region from the late 1980s following many years of publishing industries which were totally controlled by the state. The initial result was a surge in private publishing enterprises; at the same time, a number of state houses sought to diversify from their monopoly subject areas as a means of survival, and some privatised either with the help of foreign investment or through partial or total staff buy-outs.

All these developments led to a boom in rights purchases from the West throughout the 1990s, in particular of mass market titles in areas such as romance, crime and science fiction and titles which had hitherto been unavailable for political reasons; heavily illustrated information books on popular topics were also a novelty. The euphoria was short lived. Many private publishers went out of business in less than a year, in some cases leaving substantial debts to Western publishers in the form of unpaid licence royalties or invoices for co-editions. In some cases this was due to simple over-optimism combined with inexperience and unrealistic expectations of the market. Others were out to make a fast buck and move on to other forms of entrepreneurship. The more serious private publishing houses have survived, although they are now forced to be far more realistic about print runs in competitive markets.

Because of the huge desire to learn English in all countries in the region (English is often the passport to a better job with a Western company) there was a visible increase in the number of applications for local English language reprint licences for English language teaching materials and dictionaries. Here the licensing policy must depend on the individual market and the British publisher's plans for that market; for example, in Poland the licensing arrangements which had started in the 1960s and 1970s as the only means of accessing the ELT market were reduced if not terminated completely as British publishers set up distribution arrangements, agents or subsidiary companies there. As local manufacturing costs and purchasing power increased, it no longer made sense to license rights in key projects as the Polish licensee would have difficulty in producing an edition more cheaply than that of the original publisher. For some markets however it may still make sense to operate a careful licensing policy.

Although upheaval in the publishing industry has now settled down somewhat, there are still considerable variations from country to country. The boom in translating Western mass market titles slowed down as the novelty wore off and in some cases there was a perceptible backlash against the flood of Western titles appearing in the markets. In all countries in the region, the state publishers were the hardest hit; without the subsidised paper costs, printing facilities and guaranteed sales to state outlets which they enjoyed for so many years, they were forced to make radical cuts to their publishing programmes, their print runs and their staff; those which have survived have diversified their output, but many have now gone out of business. All publishers have had to face competition in the marketplace, something unknown in the time of state-controlled publishing programmes. Academic publishers faced the particular problem that paper and production costs are now at world levels, whilst their target readership – academics, professionals and the intelligentsia – are often still on salaries of less than US $200 a month. Many publishers were only able to continue to publish specialised foreign literature with the help of translation subsidy programmes such as those run by the French, German and US governments. Unfortunately, the United Kingdom has never provided a general translation subsidy programme, although the British Books for Managers programme for designated countries in the region (terminated in 2001) enabled some key management texts to be translated. The Soros Foundation (Open Society Institute) ran subsidy programmes designed to encourage the publication of Western titles to promote the concept of democracy, but has now reduced its activities in this area.

The picture in the private sector varies from country to country. Poland, Hungary and the Czech Republic have developed relatively healthy private publishing industries alongside the few remaining state houses . In countries such as Romania, Bulgaria and Albania private publishing is conducted in very difficult circumstances. In all countries in the region, the huge interest rates charged for business loans make it difficult to rely on borrowing to start or to expand a business, and some countries have had to fight against the imposition of high rates of VAT on books and tariffs on imported books which affect their ability to place print orders abroad. Almost all countries in the region have been badly affected by the current economic recession.

Copyright

With the exception of Albania, all of the former eastern bloc countries belonged to one or both of the two international copyright conventions (Berne and UCC) in communist times. Those who acquired new status (e.g., the Czech and Slovak Republics) introduced new domestic copyright legislation as a prelude to seeking convention membership as independent states. Albania finally acceded to the Berne Convention in 1994. All countries in the region introduced new domestic copyright legislation during the 1990s in order to deal with new technological developments and also to reflect movement from a command to a market economy, and indeed those countries who became new members of the European Union acceded to the WIPO Copyright Treaty much earlier than the 15 original member states, who did so only in 2010. It is, however, apparent that some vestiges of socialist copyright philosophy remain in the new legislations, in particular in the area of the very wide ‘fair dealing’ permitted for educational, academic and research purposes which is likely to be detrimental to the interests of local authors and publishers as well as to foreign copyright holders. Most of the legislations also contain quite stringent restrictions on the form of contract between creator and user, and in some cases impose very short terms on contracts between authors and publishers.

One of the penalties of the opening up of these markets was the arrival of full-scale piracy in print form, a phenomenon which had not existed when both the publishing and the printing industries were controlled by the state. The prime targets were initially translations of Western best-sellers and this was often extremely damaging not only to the foreign copyright holder but also to the legitimate licensee, who often saw pirated editions on the streets before the authorised edition had reached the market. In recent years the situation has been exacerbated by large-scale electronic piracy, with the full text of books appearing on torrent sites not only in translation but often in the original language – English bestsellers again being prime targets. Although the new bodies of domestic legislation provided for the first time for penalties against infringement, the severity of punishment varies from country to country with relatively few imposing prison sentences on offenders. The real problem is the lack of an effective enforcement mechanism, combined with the fact that the rise in violent crime and mafia influence throughout the region can be a very real deterrent to taking official action.

Method of payment

More publishers in the region are now in a position to monitor sales and returns accurately enough to be able to administer a Western-style advance and royalty system. For smaller publishing operations and new licensing contacts, it may still be preferable to work on the basis of a lump sum to cover an agreed print run, although the old communist system of paying a proportion (usually 25% of the total) on signature of the contract and the full balance on publication may now be unrealistic given the cash flow problems faced by small private publishers in all these markets, even though they aim to dispose of their print run within weeks or a few months of publication.

A key point of which Western publishers should be aware is that very few publishers in the region are able to set reliable retail prices for their books, and indeed in all these markets the same book may be seen at wildly differing prices from bookshop to bookshop or from stall to stall. The preferred unit for calculating the royalty percentage on which any lump sum is based is therefore the wholesale price, that is, the price received by the publisher from their distributors; this could be anything from 25% to 50% less than the price at which the book is on sale to the end customer. The wholesale price is often referred to by local publishers as the 'publisher's price' which can mislead Western publishers unused to the market into assuming it is the retail or the recommended retail price. It is, therefore, wise to obtain a definition of the price from each licensee and to negotiate a higher royalty percentage to allow for the discounted price.

Since inflation is unpredictable in all these markets it is also wise to include in any lump sum contract a provision to increase later instalments of the lump sum once the final price is known (**see note to Clause 2 of Precedent Eleven**).

The preferred hard currency in most countries in the region remains the US dollar and it is usually advisable to specify all amounts in this currency. Some countries favour the euro; at the time of writing, Slovakia and Slovenia have formally adopted the euro and Romanian publishers tend to find this currency preferable. Publishers in some countries may require signed and stamped invoices for all amounts due in addition to the licence contract itself, and this should be checked with the licensee.

Contracts

Most publishers in the region now seem prepared to accept licence contracts which are governed by the law of the country of the Western publisher.

It is still recommended that if copies are being manufactured by the Western publisher for a publisher in central and eastern Europe as part of a co-edition, extra care is employed to take up references on new contacts. Prepayment of a significant proportion of the total prior to commencement of manufacture can be a partial safeguard and payment against a letter of credit can also be wise.

A regulation in force in Poland requires that all licence contracts must now be signed in Polish as well as in the language of the licensor, although this requirement seems to be rather intermittently applied. Although licensees may offer to provide Polish versions themselves, this may result in inconsistency of wording in the translated versions and publishers with significant licensing business in Poland may prefer to commission official templates for their Polish contracts with the variable elements (author, title, payment terms etc) listed as a schedule at the end of the contract. The main aim of the regulation appears to be a need to make licence contracts understandable for banking staff, rather than for the staff of the licensee publisher.

Literary agents

The monopolies of the state literary agencies which operated in most countries in the region have long been abolished, although some of them still exist in the form of collecting societies for areas such as performing rights.

Whereas Western educational and academic publishers have long travelled to the region, many trade publishers have chosen instead to delegate licensing to specialist agents. The agencies of Gerd Plessl (now defunct) and Jovan Milankovic (Prava i Prevosti) entered the markets early and secured a wide range of lists containing many major Western authors.

On the whole, publishers in the region would far prefer to work direct for reasons of speed and efficiency, but many of the larger Western trade publishers continue to rely on intermediaries in markets which they still regard as volatile. A number of local agents have now been established in the individual markets (for example, Graal in Poland and Simona Kessler in Romania), and the UK agent Andrew Nurnberg has established offices in Bulgaria, Poland, the Czech Republic and Hungary.

Russia and the other former Republics of the Soviet Union

Introduction

Much of what has been covered above applies also to the territories of the former Soviet Union: now 15 independent states (the Russian Federation, the Ukraine, Belarus, Georgia, Moldova, Armenia, Azerbaijan, Uzbekhistan, Kazakhstan, Kyrgystan, Tajikistan, Turkmenistan and the three Baltic states of Estonia, Latvia and Lithuania). From December 1991, all joined the Commonwealth of Independent States (CIS) with the exception of the Baltic states, but changes of government in Ukraine and Georgia have since taken those countries out of membership whilst Turkmenistan has status as an unofficial associate member.

Most of the original state publishing houses have gone out of business or are shadows of their former selves. All those who remain were forced to cut their staff, print runs and publishing programmes, and are only able to publish academic works with the help of occasional funding from the federal subsidy programme.

A host of private publishing houses were established as soon as this was legally possible, some of which disappeared virtually overnight and some of which have survived. Those which have flourished have tended to start their programmes by publishing translations of Western bestsellers, but some have gone on to invest the profits in publishing more serious literature, or developing their own publications in areas such as illustrated children's books which they seek to license to western publishers.

Both state and private publishers have faced similar problems; the massive increase in the cost of paper and printing, the withdrawal of most state assistance either in the form of paper allocation or in guaranteed sales through the state distribution system, and the total collapse of that distribution system. In Russia in particular, publishers are often only able to guarantee distribution of their books in the Moscow and St Petersburg regions; the cost and practicalities of distributing effectively through such a vast geographical region are daunting. Some of the more enterprising and successful private publishers have invested in their own vans and trucks. This situation should be taken into account when dealing with licences to the region; it makes little sense to grant Russian translation rights to one publisher for all or even a substantial number of the former Republics if the publisher concerned has no means of covering those territories. Russian is, of course, still widely spoken throughout the former Republics and some publishers have been able to set up distribution arrangements in a small number of key states such as the Ukraine, Belarus, Kazakhstan and the Baltics as well as the Russian Federation itself. The question of defining licences by both language and geographical territory therefore needs careful thought. The entire industry was affected by the drastic collapse of the rouble in August 1998. A number of Western publishers were left with substantial debts in the area of co-edition sales. All countries in the region have been severely affected by the global economic recession which started in 2008; the Baltic states were particularly badly hit and have had to fight the imposition of far higher levels of VAT on books.

As in central and eastern Europe, there is substantial interest in the learning of English and hence an increasing number of licence requests for English language reprint rights or bilingual rights for English language teaching materials and dictionaries. Here much will depend on the overall policy of the British publisher for the region; if representation, agencies or distribution arrangements have already been set up for ELT materials then licensing may not be attractive, but in some cases there may be a need to have a joint imprint with a Russian partner to secure a course adoption. Rightsholders should be aware that there is a considerable danger of leakage of such licensed editions over borders, not just within the territory of the former Soviet Union, but also into markets such as Poland and other central and eastern European countries where distribution of the original edition may be better established.

Copyright

The Soviet Union acceded to the Universal Copyright Convention on 27 May 1973. Copyright legislation within the Soviet Union was covered by a section of the Civil Code of each Republic. Following independence, it became necessary for each newly-formed state to introduce its own domestic copyright legislation and decide whether to join the international conventions. Russia and most of the other states have introduced new domestic legislation over the last 20 years. In particular, the extension of the period of copyright protection in Russia from 25 to 50 years *post mortem auctoris* enabled that country to accede to the Berne Convention on 13 March 1995, albeit with the proviso that foreign works first published before 27 May 1973 remain in the public domain in Russia. The term of protection in Russia was further extended to 70 years *post mortem auctoris* from 2004 and Russia acceded to the WIPO Copyright Treaty from 5 February 2009. At the time of writing, all the former Republics with the exception of Turkmenistan have acceded to the Berne Convention.

The discrepancies in the levels of domestic copyright protection and international copyright recognition between individual states means that piracy can take place in one market with copies then transported across the border to larger markets such as the Russian Federation.

Piracy of books, music tapes, audio-visual tapes, DVDs and CDs is endemic in Russia and in many of the other Republics, and these countries remain high on the 301 Watch List of the International Intellectual Property Alliance; Russia is on the priority Watch List for 2010 and Belarus, Kazakhstan, Tajikistan, Turkmenistan, Ukraine and Uzbekhistan are all on the Watch List for monitoring. The revised Russian domestic copyright law of 1993 introduced penalties for copyright infringement under both civil and criminal law, but relatively few successful actions have been brought because of the high cost of a court case and the very real danger of violence from mafia connections.

Method of payment

Publishers in the region can hold hard currency bank accounts or purchase hard currency to remit abroad for the purchase of rights; the favoured currency remains the US dollar, although Estonia is expected to adopt the euro from early 2011 and may be followed by Latvia and Lithuania. The exchange rate has stabilised but the future is unpredictable, as witness the catastrophic collapse of the rouble in 1998. These are, therefore, still markets where caution is advisable; for small print runs, it is preferable to structure licence deals in the form of a lump sum to cover a designated number of copies, with as much of the total as possible payable on signature of the contract. With new publishers still appearing and disappearing overnight, it is wise to take up as many references as possible when dealing with a new contact, and to work on letters of credit or substantial prepayment if supplying printed copies or expensive printing film. A number of Western publishers now refuse to supply duplicate production material to publishers in the region because of the danger of piracy or overproduction of copies beyond the terms of the contract which are then not accounted for. Abuse of this kind has not only been undertaken by some publishers, but also by their printers. Mafia pressure (and indeed involvement) is not unknown in both the publishing and the printing sectors.

Contracts

Bureaucracy has certainly not been totally eradicated in Russia. Some Russian licensees have required that contracts must be drawn up in English and Russian, whilst others require that their own bank details must be included in the contract as well as those of the Western licensor. Some require that additional 'certificates' are signed confirming that licences have been granted and that each advance and royalty payment has been received. Again, all this documentation appears to be for the benefit of bank staff dealing with transfers rather than for the staff of the licensee publishing house.

Literary agents

The monopoly of the old state copyright agency, VAAP, was abolished from 1 January 1991 although it still exists in much reduced form as a Russian authors' organisation, RAO, and administers collective licences in areas such as performing rights. The Andrew Nurnberg agency has offices in Moscow and Riga, and there are several local agencies including the Alexander Korzhenevski Agency.

PRECEDENT TWELVE

Same-Language Low Price Reprint Agreement

The Revised 1971 Paris Texts of the Berne Convention and of the Universal Copyright Convention established new rules to facilitate the access of the developing countries to compulsory licences for translations, reprints of works in the original languages and audio-visual materials. The rules cover 'world', 'local' and other languages. Since English is, together with Spanish and French, a 'world' language, there is clearly some incentive among British publishers and authors to arrange voluntary licences whose terms can be negotiated, rather than to become subject to compulsory licences over which they have no control. For this reason, large-scale compulsory licensing has on the whole been avoided to date. Nevertheless, British publishers owe it to themselves and to their authors to remember that the word 'voluntary' conceals the granting of economic and cultural aid to developing countries not with the assistance of any government aid programme, but out of the pockets of authors and publishers.

Although the Paris Revisions date back some 40 years, it is worth flagging here that at the time of writing there has been strong lobbying from a number of developing countries, most notably in South America, for a complete copyright exception for works needed for educational purposes.

Under the terms of the Paris Revisions, a same-language compulsory licence can only be granted if the work is not available in the country concerned at a price considered sufficiently low for the market. The availability of the work in a special cheap edition produced by the original publisher for sale in developing countries, or the original edition made available at special discount terms to such countries, could be held to preclude the granting of a compulsory licence, and certainly these avenues should be fully explored before agreeing to grant a reprint licence. Sadly, the Educational Low-Priced Books Scheme (ELBS) funded by the Overseas Development Agency of the British Government and which subsidised the production of special low-priced editions of some core British textbooks for designated markets, was terminated in 1997; this removed one of the strongest lines of defence against compulsory licensing. An alternative scheme proposed by publishers, Educational Low-Priced Sponsored Texts (ELST) was dependent on charitable funding; renamed BookPower, it has not yet been able fully to replace ELBS. Some publishers have sought to fill the need for low-priced books in India by printing for local distributors in the Export Processing Zone (EPZ).

Under the compulsory licence rules, same-language reprints must be of works used in connection with 'systematic instructional activities'. The needs of the developing countries are predominantly in applied science, although there are also many applications for such works as dictionaries and books for the teaching of English as a foreign language. The period from first publication after which a compulsory licence can be enforced is for the natural and physical sciences and technical works only three years; for fiction, poetry, drama and art, it is seven years; for all other types of work, five years. Scientific and technical publishers therefore need to be especially alert to making arrangements for low-cost editions of their books soon after first publication, either under their own imprints or through the medium of carefully controlled voluntary licences to reliable partners. The demise of the ELBS scheme has undoubtedly led to an increase in the number of applications for licences for British textbooks and may have contributed to an increase in the level of piracy in countries such as India.

From the late 1980s onwards there was a significant increase in licence requests for the newly independent countries of central and eastern Europe and the former Soviet Union; many requests tended to be for reprint rights in English language teaching materials and dictionaries, with books in other categories more likely to be translated into the local language. Whilst there is undoubtedly a strong demand for foreign books as these countries have gained better access to the West, the price gap which has justified licensing has narrowed in many of the countries concerned; the removal of most government subsidies and the requirement to purchase paper at world prices makes it difficult for local publishers in some countries to undercut western prices. Direct sales of the original publisher's own edition at high discount, sales of International Student Editions (ISEs) or of a special low-cost edition such as those introduced for business and business English titles in 1991 under the British government Know-How Fund Low Price British Books Scheme (LPBB – terminated in 1998) were considered by many British publishers to be preferable to granting a licence if adequate local distribution could be assured, and this continues to be the case.

However, British publishers may still choose to license designated titles to some countries if publication under a local imprint is perceived to give better access to the market concerned or if Ministry of Education approval requires the involvement of a local partner. Multinational publishers may have the option in some countries of being able to license rights to their own subsidiary or affiliate companies, thus ensuring better control of production quality and distribution.

MEMORANDUM OF AGREEMENT made this [*number*] day of [*month*] 20 [*year*]

Between [*company name*] of [*address*] (hereinafter termed 'the Publishers') of the one part, and [*company name*] of [*address*] (hereinafter termed 'the Proprietors') of the other part

WHEREAS the Proprietors are the proprietors of a work by [*name*] (hereinafter termed 'the Author'), entitled: [*title*] [*no of*] Edition (hereinafter termed 'the Work'),

NOW IT IS HEREBY MUTUALLY AGREED AS FOLLOWS:

1. Grant of Rights

Subject to the terms detailed in this Agreement, the Proprietors hereby grant to the Publishers the exclusive licence to produce and publish a single printing of [*number*] copies only of the Work in *hardback/paperback* volume form in the English language under the Publishers' own imprint (hereinafter termed the Licensed Edition) for sale throughout [*list territories*] only. This restricted circulation is to be clearly indicated on the outside of the cover and on the reverse of the title page of the Licensed Edition by the following words: 'Licensed for sale in [*list territories*] only; not for export.'

Preamble

The licence should be specifically limited to the current edition of the book in question. This is particularly important since the majority of requests for such licences will be for educational and academic titles which will be regularly revised by the original publishers.

1. Grant of Rights

As this is a voluntary licence, the right is exclusive, but is limited to a single printing of a specified number of copies in the country concerned. No subsidiary rights of any kind are conveyed and are specifically reserved by Clause 10. The work must appear under the imprint of the licensee; this is stressed here as there have been cases of publishers in the developing countries deliberately producing reprints which externally appear to have been published by the proprietors; in other cases the reprints have been reproduced under a joint imprint without permission from the proprietors. The sales territory granted must be clearly defined and a market restriction notice must appear clearly on both the cover and title verso of the reprint; this will facilitate legal action if copies appear outside the specified territory.

2. Payment

The method of payment chosen will depend very much on the individual circumstances of each licence application, and may also be influenced by copyright or exchange control regulations in the country concerned. Ideally, it would be preferable to specify that a single lump sum should be paid for the right to produce the printing specified in Clause 1, and that the entire amount should be payable on signature of the agreement; an alternative might be half payable on signature of the agreement and the balance on publication of the licensed edition or by an agreed 'latest date' as an incentive to prompt publication.

Publishers in the countries of central and eastern Europe, the former Soviet Union and the People's Republic of China traditionally worked on the basis of a lump sum payment for a designated print run quantity, usually with an advance payment on signature of the contract and the balance on publication. This stemmed from the fact that many titles sold out immediately or within a few months of publication, making yearly or twice-yearly royalty accounting inappropriate. As these countries have moved towards a market economy with higher prices and sales no longer guaranteed through the state system, publishers there have sought to move over to a western-style advance and royalty system; however, this is only really practical where there is firm evidence that the publisher concerned has the facilities to track sales and returns accurately. In some cases it can still be wise to work on a lump sum basis. **See also the Appendix to Precedent Eleven**.

A lump sum arrangement is particularly desirable when licensing to countries where remitting payment abroad may be particularly complicated or slow. However, the amount payable for some licences (particularly if the print run is large) may exceed the maximum amount which can be remitted at any one time, and in such cases payment in instalments or an advance and royalty arrangement may be the only alternative. Again, local restrictions may apply; for example, in India (a major applicant for reprint licences) the maximum advance payment which can be remitted without special dispensation from the Reserve Bank of India is US$500. The choice of method of payment will also affect the wording of Clause 11.

As a general guide, the initial royalty rate of same-language reprint licences should not be less than 10% of the local published price, and in a number of countries considerably higher rates can be negotiated. It should be remembered that the licensee is normally acquiring rights in a well-established work; there will be no translation or editorial expenses, minimal promotion expenses and the royalty represents compensation to the proprietors and the author for the total loss of sales of the original edition in the territory once the licensed edition appears.

3. Validity of Agreement

The word 'advance' and the reference to Clause 2.1 would be omitted if a single lump sum arrangement has been negotiated.

2. Payment

The Publishers shall make the following payment/s to the Proprietors in accordance with the provisions of Clause 19 hereof:

(NB the following are alternative methods of payment)

(*Lump sum arrangement*)

The sum of [*amount*] for the right to produce the aforesaid printing of [*number*] copies of the Licensed Edition, which sum shall be payable in its entirety on signature of this Agreement. The said payment is not recoverable in the event of any default by the Publishers in carrying out the terms of this Agreement.

(*Advance/Royalty arrangement*)

2.1 The sum of [*amount*] payable on signature of this Agreement in advance and on account of any sums which may become due to the Proprietors under this Agreement. The said payment in advance is not recoverable in the event of any default by the Publishers in carrying out the terms of this Agreement.

2.2 On the recommended retail/wholesale price of all copies of the Licensed Edition sold by the Publishers:

(i) A royalty of [*number*] per cent on the first [*number*] thousand copies sold

(ii) A royalty of [*number*] per cent on all copies sold beyond the first [*number*] thousand.

2.3 On remainder copies of the Licensed Edition sold by the Publishers at or below cost no royalty shall be payable to the Proprietors but no such remainder copies shall be sold within a period of [*number*] years from the date of first publication of the Licensed Edition.

3. Validity of Agreement

This Agreement shall not come into effect until the Proprietors have received the [advance] payment detailed in Clause 2 [or 2.1] hereof.

4. Accuracy of Reproduction

The Publishers shall produce the Licensed Edition at their own expense. They shall cause it to be reproduced faithfully and accurately and shall not

5. Copyright Material from Other Sources

It may be necessary for third party permissions to be re-cleared for the reuse of copyright material in the licensed edition if the copyright owners concerned have restricted the original permission granted to use in the proprietors' edition only. It would be administratively safer for the proprietors to undertake such clearance and to recharge the cost to the publishers in addition to the terms of the reprint licence.

6. Production Quality

Production quality in developing countries can still be very poor and this clause seeks to impose the best standards possible in view of the local circumstances prevailing. Production standards in central and eastern Europe are improving; some publishers in the region are now undertaking some manufacturing in the west or the Far East to achieve higher standards.

7. Acknowledgments

The exact wording of the required copyright notice should be inserted here, together with details of the title and the name of the original publisher and/or copyright holder.

9. Failure to Publish/Out of Print

9.1 The publication time limit for a straightforward reprint edition might reasonably be expected to be short, since no editorial or translation work is involved.

9.2 This sub-clause provides for the termination of the contract when the designated print run is exhausted; however, if the licensing arrangements have been satisfactory, the contract could be extended for a further designated print run by an addendum to the contract; this provides an opportunity for a review of the financial terms.

abridge, expand or otherwise alter the Work, including illustrations where applicable, without the prior written consent of the Proprietors.

5. Copyright Material from Other Sources

The Proprietors shall be responsible for obtaining permission wherever necessary for the use in the Licensed Edition of copyright material included in the Work belonging to third parties and will advise the Publishers of any additional fees due for such permissions. The Publishers agree to reimburse the Proprietors promptly for any fees so incurred on receipt of an invoice from the Proprietors.

6. Production Quality

The Publishers undertake to ensure that, wherever possible, the printing, paper and binding of the Licensed Edition shall be of the highest quality.

7. Acknowledgments

The Publishers undertake that the name of the Author shall appear prominently displayed on the cover, spine, jacket (if any) and title page of every copy of the Licensed Edition issued and on the reverse of the title page shall appear the following copyright notice: '© [*name of copyright owner*] [*date*]' together with the following acknowledgment: 'This edition of [*title*] is published by arrangement with [*name of Proprietors*]'.

8. Complimentary Copies

The Publishers shall supply the Proprietors with [*number*] free copies of the Licensed Edition to the Proprietors on publication, together with details of the actual date of publication and the recommended retail/wholesale price of the Licensed Edition.

9. Failure to Publish/Out of Print

9.1 Should the Publishers fail to issue the Licensed Edition by [*date*] all rights granted under this Agreement shall revert to the Proprietors without prejudice to any monies paid or due to the Proprietors.

9.2 Should the Licensed Edition go out of print or off the market the rights granted under this Agreement shall forthwith revert to the Proprietors without prejudice to any monies paid or due to the Proprietors.

11. Accounts

The exact wording of this clause will be affected by the type of payment arrangement selected in Clause 2. If an advance and royalty arrangement has been chosen, regular royalties will be payable once sales have justified the initial advance payment. These may be specified as payable once or perhaps twice yearly, with appropriate accounting dates to be inserted. The details required in the sales statement are listed.

If a single lump sum arrangement has been chosen, no further payments will be due, but it may well be of interest to the proprietors to receive the same detailed sales statements which will enable them to monitor the publishers' performance.

10. Subsidiary Rights

The Publishers shall not dispose of any subsidiary rights in the Licensed Edition without obtaining the prior written consent of the Proprietors.

11. Accounts

Accounts/Statements for the sale of the Licensed Edition shall be made up yearly/twice yearly by the Publishers to [*date/dates*] and the *account/ statement* rendered (together with any sums payable under this Agreement) within three months of each accounting date. Accounts/Statements will show:

(i) the original title of the Work together with the original ISBN;

(ii) the number of copies in stock at the beginning of the accounting period;

(iii) the number of copies sold during the accounting period;

(iv) the number of copies presented free of charge during the accounting period;

(v) the number of copies remaining in stock at the end of the accounting period;

(vi) the cumulative sales of the Licensed Edition since publication;

(vii) the published price of the Licensed Edition;

[for Advance/Royalty arrangements];

(viii) the royalty rate payable;

(ix) the total payment due to (name of Proprietors);

and accounts and royalties shall be paid in accordance with the provisions of Clause 19 hereof.

Should any of the payments detailed in this Agreement be three months overdue the licence herein granted shall forthwith lapse and all rights conveyed by it shall without further notice revert to the Proprietors without prejudice to any claim the Proprietors may have for monies due, for damages or otherwise.

The Proprietors or their authorised representative shall have the right upon written request and reasonable notice to examine during normal business hours the records of accounts of the Publishers in so far as they relate to sales

15. Duration of Licence

The duration of the licence should not, it is suggested, be shorter than two years or longer than five years. When setting the period, the size of the print run, the status of the licensee and the nature of the work should be taken into account. In principle it is usually preferable to specify a short period, with a provision for renewal if the publishers' performance is satisfactory.

and receipts in respect of the Licensed Edition, which examination shall be at the cost of the Proprietors unless errors exceeding 5 per cent of such sales and receipts in the last two preceding accounting periods to their disadvantage shall be found, in which case the cost shall be paid by the Publishers.

12. Warranties and Indemnity

The Proprietors hereby warrant to the Publishers that they have the right and power to make this Agreement and that according to English law the Work will in no way whatever give rise to a violation of any existing copyright, or a breach of any existing agreement and that nothing in the Work is liable to give rise to a civil prosecution or to a civil action for damages or any other remedy and the Proprietors will indemnify the Publishers against any loss, injury or expense arising out of any breach of this warranty.

13. Restrictions on Transfer

The Licence hereby granted to the Publishers shall not be transferred in whole or in part or extended to include any other party nor shall the Licensed Edition appear under any imprint other than that of the Publishers, except with the prior written consent of the Proprietors.

14. Retained Rights

All rights in the Work, other than those specifically granted to the Publishers herein, are reserved by the Proprietors.

15. Duration of Licence

Subject to Clauses 9, 11, 16 and 22 hereof, the licence herein granted shall continue for a period of [*number*] years from the date of this Agreement and thereafter may be subject to renewal by mutual agreement between the parties hereto.

16. Termination

In the event of the Publishers being declared bankrupt or should they or anyone acting on their behalf fail to comply with any of the provisions of this Agreement and not rectify such failure within one month of having received notice from the Proprietors to do so by a registered letter sent to the Publishers at their address given at the commencement of this Agreement, then in either event this Agreement automatically becomes null and void and the licence granted to the Publishers herein shall revert to the Proprietors

18. and **20. Arbitration/Applicable Law**

Ideally, the contract should be specified as operable under English law with English arbitration provisions prevailing. In practice, local legislation in the country of the publishers may preclude this; if so, the following alternative wording could be considered:

> 'If any difference shall arise between the Proprietors and the Publishers touching the meaning of this Agreement or the rights and liabilities of the parties thereto, the same shall be referred to the arbitration of two persons (one to be named by each party) or their mutually agreed arbitrator in accordance with the provisions of the arbitration legislation for the time being in force in [*country of Publishers*]. Any dispute between the parties not resolved by arbitration or agreement shall be submitted to the jurisdiction of the courts of [*country of Publishers*].'

Another compromise form of wording which may be acceptable is the following:

> 'Unless otherwise agreed, any disputes arising out of or in connection with this Agreement shall be settled under the Rules of Arbitration of the International Chamber of Commerce by a single arbitrator appointed in accordance with such rules. The award of the arbitrator shall be final and binding on the parties and judgement upon the award rendered may be entered in any court giving jurisdiction or application may be made to such court for judicial acceptance of the award and an order of enforcement as the case may be.'

NB Licences to the People's Republic of China may require special provisions on arbitration and the prevailing law (**see Appendix to Precedent Eleven**).

19. Method of Payment

Publishers in some markets (e.g., Central and Eastern Europe, Russia and the People's Republic of China) may find it easier to remit hard currency if the financial terms are expressed in US dollars. Some central European countries which are now EU members may prefer to work in euros.

This clause seeks to ensure that any deduction of VAT on royalties remitted to licensors (imposed by countries such as Russia) is made over and above the amounts expected by the licensor (**see the note to Clause 20 in Precedent Eleven**). Many countries are obliged by law to deduct withholding tax at source from licence payments remitted abroad if no double-taxation exemption treaty exists between the two countries concerned. If adequate documentation is provided, it should be possible to recover any withholding tax deducted against UK corporation tax.

without prejudice to any claim which the Proprietors may have for damages or otherwise and without prejudice to any monies paid or due to the Proprietors.

17. Notices

Any and all notices given hereunder shall be in writing and sent by fax, e-mail, courier or registered mail to the parties at their respective addresses herein specified. The parties undertake to notify each other of any change of address within thirty days of such change.

18. Arbitration

If any difference shall arise between the Proprietors and the Publishers touching the meaning of this Agreement or the rights and liabilities of the parties hereto, the same shall be referred to the arbitration of two persons (one to be named by each party) or their umpire, in accordance with the provisions of the Arbitration Act 1996 or any subsisting statutory modification or re-enactment thereof.

19. Method of Payment

All sums which may become due to the Proprietors under this Agreement shall be paid by the Publishers in sterling/US dollars without any deduction in respect of exchange or commission to:

(i) [*address of Proprietors; appropriate accounts department*]

OR:

(ii) [*name and address of Proprietors' bank, account number, sort.code, SWIFT code and IBAN number*]

The Publishers shall not have the right to withhold any part of sums due to the Proprietors as a reserve against returns and/or credits. The amounts due are net of any withholding VAT that may be applied in the Publishers' territory and represent the sum of money that the Proprietors will receive after any withholding VAT is deducted from a VAT-inclusive figure. Should the Publishers be required by law to deduct any taxes other than VAT they shall send a declaration to this effect with the relevant statement of account showing the amount deducted.

20. Applicable Law

This Agreement shall be governed by and interpreted in all respects in accordance with the laws of England whose courts shall have exclusive jurisdiction.

21. Local Registration and Copyright Protection

This places an obligation on the publishers to protect the work in the territory they have been granted at their own expense; this would include any copyright registration procedure required under local laws. Again, the People's Republic of China has special registration procedures (**see Appendix to Precedent Eleven**).

24. Signature of Agreement

It is recommended that the Proprietors predate the Agreement before sending it to the Publishers.

21. Local Registration and Copyright Protection

The Publishers agree to take any necessary steps to register the title of the Work in the name of the copyright owner under local copyright laws at the sole expense of the Publishers. The Publishers also agree to protect such copyright and to prosecute at their own expense any person who infringes such copyright.

22. Assignment by Proprietors

The Proprietors may assign this Agreement without the consent of the Publishers in the event of the sale of all or part of the Proprietors' businesses.

23. Entire Agreement

This Agreement contains the full and complete understanding between the Parties and supersedes all prior arrangements and undertakings, whether oral or written, concerning the subject matter of this Agreement, and may not be varied except by Agreement in writing between the Parties.

24. Signature of Agreement

This Agreement shall be deemed to be legally binding only if the Publishers sign this Agreement within 6 (Six) weeks from the date of this Agreement.

AS WITNESS THE HANDS OF THE PARTIES

Signed...

For the Publishers

Signed...

For the Proprietors

PRECEDENT THIRTEEN

Illustration and Artwork Agreement

There remains some confusion about the nature of agreements with illustrators. Briefing of illustrators is still often done orally and informally, with no clear idea of exactly what rights are being acquired or retained. The mistaken belief which derived from section 4(3) of the Copyright Act 1956, that the publisher when commissioning artwork automatically owned it and the copyright stemming from it, still prevails in some quarters.

The true position, which has existed since the Copyright, Designs and Patents Act 1988 came into effect, can be set out in four propositions:

(1) When an illustration is drawn or painted, copyright automatically exists and is owned by the illustrator, regardless of whether it is commissioned or not.

(2) If the commissioner wishes to have the copyright, the illustrator has to agree to assign it to the commissioner in writing and signed by the illustrator.

(3) Unless the illustrator agrees to give the original to the commissioner it remains the illustrator's property. The fact that someone has purchased the copyright does not entitle that person to own the original artwork.

(4) Moral rights apply under the Act to artistic works as they apply to literary works.

In any contract it is always important to clarify the following:

(a) ownership of the original artwork;

(b) possession of or access to the original artwork for varying purposes, for example, art exhibitions, or promotional use or further publication in a foreign language edition of which the artwork is a part;

(c) copyright, that is, the right to grant or refuse reproduction of the artwork;

(d) exploitation of that right both for and beyond the initial publication, through the grant to the publisher of an exclusive licence from the copyright holder.

Publishers seeking to acquire ownership of original artwork need to bear in mind the possible implications of the Artist's Resale Right Regulations which came into force in the United Kingdom from 14 February 2006 following a 2001 Directive from the European Commission. The concept of *droit de suite* had long existed in continental Europe, enabling an artist to receive a royalty on the resale price of his or her work if it is resold via an agent, gallery or dealer; the first sale of the work by the illustrator and sales between private individuals will be excluded. The UK Regulations provide for a royalty payment to be made to living artists whose works are resold at a value of 1,000 euros or above, with royalty rates ranging from 4% for works valued at up to 50,000 euros and down to 0.25% for the proportion of sale over 500,000 euros. The maximum payment is capped at 12,500 euros with royalties payable via DACS (the Design and Artists Copyright Society). Concern for the impact on the strong British art market led the UK government to negotiate a derogation which deferred extending the arrangement to the works of deceased artists until at least 2010; this was extended until 1 January 2012 by the Artist's Resale Right (Amendment) Regulations which came into force from 1 December 2009.

The assumption of this Precedent is that there is a direct relationship between the publisher and the illustrator. This is not always so. In some branches of publishing, for example, in medical books, a specialist illustrator may well be recruited by a specialist author, and in educational publishing, the publisher may require the overall designer of a book to recruit the illustrators. In these situations it may be appropriate for the publisher to supply the necessary contractual documentation for the purpose of ensuring that the details with respect to ownership of artwork and grant of rights are correct.

The Association of Illustrators continues to express concern at the practice of some publishers in requiring an assignment both of copyright in and also ownership of the artwork. In the majority of cases there is no reason why the publisher, who in almost all cases is in the position of obtaining rights through the grant of an exclusive licence from the author, needs to acquire either the copyright itself or ownership of the artwork from the illustrator. Ownership of the physical artwork for the purposes of reuse in book or other form is becoming increasingly unnecessary due to advances in digital storage technology. Whatever is agreed with respect to ownership of artwork and the grant of rights, reuse of artwork in another book must in equity entitle the illustrator to further fees. There do, however, remain areas of publishing, for example, character-based publishing, where the publisher may be obliged to acquire the copyright and ownership of artwork for subsequent transfer to the owner of the rights in the character.

Throughout the Precedent, the word 'artwork' is used. Many of the points are equally relevant to the work of a photographer, as the alternative wording of Clause 1 implies; the word 'photographs' can be easily substituted throughout for 'artwork'. Photographs are treated under the Copyright, Designs and Patents Act 1988 as artistic works, and ownership and duration of copyright in them are therefore treated exactly as ownership and duration of other artistic works.

This Precedent is not intended for use when the illustrator is to be paid on a royalty basis. In those cases Precedent One is more suitable, with appropriate amendment and inclusion of promotional use and other artwork specific provisions of this precedent.

1. and 2. Provision of Artwork/Schedule for Delivery

Full details of what precisely is required from the illustrator and the form in which it is to be delivered should always be spelled out (with technical details specified in the Schedule) and agreement recorded for delivery dates for both roughs and finished artwork. Failure to deliver on time can jeopardise a project and it is advisable to provide for this with a penalty.

3. Rights Granted

This precedent provides for the Illustrator to grant an exclusive licence for use of the artwork to the publishers, including the right to sublicense to third parties. It also confirms that the Illustrator may use the artwork for portfolio and exhibition purposes.

The Association of Illustrators is concerned that illustrators should have the opportunity to exploit rights which do not directly conflict with those granted to publishers. This must be a topic for individual negotiation between illustrators and publishers, but if agreed an additional subclause 3.3 might be added:

> '3.3 Notwithstanding the rights granted to the Publishers in this clause, the parties agree that should the Illustrator have the opportunity to exploit any of the rights granted to the Publishers under this Agreement (save for the purposes set out in Clause 3.2 hereof) the Illustrator shall so notify the Publishers in writing. If in the reasonable commercial judgement of the publishers the proposed exploitation will not affect adversely the sales of the Work or any licensed editions of the Work the Publishers shall not unreasonably withhold or delay their consent to such exploitation. The Illustrator shall not proceed with such exploitation without the Publishers' written consent.'

There may be occasions when a contract requires an assignment of copyright in which case alternative wording might read as follows:

> 'In consideration of the payments hereinafter mentioned the Illustrator hereby assigns to the Publishers the entire copyright in the Artwork with full title guarantee for the legal term of copyright and any and all extensions, renewals and revivals thereof throughout the world. The Illustrator agrees that the rights include the right to produce, publish, adapt, sell and further to license the Artwork or any part of it in any and all forms (including for the avoidance of doubt all electronic forms).'

MEMORANDUM OF AGREEMENT made this [*number*] day of [*month*] 20 [*year*]

Between [*name*] of [*address*] (hereinafter termed 'the Illustrator', which expression shall, where the context admits, include the Illustrator's executors and assigns) of the one part and [*company name*] of [*address*](hereinafter termed 'the Publishers', which expression shall, where the context admits, include any publishing imprint subsidiary to or associated with the Publishers, and the Publishers' assigns or successors in business as the case may be) of the other part

Whereby it is mutually agreed as follows concerning the Illustrator's [artwork/photographs] for a work at present entitled [*title of work*] by [*name of Author/s*] (hereinafter termed 'the Work'):

1. Provision of Artwork/Photographs

The Illustrator shall provide [artwork/photographs] (hereinafter termed 'the Artwork') for the Work in accordance with a written brief from the Publishers and in a form suitable for reproduction as provided for in the Schedule to this Agreement.

2. Schedule for Delivery

The Illustrator shall provide roughs not later than [*date*] and the finished Artwork not later than [*date*]. If the Artwork is not delivered to the Publishers in accordance with the delivery date or by such other date as is subsequently agreed in writing, the Publishers may terminate this Agreement and if required the Illustrator shall repay to the Publishers all sums paid in respect of the Artwork.

3. Rights Granted

3.1 In consideration of the payments hereinafter mentioned the Illustrator hereby grants to the Publishers the sole and exclusive right and licence to produce, publish, sell and further to license the Artwork or any part of it in any and all forms (including for the avoidance of doubt all digital forms) for the legal term of copyright and any and all extensions, renewals and revivals thereof throughout the world.

3.2 The Illustrator shall be entitled to use the Artwork for personal portfolio, display or exhibition purposes and shall make due acknowledgement to the Work, its Author/s and to the Publishers.

4. Promotional Use

Publishers are now likely to store artwork in digital form (see Clause 10) so it is usually less important now for them to require access to the original artwork which will have been returned to the illustrator. Artwork in a form suitable for reproduction may be needed for exhibitions, publicity, paperback, or foreign editions.

It is one thing for the publisher to reproduce an artist's work in order to promote the book in which the work appears; here promotional use could include leaflets, inclusion in the publisher's catalogue and on the publisher's website and reproduction on material such as dumpbins. It is quite another thing for a publisher to reproduce an artist's work in order to promote other books as well. The use of a leading illustrator's work on the cover of, for example, a catalogue of children's books for the Christmas market is the kind of use which will need separate agreement.

5. Acknowledgment to Illustrator

For Public Lending Right purposes, it is particularly important to decide whether the illustrator's part in creating the total work merits the printing of his/her name on the title page. Unless it is so printed, the illustrator is likely not to be eligible to register for his/her share in PLR.

6. Copyright and Ownership of Artwork

This precedent assumes that the Illustrator has granted the publishers an exclusive licence for use of the artwork. For alternative wording in the case of an assignment of copyright, see the note to Clause 3 above.

7. Moral Rights

There may be occasions when the publishers may request a waiver of the illustrator's moral rights. This is permitted under the moral rights provisions of the 1988 UK Copyright Act (**see Appendix H**).

4. Promotional Use

The Illustrator shall permit the Publishers free of charge to use the Artwork to promote the Work in catalogues, advertisements, websites and other promotional material in any form.

5. Acknowledgement to Illustrator

The Publishers shall acknowledge the Illustrator on the title page of all print on paper editions of the Work and in any digital form edition published by the Publishers and with due prominence every time the Artwork is reproduced and shall use their best endeavours to ensure that *he/she* is given full acknowledgement in any edition of the Work sublicensed by the Publishers to a third party.

6. Copyright and Ownership of Artwork

The Illustrator shall retain ownership of and copyright in the Artwork and the Publishers shall print the following line on the reverse of the title page of print on paper copies of the Work produced by the Publishers and in an appropriate location in any electronic version published by the Publishers: 'Illustrations © (*name of Illustrator*).

7. Moral Rights

The Illustrator hereby asserts *his/her* right to be identified as the Illustrator of the Work and the Publishers undertake:

7.1 to print on every edition of the Work published by them the words: '[*The Illustrator*] has asserted *his/her* right under the Copyright, Designs and Patents Act 1988, to be identified as Illustrator of this Work';

7.2 to use all reasonable endeavours to include in any contract for volume rights with any licensee concerning any edition of the Work to be published in the United Kingdom an undertaking that a notice of assertion in the same terms shall be printed in every edition published or further licensed by such licensee.

The Illustrator on written request from the Publishers undertakes to give consent or to waive in writing the right to object to derogatory treatment of the Artwork as provided for in section 80 of the Copyright, Designs and Patents Act 1988 when such consent or waiver is an essential condition of the exercise of any of the rights granted to the Publishers under this Agreement.

8. Payment

If the agreement is for jacket artwork only, or one piece of artwork as opposed to a complete book, a single fee is in order, payable usually at a specified time, for example, within six weeks, from receipt of the invoice submitted by the illustrator after delivery of the final artwork. This Precedent assumes a more extensive supply of artwork, with payment to be made in instalments, the first on delivery and the rest dependent on delivery and approval of the artwork by the Publishers.

Clause 8.2 gives the publishers the sole and exclusive right to exploit any subsidiary rights. These may include:

paperback

book club

condensed book

first and second serial and syndication rights

anthology rights

strip cartoon rights

US hardback/paperback and book club rights

translation rights

merchandising rights

electronic rights

film and television rights

Equal division of monies for reproduction in volume or serial form is general, but must be negotiable in the circumstances of each work. Illustration fees for any of the rights should, where possible, be negotiated separately from for the use of the author's text. In the case of merchandising, film, electronic and strip cartoon rights it is not always easy to determine the contribution to these of, respectively, author and illustrator and here any monies could be divided three ways (as between author, illustrator and publisher).

9. Approval of Artwork

It is understandable that publishers will require the right to approve the artwork at both rough and finished artwork stages. This clause provides for payment of cancellation fees to the illustrator if the artwork is rejected, but draws a distinction between artwork rejected because it is unsatisfactory and artwork rejected for some other reason (which might include cancellation of the whole Work). The nearer to completion the illustrations are when the publishers cancel the commission, the greater should be the proportion of the total fee payable to the illustrator, and a higher proportion should be paid if cancellation is not because the artwork is unsatisfactory.

10. Care of Artwork

Illustrators are now more likely to deliver artwork to publishers in electronic form (see Clause 1 and Schedule) and publishers are more likely to store it in electronic form and return the originals to the illustrator. Insurance against loss of or damage to artwork in traditional paper form is a vexed problem. Illustrators sometimes have difficulty in getting cover for their own work so it is not always feasible to ask them to insure it. Some publishers may have a general insurance policy which covers them, but the conditions for secure storage required by insurers may be too stringent for other publishers. Some publishers will undertake responsibility, but limit their liability contractually to a sum equal to the original fee (i.e., the fee expressed in this Precedent under Clause 8.1). One formula reads as follows:

> 'The Publishers shall be responsible for the Artwork while it is in their custody always provided that the Illustrator shall upon delivery to the Publishers of the final Artwork state in writing the value that he/she places upon each piece of Artwork which valuation shall be mutually agreed between the parties hereto.'

8. Payment

8.1 The Publishers shall pay to the Illustrator a fee of [*amount*] payable as to [*amount*] on signature of this Agreement, [*amount*] on delivery and approval of roughs of thee Artwork and [*amount*] on delivery and approval of finished Artwork as provided for in Clauses 1 and 2 of this Agreement.

8.2 The Publishers shall further pay to the Illustrator a proportion to be mutually agreed of any net sums received by the Publishers in respect of the Artwork sublicensed by them to a third party in volume form or in newspapers or magazines or otherwise.

9. Approval of Artwork

The artwork is subject to the approval of the Publishers, who may reject any Artwork which does not conform to the Publishers' written brief, has been damaged as a result of inadequate packaging or delivery, or is in the reasonable opinion of the Publishers unsatisfactory or unsuitable. The Publishers may at their option require the Illustrator to replace or repair unsatisfactory or damaged Artwork at the Illustrator's own expense. If the Artwork is rejected as unsatisfactory at rough stage the Publishers will pay the Illustrator a rejection fee of [*number*] per cent of the total fee specified in Clause 8 hereof. If the artwork is rejected at rough stage for any other reason the Publishers will pay the Illustrator a rejection fee of [*number*] per cent of the said fee. If the finished Artwork is rejected as unsatisfactory the Publishers will pay the Illustrator a rejection fee of [*number*] of the said fee. If the finished Artwork is rejected for any other reason the Publishers will pay the Illustrator a rejection fee of [*number*} per cent of the said fee. Artwork rejected by the Publishers shall be returned to the Illustrator.

10. Care of Artwork

The Publishers shall take all reasonable steps to ensure that while in their possession the Artwork shall be properly stored. The Publishers may for ease of reproduction store the Artwork in digital format and the original Artwork shall be returned to the Illustrator. The Publishers shall not be responsible for any loss or damage to it while it is in transit.

11. Complimentary Copies

The Publishers shall send to the Illustrator on publication [*number*] complimentary copies of the Work. The Illustrator shall have the right to purchase at normal trade terms further copies for personal use but not for resale. The Illustrator shall receive [*number*] complimentary copies of any

12. Warranties and indemnity

It may be important to ensure that the artwork is original and/or has not been published before in volume form; many publishers prefer that it has not been published before in any form.

13. Recognisable Likeness

This clause is particularly important for photographic sessions with models needed for paperback covers, where print runs can be very high and damages sought for improper exploitation correspondingly so.

sub-licensed edition of the Work which includes the Artwork on receipt by the Publishers from the sub-licensed publishers of their edition of the Work.

12. Warranties and Indemnity

The Illustrator hereby warrants to the Publishers and their assigns and licensees that *he/she* has full power to make this Agreement, that *he/she* is the sole creator of the Artwork and is the owner of the rights herein granted, that the Artwork is original to *him/her* and has not previously been published in volume form in the territories covered by this Agreement, that the Artwork is in no way whatever a violation or an infringement of any existing copyright or licence, and that it contains nothing obscene, libellous or defamatory. The Illustrator will indemnify and keep the Publishers indemnified against all actions, suits, proceedings, claims, demands, damages and costs (including any legal costs or expenses properly incurred and any compensation costs and disbursements paid by the Publishers on the advice of their legal advisers to compromise or settle any claim) occasioned to the Publishers in consequence of any breach of this warranty or arising out of any claim alleging that the Artwork constitutes in any way a breach of this warranty. The Publishers reserve the right to insist that the Illustrator alter the Artwork in such a way as may appear to them appropriate for the purpose of removing any feature which on the advice of the Publishers' legal advisers may be considered objectionable or likely to be actionable by law, but any such alteration or removal shall be without prejudice to and shall not affect the Illustrator's liability under this warranty and indemnity. All warranties and indemnities herein contained shall survive the termination of this Agreement.

13. Recognisable Likeness

Should the Artwork contain a recognisable likeness of any person the Illustrator undertakes to explain to such person the use to which the Artwork will be put and to obtain from each such person a form of release and to deliver the same to the Publishers in a form satisfactory to them.

14. Out of Print

If at any time the Publishers allow the Work to become out of print and not be available in any edition in any form and if the Publishers return to the author of the text all rights granted to them under the terms of the agreement between them and the author the Publishers shall at the same time return to the Illustrator all rights in the Artwork granted under this Agreement without prejudice to all rights of the Publishers in respect of any contracts or negotiations properly entered into by them with any third party prior to the date of such reversion.

15. Termination

Either party may terminate this Agreement with immediate effect if either party is in breach of any material provision contained herein and all rights granted under this Agreement shall revert to the Illustrator, without prejudice to all rights of the Publishers to sell any remaining copies of the Work, without prejudice to any contracts or negotiations properly entered into by the Publishers with any third party prior to the date of such termination and without prejudice to any monies already paid or then due to the Illustrator from the Publishers.

16. Value Added Tax

All monies accruing to the Illustrator under this Agreement shall be exclusive of Value Added Tax (VAT). If the Illustrator is at any time registered for the purposes of VAT the Publishers shall, after notification of the Illustrator's VAT registration number, add VAT to payments made to the Illustrator in accordance with statutory regulations. The Publishers shall be notified of any change in the Illustrator's VAT status, including any alteration to the Illustrator's VAT registration number.

17. Arbitration

If any difference shall arise between the Illustrator and the Publishers touching the meaning of this Agreement or the rights and liabilities of the parties thereto, the same shall be referred in the first place to the Publishers Association's Informal Disputes Settlement Scheme, and failing agreed submission to that Scheme, to the arbitration of two persons (one to be named by each party) or their mutually agreed umpire, in accordance with the provisions of the Arbitration Act 1996 or any amending or substituted statute for the time being in force.

18. Entire Agreement

This Agreement is the entire and only agreement between the Illustrator and the Publishers concerning its subject matter and supersedes any and all prior agreements, arrangements and understandings (whether written or oral) relating thereto. No addition to or modification of any provision of this Agreement shall be binding upon the parties unless it is in writing and signed on behalf of the Illustrator and the Publishers.

19. Applicable Law

This Agreement shall be governed by and interpreted in all respects in accordance with the law of England and the parties hereto submit and agree

to the jurisdiction of the English courts whose courts shall have exclusive jurisdiction.

20. Notices

Any notice, consent or the like required or permitted to be given under this Agreement shall be in writing and shall be deemed sufficiently given as of the date delivered or mailed, postage pre-paid by registered post or the equivalent to the address of the party set out above or at such other address as any party may designate in writing to the other.

21. Assignment

This Agreement is personal to the parties. Neither party shall assign any duty or right contained in this Agreement, nor shall they delegate or sub-contract the performance of any duty or right without the prior written consent of the other, except that the Publishers may assign this Agreement to any organisation that may become the Publishers' successor or assignee in business.

AS WITNESS THE HANDS OF THE PARTIES

Signed..

The Illustrator

Signed..

For the Publishers

Schedule

The Artwork referred to in Clause 1 hereof shall consist of:

[*number*] illustrations in black and white

[*number*] illustrations in [*number*] colours

A [jacket/cover (front only/wrap-around)] for printing in colours

Medium: *in conventional paper form/in electronic form [specify format e.g. in Illustrator (version)/in Photoshop (version)]*

Size/proportion:

PRECEDENT FOURTEEN

Packaging Rights Agreement

This precedent is based on the Book Packagers Association's Standard Agreement between Book Packager and UK Publisher (Eleventh Draft, April 1996). It includes a form of contract with provisions covering the most common kind of packaging deal – the sale of finished copies of an illustrated book, royalty-inclusive, to a publisher in the UK. The Association has since disbanded as a formal entity and this precedent and the accompanying notes have been updated and modified to some extent from that last draft.

2. Price Per Copy and Date of Delivery

The appropriate staging of payments will vary according to the book and the circumstances, but the following points should be borne in mind:

(a) too many stages are administratively tiresome, since each requires invoicing and chasing;

(b) the final stage, coinciding with the payment of the printer, should be large enough to meet that payment; and

(c) the appropriate stages may include some of the following: signature of the agreement; delivery of the typescript or electronic files; galley proofs; page proofs; illustration proofs; complete ozalid or electronic files; advance bound copies; complete delivery.

As the pattern of expenditure varies from project to project, it is a good idea to draw up a cash flow before finalising stage payments.

The percentage of overs or unders given here is standard in the British book printing industry, but higher or lower percentages may be agreed.

Practices differ over the inclusion in the price of such elements as royalty, and delivery to the publisher's warehouse as opposed to 'cif a United Kingdom port' or 'ex printing works'.

Some publishers' delivery and packing requirements may be abnormal and involve expenditure in excess of what was allowed for when the unit price was calculated and agreed. In this event the extra cost of such special packing should be charged to the Publisher.

AGREEMENT made this [*number*] day of [*month*] 20 [*year*] Between [*company name*] of [*address*] (hereinafter termed 'the Publishers', which expression shall where the context admits include the Publishers' assigns or successors in business as the case may be) and [*company name of packagers*] of [*address*] (hereinafter termed 'the Proprietors'), which expression shall where the context admits include the Proprietors' assigns or successors in business as the case may be)

WHEREAS the Proprietors control the rights in a work provisionally entitled [*title*] (hereinafter termed 'the Work') [to be] written/edited by [*name*] (hereinafter termed 'the Author') of which the Proprietors have the sole and exclusive rights of manufacture and disposal of the licence to publish and have agreed to grant certain rights in the Work to the Publishers under the terms of this Agreement.

IT IS HEREBY AGREED AS FOLLOWS:

1. Sale and Purchase of Copies

The Proprietors agree to sell and the Publishers agree to purchase [*number*] copies of the Work (hereinafter termed 'the Order') in accordance with the specification set out in Appendix 1 attached to and forming part of this Agreement and subject to the terms and conditions set out in this Agreement.

2. Price Per Copy and Date of Delivery

2.1 The Publishers shall pay the Proprietors the sum of [amount] per copy (hereinafter termed the Price) and shall make such payment in the following instalments:

[*amount*] on signature of this Agreement;

[*amount*] on [agreed date];

[*amount*] on [agreed date];

[*amount*] on [agreed date];

[*amount*] on delivery to the Publishers of the Order.

2.2 The Price is inclusive of royalty and the costs of bulk packing, shipping and insurance for delivery to the Publishers' warehouse, which delivery shall be made, unless prevented by circumstances beyond the Proprietors' control, on or before [*date*] 20 [*year*], in accordance with the Publishers' delivery and packing requirements set out in Appendix 2 attached to and forming part of this Agreement. A variation of 5 per

3. Rights and Territory

The packager may wish to grant less than 'volume' rights or to provide that, for example, paperback rights should revert to it if after a certain period (e.g., 18 months) the publisher has taken no steps to exploit them.

4. Copyright

If the publisher has also bought US rights, this clause should require the filing of an application for registration within three months of publication of the work in the US in the Copyright Office, Library of Congress.

cent over or under the quantity of copies shall constitute full delivery of the Order.

2.3 The Publishers may by giving notice to the Proprietors in adequate time to enable the Proprietors to notify the printer of the Work order additional run-on copies of the Work at the price of [*amount*] per copy and such copies shall be subject to the terms of this Agreement.

3. Rights and Territory

The Proprietors hereby grant to the Publishers during the term of this Agreement the sole and exclusive licence to publish, distribute and sell the Work in [*hardback*] volume form in the English language in the Territory as defined in Appendix 3 of this Agreement. All rights in the Work other than those expressly granted to the Publishers under the terms of this Agreement are retained by the Proprietors.

4. Copyright

4.1 The Proprietors shall ensure that all copies of the Work delivered to the Publishers by the Proprietors bear the following copyright notice: '© [*name of copyright owner*], *20 [*year*] [* represents year of first publication]'.

4.2 The Publishers shall ensure that all copies of the Work published by them and licensed in the United Kingdom and in any other part of the Territory to which the Copyright, Designs and Patents Act 1988 extends shall include the above copyright notice on the reverse of the title page.

4.3 (i) If at any time during the term of this Agreement the copyright of the Work shall in the reasonable opinion of the Publishers be infringed by a third party the Publishers shall at their own expense be entitled to take such steps as they consider necessary to deal with the matter, including but not restricted to proceedings in the joint name of the Publishers and the Proprietors on giving the Proprietors a sufficient and reasonable indemnity against all liability for costs and expenses (whether of the Proprietors or of the defendants in any such proceedings) and the Proprietors shall give the Publishers all reasonable co-operation in such proceedings.

(ii) The Publishers shall be entitled to nominate the solicitors through whom such proceedings may be carried on and shall have full power to abandon compromise or settle such proceedings at their own discretion but will first consult fully with the Proprietors.

6. Proprietors' Warranties

(iv) If the indemnity given to the publisher in this clause is felt to be too much of a catch-all, it can be left out. However, some publishers may insist on a clause of this kind. At least providing a form of words gives the packager some degree of control over settlement. If packagers wish to protect themselves further, they can require publishers to print a disclaimer. Appropriate wording might be:

> 'No responsibility for loss occasioned to any person acting or refraining from action as a result of the material in this publication can be accepted by the Author, the Proprietors or the Publishers.'

(iii) Any sum recovered by way of damages and costs shall be applied first towards repayment of the costs incurred in such proceedings and any balance shall be divided equally between the parties.

(iv) Notwithstanding any other provisions of this Agreement the Publishers and their sub-licensees shall if they reasonably consider it necessary for the protection of the Work be entitled to take urgent proceedings in their sole name in any country of the world for interlocutory relief without prior notice to the Proprietors provided that the Publishers shall as soon as reasonably practicable afterwards give to the Proprietors notice of such proceedings.

(v) The provisions of this clause apply only to an infringement of the copyright in the Work which affects the interest in it granted to the Publishers under the terms of this Agreement.

5. Author's Moral Right to be Identified

5.1 The Author has asserted the Author's moral right to be identified as the Author of the Work. The Proprietors shall ensure that all copies of the Work manufactured by the Proprietors [*and the Publishers undertake to ensure that every copy of the Work licensed by the Publishers*] shall include the words 'The right of the Author to be identified as the Author of this work has been asserted by the Author in accordance with the Copyright, Designs and Patents Act 1988';

5.2 The Proprietors shall ensure that on every copy of the Work produced by the Proprietors or under licence from them [*and the Publishers undertake to ensure that on every copy of the Work licensed by the Publishers*] the name of the Author shall appear in its customary form with due prominence on the title page and on the binding.

6. Proprietors' Warranties

The Proprietors warrant to the Publishers:

(i) The Proprietors are the sole owners of the rights granted under this Agreement and have full power to enter into this Agreement and to give the warranties and indemnity contained in the Agreement.

(ii) To the best of the Proprietors' knowledge and belief the Work contains nothing obscene, blasphemous, libellous or in breach of the Official Secrets Act or otherwise unlawful and the exploitation of the rights granted under this Agreement will not infringe the copyright or any other rights of any third party.

7. Approval of Material

British publishers have varying practices as regards the checking of progress on books bought in; and book packagers have different attitudes as well. It should be borne in mind that there are advantages in securing the publisher's approval of the book at various stages of preparation, in addition to the obvious disadvantages.

It is probably best to avoid a specific time limit for checking proofs because there may be occasions when a particularly fast turnaround is required to meet the publisher's own delivery date.

8. Imperfect Copies

The revised wording of this clause is intended to provide the packager with the following safeguards:

(1) Even if the printers accept that copies of the work are defective, they are highly unlikely to credit the packager with more than the price received.

By way of example, and to keep the figures simple, consider the case of a reprint with no editorial or other plant costs.

Suppose that a packager pays the printers of the work £3.00 per copy for a printing of 10,000 copies and charges the publishers £4.00 per copy. Suppose further that all parties agree that 1,000 copies are defective. Under the previous wording of this clause, the publishers could expect to be credited automatically by the packager, who would in turn be credited by the printers. The packager would consequently lose £1,000 of gross profit as a result of the printers' errors.

(2) The revised wording should help indemnify the packager against claims by publishers for consequential loss, and go some way to make it harder for publishers to claim for tiny or imagined blemishes.

(3) Sub-clause 8.2 is designed to prevent the packager from becoming liable in a situation where the publisher discovers two or three defective copies, immediately orders a stock check, and subsequently tries to pass the cost of this exercise on to the packager.

It is important that the packager also has a written agreement with the printers setting out what happens when copies are found to be defective, and obliging the printers to repair or replace copies where more than (say) 3% of the total are found to be defective.

(iii) To the best of the Proprietors' knowledge and belief all statements in the Work purporting to be facts are true and any recipe, formula or instruction contained in it will not if followed accurately cause any injury, illness or damage to the user.

(iv) The Proprietors shall keep the Publishers fully indemnified against all losses and all actions, claims, proceedings, costs and damages, including any damages or compensation paid by the Publishers after written approval by the Proprietors on the advice of their legal advisers to compromise or settle any claim and all legal costs or other expenses arising out of any breach of any of the above warranties.

7. Approval of Material

The Publishers shall approve the typescript and proofs of the Work (*provided in a form to be agreed between the Parties*) within a reasonable time to be specified by the Proprietors, such approval not to be unreasonably withheld or delayed. Any costs incurred as a consequence of changes required to material previously approved shall be borne by the Publishers.

8. Imperfect Copies

8.1 The Publishers shall notify the Proprietors in writing within 30 days of delivery of the Order of any defects in such copies of the Work attributable to faulty materials or faulty workmanship being copies which in the reasonable view of the Publishers are unacceptable (hereinafter termed the Imperfect Copies). The parties shall forthwith attempt in good faith to agree the number of Imperfect Copies or failing such agreement the number shall be determined under Clause 8.4. Where the number so agreed or determined is less than 3 per cent of the Order, the Proprietors shall credit the Publishers with the Price of the agreed number of Imperfect Copies. Where the number so agreed is more than 3 per cent of the Order, the Proprietors shall at their option re-cover, repair or replace the Imperfect Copies or credit the Publishers the Price of the Imperfect Copies. The total liability of the Proprietors shall be limited to the Price of the Imperfect Copies, and the Proprietors shall be under no liability whatsoever for any claims for loss of profits or contracts or indirect or consequential loss or damage arising in respect of the Imperfect Copies whether by reason of negligence, breach of contract, or any other cause of action arising out of the Imperfect Copies, except as expressly provided in this Agreement.

8.2 The Proprietors shall not be liable for the cost of checking stocks of the Work in the Publishers' warehouse unless the aggregate of the Imperfect Copies is more than 100 copies of the Work or 1 per cent of the Order, whichever is the greater, and in the event of such liability

10. Undertaking to Advertise and Promote

This clause is mainly designed to ensure that the packager is kept informed on promotion plans, and to avoid inaccuracies in advertising copy. It may occasionally be possible to include an undertaking by the publisher to spend a specific sum on advertising and promotion.

11. Licences Granted by the Publishers

11.1 The following subsidiary rights are normally or often granted to British publishers under this clause: anthology, digest and quotation; first serial; second and subsequent serial; syndication; readings on radio and television; advertising; strip cartoon; digest book condensation. Trade paperback rights are also frequently granted. It is common to reserve: mass market paperback; cheap edition/reprint; film, video and television, merchandising and

the cost of the stock check must first be agreed by the parties, such agreement not to be unreasonably withheld or delayed.

8.3 The Proprietors do not exclude liability for death or personal injury caused by the Publishers' negligence.

8.4 If the parties are unable to agree the number of Imperfect Copies within seven days the matter may be referred by either party for resolution by an independent arbitrator to be nominated by the parties, and, failing agreement on such nomination within a further seven days, to such person as is appointed on the application of either party by the President for the time being of the British Printing Industries Federation. The independent arbitrator shall be deemed to act as an expert and not as an arbitrator; the independent arbitrator shall take into account the written representations of the parties; and the independent arbitrator's determination shall (in the absence of manifest error) be conclusive and binding upon the parties, and the costs of any such determination shall be borne as the independent arbitrator shall direct, or failing such direction, equally by the parties.

8.5 The express terms of this Agreement are in lieu of all warranties, conditions, terms, undertakings and obligations implied by statute, common law, custom, trade usage, course of dealing or otherwise, all of which are hereby excluded to the fullest extent permitted by law.

9. Undertaking to Publish

The Publishers shall publish the Work at their own risk and expense, unless prevented by circumstances beyond their control, within six months of the delivery to them of copies of the Work.

10. Undertaking to Advertise and Promote

The Publishers agree actively to advertise and to promote the sales of the Work in accordance with the best commercial practice, to ensure its circulation and availability throughout the Territory, to discuss their plans for promotion with the Proprietors and to provide the Proprietors with [*a reasonable opportunity to check advertising and promotional copy for accuracy* or *all advertising and promotional copy for written approval, such approval not to be unreasonably withheld or delayed.*]

11. Licences Granted by the Publishers

11.1 The Publishers shall pay to the Proprietors the following percentages of all monies received by the Publishers in respect of sub-licensing the rights set out below:

electronic rights. The percentages payable may vary between 50% (for most rights) and 90% (for first serial rights).

As regards the disposition of book club rights, which insofar as they involve manufacture are often vitally important to the packager, there are wide variations in practice. They are frequently retained wholly by the packager; often granted to the publisher; and sometimes dealt with on a profit-sharing basis between the parties.

11.2. This sub-clause provides for the circumstances where illustration rights have been cleared for volume publication but not for further exploitation. It obliges the publisher to obtain the packager's agreement to such exploitation, which can be withheld if the additional fee payable does not make the sale worthwhile.

12. Accounting for Sales

Since most packaged books are sold inclusive of royalty, and hence normal procedures regarding royalty statements are not automatically followed, it often proves difficult to obtain from publishers any information on the sales performance of the books sold to them. This clause at least makes such information a contractual obligation.

[*Category of Right*]	[*number*] per cent
[*Category of Right*]	[*number*] per cent
[*Category of Right*]	[*number*] per cent

11.2 The Publishers shall consult the Proprietors over any sale of rights under this clause. No agreement for the disposal of rights including illustrations contained in the Work shall be entered into by the Publishers without the Proprietors' prior agreement in writing. In the event that in respect of such rights additional fees are payable to sources of illustrations contained in the Work such fees shall be paid by the Publishers.

11.3 The Publishers agree to supply the Proprietors with copies of all sub-licences and agreements in connection with the sale of rights within 30 days of signature of such documents by the Publishers and copies of all statements received by them in connection with all such sales when accounting for such sales to the Proprietors. The Publishers shall pay to the Proprietors their share of any advance payments received by the Publishers in respect of sales of rights within 28 days of their receipt by the Publishers.

12. Accounting for Sales

12.1 The Publishers shall keep accurate, detailed and up-to-date accounts of sales and income from sales of copies of and exploitation of rights in the Work.

12.2 Within 90 days of each six-month accounting period ending on [*date*] and following first publication the Publishers shall submit to the Proprietors a statement showing the sales of copies and editions of the Work and of payments received under sub-licences referred to in Clause 11 during the relevant period and the relevant percentage applicable thereto and shall forthwith pay to the Proprietors such sums as are then due.

12.3 The Publishers shall allow the Proprietors (or a firm of chartered accountants appointed to act on the Proprietors' behalf) to examine the accounting records of the Publishers insofar as they relate to the Work and to take copies and extracts of the relevant parts of such accounting records. Any inspection shall take place by appointment during normal office hours after reasonable notice has been given and shall not be carried out more than twice in any calendar year. Such inspection shall be at the Proprietors' expense unless it reveals an underpayment to the Proprietors of more than 5 per cent in which event the Publishers shall bear the cost of such inspection.

13. Retention of Title

If delivery has been made but the publisher fails to pay, the packager can cancel the contract and the rights granted under it revert. But since 'possession is nine points of the law', the actual ownership of the copies (as distinct from the right to sell or exploit them) may remain vested in the publisher. This clause seeks to avoid this difficulty by including a sub-clause defining precisely the point at which ownership in the goods is transferred.

NB This clause has been drafted to meet specific legal requirements, and should not be changed without professional legal advice.

13. Retention of Title

13.1 The legal and beneficial ownership of all copies of the Work (hereinafter termed the Goods) supplied to the Publishers shall remain vested in the Proprietors until either:

(i) all sums owed to the Proprietors by the Publishers have been paid; or

(ii) (if for any reason the provision in sub-clause 13.1(i) is held to be invalid) the Publishers have paid to the Proprietors all sums due to the Proprietors in respect of the Goods.

13.2 Until the ownership of the Goods passes to the Publishers under the provisions of Clause 13.1 the Publishers shall hold the Goods as agent for the Proprietors and shall deal with the Goods only in accordance with such instructions as the Proprietors may give from time to time and in particular:

(i) The Publishers shall store the Goods in such a manner that they are separate and identifiable from all other goods and shall notify the Proprietors of the place of storage.

(ii) The Publishers shall insure the Goods against all normal insurable risks and such other items as the Proprietors may require and shall on request provide the Proprietors with details of the insurance policy.

(iii) The Publishers may dispose of the Goods as the agent of the Proprietors PROVIDED THAT:

(a) the Proprietors shall be informed in advance of the terms of any disposal and shall have approved the same in writing;

(b) the proceeds of sale of any disposal together with proceeds of any insurance claim relating to the Goods shall be held by the Publishers as trustee for the Proprietors until ownership of the Goods would have been transferred to the Publishers under Clause 13.1 and such proceeds shall be placed by the Publishers in a separate bank account which is clearly marked as a trust account;

(c) the Publishers shall on request assign to the Proprietors all the Publishers' rights against any person who purchases the Goods from the Publishers.

14. Term of Agreement

The contract as drafted is terminable only by default of either party or if (after due process) the book goes out of print. In the absence of those events it will survive the full term of copyright. However, it is not uncommon to limit such contracts to a fixed term – such as five or eight years. A time limit is a useful way of clearing the ground in advance for a promotional reprint, for example.

14. Term of Agreement

This Agreement, unless previously terminated under Clause 15, shall commence on [the date hereof] and continue for a period of [*number*] years after the date of first publication of the Work by the Publishers. This Agreement may be extended on the same terms by a period of a further [*number*] years upon written agreement by the parties, such agreement not to be unreasonably withheld.

15. Termination

15.1 The Proprietors may terminate this Agreement forthwith by notice in writing to the Publishers:

(i) if the Publishers fail to publish the Work within the time stipulated in Clause 9;

(ii) if the Publishers are in breach of any of their other obligations under this Agreement and in the case of a breach capable of being remedied fail to remedy such breach within one month of being requested in writing by the Proprietors to do so;

(iii) if the Publishers purport to assign the benefit of this Agreement without the prior written consent of the Proprietors;

(iv) if the Publishers go into liquidation either compulsorily or voluntarily (except for the purpose of and immediately followed by a solvent reconstruction or amalgamation) or if a receiver, administrative receiver, receiver and manager or administrator is appointed in respect of the whole or any part of their assets or if the Publishers make an assignment for the benefit of or composition with their creditors generally or threaten to do any of these things;

(v) if the Publishers remainder the Work under the terms of Clause 18;

(vi) if the Publishers put the Work out of print so that it is not available in the Territory in the English language unless within [*number*] months of receipt of notice in writing from the Proprietors the Publishers agree to publish in the Territory a reprint of not less than [*number*] copies or notify the Proprietors that they have licensed another publisher to publish such a reprint which will be published within that period time being of the essence.

15.2 (i) On the expiry or termination of this Agreement all rights granted to the Publishers under its terms shall automatically and immediately revert to the Proprietors absolutely;

16. Penalties

This clause deals with the important question of the penalties applicable in the case of (1) late payment and (2) late delivery of books. Book packagers should consider carefully whether to press for its inclusion. If late payment is penalised, it will be hard to resist the publisher's request for equally severe penalties for late delivery of books or other defaults. On the other hand, prompt settlement is not a common virtue among publishers. Even if the clause is omitted, it is nonetheless possible to obtain agreement for settlement of at least the final instalment by bill of exchange, which gives some protection; or even to obtain irrevocable letters of credit.

(ii) The Publishers may for a period of six months on a non-exclusive basis continue to sell any copies of the Work that are on hand as at the date of expiry or termination of this Agreement;

(iii) Termination shall not affect:

(a) the subsidiary rights (if any) of any third party under a sub-licence validly entered into by the Publishers prior to termination;

(b) the rights of the Proprietors to money accrued due to the Proprietors in respect of the Publishers' sales and exploitation of the Work up to the date of termination;

(c) any claim which either party may have against the other for damages or otherwise.

15.3 After termination or expiry of this Agreement the Publishers shall from time to time when so requested do all such things and sign and execute such documents and deeds as the Proprietors may reasonably require in order to confirm the reversion of rights to the Proprietors under the terms of this Agreement and in particular (but not by way of limitation) the Publishers shall give notice in the form specified by the Proprietors to all (if any) of the Publishers' sub-licensees of the termination of this Agreement and requesting such sub-licensees as from the date of termination to account to the Proprietors or as the Proprietors shall direct for money payable by such sub-licensees in respect of the Work.

16. Penalties

16.1 If the Publishers fail to pay to the Proprietors sums due under this Agreement within the times specified in this Agreement the Publishers agree to pay to the Proprietors interest on such sums overdue equal to [*number*] per cent above the current base rate at [*Bank*] from the due date until such payment is made.

16.2 If delivery of the Work is delayed by more than four weeks after the date provided for in Clause 2.2 unless the parties have agreed in writing upon a revised date of delivery the Publishers shall be entitled to postpone publication by a maximum of 16 weeks and the settlement of the final instalment of the purchase price herein provided for shall be postponed by an equivalent period. If delivery of the Work is delayed by more than 24 weeks after the date provided for in Clause 2.2 the Publishers shall be entitled forthwith by notice in writing to the Proprietors to cancel this Agreement and to be repaid all sums advanced to the Proprietors hereunder together with interest on such

18. Remainders

18.1 The period of two years is common, but other periods can be agreed.

18.2 The reason for the inclusion of this sub-clause is to avoid a situation whereby remaindered copies of the UK edition of the work find their way into, for example, the US, thus potentially damaging sales of any US edition.

19. Provision of Advance Material

It may be unnecessary to include this undertaking to supply materials free of charge; but if such materials as proofs and extra jackets are to be supplied, it should be clear in the agreement whether they are free, at cost, or at cost plus a handling charge.

20. Reprints

Packagers may wish to relate the unit price of any reprint to the cover price, in which case a sentence can be added to say that the price paid to the packager for any reprint shall not be less than (e.g., 25%) of the publisher's cover price.

sums equal to [*number*] per cent above the current base rate at [*Bank*] from [*date*] up to the date of cancellation.

17. Proprietors' Copies

17.1 The Proprietors shall retain twelve copies of the Work, of which six copies shall be presented to the Author.

17.2 The Proprietors shall additionally be entitled to repurchase not more than 250 copies of the Work from the Publishers at the Price and additional copies at the best UK trade discount for promotional purposes only and not for resale.

17.3 The Publishers shall supply to the Proprietors free of charge six copies of each and every edition of the Work sub-licensed by them to third parties under the terms of this Agreement.

18. Remainders

18.1 The Publishers shall be entitled no earlier than [*number, e.g., 24*] calendar months after first publication of their edition of the Work to dispose of surplus copies of that edition only as a remainder after first making an offer in writing to the Proprietors to sell such copies to the Proprietors at a price equal to the best written offer from any potential purchaser, such offer to be accepted within three months of its receipt.

18.2 The Publishers may not dispose of stocks of the Work under the provisions of this clause outside the Territory nor permit their disposal by any third party outside the Territory without the prior written permission of the Proprietors.

19. Provision of Advance Material

The Proprietors shall provide the Publishers with the advance information and material specified in Appendix 5 attached to and forming part of this Agreement and shall at the Publishers' request supply additional sales material at cost price subject to reasonable notice from the Publishers.

20. Reprints

The price of any future reprint or new edition of the Work shall be the subject of a separate agreement between the Publishers and the Proprietors.

21. Force Majeure

No failure or delay in performance of the obligations of either party to this Agreement shall be deemed a breach if such failure or delay is caused by or is due to any cause beyond the reasonable control of such party.

22. Assignment

22.1 The Proprietors may not assign the benefit of this Agreement (or any interest in the Agreement) without the prior written consent of the Publishers except to any person as part of the transfer of the relevant part of the Proprietors' business, and provided that the Proprietors procure the assignee to enter into a direct covenant with the Publishers to observe and perform all of the obligations of the Proprietors as set out in this Agreement.

22.2 The Publishers may not assign or dispose of the Publishers' rights or obligations under this Agreement without the prior written consent of the Proprietors.

23. Notices

23.1 Any notice, consent or the like (hereinafter termed the Notice) required or permitted to be given under this Agreement shall not be binding unless in writing. It may be sent to a party to this Agreement, addressed to the Company Secretary, by hand delivery, pre-paid first class post, by fax [*or by e-mail*] at the address set out in this Agreement or as otherwise notified.

23.2 Any Notice sent by post shall be deemed received on the second business day following posting.

23.3 Any Notice sent by fax [*or by e-mail*] shall be deemed given 24 hours after the time of its actual transmission.

24. Miscellaneous

24.1 This Agreement shall be binding upon and inure to the benefit of the parties, and their permitted assigns.

24.2 This Agreement contains the full and complete understanding between the parties and supersedes all prior arrangements and understandings whether written or oral relating to the subject matter of this Agreement.

24.3 This Agreement shall not be modified except in writing and signed by both parties or their duly authorised representatives.

24.4 The failure by either party to enforce at any time or for any period any one or more of the terms or conditions of this Agreement shall not constitute a waiver of any such term or of that party's right at any time subsequently to enforce any and all terms and conditions of this Agreement.

24.5 The warranties and indemnities contained in this Agreement and the provisions for payment of and accounting in respect of royalties and other monies due to the Proprietors under the terms of this Agreement shall survive the termination or expiry of this Agreement.

24.6 The headings in this Agreement are for convenience only and shall not affect its interpretation.

24.7 References to clauses, sub-clauses and schedules are to clauses, sub-clauses and schedules of this Agreement.

24.8 Nothing contained in this Agreement shall constitute or be construed as constituting a partnership or the relationship of principal and agent between the parties.

25. Jurisdiction

This Agreement shall be governed by the law of England whose courts shall have exclusive jurisdiction.

AS WITNESS

the hands of authorised representatives of the parties on the date first above written

....

for and on behalf of the Publishers

....

for and on behalf of the Proprietors

Appendix 1

It is advisable to make the description of specifications clear enough to define accurately what the publisher is buying, but not so detailed as to limit the packager's freedom to make reasonable adjustments in the course of production.

APPENDIX 1

Specification

Author:

Title:

Order No:

Quantity to be supplied:

Price per copy: FOB/CIF [*location*]

Royalty:

Total purchase price:

Delivery date:

Technical specifications

Approximate number of words:

Number of pages (*number*) pp plus (*number*) pp prelims:

Number of illustrations:

Trimmed page size:

Paper weight and type:

Jacket/cover specifications:

Manner of printing:

Binding style:

Appendix 3

There are many ways of defining the territory, including a complete listing of territories worldwide. The appropriate form will depend on the circumstances. **See especially Appendix J**.

UK publishers still often ask for exclusive UK and Commonwealth rights, in which case Canadian rights at least should be retained in order to facilitate selling rights in the US.

The question here for packagers to ask themselves is, who will sell the various rights more effectively – publisher or packager? There is no point in the packager selling rights that the publisher will not exploit. From the packager's point of view, there is an argument for starting off with the territory as suggested in the draft agreement, and asking the publisher to increase the total print quantity in exchange for concessions. It also makes sense for the packager to include a time limit in the case of at least the most important overseas markets, so that if, for example, Australian rights are licensed to the publisher, they automatically revert to the packager if after a reasonable period of time the work has not been made available, or ceases to be available, on the Australian market.

An increasingly important set of rights that packagers may prefer to retain is that of English-language sales in Europe. It is sometimes possible for a packager to deal direct with European distributors, but among the factors to consider is the possibility of competing with co-editions in other languages.

APPENDIX 2

Publishers' Delivery and Packing Requirements

APPENDIX 3

Territory

Exclusive in the Commonwealth as constituted at the date of this Agreement excluding Canada, Australia and New Zealand; non-exclusive throughout the rest of the world excluding the United States of America and its dependencies and the Philippine Islands.

APPENDIX 4

Advance Information and Material to be provided by the Publishers

Not less than (*number*) of days before commencement of production: Publishers' ISBN, barcode, logo etc

Additional Clauses

A number of other items can be dealt with in the contract. Among the additional matters which can arise are:

Prices

It may happen that a price is agreed between packager and publisher based on a percentage of a notional retail price. In theory, the publisher can make a last-minute decision to raise the cover price, while the per copy price to the packager remains unchanged. If this is perceived as a possible difficulty, it can be guarded against by using the following clause:

> 'The Price assumes a UK recommended retail price per copy for the Work of not more than [*amount*]. Should the Publishers increase the said retail price (except by reason of the addition of VAT or other tax) then the Price shall also be increased to a sum not less than [*number*] per cent of the final retail price.'

Inflation

It is not uncommon, particularly with books on a long production schedule, for provisions to be included in the agreement to protect the packager against the effects of inflation, cost increases in materials and labour, and fluctuating rates of currency exchange. Such protection is usually limited to a fixed percentage of the contract price. A possible wording is as follows:

> 'The Price is based upon rates of exchange and costs of labour and manufacture prevailing at the date of this Agreement and is subject to variation in the event of rises or falls in such rates and costs at the date of delivery. The Price shall be increased or reduced by a maximum of [*number*] per cent in proportion to such rises or falls and the Proprietors shall notify the Publishers of such increases or reductions as soon as practicable and not later than [*number*] days before the date of delivery.'

Publisher's Right to Manufacture

Publishers sometimes seek to acquire the right, in certain circumstances, to obtain from the packager film or electronic files from which to reprint the book. Such a request should usually be resisted.

Changes to the Jacket Design

The publisher may wish to make changes to the jacket design after approval of the original dummy; but such matters are better dealt with outside the context of the contract.

Prohibition on the Production of Competing Works

Some publishers attempt to prohibit the packager from producing books for other publishers which might compete with the book concerned. This should obviously be resisted.

Option on the Author's Next Work

Sometimes the publisher seeks to obtain an option on the next work by the same author in which rights are controlled by the packager. There may be a case for this. It should be remembered that options are in practice difficult to enforce.

New Edition

A situation can arise when a packager wishes to produce a new edition of a book, perhaps for an overseas customer. If the original publisher does not want to produce a new edition, it is useful for the packager to have the right to offer the new edition to a different publisher. Here is a suggested form of words:

APPENDIX 5

Advance Information and Material to be provided by the Proprietors

1. Not less than [*number*] days before delivery: full title; author's name; description of contents and illustrations; biographical details of author; jacket copy.

2. Not less than [*number*] days before delivery: [*number*] sets of complete proofs of the text.

3. Not less than [*number*] days before delivery: [*number*] advance jackets.

4. Not less than [*number*] days before delivery: [*number*] advance sets of sewn sheets with jackets/advance bound and jacketed copies.

Advance Information and Material to be provided by the Proprietors

'In the event of either (a) the rate of sale of the Work declining below 250 copies in a year, or (b) stocks of the Publishers' edition of the Work totalling less than 250 copies, the Proprietors shall have the right to offer the Publishers the first option to consider the acquisition of rights in a revised and amended edition of the Work on terms similar to those provided herein having due regard to prices of manufacture and like factors, such option to be exercised within three months of notification by the Proprietors of details of the revision and the price thereof. Should the parties fail to enter into an agreement concerning the new edition within six months of notification by the Proprietors, the Publishers' rights under this Agreement shall terminate forthwith, and any stock held by the Publishers shall be remaindered in accordance with the provisions of this Agreement, whereupon the Proprietors shall be entitled to enter into agreement with a third party to publish the new edition.'

Reprints

The same point can be made with regard to reprints:

'The price of any future reprint or new edition of the Work shall be the subject of a separate agreement between the Proprietors and the Publishers, except that the unit price paid by the Publishers to the Proprietors shall not be less than 25% of the Publishers' retail price.'

The Sale of the Publishers' Stock to Book Clubs

For obvious reasons publishers sometimes wish to sell off surplus stock to book clubs, and if the quantities involved are moderate this procedure may be acceptable. But an open-ended provision to this effect in the contract should be resisted.

Arbitration

A clause providing for arbitration is sometimes included, although rarely invoked:

'Any question or difference arising between the parties concerning the meaning of this Agreement or the rights and liabilities of the parties shall be referred to a single arbitrator in London to be agreed between the parties. Failing such agreement within 30 days of the request by one party to the other such reference shall be to an arbitrator appointed by the Chief Executive for the time being of the Publishers Association. The decision of such arbitrator shall be final and binding upon the parties. Any reference under this Clause shall be deemed to be a reference to arbitration in accordance with the provisions of the Arbitration Act 1996 or any statutory modification or re-enactment thereof.'

See also Precedent One, Clause 30.

It should be borne in mind that arbitration is costly. The arbitrators require high fees and in practice, frequently owing to other commitments, take a considerable time to determine any case referred to them. The courts have set time limits, and there are several judges experienced in publishing/copyright matters to whom publishing cases are normally referred. It is always possible for the parties to agree to arbitration where it is appropriate, but packagers have often been reluctant to agree to the inclusion of a general arbitration clause in the agreement.

PRECEDENT FIFTEEN

International Co-edition Agreement

A co-edition is normally a full-colour, illustrated project conceived by one publisher who then approaches one or more overseas partners with a view to licensing the book to them and organising the simultaneous printing of editions for all co-edition partners in order to achieve economy of scale. A simple co-edition could consist of a British publisher co-ordinating the printing of its own edition with another English language edition for a publishing partner in the USA, or a more complex arrangement whereby the originating publisher prints for several partners, perhaps including US and foreign language licensees. The following precedent covers a co-edition produced for a foreign language partner.

The originating publisher makes a substantial investment in developing the project and will carry responsibility for payment for the combined printings; it will therefore be crucial to consider carefully at what stage payments will be received from the various co-edition partners (see note to Clause 9).

Since the last edition, changes in printing and production have meant that most books are now printed from plates produced directly from electronic files, doing away with the need for film. As formats for these files will no doubt change and develop over the next few years, the specifications have been left deliberately vague in the precedent, but co-edition partners will need careful and detailed instructions on how material for their edition is to be supplied by and received by the originating publisher.

The other digital development that needs consideration is the evolution of eBooks and mobile phone or computer software applications (apps) in the area of full-colour reference material. At the time of writing, these apps are still in their infancy and it is not clear how many print publishers will wish to or have the capability to publish in this way, so originating publishers may not want to grant their co-edition partners the right to publish or sub-license in electronic formats. However, as eBooks and apps develop, the availability of an eBook or app within a territory could adversely impact upon sales of the print edition (for example, a cookery app showing recipes being cooked could reduce sales of the equivalent cookery book), so co-edition partners may need reassurance that you will not licence an eBook or app in competition with their printed edition.

Preamble

If the work does not yet exist as a finished book, or is not yet fully delivered to the proprietors, it will be necessary to add a description of the material, with detailed specifications, including the number and type of illustrations, format, paper etc. since these will be crucial to a co-edition.

Proprietors may want to reinforce the fact that the licence is limited to a specific edition of the book in question. Although it is usually preferable to continue to license subsequent editions to the same licensee, this limitation enables alternative arrangements to be made for a new edition of a book which is likely to need regular revision or updating, if the original licensee proves unsatisfactory.

1. Grant of Rights

Form

As the proprietors will be providing the publishers with printed copies under the terms of Clause 7, it is possible to specify an exact format here (e.g., hardback with or without jacket, or paperback). The publishers may, however, want to retain 'volume rights' in this clause as reassurance that you do not intend to license an alternative format to another licensee in the territory.

Territory

In the case of languages which are national languages in more than one country (e.g., Portugal and Brazil, Spain and Argentina, etc), it may be advisable to limit the licence by territory. Any licence to a US or other English language publisher will need a detailed schedule of territories to show clearly where each publisher has exclusive rights and which territories are open-market for both English language editions.

2. Duration of Licence

The aim of the contract is to enable the proprietors to supply the publishers with physical copies, and to continue to resupply further copies as required provided that agreement can be reached on timing and price. The life of the licence is therefore tied to the availability of copies: it would be unrealistic to grant a licence for the full term of copyright under these circumstances, although the term might be extended if a reprint licence is subsequently granted to the publishers under the terms of Clause 11. In practice, allowing the manufacturing control of a book of this kind to pass from the proprietors to the publishers is not desirable, although it may sometimes be a means of continuing the life of the book if agreement on the timing and pricing of manufacture by the proprietors cannot be reached (see Note to Clause 11).

3. Accuracy of Translation

No changes to the original text should be made without the prior permission of the proprietors.

In certain cases it may be advisable to reserve the right to approve the text of the translation in manuscript form prior to the proprietors commencing production of copies for the publishers, provided the proprietors or the author are competent to judge the quality of the translation. Such approval should not be unreasonably withheld or delayed. It should be established at an early stage of the negotiations whether the proprietors require such approval, as any delay may affect the co-edition production schedule for this and perhaps for other editions which are being co-ordinated with this printing.

MEMORANDUM OF AGREEMENT made this [*number*] day of [*month*] 20 [*year*] between [*company name*] of [*address*] ('the Proprietors', of the one part and [*company name*] of [*address*] ('the Publishers') of the other part

Whereby it is mutually agreed between the parties for themselves and their administrators and assigns or successors in business where the context so admits as follows concerning a translation which the Publishers wish to issue in the [*language*] language ('the Translation') of a work at present entitled [*title*] [*number*] Edition ('the Work') by [*name*] ('the Author') which is/is to be published in the [*language*] language by the Proprietors.

1. Grant of Rights

In consideration of the payments set out in the attached purchase order ('the Purchase Order') which shall form part of this agreement ('the Agreement') and in Clause 12 below the Proprietors grant to the Publishers the exclusive right and licence to publish the Translation in [*hardback/paperback/volume*] form and to sell copies of the Translation throughout the following territories: [*list territories*].

2. Duration of Licence

Subject to the terms of Clauses 11, 13, 14, 17, 19 and 23 hereof, the licence granted in this Agreement shall last for a period of [*number*] years from the date of this Agreement. The Agreement may be renewable thereafter subject to the mutual agreement of terms between the parties.

3. Accuracy of Translation

The Publishers shall arrange for the translation of the Work to be made at their own expense faithfully and accurately by a qualified and competent translator, whose name and qualifications shall be sent to the Proprietors for approval. The Publishers undertake that no abridgement of, alterations and/ or additions to the Work shall be made without the prior written consent of the Proprietors. The Publishers, if requested to do so, shall submit the text of the Translation to the Proprietors for approval prior to the commencement of production of the Translation.

4. Content of the Work and Clearance of copyright material

This clause is intended to alert both parties to the need to agree which party is to obtain permission from and pay any required permissions fees due to third parties, and indeed to remind them in the first place that such costs may have to be paid. Given the time constraints of the production schedule for a heavily-illustrated co-edition project where other foreign publishers may also be involved, it would seem advisable for the proprietors to be responsible for the work of all permissions clearance required, rather than to be dependent on each licensee undertaking the clearance work for his own market. However, the proprietors must then decide whether the full cost for clearance for each market should be quoted to the licensees in each country as a separate item, or whether it should be included in the unit cost quoted to each customer.

5. Acknowledgments

While the proprietors will be manufacturing copies for the publishers, the correct form of acknowledgment to the author and the proprietors, plus a correct copyright line should be set out for inclusion in the translated text which the publishers will supply to the proprietors.

6. Provision of Translated Text and Approval of Proofs

The proprietors will need to brief the publishers carefully on the exact form in which the text of the translation is to be supplied; it is likely that the exact details for this will be agreed separately from the contract. The question of whether items such as black rules or decorations within the text are part of the illustration layout or of the text to be supplied by the publisher must be made clear in advance. The publishers will need to be supplied with the UK text and illustrations (low resolution images) in position as an electronic file, to prepare the layout of their translation. The publishers will then overwrite the UK text in the file with their typeset translation, working round the illustrations, or will have their translation typeset using the grid provided. They will then supply the proprietors with a file with the translated text set and in position round the illustrations together with a printout of the translated version. When supplying fonts for use by the publishers you need to ensure that the publishers (and not just the proprietors) have the proper licence to use such fonts. The deadline for the supply of material to the proprietors should be a contractual matter since late supply of material from one foreign partner could jeopardise the whole schedule for a multi-language co-edition.

The proprietors should supply the publishers with proofs or ozalids of the translation by an agreed date and the publishers must in turn approve those proofs or identify and correct any errors within an agreed period from their receipt so that final production may go ahead on time.

4. Content of the Work and Clearance of Copyright Material

All detail as to the manner of illustration, design and production of the Work will be left to the sole discretion of the Proprietors in consultation with the Publishers, subject to the approval stages specified below and in the Purchase Order. [*The Proprietors/the Publishers*] shall be responsible for obtaining, wherever necessary, permission for the use in the Translation of copyright literary or artistic material incorporated in the Work, and [*the Proprietors/ the Publishers*] shall be responsible for paying any fees required for such permissions and for ensuring that appropriate acknowledgment is made in the Translation.

5. Acknowledgments

The Publishers undertake that the name of the Author shall appear in its customary form with due prominence on the title page and on the binding and jacket/cover of every copy of the Translation. On the reverse of the title page shall appear the following copyright notice: '© [*name of copyright owner*] [*date*]' together with the title of the Work in English, and the following acknowledgment: 'Published by arrangement with [*name of Proprietors*]'.

6. Provision of Translated Text and Approval of Proofs

6.1 Following receipt of the text of the Work for translation, the Publishers shall supply the Proprietors with the text of the Translation typeset and in position and their complete jacket/cover artwork to the Proprietors' required specifications no later than the date specified in the Purchase Order. The Publishers shall have the right to design an alternative jacket/cover for the Translation, and shall submit the jacket/cover design to the Proprietors for prior approval. Any costs incurred by the Proprietors in originating and proofing the Publishers' jacket shall be charged to the Publishers.

6.2 The Proprietors shall supply the Publishers with low resolution proofs/ozalids of the Translation for their approval in accordance with the dates laid out in the Purchase Order. The Publishers shall confirm their approval by fax or e-mail or supply any amendments to the Proprietors within [*number*] working days of the receipt of the proofs/ozalids. Corrections or amendments to material previously approved by the Publishers shall be charged to the Publishers.

7. Supply of Copies

The exact details of pricing, number of copies, delivery dates etc are, in this contract precedent, shown in an attached purchase order alongside exact physical specifications for the translation (details of format, extent, paper, binding, packing etc). This purchase order forms part of the agreement, but allows for simple changes to order quantity or dates to be reflected in a replacement purchase order without a complicated addendum to the agreement. It also makes the addition of purchase orders for subsequent reprints easier.

In some cases the proprietors may agree to supply an additional quantity of books free of charge, for promotional use by the publishers, or to add further copies at the run-on price (i.e., not including a contribution to the proprietors' plant costs).

The exact terms of supply are crucial and must be clearly agreed between the parties and set out in the purchase order: whether the price is royalty inclusive or exclusive (an exclusive deal will necessitate the inclusion of Clause 12 and modifications to several other clauses); whether export packing is included; whether the price is ex-works (if so, the printing location must be specified); FOB (free on board) a designated port in the country of manufacture, in which case the proprietors' responsibility will end on delivery into the publishers' nominated shippers; CIF (cost, insurance and freight) a designated port in the country of the publishers, who will then be responsible for the cost of offloading, customs clearance and onward transport into their own warehouse. It is less usual for the proprietors to quote a price delivered into the publishers' warehouse as the proprietors are not normally familiar with local transportation facilities, but this is becoming more common when a co-edition is being printed in and delivered to a location in mainland Europe, and does not require shipment by sea. This is often defined as DDU (delivered duty unpaid): responsibility for any customs clearance payments still lies with the publishers.

It is vital that if the proprietors alter the printing location all the co-edition partners should be warned immediately, since it may adversely affect shipping costs.

It is also vital that before a price per copy is agreed any specific requirements by the publishers which would not normally be provided (e.g., a different jacket design, shrink-wrapping or individual cartoning, if this is not standard) are discussed since they will affect the price.

It is important for the proprietors to specify how long the price quoted is valid for; if the publishers fail to deliver the film or disk or approve ozalids of the translation by the required deadlines, their order may not be included in the co-edition and any reduction in the total print run may affect the price quoted to all participants. A licensee who fails to meet required deadlines cannot expect the proprietors to hold to the same unit price if he is to supply the copies at a later date.

This clause may include a provision for the publishers to increase their order provided that this is confirmed before the paper cut-off date. Such copies may be supplied at a run-on price which would facilitate the onward sale of copies to a book club or special customer by the publishers.

Paper prices can escalate suddenly, which is particularly risky for proprietors quoting prices as much as two years ahead of the date of printing. If there is a substantial period between quoting and delivery, proprietors may be able to include the following clause in their contracts:

> 'The unit price specified per copy is current, but if, due to circumstances beyond the Proprietors' control, increases in the costs of paper and printing come into effect between this date and the date of printing copies of the Translation then the unit price may be revised to an upward limit of [number] per cent to cover the actual increases.'

Over- or Under-Supply

Since the final quantity produced by the printer may be over or under the exact quantity ordered, provision is made for the acceptance of up to an agreed percentage variance. A variance of 5% is generally considered acceptable. It is important to note that a distinction

7. Supply of Copies

The Proprietors undertake to supply to the Publishers copies of the Translation in the quantities, in the format and at the cost specified in the Purchase Order with the Publishers' imprint *plus a further* [*number*] *copies free of charge/at the run-on price specified in the Purchase Order*, all such copies to conform substantially to the specifications in the Purchase Order. The Proprietors will also supply an additional [*number*] of jackets free of charge as specified in the Purchase Order.

The price agreed for the copies will hold provided that the Publishers supply all necessary material for the Translation and approvals by the relevant dates specified in the Purchase Order. The Proprietors shall endeavour to deliver the exact quantity ordered of the Translation, but a variance over or under of [*number*] per cent of this quantity shall constitute full delivery and shall be charged for at the agreed price.

The price per copy is based on the exchange rate specified in the Purchase Order. Should the exchange rate at the time that payments from the Publishers to the Proprietors become due vary from this by more than 5 per cent the net difference between the 5 per cent and the actual currency alteration will be divided equally between the Proprietors and the Publishers.

Should the Publishers wish to increase their order above the agreed number of copies they shall inform the Proprietors by the paper cut-off date specified in the Purchase Order and such copies shall be supplied *at the run-on price specified per copy/a price to be agreed.*

The price specified includes the provision to the Publishers of the advance material specified in the Purchase Order free of charge. The Proprietors will, on request and where possible, provide advance jackets and other promotional materials for sales purposes in advance of bulk shipment of the Translation at a price to be mutually agreed.

---

should be drawn between an additional allowance of 'free' copies (usually provided to cover review copies or a small number of damaged copies) and a true over- or under-supply by the proprietors' printers.

When prices and profit-margins are tight, a fluctuation in the exchange rate can cause problems for either proprietors or publishers. The safest way for the proprietors to protect their margins is to quote the unit price in the currency of the country in which the translation is being printed, but this may not always be practical. The range of printing locations used today may mean that in any single co-edition deal three currencies are involved: that of the proprietors, that of the publishers, and that of the printing location. A fluctuation of more than 5% in either direction would seem a fair point for the parties to share the differential.

8. Approval of Advance Copies and Delivery of Bulk Shipment

8.1 Provision should be included here for the supply of an agreed number of advance copies and the parties should agree on whether these will be standard copies as they come off the production line or early handbound copies if the production schedule is particularly tight. The method of despatch of these copies should be agreed and the publishers required to inform the proprietors of their approval or of any problems immediately on receipt of the advance copies and before the bulk shipment date outlined in 8.2.

8.2 A realistic schedule for bulk shipment must be agreed between the parties, although the proprietors would be unwise to agree to a date 'not later than … ', particularly if several partners are involved in the co-edition. A firm deadline should, however, be imposed for the provision of shipping and documentation instructions by the publishers. The proprietors are further protected in the following Clause 8.3 against delays that are outside their control, though some publishers may insist on a final delivery deadline within a number of months.

9. Payment

The payment terms for a deal may vary greatly according to the title in question, the level of investment by the proprietors, and the relationship between the parties. One arrangement might be one-third of the total amount on signature of the contract, one-third on commencement of production, on receipt of the translation or by an agreed date, and one-third on shipment of the copies. An alternative might be half on signature of the contract and half an agreed number of days after shipment. Some proprietors may be prepared to agree to accept full payment an agreed number of days after receipt of the copies by the publishers. However, as considerable investment is often involved on the part of the proprietors, in origination costs, paper purchase and printing costs, it is reasonable for the publishers to offset some of those costs by paying a proportion of the total at an early stage. It is always wise to obtain both bank and trade references when dealing with a new licensee; if there is any doubt, payment could be required against an irrevocable letter of credit drawn on a bank in the country of the proprietors. It may be wise to ensure that the stage payments received by the time that printing commences are sufficient to cover the printing cost. For added protection against a publisher defaulting on payments proprietors may want to add a clause specifying that legal title in the books passes to the publisher only on receipt of payment for the copies, although the risk of loss or damage should pass to the publishers on delivery.

10. Complaints

While it is hoped that the publishers will have reported any problems on quality as soon as the advance copies are received, it is nevertheless essential that any problems with the bulk consignment, for example, shortages, printing or binding faults or damage in transit, should be reported to the proprietors promptly so that they can take up any such problems with the printer or the shipping agent.

8. Approval of Advance Copies and Delivery of Bulk Shipment

8.1 The Proprietors shall supply the Publishers with [*number*] advance copies of the Translation by post/courier/airfreight as soon as production is completed. The Publishers shall confirm their approval or notify the Proprietors of any complaints immediately on receipt of such advance copies and in advance of shipment of the bulk of the copies of the Translation.

8.2 The Proprietors undertake to deliver the copies of the Translation in bulk to the delivery address specified in the Purchase Order on or around the delivery date agreed in the Purchase Order provided that the Publishers supply full packing, documentation and shipping instructions by the dates agreed in the Purchase Order. Delivery shall be to one address only unless agreed in advance with the Proprietors.

8.3 If the Proprietors cannot meet the agreed delivery date due to circumstances beyond the Proprietors' control, the delivery date may be extended by the period of the delay. The Proprietors will endeavour to keep the Publishers advised promptly of any variation in the delivery date.

8.4 The prices and delivery schedule set out in the Agreement and Purchase Order are based on the Publishers' participation in a co-edition of the Work. If the Publishers fail to deliver or approve material within the agreed time, the Proprietors shall be at liberty to amend the delivery date for the copies and/or to pass on any additional costs incurred in producing the copies of the Translation separately, without prejudice to any claim which the Proprietor may have for damages or otherwise.

9. Payment

Payment for the copies shall be made according to the schedule laid out in the Purchase Order. If the Publishers shall fail to pay to the Proprietors sums due by the dates specified, the Publishers agree to pay to the Proprietors interest on such sums overdue equal to [*number*] per cent above the current base rate until such payment is received.

10. Complaints

Any complaint regarding the quality or condition of the bulk shipment of copies of the Translation or any shortage in delivery of copies must be submitted in writing to the Proprietors within one month of receipt of the shipment. In the absence of any notification within this period the Proprietors have the right to assume that the Publishers have accepted full delivery of the shipment to their satisfaction.

11. Re-orders

It is obviously in the interests of the proprietors to continue to manufacture copies for the publishers if sales of the translation prove successful, and it will be necessary to canvass each co-edition partner regularly so that their needs can be co-ordinated, either with the proprietors' own reprint needs or so that several overseas editions can be printed together.

Provision is, however, included here for production material to be provided to the publishers to enable them to continue printing the translation themselves if it proves impossible to reach agreement on price and delivery date for future orders. This switch of manufacturing responsibility is usually only allowed as a last resort, since it reduces the potential number of partners in the co-edition; it has also been known to lead to a situation where the publishers then offer to print for other co-edition partners. Although they could not proceed with this without permission from the proprietors, a licensee might be able to undercut the printing prices offered by the proprietors and it would then be difficult to justify maintaining control of the production. On the other hand, if the proprietors cannot offer satisfactory prices and schedules on reprints to the co-edition partners, the proprietors may on occasion be able to join a co-edition organised by a licensee.

12. Royalties

This clause should be inserted only if the price agreed is royalty exclusive. A royalty-inclusive price would require no further accounting to the proprietors, who would receive full payment whether the translation sold well or not. There is still, however, an argument for the proprietors being kept informed on sales of the translation, if only to keep track of when further copies might be required (see Clause 13).

If royalties are payable, an advance should be paid; this would usually be paid in full on signature of the contract, although a larger advance could perhaps be split half on signature and half on publication or by an agreed date. It is important to make it clear that this advance relates only to royalty payments and not to payment for the copies supplied. The royalty advance is forfeit if the publishers breach the contract in any way.

Any variation agreed between the parties (e.g., the royalty being calculated on the net amount received by the publishers rather than on the catalogue retail price) would have to be specified in this clause. The wording 'catalogue retail price' is aimed to allow for any system of pricing, whether minimum price, fixed price or not. In some countries the price on which the royalty is based will be less VAT (value added tax) or similar local sales tax.

Royalty rates are often lower than UK rates to allow for the cost of translation. It is customary for the royalty rates to escalate after an agreed level of sales. The royalty percentages and the level and number of escalation points are, of course, open to negotiation between the parties. It is customary for different royalty rates to apply for hardback and paperback editions.

11. Reorders

11.1 Should the Publishers require further copies of the Translation in the original format or in any other format the Proprietors agree to supply such copies at a price to be mutually agreed between the parties on a date to be agreed when the order for such copies is placed. The Proprietors agree to supply additional copies of the Translation to the Publishers for sale to book clubs or other special customers within the Publishers' territories at a price to be mutually agreed, provided such quantities are confirmed before the paper cut-off date specified in the Purchase Order.

11.2 The Publishers shall not cause the Translation to be printed for themselves or any sub-licensee or cause the Translation to be produced or printed in any form in whole or in part without the prior written consent of the Proprietors.

11.3 If the parties are unable to agree on the price or delivery date for such copies, the Proprietors may at their sole discretion supply the Publishers with production material for the Work at a price to be mutually agreed, and grant the Publishers the right to arrange for printing of copies of the Work for themselves, and the Publishers shall pay royalties to the Proprietors on all copies of the Work sold by them from any subsequent printing at a rate to be mutually agreed.

****For Royalty Exclusive Deal*

12. Royalties

The Publishers shall make the following payments to the Proprietors in accordance with the terms of Clause 24 below:

12.1 The sum of [*amount*] which shall be in advance and on account of any royalties which may become due to the Proprietors under this Agreement, payable on signature of this Agreement by the Publishers. The said payment in advance is not recoverable in the event of any default by the Publishers in carrying out the terms of this Agreement.

12.2 On the Publishers' catalogue retail price excluding any sales tax of all copies of the Translation sold by the Publishers:

(i) a royalty of [*number*] per cent on the first [*number*] thousand copies sold;

(ii) a royalty of [*number*] per cent on all copies sold beyond the first [*number*] thousand;

13. Accounts

The exact wording of this clause will vary depending on whether the price quoted is royalty inclusive (in which case this clause is intended to secure regular sales reports) or exclusive (in which case this clause sets out payment requirements).

Accounting is commonly half-yearly in the Anglo-American tradition, although some academic publishers in these markets tend to account yearly. The tradition in mainland Europe is yearly accounting. This clause makes provision for examination of the publishers' books if required, although this is an expensive exercise and likely to be undertaken only if there is serious reason to believe that royalties are being under-reported.

12.3 No royalties shall be payable on copies of the Translation sold at cost price or less, given free of charge to the Proprietors, given away in order to promote the sale of the Translation, lost through theft or damaged or destroyed by fire, water, in transit or otherwise.

13. Accounts

Accounts/Statements for the sale of the Translation shall be made up *yearly/ half-yearly* by the Publishers to [*date/dates*] and the *account/statement* must be rendered (***together with any sums payable under the terms of Clause 12.2 above***) within three months of the accounting *date/s*. Accounts will show:

(i) the number of copies in stock if any at the beginning of the accounting period;

(ii) the number of copies sold during the accounting period;

(iii) the number of free copies given away during the accounting period;

(iv) the number of copies remaining in stock at the end of the accounting period

(***and accounts shall be paid in accordance with the terms of Clause 24 hereof***).

Should the Publishers default in the payment of any sums due from the Publishers to the Proprietors under this Agreement or Purchase Order and the Publishers have not within one month of written notification from the Proprietors paid any sums due this Agreement will automatically terminate and all rights granted by it shall, without further notice, revert to the Proprietors, without prejudice to any claim which the Proprietors may have for moneys due, for damages or otherwise.

The Proprietors or their authorised representative shall have the right upon written request to examine the records of account of the Publishers in so far as they relate to the sales and receipts in respect of the Translation, which examination shall be at the cost of the Proprietors unless errors exceeding 2 per cent of such sales and receipts in the last two preceding accounting periods to their disadvantage shall be found, in which case the cost shall be paid by the Publishers.

14. Failure to Publish

It should be remembered that the publishers will be receiving finished copies ready for sale and the publication time limit permitted may therefore be reasonably short, probably allowing no more than six months calculated from the expected delivery date of the books to the publishers. While there is a provision for cancellation of the contract in the case of failure to publish, in practice the interest of both parties must lie in the translation being published. Any exceptional circumstances which might lead to delay in publication should therefore be discussed between the parties at the earliest possible stage: for example, late delivery by the proprietors might lead to the publishers wishing to hold off publication until the next appropriate selling season. A postponement of publication for a deal negotiated on a royalty-exclusive basis will, of course, result in a delay of revenue to the proprietors.

15. Publication Details

This clause provides for the publishers to confirm details of the exact publication date and price to the proprietors, and also permits the proprietors to repurchase a limited number of copies of the translation. This can be a lifeline for proprietors trying to set up further printings of the work when copies of the proprietors' own edition are out of stock, pending a reprint or paperback edition.

It is suggested here that the proprietors will retain a number of copies for their own records and for the author before shipping copies to the publishers, so there should be no need for the publishers to send back copies of their edition for the author or proprietors.

16. Control of Publication

The overall management of the publication of the translation is controlled by the publishers.

17. Remainders

A publisher who has purchased a large quantity of a co-edition and then finds it very slow to sell may want to cut their losses and dispose of excess stock fairly rapidly, so the common limitation of 18 to 24 months may be resisted by the publishers. However, the proprietors should beware of overstocks being disposed of in other markets which could harm both their own sales and other licensees' sales of the work. For a remaindered edition of a co-edition the net amounts received are highly unlikely to exceed cost price. It should be remembered that no royalties will be due in the event of remaindering if the copies were supplied to the publishers on a royalty-inclusive basis.

14. Failure to Publish

The Publishers shall, unless prevented by circumstances outside their control, publish the Translation within [*number*] months of receipt of the bulk delivery of the Translation. If the Publishers fail to issue the Translation within that period all rights granted by this Agreement may at the sole option of the Proprietors and on notice in writing from the Proprietors to the Publishers revert to the Proprietors and on such notice any advance payments provided for in Clauses 9 and 12.1 above (including any outstanding unpaid portions) shall be forfeited, without prejudice to any claim which the Proprietors may have for moneys due, for damages or otherwise.

15. Publication Details

The Publishers shall provide the Proprietors with details of the actual date of publication and the catalogue retail price of the Translation. The Proprietors shall have the right to repurchase up to 50 copies of the Translation from the Publishers at the original purchase price and further copies at normal trade terms for internal or publicity use by the Proprietors, but not for resale. The Proprietors shall also be entitled to retain ten copies of the Translation at the Publishers' expense for presentation to the Author.

16. Control of Publication

The promotion, the manner and extent of advertisement, the number and distribution of free copies for the press or otherwise, pricing and terms of sale of the Translation issued by the Publishers shall be in the sole discretion of the Publishers who shall in all other respects (except as otherwise provided for in this Agreement) have the entire control of the publication.

17. Remainders

If, after a period of [*number*] months from the date of first publication of the Translation by the Publishers, the Translation shall in the opinion of the Publishers have ceased to have a remunerative sale, the Publishers shall, on giving notice in writing to the Proprietors, be at liberty to dispose of any copies remaining on hand as a remainder or overstock (***and shall pay to the Proprietors on such copies [*number*] per cent of the net amounts received by the Publishers, except that on any copies sold at cost price or less no royalty shall be payable***). In the event of the disposal of the Publishers' entire remaining stock under this provision, all rights in this Agreement shall revert to the Proprietors immediately without prejudice to any monies due to the Proprietors from the Publishers.

18. Subsidiary Rights

Care needs to be taken that the rights granted under this clause do not exceed those acquired in the head contract. The range of rights granted to a publisher may be more limited than in a normal US or translation sub-licence because the publishers are buying finished copies of the book.

The rights included in this clause do not include any licence involving the manufacturing of copies by a sub-licensee, for example, a book club or a paperback publisher in the publishers' market. This is logical since the contract presumes that all manufacture is controlled by the proprietors, at least initially. If additional copies were required for such purposes, the proprietors would expect to be asked to quote for the supply of those copies (see note to Clause 7 re increasing the order prior to the paper cut-off date).

It is important that the grant of these rights is subject to the approval of the proprietors, such approval not to be unreasonably withheld. Swift clearance would undoubtedly be necessary for a deal with a book club or for serial rights.

The share of income to the proprietors from the sale of such rights should be agreed with the publishers in advance. It is common for the revenue to be more equally split between publishers and proprietors than in normal translation or US licences. This clause requires that accounting for the income from subsidiary rights shall be made to the proprietors within an agreed number of days from the receipt of income by the publishers from their sub-licensees, as, if the contract is for books supplied royalty inclusive there will not be a regular accounting to the proprietors in which to include subsidiary rights income.

For book club deals it should be remembered that if copies have been sold to the publishers on a royalty-inclusive basis, there will be further royalty payment if those copies are sold on to a book club. If, however, copies have been supplied to the publishers on a royalty-exclusive basis, payment is due and will depend on the proposed arrangement between the publishers and the book club. If the book club buys copies from the publishers on a royalty-exclusive basis, the proprietors should receive a share of the royalty paid by the club to the publishers. If the book club buys copies from the publishers on a royalty-inclusive basis, the proprietors should receive a royalty on the unit price paid by the club to the publishers.

Both publishers and proprietors should be aware that whilst one or other party will have cleared rights and paid permission fees for illustrations and text for use within the book (see notes to Clause 4), such rights do not normally extend to use by a third party such as a newspaper. Consideration also needs to be given to the fact that the publishers will not have illustrative material that they can supply to a periodical – any request to use photos or artwork will have to be referred back to the proprietors.

19. Out of Print

A clear understanding between the parties as to exactly what 'out of print' means in the contracts they sign is important. If the translation is unavailable, no re-order has been placed with the proprietors and no arrangements have been made to supply production material to the publishers to enable them to manufacture themselves (Clause 11) the contract can be cancelled.

It is important to remember that the copyright in the translated text will normally lie with the publishers or in some cases with the translator. Unless arrangements are made for the proprietors to negotiate a transfer of the right to use that translation, any subsequent alternative arrangements made by the proprietors for an edition of the work in the same language would normally require the proprietors to refer any new licensee to the publishers or the translator for the reuse of the text of the translation.

18. Subsidiary Rights

The Proprietors grant to the Publishers the right to sub-license the following rights, subject to the payment to the Proprietors of the specified percentages:

(i) ***Book club rights where copies produced by the Proprietors are supplied by the Publishers on a royalty exclusive basis: [*number*] per cent of the royalty paid by the book club to the Publishers

(ii) ***Book club rights where copies of the Translation produced by the Proprietors are supplied by the Publishers on a royalty inclusive basis: [*number*] per cent of the price paid by the book club to the Publishers

(iii) Serial rights to newspapers and other periodicals:

- (a) First serial rights: [*number*] per cent
- (b) Second serial rights: [*number*] per cent

(iv) Text quotation rights: [*number*] per cent

(v) Anthology rights: [*number*] per cent

(vi) Digest and condensation rights: [*number*] per cent.

Any sub-licences granted under this clause are subject to the prior written approval of the Proprietors, such approval not to be unreasonably withheld and shall be limited to the language, territories and licence period specified in this Agreement. Any payment due to the Proprietors under this clause shall be remitted to the Proprietors within [*number*] days of receipt by the Publishers of such sums.

In the event that additional fees are payable to the sources of illustrations for their use in this respect or for publicity or other purposes, such fees shall be paid by the Publishers. Nothing in this Agreement will be construed as granting to the Publishers any rights in or to the illustrations, design, layout or artwork used in the Translation.

19. Out of Print

In the event of the Translation going out of print or off the market at any time during the period of this Agreement the Proprietors shall be at liberty to terminate this Agreement on giving the Publishers six months' notice to re-order copies of the Translation/purchase production material as provided for in Clause 11 above. If on the expiration of such period of six months no such arrangements have been made all rights granted under this Agreement shall revert to the Proprietors without prejudice to any moneys paid or due to the Proprietors.

20. Restrictions on Transfer

The rights cannot be transferred in any way except in the case of sub-licences properly granted under the terms of Clause 18.

21. Retained Rights

All rights not specifically granted in the contract are reserved by the proprietors. In the case of any book with potential as the basis for a film where those rights are not controlled by the proprietors, it would be advisable to add the following wording to this clause:

> 'The Publishers, who have no interest in or control of film rights, agree that a film company shall have the right, without compensation to the Publishers, to print and publish in the [*language*] language synopses (including quotations) of not more than 10,000 words for use in promoting the film but not for resale.'

22. Warranties and Indemnity

The proprietors here warrant that they control the rights in the language in question and that the book contains nothing likely to lead to legal action in terms of defamation, libel or breach of copyright. It is important that this warranty is limited to liability under the legislation in the country of the proprietors, since few publishers could be expected to have at their fingertips the detailed knowledge required to make such warranties under legislation worldwide.

This clause makes provision for the publishers to make changes if the contents of the book are deemed likely to lead to legal action in their own country.

23. Termination

This makes provision for cancellation following material breach of the contractual terms by the publishers or in the case of bankruptcy or cessation of business on the part of the publishers.

20. Restrictions on Transfer

This Agreement and the licence hereby granted may not be assigned or transmitted in whole or in part by the Publishers (with the exception of any authorised arrangements under the terms of Clause 18 above), nor shall the Translation be published under any imprint other than that of the Publishers as set out in this Agreement, without the prior written consent of the Proprietors.

21. Retained Rights

All rights in the Work whether now existing or which may hereafter come into existence which are not specifically granted to the Publishers in this Agreement are reserved by the Proprietors.

22. Warranties and Indemnity

The Proprietors hereby warrant to the Publishers that they have the right and power to make this Agreement and that according to English law the Work will in no way whatever give rise to a violation of any existing copyright or a breach of any existing agreement and that nothing in the Work is liable to give rise to a criminal prosecution or to a civil action for damages or any other remedy and the Proprietors will indemnify the Publishers against any loss, injury or expense arising out of any breach or alleged breach of this warranty by reason of publication or sale by the Publishers of the Translation pursuant to this Agreement. If in the opinion of the Publishers and on the advice of their legal advisers the Work contains any passage that may be reasonably considered actionable at law in the territories granted to the Publishers under this Agreement, the Publishers shall have the right upon prior written notice to the Proprietors to modify or to remove such passage from the Translation.

23. Termination

23.1 Should the Publishers at any time by themselves or anyone acting on their behalf be in material breach of any of the clauses or conditions set forth in this Agreement within [*number*] months after written notice from the Proprietors to rectify such breach, or

23.2 Should the Publishers be declared bankrupt, or make an assignment for the benefit of their creditors, or take advantage of any insolvency law in their jurisdiction, or if a receiver or trustee is appointed for their property, or if they liquidate their business (otherwise than in a voluntary liquidation for the purpose of and followed by reconstruction

24. Method of Payment

This clause provides instructions on the exact method of payment to the proprietors. If the currencies required for payment for copies of the translation (Clause 7) and any advance and royalty payments (Clause 12) are different, this will have to be specified in this clause. Advance and royalty payments may be taxed at source in some countries, in which case the publishers must provide appropriate documentation to substantiate this and to enable the proprietors to recover the deduction if fiscal legislation permits.

25. Notices

This clause specifies the form in which notice must be given and requires the parties to notify each other of any change of address.

26. Arbitration

Provision is made for arbitration in the initial stages of a dispute; if the problem cannot be resolved in this way, the ideal situation would be for any legal action to take place in the jurisdiction of the country of the proprietors. This is an important consideration during the early stages of negotiations with a new customer. The legislation of some countries does not permit a contractual requirement of this kind.

An alternative (but less satisfactory) provision might read as follows:

> 'Any legal action brought by either party to this Agreement against the other shall be brought in the jurisdiction of the registered business offices of the party against whom the action is brought and the laws of that jurisdiction shall apply.'

27. Applicable Law

Again, ideally the contract should specify that the contract is governed by the legislation of the country of the proprietors, but this may not always be possible.

within [*number*] months), or if they cease their usual operation for any reason, should a petition be presented or a meeting be convened for the purpose of considering a resolution for the making of an administrative order, the winding up or dissolution of the Publishers (otherwise than a voluntary liquidation for the purpose of reconstruction) then in such events all rights granted under this Agreement shall revert to the Proprietors forthwith and without further notice, without prejudice to all rights of the Publishers in respect of any contracts properly entered into by them with any third party prior to the date of such reversion, without prejudice to any claim which the Proprietors may have for damages or otherwise and without prejudice to any moneys already paid or then due to the Proprietors from the Publishers.

24. Method of Payment

All sums which may become due to the Proprietors under this Agreement shall be paid by the Publishers in [*currency*], without any deduction in respect of exchange, commission or any other cause by direct bank transfer to [*details of Proprietors' bank account*]. Should the Publishers be obliged by law to deduct tax they shall send a declaration to this effect with the relevant statement of account showing the amount deducted.

25. Notices

Any and all notices given hereunder shall be in writing and sent by telex, fax, e-mail, registered or certified mail, return receipt required, to the parties at their respective addresses herein specified. The parties undertake to notify each other of any change of address within thirty (30) days of such change.

26. Arbitration

If any difference shall arise between the parties touching the meaning of this Agreement or the rights and liabilities of the parties hereto, the same shall be referred to the arbitration of two persons (one to be named by each party) or their umpire, provided that any dispute between the parties hereto not resolved by arbitration or agreement shall be submitted to the jurisdiction of the [*territory*] courts.

27. Applicable Law

This Agreement shall be governed by and interpreted and construed in accordance with the laws of [*territory*].

28. Local Registration and Copyright Protection

This clause firmly places the responsibility for and expense of complying with any required local copyright registration procedures and the subsequent protection of rights on the shoulders of the publishers.

29. Restriction to Current Edition

It is recommended that the preamble limits the contract to the current edition of the work. In practice a co-edition for any subsequent edition could only be undertaken by arrangement with the proprietors since they will control the manufacturing; however, this clause reinforces the limited nature of the licence granted.

If, however, the relationship between the partners is good, the proprietors may wish to consider as an alternative the inclusion of an option clause which might read as follows:

> 'The Proprietors agree to grant to the Publishers the first option on the [*language*] language rights in the next edition of the Work. The Publishers undertake to give a decision within [*number*] days of receipt of a copy of the [manuscript/proofs/adequate advance material] for the new edition from the Proprietors. The terms for any licence for the next edition are to be the subject of separate negotiations between the parties.'

28. Local Registration and Copyright Protection

The Publishers agree to take all necessary steps to register the title of the Work in the name of the copyright owner under any national copyright laws at the sole expense of the Publishers. The Publishers also agree to secure the benefits of copyright protection under international copyright conventions that are available for such protection, and at their own expense to pursue all relevant rights at civil and criminal law against any person who infringes such copyright.

29. Restriction to Current Edition

This Agreement does not grant any rights with respect to subsequent editions of the Work.

AS WITNESS THE HANDS OF THE PARTIES

Signed...

Name (printed):.......................................

Position...

Date..

for the Publishers

Signed...

Name (printed):.......................................

Position...

Date..

for the Proprietors

Schedule

The purchase order to be attached to the co-edition contract lists all the details of the supply of the physical copies of the work to the publishers. It is important that any details that were 'approximate' at earlier stages of the negotiation – for example, the exact number of illustrations, or the exact dates for supply of material are tied down here. A co-edition publisher, for example, needs to be able to compare the final bound copies with the agreed specifications laid out here in order to approve or reject the books. Any proposed changes to, for example, the weight of paper to be used or the binding style, must be approved by the participating co-edition publishers. If necessary, samples of paper and binding material may be attached to the schedule. A sample schedule might read as follows:

The Translation	
Author:	J R Jones
Title:	An Illustrated Guide to Aircraft
Specifications	
Number of pages:	232pp plus xii pages of prelims
Number of illustrations:	420 colour photographs, 120 black and white line drawings
Trimmed page size:	234mm × 156mm (portrait)
Paper weight and type:	100gsm wood-free machine finished (sample attached)
Jacket/cover specifications:	4-colour laminated
Manner of printing:	4/4
Binding style:	Sewn in 16pp sections, cased, artificial cloth over 3mm boards, head and tail bands, coloured end-papers, imitation gold blocking on spine
Quantity to be supplied:	5,000 copies
Price and payment schedule	
Price:	GBP4.25 per copy
Run-on price:	GBP3.40 per copy
Royalty inclusive	
Shipping:	CIF Oakland, California, USA
Total purchase price:	GBP21,250 (twenty-one thousand, two hundred and fifty pounds sterling)
Payment stages and credit terms:	£5,312.50 payable on signature of contract and purchase order £5,312.50 payable on receipt of translated text £5,312.50 payable on notification of shipping of bulk copies £5,312.50 (to be adjusted for over- or under-delivery) sixty days from notification of shipping
Exchange rate:	£1. = US$1.60
Material to be provided by Proprietor:	Files in Quark or InDesign format with low-resolution images in place supplied by Proprietor
Files of translation to be supplied by Publisher:	Quark or InDesign format with text typeset in position, together with print resolution PDF of separate pages with all fonts embedded. Each page must include at least 3mm bleed.

Purchase Order

The Translation

Author:

Title:

Specifications

Number of pages: [*number*] pp plus [*number*] pp prelims

Number of illustrations:

Trimmed page size:

Paper weight and type:

Jacket/cover specifications:

Manner of printing:

Binding style:

Quantity to be supplied:

Price and payment schedule

Price: [*amount*] per copy run-on price: [*amount*] per copy

Royalty exclusive/inclusive

Shipping: *FOB [named place of printing]/CIF[named port of entry]/DDU [named delivery point]/ex-works [named place of printing]*

Total purchase price:

Payment stages and credit terms:

Schedule

Date of delivery of Proprietors' disks to Publishers for translation:	31 January 2012
Date of delivery of Publishers' translation:	31 March 2012
Date of delivery of proofs/ozalids for approval by Publishers	30 April 2012
Date shipping/packing/ invoicing instructions required:	31 May 2012
Paper cut-off date:	31 May 2012
Bound copy date:	31 August 2012
Delivery of bulk stock:	31 October 2012

Advance material

Advance material supplied free of charge:	Two hand-bound copies by courier on completion of printing; 5% extra jackets supplied with bulk shipment
Additional advance material required by Publisher:	50 advance copies by air-freight by 30 September 2012 (to be supplied at cost plus cost of freight)

Delivery instructions

Publishers' address:

Flypast Press, Pittsburgh, PA 01786; Contact: Bob Jones; Tel: 001 XXX XXXX; Fax: 001 XXX XXXX; E-mail: rjones@flypastbooks.com

Invoicing address and document requirements:

One set of original documents by courier to publishers' address above, second set of original documents to customs clearance agent below. Copy to be sent by fax to Bob Jones at fax number above.

Publishers' customs clearance agent:

Book Clearance House, 11935 Dock Drive, Oakland, CA 80289; Contact: Arlene Brown; Tel: 001 XXX XXXX; Fax: 001 XXX XXXX; E-mail:arlene@bookclear.com

Packing and labelling instructions (any special requirements at additional charge):

Binder's parcels with ten copies per parcel, stacked on pallets and crated. All parcels to be marked with Title and ISBN.

Exchange rate:

Material to be provided by Proprietor and Publisher

Text for translation/disk/electronic files etc to be supplied by Proprietor [*exact specifications of format etc*]

Disk/electronic files of translation to be supplied by Publisher [*exact specifications of format etc*]

Schedule

Date of delivery of Proprietors' text to Publishers for translation

Date of delivery of Publishers' translated text:

Date of delivery of proofs/ozalids for approval by Publishers:

Date shipping/packing/ invoicing instructions required:

Paper cut-off date:

Bound copy date:

Delivery date for bulk stock:

Advance material

Advance material supplied free of charge:

Additional advance material required by Publisher (to be supplied at price to be mutually agreed):

Delivery instructions

Publishers' address, contact names and details

Invoicing address and document requirements

Publishers' customs clearance agent (if CIF) or nominated shipper (if FOB) (address and contact names and details)

Packing and labelling instructions (any special requirements at additional charge):

PRECEDENT SIXTEEN

Film, Television and Allied Rights: Option and Assignment Agreements

Since a publisher acts very largely as an agent for his (or her) author there is a special responsibility on the publisher to understand at least the basic elements of film rights dealings.

When the publisher handles subsidiary rights, he is on home ground, with a fairly sure sense of the extent and the value of the rights for which he is negotiating on his and his author's behalf. That sense may be conspicuously absent when the publisher deals with film rights: neither the extent nor the value of the rights may be at all clear to him. Many literary agents seek to exclude any dramatisation and documentary rights, **(see Precedent One, Clause 14 (xvi) for a definition)** from the package of rights granted to publishers. Not all authors, however, have agents and the publisher may find himself at times in the happy but embarrassing position of having acquired 'film, TV and allied rights' (see especially the note to Clause 1 of the Assignment below), of receiving strong (and perhaps unexpected) interest in those rights from a film or television company, and of having, in truth, little idea how to proceed.

To all such publishers and equally to their authors, this Precedent is dedicated. It has, together with the Notes, been drafted by Michael Ridley and Alan Williams of DLA Piper, Solicitors.

Introduction: who should enter into the film agreement?

Under the publishing agreement, the publisher's involvement in the film rights may come in a number of ways: the right to control; the right to negotiate; or, with the author retaining no interest other than a financial one, a full grant of the rights. All of these will last only as long as the publishing agreement or a properly drawn sub-licence is in force **(for such a grant, see Precedent One, Clause 14 (xvi))**. The former two (i.e., the right to control or the right to negotiate) are more often found than the last (a full grant of rights) and they leave the publisher in a far from satisfactory position. He does not then actually own the rights, but is left to negotiate for their exploitation without either being formally appointed an agent or being able to conclude the deal himself. Film rights (and this is the important point) involve the investment of such large sums of money into the film that purchasers and their financiers look very carefully at the legal title and the publisher's right to contract.

Unless the publisher has obtained a full grant of the rights (in the last of the three senses mentioned above) he should go back to the author for consent. In most cases, irrespective of whether consent is or is not required, the contract with the purchaser should actually be signed by the author (as the copyright owner) rather than by the publisher (as licensee or quasi-agent). The publisher, anyway, will not want or be able to contract as principal. First, he should not want to give the warranties usually required from the author/owner of the work, such as originality, defamation and so on, which impose material potential liability. Secondly, the publisher will not be the copyright owner. There are two final, cogent, reasons for ensuring that it is the author who actually signs the option/assignment to the film or television company: first, the usual form of publishing agreement is a licence which is terminable on the happening of a number of events – not only insolvency or breach of contract can cause termination, but also the title going out of print and, although there is usually a 'savings' clause to protect publishers in this situation, there should be no possibility that the ensuing reversion of rights can affect the film rights grant, particularly if that exposes the publisher to liability.

The second reason is that the Copyright, Designs and Patents Act, 1988 ('the CDPA') introduced moral rights into English law – the rights of paternity and integrity (**see in general Appendix H**). Those rights can be waived; not all publishers will seek such a waiver, nor all authors grant it, in respect of publishing rights. However, the film rights will hardly be marketable without such a waiver. At the very least, the author will have to join in the film rights grant not only as copyright owner, but in order to give such a waiver.

Putting the film proposal package together

Film and television producers rely upon a number of sources of material for their films: public domain material, copyright literary material and work specially commissioned. For present purposes, it is the second source which is relevant. Having acquired the copyright literary material, the prospective film producer will then arrange for a screenplay or teleplay writer to write a screenplay or teleplay based on it, that is, there will be an adaptation of the work. Section 21 of the CDPA contains a full definition of the word 'adaptation': it includes making a dramatic version of a literary work.

Because of the enormous production costs involved in making films and because of the large acquisition prices commonly paid, it is customary for a film producer to seek an option on the work; and for the rights owner to seek payment for that option in a sum usually around 10% of the purchase price.

The essence of an option agreement is that the producer buys the sole and exclusive option to acquire certain specific, pre-negotiated rights. It is essential that the terms of the assignment of those rights are not left to the future but are settled with, and at the same time as, the option agreement. An option to buy 'rights to be negotiated' and/or 'for a price to be agreed' is a present ticket to future confusion, uncertainty and expense.

The option period will normally run for around a year to 18 months and is often renewable for a further six months to a year on payment of a further fee. The first fee is usually paid in advance and on account of the final purchase price but not returnable, whereas the second fee (often about 5% of the purchase price), whilst still not returnable, is often *not* on account of the purchase price. There is no reason why this extension fee should not also be on account: if it is not, it is in effect a small penalty or price increase paid by the producer for 'overstaying his welcome'.

The package which the producer will want to put together before he can look for development or production finance is an option on the literary material; a screenwriter to make an adaptation into the screenplay; a director, a provisional budget and shooting schedule (which can only be prepared from the screenplay itself); and possibly, lead artists. The period of grace represented by the option period enables the producer to try to put that package together without having to commit large sums of money to the rights. If he is not successful in putting his package together and finding production finance, then his financial loss is limited to the option fee (and any screenwriters' fees) and, incidentally and not immaterially, the publisher and author are free to negotiate with third parties in the future, which they would not have been if the rights had been sold outright.

The rights

It is necessary at this stage to examine very briefly some of the relevant definitions contained in the CDPA and the way in which it approaches copyright. It extends protection to material in a number of specified categories, including literary, dramatic and musical works (defined in s 3), film and sound recordings (s 5), and broadcasts (s 6). Restricted acts are those acts in relation to a copyright work which, if done without the authorisation of the copyright owner, constitute an infringement of copyright. The restricted acts are set out in s 16. Briefly, they include copying the work, renting or lending it to the public, performing, showing or playing it in public, or communicating it to the public.

Section 5B of the Act defines a 'film' as a recording on any medium from which a moving image may by any means be produced. This could include a work produced electronically on CD-ROM or online, so there is scope for conflict here. See later on in the Introduction for further commentary on this.

Section 6 of the Act defines a 'broadcast' as a transmission by wireless telegraphy of visual images, sounds or other information which:

(a) is transmitted for simultaneous reception by members of the public and capable of being lawfully received by them; or

(b) is transmitted at a time determined solely by the person making the transmission for presentation to members of the public. Excepted from this definition, amongst other things, is any internet transmission unless it is a transmission taking place simultaneously on the internet and by other means; and a concurrent transmission of a live event.

The agreement by which film rights are acquired should, therefore, ideally be expressed in the above terms and grant or exclude rights according to the rights intended to be granted or excluded. For instance, it may be intended only to grant feature film rights, or only television rights (including or excluding cable and satellite rights), and so it is possible to seek great flexibility in the contract. The financier seeks somewhat less flexible ends: he wants as much as he can get in return for his potentially large investment.

Please note when referring to this precedent that it is drafted from the perspective of granting theatric film rights, i.e. an audio visual version of a book primarily intended to be shown in cinemas but also then to be exploited by other means. As a matter of copyright law the principles that apply to films are the same as those that apply to television film versions but the commercial practice for television film rights is quite different. We summarise some of the principal differences at the end of this introduction. This document does not attempt to deal with 'straight to DVD' or internet-only productions. The distinction is a fine but important one.

Distribution

Cable, satellite, DVD, Internet Protocol Television (IPTV) and Video on Demand (VOD) are methods of exploitation which have revolutionised the distribution of films to the public.

Very few channels are cable-exclusive and these rights will usually be treated as part of the package of television rights. Many channels are broadcast simultaneously today over terrestrial and satellite – and often cable – platforms, too.

Satellite transmission has a number of advantages including a high bandwidth or spectrum of frequencies and (many will say its disadvantage) a large transmission area or 'footprint'. Satellites beam to areas larger than national boundaries, a problem with which national governments, programme and copyright licensors and talent unions (among many others), have yet fully to grapple. Digital terrestrial television, which in the UK operates over the Freeview platform, is just the latest form of television transmission to a rooftop receiver, but is frequently referred to as a subset of television rights.

Internet exploitation is often captured by reference to online or IPTV usage. It is now a standard requirement of producers to be able to exploit their films by this means. Whilst this presents a number of issues both technical and legal for the producers and distributors, as far as authors are concerned this should be regarded as another revenue-generating opportunity in which they should expect to participate.

DVDs and VOD are beating the most immediate path to the consumer's door. While the idea of a rental right is already covered by the Act and the concept of a *droit moral* has long been established, the issue of an author's work being released on DVD has been specifically dealt with in the European Directive on Rental and Lending Rights. The aim of the rental right is to give both authors and actors a continuing remuneration from the later stages of the exploitation of their labour. The implementation of the law caused problems of interpretation and implementation for all those concerned in the licensing and exploitation of both the underlying and derivative works of a film released on DVD.

From implementation, performers, composers and authors of screenplays and underlying literary works as well as individual producers and principal directors of films all (for the sake of brevity now referred to as 'talent') have the exclusive right to prohibit the rental of copies of their work to the public (or at least to receive equitable remuneration in respect of rental).

The creation of this right should not necessarily be regarded as an additional bargaining tool in negotiating terms of involvement in a film because, in any agreement between talent and the corporate film producer and in the absence of any intention to the contrary, talent will be presumed to have transferred their rental right in relation to the film in return for the right to receive equitable remuneration, which will be payable by the person to whom the rental right has been transferred.

There has been much discussion about how the calculation of 'equitable remuneration' will be made. The Regulations fail to offer any specific guidance. It is not within the remit of these notes to provide that guidance in what is a complicated area. The introduction of rental and lending rights has taken place, in fact, with a much lesser impact than originally anticipated and 'equitable remuneration' has tended to be addressed by including acknowledgments by the rights owners that payments are inclusive of such entitlement.

All forms of exploitation are simply another way of bringing the product to the public. The standard grant of literary film rights in the past was usually wide enough to grant to the producer the right to use all forms of exploitation of the original which in essence are just other ways of reproducing or copying the original film, that is by exhibiting it to the public, broadcasting it, communicating it to the public or distributing it to the public by way of DVD or VOD (the acts, that is, restricted by copyright in a film). Whether that traditional grant was wide enough to include exploitation using the new technologies will depend, amongst other things, on the precise wording of the grant and the date of the grant.

The modern option agreement/assignment should now deal head-on with the question of the so-called electronic rights in so far as the publisher sees this form of exploitation as something that they can retain and exploit as a right in the text quite separate to the electronic exploitation of an audio visual version of the book. If they are *not* included in the grant but are reserved, it will be essential (for the producer) to ensure that their manner and timing of exploitation by the rights owner are controlled in order to reduce the risk of competitive marketing; and it will be necessary to face the question of whether some forms of electronic exploitation fall within the definition of 'film' under the CDPA, which might give rise to complications!

The Precedent offers a typical form of option agreement and, to show the essential elements, a simple form of assignment. It is not intended to be relied on without further, specialist advice. An assignment of film, (TV and allied) rights would normally be expected to be very much fuller and more complex, particularly if an American financier was involved or a multimillion dollar production budget was envisaged. Also, it should be anticipated that the warranties as to title, etc would be fuller, the wording of the grant much expanded, and so on. A licence only of television rights takes a different form, other considerations applying.

The detailed drafting of agreements for the grant of film (TV and allied) rights contains many pitfalls for the unwary. It is, therefore, always advisable where there is any doubt, whether about the form or the detail, to seek legal advice and preferably from a solicitor specialising in the business.

Television Film Rights

The main differences between grants of rights for television adaptations and those for films can be summarised as follows:

(1) The grant is usually by way of exclusive licence and not assignment.

(2) The licence is subject to a period as regards the right to make TV adaptations usually of between 10–15 years but is unlimited (though non-exclusive after the initial licence period) as regards the right to exploit that adaptation. This allows the rights owner to license future remakes of TV adaptations and for the maker of the original version to continue to exploit their doubtless by then 'classic' version.

(3) The grant does not usually allow for theatric exploitation – unless it is, for example, a one-off 90 minute adaptation and the parties specifically want to provide for the possibility of such use if the adaptation is a major success.

(4) Payment is not usually a percentage of the budget, as in the case of a theatric film, but a sum per hour (or relevant episode slot length) to accommodate varying numbers of episodes. Further income would typically either be a share of net receipts or residuals and repeat fees similar to those contained in the broadcasters' collective agreements with the Writers Guild of Great Britain.

(5) There should also be provision for either author-written or producer-created sequels to the narrative of the original book and a similar price per hour should be paid as for the rights to the main book as opposed to the reduced figures that are typically paid for film rights.

Preamble

'The Owner' will be the rights-owner, the owner of the copyright in the work; as explained in the introduction to this precedent this will not usually be the publisher. It will be the author or, in some cases, the company that owns his services. There is no reason why the publisher should not be joined into the agreement, first to give his/her consent to it and secondly to ensure that all payments are channelled through him/her; but not to give the grant or warranties other than limited warranties, for example, that he/she has not previously dealt with the rights.

The Option Agreement

1. and **2. Option/Extension/Exercise**

The initial option fee and period and extension fee and period, and the mechanics of how the period can be extended, should be clearly specified, and the rights assignment identified. There is no reason why further extensions, beyond the initial one, should not be negotiated but Owners usually want to caveat any additional extension beyond the first by requiring the purchaser to be able to demonstrate that material progress is being made towards production as a condition of the further extension i.e. the purchaser has raised development funding or can demonstrate that active negotiations are in progress with a production funder.

3. On Account

Whether or not the option fees are on account of the purchase price is negotiable and may depend on the circumstances. Option fees are rarely, if ever, returnable. The initial fee is usually 10% of the final purchase price, but can be any percentage. If the purchase price is itself a percentage of an unknown amount (i.e. the budget) then the option fee will be an agreed figure. An extension fee is often 5% and usually *not* on account.

THIS OPTION AGREEMENT is made the [*number*] day of [*month*] 20 [*year*]

BETWEEN:

(1) [*name*] (hereinafter termed 'the Owner', which expression includes his/her administrators, executors and successors in title), of [*address*]; and

(2) [*company name*] (hereinafter termed 'the Purchaser', which expression includes its successors in title and assigns) whose registered office is at [*address*].

NOW IT IS HEREBY AGREED as follows:

1. Option

In consideration of the sum of [*amount*] paid by the Purchaser to the Owner (receipt whereof the Owner hereby acknowledges) the Owner grants to the Purchaser the sole and exclusive option to acquire the rights specified in the draft Assignment annexed hereto as Exhibit A (referred to as the Assignment and identified by initials of the Purchaser and the Owner) on the terms therein specified in a [*story/novel/play*] written by [*the Owner*] ('the Author') entitled [*title*] ('the Work').

2. Extension/Exercise

2.1 At any time before the end of [*number of months*] from the date hereof the Purchaser may either:

(i) exercise this option by notice in writing to the Owner; or

(ii) extend the option for a further period of [*number of months*] by notice in writing to the Owner accompanied by payment of a further sum of [*amount*] and if the Purchaser so extends the option it may exercise the same by notice in writing to the Owner at any time before the end of the said further period.

2.2 Simultaneously with or as soon as practicable after exercise of the option the Purchaser shall at its expense deliver to the Owner engrossments of the documents required under Clause 4.1 below.

3. On Account

Sums paid to the Owner under Clause 1 hereof shall be on account of the monies specified in Clause 2 of the Assignment; sums paid under Clause 2 shall not be on account. Neither of the sums shall be returnable in any event.

4. Completion

Before getting the full payment on exercise of the option, the owner will be asked to deliver an executed engrossment of the assignment, and (if the copyright is registered in the US or if distribution in the US is anticipated and there is any likelihood that the US distribution may require registration) a short-form assignment which will be used for registration of the assignment in the US copyright register in Washington. Registration is no longer an essential prerequisite to maintenance of copyright in America, but is a sensible prerequisite to successful actions against copyright infringement there. Often, for the sake of tidiness and ease of administration, the short-form assignment is annexed to the main assignment when the option is signed but it is not essential that it should be. It reflects the main terms of the assignment and can, therefore, be prepared at any time. An example has *not* been included in this precedent.

A quitclaim is confirmation by a publisher that he/she does not maintain any claim over the film rights, that is, that the owner is entitled, so far as that publisher is concerned, to enter into the agreement. Strictly, this is not required where the original publisher enters into the assignment as owner of the rights (since in that case the publisher *does* have an interest in the rights and signifies his/her consent by the act of entering into the agreement), but in all other cases a prudent purchaser will demand quitclaims from all English language publishers. The form of the quitclaim is usually very standard and, provided there is authority in both the option agreement and the assignment for payment of all moneys to the publisher, there is no reason why it should not be given. Once again, it is usual (but not essential) that the wording of the quitclaim should be settled at the same time as the option.

Unusually, the purchaser does sometimes ask for quitclaims from the major foreign-language publishers also, but English language quitclaims will more often than not be sufficient.

5. Before Completion

Since this is only an option and *not* a grant of rights, this clause is required by the purchaser to allow him/her to prepare a screenplay. Otherwise, technically, he/she would be in breach of copyright in making an adaptation without the owner's consent. That consent is, of course, implied in the whole nature of the option agreement, but why leave anything open to argument? Conversely, the publisher should ensure that sufficient authority is given only to the extent necessary; what rights are included (i.e., film or TV or both) will depend on the deal.

6. Owner's Obligations

These warranties are the least that can be expected of the owner. The purchaser may require an *absolute* defamation warranty.

4. Completion

4.1 Within seven days of receipt of the said engrossments the Owner will at *his/her/its* expense:

(i) execute and deliver to the Purchaser an engrossment of the Assignment;

(ii) procure the execution of and delivery to the Purchaser of quitclaims in [the form annexed hereto as Exhibit B or] such [other] form as the Purchaser may approve by all English language publishers of the Work.

4.2 Upon receipt of the documents specified in paragraphs (i) and (ii) of Clause 4.1 above the Purchaser will:

(i) pay the consideration specified in Clause 2 of the Assignment to the extent that it is due at that date;

(ii) at the Purchaser's expense execute and deliver to the Owner a counterpart of the Assignment.

4.3 If the Owner fails to execute and deliver the said documents in accordance with Clause 4.1 above the Purchaser is hereby authorised by the Owner to execute the same on its behalf.

5. Before Completion

During the subsistence of this option and any extension thereof:

5.1 the Purchaser shall be entitled to make adaptations of the Work in the form of film treatments and scripts and to show the same to third parties who may be interested in the production and/or exploitation of a film based on the Work;

5.2 the Owner will at the request of the Purchaser deduce his/her/its title to the rights that are the subject of this option.

6. Owner's Obligations

6.1 The warranties and undertakings set out in Clause 3 of the Assignment shall be deemed incorporated herein and shall be binding on the Owner throughout the subsistence of this option.

6.2 During the subsistence of this option the Owner shall not dispose of or encumber the said rights or do anything that would if the option is

7. Exercise and Expiry of Option

7.1 This clause, if included, will allow the owner to buy in all scripts or treatments if the option expires without being exercised. He/she will only want to do this if there is someone else interested in using that material. At this stage there will be two separate copyrights involved, the copyright in the underlying literary work (i.e., in the published work itself) and the copyright in any script or treatment. The purchaser cannot exploit his/her copyright in the script or treatment without acquiring the underlying copyright and the owner cannot use the script or treatment without first acquiring the rights therein. It follows that the purchaser, if his/her option has expired, will usually be only too willing to sell any scripts or treatments and the only purpose of this clause is to give a contractual right to the owner (which he/she would not otherwise have) and to set a limit to the price demanded. The latter can, of course, work both ways.

7.2 The period during which this buy-in option should run is negotiable. If the principle of the option is conceded, then the period might as well be long as short. After 80 years (the maximum period to avoid offending the risk against perpetuities) the material could well be in the public domain, simply through the passage of time.

8. Assignment

(1) The purchaser will seek to insist on the right to assign. Under English law he/she will remain liable for his/her obligations notwithstanding the assignment; he/she cannot escape those obligations unless the contract specifically so provides, that is, unless there is a novation – a new contract. Provision is not necessary (though it is often found) in this clause that the purchaser will remain liable.

(2) Some owners seek to limit the right to assign in an effort to control the ownership of their rights. This would be relevant where the option was being granted to a particular producer with the intention that only he/she may make the film. Even he/she will need the limited right to assign the option to his/her financiers. Sometimes the qualification 'no assignment without the owner's prior written consent, such consent not to be unreasonably withheld' is seen. That compromise rather begs the issue – there is plenty of scope for argument over 'unreasonably' in that context.

9. Agent

The agency clause is most important if, as will usually be the case, the publisher wants all moneys paid to him, so that he can deduct his share before passing the balance on to the owner (i.e., usually, the author of the original work). In the absence of the agency clause a purchaser would have to pay monies direct to the owner. If the publisher is not a party, then he/she only has an action in damages against the owner if the monies are not paid to the publisher. But the publisher would be able to enforce the payment if he/she were a party.

The purchaser should not be too ready to accept the agent's signature on the Assignment, because that would bring the option agreement on to the purchaser's title documents to the film rights to prove valid execution of the assignment. In any event, if a US short-form assignment is required (see note 4) it should be signed by the owner personally because signature by an agent may not comply with US regulations.

In practice option agreements are often varied, especially by extension, and such variations are often agreed on behalf of an owner by his agent. It may be vital for a purchaser to be able to prove that the owner is bound by an extension. The proviso permitting revocation of the agency is desirable in the interest not only of the owner, but also the purchaser because otherwise the purchaser might be placed in a dilemma if the owner did revoke the agent's authority. In that case, unless the authority for payments under the next clause was expressed to be irrevocable, the purchaser would be bound to pay in accordance with the owner's new instructions, but the original agent might feel aggrieved and, under some laws (e.g., US), might claim that he had a third-party interest entitling him to continued payments so that he could continue to deduct his commission before accounting to the owner.

exercised prevent *him/her/it* assigning them to the Purchaser or cause the warranties in the Assignment to be untrue.

7. Exercise and Expiry of Option

7.1 If this option expires without being exercised the Owner shall have an exclusive option to purchase all the Purchaser's rights in any treatments or scripts based on the Work subject to the terms on which the Purchaser may hold such rights.

7.2 The Owner's option under sub-clause 7.1 may be exercised by written notice at any time before the end of [*number*] years from the date of this Agreement.

7.3 The price payable by the Owner upon exercise of the option under sub-clause 7.1 shall be a sum equal to all sums paid by the Purchaser in connection with the acquisition of the relevant rights plus interest thereon at [*number %*] over the [*name of bank*] base rate from time to time and the Owner shall indemnify the Purchaser against liability for any future payments that may become due in respect of such rights.

8. Assignment

The Purchaser shall be entitled to assign the benefit of this Agreement to any third party.

9. Agent

The Owner hereby appoints [the Publisher] ('the Agent') as his agent in all matters relating to this Agreement including any variation or extension hereof [and execution and delivery to the Purchaser of the Assignment under sub-clause 4.1(i) above].

[PROVIDED THAT this appointment may be revoked or varied at any time by written notice from the Owner to the Purchaser.]

10. Payment Instructions

The Owner hereby [irrevocably] instructs the Purchaser to pay all monies due to him hereunder to [*name of Agent*] whose receipt shall be a good discharge to the Purchaser [, unless the Purchaser has previously received written notice of revocation of such instructions].

11. Notices

Any notice to be given hereunder shall be duly given if:

(i) delivered personally; or

(ii) mailed by first class pre-paid mail to the address stated in this Agreement of the party to be served which notices shall be deemed to have arrived in due course by post; or

(iii) sent by facsimile to the addressee's number notified to the sender by the addressee or recorded in any official index of facsimile numbers which notices shall be deemed to have arrived on the date of transmission if not later than one hour before close of business at the addressee on a business day or otherwise on the next business day at the addressee provided the sender does not receive any indication that the message is incomprehensible.

12. Rights of Third Parties

This Agreement does not create any right under the Contracts (Rights of Third Parties) Act 1999 which is enforceable by any person who is not a party to it.

13. Governing Law

13.1 This Agreement shall be governed by and construed in all respects in accordance with English law and the parties agree to submit to the non-exclusive jurisdiction of the English courts as regards any claim or matter arising in relation to this Agreement.

13.2 [*name of Owner*] hereby appoints [*name of Agent*] of [*address*] (marked for the personal attention of [*name*] or [*name*]) as its authorised agent for the purpose of accepting service of process for all purposes in connection with this Agreement.

SIGNED by the Owner

....

SIGNED on behalf of the Purchaser by its director/duly authorised representative)

....

The Assignment

'The Assignor' will in almost all cases be the same party as the owner in the option agreement.

'The Assignee', however, may well be different, depending on whether the purchaser of the option has assigned his/her rights in the option to a production company, to financiers or to another entrepreneur. Options sometimes do change hands many times as producers struggle to put finance packages together.

The recitals record the legal title to the work.

1. Rights Granted

See Introduction to this precedent for a summary of the issues where the rights are for a television production

Exhibit A

THIS ASSIGNMENT is made on the [*number*] day of [*month*] 20 [*year*]

BETWEEN:

(1) [*name*] (hereinafter termed 'the Assignor') of [*address*]; and

(2) [*company*] LIMITED (hereinafter termed 'the Assignee' which expression includes its successors in title, licensees and assigns) whose registered office is at [*address*].

WHEREAS:

[(A) The Assignor is the sole author of the original [*story/novel/play*] entitled '[title]' ('the Work') and the beneficial owner of the entire copyright in the Work throughout the world [subject only to the publishing agreements of which details have been given to the Assignee].

OR

(A) The Assignor is by virtue of the documents specified in Schedule A hereto the beneficial Owner of the entire copyright throughout the world in the original [*story/novel/play*] by [*name*] ('the Author') entitled '[*title*]' ('the Work') [subject only to the publishing agreements of which details have been given to the Assignee].

(B) Words used herein shall where appropriate have the meanings given to them by the Copyright, Designs and Patents Act 1988, as amended or re-enacted.

TERMS:

1. Rights Granted

1.1 For the consideration specified in Clause 2 hereof the Assignor with full title guarantee hereby assigns to the Assignee for the full period of copyright and all renewals and extensions the whole of the film [television] and allied rights in the Work throughout the world

(ii) The wording of the grant needs careful scrutiny; is it to be for *one* film only (increasingly the 'norm' except for big Hollywood-style projects) or for any number and if the latter, is there to be payment of further consideration on the making of each subsequent film? (Yes, there should be!)

(v) Please see the Introduction for a discussion of this right.

(vi) This specific reference is required as a result of the EU Directive on Rental and Lending Rights.

(vii) This right can be confined to live performances because filmed performances are permitted under sub-clause (iv).

including but not by way of limitation the sole and exclusive right to do or to authorise the following acts:

(i) Adapt into Screenplays: to adapt the Work into film treatments, screenplays or similar dramatic works in all languages;

(ii) Reproduce as Films: to copy the Work by reproducing it in the form of an unlimited number of films and their soundtracks recorded on any medium [Provided that the Assignee shall not without the prior written consent of the Assignor make more than one such film and the Assignor may give or withhold such consent in its absolute discretion and upon such terms including payment of further consideration as the Assignor thinks fit];

(iii) Perform by Films: publicly to present such films by all media and means now known or hereafter to be invented;

(iv) Broadcast: to broadcast such films to the public;

(v) Communicate such Films to the Public: communicate such films to the public in such a way that members of the public may access it from a place and at a time individually chosen by them;

(vi) Issue Copies: to issue to the public copies of such films (including by way of rental or loan) and generally distribute or transmit electronic or other recordings of such films by all methods now known or hereafter to be devised or invented;

[(vii) Television Spin-Offs:

(a) to adapt the Work by converting it into treatments, scripts or similar dramatic works, in any languages for television programmes;

(b) to make audio-visual recordings of such scripts in the form of films and their soundtracks recorded on any medium or by storing performances of them by electronic means;

(c) to broadcast such audio-visual recordings and to include them in cable programme services and/or transmit them by any and all means now known or hereafter devised including without limitation by means of any online system such as the Internet and/or interactive service;]

(viii) Publicity Excerpts: for advertising and publicity purposes only to broadcast and to include in cable programme services

(xii) That is, a waiver of moral rights. It was always customary to exclude *droit moral* prior to the CDPA in an effort (not always successful) to reduce the chances of argument in a jurisdiction which did not recognise the concept. It is now essential to address the problem, but there remains the possibility that some jurisdictions (for example, the French) will not accept a waiver of moral rights.

Not all of the foregoing are always included in any grant of the 'film' rights. Each grant is a matter for individual negotiation and this may or may not include television, satellite, cable, DVD, or online exploitation, such as video on demand though most producers will expect to be able to exploit their film in all media in which it is capable of being exploited and indeed future media not yet currently known. A general exclusion of all rights that are not being granted should be incorporated in the draft to ensure that rights are not included by omission.

The period of the grant is invariably for the full period of copyright except in connection with films made for television where different principles are likely to apply, in respect of which please refer to the introduction to this precedent.

2. Payments

Credit will be given against the purchase price for the relevant parts of the option fee (those that were paid on account of the purchase price). The price may be payable in one sum on exercise of the option, or in instalments; for instance, the first on exercise and the second, for example, on start of principal photography. Avoid the latter – photography may never start, in which event the payment would never be made. Opt instead for a period of time (say, five years) or the start of photography, whichever is the earlier.

Where payment is to be a percentage of the budget it is sometimes subject to a specified minimum and maximum amount known as a 'floor' and a 'ceiling' respectively to protect the author in the case of the former and the producer in the case of the latter.

(whether live or by film or other recording) excerpts of the Work or any adaptations thereof (with such alteration as the Assignee may think fit) not exceeding 15 minutes in duration;

(ix) Synopses: to write, print, publish and sell synopses and résumés of the Work not exceeding [*number*] words in length but only for the purpose of publicity and exploitation of such films [and television programmes];

(x) Sound Recordings: to make sound recordings from the soundtracks of such films [or television programmes] on any medium or by any method whereby the same may be separately performed and to issue copies of such sound recordings to the public (whether by way of sale or otherwise) and by use of such sound recordings to perform the Work in public, to broadcast it and to include it in cable programme services;

(xi) Merchandising: to exercise all so-called 'merchandising rights' as that expression is understood in the film [and television] industries of the United Kingdom and the US;

(xii) Moral Rights: to make additions to, deletions from or alterations to or adaptations of the Work or any part thereof for the purposes of or in the course of exercising the rights hereby granted and to do the acts specified above in relation to the Work or any part thereof with such additions, deletions, alterations or adaptations notwithstanding any moral right or 'droit moral' or similar right to which the Assignor may be entitled in any country;

(xiii) Customary Rights: to do all other acts customarily comprised in grants of full film [and television] rights;

(xiv) Assigns: to assign or license to any third party the rights specified above [but excluding the reserved rights specified in Clause [*number*]].

2. Payments

In consideration of the foregoing assignment the Assignee:

2.1 Cash: has on or before the date hereof paid to the Assignor the sum of or sums amounting in the aggregate to [*amount*] (the receipt of which the Assignor hereby acknowledges);

2.2 shall pay to the Assignor the following further sums on the dates or in the manner mentioned below:

Deferments are payments deferred to what would otherwise be first profits, so the payment may never be made – it is contingent on the success of the film and can be equated to profits. It is unusual for literary rights to be paid for out of deferments.

The difference between a share of profits and a deferment is that the latter is usually expressed as a quantified sum of money and is paid out before the profits actually arise. 'Profits' is an expression that is as long as the proverbial piece of string. Great care should be taken over the definition. None is included here in any detail because each definition should be tailor-made for each circumstance. Very briefly, 'profits' arise once the gross receipts from the exploitation of the film in the relevant media exceed:

(a) the cost of production including the cost of financing;

(b) the cost of distribution including fees, commissions and expenses;

(c) deferments.

That simple formula can take several pages to expand in detail. Once again, great care must be taken that the definition is adequate. Gross receipts should be defined as including all income and at source rather than in the hands of a recipient, because receipts have an unfortunate habit of getting very much smaller the longer they travel. It should be *all* income, not just income from the first film but also from secondary exploitation; for example, by way of disc, broadcast television, cable and also remakes and sequels (see the Special Notes below). The cost of production should be the actual cost as certified by the production company's auditor. Net profit definitions usually also define the recipients' right to inspect the books of account (once annually) and to receive statements (typically, quarterly for two years from the first release of the film, then half-yearly for three years, then annually). Once again, the subject is sufficiently complicated to justify taking expert advice. While it is unfortunately true that more films do not achieve profits than do, when a film is successful, it is worth having the protection of a tight definition.

As a result of the implementation of the Rental Rights Directive, it is now necessary to address this question. See the introductory notes to this Precedent.

3. Warranties

The purchaser will often reasonably ask for a wider range of warranties, including warranties for further assurance and for extension of copyright (in those jurisdictions where there are separate periods of copyright). The purchaser may also ask for specific authority to act in the owner's name in protecting the rights granted. He may also ask to inspect title documents.

(i) Purchase Price: the sum amounting in the aggregate to [*number*] per cent of the Final Budget of [the first and only [film] that may be produced hereunder and for the purposes of this Clause 'Final Budget' shall mean the production budget as approved by financiers, distributors and completion guarantors [but excluding the items for contingency financing fees, interest, completion guarantors fee, insurance costs, legal fees, deferments, story costs and [other finance charges]];

(ii) [Deferment: the sum of [*amount*] as a deferment payable only out of the 'First Profits' (as defined in Schedule A/B hereto) from the first or only film that may be made pursuant to the rights hereby granted proportionately with any other deferments that may be payable out of the First Profits;]

(iii) Profits:

(a) sums from time to time equal to [*number*] per cent of Net Profits (as defined in Schedule A/B hereto) from the first or only film that may be made pursuant to the rights hereby granted;

(b) if any television programme or episode (not being a film made pursuant to sub-clause 1.i(ii) hereof) is made pursuant to sub-clause 1.1(vi) hereof the Assignee shall pay to the Assignor not later than 28 days after the first broadcast or cable programme services transmission for each programme or episode not exceeding 30 minutes in duration an initial fee of [*amount*] or twice that amount for a programme exceeding 30 minutes but not exceeding 60 minutes or thrice that amount for a programme exceeding 60 minutes and a further sum equal to one quarter of such initial fee 28 days after each of up to four repeat broadcasts or transmissions but after four repeats no further fees shall be payable.

3. Warranties

The Assignor hereby warrants to and undertakes with the Assignee that:

3.1 the Work is original to [*the Assignor*] [*the Author*] and nothing therein infringes the copyright or any other rights of any third party and so far as the Assignor is aware it is not defamatory;

3.2 the Assignor is not aware of any claim that the Work infringes any right of any third party;

4. Hold-backs

This is relevant where only the film rights are granted so that others, such as stage or TV drama, are retained; the purchaser will seek to insist that the latter rights are not exploited for a sufficient period to allow him to turn the film rights into profit.

5. Credit

It is important that the credit obligations should be fully set out.

7. Turnaround/reversion

It is highly unlikely that a film-maker who is considering investing millions in a project will allow the original owner of the rights any right to rescind the agreement: actions for breach are usually specifically limited to actions for damages – after all, the concept is a sale and purchase. The position is otherwise in TV-rights-only deals where a licence for 10 to 15 years is common, all rights in the underlying material reverting at the end of the licence period.

3.3 copyright in the Work subsists and *he/she* will procure if and when appropriate the renewal or extension of the copyright in the Work under the laws of all countries that afford renewal or extension rights and assign to the Assignee for such renewal or extension term the rights defined by Clause 1 hereof and the Assignor hereby authorises the Assignee to execute all documents and to do all acts that may be necessary to procure such renewal or extension and assignment;

3.4 he/she has not granted any assignment or licence in relation to the Work [other than the publishing agreements referred to above];

4. Hold-backs

The Assignor agrees that *he/she* has not granted and will not until the [*number*] day of [*month*] 20 [*year*] grant any licence for or permit any broadcast or public performance of the Work or any adaptation thereof.

5. Credit

5.1 If the Assignee makes a film [or television programme] based on the Work it will give the original author credit on all copies delivered by it to its distributors or licensees [and in all major paid advertising and publicity issued by or under its control except group, list, teaser and trailer advertising and newspaper advertising of less than eight column inches] in some such form as 'Based on [*title*]' mentioning the name of the Work if different from the film or programme.

5.2 No casual or inadvertent failure to afford credit as aforesaid shall constitute a breach hereof and the Assignor's remedies for a breach shall be confined to damages.

6. Moral Rights

The Assignor hereby unconditionally and irrevocably waives in favour of the Assignee the Assignor's rights under section 80 of the Copyright, Designs and Patents Act 1988 and any moral right or 'droit moral' or similar right to which the Assignor may be entitled in any country to the extent such a waiver is permitted by the laws of such country.

7. Turnaround

If principal photography of the first or only film to be made hereunder has not commenced within [X] years of the date hereof, the Assignor shall have the right to require the assignment back to him of all rights assigned hereunder on

Rarely, a turnaround, or reversion, provision is found providing for the rights to revert – on repayment of the purchase price – if a production has not commenced within an agreed period from the date of the assignment, say 5 years.

8. Agents

The agency clause is as important here as in the option agreement.

Sequels and Remakes Because a concise version of a film rights assignment has been included in this book, incorporating a comprehensive grant of rights, there is no specific reference to another aspect frequently found in a film deal: the right to make sequels and remakes. Where the main grant is for *one* film only, provision can be made for sequels and remakes which are traditionally paid for at 50 and 33⅓% of the original purchase price respectively. There are two kinds of sequels: author-written and producer-written. The purchaser will be keen to acquire such rights if he thinks the subject-matter will bear more than one film, as he will wish to be protected against the situation where his film is successful and leads to a considerable increase in the value of the author's works.

repayment to the Assignee of all sums paid by the Assignee to the Assignor hereunder, less only that part paid by way of option fee.

8. Agents

The Assignor hereby [irrevocably] authorises *his/her* Agents, [*name of Agent*], to collect and receive all moneys payable to the Assignor hereunder and declares that their receipt shall be a good discharge for such moneys [and that they shall be empowered to act in all matters arising out of this Assignment] [unless the Assignee has previously received written notice of revocation of such authority].

9. Rights of Third Parties

This Assignment does not create any right under the Contracts (Rights of Third Parties) Act 1999 which is enforceable by any person who is not a party to it.

10. Governing Law

This Assignment shall be governed by and construed in all respects in accordance with English law and the parties agree to submit to the non-exclusive jurisdiction of the English courts as regards any claim or matter arising in relation to this Assignment.

SCHEDULE A

Title Documents of Assignor

Date	*Description of Document*	*Parties*

SCHEDULE A/B

Definitions of Receipts and Profits

SIGNEDby..

duly authorised for and...

onbehalfoftheAssignor...

SIGNEDby..

duly authorised for and...

onbehalfoftheAssignee...

PRECEDENT SEVENTEEN

Merchandising Rights Agreement

> *'The world moves on, and the following precedent attempts to move with it. The exploitation of merchandising rights may stretch out to tea towels, to soft toys, to jigsaw puzzles, to coffee mugs, to T-shirts, and to many other forms of merchandising in ways which may not be familiar to all publishers, authors and artists.'*

The paragraph reproduced above introduced a Precedent for Merchandising Rights in the First Edition of *Publishing Agreements*, published in 1980. Now, in 2010, the world has moved on further. I see, regularly, merchandising rights agreements extending to 75 pages and more. If what you are looking for is to be that 'sophisticated', leave the following precedent well alone and go straight to a specialist lawyer in this field. Even though what we have presented here is a relatively simple document intended to 'flag' the more important of the issues, there is no substitute for specialist advice. Hopefully however, when you go for that advice, this document will have enabled you to do so more efficiently!

Precedent One, Clause 14(xix) sets out a range (not, however, a definitive range) of ways of exploiting, through merchandising, characters, items and events in the work which the publisher is publishing in book form. Such merchandising rights may, or may not, be granted to the book publisher.

This precedent can be adapted to cover many types of merchandising, but it does not cover electronic merchandising, for instance, the establishment of a website dedicated to exploiting the image of a fictional character, or the development of electronic games or other spin-offs from a character. Merchandising of this nature is most commonly carried out by divisions specialising in the development and exploitation of digital media, and great care is needed to ensure that control is maintained on every aspect of the merchandising.

Electronic media such as the Internet or mobile telephones may, however, be used to exploit the merchandising rights granted under this agreement. The precedent allows for this: rights to use Internet domain names are included within the definition of trademarks, and promotions on e-commerce websites are covered by the general merchandising rights.

The general point, made elsewhere in *Clark's Publishing Agreements*, that if the publisher wishes to acquire a right, he must make sure that he has the skills necessary to exploit it, applies especially to merchandising rights. If the publisher is sure that he has those skills, then he will negotiate to acquire merchandising rights from the author and/or illustrator. The publisher may have his own merchandising division using sub-contractors to undertake the manufacturing, marketing and distribution functions while maintaining control over the merchandising programme for a particular work. Alternatively, the publisher may hand over this responsibility to a merchandising agent which has the know-how to design and develop a merchandising programme and enter into sub-licences with manufacturers of particular items or sub-contract manufacture, thus maintaining direct control over each product.

This precedent consists of the grant from the rights owner (licensor) to the licensee of the rights in all or only some aspects of a particular work to be applied to an identified category or categories of product. In many cases the licensee will need to grant sub-licences and here the chain of control, which is critical to the whole merchandising operation, can be put at risk. The main licensee must owe basic obligations towards the licensor in relation to the quality of the licensed products which will be backed up by its agreements with sub-licensees and manufacturers. It is advisable for the licensor to dictate the precise terms of any sub-licence agreement entered into by the licensee, as Clause 4.3 contemplates.

The length and complexity of merchandising agreements frequently depend upon how keen the licensor is to preserve and enhance the reputation attaching to the work and secure its value in the long term or whether he simply wants a healthy short-term royalty income. Control by the licensor over the quality of merchandise is essential, as is the maintenance of the goodwill attached to the work. If the material is exploited in the right way, goodwill will increase and, with it, the likely royalty income.

This precedent sets out a framework for the key merchandising rights and obligations. Most clauses can be developed and made more detailed if necessary. In particular, it does not deal with the detailed mechanics of quality control since they differ in every case. In any merchandising arrangement where the licensee is required to seek approvals from the licensor, he should be required to build into the manufacturing timetable sufficient time to secure such approvals and, if necessary, to make adjustments to the product to reflect the licensor's comments. All too frequently, the licensor is presented with a proposition on a 'take it or leave it' basis and, with an eye to securing his royalty stream, the licensor may be reluctant to delay manufacture and distribution of a product with which he is unhappy.

This precedent is fairly even-handed, but it slightly favours the licensor. For instance, there are no warranties in relation to the rights being licensed.

Finally, this precedent should be used with caution and an open mind. It will not suit all situations, but applies to a relatively straightforward and typical arrangement. It is designed to be adapted and fleshed out as appropriate. Legal advice should be obtained on any potential problem areas, particularly the securing of intellectual property rights (Clause 3), approvals and controls (Clauses 4 and 5), the licensee's covenants (Clause 7), and product liability and litigation (Clause 8). If either of the parties is a major player in its field or if this agreement could have an effect on trade between EU Member States, then competition law advice should be sought.

This precedent and the accompanying notes have been drafted by Alan Williams and Nick Fitzpatrick of DLA Piper, Solicitors.

AGREEMENT made this [*number*] day of [*month*] 20 [*year*] between [*company name*] of [*address*] ('the Licensor'), of the one part and [*company name*] of [*address*] ('the Licensee') of the other part.

Whereby it is agreed as follows:

1. Definitions

In this Agreement the following definitions shall apply:

(i) 'Licensed Products' shall mean the products listed in Schedule II (as amended from time to time by agreement in writing between the parties) which are approved by the Licensor pursuant to this Agreement.

(ii) 'Net Invoice Price' shall mean the price of any Licensed Products invoiced by the Licensee or any Sub-Licensee after deduction of freight, insurance, packaging costs and any value added or other sales tax charged thereon.

(iii) 'Quarter' shall mean each consecutive three-month period that this Agreement remains in force, the first such period beginning on the first day of the Term.

---

1. Definitions

The work is to be defined in Schedule I and the licensed products or services, derived from the work, in Schedule II. As much detail as possible should be included. The drafting leaves scope for full details of the licensed products to be inserted (and added to from time to time) accompanied by an indication of what aspect of the work is going to be used in connection with each product (e.g., character, names, illustrations). The term of the licence should initially be short, but it is often appropriate to provide for continuation of the term at the licensor's option on a year-by-year basis.

There may be registered trade or service marks already in existence or the licensor may intend to register trade or service marks derived from the work in respect of the goods or services licensed. There may also be Internet domain names which may be used by the licensee for promotional purposes. These have been included in the definition of trademarks, but if there are many they could conveniently be listed in a separate schedule and dealt with in a separate definition.

The definition of Net Invoice Price could be amended to allow for discounts, refunds for returns and the like. This will follow negotiations between the parties.

2. Appointment

The agreement will generally be 'exclusive' to the licensee in respect of the identified categories of licensed products. The term 'exclusive' in this context means that the licensor excludes himself and any third parties from the rights granted to the licensee. A 'sole' licence merely excludes third parties so that the licensor can undertake the licensed activities himself. If third parties are to be appointed, the appointment should be 'non-exclusive'. Legal advice should be taken when assessing the various options.

It is important to define the scope of the rights and who owns characters, symbols and other elements, particularly those developed by the licensee during the term of the licence. See also the note to Clause 3.

Note that, for EU competition law reasons, the limitation of the appointment to the Territory cannot be used (where the Territory involves one or more, but not all, EEA member states) to prevent the licensee making passive sales (i.e., responding to unsolicited orders for the product) from customers located outside the Territory. The licensee can, however, be prevented from *actively* marketing the products outside the Territory.

3. Intellectual Property Rights

The licensor may not own all the relevant intellectual property rights, but rather may have an exclusive licence from the author/illustrator or some intermediary which includes the merchandising rights. The precise position in respect of all aspects of the work should be checked in each case and reflected in the wording of the agreement. The moral rights of the author/illustrator may survive despite such licence or assignment. Ideally moral rights will have been expressly waived when the author/illustrator originally agreed to prepare the work. Alternatively, a waiver could be obtained prior to the grant of the merchandising rights so that the author/illustrator cannot inhibit their exercise. For moral rights in general, **see Appendix H**.

It is usually in the licensor's interests to become the owner of the intellectual property rights in any new materials derived from the work. A new work may, though derivative, be sufficiently 'original' to enjoy its own intellectual property rights. The precedent provides for this (see Clause 3.2).

The 'further assurance' (see Clause 3.3) is vital to perfect the licensor's interest in any newly generated works.

(iv) 'Sub-Licensee' shall mean any individual, company or firm with whom the Licensee enters into an agreement for the manufacture or marketing of Licensed Products following consultation with the Licensor pursuant to this Agreement.

(v) 'The Term' shall mean the term of [*specify period*] from the date of this Agreement which period may be extended by agreement in writing between the parties.

(vi) 'The Territory' shall mean the territory set out in Schedule III.

(vii) ['The Trademarks' shall mean the trademarks, service marks [Internet domain names] and applications for any of them identified in Schedule IV.]

(viii) The 'Work' shall mean the work details of which are set out in Schedule I.

2. Appointment

The Licensor hereby appoints the Licensee as its [sole and] [exclusive] licensee in the Territory for the manufacture, marketing, distribution and sale of Licensed Products derived from or relating to the Work for the Term subject to the terms and conditions of this Agreement.

3. Intellectual Property Rights

3.1 The Licensor is the [proprietor]/[exclusive licensee] of copyright in the Work [and is the registered proprietor of the Trademarks]. Any alteration for the purposes of this Agreement of [the Trademarks or] any material comprised in the Work shall be subject to prior approval in writing by the Licensor.

3.2 The Licensee hereby, with full title guarantee, assigns to the Licensor (by way of present assignment of future rights) the copyright and any other intellectual property right subsisting in any material created by or for the Licensee derived from the Work or any aspect thereof throughout the world for the full period of such rights (together with any extension, revival or renewal thereof). The Licensee shall not do or refrain from doing any act which may prejudice the subsistence of any relevant intellectual property rights or their ownership by the Licensor.

3.3 The Licensee shall at the Licensor's expense do all such acts and execute such documents as the Licensor shall reasonably require to confirm the assignment of any rights created pursuant to this Agreement or to secure the registration of the Trademarks.

4. Product Development

Clause 4.1 contemplates that at the date of the agreement the licensee has not put forward its proposals for a manufacturing programme. This is often agreed before the merchandising agreement is signed, in which case it should be included as a schedule. Quality control over every aspect of licensed merchandise is essential to maintain the value of the work in its own right, the image and reputation of the licensor and the validity of any registered trademarks.

Where the licensee is merely managing a merchandising operation and engaging sub-licensees in different areas the licensor should at least review, if not dictate, the terms of the sub-licence agreement to be used and to approve the identities of any sub-licensees involved. In such a case the licensor may be less concerned to oversee the merchandising programme that Clause 4.1 contemplates.

Ideally the copyright notice (see Clause 4.4) will include an acknowledgment for the book's author/illustrator etc, but this is a matter of policy for the licensor depending both on his agreement with the author/illustrator and on the moral rights position.

Clause 4.1: Specify frequency of proposals.

Clause 4.3: Where possible specify timetable.

5. Packaging, Marketing and Distribution

The respective contributions of the parties to these functions can vary enormously depending upon the commercial circumstances. This clause sets out a typical arrangement favourable to the licensor, but further protection could be obtained by specifying in more detail the sale outlets, including Internet and mail order shopping outlets.

4. Product Development

4.1 The Licensee shall devise a programme for the manufacture of Licensed Products and shall from time to time present to the Licensor a range of proposals for Licensed Products including details of the proposed manufacturers or any other Sub-Licensees who may be involved in their development. The Licensor shall within [*number, e.g., 14*] days of receipt of such proposals indicate in writing its approval or otherwise of the said programme [and where appropriate shall require the Licensee to enter into sub-licence agreements with Sub-Licensees substantially in the form of the sub-licence set out in Schedule V to this Agreement].

4.2 In relation to each Sub-Licensee the Licensee shall provide such creative and technical assistance as shall be reasonably required and shall liaise between the Licensor and the Sub-Licensee with a view to securing appropriate access to any materials which may be of use to the Licensee.

4.3 The Licensee shall oversee the performance by the Sub-Licensee of its sub-licence obligations. Whether or not a Sub-Licensee is involved the Licensee shall ensure that the Licensor is supplied with pre-production designs and samples of the Licensed Products and the packaging and promotional materials for them for approval at key stages [or specify stages] in the development and manufacturing process. The Licensor shall within [*number, e.g., 14*] days after presentation of such designs and samples communicate its approval or otherwise and the Licensee shall not proceed with the development of any Licensed Product without the relevant approval of the Licensor. Allowance for this approval period shall be built into the timetable for the manufacture of Licensed Products. [Such approval shall not be unreasonably withheld.]

4.4 The Licensee shall ensure that all Licensed Products [and the packaging therefore] carry a copyright notice [and trademark notice] in a form and applied in a manner [approved by the Licensor]/[set out in Schedule VII].

5. Packaging, Marketing and Distribution

5.1 The Licensee shall ensure that all Licensed Products, their packaging and any promotional material relating to them shall conform with the samples previously supplied to and approved by the Licensor pursuant to Clause 4 above.

5.2 The Licensee shall be responsible for advertising, distributing and marketing the Licensed Products in the Territory.

6. Payment

It is usual for the licensee to make a down payment at the start of the contract which may or may not be set against future royalties (see Clause 6.1).

Quarterly accounting is usual in the merchandising field. Although this is inconsistent with practice in publishing, it can provide the licensor with a steady income source (see Clause 6.2).

It is often appropriate to provide for a lot of detail about sales in the statements of account. Allowance could be made for withholding tax: if it has to be deducted, then a valid tax deduction certificate should be provided. Note that royalty payments are subject to VAT.

5.3 The Licensee shall not without the prior written consent of the Licensor distribute, sell or authorise the distribution or sale of the Licensed Products to any third party which is not a bona fide wholesale or retail firm or company. If so required by the Licensor the Licensee shall stop trading immediately in relation to Licensed Products with any person, firm or company of whom the Licensor shall disapprove on any reasonable grounds.

5.4 [The Licensee shall meet the sales targets set out in relation to the Licensed Products in Schedule VI.]

6. Payment

6.1 The Licensee shall pay the Licensor on the signing of this Agreement the sum of [*amount*] [which shall be on account of royalty payments due during the currency of this Agreement]/[which shall be a non-returnable down payment in consideration for the Licensor entering into this Agreement].

6.2 The Licensee shall supply to the Licensor within [*number*] days of the end of each Quarter a statement setting out details of all Licensed Products sold in the Territory during that Quarter and shall pay to the Licensor a royalty equal to [*number*] per cent of the Net Invoice Price on all such sales irrespective of whether payment has been received by the Licensee [subject to deduction of the advance referred to in sub-paragraph 6.1 from the payments due in each Quarter until it is absorbed]. [The Licensor's acceptance of a statement shall not preclude the challenge of any mistakes or inconsistencies found subsequently.]

6.3 No royalties shall be paid in respect of Licensed Products provided for promotional purposes or otherwise. The Licensee shall deliver to the Licensor, free of charge, up to a maximum of [*number*] of each of the Licensed Products.

6.4 The Licensee shall keep full and accurate accounts and records of all dealings in the Licensed Products.

6.5 The Licensor or its authorised representative shall have the right upon reasonable notice to the Licensee to enter upon the premises of the Licensee to examine the accounts and records of the Licensee and where appropriate of any Sub-Licensees insofar as they relate to dealings in Licensed Products. Such examination shall be at the expense of the Licensor unless, in the statement referred to in sub-paragraph 6.2 above, errors of more than five (5) per cent are disclosed in which case the said costs shall be met by the Licensee.

7. Licensee's Covenants

The extent to which a licensee is willing to assume liability will vary with the nature of the deal. Read this clause in conjunction with Clause 8.

6.6 It shall be the exclusive responsibility of the Licensee to recover any money due from Sub-Licensees and purchasers of the Licensed Products and no account shall be taken by the Licensor of any bad debts incurred by the Licensee.

6.7 On the expiration or termination of this Agreement the Licensee shall for a period of [two months] be entitled to sell off any Licensed Products which have at the date of such expiration or termination been manufactured in accordance with this Agreement and all royalties in respect thereof shall be accounted for and paid to the Licensor within fifteen (15) days of the expiry of the said [two-month] period.

7. Licensee's Covenants

The Licensee covenants with the Licensor that:

7.1 Quality: the Licensed Products shall be of a high standard and of a style, appearance and quality as to be suited to the exploitation to the best advantage of the Work [and the Trademarks] and to enhance their value and the goodwill relating to them.

7.2 No Representations: the Licensee shall not make any representation or give any warranty on behalf of the Licensor.

7.3 No Impairment: the Licensee shall not at any time do or suffer to be done any act or thing which will in any way impair or affect any intellectual property rights in the Licensed Products or the rights and interests of the Licensor therein.

7.4 No attacks: if the Licensee shall attack, question or deny the title of the Licensor in and to the Work or any intellectual property rights to them or attack the validity of the [Trademarks or] licensed rights, the Licensor shall be entitled to terminate this Agreement forthwith by notice in writing.

7.5 No harm: it will not harm, misuse or bring into disrepute the Work [or the Trademarks].

7.6 No expense: it will not create or incur any expenses chargeable to the Licensor.

7.7 Protect: it will protect to the best of its ability its rights to manufacture, sell and distribute the Licensed Products hereunder.

7.8 Combination Sales: it will not use the Licensed Products for combination sales or as premiums, giveaways or for any similar

8. Liability and Litigation

The strategy for conducting litigation and the respective responsibilities of the parties can be adjusted in various different ways. This clause sets out a traditional approach which gives each party liability and responsibility for litigation arising from matters within their control. The licensee here is expected to take out insurance to cover his liabilities. The insurance provisions could be made reciprocal.

9. Termination

The reference in Clause 9.1(iii)(a) to s 123 of the Insolvency Act 1986 relates to corporate insolvency: substitute s 268 for parties who are individuals. This clause will need to be adapted when the licensee is an individual or a partnership as opposed to a company.

method of merchandising and will ensure that its customers likewise will refrain from making such use of the Licensed Products.

7.9 No Commercial Tie-ups: it will not enter into any agreement relating to the Work [or the Trademarks] for commercial tie-ups or promotions with any company engaged wholly or partly in a business similar to the Licensor's business [or specify business].

8. Liability and Litigation

8.1 The Licensee shall give the Licensor prompt notice of any unauthorised use of the Work or of any products or services unfairly competing with the Licensed Products which comes to its attention. The Licensor shall in its own discretion determine what action should be taken in relation to each such use and the Licensee shall co-operate fully in that action [at its own expense].

8.2 The Licensor will indemnify the Licensee in relation to any action or claim by any third party in which it is alleged that the use of the Work or any part of it in relation to the Licensed Products pursuant to this Agreement infringes the rights of any third party provided that the Licensee gives the Licensor prompt notice of such claim or action and does nothing to prejudice the Licensor's conduct thereof.

8.3 The Licensee shall indemnify the Licensor and shall be responsible for defending or settling any claims or proceedings brought by third parties arising from any use of the Work in relation to products not approved by the Licensor or the distribution or sale of Licensed Products in any territory other than the Territory or in relation to the safety of the Licensed Products, their conformity with any statute or regulations, their design, materials or method of manufacture. The Licensee shall take and maintain a policy of insurance with an insurance office of repute for a minimum of [*amount*] in respect of its liabilities for the Licensed Products and shall make that policy available for inspection by the Licensor at the Licensor's request from time to time.

9. Termination

9.1 The Licensor shall have the right at any time to give notice in writing to the Licensee to terminate this Agreement and any sub-licences made pursuant to it on the occurrence of any of the following events:

(i) [if within [*agreed period, e.g., 12 months*] of the date of this Agreement the target sales set out in Schedule VI shall not have been met by the Licensee;]

10. Partnership, Assignment etc

Either or both parties can be prevented from assigning rights under the contract. The formula at Clause 10.2 is the most common.

(ii) if the Licensee commits any material breach of any of the terms of this Agreement which, if capable of being remedied, shall not have been remedied within 30 days of the Licensor serving written notice upon the Licensee to do so;

(iii) if the Licensee enters into liquidation whether compulsory or voluntary (other than for the purpose of a reconstruction or amalgamation not involving an insolvency of the Licensee);

(a) if the Licensee is deemed unable to pay its debts within the meaning of section 123 of the Insolvency Act 1986 (as amended from time to time);

(b) if an administrator, administrative or other receiver in respect of the Licensee or any of its assets is appointed;

(c) any steps are taken with a view to proposing or applying for any kind of composition, interim order, scheme of arrangement, compromise or arrangement involving the Licensee and any of its creditors (including a voluntary arrangement with its creditors);

(d) any steps are taken with a view to the dissolution of the Licensee; or

(iv) if the Licensor shall serve notice pursuant to Clause 7.4.

9.2 Termination of this Agreement shall not affect the rights or liabilities of the parties acquired or incurred up to the date of termination.

10. Partnership, Assignment etc

10.1 The licence hereby granted shall not create a partnership between the parties.

10.2 This Agreement shall not be capable of assignment or transmission in whole or in part by the Licensee without the prior consent in writing of the Licensor.

11. Rights of Third Parties

This Agreement does not create any right under the Contracts (Rights of Third Parties) Act 1999 which is enforceable by any person who is not a party to it.

12. Governing Law and Arbitration

This clause is common in the publishing business. It may be appropriate to have a different arbitration mechanism, and to provide for internal escalation procedures or other forms of alternative dispute resolution. For details of the Informal Disputes Arbitration Service offered by the Publishers' Association, see Note 30 to Precedent One.

12. Governing Law and Arbitration

This Agreement shall be governed by and construed in all respects in accordance with English law. If any dispute or difference arises between the parties in connection with this Agreement it shall be referred to arbitration in London [*specify arbitration rules*] before a single arbitrator. If the parties are unable to agree as to the appointment of such arbitrator within [*period, e.g., 30*] days of one party serving notice on the other calling for the appointment of an arbitrator then such arbitrator shall be appointed on the application of either party to the President for the time being of the [Publishers Association]. The award of the arbitrator shall be final and binding on the parties and judgment upon the award may be entered in any court having jurisdiction, or application may be made to such court for judicial acceptance of the award and order for enforcement as the case may be.

Schedules

I The Work

Title, Author/Illustrator (and description)

II Licensed Products

(Identify aspect of the Work, e.g., name or illustration, to be used in relation to each product.)

III Territory

Registered trademarks

Trademark applications identifying relevant countries, use classes and goods

[V Sample Sub-Licence Agreement]

If used, this sub-licence should mirror the obligations in the head licence.

[VI Targets]

[VII Copyright and Trademark Notices]

Introduction to Electronic Precedents

Surely not since Allen Lane perfected the exploitation of the paperback medium has the industry found itself in such a state of uncertainty. What does the electronic medium do to publishing; is it competitive or is it complementary? Will the investment needed for digital delivery pay for itself – or will it pay someone else entirely: whether that is Google, Amazon, Apple or Facebook or even some other, as yet unknown, Web 3.0 operator? Must the lessons learnt by the music business and other sectors be applied by publishers or are the challenges and solutions in digital media content-specific?

The publishing industry has at least had time to consider these questions. Indeed, the fifth edition of *Publishing Agreements* in 1997 was the first to dip its toe into the water of electronic publishing by incorporating two precedents – one a licence to a software developer/producer to utilise existing printed material in carrier form (e.g. as a CD-ROM) and the other a licence to an institution to make existing printed material available by local network to end users within its own site. The sixth edition, in 2002, added several further precedents reflecting the rise of the Internet as a distribution medium in the intervening years and the continued growth of electronic publishing, particularly within the STM, academic and other specialist sectors.

By the previous seventh edition in 2007 there were six precedents dealing with electronic publishing and digital content distribution. Four years on again, this eighth edition also includes six precedents. The original hard carrier licence referred to above has been retained and updated as Precedent Eighteen (although today as likely to be used for distributing material on a flash drive or for a Nintendo handheld as the traditional CD/DVD-ROM). The original local network licence for printed material is also retrained and updated as Precedent Nineteen [along side Precedent Twenty, the latest version of the model online licence for material supplied in electronic form produced by the Publishers Association and Joint Information Systems Committee (JISC), representing the higher and further education sectors in the UK.

In contrast to the previous two agreements, which are designed mainly for use with specific works, an updated Precedent Twenty-One is intended for use with wider digital publishing projects by providing an agreement for online access to a database or similar digital content service. Precedent Twenty-

Three is an agreement for the distribution of content on a Website, primarily for use with the fixed Internet but with suggestions for use in connection with wireless distribution such as via the portal of a mobile phone network. In recent years, online traffic has moved away from traditional portals to the search engines and to other sites such as the social networks. There will no doubt be further shifts to come but many of the same concepts and issues in these documents will continue to apply.

As the above suggests, some publishers could have had 15 or more years experience of electronic publishing. However, those publishers, at least since the earliest experiments with CD-ROM, have largely been confined to the STM and limited other sections of the publishing industry. What has changed in the last five years is the appearance, at last, of serious eBook devices with mainstream appeal. eBooks have been around before of course. A wide array of technologies from the CD-based Sony Bookman in 1990 onwards have come and, often soon after, gone as manufacturers have tried to provide a digital alternative to the bound book. Only since the last edition, however, has it finally seemed that there are credible devices available with a public – and the publishing industry – willing to support them. Indeed, at the time this introduction is being written, eBook sales figures claimed in the US are beginning to challenge online hard-back sales.

As a result, the fifth electronic precedent in this edition, Precedent Twenty-Two, is an agreement for the sale of eBooks. It must be stressed, however, that there is no such thing as a standard form of eBook agreement. The larger players in the market do, of course, operate with their own standard agreements but we have obviously not attempted to replicate those just as we have not previously attempted to include the terms of leading aggregators or database publishers. Instead we have used a form of agreement from earlier editions which licensed a hand-held electronic device manufacturer. As such, we have largely upgraded what previously would have been used to make material available on a PDA or other predecessor to today's eBook readers. Now, however, we are clearly dealing with something which is identifiable as the publisher's own eBook edition, i.e. a stand-alone digital product, or an 'app', published alongside print versions of the same title.

The road of technology development and adoption is never straightforward, and the eBook has much further to go. The parameters of eBook distribution have yet to be settled. There is much current debate over issues such as the co-called 'agency-model' as discussed further in Precedent Twenty-Two. Commentators regularly talk of the need to create an inclusive and mutually beneficial ecosystem but commercial tensions between the hardware manufacturers/sales platforms and the publishers (and in turn authors and content creators) are hard to avoid. The economics of eBooks (as for other digital content) are a particular concern and both pricing and usage models. It remains to be seen whether rental and subscription models might work as well as downloads and pay-per-view. Indeed some might argue that, at least for certain publishers, concentrating solely on the eBook is too narrow a focus within the wider opportunities, and challenges, of digital media.

Certainly, however, this collection of precedents will provide a strong illustration, if one were needed for any publisher working in digital media, of the pace of technical change and the need for commercial and legal practice to be able to adapt accordingly. As previously noted, each of the digital precedents in this eighth edition remain documents where further tailoring and alteration should be expected. As a result, to assist reader further, some additional background commentary is provided below on the key issues of digital rights, digital rights management (DRM), territory, post-termination use and the act of digitisation itself.

(1) *Rights*

Clearly, for a publisher to be able to enter into the sort of arrangements contemplated by these documents it must first have ensured that it has the necessary rights to do so. The old adage that publishers should buy in rights 'wide and long' and then license them out 'narrow and short' remains sensible, if admittedly simplistic, advice in today's sophisticated digital content market. A discussion on acquiring rights for these forms of electronic use in the specific context of an author agreement is set out in some detail in **Precedent One, Note 2 to Clause 1**. Described below is how those digital rights may then be licensed and exploited.

Rights owners in all sectors of the media industry, from music to sports, have been struggling to fit new digital distribution methods with existing licence structures. In many cases their ain has been to develop so-called 'non-disruptive rights templates' that introduce new markets without harming existing ones. In some cases a more radical solution has been adopted with licensing structures being completely re-engineered. As digital publishing markets develop, legal and commercial lessons learnt in some of those other sectors may also have value to publishers, something we have already seen in discussion of where an eBook edition should appear within the traditional hardback and paperback publication windows.

Publishers certainly need to define the rights which are licensed or exploited in a manner which does not conflict with existing rights grants nor unduly restrict future activities. Care must be taken, even where non-exclusive rights are being granted. Distinguishing between physical hard carrier formats and online media is not without its difficulties (see the comments in Precedent Eighteen regarding CD-I and CD-ROM), it is, though, advances in online technology: the long promised 'convergence' effect, that have produced most concerns. With developments in broadband, broadcast to mobile and digital TV, it has become increasingly difficult to distinguish between existing Internet, mobile phone/wireless and television/radio markets and to draft robust rights definitions to match.

It is not just a matter of technology. In some cases it is a question of thinking through the possible uses of a product or service. For instance, the right to distribute for use on hand-held devices by hard carrier or by pre-loading in the device (a right included in Precedent Twenty-Two) can be distinguished from the right to supply to that same hand-held device purely via an online network (see Precedent Twenty-Three). A publisher may be prepared to grant both rights together but it should do so having considered the distinction, not as an oversight in a grant of 'handheld device rights'. It may be that a longer term solution for rights owners will be to focus less on platforms and types of technology: be it paperback books or websites, and more on specific functionality and form.

The industry spat over e-reader devices with a 'read aloud' function is a recent twist on this licensing consideration (see **Note to to Clause 1 in Precedent One**). Indeed e-reader and other devices and digital platforms are likely to continue to offer functionality in advance of what publishers will want or are able to grant the rights to exploit in the short to medium term. Establishing rules for digital content, e.g. how it may be used and on which devices, whether these merely attempt to replicate – or actually try to extend or limit – the equivalent hard copy usage is a creative and commercial challenge. It also impacts upon the legal rights that the publisher acquires from its authors and other creative partners and suppliers. These link to further technical considerations which are discussed below.

(2) *DRM*

Whatever the scope of rights in question, control of the use of those rights is no longer a matter of just contract and copyright (or other intellectual property). Technology might itself provide a solution if, in Charles Clark's famous phrase, 'the answer to the machine is in the machine'. Reference to use of some form of digital rights management (DRM) implementation is made in most of the precedents in this section. DRM systems essentially have two elements.

First, they identify content, in a similar way to ISBN numbers. The digital object identifier (DOI) initiative is one of the most well used identifier schemes in the publishing world – but there are others. The system must describe the work (its author, its date of publication etc.) and its uses so that usage rules can be set. The second element is the provision of the content in such a way that those rules can be enforced. This is often achieved through 'locking' technology which effectively tries to wrap and unwrap content and so restrict how it may be viewed, copied, printed etc. in support of the agreed usage model discussed above. Many content owners are also just as interested in so-called 'watermarking' and 'fingerprinting' i.e. the use of a label marked on the content, in order to identify and track it.

DRM systems raise a number of legal and commercial issues. These include the extent to which they can: respect copyright (or equivalent) expectations such as 'fair dealing' or private copying provisions (which may not amount to a legal right under existing law), protect privacy (EU law specifically makes clear that support for DRM technology does NOT override the need to comply with data protection law) and delivery interoperability e.g. will eBook content with one type of DRM work on an eBook designed for a different type of DRM? These are topics which, even if not dealt with specifically in the contracts set out here, should be considered when DRM systems are selected or specified for licensees' use.

Since the last edition of this book was published, the music industry has retreated from the use of DRM as a means of controlling access to digital content. Following market resistance, and a very public debate between the record labels and the market-leading Apple iTunes store, DRM-free tracks were first made available at a higher price point and then iTunes and other sales platforms were able to sell all music DRM-free. Some audio-book publishers have followed this lead. Yet many other forms of digital content, including eBooks, continue to be supplied with DRM protection. New developments in DRM technology include so-called 'rights lockers' that allow purchasers of content to assert their usage rights on different devices, and potentially even in different formats – ultimately with different retail suppliers.

(3) *Territory*

Discussion of Internet and online distribution often focuses on the relative ease with which material can pass across territorial borders. Whilst this is certainly true it would be a mistake to think that online rights are not regularly granted and exploited subject to territorial limits.

Where material is licensed for use on a local area network (LAN), or even a virtual private network (VPN), the licensee will normally have sufficient control over access to and use of that network to be able to comply with a publisher's territorial restrictions. Where access is being granted to content over the public Internet it may still be limited, through passwords etc., to authorised users (i.e. employees, registered students etc.) who are located within a specific place/territory. Where users are not from a limited group they may still be registering with credit card authorisation or some other criteria that link them to territory.

Even with free-to-Web content the IP address (i.e. the unique number that is assigned to each computer accessing the Internet) of each user can be traced with a fair degree of accuracy (but not 100%) to determine where that user is situated. Mobile networks are themselves limited to territorial infrastructure and licensing regimes so again territorial grants are common, although provision may need to be made for 'roaming' i.e. the ability to access a home network from overseas via a local network. Finally, use of language and a distinction between active and passive targeting of any given audience may provide some practical limitations too.

(4) *Post-termination use*

One topic that has received increasing attention is the question of continued use of online content by a license following termination of a supply agreement for that content. The basic issue is straightforward: when a user buys a work from a publisher in print form the user has permanent access to that work, yet where the user buys access to that work under an online agreement the user's ability to access that work may end when the agreement ends. Where the user has paid considerably less for the online access than the hard copy this may seem an acceptable trade-off. Where this is not the case, the user may push for continued access. This is particularly so with libraries and other institutional licensees who are keen not to be prejudiced by migrating from print to digital content.

So, for example, if a user subscribes to one year's online access to journal content published on a monthly basis, when that subscription period ends the user may receive continued access to the journal content published during that year as if it had received hard copy versions. Access to any future editions would not be permitted unless the subscription period was renewed. Access to any archive of past editions pre-dating the one year subscription period might also be restricted. Any continued access would also remain subject to terms and conditions of use in order to prevent misuse of the content. So the phrase 'post-termination' should be used with care. The relevant agreement would need to distinguish between expiry of any supply or new/archive content and termination of the agreement, and any continued right, as a whole.

This issue has also arisen where an eBook purchaser attempts to obtain a replacement copy of a title when, for example, their eBook reader is lost or damaged. If a publisher permits online eBook sellers to provide such copies should and can such rights continue indefinitely – and from any location? The wider notion of whether an eBook is as permanent as a printed copy was challenged by the remote removal by Amazon of certain George Orwell titles from customer devices following a problem over rights. The customers were refunded but Amazon's CEO ultimately apologised for the action. The press made much of the fact that '1984' was one of the titles but Orwell's essay 'Books v. Cigarettes' has more resonance. In that Orwell audited the retail costs – and relative value – of his reading habits. Whilst written in 1946 any publisher pricing eBooks and other digital reading experiences would recognise the factors discussed.

(5) *Digitisation*

These precedents are no longer predicated on the supply of material by a publisher to a digital distribution partner in print form. Yet in some cases that will continue. Indeed, in Precedent Nineteen explicit reference is still made to the process of taking print content and 'converting into machine-readable form', or in other words: digitisation.

That process could actually prove to be as valuable for the publisher as the act of distribution itself for the reasons explained below. It may, of course, become an increasingly unnecessary process for new works. Today, production technology for many publishers is firmly digital with books and journals now largely written, delivered, edited, typeset and produced on computer – even where the delivery of that content to the reader remains stubbornly in print-on-paper format. By contrast, older pre-existing content will usually be held in analogue form.

Many publishers and other content owners have so far resisted digitising their archives of content because of both the resource and rights clearance issues involved. Therefore, any form of arrangement where a distributor digitises content as part of the distribution agreements can be of great benefit to the licensing Proprietor. In such cases it would, however, be preferable to building in agreed terms clarifying ownership and requiring the supply of a copy of the digitised material back to the Proprietor.

Of course, as digital distribution methods develop the revenue potential for both new digital content and the exploitation of archives increases and the implementation costs of publisher digitisation programmes become more worthwhile. Such a programme could itself be the subject of a detailed commercial agreement with service level and ownership issues being dealt with alongside costs and timing. It might be undertaken in-house or out-sourced to a third party. That third-party may be prepared to incur some or all of the costs in return for rights in the digitised material. This of course is a model used by Google, which is probably doing more digitising of books than most. (See **Legal Developments: An Introduction** for reference to the Google Settlement, as yet unresolved at the time of writing).

An added complication is the format in which the digital material is held and supplied. Notwithstanding industry attempts to establish an agreed open standard, the range of proprietary file formats for eBooks is extensive and creating material to fit can be expensive. Accordingly the closing statement made in this Introduction in the last edition: that the development of digital repositories that are able to hold and deliver content for new media distribution is likely be one of the key challenges for publishers in the next five years, has proved apposite. Putting in place those technical supply arrangements remains as important as the need to establish the licensing and contractual framework to match.

PRECEDENT EIGHTEEN

Licence to Digital Media Producer to Utilise Existing Print Material in Carrier Form

This precedent is an agreement licensing a pre-existing literary work to a digital media, apps or software producer for distribution in carrier form (e.g., as a CD-ROM, DVD-ROM, USB flash drive or a proprietary handheld format), though with little alteration it could equally well apply to such licensing works combining literary and artistic elements. It has been drafted on the premise that either the original work will form the basis for the electronic product (which would be the case for an electronic encyclopaedia, for instance – visual and audio materials being subsidiary in intellectual property terms to the main work), or that the original work will be one of a few of equal importance included in the product – for example, a digital bookshelf presented for a proprietary games device (on, say, a Nintendo DS game card or Sony PSP universal media disc) featuring a dictionary, a thesaurus and an encyclopaedia. Where the licensed material does not form a substantial part of the electronic product (measured either by volume or by importance), the licensor's ability to insist on comprehensive approval and consent provisions is likely to be considerably diminished and the contract will need to be modified accordingly. For uses of relatively insignificant portions of existing works a permissions-type agreement may be more appropriate. The document could be adapted for applications developed for online and mobile delivery but the other electronic precedents presented in this book will probably be a better starting point.

Preamble

Recital 1: It is vital for licensing publishers to ensure that they *do* control electronic rights under their agreement with the copyright holder before seeking to exploit those rights in any way. It is to be hoped that head contracts being made today make the position perfectly clear; **see Precedent One, Clause 14 (xxi) and (xxii).** The situation may be less clear-cut with older contracts; a grant of 'mechanical reproduction rights', for instance, is unlikely to be sufficient. One criterion that must be borne in mind in interpreting contracts which are not specific over electronic rights is the intentions of the parties at the time of signature. If it is unambiguous that the contract was intended to grant rights to the publisher in future technological developments which could not have been anticipated when the contract was made then all may be well. Even if the licensing publisher has taken an assignment of the entire copyright in the work it has been held that the foregoing still applies. In any case of doubt professional advice should be sought.

Recital 2: If the licensed work is one of several to be included in the product this should be changed to something along the lines of '... based upon the Work, the X English Dictionary and the Y Encyclopaedia and the Proprietor is willing to license the Licensee to utilise the Work so as to do so ...'.

1. Licence

1.1 (1) In most licensing situations it is prudent to license rights for as short a time as possible. Nowhere is this more true than in licensing electronic rights: extraordinarily rapid advances in the technology (methods of distribution, transmission, software and hardware) mean that this year's licensed products may be next year's memories. Most licensors are now aware of the need to license (particularly in terms of the platform) as narrowly as possible, since it is impossible to predict what the effect of previously-licensed products may be on the ability to license for applications as yet unknown. Platforms are dealt with in sub-clause (3) of this clause. A performance criterion (see Clause 17.1) is worth considering, since it will enable recovery of rights if insufficient sales are being made by a licensee. A short licence term is also a desirable inclusion. Clearly, the willingness of licensees to agree a licence term of perhaps three years will depend in part on their initial investment in the electronic product concerned and, in the case of proprietary formats, the life-cycle of the platform on which it is presented; it might be unrealistic to expect the producer of a full multimedia product (with the attendant investment that implies) to accept a three-year licence – though a performance criterion may be more easily achievable or it may be possible to build in a three-yearly review provision. In situations involving more modest investment, or limited platforms, a licence term of three to five years is often reasonable – possibly with a provision for renewal either by mutual agreement or for automatic renewal if sales (or revenue) exceed a stipulated figure during the final year of the licence.

(2) Whether an exclusive or non-exclusive licence is to be granted is, of course, a matter for negotiation between licensor and licensee. Much will depend on the extent of the material being licensed: if the licence is on a permission-type basis for a modest amount of material non-exclusive rights are generally all that will be required. If a multimedia work is to be developed out of an existing literary work, it is likely that the licensee will want some form of exclusivity over its rights. As in sub-licensing rights in print form it is important to ensure that the contract is specific as to the actual rights being licensed, whether exclusively or non-exclusively. For instance, an exclusive licence to utilise a dictionary for production of an electronic product to include also a thesaurus and an encyclopaedia would not in itself preclude the licensor from licensing rights in the same work for electronic exploitation in a product which did not also include a thesaurus and encyclopaedia.

MEMORANDUM OF AGREEMENT made this [*number*] day of [*month*] 20 [*year*] between [*company name*] of [*address*] (hereinafter termed 'the Proprietor', which expression shall be deemed to include the Proprietor's assigns or successors in business as the case may be) of the one part, and [*company name*] of [*address*] (hereinafter termed 'the Licensee') of the other part,

WHEREAS, pursuant to an agreement between the Proprietor and the owner of the copyright, the exclusive rights of exploitation in a literary work written by [*name*] (hereinafter termed 'the Author') and entitled [*title*] (hereinafter termed 'the Work') are vested in the Proprietor and

WHEREAS the Licensee wishes to create and develop a digital media product at present known as [*title*] (hereinafter termed 'the Product') based upon the Work and the Proprietor is willing to license the Licensee to do so on the terms and conditions of this Agreement

NOW IT IS HEREBY MUTUALLY AGREED as follows:

1. Licence

1.1 In consideration of the payments hereinafter mentioned and subject to the terms and conditions hereof the Proprietor hereby grants to the Licensee for a period of [*number*] years from the date of this Agreement (hereinafter termed 'the Licence Term') the exclusive

---

(3) The territory in which rights can be granted may be limited by the head contract. Even if it is not, there may be good reasons (such as a pre-existing licence to a US publisher which includes electronic rights) for restricting a licensee to less than world rights. Such a restriction is practicable for carrier-based products (subject, of course, to the same EC single market and other provisions as apply to books) and local networks, but is more problematic for exploitation on the Internet where territorial limits are less easily applied – but see comments regarding online territorial rights in the **Introduction to Electronic Precedents** which precedes this Precedent.

(4) The language to be included here is the human language involved. Licensees of multimedia products may intend to make them available in multi-language editions or to issue local language editions. Again the head contract (possibly together with existing sub-licensing agreements) will determine the availability of different languages for licensing.

1.3 It is very advisable to restrict the licensed platform. As described in the Introduction to electronic precedents, there is a danger that developments in technology can allow ambiguity to creep into the scope of rights granted. For instance, versions of this Precedent in earlier editions described how a licensee might license the open standard form of CD-ROM separately from the proprietary CD-I platform. CD-I was one of a number of mainly TV-based, multimedia disc systems, that were launched alongside CD-ROM. CD-I was heavily promoted by electronics giant Philips during the 1990s and reference to it still appears in some rights contracts, even though it is now no longer produced. In fact, before CD-I was discontinued, Philips attempted to re-launch the technology as an online platform – which would have been a challenge to all those rights contracts that had included the platform on the basis that it was for carrier use only. Clearly, both drafting skills and technological knowledge are needed to develop effective definitions for digital rights.

In practice many producers are likely to wish to prevent the licensing publisher from granting electronic rights to another party for what could be an opposing platform. In these circumstances, rather than tying up other platforms by licensing them to the licensee for purely defensive reasons, a licensor can either seek to include in the contract a commitment by the licensee to exploit in such a platform or to include an option and matching rights provision for other platforms. If none of these can be agreed a time limit during which licensing others for different platforms without the licensee's consent (not to be unreasonably withheld or delayed) is precluded could be included.

It is still common to license carrier-based electronic rights (whether for open formats such as CD /DVD or for proprietary ones) separately from online distribution rights and the technical format of currently popular eBook readers has effectively maintained that distinction. There are, however, some hybrid carrier/online products (particularly in the video games sector but also the so-called digital or managed copy features on feature film DVDs).

1.4 For more information on rental and lending, see the Introduction.

2. Reserved Rights

2.1 Precedents for licensing online transmission will also be found in this section – **see Precedents Nineteen, Twenty and Twenty-Three**.

2.2 (1) It is advisable to make any proposed 'bundling' of an electronic product (i.e., software which is included with the sale price of hardware) subject to consent. The prices paid by hardware manufacturers for software to be bundled is low in comparison with the prices paid by consumers for the same software sold separately (and is therefore likely to have an effect on royalties paid to the licensor); and there is a perception that some bundled software is bundled because it does not enjoy sufficient sales in stand-alone form. On the other hand bundled software, at whatever reward to the licensor, can promote enhanced future stand-alone sales of associated software and upgrades of the existing software. If consent to bundling is given a licensor may wish to impose restrictions over such matters as quantities and timing.

(2) Sales can also be enhanced as the result of cover disks supplied free to purchasers of computer magazines and, increasingly, newspapers and the general press. Such disks often include only a sample of an electronic product and frequently are supplied to the magazine or other print publication at a nominal price, free of charge or accompanied by payment (because of their promotional value). Depending on the nature of the work being licensed there may be no reason to prohibit such cover disks; but see note on Clause 8.2.

(3) One of the more common bundles of disk-based works today is with printed copies of the same work and it may be necessary to use elements from this Precedent Seventeen in the relevant print agreement. The development of hybrid carrier/online products, as described above in relation to Clause 1.3, might require a combination of elements from this Precedent Seventeen and the online agreements (**Precedents Nineteen, Twenty and Twenty-Three**) which follow.

licence to develop the Work for inclusion in the Product and to manufacture and distribute the Work in the form in which it is included in the Product throughout [*territory or territories*] (hereinafter termed 'the Territory') for retrieval in the [*language*] language.

1.2 The licence hereby granted shall entitle the Licensee to utilise the Work only in connection with the Product.

1.3 The Product shall be manufactured and distributed and made available by the Licensee only in the form of [*specify platform*].

1.4 Before making the Product available for rental or authorising third parties to do so the Licensee shall obtain consent from the Proprietor in accordance with sub-clause 5.1 of Clause 5.

2. Reserved Rights

2.1 All rights in the Work other than those licensed to the Licensee under sub-clauses 1.1 and 1.2 of Clause 1 are reserved by the Proprietor for exploitation by itself or in conjunction with other parties or by licence to other parties or for non-use as at its sole discretion it shall see fit. Without prejudice to the generality of the foregoing the licence hereby granted to the Licensee is solely in respect of the carrier form specified in sub-clause 1.3 of Clause 1 and expressly excludes any right to make the Product available to any third party by any electronic delivery service or by any means of online, satellite or other transmission.

2.2 Save as otherwise may specifically be permitted herein the Licensee shall not without the prior consent of the Proprietor permit the Product to be included with any other work and/or any computer software nor without the prior consent of the Proprietor shall the Licensee permit the Product to be sold or bundled or otherwise distributed as part of a package with any other computer software or hardware or with any other material of any description.

3. Release

3.2 Before licensing exclusive rights to produce an electronic product it is necessary that the licensor should satisfy itself of the licensee's competence to develop, market and sell the product. This provision is intended to ensure that this competence is translated into actuality. Some licensees may be wary of accepting an obligation as strong as best endeavours, in which case the wording may need to be modified.

4. Alterations

4.1 (1) The moral right of the author to object to derogatory treatment (the right of integrity) might be infringed by electronic (or any other) adaptation. This provision seeks to prevent such infringement. Verbatim use of an author's previously-published work in an electronic product should not cause problems, but many electronic products require the original work to be adapted considerably. If that is the case then this provision will need to be amended accordingly.

(2) It is now relatively common for those acquiring rights for full multi-media exploitation to seek a full waiver of the author's moral rights (to the extent permitted by applicable local laws), in the same way as do film and television producers. **See General Proviso of Clause 14 in Precedent One and accompanying note**. If a waiver of moral rights or consent for a particular application has to be obtained (from the author: the publisher has no moral rights, whether or not it controls electronic rights by way of assignment of copyright or licence) the author may wish to have the right to approve of or at least to be informed of changes and may also want the right to prevent the electronic work being credited to him/her if it is unacceptable to the author. This latter provision would require Clause 6.1 to be amended.

4.2 Is an attempt to protect the author's moral right of integrity from being infringed by users of the product. It is likely that the 'methods, processes and devices' which prevent users from altering the content will be the same as those used to implement any digital rights management solution in accordance with Clause 14.

5. Consultation and Approval

The licensor should endeavour to include as many approval and consultation provisions in the contract as are reasonable in the circumstances: see the first paragraph of the notes to this Precedent and Note (1) to Clause 4.1. Some of those included here are quite onerous for the licensee; but wherever an electronic product is to be based on a published work or is to utilise a substantial part, the licensor should be concerned at least to have some input into the use of the original material, the quality of the product and the plans for marketing it. If the approvals and consultation provisions are sparse, the licensor may wish to include in the contract the

3. Release

3.1 Subject to the Licensee obtaining approvals from the Proprietor in accordance with Clause 5 the Licensee shall release and market the Product at the sole cost, expense and risk of the Licensee in all significant parts of the Territory within [*period*] from the date of this Agreement. The Licensee shall notify the Proprietor in writing of the date of release of the Product in each part of the Territory no later than two months prior to such release.

3.2 The Licensee shall use its best endeavours to exploit the rights granted to the Licensee hereunder to their optimum commercial potential and shall ensure that the Product is given fair and equitable treatment and is not discriminated against in favour of any computer software or other similar products which the Licensee may publish or distribute.

4. Alterations

4.1 Save as shall be necessary for the purpose of adaptation into electronic form the Work shall not be abridged, expanded or otherwise altered in any way for the Product without the prior consent of the Proprietor. The foregoing notwithstanding (but subject to the Proprietor's right to be consulted under sub-clause 5.2 of Clause 5) the Licensee shall be at liberty to include search and other apparatus in the Product so as to increase the usefulness thereof. The Licensee undertakes that the Product shall be faithful to the overall tone and character of the Work.

4.2 The Licensee shall include in the Product any and all programs, methods, processes and devices, including any specifically agreed with the Proprietor in accordance with sub-clause 5.2, as shall be available and appropriate in order to ensure (in so far as it is possible so to ensure) that users of the Product are unable to manipulate its contents so as to degrade or to subject to derogatory treatment the Work as included in the Product.

5. Consultation and Approval

5.1 The Licensee shall consult the Proprietor at all times during development of the Product in respect of the Work and shall implement the reasonable requests of the Proprietor regarding use of the Work and parts of the Work and regarding preservation of the overall tone and character of the Work.

proviso that it reserves the right to require the licensee to omit the names of the proprietor and/or the author from the product, its packaging etc.

5.2 Where the product is being released 'into the wild' to members of the public, licensors may be particularly concerned to ensure that it is not possible for users to extract all or part of their works, and they may reasonably require the licensee to implement appropriate digital rights management controls into the final product. The licensor may wish to stipulate whether the work can be printed out in hard copy or whether files can be copied, transmitted or burned to CD. For more detail on these types of controls see the online agreements (**Precedents Nineteen, Twenty and Twenty-Three**) which follow. Aside from the technical restrictions there may or may not be a requirement to include an end-user licence by which express usage rights are granted to the final user of the product. Such an end-user licence could be in a form appended to the agreement or as approved by the licensor or left to the licensee providing it reflects these provisions. Traditionally, software end-user licences were included in paper form with the disk packaging as so-called 'shrink-wrap' agreements: entered into when the wrapping around the disk was broken. In some cases on-screen warnings may now be considered sufficient. Where the end-user is a consumer, particular care must be taken with the terms of that licence as the provisions must comply with consumer protection legislation (**see the introduction to Precedent Twenty-Two**).

5.6 Interim reviews/approvals may be appropriate for more complex products, perhaps via secure online access rather than physical attendance.

5.2 The Licensee shall consult the Proprietor about any reasonable digital rights management implementation ('the DRM Implementation') required by the Proprietor with respect to the Work and shall incorporate such into the Product.

5.3 The Licensee shall consult the Proprietor and shall give bona fide consideration to the views of the Proprietor regarding the proposed inclusion of apparatus and works and other materials additional to the Work in the Product. If in the opinion of the Proprietor any such additional works and/or other materials are unsuitable for inclusion with the Work the Licensee shall not include them in the Product.

5.4 Within thirty days after the date of this Agreement the Licensee shall submit for the approval of the Proprietor (such approval not to be unreasonably withheld) an outline of the Licensee's marketing plans for the Product together with details of the budget therefor.

5.5 The Licensee shall submit for the approval of the Proprietor (such approval not to be unreasonably withheld) the following materials as soon as they shall be available:

(i) the design and specification for the Product;

(ii) the prototype of the Product, incorporating any agreed DRM Implementation;

(iii) the design, labelling, inlay card, user's guide, packaging, informational and promotional materials for the Product.

5.6 The Licensee shall show the final master of the Product to the Proprietor on screen (at the Proprietor's offices, the Licensee supplying all necessary equipment therefore if requested by the Proprietor so to do) for approval prior to release and such approval shall not be unreasonably withheld or delayed.

5.7 No later than three months prior to the proposed release date for the Product the Licensee shall submit for the approval of the Proprietor (such approval not to be unreasonably withheld):

(i) details of the Licensee's plans for publicising and promoting the Product and of the budget therefore;

(ii) a list of those persons and organisations to whom and to which the Licensee proposes to send units of the Product free of charge for the purposes of publicising and promoting the Product.

5.8 The Proprietor shall notify the granting or the withholding of approval under sub-clauses 5.3, 5.4 and 5.6 of this Clause within fourteen days of

5.10 Rental markets have never been strong in the publishing sector, but emerging digital products and services are currently re-exploring a range of distribution models.

6. Credits and Copyright Notice

6.2 (1) It may, of course, be a requirement of the head contract (**see Precedent One, Clause 19**) that the copyright notice is reproduced in sub-licensees' editions; and in any event a provision such as this should be included in all contracts for sub-licensed editions: There may be a similar provision regarding an assertion of the moral right to be identified as the author (**see Precedent One, Clause 28**), in which case, unless that moral right has been waived or consent has been given (see Note (2) to Clause 4.1), that too will need to be reflected in the licensing contract.

(2) In some cases, the licensee will wish to use a trade mark owned or controlled by the licensor; for instance, if the title of an established printed encyclopaedia includes the name of the publishing house, a licensee of CD-ROM rights is likely to wish to use the same title. Either in the contract for licensing electronic rights or elsewhere, the non-exclusive right to utilise the trade mark in connection specifically and only with exploitation of the licensed electronic product will need to be granted. It is most important that such licensed use of a trade mark is confined only to the use intended and that it terminates as soon as the electronic licence ceases. Before licensing a *registered* trade mark ensure that its registration covers the relevant classes; for example, electronic products fall within class 9, whereas printed books are in class 16. It is desirable, though under the Trade Marks Act 1994 no longer a requirement, for licences to be registered in the Register of Trade Marks so that they have some protection against a subsequent purchaser of the trade mark.

receipt of the respective materials and under sub-clause 5.5 of this Clause within seven days of viewing the final master. If any such approval shall be withheld by the Proprietor the Licensee shall not proceed with further development or release of the Product unless and until it shall have re-submitted amended versions of such materials and/or shown an amended version of such final master to the Proprietor and/or re-submitted an amended list and/or outline respectively and shall have obtained the approval of the Proprietor in accordance with these provisions.

5.9 If after first release of the Product the Licensee shall propose to issue a revised or new version thereof the Licensee shall obtain the Proprietor's written consent thereto (such consent not unreasonably to be withheld) and such revised or new version shall be subject to the consultations with and approvals and consents of the Proprietor as provided hereunder in respect of the original edition of the Product, in so far as such consultations, approvals and consents are capable of applying to such revised or new edition.

5.10 The Licensee shall obtain the consent of the Proprietor to any proposal for renting the Product prior to implementing or agreeing such proposal and shall not proceed with such proposal unless and until such consent (which if granted shall be upon terms and conditions subject to mutual agreement) shall have been received.

5.11 No consent or approval which may be given by the Proprietor to the Licensee under this Agreement shall be deemed to constitute any certification or compliance required of the Licensee pursuant to sub-clause 13.3 of Clause 13.

6. Credits and Copyright Notice

6.1 The Licensee shall include the name of the Author and the title of the Work and the words 'Licensed by [*name of Licensee*]' with due prominence on the inlay card and user's guide for every unit of the Product and its packaging and shall arrange for the name of the Author to appear on each occasion when the Product (or any part thereof) is displayed on screen by a user and on each occasion when the Product (or any part thereof) is printed out by a user.

6.2 The Licensee shall include in some prominent place on every unit of the Product and its packaging the following copyright notice:

© [*name of copyright owner*][*date*]

and shall arrange for such copyright notice to appear on each occasion when the Product (or any part thereof) is displayed on screen by a user and on each occasion when the Product (or any part thereof) is printed out by a user.

7. Financial Responsibility, Production and Discounts

7.2 This provision presupposes that the licensee will be responsible for manufacture of the product. Some licensees license their distributors to manufacture, in which case this provision will need to be changed accordingly (i.e., so that the licensee is to require the distributor to notify the manufactured quantities, in order that the licensor can in turn be notified). If the licensee's distributor is empowered to manufacture copies the provisions of Clause 9.1 and 9.4 relating to the distributor's affairs assume added importance.

8. Royalties

8.1 The basis of remuneration for licensors of electronic products is by no means standardised as yet as the **Introduction to Electronic Precedents** which precedes this Precedent makes clear. As long as the original work constitutes a substantial part of the electronic product some form of royalties can normally be expected. These may be based on the recommended retail price (excluding VAT) or on the dealer price; but, particularly where the licensee's distributor is responsible for manufacturing the product, there may be no recommended retail price or dealer price set. Royalties based on net receipts are therefore common. As with film contracts it is vital to establish and list what deductions, if any, are permitted to be made. It may be possible to get the licensee to agree to pay a percentage of all monies actually received by it in respect of a product, as opposed to a percentage of net receipts – in which case (subject to the proviso that the licensee has no other financial interest in the distributor's performance) the licensee's and licensor's interests in the veracity of such receipts should be identical. Royalty percentages can vary from as little as 5% up to perhaps 30 or 35% – possibly on a rising scale. Profit-sharing is another method of remuneration sometimes encountered.

As to advances, some licensees will be willing to pay reasonable amounts in anticipation of subsequent earnings; others may be prepared to pay lump sums in advance in addition to (probably rather lower) royalties.

8.2 Licensees may also wish to provide for product supplied as cover disks at cost or less to be free from royalty payments. See also Note (2) to Clause 2.2.

7. Financial Responsibility, Production and Discounts

7.1 Cost of development, manufacture, marketing and promotion and all other expenses in connection with the Product and the inclusion of the Work in the Product shall be borne by the Licensee.

7.2 The Licensee shall first manufacture [*number*] units of the Product unless a different quantity shall be mutually agreed between the Licensee and the Proprietor. The Licensee shall notify the Proprietor promptly of the quantities of any and all further units of the Product manufactured.

8. Royalties

8.1 In consideration of the licence hereby granted the Licensee shall make the following payments to the Proprietor:

(i) the total sum of [*amount*] on account of the royalties specified in (ii) below payable as follows: [ ];

(ii) on all units of the Product sold by the Licensee royalties as follows: [ ].

8.2 No royalties shall be payable on units of the Product given away to the Proprietor or given away to publicise and promote the Product to such persons and organisations as shall have been approved by the Proprietor in accordance with sub-clauses 5.6 and 5.7 of Clause 5.

9. Accounts

9.1 The Licensee shall prepare accounts showing manufactured quantities, sales and stocks of the Product and of royalties due to the Proprietor to the 31 March or 30 June or 30 September or 31 December (whichever shall occur first) following first release of the Product and thereafter quarterly to the aforementioned dates and shall deliver such accounts to the Proprietor, together with any payments thereby shown due, within thirty days of the respective accounting date. At the time of delivering such accounts to the Proprietor the Licensee shall send to the Proprietor copies of the Licensee's distributor's statements relating to the Product during the period concerned. All payments shall be remitted in pounds sterling and (except as otherwise specifically provided herein) shall be made without deductions in respect of exchange or taxation or otherwise.

9. Accounts

9.4 For a note on accounts inspection clause percentages, **see Note (5) to Clause 17, Precedent One**.

9.2 The Licensee shall not have the right to withhold any part of royalties due to the Proprietor as a reserve against returns and/or credits.

9.3 If any withholding or other taxes or levies are required by law to be deducted from payments due to the Proprietor hereunder the Licensee shall provide the Proprietor with such documentary evidence of such deductions as may reasonably be required by the Proprietor.

9.4 Upon reasonable written notice and during the Licensee's normal business hours the Proprietor or the Proprietor's appointed representative shall have the right to examine the Licensee's records of account at the place at which they are normally kept, in so far as such records relate to stocks, sales and receipts in respect of the Product. Such examination shall be at the expense of the Proprietor unless errors shall be found, to the Proprietor's disadvantage, in excess of [*number*] per cent of the amount due to the Proprietor in respect of the last preceding accounting period, in which event the expense of such examination shall be borne by the Licensee. Any amount thereby shown to be due to the Proprietor shall be paid on receipt by the Licensee of the Proprietor's invoice therefor. No more than one such inspection shall be made in any one twelve-month period. The Licensee shall include in its agreement with its distributor a provision similar to this provision, in order that the Licensee may examine and verify such distributor's records of account in respect of the Product.

10. Value Added Tax

All monies due to the Proprietor hereunder are exclusive of Value Added Tax, which shall be added to and paid with such monies in accordance with statutory regulations. The Proprietor's VAT registration number is [*number*].

11. Complimentary copies

The Licensee shall send to the Proprietor on or before the day of first release [*number*] complimentary units of the Product in its packaging and the Proprietor shall be entitled to purchase further units at best trade terms. As soon as they shall be available the Licensee shall send to the Proprietor [*number*] complimentary units of each revised or new version of the Product in its packaging issued by the Licensee in accordance with the conditions hereof.

12. Proprietor's Warranties to Licensee

The warranties which can be extended to sub-licensees will depend on the warranties given to the licensor in the head contract. Note that this warranty specifically excludes third-party copyright materials included in the original work. Unless electronic use of such materials was envisaged from the outset it is unlikely that permissions licences will cover it. Thus, if such material is required for the electronic product somebody (the author, the licensing publisher or the licensee) will need to obtain further permission to use it. As worded here, such clearance would be the responsibility of the licensee (see Clause 13(i)).

Where the original work includes personal data relating to third parties, the licensee may require the licensor to warrant that such data was obtained fairly and lawfully, and that the appropriate consents have been acquired to allow that data to be transferred to, and processed by the licensee. This provision is complemented in Clause 13(iv) where the licensee warrants that it complies with relevant data protection law itself (e.g., maintaining an appropriate notification with the Information Commissioner).

As is traditional in publishing contracts, reference is made only to copyright. In digital distribution, however, it is increasingly common to refer to a wider bundle of 'intellectual property rights' reflecting the fact that other rights, for example, database rights, trade mark rights, even patents, can become relevant to the way in which works are developed and exploited in digital media.

12. Proprietor's Warranties to Licensee

The Proprietor hereby warrants to the Licensee that:

(i) the Proprietor is entitled to enter into this Agreement and to grant the rights in the Work hereby licensed to the Licensee and that (except in respect of other copyright works or parts thereof included in the Work) the Work neither infringes any copyright or other rights belonging to any other party nor is it defamatory, indecent, capable of causing religious or racial hatred or otherwise unlawful;

(ii) to the extent that the Work incorporates personal data of third parties, the Proprietor has complied with the provisions of the Data Protection Act 1998 and any other applicable statutory obligations or guidelines relating to the processing of personal data.

13. Licensee's Warranties to Proprietor

The Licensee warrants to the Proprietor that:

(i) in respect of other copyright works and parts thereof included in the Work which the Licensee wishes to include in or adapt for the Product, the Licensee shall obtain prior written permission from the respective copyright owners and shall pay any and all fees required by such copyright owners;

(ii) the Licensee shall not by any act or omission derogate from or prejudice the copyright or any other right in the Work or infringe any moral right of the Author;

(iii) the Licensee shall submit the Product for censorship and/or age classification certification, product certification and any other purposes for which submission shall be required and shall obtain any such certification from the appropriate authorities and shall comply with all rules, regulations and other formalities prior to exercise of the rights granted to the Licensee hereunder in each territory in which the Product is to be distributed or sold;

(iv) to the extent that the Product incorporates personal data of third parties, the Licensee has complied with the provisions of the Data Protection Act 1998 and any other applicable statutory obligations or guidelines relating to the processing of personal data;

(v) the Licensee shall indemnify and keep the Proprietor indemnified against all actions, suits, proceedings, claims, demands and costs (including any legal costs and expenses properly incurred and any compensation costs and disbursements paid by the Proprietor on

14. Copyright Infringement

Notwithstanding that the parties may have agreed on the implementation of a specific digital rights management solution in accordance with Clause 5, it is always possible that encryption methods will be broken in time, rendering such useless. This clause therefore recognises that there is nevertheless an ongoing obligation on the licensee to prevent and report instances of copyright infringement. As mentioned above in relation to Clause 5.2, this may include reference to use of an end-user licence agreement.

the advice of its legal advisers to compromise or settle any claim) occasioned to the Proprietor in consequence of any breach of these warranties, or arising out of any claim alleging that the Product constitutes in any way a breach of these warranties.

14. Copyright Infringement

The Licensee shall use its best endeavours to prevent the unauthorised duplicating, copying or any pirating of the Product. If at any time during the subsistence of this Agreement in the reasonable opinion of the Licensee or the Proprietor the copyright in the Product is being infringed, the party holding such opinion shall at once inform the other. If the Proprietor shall refuse or neglect to take action in respect of such infringement the Licensee may take such steps as it considers necessary for dealing with the matter; and if it so desires it shall be entitled (after providing the Proprietor with an undertaking in writing to pay all costs and expenses and to indemnify the Proprietor against all liability for further costs) to take proceedings in the joint names of the Licensee and the Proprietor. Any profits or damages which may be received in respect of any infringement of copyright in the Product shall, after the deduction of all costs and expenses, be divided equally between the Licensee and the Proprietor. The provisions of this Clause are intended to apply only to any infringement of the copyright in the Product affecting the interest in the Work licensed to the Licensee under this Agreement.

15. Disposal of Product

The Licensee shall not dispose of or destroy the Product prior to eighteen months from its first release and then only after offering to the Proprietor the written option for sixty days to purchase units at the disposal price or to obtain units intended for destruction without charge.

16. Assignment

This Agreement is personal to the Licensee and the Licensee shall not assign, transfer, charge, license, sub-license or otherwise part with possession of the benefit or burden of this Agreement or any part of it without the prior consent of the Proprietor, nor shall the Licensee attempt to do so.

17. Termination

17.1 The licence hereby granted shall terminate without further notice and all rights hereunder shall revert forthwith to the Proprietor in any of the following circumstances:

17. Termination

17.1 (ii) Performance criteria may be (as here) in respect of sales or can require the licensee to pay a minimum amount to the licensor over a specified period (e.g., at least £1,000 over two consecutive accounting periods, failing which the contract terminates). The latter method gives a licensee wishing to retain a licence the opportunity to make the amount due to the licensor up to the specified minimum even though that figure may not have been earned by the number of sales made. A performance criterion is most desirable; sales of many electronic products are pathetically small at present. See also Note (1) to Clause 1.1.

17.1 (iii) See Note to Clause 17.2.

17.1 (viii) and (ix) These provisions are particularly important in the context of electronic licensing agreements: the casualty rate for companies in this area tends to be high.

17.2 The Proprietor may also require the licensee to destroy masters of the product on termination and to provide a certificate of such destruction.

(i) on expiry of the Licence Term;

(ii) if sales of the Product fall below [*number*] units in each of two successive accounting periods (as provided in Clause 9.1);

(iii) if the Licensee shall allow the Product to become unavailable to the extent that there are fewer than twenty-five units in stock (as to which the Licensee shall notify the Proprietor promptly) and to remain at or below such stock level for three months;

(iv) on completion of disposal or destruction of the Product in accordance with Clause 15;

(v) if any payment due hereunder to the Proprietor shall have become overdue by thirty days;

(vi) if the Licensee shall at any time by itself or anyone acting on its behalf fail to fulfil or comply with any other terms or conditions accepted by it hereunder and shall not rectify such failure within thirty days of written notice from the Proprietor to do so;

(vii) if the Licensee shall fail to release the Product within the period specified in Clause 3 in which case any balance of the total advance sum provided under sub-clause 8.1(i) of Clause 8 then unpaid shall at once become due and payable to the Proprietor;

(viii) if the Licensee shall be declared bankrupt or shall go into liquidation (other than voluntary liquidation for the purpose of reconstruction) or shall have a receiver or administrator or administrative receiver appointed of its business or shall attempt to come to arrangements with its creditors. The equivalent of any of the foregoing, though known by different terminology, shall likewise be grounds for termination under this provision;

(ix) if the Licensee shall cease to carry on business as a producer and distributor of materials in the form specified in Clause 1 or if the Licensee shall otherwise cease to be in a position fully to perform its obligations hereunder.

Termination of this Agreement shall be without prejudice to the right of the Proprietor to receive any monies due from the Licensee and without prejudice to any entitlement of the Proprietor to damages and/or otherwise.

17.2 Upon termination of this Agreement for any cause the Proprietor shall have the right for thirty days thereafter to purchase (at the Proprietor's discretion either for sale by the Proprietor or for any other purpose) units of the Product then remaining at a price to be subject to negotiation, which price shall not exceed cost. If this Agreement

shall terminate pursuant to (i), (ii) or (iii) of sub-clause 17.1 of this Clause the Licensee shall have the non-exclusive right for a period of three months from the date of termination to dispose of any units of the Product manufactured by the Licensee during the Licence Term and not required by the Proprietor, subject to the terms and conditions hereof; provided that the Licensee shall not manufacture or permit to be manufactured during the three months prior to expiry of the Licence Term more units of the Product than could reasonably be anticipated as necessary to fulfil orders during the remainder of the Licence Term.

17.3 After termination of this Agreement:

(i) the Licensee shall not manufacture any further units of the Product including or utilising the Work;

(ii) the Licensee shall not attempt to delay or frustrate further exploitation of the Work by the Proprietor.

18. Relationship between Parties

This Agreement does not constitute a partnership or joint venture between the parties hereto. The Licensee is not the agent of the Proprietor and shall not hold itself out as such by advertising or otherwise to the public or to any particular third party and the Proprietor shall not be bound by any representation, act or omission whatsoever of the Licensee.

19. Confidentiality

The Licensee undertakes at all times during the subsistence of this Agreement and thereafter to keep confidential (and to ensure that its officers and employees and agents shall keep confidential) the terms of this Agreement and any and all confidential information which it may acquire in relation to the business or affairs of the Proprietor, save for any information which is publicly available or becomes publicly available through no act of the Licensee; provided that the Licensee shall be at liberty to disclose such terms and confidential information under a duty of confidence to its professional advisers and to others if and when required to do so by force of law.

20. Approvals, Consents and Notices

20.1 No approvals or consents given to the Licensee under this Agreement shall be valid unless they are given in writing and signed by a duly authorised representative of the Proprietor.

20.2 Each party shall notify the other promptly of any change of address. Any notice required hereunder shall be deemed to have been served properly if delivered personally or sent by facsimile or pre-paid first class recorded delivery post to the last-known address of the party to be served with such notice. A hard copy of any notice served by facsimile shall at once be sent by pre-paid first class post to the party to be served with such notice.

21. Waiver of Remedies

No forbearance, delay or indulgence by either party in enforcing the provisions of this Agreement shall prejudice or restrict the rights of that party nor shall any waiver of its rights operate as a waiver of any subsequent breach and no right, power or remedy herein conferred upon or reserved for either party is exclusive of any other right, power or remedy available to that party and each such right, power or remedy shall be cumulative.

22. Third Parties

The parties do not intend that any term of this Agreement shall be enforceable solely by virtue of the Contracts (Rights of Third Parties) Act 1999 by any person who is not a party to this Agreement.

23. Disputes

If any difference shall arise between the Proprietor and the Licensee concerning the meaning of this Agreement or the rights and liabilities of the parties hereto such difference shall in the first instance be referred to the Informal Disputes Settlement Scheme of the Publishers Association and, failing agreed submission by both parties to such Scheme, shall be referred to the arbitration of two persons (one to be named by each party) or to a mutually-agreed umpire in accordance with the provisions of the Arbitration Act 1996, or any amending or substituted statute for the time being in force.

24. Interpretation

References herein to Clauses are to Clauses of this Agreement. The headings to the Clauses are for ease of reference only and shall be disregarded in their interpretation or construction.

25. Governing Law

This Agreement shall be subject to and shall be interpreted in all respects in accordance with English law and the parties hereto submit and agree to the non-exclusive jurisdiction of the courts of England as regards any claim or matter arising in relation to this Agreement.

26. Entire Agreement

This Agreement is the entire and only agreement between the Proprietor and the Licensee concerning its subject matter and supersedes any and all prior agreements, arrangements and understandings (whether written or oral) relating thereto. Neither party has relied upon any statement, representation or warranty of any person other than as expressly set out in this Agreement but nothing in this Agreement shall limit or exclude either party's liability for fraud. No addition to or modification of any provision of this Agreement shall be binding upon the parties unless it is in writing and signed on behalf of the Proprietor and the Licensee.

AS WITNESS the signatures of duly authorised representatives of the parties.

For and on behalf of	For and on behalf of
....	....
Licensee	Proprietor

PRECEDENT NINETEEN

Licence to Institution to Make Existing Print Material Available by Local Networks to End Users within its Own Site

This precedent is an agreement licensing a pre-existing literary work supplied in print form (in contrast to **Precedent Twenty** where content is supplied electronically) to a licensee as a site licence for online distribution via a closed local area network. It could, with relatively modest changes, be adapted as a site licence for a publisher's existing electronic database (although **Precedent Twenty-One** provides a more standard form of access agreement for a wider database-style service). If appreciably less than a complete work is being licensed for use on such a network a permissions-type agreement may be more appropriate. Online licensing of journals is frequently provided by journal publishers or specialist providers on a subscription basis and different criteria tend to apply, again generally closer to **Precedent Twenty**. This document is in effect a digitisation agreement, although for mass conversion of older print archives into digital format a rather different form of services agreement is usually put in place as discussed further in the **Introduction to Electronic Precedents** and the commentary for the Precedent below.

Preamble

Recital 1: **see the note to Recital I of Precedent Eighteen** regarding the licensing publisher's right to control electronic rights.

Recital 3: note that the definition of 'Site' in the Schedule to the agreement may have to take account of a situation in which the licensee's local area network covers more than one geographical location (for example, a corporate intranet or virtual private network (VPN) may be accessible in one or more regional and/or foreign offices). This may have implications where the licensor is unable to license in certain territories.

1. Licence

(1) Given that this is a licence to one institution for a specific site (and similar licences may be granted to other institutions), it is normal to grant non-exclusive rights.

(2) In (i) the process of 'converting into machine-readable form', or digitisation, could actually be as valuable to the publisher as the distribution of content for the reasons described in the **Introduction to Electronic Precedents**.

(3) For more sophisticated digital services, reliance on one 'backup copy' is likely to be replaced by a complex disaster recovery plan featuring mirror sites, secure archives and, potentially, third-party service providers. The scope of this clause would then need expanding accordingly.

(4) The scope of permitted acts will often be expanded to cover other uses, as described in **Precedent Twenty, Clause 3**. JISC recommend certain minimum requirements for the higher and further education sectors, for example, from use in traditional 'chalk and talk' settings to more cutting-edge 'virtual learning environments'. Where the scope of use is expanded, the licensor may be advised to clarify the permitted purposes for which such uses may be put, for example, 'internal business use', 'non-commercial use' (perhaps as defined further) in a similar way to Clause 3 which currently limits hard copying.

(5) With regard to 1 (iii), a licensing publisher may not wish end-users to print out hard copies – even of modest proportions of the complete work (**although see Appendix D on the criteria for fair dealing**). If that is the case this sub-clause should be omitted. Even if hard copies are permitted the licensor may wish to clarify exactly how those copies can be used, for example, in internal/external presentations, course packs, and whether additional restrictions should apply to that use, for example, additional labelling/acknowledgement, audit/reporting. Again, **see Precedent Twenty, Clause 3 and notes for further comments**.

On the other hand a licensing publisher may be willing to permit end-users to go beyond printing out extracts – for example, by downloading to local hard drives (that is, explicitly downloading to a distinct location as opposed to the cache downloading necessarily invoked by mere browsing). If downloading is to be permitted under the contract it will be necessary to decide (i) the maximum portion that may be downloaded;

MEMORANDUM OF AGREEMENT made this [*number*] day of [*month*] 20 [*year*] between [*company name*] of [*address*] (hereinafter termed 'the Proprietor', which expression shall be deemed to include the Proprietor's assigns or successors in business as the case may be) of the one part, and [*name of institution*] of [*address*] (hereinafter termed 'the Licensee') of the other part

WHEREAS the Proprietor controls the exclusive rights of exploitation in a literary work written by [*name*] (hereinafter termed 'the Author') entitled [*title*] (hereinafter termed 'the Work') and

WHEREAS the Proprietor has issued the Work in printed book form and

WHEREAS the Proprietor wishes to make the Work available to end users (hereinafter termed 'End Users') as specified in Schedule 1 within the limits of the site (hereinafter termed 'the Site') specified in Schedule 1 and the Proprietor is willing to license the Licensee to do so on the terms and conditions of this Agreement

NOW IT IS HEREBY MUTUALLY AGREED as follows:

1. Licence

In consideration of the payments hereinafter mentioned and subject to the terms and conditions hereof the Proprietor hereby grants to the Licensee a non-exclusive licence:

(i) to convert the Work into machine-readable form and to store it electronically on the Licensee's database (hereinafter termed 'the Database', the Work as stored on the Database hereinafter being termed 'the Licensed Edition'), and to make one copy of the Licensed Edition for backup and disaster recovery purposes;

(ii) to make the Licensed Edition available for access, searching and viewing by means of electronic data transmission to End Users within the limits of the Site via remote terminals on the Licensee's local area network;

(ii) whether downloading is permitted only for research and private study; (iii) whether it must only be temporary; and (iv) whether to allow downloading in the form of text which is capable of being edited and, therefore, otherwise manipulated or whether the downloading is allowed only in the form of bitmapped images.

It may be the case that the licensor requires the implementation of a digital rights management solution to achieve these and other restrictions on handling of the work by the end-users. The provision should be changed according to the circumstances, which in turn will probably result in consequential changes elsewhere in the contract.

(6) Licensors may also have to consider whether material from the licensed edition may be reused in original documents for internal circulation within the licensed institution (only not for sale or distribution to third parties).

2. Reserved Rights

(1) Ideally the grant of rights should be sufficiently clear to define the limits of what the Licensee is receiving, but where new technology is involved we recognise that may well be a counsel of perfection. It is always good practice, therefore, particularly with new forms of distribution, to clarify what rights the Proprietor is reserving. Also, as mentioned in the Introduction to Electronic Precedents, an additional goal may often be to develop non-disruptive rights templates that prevent new forms of digital use conflicting with existing rights grants. Even if this licence is non-exclusive the risk of disruption could exist where the Proprietor has granted exclusive rights to the same content in another media.

(2) As discussed above, receipt of a digitised version of the work from the digitisation process could be important to the licensing publisher. In which case, the licensor might want clarification as to ownership of any rights in that digitised version (to the extent any separate rights from the original work are created) and also physical access to that material (even if no rights are created).

(3) The wording here seeks to restrict the licensee as far as possible to the usage intended. It may of course need to be amended, depending on individual circumstances. In particular, the drafting of the definition of 'Site' will be key to setting the parameters of acceptable use by the Licensee. Corporate intranets and VPNs are commonly accessible not only from remote office locations, but also by employees accessing the intranet on-site using wireless networking, or from home over the public Internet. In all cases there may be varying degrees of security associated with the connection which may cause concern for licensors of sensitive content.

(4) In 2.1 reference to 'online, broadcast or other means of transmission' covers both Internet and broadcast-based systems. An alternative common phrase currently used is 'wired and/or wireless means' reflecting the wording of copyright legislation attempting to provide a technology-neutral definition of a communication to the public.

3. Hard Copying

See Note (5) to Clause 1. If printing out is to be permitted then limiting it to 5% of the total text may be appropriate, in line with the Copyright Licensing Agency's photocopying licensing scheme. Alternatively, the limit on printing could be expressed as up to a specified number of pages or screens.

Certainly, if there was any question of all or substantially all of the original work being printed out as hard copy, most publishers would wish the end-user instead to buy a copy of the printed book. See, however, the issue of post-termination licences in the **Introduction to Electronic Precedents** and below at Clause 17.

4. Release

Committing a licensee of online rights to a release date may seem to be of less importance where there is a non-exclusive grant of rights and/or there is no access use payment of any kind (see comments on Clause 9). Regardless, though, of how far the licensor may be at a disadvantage if the work is not released on a timely basis, it is a common requirement in any form of online rights licence that the licensee should have a contractual commitment to make the content available. In certain contracts – particularly those targeted at consumer users – that might be extended into more detailed requirements as to where and how it is featured within the relevant online service (for more details on such 'placement' provisions, **see Precedent Twenty-Three**).

(iii) to permit End Users to print hard copies of extracts from the Licensed Edition as stipulated in Clause 3.

2. Reserved Rights

2.1 All rights in the Work other than those specifically licensed to the Licensee under Clause 1 are reserved by the Proprietor for exploitation by itself or in conjunction with other parties or by licence to other parties or for non-use as at its sole discretion it shall see fit. Without prejudice to the generality of the foregoing the licence hereby granted to the Licensee is solely in respect of the uses specified in Clause 1 and expressly excludes any right to make the Work or the Licensed Edition available by electronic or any other means to any party other than End Users or outside the Site or as an electronic carrier product or by any other electronic delivery service or by any other online, broadcast or other means of transmission.

2.2 The Licensee shall not exploit the Licensed Edition or any part of it commercially nor sell, rent, loan (with or without payment), hire out or license the Licensed Edition or any part of it to any third party nor post any of the contents of the Licensed Edition to any website, electronic bulletin board, wide or local area network or other online environment without the prior consent of the Proprietor.

3. Hard Copying

The Licensee may permit End Users to print hard copies of up to [*number*] per cent of the Licensed Edition (measured by wordage) for the purposes of research and private study only.

4. Release

The Licensee shall make the Licensed Edition available as stipulated in sub-clause 1.2 of Clause 1, at the sole cost and expense of the Licensee, within [*period*] from the date of this Agreement.

5. Alterations

Much of **Note (1) to Clause 4.1 of Precedent Eighteen** is relevant here, though the kind of use envisaged in the present precedent is likely to involve far less radical change (if any at all) than is the case for many carrier-based products. Clearly, some online use could involve extensive re-formatting of the work, even if the work is still prevented in verbatim form without additional multi-media content; for instance, where content is presented on a mobile platform where a smaller screen size automatically requires alteration and re-presentation.

6. Revisions

Especially if the period of years stipulated as the minimum duration (Clause 16) is reasonably lengthy, it is wise to provide for revisions to the work in book form to be incorporated in the licensee's online version. If the licensee should fail to comply with the provisions of this clause, Clause 17.1(ii) can then be invoked. The availability of online content is increasing the need for revisions on an ever more regular basis. Well-known print reference works that were previously revised in new editions around a print cycle based on years are now updated online on a far more regular basis. Revisions may also be made for legal reasons and in those cases the licensor may want the material to be updated more urgently and/or qualify the warranty protection given at Clause 13 if the licensee fails to do so. For more detail see the **Notes to Clause 4 of Precedent Twenty-Three**.

7. Inspection

Audit provisions such as this are beginning to be extended into wider compliance clauses linked to the DRM requirements of a licensor (see the **Introduction to Electronic Precedents**).

8. Credits and Copyright Notice

See notes to Clause 6 of Precedent Eighteen.

5. Alterations

5.1 The Licensee shall not abridge, expand or otherwise alter the Work in any way for the Licensed Edition without the prior consent of the Proprietor.

5.2 The Licensee shall include in the Database (and elsewhere, as may be relevant) any and all programs, methods, processes and devices as shall be available and appropriate in order to ensure (in so far as it is possible so to ensure) that End Users are unable to manipulate the content of the Licensed Edition so as to degrade it or to subject it to derogatory treatment.

6. Revisions

If at any time during the currency of this Agreement the Proprietor shall issue a revised edition of the Work and shall send details of such revisions to the Licensee the Licensee shall within 30 days after receipt thereof incorporate such revisions into the Licensed Edition and shall send written confirmation thereof to the Proprietor.

7. Inspection

Upon reasonable written notice the Proprietor or the Proprietor's appointed representative shall have the right to examine the Licensed Edition at the Site so as to satisfy itself that the Licensed Edition and the uses permitted and the restrictions imposed in relation to the Licensed Edition conform to the provisions of this Agreement. If the Proprietor shall determine that they (or any of them) fail to do so the Proprietor shall be entitled to give notice to the Licensee in accordance with paragraph (ii) of sub-clause 17.1 of Clause 17.

8. Credits and Copyright Notice

The Licensee shall include the name of the Author, the title of the Work, the following copyright notice:

© [*name of copyright owner* [*date*]]

and the words 'Licensed by [*name of Licensor*]' with due prominence at the beginning and end of the Licensed Edition and shall arrange for the name of the Author and the aforesaid copyright notice to appear on each occasion when the Licensed Edition (or any part thereof) is displayed on screen by End Users and on each occasion when an extract from the Licensed Edition is printed out by End Users.

9. Payments

There are several different options available for remunerating licensors of online rights for local networks, including:

1. *A single outright payment.* This would be inappropriate for a licence such as this (see Clause 16) which continues, after an initial specified period, until terminated. Even where the duration is fixed, it is difficult to assess how much such an outright payment should be unless there are relevant prior usage statistics available. It does, of course, have the advantage (possibly to both parties) of certainty; and it benefits the licensee in that it may not be necessary to render statements of usage to the licensor (see Clause 10.1) – though a licensing publisher will usually require such statements anyway, for statistical purposes.
2. *An initial outright payment followed by a further outright payment for each year during which the licence continues in force.* This arrangement surmounts the first problem mentioned under 1 above. The second problem still remains, but many online publishers have now had sufficient experience to be able to gauge pricing levels more effectively. This approach has been common with journal publishers who have found it easiest to replicate the subscription model of print material (indeed online access has often been provided alongside provision of a print version). Although publishers will clearly prefer a full payment in advance, in some cases this has been developed into a pay-as-you-go model with a year's (or other subscription period) payment split into regular instalments.
3. *A fee for each occasion an end user accesses the work.* This can be extended to provide for separate, additional fees for each occasion an end user downloads or prints out a portion of the work (assuming those activities to be permitted under the rights granted). Such a pay-per-view approach has become more common as more sophisticated online payment systems have been developed and can be attractive to licensees with limited usage patterns.
4. *A fee based on the time spent by end-users accessing the work.* As network bandwidth has increased and 'always-on' connections have replaced metered dial-up access, content models which effectively ration online time have become far less popular.

The clause wording as drafted combines options 2 and 3. Note that the sums due under Clause 9(i) and (ii) are outright payments and are not an advance against/on account of royalties due under (iii), although they could be expressed to be. It is envisaged that if they are not on account of royalties the outright sums (representing payment to the licensor even if no online access occurs, for example, an access licence fee) may be relatively modest. Outright sums payable from the second year onwards could be expressed as related to the amount paid in the first year – for example, the sum payable on each anniversary could be 50% of the total amount paid to the licensor during the preceding year.

10. Accounts

10.3 For a note on accounts inspection clause percentages, **see Note (5) to Clause 17, Precedent One**.

9. Payments

In consideration of the licence hereby granted the Licensee shall make the following payments to the Proprietor:

(i) the sum of [*amount*] payable on signature of this Agreement by both parties;

(ii) the sum of [*amount*] payable on each anniversary of the date of this Agreement during the continuance hereof;

(iii) the sum of [*amount*] on each occasion the Licensed Edition is accessed by End Users.

10. Accounts

10.1 The Licensee shall prepare accounts showing the number of occasions on which the Licensed Edition has been accessed by End Users during the accounting period concerned and monies due to the Proprietor in respect thereof to the 30 June or 31 December (whichever shall occur first) following first release of the Licensed Edition and thereafter half-yearly to the aforementioned dates and shall deliver such accounts to the Proprietor, together with any payments thereby shown due, within 30 days of the respective accounting date. All payments shall be remitted in pounds sterling and (except as otherwise specifically provided herein) shall be made without deductions in respect of exchange or taxation or otherwise.

10.2 If any withholding or other taxes or levies are required by law to be deducted from payments due to the Proprietor hereunder the Licensee shall provide the Proprietor with such documentary evidence of such deductions as may reasonably be required by the Proprietor.

10.3 Upon reasonable written notice and during the Licensee's normal business hours the Proprietor or the Proprietor's appointed representative shall have the right to examine the Licensee's records at the place at which they are normally kept, in so far as such records relate to the Licensed Edition and payments due to the Proprietor in connection therewith. Such examination shall be at the expense of the Proprietor unless errors shall be found, to the Proprietor's disadvantage, in excess of [*number*] per cent of the amount due to the Proprietor in respect of the last preceding accounting period, in which event the expense of such examination shall be borne by the Licensee. Any amount thereby shown to be due to the Proprietor shall be paid on receipt by the Licensee of the Proprietor's invoice therefor. No more than one such inspection shall be made in any one twelve-month period.

12. Proprietor's Warranties to Licensee

See note to Clause 13 of Precedent Eighteen.

13. Licensee's Warranties to Proprietor

As discussed in the **notes to Clause 5.2 in Precedent Eighteen**, provisions relating to a specific end-user licence may be added to ensure that end users that are explicitly licensed in accordance with the relevant restrictions – and therefore actively made aware of those restrictions – in addition to any technical enforcement of the restrictions. More detail could also be added on the way in which passwords, or other technical devices, are used to control and monitor use.

The publisher licensee should be aware that it is likely that any licensee might push for an indemnity similar to that provided for at (v) to be included in Clause 12 from the licensor for benefit of the licensee.

11. VAT

All monies due to the Proprietor hereunder are exclusive of Value Added Tax, which shall be added to and paid with such monies in accordance with statutory regulations. The Proprietor's VAT registration number is (*number*)

12. Proprietor's Warranties to Licensee

The Proprietor hereby warrants to the Licensee that:

(i) the Proprietor is entitled to enter into this Agreement and to grant the rights in the Work hereby licensed to the Licensee and that (except in respect of other copyright works or parts thereof included in the Work) the Work neither infringes any copyright or other rights belonging to any other party nor is it defamatory, indecent, capable of causing religious or racial hatred or otherwise unlawful;

(ii) to the extent that the Work incorporates personal data of third parties, the Proprietor has complied with the provisions of the Data Protection Act 1998 and any other applicable statutory obligations or guidelines relating to the processing of personal data.

13. Licensee's Warranties to Proprietor

The Licensee warrants to the Proprietor that:

(i) in respect of other copyright works and parts thereof included in the Work the Licensee shall obtain prior written permission for their inclusion in the Licensed Edition from the respective copyright owners and shall pay any and all fees required by such copyright owners

(ii) the Licensee shall not by any act or omission derogate from or prejudice the copyright or any other right in the Work or infringe any moral right of the Author;

(iii) the Licensee shall use all reasonable endeavours to ensure that the Licensed Edition is used in accordance with the terms and conditions of this Agreement and shall advise all End Users of the permitted uses and restrictions under this Agreement. In particular (and without prejudice to the generality of the foregoing) the Licensee shall use all reasonable endeavours to ensure that End Users keep their respective passwords confidential and do not make such passwords available to others

(iv) to the extent that the Licensed Edition incorporates personal data of third parties, the Licensee has complied with the provisions of the Data Protection Act 1998 and any other applicable statutory obligations or guidelines relating to the processing of personal data;

(v) the Licensee shall indemnify and keep the Proprietor indemnified against all actions, suits, proceedings, claims, demands, losses and costs (including any legal costs and expenses properly incurred and any compensation costs and disbursements paid by the Proprietor on the advice of its legal advisers to compromise or settle any claim) occasioned to the Proprietor in consequence of any breach of these warranties, or arising out of any claim alleging that the Licensed Edition constitutes in any way a breach of these warranties.

14. Copyright Infringement

The Licensee shall use its best endeavours to prevent misuse or unauthorised duplicating, copying or any pirating of the Licensed Edition. If at any time during the subsistence of this Agreement in the reasonable opinion of the Licensee or the Proprietor the Licensed Edition is being misused or the copyright in the Licensed Edition is being infringed, the party holding such opinion shall at once inform the other. If the Proprietor shall refuse or neglect to take action in respect of such misuse or infringement the Licensee may take such steps as it considers necessary for dealing with the matter; and if it so desires it shall be entitled (after providing the Proprietor with an undertaking in writing to pay all costs and expenses and to indemnify the Proprietor against all liability for further costs) to take proceedings in the joint names of the Licensee and the Proprietor. Any profits or damages which may be received pursuant to proceedings taken in the joint names of the Licensee and the Proprietor in respect of any misuse of the Licensed Edition or any infringement of copyright in the Licensed Edition shall, after the deduction of all costs and expenses, be divided equally between the Licensee and the Proprietor. The provisions of this Clause relating to any infringement of copyright are intended to apply only to any such infringement in the Licensed Edition affecting the interest in the Work licensed to the Licensee under this Agreement.

15. Assignment

This Agreement is personal to the Licensee and the Licensee shall not assign, transfer, charge, license, sub-license or otherwise part with possession of the benefit or burden of this Agreement or any part of it without the prior consent of the Proprietor, nor shall the Licensee attempt to do so.

16. Duration

The licence period can, of course, be a fixed period of years or months, which may or may not be stipulated as being subject to renewal by mutual agreement or at the licensor's discretion; or, as here, it can continue after the initial period until one or other party wishes to terminate it.

17. Termination

17.1 (iv) If the site licence is to a non-commercial organisation (for example, a university) this wording may be largely irrelevant – though if the licence is granted to a company controlled by a university it will be needed.

17.1 (v) the relevant deletion must be made (and indeed something more specific could be substituted – pharmaceuticals for business, for instance).

17.2 If downloading has been permitted under the licence (see Clause 1, Note (2)) the words 'and shall arrange for any portions of the Work which have been downloaded to individual hard disks to be deleted' should be added at the end of the first sentence. To strengthen the second sentence, 'statutory declaration' could be substituted for 'written declaration'. As described in the **Introduction to Electronic Precedents**, however, there is pressure on licensor publishers from licensees (especially those who have paid material amounts in licence/access fees) to receive ongoing access to the content which they have received during the term of their licence when that agreement ends, in the same way that they would have done with hard copy. The suitability and implementation of such a concept will obviously vary greatly from case to case, but is something that a licensor should be ready to address.

16. Duration

Subject to the provisions of Clause 17 the licence hereby granted shall subsist for a period of [*number*] years from the date of this Agreement and thereafter until terminated by at least ninety days' notice providing for termination at the next-following anniversary of the date of this Agreement.

17. Termination

17.1 The licence hereby granted shall terminate without further notice and all rights hereunder shall revert forthwith to the Proprietor in any of the following circumstances:

(i) if any payment due hereunder to the Proprietor shall have become overdue by thirty days;

(ii) if the Licensee shall at any time by itself or anyone acting on its behalf fail to fulfil or comply with any other terms or conditions accepted by it hereunder and shall not rectify such failure within thirty days of written notice from the Proprietor to do so;

(iii) if the Licensee shall fail to release the Licensed Edition within the period specified in Clause 4;

(iv) if the Licensee shall be declared bankrupt or shall go into liquidation (other than voluntary liquidation for the purpose of reconstruction) or shall have a receiver or administrator or administrative receiver appointed of its business or shall attempt to come to arrangements with its creditors. The equivalent of any of the foregoing, though known by different terminology, shall likewise be grounds for termination under this provision;

(v) if the Licensee shall cease to operate in business/education.

Termination of this Agreement shall be without prejudice to the right of the Proprietor to receive any monies due from the Licensee and without prejudice to any entitlement of the Proprietor to damages and/or otherwise.

17.2 Upon termination of this Agreement for any cause the Licensee shall cease to make the Licensed Edition available to End Users and shall delete the Work from the Database and shall destroy any copy of the Licensed Edition made pursuant to sub-clause 1.1 of Clause 1 for back-up and disaster recovery purposes. Within seven days of termination of this Agreement the Licensee shall send to the Proprietor a written declaration that the foregoing provisions of this Clause have been effected.

18. Relationship between Parties

This Agreement does not constitute a partnership or joint venture between the parties hereto. The Licensee is not the agent of the Proprietor and shall not hold itself out as such by advertising or otherwise to the public or to any particular third party and the Proprietor shall not be bound by any representation, act or omission whatsoever of the Licensee.

19. Confidentiality

The Licensee undertakes at all times during the subsistence of this Agreement and thereafter to keep confidential (and to ensure that its officers and employees shall keep confidential) the terms of this Agreement and any and all confidential information which it may acquire in relation to the business or affairs of the Proprietor, save for any information which is publicly available or becomes publicly available through no act of the Licensee; provided that the Licensee shall be at liberty to disclose such terms and confidential information under a duty of confidence to its professional advisers and to others if and when required to do so by force of law.

20. Approvals, Consents and Notices

20.1 No approvals or consents given to the Licensee under this Agreement shall be valid unless they are given in writing and signed by a duly authorised representative of the Proprietor.

20.2 Each party shall notify the other promptly of any change of address. Any notice required hereunder shall be deemed to have been served properly if delivered personally or sent by facsimile or pre-paid first class recorded delivery post to the last-known address of the party to be served with such notice. A hard copy of any notice served by facsimile shall at once be sent by pre-paid first class post to the party to be served with such notice.

21. Waiver of Remedies

No forbearance, delay or indulgence by either party in enforcing the provisions of this Agreement shall prejudice or restrict the rights of that party nor shall any waiver of its rights operate as a waiver of any subsequent breach and no right, power or remedy herein conferred upon or reserved for either party is exclusive of any other right, power or remedy available to that party and each such right, power or remedy shall be cumulative.

22. Third Parties

The parties do not intend that any term of this Agreement shall be enforceable solely by virtue of the Contracts (Rights of Third Parties) Act 1999 by any person who is not a party to this Agreement.

23. Disputes

If any difference shall arise between the Proprietor and the Licensee concerning the meaning of this Agreement or the rights and liabilities of the parties hereto such difference shall in the first instance be referred to the Informal Disputes Settlement Scheme of the Publishers Association and, failing agreed submission by both parties to such Scheme, shall be referred to the arbitration of two persons (one to be named by each party) or to a mutually agreed umpire in accordance with the provisions of the Arbitration Act 1996, or any amending or substituted statute for the time being in force.

24. Interpretation

References herein to Clauses are to Clauses of this Agreement. The headings to the Clauses are for ease of reference only and shall be disregarded in their interpretation or construction.

25. Governing Law

This Agreement shall be subject to and shall be interpreted in all respects in accordance with English law and the parties hereto submit and agree to the non-exclusive jurisdiction of the courts of England as regards any claim or matter arising in relation to this Agreement.

26. Entire Agreement

This Agreement is the entire and only agreement between the Proprietor and the Licensee concerning its subject matter and supersedes any and all prior agreements, arrangements and understandings (whether written or oral) relating thereto. Neither party has relied upon any statement, representation or warranty of any person other than as expressly set out in this Agreement but nothing in this Agreement shall limit or exclude either party's liability for fraud. No addition to or modification of any provision of this Agreement shall be binding upon the parties unless it is in writing and signed on behalf of the Proprietor and the Licensee.

AS WITNESS the signatures of duly authorised representatives of the parties.

For and on behalf of	For and on behalf of
....	....
Licensee	Proprietor

PRECEDENT TWENTY

Licence to Institutions to Use Material Supplied in Electronic Form

The original version of this licence was developed by a working party of representatives from the UK Publishers Association and the Joint Information Systems Committee (JISC) in the mid 1990s. It, and variants of it negotiated between publishers and JISC is used by publishers licensing electronic journal content to UK higher education (and other) institutions under the National Electronic Site Licence Initiative 2 (NESLi2) scheme.

Variations of this licence are also used by some other national negotiating bodies for their licensing of electronic journal content from publishers.

It is important to note that many publishers have their own forms of licence, as do some larger institutions and consortia. In addition, there is a scheme called Shared E-Resource Understanding (SERU) (http://www.niso.org/workrooms/seru) which provides an alternative to a formally negotiated licence.

THIS AGREEMENT is made this [*number*] day of [*month*] 20 [year]

BETWEEN: [*full legal name of institution*] having its registered office at [*address*] ('Licensee').

AND [*full legal name of publisher*] a company having registered number [*registration number*] and having its registered office at [*address*] ('Publisher') or not-for-profit organisation whose principal place of business is at [*address*].

RECITALS

WHEREAS [*insert brief product description*];

AND WHEREAS the [*product name*] and all intellectual property rights therein are owned by or duly licensed to the Publisher;

AND WHEREAS this License is based on the PA/JISC and the NESLI model licence for journals;

AND WHEREAS the terms of this Licence and the offer for [*product*] were negotiated and agreed under the [*product name*] agreement between the Publisher and the JISC Content Procurement Company Limited (trading as JISC Collections) ['JISC Collections'] dated [*date*] as part of NESLi2, the electronic journals licensing initiative for UK higher and further education institutions, their users and others;

AND WHEREAS the parties are desirous to contract on the basis of the terms and conditions of this Licence.

IT IS AGREED AS FOLLOWS

1. Definitions

Authorised Users: those people who are allowed to use the material as a result of the licence agreement. This will usually cover any individuals who would ordinarily be allowed to use the institution's library. This will often include walk-in users, and may also include certain commercial users (including those who are off site) who have a contractual arrangement with the institution.

Commercial Use: this was developed as a non-commercial licence. Use by commercial licensees, e.g. pharmaceutical companies may require some modification of terms, but a publisher would probably want to include a principle that any commercial use shall not compete with the publisher's use.

Fee: for national licences, such as NESLi2, the fees are usually agreed between the publisher and a central body. They may or may not be paid to the publisher by this central body or by the individual institutions, but the licence will be signed by each institution on its own behalf.

JORUM Repository: applies specifically to licences covering UK institutions.

Subscription Period: it is usual to define subscription periods according to the volumes and issues acquired in order to cover any early or late publication.

1. Definitions

1.1 In this Licence, the following terms shall have the following meanings:

'Authorised Users'	means individuals who are authorised by the Licensee to access the Licensee's information services whether on-site or off-site via Secure Authentication and who are affiliated to the Licensee as a current student (including but not limited to undergraduates and postgraduates), member of staff (whether on a permanent or temporary basis including retired members of staff and any teacher who teaches Authorised Users in the United Kingdom) or contractor of the Licensee. Persons who are not a current student, member of staff or a contractor of the Licensee, but who are permitted to access the Licensee's information services from computer terminals or otherwise within the physical premises of the Licensee ['Walk-In Users'] are also deemed to be Authorised Users, only for the time they are within the physical premises of the Licensee. Walk-In Users may not be given means to access the Licensed Material when they are not within the physical premises of the Licensee. For the avoidance of doubt, Walk-In Users may not be given access to the Licensed Material by any wireless network provided by the Licensee unless such network is a Secure Network.
'Commercial Use'	means use for the purpose of monetary reward (whether by or for the Licensee or an Authorised User) by means of the sale, resale, loan, transfer, hire or other form of exploitation of the Licensed Work. For the avoidance of doubt, neither recovery of direct cost by the Licensee from Authorised Users, nor use by the Licensee or Authorised Users of the Licensed Work in the course of research funded by a commercial organisation is deemed to constitute Commercial Use.
'Educational Purposes'	means for the purpose of education, teaching, distance learning, private study and/or research.
'Fee'	means the fee as set out in Schedule 1. The fee shall be in line with the Offer negotiated and agreed under the [*insert product name*] Agreement between JISC Collections and the Publisher dated [*date*] as set out in Annex 1 hereto as part of NESLi2.
'Intellectual Property Rights'	means patents, trademarks, trade names, design rights, copyright (including rights in computer software and moral rights), database rights, rights in know-how and other intellectual property rights, in each case whether registered or unregistered and including applications for the grant of any of the foregoing and all rights or forms of protection having equivalent or similar effect to any of the foregoing which may subsist anywhere in the world.
'JORUM Repository'	means the central repository of learning and teaching material funded by the UK funding bodies.
'Licensed Material'	means the material listed in Schedule 2.
'Offer'	means the offer agreed between JISC Collections and the Publishers for [*insert product name*] within the framework of NESLi2 which is attached hereto in Annex 1.
'Secure Authentication'	means access to the Licensed Material by UK Access Management Federation compliant technology, Internet Protocol ('IP') ranges or by a username and password provided by the Licensee or by another means of authentication agreed between the Publisher and the Licensee.

2. Licence Grant

The licence is, of course, non-exclusive. Although it does not state so in this clause, the licence is almost always non-transferable.

3. Permitted Uses

3.1.3.4 and 3.1.3.5 Although these uses are ones that a publisher might expect to license separately or grant permission for (in a print world) it is standard to include these in electronic content licences.

'Secure Network'	means a network which is only accessible to Authorised Users by Secure Authentication.
'Subscription Period'	means the period nominally covered by the volumes and issues of the Licensed Material as identified in Schedule 2, regardless of the actual date of publication. The Subscription Period for the Licensed Material listed in Schedule 2 is from [*date*] until [*date*].

1.2 Headings contained in this Agreement are for reference purposes only and shall not be deemed to be an indication of the meaning of the clause to which they relate.

1.3 Where the context so implies, words importing the singular number shall include the plural and vice versa and words importing the masculine shall include the feminine and vice versa.

2. Licence Grant

2.1 The Publisher hereby grants to the Licensee, subject to and in accordance with the terms of this Licence, a non-exclusive licence to access and use the Licensed Material and to allow Authorised Users to access and use the Licensed Material via Secure Authentication for Educational Purposes.

2.2 In consideration for the Publisher's licensing of the Licensed Material pursuant to Clause 2.1, the Licensee undertakes to pay to the Publisher the Fee in accordance with the provisions of Schedule 1.

3. Permitted Uses

3.1 The Licensee may:

3.1.1 make such local temporary copies of the Licensed Material as are necessary to ensure efficient use of the Licensed Material by Authorised Users, provided that such use is subject to all the terms and conditions of this Licence;

3.1.2 provide Authorised Users with integrated access and an integrated article author, article title and keyword index to the Licensed Material and all other similar material licensed from other publishers;

3.1.3 allow Authorised Users to:

3.1.3.1 access the Licensed Material by Secure Authentication in order to search, retrieve, display and view the Licensed Material;

3.1.3.6 Variants on this may include Licensees wishing to offer interlibrary loan by more direct electronic means (for example, sending a PDF via email but requiring the recipient to print it out and delete the email) or offering interlibrary loan to institutions in different countries. Publishers may wish to negotiate on this.

3.1.3.9 as 3.1.3.4

3.1.3.2 electronically save parts of the Licensed Material;

3.1.3.3 print out single copies of parts of the Licensed Material;

3.1.3.4 incorporate parts of the Licensed Material in printed and electronic course packs, study packs, resource lists and in any other material (including but not limited to multi-media works) to be used in the course of instruction and/or in virtual and managed environments (including but not limited to virtual learning environments, managed learning environments, virtual research environments and library environments) hosted on a Secure Network. Each item shall carry appropriate acknowledgement of the source, listing title and copyright owner. Course packs in non-electronic non-print perceptible form, such as Braille, may also be offered to Authorised Users;

3.1.3.5 incorporate parts of the Licensed Material in printed or electronic form in assignments and portfolios, theses and in dissertations ('the Academic Works'), including reproductions of the Academic Works for personal use and library deposit. Reproductions in printed or electronic form of Academic Works may be provided to sponsors of such Academic Works. Each item shall carry appropriate acknowledgement of the source, listing title and copyright owner;

3.1.3.6 supply to an authorised user of another library (whether by post, fax or secure electronic transmission, using Ariel or its equivalent, whereby the electronic file is deleted immediately after printing) a single paper copy of an electronic original of an individual document;

3.1.3.7 provide single printed or electronic copies of single articles at the request of individual Authorised Users;

3.1.3.8 display, download and print parts of the Licensed Material for the purpose of promotion of the Licensed Material, testing of the Licensed Material, or for training Authorised Users;

3.1.3.9 publicly display or publicly perform parts of the Licensed Material as part of a presentation at a seminar, conference, or workshop, or other such similar activity;

3.1.3.12 The JORUM repository holds course pack and other teaching material.

3.1.3.13 These apply to UK licences. In some cases, funding of research by a UK funding body may require that the funding body has access to the outputs from that research.

3.1.3.14 This covers inclusion of material written by authors at the institution in the institution's repository, even when the repository is open to people other than authorised users. Publishers may wish to exclude or limit this clause, or at least consider its implications in relation to their contributor agreements and society journal contracts.

3.1.3.15 Publishers may wish this to be defined more narrowly or specifically.

3.2 Publishers will need to decide whether they wish to accept this clause as it stands, modify it or remove it. For example, publishers may wish the institution to define the rights that they are specifically concerned about that this clause is meant to protect, and to capture those as positive terms within the licence. Variants of this clause, from other countries, which replace the UK copyright act with the relevant national legislation, do appear. Publishers will need to decide how to respond, depending on their knowledge of the relevant legislation.

3.1.3.10 make such copies of training material and network such training material as may be required for the purpose of using the Licensed Material in accordance with this Agreement;

3.1.3.11 deposit in perpetuity the learning and teaching objects as referred to in Clause 3.1.3.4 in electronic repositories operated by the Licensee on a Secure Network. The access and use of such learning and teaching objects shall be governed by the terms and conditions of the applicable repository;

3.1.3.12 deposit in perpetuity the learning and teaching objects as referred to in 3.1.3.4 in the JORUM repository. The access and use of such learning and teaching objects shall be governed by the terms and conditions of the JORUM depository;

3.1.3.13 save and/or deposit in perpetuity parts of the Licensed Material in electronic repositories operated by the Licensee and/or by an Authorised User on a Secure Network. Access to and use of such repositories shall be limited to Authorised Users and the UK funding bodies;

3.1.3.14 save and/or deposit in perpetuity parts of the Licensed Material of which they are the authors on any network including networks open to the public and to communicate to the public such parts via any electronic network, including without limitation the Internet and the World Wide Web, and any other distribution medium now in existence or hereinafter created; and

3.1.3.15 use the Licensed Material to perform and engage in textmining/datamining activities for academic research and other Educational Purposes.

3.2 This Licence shall be deemed to complement and extend the rights of the Licensee and Authorised Users under the Copyright, Designs and Patents Act 1988 and the Copyright (Visually Impaired Persons) Act 2002 and nothing in this Licence shall constitute a waiver of any statutory rights held by the Licensee and Authorised Users from time to time under these Acts or any amending legislation.

4. Restrictions

4.1.4 Publishers should bear in mind clauses 3.1.3.11–3.1.3.13 in considering this clause.

4.5 This will probably require modification if the licensee is a commercial organisation. However, other clauses (e.g. 3.1.3.11–3.1.3.13) are unlikely to apply.

5. Responsibilities of the Publisher

5.1.2 Publishers may wish to guard against anything stronger than 'reasonable efforts' in order to allow for occasional production errors or indeed special requirements of particular titles unknown at the time of signing the licence. However, it is considered normal practice for the electronic version of a journal to be made available before the print version.

5.1.3–5.1.6 These cover the necessary points to enable to institution to make proper use of the material, which is clearly in the interests of a publisher expecting to renew the licence at the end of the term.

4. Restrictions

4.1 Save as provided herein, the Licensee and Authorised Users may not:

4.1.1 sell or resell the Licensed Material unless the Licensee or an Authorised User has been granted prior written consent by the Publisher to do so;

4.1.2 remove, obscure or modify copyright notices, text acknowledging or other means of identification or disclaimers as they appear;

4.1.3 alter, adapt or modify the Licensed Material, except to the extent necessary to make it perceptible on a computer screen, or as otherwise permitted in this Agreement. For the avoidance of doubt, no alteration of the words or their order is permitted;

4.1.4 display or distribute any part of the Licensed Material on any electronic network, including without limitation the Internet and the World Wide Web, and any other distribution medium now in existence or hereinafter created, other than by a Secure Network unless permitted in this Agreement; or

4.1.5 use all or any part of the Licensed Material for any Commercial Use or for any purpose other than Educational Purposes.

4.2 This Clause shall survive termination of this Agreement for any reason.

5. Responsibilities of the Publisher

5.1 The Publisher agrees:

5.1.1 to make the Licensed Material available to the Licensee and Authorised Users from the commencement of the Subscription Period;

5.1.2 to use all reasonable endeavours to make the electronic copy of each journal covered by this Agreement available, not later than the start of business hours on the day of publication of the printed version. In the event that for technical reasons this is not possible for any particular journal, as a matter of course, such journal shall be identified at the time of licensing, together with the reasons therefore;

5.1.3 to use all reasonable endeavours to make the Licensed Material available to the Licensee and Authorised Users at all times and

5.1.7 and 5.1.8 These are standard for most journal platforms and these clauses are about enabling the institution to make proper use of the licensed materials.

5.1.9 This is likely to be a non-negotiable requirement of any journal content licence, and increasingly may appear in licenses for other content.

5.1.10 Some licenses which cover multiple years allow the licensee to substitute some titles within the package of content, or to cancel a certain number/percentage/value. These details will need to be agreed between the parties as part of the overall negotiation.

5.1.11 Institutions will probably expect individual publishers to have made arrangements for the long-term archiving of the material in the event of the publisher's demise.

5.1.12 Project Transfer covers the movement of journals between publishers and attempts to give clarity to all parties (and guide best practice) on access rights etc following the move of a journal to a new publisher. How it works in any particular case will be governed by the contracts (both past and present) that cover ownership and publication of the individual title. Publishers that are not signed up to the Transfer Code of Practice may wish to consider doing so.

on a twenty-four hour basis, save for routine maintenance, and to restore access to the Licensed Material as soon as possible in the event of an interruption or suspension of the service;

5.1.4 to provide for customer support services to Authorised Users via email or phone, including answering email inquiries relating to the use, functionality and content of the Licensed Material within 24 hrs of request;

5.1.5 to use all reasonable endeavours to ensure that the relevant server or servers have adequate capacity and bandwidth to support the usage of the Licensee at a level commensurate with the standards of availability for information services of similar scope operating via the World Wide Web, as such standards evolve from time to time over the term of this Agreement;

5.1.6 to provide electronic product documentation to the Licensee free of charge. The Publisher will allow copies of all documentation to be made and distributed by the Licensee to Authorised Users provided it is either duplicated in full, or a proper ownership acknowledgement is included;

5.1.7 to use all best efforts to comply with the OpenURL Standard (http://www.niso.org./kst/reports/standards?step+2&gid+&project_key=d5320409c5160be4697dc046613t71b9a773cd9e);

5.1.8 to use all best efforts to comply with the W3C standards (http://www.w3.org/WAI/Resources/#in and http://jisc-collections.ac.uk/Guide-for-Publishers/Publisher-guidelines/Accessibility-standards/);

5.1.9 to make available to the Licensee COUNTER-compliant usage statistics, on at least a quarterly basis (http://www.projectcounter.org and http://www.jisc-collections.ac.uk/Guide-for-Publishers/Publisher-guidelines/User-statistics/);

5.1.10 to permit the Licensee to make cancellations and substitutions of the Licensed Material per annum [*only applicable for multi-years agreement*];

5.1.11 to archive the Material in the [*insert names of services*] archiving services with an indication of the date that archiving commences. The URL that provides details of trigger events that allow access to the archive is at [*insert URL*];

5.1.12 use all best efforts to comply with the Code of Practice of Project Transfer relating to the transfer of titles between publishers http://www.uksg.org/transfer;

5.1.13 and 5.1.14 These are good practice and aid the 'discoverability' of the Licensed Materials.

5.2 This covers the publisher in the case of either content that needs to be removed because of potential legal problems and also content that leaves the publisher because a journal moves to a new publisher. Publishers may wish to include a right to replace lost content with new content at their own discretion.

6. Responsibilities of Licensee

This covers the Licensee's responsibilities to keep the material secure and access restricted to those authorised to use the material. Publishers may wish to consider whether a higher standard than 'all reasonable efforts' is appropriate, given, for example, the requirement for 'all best efforts' in clause 5. Publishers will no doubt be aware that academic institutions do tend to take intellectual property rights very seriously and are likely to apply high standards whatever the licence wording.

5.1.13 provide link resolver and A-Z vendors ideally monthly, or as agreed between the parties, with the following information about each title in the Licensed Material: Title, ISSN or eISSN, previous title(s) if appropriate, previous ISSN or eISSN if appropriate, first volume and issue made available as part of the Offer, or (if volume/issue is not available) first year, final volume/issue or year (if volume/issue not available) and URL. Information on the names of the link resolver companies can be obtained from Content Complete Limited; and

5.1.14 provide the link resolver vendors with the algorithm or syntax for constructing an article-level link from an article's metadata within the Licensed Material.

5.2 The Publisher reserves the right at any time to withdraw from the Licensed Material any item or part of an item for which it no longer retains the right to publish and for which the Publisher has been unable to secure the provisions as set out in Clauses 8.7 and 8.8, or any item or part of an item for which the Publisher has reasonable grounds to believe it infringes copyright or is defamatory, obscene, unlawful or otherwise objectionable. The Publisher shall give written notice to the Licensee of such withdrawal. If the withdrawn material represents more than ten per cent (10%) of the Licensed Material the Publisher shall make a pro rata refund of part of the Fee to the Licensee, taking into account the amount of material withdrawn and the remaining unexpired portion of the Subscription Period.

6. Responsibilities of Licensee

6.1 The Licensee agrees to:

6.1.1 issue passwords or other access information only to Authorised Users and use all reasonable efforts to ensure that Authorised Users do not divulge their passwords or other access information to any third party;

6.1.2 provide lists of valid IP addresses to the Publisher and update those lists on a regular basis the frequency of which will be agreed by the parties from time to time;

6.1.3 use all reasonable efforts, including without limitation by use of Secure Authentication, to ensure that only Authorised Users are permitted access to the Licensed Material;

6.1.4 use all reasonable efforts to ensure that all Authorised Users are made aware of and undertake to abide by the terms of this Agreement; and

7. Fee

This covers the fees payable, which in the case of a national licence, such as NESLi2, are likely to have been negotiated between a central body and the publisher, rather than directly between publisher and licensee.

8. Term and Termination

8.2 As the licence may be for multiple years, it is increasingly common to see a clause such as this, which enables to licensee to terminate early because of a lack of funds. In practice, publishers have little option but to accept these clauses, though they can be simply a means to trigger a renegotiation – neither party will necessarily want to cancel the licence.

6.1.5 use all reasonable efforts to monitor compliance with the terms of this Agreement and notify the Publisher immediately and provide full particulars on becoming aware of any of the following (a) any unauthorised access to or use of the Licensed Material or unauthorised use of any of Licensee's password(s); or (b) any breach by an Authorised User of the terms of this Agreement. Upon becoming aware of any breach of the terms of this Agreement, the Licensee further agrees promptly to fully investigate and initiate disciplinary procedures in accordance with the Licensee's standard practice and use all reasonable effort to ensure that such activity ceases and to prevent any recurrence.

6.2 The Licensee undertakes to the Publisher that the computer system through which the Licensed Material will be used is configured, and procedures are in place, to prohibit access to the Licensed Material by any person other than an Authorised User, that it shall inform the Authorised Users about the conditions of use of the Licensed Material, and that during the term of this Agreement, the Licensees will make best efforts to bar non-permitted access and to convey appropriate use information to its Authorised Users.

7. Fee

7.1 The Publisher will invoice the Licensee or their agent for the Fee payable at the address set out below:

[*address of Licensee or agent*]

7.2 The terms of payments to the Publisher are set out in Schedule 1 hereto.

8. Term and Termination

8.1 This Agreement shall commence at the beginning of the Subscription Period and, unless terminated earlier as provided for in this Clause 8, will remain in full force and effect until the end of the Subscription Period.

8.2 The Licensee may terminate this Agreement at any time if sufficient funds are not provided or allotted in the library budget by the appropriate body in Licensee's institution for the Licensed Material. The Vice Chancellor of Licensee's institution shall provide a written statement to the Publisher in which the Vice Chancellor confirms the significantly decreased budget allocation to the library. In the event that the Licensee wishes to terminate this Agreement after the first

8.5 Institutions take ongoing access very seriously. It is usual for electronic content licences to include provision for continued 'ownership' of the licensed content after termination, and it is unlikely that an institution would sign a licence without such a provision. Because the material licensed to an institution during the term of the licence may include material such as back issues of journals published before the licence period, it is usual to define what content the institution retains access to as that content published and paid for within the period. In this way publishers provide institutions with an incentive (access to extra material) to continue subscribing.

8.6 Knowing that they will have archival access should the publisher vanish is important for institutions. Publishers may wish to clarify what their arrangements are in negotiation with customers so that wording that reflects actual circumstances is included in the agreement.

8.7 This enables the institution to keep the material it 'owns' accessible to Authorised Users after termination, consistent with clause 8.5.

twelve months of the term of this Agreement, the Licensee should notify the Publisher three months prior to the first anniversary date of this Agreement. The same applies for terminations for subsequent years. Any such termination will become effective on 1 January of the relevant year.

8.3 Any party may terminate this Agreement at any time on the material breach or repeated other breaches by the other of any obligation on its part under this Agreement by serving a written notice on the other identifying the nature of the breach. The termination will become effective thirty days after receipt of the written notice unless during the relevant period of thirty (30) days the defaulting party remedies the breach forthwith by written notice to the other party.

8.4 Upon termination of this Agreement by the Publisher due to a material breach or repeated other breaches by the Licensee, the Publisher shall cease to authorise on-line access to the Licensed Material by the Licensee and Authorised Users.

8.5 After termination of this Agreement (save for a material breach by the Licensee of its obligations under this Agreement) the Publisher will provide (at the option of the Licensee) the Licensee and its Authorised and Walk-in Users with access to and use of the full text of the Licensed Material which was published and paid for within the Subscription Period, either by i) continuing online access to archival copies of the same Licensed Material on the Publisher's server which shall be without charge; or ii) by supplying archival copies of the same Licensed Material in an electronic medium mutually agreed between the parties which will be delivered to the Licensee or to a central archiving facility operated on behalf of the UK HE/FE community or other archival facility (excluding an archival facility of a STM publisher) without charge; or iii) supplying without charge archival copies via ftp protocol of the same Licensed Material.

For the avoidance of doubt access and use of archival copies shall be subject to the terms and conditions as set out in Clauses 3 and 4 of this Agreement.

8.6 The Publisher will provide two options for archival access, and the Licensee may select either: i) the Licensed Material as subscribed to during the term of the Subscription Period or ii) the Licensed Material subscribed to on the day prior to termination of this Agreement.

8.7 The Licensee is permitted to mount the archival copies of the Licensed Material supplied by the Publisher in accordance with Clauses 8.5 (ii) and 8.5 (iii), communicate, make available and provide access to such Licensed Material via a Secure Network to Authorised Users in accordance with the terms of this Agreement. The Licensee is further permitted to make such copies or re-format the Licensed Material

8.8 When making use of this clause, publishers will need to be aware of their obligations under any contracts with the materials' owners (if a learned society) or new owners (if the material has been sold or transferred to another publisher).

8.9 This ensures that the licensee retains the ability to access any material that was published.

8.10 This recognises that features of an online platform are not necessarily replicable when delivering 'flat' files of content, and that it is the content that is key.

9. Acknowledgement and Protection of Intellectual Property Rights

9.1 Note: the licence as it stands states clauses 9.1 and 9.2 in the opening line of clause 9.1 but these should probably be 9.2 and 9.3.

contained in the archival copies supplied by the Publisher in any way to ensure their future preservation and accessibility in accordance with this Licence.

8.8 In the event that ownership of a part or parts of the Licensed Material is sold by the Publisher or otherwise transferred to another publisher, the Publisher will use all reasonable efforts to retain a non-exclusive copy of the volumes published and make them available free of charge through the Publisher's server or by supplying such material free of charge to the Licensee in accordance with the procedure described in Clause 8.5.

8.9 In the event that the Publisher ceases to publish a part or parts of the Licensed Material, a digital archive will be maintained of such Licensed Material and be made available free of charge through the Publisher's server or via a third party server or by supplying such material free of charge to the Licensee in accordance with the procedure described in Clause 8.5.

8.10 The archival copies supplied in accordance with Clause 8.5 (ii) and (iii) will contain all textual content of the Licensed Material but may not contain all links and other features and functionality associated with the online version available via the Publisher's server. Access and use of such copies will not attract a fee charged by the Publisher.

8.11 On termination of this Agreement by the Licensee due to a material breach or repeated other breaches by the Publisher, the Publisher will reimburse the Licensee a pro rata proportion of the then remaining Fee for the unexpired part of the Subscription Period. The Publisher shall not be obligated to return any portion of the Fee for termination by the Publisher due to the Licensee's breach pursuant to Clause 8.3.

9. Acknowledgement and Protection of Intellectual Property Rights

9.1 Save as provided for in Clauses 9.1 and 9.2, the Licensee acknowledges that all Intellectual Property Rights in the Licensed Material are the property of the Publisher or duly licensed to the Publisher and that this Agreement does not assign or transfer to the Licensee any right, title or interest therein except for the right to access and use the Licensed Material in accordance with the terms and conditions of this Agreement.

9.2 For the avoidance of doubt, the Publisher hereby acknowledges that any database rights created by the Licensee as a result of local mounting of the Licensed Material as referred to in Clause 8.6 shall be the property of the Licensee.

10. Representation, Warranties and Indemnification

10.1 The Publisher may wish to seek some modification of the warranty, or indemnity provision, for example the inclusion of 'to the best of its knowledge' or some similar wording.

10.2 The Publisher should ensure that it has a mechanism for communicating changes in the platform or specifications to its customers.

9.3 For the avoidance of doubt, the Publisher hereby acknowledges that any database rights created by Authorised Users as a result of textmining/datamining of the Licensed Material as referred to in Clause 3.1.3.14 shall be the property of the Authorised User that has created the database.

10. Representation, Warranties and Indemnification

10.1 The Publisher warrants to the Licensee that the Licensed Material and all Intellectual Property Rights therein are owned by or licensed to the Publisher and that the Licensed Material used as contemplated in this Agreement does not infringe any Intellectual Property Rights of any natural or legal person. The Publisher agrees that the Licensee shall have no liability and the Publisher will indemnify, defend and hold the Licensee harmless against any and all damages, liabilities, claims, causes of action, legal fees and costs incurred by the Licensee in defending against any third party claim of Intellectual Property Rights infringements or threats of claims thereof with respect of the Licensee's or Authorised Users use of the Licensed Material, provided that: (1) the use of the Licensed Material has been in full compliance with the terms and conditions of this Agreement; (2) the Licensee provides the Publisher with prompt notice of any such claim or threat of claim; (3) the Licensee co-operates fully with the Publisher in the defence or settlement of such claim; and (4) the Publisher has sole and complete control over the defence or settlement of such claim.

10.2 The Publisher reserves the right to change the content (including removal of an entire journal on ceasing to have the right to publish), presentation, user facilities or availability of parts of the Licensed Material and to make changes in any software used to make the Licensed Material available at their sole discretion. The Publisher will notify the Licensee of any substantial change to the Licensed Material.

10.3 While the Publisher has no reason to believe that there are any inaccuracies or defects in the information contained in the Licensed Material, the Publisher makes no representation and gives no warranty express or implied with regard to the information contained in or any part of the Licensed Material including (without limitation) the fitness of such information or part for any purposes whatsoever and the Publisher accepts no liability for loss suffered or incurred by the Licensee or Authorised Users as a result of their reliance on the Licensed Material.

10.4 In no circumstances will the Publisher be liable to the Licensee for any loss resulting from a cause over which the Publisher does not have direct control, including but not limited to failure of electronic

10.5 This clause recognises the seriousness with which institutions view intellectual property, and may give publishers some comfort when considering the wording of clause 10.1.

11. Force Majeure

Covers events outside the control of either party.

or mechanical equipment or communication lines, telephone or other interconnect problems, unauthorised access, theft, or operator errors.

10.5 The Licensee agrees to notify the Publisher immediately, provide full particulars in the event that it becomes aware of any actual or threatened claims by any third party in connection with any works contained in the Licensed Material and do all things reasonably required to assist the Publisher in such claims. It is expressly agreed that upon such notification, or if the Publisher becomes aware of such a claim from other sources, the Publisher may remove such work(s) from the Licensed Material. Failure to report knowledge of any actual or threatened claim by any third party shall be deemed a material breach of this Agreement.

10.6 Nothing in this Agreement shall make the Licensee liable for breach of the terms of this Agreement by any Authorised User provided that the Licensee did not cause, knowingly assist or condone the continuation of such breach after becoming aware of an actual breach having occurred.

10.7 Save as provided for in Clause 10.1, neither the Licensee nor the Publisher will be liable to the other in contract or negligence or otherwise for (i) any special, indirect, incidental, punitive or consequential damages (ii) loss of direct or indirect profits, business, contracts, revenue or anticipated savings or for any increased costs or expenses.

10.8 No party limits its liability for (i) death or personal injury to the extent it results from its negligence, or of its employees or agents in the course of their engagement; and (ii) its own fraud or that of its employees or agents in the course of their engagement.

11. Force Majeure

11.1 Either party's failure to perform any term or condition of this Agreement as result of circumstances beyond the control of the relevant party (including without limitation, war, strikes, flood, governmental restrictions, and power, telecommunications or Internet failures or damages to or destruction of any network facilities ['Force Majeure'] shall not be deemed to be, or to give rise to, a breach of this Agreement.

11.2 If either party to this Agreement is prevented or delayed in the performance of any of its obligations under this Agreement by Force Majeure and if such party gives written notice thereof to the other party specifying the matters constituting Force Majeure together with such evidence as it reasonably can give and specifying the period for

12. Assignment

Given that the licence is for particular content licensed to a particular institution, it is reasonable that assignment requires the agreement of the other party.

13. Governing Law and Dispute Resolution

13.1 Either party (if not in the UK) might wish for the licence to be governed by their national law, in which case the other party will need to decide whether they can accommodate that. Alternatively, both parties may agree to remove mention of national law from the agreement, which in practice would mean that any dispute would be dealt with under the laws of the country in which the party that raises the dispute is based.

13.2–13.5 The parties may wish to include more formal dispute resolution clauses instead, for example binding arbitration. In any event is it worthwhile to include at least the principle that the parties will seek to resolve disputes without resort to law.

which it is estimated that such prevention or delay will continue, then the party in question shall be excused the performance or the punctual performance as the case may be as from the date of such notice for so long as such cause of prevention or delay shall continue.

12. Assignment

12.1 Save as permitted for under this Agreement, neither this Agreement nor any of the rights and obligations under it may be assigned by either party without obtaining the prior written consent of the other party, such consent shall not unreasonably be withheld or delayed. In any permitted assignment, the assignor shall procure and ensure that the assignee shall assume all rights and obligations of the assignor under this Agreement and agrees to be bound to all the terms of this Agreement.

13. Governing Law and Dispute Resolution

13.1 This Agreement shall be governed by and construed in accordance with English law and the parties irrevocably agree that any dispute arising out of or in connection with this Agreement will be subject to and within the jurisdiction of the English courts.

13.2 The parties agree to use best efforts to resolve disputes in an informal manner, by decision of the Managing Director of the Publisher and the current Vice Chancellor of the Licensee. Where the parties agree that a dispute arising out or in connection with this Agreement would best be resolved by the decision of an expert, they will agree upon the nature of the expert required and together appoint a suitable expert by agreement.

13.3 Any person to whom a reference is made under Clause 13.2 shall act as expert and not as an arbitrator and his decision (which shall be given by him in writing and shall state the reasons for his decision) shall be final and binding on the parties except in the case of manifest error or fraud.

13.4 Each party shall provide the expert with such information and documentation as he may reasonably require for the purposes of his decision.

13.5 The costs of the expert shall be borne by the parties in such proportions as the expert may determine to be fair and reasonable in all circumstances or, if no determination is made by the expert, by the parties in equal proportions.

15. General

15.1 If this is not included, then any offers or other communications made prior to the licence may be considered to form part of it, which could cause problems later on.

15.4 without this clause a party might lose the right to object to something under the terms of the licence because they had previously failed to object to it.

14. Notices

14.1 All notices required to be given under this Agreement shall be given in writing in English and sent by courier, or special delivery to the relevant addressee at its address set out below, or to such other address as may be notified by either party to the other from time to time under this Agreement, and all such notices shall be deemed to have been received three (3) days after the date of posting in the case of special delivery or despatch in the case of courier:

if to the Licensee: [*insert details of addressee and address*]

if to the Publisher [*insert details of addressee and address*]

15. General

15.1 This Agreement, its Schedules and Annex constitute the entire agreement between the parties relating to the Licensed Material and supersede all prior communications, understandings and agreements (whether written or oral) relating to its subject matter and may not be amended or modified except by agreement of both parties in writing.

15.2 The Schedules and Annex shall have the same force and effect as if expressly set in the body of this Agreement and any reference to this Agreement shall include the Schedules and Annex.

15.3 The invalidity or unenforceability of any provision of this Agreement shall not affect the continuation in force of the remainder of this Agreement.

15.4 The rights of the parties arising under this Agreement shall not be waived except in writing. Any waiver of any of a party's rights under this Agreement or of any breach of this Agreement by the other party shall not be construed as a waiver of any other rights or of any other or further breach. Failure by either party to exercise or enforce any rights conferred upon it by this Agreement shall not be deemed to be a waiver of any such rights or operate so as to bar the exercise or enforcement thereof at any subsequent time or times.

Schedule 1: Fee

Note: The NESLi2 licence is negotiated between the publisher and JISC Collections, and it is important that this is respected. Similar conditions may apply to licences in other countries where these are negotiated centrally.

Schedule 1: Fee

[*Include here details of the Offer as set out in Annex 1 plus the final fee to be paid by the Licensee.*]

1. The Licensee shall cause the Publisher to be paid a Fee for the period [*dates*] of £ [*amount*] (exclusive of VAT) as payment for the rights granted in this Agreement. Such Fee shall fall due and payable by the Licensee within 45 days on receipt by the Licensee of the Publisher's invoice. The Fee is shown exclusive of VAT, which will be payable in addition by the Licensee where applicable.

[*The above clause can be repeated for multi-annual contracts.*]

[*Note: Please do not include in this Agreement or ask the Licensee to sign any further terms and conditions other than after consulting JISC Collections.*]

Schedule 2: Licensed Material

It is good practice to include not only titles, volume and issue numbers but also ISSNs (ideally print and electronic ISSNs where these differ) or other unique identifiers.

Schedule 2: Licensed material

The Licensed Material consists of the following: [*Do not forget to indicate the number of volumes and issues for each title.*]

Annex 1: Offer

This will be the formal offer made by the publisher to the central body or licensee.

Signatures

It is advisable to get a signature from each institution that agrees to a licence, even if the deal is a national one where licensees are automatically included.

Annex 1 – Offer

This Offer is identical to the offer included in Schedule 1 of the [*insert product name*] Agreement between [*name of publisher*] and JISC Collections dated [*date*].

IN WITNESS the hands of the above parties on the date first above written:

SIGNED by: ______________________________

Name: (Signature)

Position:

for and on behalf of

[INSTITUTION]

SIGNED by: ______________________________

Name: (Signature)

Position:

for and on behalf of

[PUBLISHER]

PRECEDENT TWENTY ONE

Online Access to Database Agreement

This is a simple form of user agreement for accessing a publisher's, aggregator's or other operator's online database service. It is intended for use where a publisher is making a range of works available within a wider database, rather than individual works on a bespoke basis (where **Precedent Nineteen** would be more suitable). It could, however, be used as the basis for the legal provisions of any website or other online based product.

It is drafted as terms and conditions, in the form commonly used by many electronic publishers, for a business or educational publishing application, with the licensee customer (probably a corporate or institutional entity) procuring access for its individual employees, students or other personnel ('Authorised Users'). It is drafted in a straightforward style to aid and encourage swift agreement and as such the structure is also suitable for consumer use. It should, however, be stressed that in such case, as with any consumer contract, the additional protections provided by consumer legislation must be taken into account. In addition to general rules which are applicable to any consumer contract (which essentially require more fair and balanced provisions between supplier and consumer than might be permissible in a business to business document and for those provisions to be free of jargon and legalese) there are also separate requirements for dealing with consumers online. In recent years the relevant regulatory authorities have become far more active in enforcing both types of legislation and it is no longer possible for consumer contracts simply to follow identical wording to business contracts. We would recommend that specialist professional guidance is sought in order to ensure compliance with such requirements.

This type of document is intended for online use: as part of a so-called 'click-wrap' or 'click-through' contract where the customer agrees to the terms electronically, usually by clicking an 'accept' button or otherwise completing an online application process (and perhaps paying any licence fees online too). More publishers are aiming to introduce such contracts in order to encourage a faster, more streamlined customer acquisition programme. In some cases, however, access agreements can still be heavily negotiated. The library sector in particular is keen to establish that any move from paper to online does not involve the application of contractual terms which reduce benefits

1. Definitions

You (and Your)/Authorised User definition: Whether the customer is a corporate entity, an institution or an individual, it is common to detail, in addition to the customer who is entering into the contract, the specific users who can access the service (they might be limited to employees, students or family members etc.) and to confirm that the customer will be responsible for their use of the service. As stated in the introduction to this Precedent this document is drafted in a form suitable for use with a customer ('You') which is a business, even if the 'Authorised Users' are individuals (rather than, say, subsidiaries of the contracting entity). Where the customer is acting as a consumer then specific UK and EU rules will apply. Although the general structure of this agreement will still be suitable in that case, as will much of the wording, which is intentionally drafted in a straightforward style, the publisher would need to ensure that the specific requirements of those rules are taken into account. This is often not the case in practice and publishers should be cautious about relying on the approach taken in other terms and conditions available online, especially by suppliers outside the EU where different laws apply.

Account definition: The concept of an 'Account' is not strictly necessary where the 'Fees' (see below) are relatively straightforward, for example, for a flat-rate subscription, but is useful where variable/pay-per-view charges can be incurred and is a common feature.

Agreement definition: As is common, the contract is actually formed by a number of documents. These terms and conditions are designed to be entered into online with an electronic registration form and price list (see below) but many electronic publishing agreements are negotiated in paper form with the different documents attached as schedules or appendices. Note that special rules apply to online contracts entered into with consumers. The customer may want flexibility if, say, their business and use of service alters.

Fees definition: As online publishing has developed, the pricing structures have become more sophisticated to match the relevant product, the market and particular customers. In addition to the comments in the **Introduction to Electronic Precedents** an overview of some of the different methods and models used are set out in the **note to Clause 9 of Precedent Nineteen** but, broadly, the agreement will either refer, as here, to a standard price list or the publisher will have given a specific quote to a customer. If the latter, care may be needed over the confidentiality and continued validity of the offer made.

Service definition: The particular publishing service offered can be set out here or defined by reference to a separate specification. The publisher will usually want to limit the detail, or at least provide for flexibility, in what it is to provide (see Clause 2.4), while the customer will often look for more certainty.

for, or place unreasonable additional obligations on, users. Content owners of all types are, of course, keen to ensure that their more valuable products are only made available in digital form subject to appropriate protection.

1. Definitions

In these terms and conditions the following meanings shall apply:

'Publisher':	[*name*];
'You (and Your)':	the customer, with whom Publisher enters into the Agreement, and any person who Publisher reasonably believes is acting with the customer's authority or knowledge including the Authorised Users;
'Account':	the facility extended under this Agreement allowing You to access and use the Service;
'Agreement':	the entire contract between Publisher and You for the provision of the Service incorporating these terms and conditions, the Registration Form, and the documents referred to in them, to the exclusion of all other terms in accordance with Clause 9.7;
'Approved Use':	Your private and internal business use only;
'Authorised Users':	the users notified to Publisher in the Registration Form;
'Data':	the information and other materials in whatever form from time to time available through, on or otherwise forming, the Service;
'Fees':	the charges for the Service as set out and amended from time to time in the Publisher's price list;
'Password':	a unique user name and code;
'Registration Form':	the Service registration form displayed and completed online;
'Rights':	Data which is protected by copyright, database and other intellectual property and related rights of Publisher and its licensors;
'Service':	[*insert details of publishing service*];
'Start Date':	[*date*]; and
'Term':	[*period*].

2. Registration

2.2 The collection and use of personal data can be highly valuable, but is subject to complex regulation. Active enforcement action and the penalties for non-compliance have increased in recent years as has the general awareness on the part of the public over privacy and data protection. Any publisher developing a database of customer information, whether for advanced CRM activities or simply to provide its service to customers, ought to build in some form of privacy policy and consent wording into its contracting process. This clause reflects that and is drafted on the basis of an opt-out which remains lawful and relatively common in the UK for business to business marketing and for consumer postal marketing and for electronic contact with consumers for an existing supplier's 'similar' goods and services. An opt-in is often seen as best practice, however, and may be deemed legally necessary in some cases. Note that different rules apply to individuals and to corporate recipients and employees so this form of wording may not be suitable or appropriate in all situations. The law and regulation of marketing and commercial communications continues to develop and publishers are advised to take legal advice to ensure their commercial approach, and legal documentation, remain up-to-date. Other territories, even within Europe, apply different rules.

2.4 As discussed above, publishers often seek to build in flexibility over what is included within the service, particularly where they are providing third-party material as part of an aggregated service. A customer will often not accept such a blanket disclaimer where it is paying for a set term. A right to cancel or agree a reduced fee may be a compromise.

3. Provision of the Service

3.2 The Internet has, of course, become the standard platform of distribution for many publishers usually with the benefit of not requiring any bespoke supporting software or hardware. Proprietary online services, broadcast and other platforms will often require the use of special equipment or computer programs and these will require additional leasing and licensing provisions.

2. Registration

2.1 In order to register for the Service and set up Your Account You must complete the Registration Form. You confirm that all the details supplied by You when You register are accurate and complete. You agree to notify the Service help desk promptly of any changes. Publisher may refuse any application to register at its sole discretion. The Agreement shall not be binding until Publisher has issued its acceptance to You.

2.2 The details You provide to Publisher will be stored on computer and used to provide the Service to You. Your details including those of your Authorised Users will not be supplied to any other third parties except with consent or where required by law. Publisher may from time to time use Your details to provide You and your Authorised Users with information about the Service and other similar products and services which it provides. If You do not wish to receive this information click the opt-out box when You register or contact the Service help desk at any time. For more information please read Publisher's privacy policy.

2.3 In order to operate Your Account You will be issued with a Password. You are responsible for the security and proper use of Your Passwords and Your Account, including all charges incurred through them. You must inform the Service help desk immediately if You have any reason to believe that Your Passwords have become known to someone not authorised to use them. If Publisher reasonably believes that there is likely to be a breach of security or misuse of the Service or Your Account it may change Your Passwords immediately and will notify You accordingly.

2.4 All Data advertised on the Service is subject to availability and may be amended or replaced without notice at any time.

3. Provision of the Service

3.1 Publisher will provide the Service and Your Account in accordance with the terms and conditions of the Agreement.

3.2 The Service is accessed via the Internet. You are responsible for the provision of and payment for the telecommunications services plus a suitable computer, browser, modem and any other items of hardware, software or communications equipment necessary to enable You to access the Service and receive the Data. Contact the Service help desk for further details of minimum technical requirements. Publisher will not be able to issue refunds against these charges or accept responsibility for any delay or inability to access any part of the

3.3 Again, these are more or less standard limitations on the obligations of the publisher. But note that the customer may demand more stringent service levels with minimum guarantees, credits/refunds for under performance etc. Obviously the publisher should seek to resist accepting onerous obligations and in particular should not take responsibility for service elements (e.g. the Internet) over which it can have no control.

4. Use of the Data

4.1 This is a crucial clause. It sets out the purposes for which the customer may use the service and its contents. Some agreements provide for much more detail confirming what is and is not allowed. Publishers should think carefully about their service and their customers when drafting the terms of the licence and not just rely on precedent. Additional issues to consider include specifying certain premises or equipment, specifying certain uses, for example, research, quotation and citation, allowing downloaded material to be included in external work product subject to agreed restriction etc.

4.2 These are a range of acts that a publisher may or may not seek to restrict. Some elements of a service may have different restrictions to others. Realistically, being able to police these controls may be difficult, although some publishers include physical audit rights in order to improve their ability to do so (**see further discussion of this in the Introduction to Electronic Precedents**).

4.4 Most publishers are prepared to warrant that they have the rights to supply; some publishers just agree to indemnify if there is an infringement. Depending upon the type of service, other warranties regarding, for example, defamation or obscenity may be given. Whatever the position, a publisher must ensure that it does have the necessary rights – whether by way of purchase or licence – to use the data for these purposes.

Service or the Data due to any faults of, or Your means of access to, the Internet.

3.3 Publisher cannot guarantee that the Service will never be faulty or that it will be available at all times but Publisher will endeavour to correct reported faults as soon as Publisher reasonably can. If a fault occurs You should report the fault to the Service help desk. Publisher may need to vary the technical specification, or temporarily suspend the whole or any part, of the Service from time to time but shall give You as much notice as is reasonably practicable in the circumstances.

4. Use of the Data

4.1 The Service enables You to download Data. Publisher grants You a non-exclusive, non-transferable licence to use the Data on the following terms. Subject to payment of the appropriate Fees and to the excluded uses set out in Clause 4.2 below, and unless indicated to the contrary on the Service, any Data You download may be viewed on screen and printed out in hard copy for Approved Use.

4.2 You must not, nor attempt to, (i) resell; (ii) make available on a local or wide area network; (iii) link to or frame; (iv) make mass, automated or systematic extractions from; (v) include within an archival or searchable database; (vi) access remotely or (vii) distribute externally the Service or the Data (in whole or in part). Any Data which You download must be held securely within Your possession and control free from any third-party access and with all credits, legends, notices or markings maintained.

4.3 You may make such temporary electronic copies of the Data as is reasonably necessary to enable the Approved Use only. All other Rights are reserved by Publisher and its licensors. Any copying, storage, transmission, publication or use, other than as set out above, is prohibited.

4.4 Publisher warrants and undertakes to You that Your use of the Data in accordance with the terms of this Agreement shall not infringe the Rights of any third party. You must contact Publisher immediately if anyone makes or threatens to make a claim against You relating to Your use of the Data and You will comply with any reasonable request from Publisher in relation to such claim.

5. Charges

5.1 You must pay the Fees due for the access and use of the Service and the Data through Your Account in accordance with this clause.

5. Charges

5.3 As mentioned in the **Introduction to Electronic Precedents** and some of the other Precedents, customer demand for continuing access following the end of the contract to some or all of the content supplied during the term has increased. In some cases publishers have always permitted some post-termination use, for example, where downloaded material has been used as part of the customer's work product; but that concept is now being extended more often to allow continued access to content supplied during the original supply period to replicate the experience – and commercial value – of having subscribed to a hard copy journal or purchased a hard copy book. In either case, care must be taken to ensure that any post-termination licence is recognised as such, that is, that post-term use is subject to the same or similar restrictions as during the term (and that access and use can be ended if the licensee is in breach).

6. Term and Termination

6.1 Some publishers include rolling renewal to encourage extension for further terms, although setting prices for these can be difficult.

7. Liability

Publishers are not alone in wanting to limit their potential liability, so licensors should not be surprised when licensees seek to make elements of such a clause mutual. This clause seeks to limit the warranties made, exclude financial losses and all indirect losses and cap direct loss to the level of fees paid. The suitability and enforceability of any such clause needs careful consideration on a case-by-case basis. Liability in relation to printed material is rarely expressly limited or excluded since detailed contractual licence terms have traditionally not been entered into with the reader; however, with online publications, changes to the types of material published, wider geographical coverage and additional risks in relation to software and equipment do make liability considerations more important.

5.2 You will be invoiced monthly in arrears for the Fees due. Each invoice will be payable within 30 days of the date stated on the invoice. If You do not pay an invoice in cleared funds within that period, Publisher may: (i) charge interest on any outstanding moneys due at a rate of four per cent (4%) above the [*e.g., HSBC*] plc base rate from time to time in force calculated on a daily basis; and/or (ii) suspend Your Password and Your Account, until payment in full is made.

5.3 On expiration or termination of this Agreement for whatever reason: (i) Publisher shall terminate Your access to the Service; (ii) You and Your Authorised Users shall have no further right to access or use the Data; and (iii) You must permanently delete or otherwise destroy any copies of the Data in Your possession or control.

5.4 All Fees are quoted exclusive of any applicable value added tax which shall be payable by You in addition.

6. Term and Termination

6.1 The Agreement shall commence on the Start Date and continue for the Term unless terminated earlier in accordance with the following provisions.

6.2 In addition to any other rights Publisher may have, Publisher can terminate the Agreement, Your Passwords and Your Account immediately without notice if You: (i) breach any provision of this Agreement and fail to remedy that breach within seven days upon notice from Publisher; or (ii) are made bankrupt, enter into liquidation or any arrangement or composition with Your creditors or if a receiver or administrator or administrative receiver is appointed against any of Your assets or business or if You suffer any equivalent or analogous event to any of the foregoing in any jurisdiction.

6.3 If Publisher delays in acting upon a breach of this Agreement by You, that delay will not be regarded as a waiver of the breach. If Publisher does waive a breach of this Agreement by You, that waiver is limited to that particular breach.

7. Liability

7.1 Whilst Publisher will use all reasonable skill and care in the creation and supply of the Service and the Data Publisher does not give any warranty as to its suitability, accuracy or fitness for any purpose.

7.2 Subject to Clauses 7.3 and 7.4 Publisher excludes all liability whether in contract, tort (including liability for negligence) or otherwise for

the suitability, accuracy or fitness for any purpose of the Service and any Data and limits its liability for any other liability under this Agreement to the Fees payable by You for the element of the Service or the Data in dispute.

7.3 Subject to Clause 7.4 Publisher excludes all liability for loss of business revenue or profits, anticipated savings or wasted expenditure, corruption or destruction of data and for any indirect or consequential loss whatever.

7.4 Publisher does not limit or exclude its liability for death or personal injury caused by its negligence or any other liability the limitation or exclusion of which is prohibited by law.

7.5 Save as expressly permitted in this Agreement, all warranties, conditions or other terms implied by statute, common law or otherwise are excluded to the fullest extent permitted by law.

8. Indemnity

You agree to indemnify Publisher against any costs, claims, damages or expenses arising from any use by You of the Service and the Data under this Agreement which are brought or threatened against Publisher by another person.

9. General

9.1 You agree to keep confidential (both during and after the Term) the contents of the Agreement and all information concerning the business or affairs of Publisher. This does not apply to any disclosure required by a court or regulatory body of competent jurisdiction, trivial information or information already publicly available or demonstrably in Your possession at the time of disclosure (other than as a result of breach of any confidentiality obligation).

9.2 Publisher may modify the Agreement at any time, such modifications becoming effective immediately upon either posting of the modified Agreement on the Service or notification to You. By continuing to use the Service following any such modification You will be deemed to accept such modification.

9.3 You are not allowed to transfer or attempt to transfer this Agreement in whole or in part.

9.4 Publisher will not be liable if Publisher cannot perform its obligation under this Agreement because of circumstances beyond its reasonable

control such as technical failure, severe weather, fire or explosion, civil disorder, war, or military operations, natural or local emergency, anything done by government or other competent authority or industrial disputes of any kind.

9.5 Notices given under the Agreement may be given by Publisher to You online through the Service or in writing to the address as currently stated in Your Account details and by You to Publisher through the Service help desk.

9.6 The parties do not intend that any term of this Agreement shall be enforceable solely by virtue of the Contracts (Rights of Third Parties) Act 1999 by any person who is not a party to this Agreement.

9.7 This Agreement is the entire and only agreement between the parties concerning its subject matter and supersedes any and all prior agreements, arrangements and understandings (whether written or oral) relating thereto. Neither party has relied upon any statement, representation or warranty of any person other than as expressly set out in this Agreement but nothing in this Agreement shall limit or exclude liability either party's liability for fraud.

9.8 This Agreement is governed by, and construed in accordance with, English Law and You and Publisher submit to the non-exclusive jurisdiction of the English courts as regards any claim or matter arising in relation to this Agreement.

PRECEDENT TWENTY-TWO

EBook Distribution Agreement

As described in the **Introduction to Electronic Precedents,** there is no such thing as a standard 'eBook agreement'. What we have provided here is a form of agreement reflecting some of the issues currently being considered in the distribution and sale of eBooks. It is based upon a form of precedent which appeared in earlier editions of this book for licensing a producer of a hand-held electronic device and as such simply takes what might previously been used to make material available on earlier generation *Palms, Psions* or *Franklins* (with content delivered in physical form or pre-loaded) and upgrades it for the current crop of eBook reader devices (with content delivered online). It is described as a 'Distribution' rather than a 'Licence' Agreement to comply with the traditional publishing concern that any arrangement labelled a licence might be viewed as an exploitation of subsidiary rights. It should be clear, however, that under this arrangement the publisher is still publishing the works in question, albeit in eBook rather than print form, rather than licensing a third party to publish. **See Note 2 to Clause 1 in Precedent One and Note to Clause 3.3.1 in Precedent Two**. As described in the **Introduction to Electronic Precedents,** the arrangements set out in this document can be distinguished from delivery of a publisher's digital content other than as a standalone eBook which is dealt with in **Precedent Twenty-Three**, although we do also include suggestions in the **commentary to Precedent Twenty-Three** regarding mobile/wireless distribution of that form of content.

Preamble

Under this agreement the publishers grant the operators of a website the rights to sell the publishers' eBooks on that website. The website operators sell the books on their own account in the normal way. They set the price of the eBooks for the customers of the website and pay an agreed wholesale price to the publishers. Accordingly this agreement does not adopt the so-called 'agency model' where the publishers would seek to appoint the website operators as the publishers' agent, something that becomes more possible as physical stock is replaced with digital files. That model allows the publishers to set the retail price as, in effect, the publishers are selling directly to the customers through the website operator and thus there is no attempt to fix prices within a chain of distribution (such resale price maintenance would be unlawful). The website operators are paid an agency commission from the moneys received. In such circumstances the agreement between the publishers and the website operators must be drafted with care to ensure that it reflects a genuine agency relationship. In essence the website operators must not bear material commercial risk in the activities they undertake on the publishers' behalf. The actual activities of the parties must then of course comply with those terms in practice. Specialist legal advice should be obtained by any publishers contemplating adopting an agency-model. Whether or not the agency model is used the publishers could be just as likely to be entering into this form of arrangement with some form of middleman – a wholesaler/aggregator – rather than the website store itself. The agreement will still contain very similar material, although its format may vary in different circumstances. For the larger players, a set of standard terms, perhaps entered into online, may well be used.

As mentioned in the **Introduction to Electronic Precedents** and in the introduction to this Precedent the market is far from settled and many aspects of eBook deals discussed here will be subject to further development and new elements will no doubt appear. As in any new and uncertain environment either party to a commercial agreement may look to include commitments from the other that the provisions will be no less favourable than those given to third parties. Here both the publishers and the licensees might attempt to include such provisions and again specialist advice may be needed to ensure the legality and enforceability of those.

1. Rights Granted

1.1 The licence permits the licensees to promote, sell and digitally-deliver the electronic book editions of specific works listed in a schedule. The parties may prefer the flexibility of an arrangement extending to the publishers' eBook list on an ongoing basis. There may be issues over which titles are or are not included, although this may be less of a concern if the publishers make all their eBooks available on a non-exclusive basis, as here. There are a number of key control points within the grant. Duration is discussed below. The rights are limited to sales from a specified website to specific eBook reader devices listed in a schedule. Each eBook must be sold subject to an agreed usage model and digital rights management solution both of which might well be set out in more detail in schedules or additional documents – for more details see **Introduction to Electronic Precedents.** This is still a relatively wide grant, the reference to 'digitally-delivered' could include a number of transmission means in addition to standard downloads such as a so-called cloud-style 'content-locker', and so the publisher may wish to limit to very specific delivery means and networks. Alternative physical delivery means, for example, by preloading to a device prior to sale are expressly excluded at Clause 9. The rights are granted on a world-wide basis although crucially that is subject to the specific territorial limitations of each eBook (see Clause 2.4). To the extent that most bookstore websites will be available free-to-web on an international basis but specific sales and downloads can be limited by territory that is logical but publishers may want to limit the overall grant to match the titles and the rights they hold. It also implies accuracy of metadata and the agreement could make specific provision for correcting and updating errors! Where the licensees are re-formatting they may look to exclude liability for errors.

1.2 The licensees are also permitted to reproduce the Publishers' trade marks where appropriate, to allow reference to applicable imprints and branding, as well as promotional materials provided by the publishers (for large amounts of additional content or significant promotions a version of **Precedent Twenty-Three** might be used in addition). Additional promotional materials are distinguished from previews of the eBooks themselves which are

MEMORANDUM OF AGREEMENT made this [*number*] day of [*month*] 20 [*year*] BETWEEN [*company name*] of [*address*] (hereinafter termed 'the Licensees', which expression shall where the context admits include the Licensees' assigns or successors in business as the case may be) of the one part and [*company name*] of [*address*] (hereinafter termed 'the Publishers', which expression shall where the context admits include the Publishers' assigns or successors in business as the case may be) of the other part

WHEREAS the Publishers are the proprietors of the work/s listed in Appendix 1 to this Agreement (hereinafter termed 'the Work/s') and the publishers of the electronic book editions of the Work/s (hereinafter termed 'the EBook/s').

AND WHEREAS the Licensees are the operators of the Internet website electronic book store [*name and URL of website*] which promotes, sells and digitally-delivers electronic books to the public (hereinafter termed 'the Web-Store')

AND WHEREAS the Licensees are desirous of making available the Work/s in the form of the EBook/s within the Web-Store)

IT IS HEREBY MUTUALLY AGREED between the parties as follows:

1. Rights Granted

1.1 The Publishers hereby grant to the Licensees for the duration of this Agreement as outlined in Clause 3 hereof the worldwide non-exclusive right to promote, sell and digitally-deliver the English-language Work/s in the form of the EBook/s on the Web-Store for viewing on the hand-held electronic book reading devices specified in Appendix 2 and such other systems as the parties may from time to time agree in writing (the 'Devices') at all times subject to the agreed usage model [*specify the limitations on use*] and secured using [*specify digital rights management system*] in accordance with the term and conditions of this Agreement.

1.2 The Publishers also grant to the Licensees the non-exclusive non-transferable right to use the trade marks and the trade names of the Publishers detailed in Appendix 3 to this Agreement and any associated marketing copy, reviews, author photographs and biographical details and other promotional material provided by or on behalf of the Publishers in connection with the use and/or promotion of the EBook/s. The trade marks shall be used in such a way as to allow users to recognise the Publishers as the publishers of the EBook/s. The final form of the trade marks and the promotional materials used will be subject to specifications agreed upon by the parties in writing

limited to agreed amount of text. Clearly it would be necessary for the publishers to ensure that they had the appropriate permissions from their authors for these activities where necessary. The publishers may want to provide for more input in, or control over, any marketing activities.

2. Delivery, Hosting and Sale of EBooks

2.1 The method of delivery of material to the licensees may vary, indeed the files could continue to be held by the publishers (see Clause 2.3). The file format, e.g PDF, EPUB or a proprietary device standard, may also vary. Unless the publishers can convert to and deliver every format required by the licensees, it may be preferable to allow the licensees to undertake the necessary work. Where a number of different devices and/or where more complex content types are involved, a separate testing and acceptance procedure may need to be added to deal with this. The main concern will be cost and the agreement might clarify more clearly which party will be expected to incur that. Anti-virus protection might be raised by the licensees. With an ongoing supply arrangement the timing may need amending for a regular arrangement. In any event, the publishers will want a commitment that the content of the eBooks will not be amended other than for technical purposes save where the publishers actively request changes to be made. In the case of legal amendments in particular the publishers may want to impose specific timescales for these to be implemented. A publisher should look for turn-around times of 24–48 hours and certainly expect action within a working week. This may involve a title being suspended or withdrawn completely.

2.2 The eBook edition will include associated metadata, i.e. descriptive data for that work including title, authors, publisher and relevant identifiers (e.g. BISAC, ISBN, eISBN) etc., as well as, potentially, additional content which might be anything from an additional text chapter to multi-media content and links to online sources. Equally there may be cuts from other editions of the works.

2.3 This agreement assumes that the licensees will host the files on their or their third party hosting centre's servers and the publishers will want re-assurances as to the security of these arrangements and an alert when a breach takes places. The publishers may well want to amplify the provisions set out here perhaps referring to specific security policies and an audit right permitting physical and technical review access is not uncommon. If the publishers and the licensees had the appropriate arrangements in place the publisher could store the files itself and only supply those via the website in response to sales requests. That would require integration between the parties technical environments and probably both sides working with the same or standardised delivery platforms.

2.4 The publishers have included date and territorial restrictions in the metadata. They may also want to include specific references to the geo-blocking that the website is expected to implement in support of this e.g. checking IP addresses as well as physical billing details. The eBooks are to be sold as standalone titles only. The publishers would ideally go further and ensure that the eBook/s were made available with specific carriage and promotion commitments (see **note to Clause 2 of Precedent Twenty-Three**) but the licensees may well see this as a separate marketing commitment – and revenue stream.

in advance. Excerpts of up to [*specify amount*] from the text of any EBook may be made available for preview on the Web-Store unless otherwise specified by the Publishers.

2. Delivery, Hosting and Sale of EBooks

2.1 The Publishers agree to deliver to the Licensees the EBook/s in an agreed file format and by an agreed delivery medium on a timely basis on or before [*number*] days from the date of this Agreement. The Licensees may not make any subsequent deletions, changes, modifications or updates to the EBook/s without the prior written permission of the Publishers except where this is technically necessary to facilitate the digital-delivery of the EBook/s on the Web-Store to the Devices. The Licensees shall make subsequent deletions, changes, modifications or updates to the EBook/s (and the trade marks and any promotional materials) when requested to do so in writing by the Publishers including without limitation when a new version of an EBook is published and/or when this is required for legal reasons. If necessary the Publishers may suspend and/or permanently withdraw any EBook (or trade mark or promotional material) from this Agreement at any time on written notice to the Licensees.

2.2 Each EBook shall be delivered with its associated metadata as well as its non-text content and cover artwork (if any) which for the purposes of this Agreement shall be deemed part of the EBook. The Publishers may add content to or exclude content from the original Work/s in its respective EBook edition at the Publishers sole discretion.

2.3 The Licensees shall store the EBooks at a hosting facility approved in writing in advance by the Publishers and the Licensees shall ensure that agreed minimum technical and physical security protections are applied in respect of the facility and the Web-Store. The Licensees must notify the Publishers immediately on discovery of any breach of those security protections or the DRM security referred to in Clause 1.1 above.

2.4 The Licensees shall not make the EBook/s available for sale on the Web-Store in breach of the territorial limitations and first publication dates as set out in the EBook/s metadata or as is otherwise specified by the Publishers. The Licensees shall not bundle the EBook/s with other eBooks or any other products or services without the prior written permission of the Publishers. The Licensees shall ensure the EBook/s are sold subject to terms of use in compliance with the agreed usage model and the DRM security referred to in Clause 1.1.

2.5 The licensees undertake to provide the website in accordance with all applicable law and regulation including data protection. Beyond the accounting provisions there is no provision for information sharing between the parties. The licensees are likely to resist any obligation to pass on the personal data of its customers but if the agreement were that the publishers could market to those individuals directly then provisions would needed to be added here to ensure that this was done in accordance with privacy regulations (see **note to Clause 2.2 of Precedent Twenty-One**). More commonly the publishers might be given generic data regarding the customer demographics.

3. Duration of Agreement

As drafted the agreement has a specific term with any extension to be agreed – alternatively some kind of review provision could be added, although the danger with such provisions is that they create uncertainty as to either side's ability to depart cleanly. In fact, the agreement might have a more flexible term – with either side being able to walk away on limited notice (days rather than months) – unless specific expenditure was being undertaken for this particular deal, e.g. particular formats or eBooks are being created, when exclusive rights might be agreed. Indeed if neither side had a commitment to offer or accept particular titles then the duration of the agreement may have less impact anyway but see the comments on Clause 10 below.

4. Payment

4.1 The wholesale price could be reframed as a discount from an RRP list price or even replaced with an agreed percentage of revenue received, although there some other mechanism such as an advance or minimum guarantee might be needed to protect the publisher (the licensees may in turn seek protection and limit the wholesale prices through agreed bands or calculations linked back to the retail price). The agency model referred to above seeks to avoid the difficulty of the latter by allowing the publisher to work from its own retail price. The agency model arose, in part, as a reaction to concerns that the price of eBooks set by the website stores selling them – for various reasons – might not reflect the value of the underlying work and digital investment costs of the publishers. The music industry has struggled after the first successful lawful digital services set the price aggressively low (albeit at a time and in an environment when unlawful sources of online music were dominant and the services were 'competing with free'). The actual price levels of eBooks is not a topic for discussion here but as mentioned in the **Introduction to Electronic Precedents** all sides are looking to establish a viable 'ecosystem' for digital content. That raises the question of what other revenues may be available for sharing, e.g. from advertising and sponsorship activities on the website? At a more practical level it may be worth clarifying when a sale is made, e.g. after credit card clearance and completion of a successful download – and the licensees may want to confirm when a wholesale price is not payable, e.g. for credit card charge-backs and refunds etc. For international deals currency and withholding issues will also be addressed.

4.2 With new forms of distribution the publishers might want more regular audit scrutiny. The publishers might add specific provision for late payment (see **Clause 3 of Precedent Twenty-Three**) or rely on the provisions of the general law.

2.5 The Licensees are responsible for all aspects of the operation of the Web-Store including digital-delivery, billing and collection, VAT payments and customer support and shall do so in accordance with all applicable law and regulation including all relevant consumer and e-commerce provisions and the Data Protection Act 1998 and any other applicable statutory obligations or guidelines relating to the processing of personal data.

3. Duration of Agreement

The duration of this Agreement shall commence on the date of this Agreement and shall continue for [*number*] years from that date unless terminated earlier under the terms of Clause 10 hereof.

The Agreement may be renewed beyond the initial term of duration on terms to be agreed between the parties.

4. Payment

The Licensees shall pay to the Publishers:

4.1 The applicable wholesale price set out in Appendix 4 in respect of each copy of the EBook/s sold via the Web-Store under this Agreement, payable quarterly on the [*number*] day of March, June, September and December of each year for all EBook/s sold during the preceding calendar quarter. The Licensees shall submit to the Publishers any royalty and sales information required by the Publishers to verify the accuracy of such royalty payments. All monies due to the Publishers hereunder are exclusive of Value Added Tax, which shall be added to and paid with such monies in accordance with statutory regulations. The Publisher's VAT registration number is [*number*].

4.2 The Licensees shall keep complete and accurate records of all sales of EBook/s and shall make such records available to the Publishers for inspection during office hours on one occasion only during each year of the duration of this Agreement. Any such inspection shall be at the expense of the Publishers unless errors shall be found to the disadvantage of the Publishers in excess of five per cent of the amount due to the Publishers in respect of the preceding annual accounting period, in which case the Licensees shall bear the cost of such inspection. Any amount thereby shown to be due to the Publishers shall be paid immediately to the Publishers.

4.3 One key aspect of any digital content offering is whether a consumer may be permitted to obtain replacement copies of purchased content, for example, when the consumer loses or damages the device on which that material is stored. Most operators have some form of policy on this and will seek to reflect that in their agreements with their content suppliers. The ultimate solution for this, and indeed for digital rights management concerns (see **Introduction to Electronic Precedents**), may be the cloud-based 'rights-locker' concept that allows the consumer to allocate the content they buy (or at least the rights to that content which they have purchased) to their designated online account. The consumer can then pull down or transfer content to nominated devices as necessary in compliance with those rights. Where the publishers have amended, replaced or withdrawn the eBook originally sold to the consumer then they will want the agreed approach to reflect this.

6. Acknowledgments

There should be a clear requirement for the licensees to acknowledge the publishers and display the appropriate copyright notices etc. to enable the publishers to comply with their obligations to authors and others. In practice the terms of use, DRM implementation and limited usage rights being sold (see Clauses 1.1 and 2.4) are the key copyright protections. It is likely the devices will have functionality that extends well beyond the usage rights that the publisher is willing or able to grant.

7. Warranties and Indemnities

Some licensees, if located and/or selling outside the UK, may not wish to accept the restriction of the warranties to English law. As with all licences, the publishers can only provide warranties and indemnities in line with what they themselves have from the author and their other relevant suppliers. Save for the territorial restriction these are framed in relatively generous terms given the warranties and indemnities also requested from the licensees – but they in turn may not be comfortable with effectively guaranteeing their sales platform in this way. As ever the scope of the warranties, the terms of the indemnity, including the ability of the indemnifying party to control the handling of any relevant dispute, and the overall levels of liability of either side under the agreement could be the subject of negotiation – and limitation – in accordance with applicable law.

4.3 The Licensees may make available for free digitally-delivered replacement copies of deleted or defective EBooks purchased by customers of the Web-Store in accordance with the Web-Store's reasonable standard policy for replacements as agreed with the Publishers. No moneys will be payable by the Licensees to the Publishers in respect of such copies.

4.4 The Licensees shall be free to set the retail price of the EBooks on the Web-Store at their sole discretion.

5. Copyright and Intellectual Property Rights

5.1 The copyright and all related rights in the Work/s, the EBook/s and any promotional or additional material provided by or on behalf of the Publishers shall remain vested in the Publishers, including for the avoidance of doubt when any approved amendments are made by the Licensees.

5.2 The Licensees shall acquire no rights in the trade marks, and all goodwill in the trade marks shall inure to and remain with the Publishers. The Publishers shall have the right of prior approval over the form and manner of public display of the trade marks. The Licensees shall not remove, alter or otherwise modify the trade marks displayed in connection with the EBook/s.

6. Acknowledgments

The Licensees shall provide proper copyright and author acknowledgment for the EBook/s in the form specified by the Publishers in Appendix 1 to this Agreement.

7. Warranties and Indemnities

7.1 The Publishers hereby warrant that they have the right and power to make this Agreement, including the right to license the EBook/s and to authorise use of the trade marks and any promotional material, and that according to English law the Book/s if made available strictly in accordance with this Agreement will in no way give rise to a violation of any existing copyright, or a breach of any existing agreement and that nothing in the Work/s is likely to give rise to a criminal prosecution or to a civil action for damages or any other remedy and the Publishers will indemnify the Licensees against any loss, injury or expense arising out of any breach of this warranty.

8. Restrictions on Transfer

The business of digital content is rarely provided on a solely in-house basis. Both sides are likely to use technical partners in support of these arrangements and the licensees may well use third parties to deliver its e-commerce solution and hosting of the website and the eBook content. The publishers may want the right to pre-clear and audit these parties.

10. Termination

On termination for expiry or under Clause 10.2 the same provisions at Clause 10.3 apply – effectively the immediate end of sales, the return of all materials (which could be very valuable to the publishers if they did not hold the relevant file formats themselves) and deletion of copies in the licensees' control. As ever, the licensee might argue for different post-termination results in response to different termination triggers e.g. where they are are not 'at fault'. The replacement policy discussed at Clause 4.3 above will also need to consider consumer access following termination. These issues are discussed further in the **Introduction to Electronic Precedents**.

7.2 The Licensees hereby warrant that they have the right and power to make this Agreement, that the EBook/s shall only be promoted, sold and delivered in accordance with this Agreement and the Licensees will indemnify the Publishers against any loss, injury or expense arising out of any breach of this warranty.

8. Restrictions on Transfer

The licence and other rights hereby granted to the Licensees shall not be transferred to or extended to include any other party without the prior written consent of the Publishers save that the Publishers acknowledge that such rights may be sub-licensed to the Licensee's service providers to the extent technically necessary for them to operate the Web-Store for the Licensees provided that the Licensee remains responsible for their activities and the Licensees are not relieved of their obligations hereunder.

9. Retained Rights

All rights in the Work/s, the EBook/s and any promotional or additional material provided by or on behalf of the Publishers other than those specifically granted to the Licensees under this Agreement, are reserved by the Publishers. The Licensees may only distribute the EBook/s and the Work/s in the form provided by the Publishers. The Licensees may not distribute the EBook/s or the Work/s in any other form or by any other media including without limitation pre-loaded in any device, on a physical carrier or in print form.

10. Termination

10.1 Termination of this Agreement may occur following expiry of the initial term as outlined in Clause 3 hereof.

10.2 Termination may also occur in the event of either party to this Agreement being declared bankrupt, entering into liquidation or any arrangement or composition with its creditors or if a receiver or administrator or administrative receiver is appointed against any of its assets or business or if it suffers any equivalent or analogous event to any of the foregoing in any jurisdiction or should either party fail to comply with any of the provisions of this Agreement and not rectify such failure within seven days written notice from the other party to do so. In either such event this Agreement automatically becomes null and void and the licence granted to the Licensees herein automatically becomes null and void and the licence granted to the Licensees herein shall revert to the Publishers without prejudice to any monies paid or due to the Publishers.

11. Notices

Such licensees may require a confidentiality clause binding on both parties.

10.3 Save as otherwise provided for in this Agreement, on termination the Licensees shall (i) return to the Publishers within thirty days of termination all copies of the EBook/s and any promotional or additional material provided by or on behalf of the Publishers then in the possession of or under the control of the Licensees and (ii) immediately cease to make the EBooks available for sale on the Web-Store and remove reference to the EBook/s on the Web-Store; (iii) immediately cease use of the promotional material and the Publishers' trade marks; and (iv) permanently delete all copies of the EBook/s, any promotional or additional material and the Publishers' trade marks in the possession of or under the control of the Licensees and certify to the Publishers in writing that all such copies have been destroyed.

11. Notices

Any and all notices given hereunder shall be in writing and sent by fax, email, courier or registered letter to the parties at their respective addresses herein specified. The parties undertake to notify each other of any change of address within thirty days of such change.

12. Confidentiality

Each party shall keep confidential and shall not use or disclose to any third party confidential information it may acquire concerning the other party's business, save for any information which is publicly available. In particular, each party will keep confidential, and will not itself or disclose to any third party (except as necessary for the performance of the terms of this Agreement) the identity of the other party's customers and the uses made by the customers of the Work/s. The content of this paragraph shall survive the termination of this Agreement.

13. Arbitration

If any difference shall arise between the parties touching the meaning of this Agreement or the rights and liabilities of the parties hereto, the same shall be referred to the arbitration of two persons (one to be named by each party) or their umpire, in accordance with the terms of the Arbitration Act 1996 or any amending or substituted statute for the time being in force.

14. Relationship between Parties

This Agreement does not constitute a partnership or joint venture between the parties hereto. The Licensees are not the agent of the Publishers and shall not hold themselves out as such by advertising or otherwise to the public or

20. Applicable Law

Licensees located outside the UK may not accept the contract being operable under English law; US licensees may insist on the law of the state in which they are incorporated. The jurisdiction of the English courts is non-exclusive to allow for enforcement outside the UK.

to any particular third party and the Publishers shall not be bound by any representation, act or omission whatsoever of the Licensees.

15. Approvals and Consents

No approvals or consents given to the Licensees under this Agreement shall be valid unless they are given in writing and signed by a duly authorised representative of the Publishers.

16. Waiver of Remedies

No forbearance, delay or indulgence by either party in enforcing the provisions of this Agreement shall prejudice or restrict the rights of that party nor shall any waiver of its rights operate as a waiver of any subsequent breach and no right, power or remedy herein conferred upon or reserved for either party is exclusive of any other right, power or remedy available to that party and each such right, power or remedy shall be cumulative.

17. Third Parties

The parties do not intend that any term of this Agreement shall be enforceable solely by virtue of the Contracts (Rights of Third Parties) Act 1999 by any person who is not a party to this Agreement.

19. Interpretation

References herein to Clauses are to Clauses of this Agreement. The headings to the Clauses are for ease of reference only and shall be disregarded in their interpretation or construction.

20. Applicable Law

This Agreement shall be subject to and shall be interpreted in all respects in accordance with English law and the parties hereto submit and agree to the non-exclusive jurisdiction of the courts of England as regards any claim or matter arising in relation to this Agreement.

21. Entire Agreement

This Agreement is the entire and only agreement between the Publishers and the Licensees concerning its subject matter and supersedes any and all prior agreements, arrangements and understandings (whether written or oral)

relating thereto. Neither party has relied upon any statement, representation or warranty of any person other than as expressly set out in this Agreement but nothing in this Agreement shall limit or exclude either party's liability for fraud. No addition to or modification of any provision of this Agreement shall be binding unless it is in writing and signed on behalf of the Publishers and the Licensees.

AS WITNESS THE HANDS OF THE PARTIES

Signed..

For the Licensees

Signed..

For the Publishers

APPENDIX 1

The Work/s

Title of Work | Copyright notice

APPENDIX 2

The Devices

APPENDIX 3

Trade Marks

APPENDIX 4

Wholesale Price List

PRECEDENT TWENTY THREE

Website Content Distribution Agreement

The opportunities for publishers in distributing material via websites continue to grow. The range and scale of those opportunities can vary enormously, however, depending on the nature of the material and the website operator. Certainly, wherever publisher 'content' is being supplied as part of a commercial arrangement, for example, in return for payment or a share of revenue generated, then a written agreement should be used. This precedent is designed for the distribution of shorter form web-based content, rather than an e-book or other stand-alone digital product, and is intended to be, to use a technical phrase, 'scaleable', that is, further detail can be added where required for more complex and/or financially significant deals. The starting point in its design, though, was to provide a relatively simple and straightforward document which encourages swift agreement between the parties. It is in the form which has become standard, both amongst content providers of all kinds as well as online distributors themselves – be they websites, portals or aggregators, i.e. a front signature sheet with terms and conditions attached with any technical details added in Schedules. It is designed for websites on the Internet, but could be used with proprietary online services, broadcast and other platforms with some development. It could, for instance, be adapted relatively easily for wireless distribution – perhaps with the Website Operator's service being not a fixed Internet website, but the portal of a mobile phone network or mobile content aggregator and this format of agreement is commonly used in the mobile industry.

The Term Sheet: This is intended to allow all the 'variables' in any deal to be inserted into, and found in, one place. Website distribution arrangements vary enormously in both technical and commercial detail. The aim would be for the Terms and Conditions to remain as standard as possible, ideally with little negotiation, with only the Term Sheets changing. Obviously this is not always achievable, but for many sites – and publishers – the speed with which such deals need to be agreed and the relatively limited revenue that some might provide do require the process of agreeing terms to be as streamlined as possible. Indeed, agreements for distributing content on and/or linking between websites are increasingly presented by the larger players as standard terms to be agreed online on a click-through basis. The ability to do so may, however, be more dependent on the relative commercial strength of parties rather than the even-handedness of the terms. Here, provisions are made mutual where possible, although as explained below that may not always be appropriate.

Branded Pages: It is assumed that the material will be delivered by the Publisher – either online or by disc or even in print on-paper-format – to the Website Operator and physically uploaded to the relevant website server and held by or on behalf of the Website Operator. Larger players who are providing or receiving a large amount of content in this way will usually seek to automate this process. Some content providers now allow access to their material though an API (application programming interface) – a mechanism that allows websites to select and post material automatically – and which may in some cases require a separate set of standard terms. An even more streamlined alternative are news or RSS (often cited as 'really simple syndication') feeds which allow machine readable web content to be distributed to 'reader' software which the recipient can imbed within its own website. Again a simple set of standard terms may apply. In some cases the distributing website will simply link through to content held on the Publisher's server or to some third party digital distributor acting on the Publisher's behalf. That content can be styled or 're-skinned' as preferred to maximise integration with the look-and-feel of the linking website (see further discussion below). This provides the advantage of the content not leaving the Publisher's control and has grown in importance as digital repositories begin to offer publishers, of all sizes, the ability to outsource elements of their online distribution strategy. In that case the need for some form of branded pages, jump-off/landing point or other environment within the Website Operator's service would not necessarily change.

Charges: As mentioned above there are many, many ways that a deal could be structured from no payment at all – with the commercial benefit delivered being online exposure itself: page impressions, return traffic, further viral distribution etc. – to complex combinations of fees, 'bounty' shares of advertising and/or e-commerce revenue and in-kind payments - perhaps further content or marketing assistance or print/other media tie-ins. Publishers, of course, would ideally look to receive set licence fees – maybe linked to actual traffic levels – but economics may not always allow this. The continuing dynamism, and uncertainty, of this sector means that there is no such thing as a 'standard' approach. A separate schedule might be used for complicated deals.

Note that as drafted the publisher receives the first payment even before Launch, encouraging the partner to implement the delivery of the content sooner than later.

Contract Period: The term of online deals can vary enormously too, from short promotions of a few days or weeks to longer arrangements. That said, few deals are agreed for longer than, or without some option of a break after, a year or so.

Launch: In some cases, reference to the public might need to be replaced by reference to subscribers or particular types of user, for example, where sites are restricted in access or particular users need to be distinguished and/or tracked. It may be appropriate to provide for a termination right for one or both parties if launch is delayed beyond a fall-back date of *x* weeks after the Start Date.

If the Launch Date is critical it would be sensible to specify a firm date here, but that is not always possible.

A. TERM SHEET

Dated:

Parties:

[Publisher] ('the Publisher') of [*insert details*]; and

[Website Operator] ('the Website Operator') of [*insert details*].

Key Terms:

The following terms shall have the following meanings:

Branded Pages:	The [co-branded] page or pages and/or user interface screens of the Website Operator Service incorporating and/or linking to the Publisher Content which are to be developed in accordance with this Agreement.
Charges:	[The monthly distribution fee of £[*insert amount*] [to be first invoiced on the Start Date and thereafter on the first working day of each calendar month during the Contract Period]].
Contract Period:	From the Start Date and continuing until the end of [*insert period*] from Launch.
Launch	The date on which the public may first access the Publisher Content on the Website Operator Service via the Branded Pages [which date is to be agreed by the parties and which the parties provisionally intend to be [*insert date*]].
Liability Limitation:	For the purposes of Clause 6.4, the sum of £[*insert amount*].
Publisher Content:	[*insert description of material*].
Report:	A report detailing the number of users accessing the Publisher Content through the Branded Pages].
Start Date:	[*insert commencement date*]
Website Operator Service:	www.[ ] [*insert description of service/website*].

Contact Details:

Contract Managers:	[*insert name, tel, fax and e-mail details for each party*].

Liability Limitation: The clause to which this definition applies, Clause 6.4, seeks to limit the warranty made, exclude financial losses and all indirect losses and cap direct loss to the level of fees paid. The suitability and enforceability of any such clause needs careful consideration on a case-by-case basis. The indemnity may be too wide for some.

Report: Even if access numbers and other traffic metrics and variables do not impact on the Charges, the Publisher will commonly want at least some feedback on usage of the content. A specimen report might be attached as a schedule.

Website Operator Service: The level of detail used to describe the services, sites and their content will vary. A one-line description or reference to just a URL is common, but for longer term or more important deals that might not provide sufficient certainty. As discussed in the **Introduction to Electronic Precedents**, the cross-over between converging technologies may require a publisher to ensure that all its contracts contain far more detailed descriptions. This precedent is drafted on the basis that the Website Operator is the operator of an easily identifiable website destination. This definition could however be adapted for, say, the content portal of a mobile phone network. In such circumstances additional definitions, such as the type of mobile devices the content can be accessed by, and the specific network the content can be distributed over, would probably be added.

Contract Managers: Digital distribution deals need 'hands-on' management to ensure they work well – from technical matters to financial or legal problems it is a good idea for both sides to be able to contact each other through a designated contact, maybe with deputies or other team members.

Schedules: If the Term Sheet cannot define the key deal terms with sufficient detail, schedules can be added.

1. Development and Management of Branded Pages

1.2 As described above, arrangements such as this can be in many forms and the specification might be complex or quite simple. If the latter it might be better to agree it in advance and attach it to the agreement. This clause sets up a simple procedure for agreeing, then implementing, the Branded Pages which will include and/or link on to the content. With more complex arrangements the testing aspects may be less of a simple sign-off and more of a detailed technical exercise, for instance with mobile content the Website Operator may want to test the functioning of the content on specific models of handset to ensure that end users will not have difficulty accessing and using the material. With different platforms the content may need to be re-configured quite considerably.

1.3 Obviously the Publisher may assist to a lesser or greater extent in the development process. The level of integration work will, of course, increase dramatically if content is not being physically delivered to the Website Operator. What additional material goes on to the Partner's site in support of the main material might need careful review. The Publisher may want to control under what terms of use the end user is allowed access or is sold access. More detailed DRM provisions could be included too. Here the Publisher will seek certainty tempered with some flexibility.

1.4 This assumes there may be some 'refreshing' of the content, or the pages accessing it, during the term of the Agreement – see also Clause 2.2.

1.5 User traffic needs generating and promotions on the partner's homepage, in its emails to users or on its other platforms, might be included in the agreement, or left to be agreed – especially where the content itself might feature. The publisher might provide its own marketing support too. This might include an agreed stance on how search engines and other key online destinations are to be dealt with.

The parties each agree to the terms of this Agreement (which expression includes this Term Sheet, the attached Terms and Conditions [and the attached Schedule(s)]).

Signed by:____________________	Signed by:____________________
For and on behalf of	For and on behalf of
[*Publisher*]	[*Website Operator*]

B. TERMS AND CONDITIONS

1. Development and Installation of Branded Pages

1.1 This Agreement shall continue for the Contract Period unless terminated earlier pursuant to Clause 8.

1.2 Following signature of this Agreement the Website Operator will prepare and agree a written design specification ('the Specification') for the Branded Pages with the Publisher. The Website Operator will allow the Publisher access to electronic copies of the Branded Pages prior to Launch for testing and written approval by the Publisher [(approval not to be unreasonably withheld or delayed)]. Following such approval, the Website Operator will promptly instal and integrate the Branded Pages within the Website Operator Service for public access and notify the Publisher in writing immediately upon implementation.

1.3 The Publisher agrees to supply the Website Operator with the Publisher Content and such ancillary information, terms and conditions, branding and other materials required for the Website Operator's creation and incorporation of the Branded Pages within the Website Operator Service as are set out in the Specification ('the Materials') in an agreed format and medium along with such reasonable assistance as is necessary for installing and testing the correct functioning of the Branded Pages.

1.4 The parties will regularly review the design and content of the Branded Pages and make any changes or additions to those Branded Pages on terms to be agreed.

1.5 The parties will discuss any joint marketing opportunities and agree in writing the terms on which these will be undertaken.

2. Service Levels

The current wording does not establish an onerous obligation on either party. This is not uncommon where it is in a distributor's interest to keep its own site online and the publisher is receiving the fee regardless of 'uptime' performance. Where the ongoing availability of the material is crucial, highly detailed service levels and compliance provisions may need to be inserted – service credits might be paid for excessive downtime or for 'dead links' within the pages on the site, for example, caused by content updates. The Publisher will, however, usually want some form of carriage commitment, that is, that the Website Operator is under some obligation to include the content and cannot simply decide not to use the material. The Publisher may also want some commitment as to where the content will feature. In this case this information could be included in the Specification, but it is also common to include a placement provision agreeing where on the Website Operator's Service the content will appear and also whether there are any limitations as to what can appear in proximity to it, for example, advertising, competitor material, unsuitable material etc. – even whether the content is appearing within a 'premium' area of the site. This can all develop into a wider content use policy that describes how content must be used by a licensee. In mobile distribution, the end-user screen size can make placement issues very important. Of course, as with window displays and shelf space in a physical store or promotion within an online bookshop, obtaining prominence commitments often comes at a price.

3. Charges

This precedent is based upon a relatively simple deal for distribution; for example, where a publisher provides samples from one of its author's recipe books and a newspaper or general portal site wishes to include this in a regular cookery feature on its pages or in a fiction context where sample chapters or original specially written material are made available for a promotion of a new edition. With the Branded Pages concept the site would seek to integrate the Publisher's material within its own content quite closely, redeveloping whole pages and their branding and 'look-and-feel'. The site gets the benefit of this additional content and it may boost advertising on its site. The Publisher gets a fee (as mentioned above, the Publisher may agree a revenue share perhaps with some form of advance and minimum guarantee, or it may use a wholesale model charging a set fee per end-user). The Publisher may, of course, settle for the benefit of promotion of its book and author. If it also has its own Publisher website or there are links to a third party online bookstore it may even increase online sales of the book. Indeed it might be difficult to persuade the host site to make a payment if the content is normally free to access on the Publisher's site where a no-fee linking arrangement might be more appropriate. In fact the Publisher might actually pay the site for the traffic, like an advertising deal, or at least a share any of revenue generated by that traffic. The aim then would be for the site's user 'traffic' to flow to the Publisher site. There the site might seek to ensure that users return to its site by linking to the Publisher's site within a screen frame which includes a return link (and maybe advertising too). In this instance, however, we assume that the Publisher's revenue opportunities from advertising or e-commerce are limited and that either the content is not otherwise made available online, or if so is normally available behind a pay-wall or on a pay-to-download basis when accessed directly (or the Website Operator seek to include an exclusivity restriction).

3.3 If, unlike here, the Report's contents are linked to fee levels, for example, share of revenue received, payment per new subscriber etc. then invoices would be issued after receipt. Audit provisions might then be necessary along with more detail on tax and withholdings where international payments are involved.

4. Operation and Management

Some website content can be particularly high risk in terms of defamation, intellectual property rights infringement and other content liability, especially where users are allowed to post their own content through different types of interactive functionality. As a result suspension and so-called 'notice and take down' rights on both sides are usually set out, often with more detail than this, establishing what the procedures and implications of certain content appearing will be. Most website operators are used to swapping content quickly. Indeed with the

1.6 Each party agrees to perform its respective obligations under this Clause 1 at its own cost and expense.

2. Service Levels

2.1 Following Launch the Website Operator shall use reasonable endeavours to ensure that the Branded Pages and the Website Operator Service are available at all times, that any faults are rectified as soon as possible and that after any suspension the Website Operator Service is re-instated as soon as possible.

2.2 Following Launch the Publisher will provide updates for the Publisher Content [on a regular basis] during the Contract Period and shall respond to any reasonable requests regarding, and rectify, any faults within the Publisher Content as soon as possible. Any such updates and amendments shall, once delivered to the Website Operator, be deemed Publisher Content.

3. Charges

3.1 The Publisher will invoice the Website Operator for, and the Website Operator will pay to the Publisher, the Charges as set out on the Term Sheet.

3.2 The Website Operator will pay each invoice in cleared funds within fourteen (14) days of the date of the invoice.

3.3 The Publisher will on the first working day of each month following Launch submit to the Website Operator the Report in [an agreed format and medium][the format and medium set out in the Schedule].

3.4 The Website Operator will pay on demand interest on all overdue amounts from the date any payment fell due to the date of actual payment at the rate of 4 per cent above the base lending rate of [*insert name*] Bank Plc from time to time in force.

3.5 The Website Operator will pay value added tax on any of the payments due under this Agreement at the applicable rate against delivery of a valid value added tax invoice.

4. Operation and Management

4.1 The Contract Managers will be the primary point of contact between the parties and will meet or communicate via e-mail or telephone not less than once a month to review and monitor performance of this Agreement, feedback from users and marketing activities in relation to the Branded Pages.

notion of take down enshrined within the protections for service providers under liability provisions of both US and European law, such provisions are usually largely uncontroversial (but see **Legal Developments: An Introduction** for reference to the obligations on ISPs under the UK Digital Economy Act 2010). It should be noted, however, that operators of aggregated electronic products often used to resist accepting obligations to remove and/or replace content in their archives. That was largely a technical issue: material made available on microfiche or disc was difficult and expensive to replace. In some cases it was also an editorial decision by the operator to maintain control over the way in which revisions and corrections were issued and presented. Even with the decline of physical delivery and the increased use of online products on web based platforms some operators can still resist such requests from licensor suppliers. That is often from operators outside of the UK where a different approach to libel in particular may mean that there is not the same need to act in respect of archive material; see *Coming Attractions* in **Legal Developments: An Introduction.** Ideally in such cases a licensor would look to limit the protection being given to the operator under the warranties and indemnities so that if the operator resisted a contractual obligation, or failed in practice, to make changes within a reasonable period when requested to do so the operator would do so at its own risk and would no longer be able to recover any costs or other liabilities which it incurred from the licensor.

5. Intellectual Property Rights

General wording such as this is probably sufficient. If necessary one of the more formal grants of rights from one of the other precedents could be used. Where the Publisher is delivering content to the Website Operator and the Publisher has no further involvement in the delivery of the content to the user, the Publisher may not itself need any licence of rights. However, where there is any kind of link back to the Publisher's or its author's website or any aspect of the content which is being hosted by or on behalf of the Publisher then the mutual licence of rights is sensible.

Note that an agreement between two parties merely to implement a hypertext link between their respective Internet websites can be established very simply through an exchange of letters or just a telephone call. In some cases there may be no agreement at all and many links are set up by one site (the 'linking site') to another (the 'linked site') without the linking site being granted, or even seeking, permission from the linked site. Commonly, of course, this is not something that the linked site will object to and the Internet would probably not have developed in the way it has if objections were common. Whether a linked site can take action against a linking site if it does object remains a matter of debate. There is insufficient space here to set out the issues of intellectual property rights and other law that have been debated in many countries' courts around the world when this issue has been raised. From the cases that have been considered to-date, however, it is at least arguable that under many countries' laws (which were probably not created with hypertext linking in mind) copyright, database rights (in the EU) and/or trade mark rights can be infringed by certain types of links.

4.2 The Publisher shall have the right to require the Website Operator to block access to or remove any Branded Pages, Publisher Content or Materials on the Website Operator Service on immediate notice to the Website Operator if:

(a) the Website Operator is, or if the Publisher has reasonable grounds to suspect that the Website Operator is, in breach of its warranties given in Clause 6 below; or

(b) the Publisher itself, or if the Publisher has reasonable grounds to suspect that it is, in breach of its warranties given in Clause 6 below.

4.3 The Website Operator shall have the right to block access to or remove completely any Branded Pages, Publisher Content or Materials on the Website Operator Service on immediate notice to the Website Operator if the Publisher itself is, or if the Publisher has reasonable grounds to suspect that it is, in breach of its warranties given in Clause 6 below.

4.4 The parties will promptly discuss the reasons for such blocking or removal and co-operate in good faith to re-instate any Branded Pages, Publisher Content or Materials where it can be reasonably demonstrated that no warranty has been breached or that any breach has been remedied to both parties' reasonable satisfaction including through the provision of equivalent replacement content.

5. Intellectual Property Rights

5.1 As between the Publisher and the Website Operator, the Website Operator is the owner of all intellectual property rights in the Website Operator Service and the design and content of the Branded Pages (with the exception of any of the Publisher Content and the Materials), the Website Operator's name and trade marks or any other content supplied by the Website Operator. The Website Operator grants the Publisher a non-exclusive, non-transferable licence of these rights (at no cost) to the extent and in so far as are reasonably necessary for the Publisher to comply with its obligations under this Agreement.

5.2 As between the Publisher and the Website Operator, the Publisher is the owner of all intellectual property rights in the Publisher Content, the Material, the Publisher's name and trade marks, any other content supplied to the Website Operator by or on behalf of the Publisher and the Reports. The Publisher grants the Website Operator a non-exclusive, non-transferable licence of these rights (at no cost) to the extent and insofar as is reasonably necessary for the Website Operator to comply with its obligations under this Agreement.

Much depends on the context of the link and in many cases there is some other ancillary content usage: the copying of a title, headline or introductory paragraph or the creation of an abstract or summary which can be more important legally than the act of linking itself. In the US the 'hot news' doctrine has been successfully reinvented to protect the re-use of time sensitive content on websites and provided an alternative to intellectual property rights. There have been a number of conflicting decisions in several jurisdictions on the activities of search engines in particular. Linking sites should certainly consider obtaining some form of permission wherever the linking planned involves more than a straightforward link to the linked site's homepage, for example, where it is 'deep-linking' to within the linked site and by-passing advertising and other content, or using framing techniques to 're-skin' the linked site to make it appear to the user that the linked site is part of the linking site, and also where it may be difficult to disable the link quickly if the linked site did object for technical or commercial reasons. Technical measures can of course be used to regulate access to sites in the first place. Simple access rules are communicated to automated search software (so-called 'spiders' or 'robots') using a protocol called the Robots Exclusion Standard but a more sophisticated alternative called ACAP (the Automated Content Access Protcol) which seeks to apply more detailed licence terms has been proposed by a group of leading publishers. In addition, website terms and conditions often seek to restrict linking as a matter of contract.

6. Warranties

Most publishers are prepared to warrant – and a paying distributor will often insist that they do warrant – that they have the rights to supply; although some online publishers may just agree to indemnify if there is an infringement. Depending upon the type of service, other standard print warranties regarding, for example, defamation or obscenity may also be given (territory will, of course, be relevant – here there is no provision for any kind of restriction on access). A mutual position where possible will encourage agreement. Of course, whatever the position, a publisher must ensure that it does have the necessary rights – whether by way of purchase or licence – to allow the content to be distributed in this way. For more discussion **see the Introduction to Electronic Precedents**.

5.3 Both parties agree:

(a) to comply with any reasonable usage guidelines provided by the other in respect of the use of the other''s name, trade marks, logos and branding ('the Brands');

(b) not to do or authorise the doing of any act or omission which brings the Marks into disrepute or damage the good will and reputation attaching to them or in a manner likely to dilute their value, strength or registration; and

(c) that any goodwill arising from such use shall accrue, as between the parties, to the licensing party.

6. Warranties

6.1 The Website Operator warrants and undertakes to the Publisher that:

(a) it is entitled to grant the licence of rights pursuant to Clause 5.1 free from any third party claim;

(b) it will use reasonable skill and care in developing and installing the Branded Pages and the Publisher Content on the Website Operator Service and in operating the Website Operator Service; and

(c) the Website Operator Service and the Branded Pages shall contain nothing that is defamatory, blasphemous or indecent or that infringes the rights of any third party or is otherwise unlawful.

6.2 The Publisher warrants and undertakes to the Website Operator that:

(a) it is entitled to grant the licence of rights pursuant to Clause 5.2 free from any third party claim;

(b) the Publisher Content and the Materials will be supplied in a manner suitable for inclusion within the Links in accordance with the Specification; and

(c) the Materials and the Publisher Content shall contain nothing that is defamatory, indecent or may cause religious or racial hatred or that infringes the rights of any third party or is otherwise unlawful.

6.3 Each party agrees to indemnify the other and keep it indemnified at all times against all claims, proceedings, demands, damages, liabilities and costs, including legal costs, incurred in consequence of any breach or alleged breach of the former's warranties given in this Clause 6.

7. Confidentiality and Data

Privacy is very important for all websites. The Website Operator and/or the Publisher might well seek more detailed assurances regarding the collection and use of user and privacy and data protection law compliance generally. What appears here is the bare minimum – a recognition by each party that they must comply with applicable law. This in turn might develop into discussion of who 'owns' the user/customer. For example, does the Publisher get access to the Website Operator users? After the Contract Period can the Website Operator publisher continue to market to these users? What data can either side collect and use regarding them? If such additional usage is agreed commercially then that must still be implemented in accordance with data protection law and it will usually be necessary to obtain appropriate consents from the users. This should be reflected by specific obligations in the contract as to the form and placement of data collection notices. Special rules apply to the use of these notices (see discussion of opt-in and opt-out in **Precedent Twenty-One, Notes to Clause 2.2**). There are also other controls on the supply of personal data to third parties especially when data is passing outside of the EEA. These may require further contractual detail and in some cases it is sensible to use the model terms proposed by the relevant data protection authorities in the UK and EU.

8. Termination

A pretty standard approach to termination. More complex deals may require more detail on both reasons and consequences of termination.

6.4 Subject to Clause 6.5 and 6.6, the liability of either party under this Agreement for any one event (or series of connected events) shall not exceed the Liability.

6.5 Subject to Clause 6.6, neither party shall be liable to the other for loss of profits, business, production, revenue, goodwill, anticipated savings and any kind of indirect, special or consequential loss or damage.

6.6 Notwithstanding any other provisions of this Agreement, neither party excludes or limits liability to the other for death or physical injury resulting from its own negligence or any other liability the exclusion or physical limitation of which is expressly prohibited by law.

6.7 Save as expressly permitted in this Agreement, all warranties, conditions or other terms implied by statute, common law or otherwise are excluded to the fullest extent permitted by law.

7. Confidentiality and Data

7.1 Each party agrees to keep confidential (both during and after the Contract Period) the terms of this Agreement and all information concerning the business or affairs of the other. This obligation will not apply in the case of any disclosure required by a court or regulator of competent authority, trivial information or information which is already publicly available or in the possession of a party at the time of disclosure by the other (other than as a result of a breach of any confidentiality obligation).

7.2 Each party will comply with its obligations under the Data Protection Act 1998 (as amended or replaced) and any associated legislation or regulations regarding personal data.

7.3 Each party will implement and maintain appropriate security procedures to prevent damage, loss or corruption of, or unauthorised access to confidential information or other data and materials.

8. Termination

8.1 Either party may terminate this Agreement on immediate written notice to the other:

(a) if the other commits any material or persistent breach of its obligations under this Agreement which, in the case of a breach capable of remedy, is not remedied within fourteen (14) days of service of a notice specifying the breach and requiring it to be remedied;

9. Disputes Procedure

Alternatively, use the arbitration wording in some of the other precedents or the Publishers Association's informal disputes procedure (**see Precedent One, Clause 30**).

(b) if the other holds any meeting with or proposes to enter into or has proposed to it any arrangement or composition with its creditors (including any voluntary arrangement as described in the Insolvency Acts 1986 and 2000 or amendments made to the same); has a receiver, administrator, or other encumbrancer take possession of or appointed over or has any distress, execution or other process levied or enforced (and not discharged within seven (7) days) upon the whole or substantially all of its assets; ceases or threatens to cease to carry on business or becomes unable to pay its debts within the meaning of Section 123 of the Insolvency Act 1986; and

8.2 Either party may terminate this Agreement pursuant to Clause 10.

8.3 The Publisher may also terminate this Agreement on thirty (30) days' written notice to the Website Operator at any time during the Contract Period if the Publisher ceases or intends to cease to publish the Publisher Content.

8.4 Forthwith on termination of this Agreement:

(a) the Publisher will cease to supply the Publisher Content to the Website Operator;

(b) the Website Operator will remove the Branded Pages and any Publisher Content and any Materials from the Website Operator Service; and

(c) the Website Operator will permanently delete or return all copies of the Publisher Content and the Materials in its possession or control at the date of termination.

8.5 Termination of this Agreement shall be without prejudice to any rights of a party accrued before termination, including any Charges payable.

9. Disputes Procedure

Any dispute under this Agreement will in the first instance be referred to the parties' respective Contract Managers for discussion at their next meeting, or where necessary at an earlier meeting. The Contract Managers will attempt to resolve the dispute to the satisfaction of both parties, but if they fail to do so, it will be referred to the managing directors of the parties. If the managing directors fail to settle the dispute within fourteen (14) days from referral either party may pursue any remedies available to it pursuant to Clause 12.8.

10. Force Majeure

Neither party will be liable to the other for any failure or delay in performing its obligations under this Agreement to the extent that this failure or delay is the result of any cause or circumstance beyond the reasonable control of that party and that failure or delay could not have been prevented or overcome by that party acting reasonably and prudently. If by reason of force majeure either party is unable to perform all or any part of its obligations under this Agreement for a continuous period of thirty (30) working days, the other party may terminate this Agreement immediately by written notice.

11. Assignment

The Website Operator may not assign or transfer any of its rights or obligations under this Agreement without the written consent of the Publisher.

12. General

12.1 Nothing in this Agreement will be deemed to create a partnership or joint venture between the parties.

12.2 Each party confirms that this Agreement sets out the entire agreement and understanding between the parties regarding its subject matter and that it supersedes all previous agreements, arrangements and understandings (whether written or oral) between them relating thereto. Neither party has relied upon any statement, representation or warranty of any person other than as expressly set out in this Agreement but nothing in this Agreement shall limit or exclude either party's liability for fraud.

12.3 No failure or delay by any party in exercising its rights under this Agreement will operate as a waiver of that right nor will any single or partial exercise by either party of any right preclude any further exercise of any other right.

12.4 The rights and remedies of the parties under this Agreement are cumulative and in addition to any rights and remedies provided by law.

12.5 The parties do not intend that any term of this Agreement shall be enforceable solely by virtue of the Contracts (Rights of Third Parties) Act 1999 by any person who is not a party to this Agreement.

12.6 Any variation to this Agreement must be in writing and agreed by the parties.

12.7 Any notice given under this Agreement will be in writing and may be delivered to the other party or sent by pre-paid post or facsimile transmission to the address or transmission number of that party specified in the Terms Sheet or such other address or number as may be notified under this Agreement by that party from time to time for this purpose.

12.8 This Agreement will be governed by and construed in all respects in accordance with English law and the parties agree to submit to the non-exclusive jurisdiction of the English Courts as regards any claim or matter arising in relation to this Agreement.

APPENDIX A

The US Market

The familiar division of English language publishing rights between the two chief players, British publishers and US publishers, has been a major element of publishing since the market and appetite for English language books in the 'new world' began to grow into an economic powerhouse. Many years later, with their huge domestic market and print runs that most British publishers can only envy, US publishers usually have the upper hand when it comes to contract negotiations. US publishers typically pay bigger advances; they print and sell more copies than their British counterparts; their business can survive on their domestic market alone, and yet many have vigorous international sales departments which aggressively sell the US edition throughout the world. Agents and British publishers licensing rights to US publishers are often reluctant to risk alienating the US publisher (and possibly lose a lucrative and influential US deal) by trying to gain better terms, so negotiations can often be a challenging experience. Nevertheless, even in the toughest situations, there are improvements that can be made.

Often the first place where differences of opinion emerge is over territories. There is sometimes a tendency to try and skim over this important area by addressing it in the most general terms and using phrases like 'usual open market rights' or 'standard British Commonwealth territories'; unfortunately, many US publishers have a different interpretation of such phrases. Territory schedules outlining the territories to be shared and those to be retained exclusively by each party should always be provided and attached to contracts (**for sample UK schedule, see Appendix J, Schedule 2**). The schedule attached to the British publisher's contract should mirror (rather than contradict) the one attached to the US publisher's contract. Failure to grasp the nettle and attend to this in detail can cause considerable problems later on when both publishers claim the right to sell into specific territories (exclusively as far as the British publisher is concerned). If contradictory schedules back up those opposing claims, the result is two angry and misled publishers and an author who may be asked to compensate the 'loser' by repaying some part of the advance. Certain territories, such as Israel, Iraq, India, Hong Kong, Malaysia, New Zealand and Singapore, come and go from territory schedules depending on the position taken by each party, but in this area there is usually some leeway for give and take. The discussion becomes considerably more heated when the territories of the EU are the subject (**see list of European Economic Area territories in Appendix J, Schedule 3A and note 6 to Clause 1 in Precedent One**). Although most US publishers reject the British rationale for why these territories should be exclusive to the British publisher (the vigorous European market for English language books is a major factor in their desire to retain non-exclusive access to these markets especially when economic factors often give the edge to America in terms of pricing), in the last few years there has been a significant relaxation in the attitude of many of the big US publishers (particularly those with strong affiliated British companies) and an increased willingness to accept the British publisher's exclusive control of the EU territories, especially where there is already a British deal pending or finalised or where the British publisher is the licensing entity. In contrast, or maybe as a direct result of the pressure to cede the EU territories, the likelihood of the US publisher insisting on retaining or acquiring Canadian rights has greatly increased. It should also be noted that recently there has been an increased push by some of the large US publishers to gain access to the big English speaking markets traditionally controlled exclusively by the British publisher (e.g. India, Pakistan and Australia). Many US publishers have offshoot offices and strong business relationships in these countries and are increasingly seeking to include these territories within their granted rights on a non-exclusive, or even an exclusive, basis.

Many US publishers also add two additional clauses to their schedules (or include them in the body of the contract). One (which will be hard to have deleted, because it reflects US trading laws) is language to the effect that the publisher is not responsible for sales by third parties in contravention of the agreed territorial grant. The second is language to the effect that any country which declares itself non-exclusive (or becomes non-exclusive via its national laws) automatically becomes part of the open market. It may be possible to have this deleted and such deletion serves to strengthen the British publisher's contractual claim to exclusivity with regard to territories which may declare themselves open markets (such as Singapore).

In the last few years the idea of eBooks as a viable commercial product has become a reality in the US. The popularity and visibility of hand held electronic reading devices such as the Kindle and the iPad have fundamentally changed the US publishing environment and forced publishers to confront a future where the continued existence of bookstores and paper product is in question. Although the UK and Europe are experiencing a similar shift in focus the power and promise of the new digital products is more evident in the US than anywhere else. Most of the trade (i.e. non-academic) US publishers now publish virtually their entire list in both print and eBook formats simultaneously. It seems that the possible cannibalisation of hardcover sales by the cheaper eBook edition has proved a weak opponent to the demands of the market and the fear of piracy if a work is not made available digitally. Now many US publishers are setting their sights on producing what are coming to be known as 'enriched' or 'enhanced' or 'deluxe' eBooks – eBooks with added materials or with improved functionality that can make use of the possibilities offered by devices that can handle video and audio materials embedded within an eBook file. Since it is extremely unlikely that you will be able to retain the electronic rights when you enter into a deal with a US publisher (or retain the audio rights that are now allied even more closely to the eBook rights), the best advice is to focus on the basics. Make sure that any territorial and publication date restrictions in place apply to eBook and digital audio editions as well as to the physical products, make sure that your royalty statements provide separate information regarding eBook sales, and ensure you can regain rights if the print book is no longer in stock (or you are no longer receiving a reasonable level of remuneration with respect to the eBook edition and/or digital audio editions that are still available for sale). You may be able to negotiate for a return of the eBook (and/or audio) rights if they are not exercised by the publisher within a stipulated period, but some US publishers will not agree to this. A few important additional issues you may want to consider asking for are as follows: the right to control/approve any advertising that the publisher may allow to be included in its eBook editions and a right to share in any revenues received from such advertising; approval of any changes to the eBook edition (which should include approval of digests and condensations and approval of any sale of portions of the work); and approval of any material added to the eBook to create an enriched or enhanced eBook edition (the publisher should also provide you with warranties and an indemnification covering any such added materials). Finally, it seems that there is quite a wide range of different royalty rates on offer from US publishers for the eBook and digital audio editions, although there is some coherence around the 25% of net receipts that is offered by several of the larger US publishers; whatever the rate offered, it is hard to negotiate 'up' from whatever rate the is the publisher's 'standard' so a compromise position should be an option to review or renegotiate the rate after a period of years (which could be anywhere between two and five years). On the bright side the royalty rates offered for – and actual monies earned by – eBooks and digital audio editions in the US are generally higher than what is being either offered or paid in the UK. If you get a chance to meet or to talk with the people handling the digital side of the US publisher's business you should take the opportunity to ask them where they expect this market to be in two or five or ten years' time; they are usually willing to propose some thoughts and you may hear things that will surprise or terrify you depending on your opinion of eBooks. The one thing that cannot be denied is that they are here to stay!

US publishers tend to see themselves as the primary publisher (regardless of the order in which the British and the US rights were acquired and regardless of the nationality of the author) and they also tend to expect that delivery to the US publisher should be pre-eminent. Any agreement with a US publisher for a book which is not yet complete needs to establish firmly that delivery will be simultaneous, otherwise the British publisher may run into problems fulfilling availability requirements in Australia (and risk losing its exclusivity there – **see *Australia: Parallel Importation* in Legal Developments: An**

Introduction to this edition) and may find the US edition released first in the competitive open market. With respect to any deal where the US publisher is acquiring rights, the contract will typically include the usual US review and acceptance terms. This could mean that (in the best case) the author will have to work through two sets of editorial comments, and (in the worst) may have a book accepted on one side of the Atlantic and rejected on the other. In reality, editors usually find a way to work together to ensure that comments are collated and it is unusual to have radically different versions of the same book on sale in each market. Where the US publisher is licensing rights to a British publisher it is very common to be presented with terms that in effect say, 'our acceptance is your acceptance'. It is worth trying for a review period and for acceptance criteria; however, the more celebrated the author, the less likely it is that these can be achieved (the pragmatic US view being that the book has been bought because of the reputation of the author rather than the content of the book!).

With regard to publication dates, many US publishers seek to stipulate that the work may not be published anywhere prior to publication by the US publisher. No language that seeks to synchronise or control the publication dates in the UK should be accepted. It should be possible to limit any US control of British publication plans to the release date for the work in the Open Market, which may be stipulated as 'no earlier than the earliest domestic publication date for either the US or the comparable British edition' or which may be mutually agreed. For important authors, publishers on both sides of the Atlantic may be amenable to setting joint publication/release dates for all territories. Release dates for first serial extracts can also be an area that the US publisher will seek to control (on the basis that a British extract may damage the exclusivity granted by it to its US serial licensee). Whilst it may be possible to limit the rights of a serial licensee to the publisher's exclusive territories (but most publications will at least want casual/incidental sales outside such territories acknowledged) and establish a joint mutually-agreed first serial release date/period, the UK rights holder should be aware that the UK market for serials is still relatively lucrative and usually more likely to generate a serial deal than the US; for this reason, the UK rights holder needs to be very wary that any US release/publicity does not harm potential for a UK serial deal (**for a detailed account of serial rights, see Precedent Nine**). It is worth noting that first serial deals are becoming harder and harder to achieve in the US as so much material is now available online for free and the price tag attached to such deals continues to shrink.

An area that concerns some British publishers is the absence of any copyright protection in the USA for the typographical arrangements created by the publisher. A British publisher licensing to a US publisher will normally own the copyright in the typesetting arrangement. If this is the case and the licence permits the US publisher to use the proprietary typographical arrangement, it may be advisable for the US publisher to include language in its agreement which will prevent it from allowing its own licensees to use such typography without the British publisher's approval; in that way it may be possible to extract an additional fee from the US publisher's licensee (which should not be shared with the US publisher!). If it is not the intention for the US publisher or its licensees to use the original UK typographical setting, this must be made a contractual restriction in order for the rights in the setting to be protected.

Warranties, representations and indemnities are notoriously problematic areas for US and British publishers. US publishers are part of a very litigious society and, although British publishers are beginning to pay much more attention to this area of the contract, they are still some way from insisting on the broad and far-reaching 'warranties and reps' expected of most American authors. Differences between the two countries increase the difficulty of negotiating these terms. Not only do the laws governing such matters as libel and privacy vary between the US and the UK, but terminology also differs. US publishers do not understand moral rights (which for literary works are not enshrined in US copyright law), or see why they need to submit to the terms of the Official Secrets Act. British publishers react against the apparently endless verbiage that seems to want to cover every possible legal adversity. The following brief pointers may assist in achieving slightly more satisfactory terms in this difficult area. The warranties made by the granting party should always be limited to the material or work 'as published' by such party. In this way any changes, deletions or insertions are not covered (e.g. material or changes which the US publisher introduces into its edition will not be covered by the UK licensor's warranties and indemnities – which is beneficial if a claim arises from such material or from such changes). The link between the warranty and the indemnity undertakings needs to be as tightly defined as possible – on close examination some US contracts contain very broadly expressed criteria, which can leave the indemnifying party overly exposed. The indemnity should be able to be invoked only on account of breaches or alleged breaches of the warranties or on account of actions inconsistent with the warranties. It is very unlikely that a UK publisher when licensing will be able to persuade a US publisher to preface the entire warranty with the words 'to the [best of the] author's knowledge', but it is sometimes possible to have these words included in front of some non-core warranties (picked from what is often a seemingly endless list). Conversely, it may be difficult for US publishers to agree to drop the phrase 'to the best of their knowledge' when a UK publisher is acquiring rights – but retention in this case has potential consequences in relation to protection of the UK publishing house in the event of, for example, a libel claim made against it (**see Precedent One note 1**). Many US contracts require that warranties are made with respect to use of the title – it is important to make sure that the language makes it clear that the UK publishers are only responsible for a title they have provided. As in the UK, there is no copyright in titles in the US; however, the parameters there for registration of trademarks are more generous and titles (such as Chunky Board Books) which would be too generic or descriptive for trademark registration in the UK can be registered in the US, so there is a danger of unknowingly risking a trademark infringement issue. With regard to financial matters, it should be possible to set limits on how long sums due to an author may be withheld to cover legal costs (a cut-off of 12 months from the date a claim is made, provided no action has been instituted or taken during that period, is reasonable) and on how much is held (the sum should be proportionate to the size of the claim). If a UK publisher is licensing rights to a US publisher, it is generally not worth insisting on retaining the right to defend an action (far better to have the American experts handle!), but it is advisable to try for approval of settlements (still by far the most common means of resolving a publishing claim), at least for any settlement where the amount of the claim is less than the US publisher's insurance deductible. Failing that, it is certainly advisable to seek full consultation prior to any settlement being agreed upon. In a reverse situation, the UK publisher should resist US demands for control of defence/approval of settlement, where rights are being licensed to a UK publisher. It should be possible to persuade the US publisher to settle for consultation in both areas.

Although an author is almost certain to be required to make his/her warranties and representations under US law, in terms of the legal jurisdiction of the contract (the law under which the terms of the agreement will be interpreted), it may be possible to persuade the US publisher to agree to a compromise whereby the 'law of the defending party' will apply. This will be most achievable where the contracting party is a British company rather than an individual. Although this change provides some comfort in the event the contracting parties are at legal odds with each other, it will not assist the defence of a claim made by a third party citing a breach of warranty.

US contracts sometimes seem to conjure terms from early British contracts in the areas of royalties and reserves against returns. It is still very common to see royalties in all areas except for full-price trade sales being calculated on 'net receipts' but royalties based on a fraction of the retail price (4/5ths or 3/5ths) that are common in British publishers' contracts and making a more frequent appearance and it is certainly worth exerting some pressure to achieve these better rates; it should at least be possible to get them applied to some areas of high discount sales (e.g. copies sold at less than 60% off the retail price), but do be aware that, unlike the UK market, US publishers still operate within certain discount restrictions and a surprisingly high quantity of sales still provide the author with full catalogue/retail price royalties. Many US contracts propose no percentage or time limits on reserves but it is becoming a little easier to get some limitations inserted into American agreements. It is advisable to seek a maximum percentage limit of between 30% and 40% and it may be a workable compromise to propose or agree that such percentage limitation will not be applicable in the first year following publication as returns tend to be very unpredictable and high during that period. Some US publishers will agree to limit reserves to four periods (separately for hardcover and paperback editions) so this is also worth seeking. However, if you find that your efforts are unsuccessful (such limitations are still not generally found in many US publishers' contracts) remember that, despite the draconian contractual wording, it is quite typical for no reserve to be held after the fourth accounting period for each edition.

The terms that govern the out-of-print language can vary hugely between US publishing houses, but all of them are much more attuned to holding on to rights than their British counterparts, at least in the trade sector. With eBooks and the possibility of creating single editions via print-on-demand now a reality, failure to achieve tight language in this area may mean that a term of copyright grant will result in US rights being tied up for that entire period with no possibility for early reversion based on a work being 'out of print' since, technically, the work will always be 'available for sale', which is how many US contracts define the 'in print' status. In order to sidestep this possibility it is important to focus on the definition of 'in print'; it should provide for either the US publisher or its licensee to have stock of a full-length, paper printed, English language edition, which is generally available for sale in the US. The language should also provide for minor licensed editions (e.g. large print, book club, deluxe hardcover) and editions not produced for sale by bookstores (e.g. premium and proprietary editions), and non-print media editions (e.g. audios and any licensed eBook editions), to be excluded from fulfilling the 'in print' requirement. It should also be possible to achieve specific sales quotas, stock quantities or a dollar amount remittance per year (or per accounting period) as a way of qualifying the 'in-print' requirements. It is worth noting that most American publishers, at least at present, seem reluctant to stick rigidly to terms that could be seen as denying a rights-holder the right ever to terminate an agreement and regain rights based on a work being out of print. All rights should revert after a limited notice period if the 'in print' terms are not fulfilled and no licences should be able to be renewed or extended after rights have reverted.

Most US publishers will expect the full range of subsidiary rights to be granted to them. It is certainly reasonable to insist on approval of any subsidiary right which involves material changes to the licensed book (such as abridgements, condensations, digests) or where the licensed book is being combined with other works (such as anthologies or omnibuses), but it may be difficult to get approvals on 'standard' rights like reprints, serialisations and audio, although it should be possible to achieve 'consultation'. However, US publishers do vary greatly in their attitude to subsidiary rights approvals/ consultations and with a little tenacity it may be possible to achieve more than was expected. Attitudes to eBook licensing are a little unpredictable; although currently these rights are rarely licensed, some publishers (perhaps still unsure of what the future holds) are unwilling to give approval over the exercise of these rights.

One of the areas of US agreements that can seem very draconian is the language that deals with bankruptcy issues. Whether they are lengthy and detailed or sharp and terse, bankruptcy clauses all have the same meaning: if the licensee company goes bankrupt or files for Chapter 11 (basically the same thing), there will be no automatic reversion of rights and in order to get the rights licensed back, it will be necessary to go through a lengthy legal process handled by the company's receivers or administrators. Some companies do seem willing to include automatic reversion of rights language and it is certainly worth having, if only for the moral weight it may provide in correspondence with the receivers; however, in terms of reversing the course of American bankruptcy legislation such language will not prevail – contract law is always superseded by federal and state law which does not allow for such an automatic return of the bankrupt company's assets (which include the rights licensed to them).

Earlier in this Appendix, it was mentioned that reciprocity is a tool that may be used to good effect. Some US publishers are willing, to a greater or lesser degree, to consider contract negotiations on that basis; others will reject such requests for reciprocal terms out of hand. They may cite differences in basic business practice between the two countries, which is a valid point. For example, UK publishers have long been used to accepting limits specified by UK agents which restrict their ability to hold reserves; many US publishers do not accept such limits from US agents. Many US publishers class the processes and terms for acquisition and licensing of rights as two separate areas of business. Nevertheless, at the end of the day, when some seemingly reasonable request for reciprocity has been firmly repudiated, one may wonder 'Why are they so unfair?' And the answer to that question, at least for the time being, is, simply, 'because they can be!'

APPENDIX B

Paperback Rights

The Background

Until the late 1980s, most publishing companies published books either only in hardback or only in paperback editions. The paperback publishers were primarily reprint publishers, taking a licence from the original hardback publisher to issue the book in a cheaper paperback edition at an agreed time after publication of the hardback version. Their sales and marketing techniques differed from those used by hardcover houses, as the paperback publishers were able to take advantage of the wider range of outlets that could sell these 'mass-market' editions.

Licensing paperback rights was an important source of rights income for hardback publishers, although sales of their own hardback edition would slow down or stop completely once a paperback edition was on the market. This arrangement continued even after mergers within the publishing industry meant that hardback and paperback imprints existed within a single publishing group. A hardback imprint might license paperback rights to its sister company on an arm's-length basis, as well as selling rights in other titles to an outside company. Gradually, as some authors or projects were able to command higher and higher advances, and it became recognised that most of the money was to be made on the mass-market edition, larger publishers began to operate in a 'vertical' manner, acquiring rights for both their hardback and paperback imprints. It became almost impossible for a hardback publisher without a paperback arm to compete for the high-profile authors.

The Current Situation

Nowadays, all large trade publishing groups in the UK have both hardback and paperback imprints; they publish in both formats in a wide variety of sizes, styles and at varying prices, and value the flexibility that this offers them. As a result, there is now very little trading in rights between the major groups in this country (unlike France, for example, where some hardback publishers still license paperback reprint rights to the paperback arm of a rival company). Many hardback publishers have not renewed contracts with outside paperback companies at the end of the licence period, choosing instead to recover the rights and to publish in paperback themselves. The royalty structures set out in **Precedent One (General Book Author – Publisher Agreement)** reflect this vertical arrangement by showing a full range of paperback royalties.

An author contract should still allow the licensing of paperback reprint rights by the original publisher, however, as there are some publishers who predominantly publish only in hardback or high-priced paperback editions, including smaller independent houses, specialist or regional publishers with limited access to the wider sales that can be achieved by a mass-market paperback imprint.

There is still, therefore, a need for a contract for the licensing of paperback rights, and, at first sight, this should be one of the easier contracts to prepare, as the grant of rights is one of the most straightforward: the licence relates to the same language and the same territories as the original edition and is not required (as a film rights contract might, for example) to reflect the workings of an unfamiliar medium.

There are three important issues to address: the licence granted by the original publishers must be limited to the rights acquired by them in the author contract, and not conflict with any contractual arrangements that have been entered into subsequently; neither edition must spoil the intended market for the other as both publishers are operating within the same marketplace; there are also some provisions regarding revisions, licence periods, royalties and advances that are specific to the business of paperback publishing.

It is assumed in the text that follows that 'you' are the licensing hardback publisher.

Limiting the Licence

To avoid licensing beyond your own grant of rights from the author, you need to look carefully at the following areas:

Territories

The exclusive and non-exclusive territories that you grant to a paperback publisher must reflect the territories that you have within your head contract, and reflect restrictions imposed by other contracts you may have made. If, for example, you have exclusive rights throughout the world but have subsequently sold (or intend to sell) US and/or Canadian volume rights to another company, then you must exclude those territories from your contract with a UK paperback publisher (**for further details on US rights, see Appendix A**). Similarly, the grant of paperback reprint rights to an English language publisher in India would prevent you from including this territory in an exclusive licence to a UK paperback publisher. Even the licensing of hardback reprint rights to India, where retail prices are very cheap, could conflict with a paperback licence as India is a major export market for UK paperback publishers (**for details on low-price reprint agreements, see Precedent Twelve**).

Length of Licence

If your head contract is for less than the full term of copyright, you cannot grant a licence, or a subsequent renewal of a licence, for a longer period than the remaining term of the licence period granted to you in your head contract.

Warranties and Indemnities

You need to check the wording of warranties and indemnities in a paperback licence carefully to ensure that you are not granting anything for which you are not protected in your warranty and indemnity from the author.

Permissions in Text, Illustrations and Jacket Design

Permission to use extracts from another author's work or illustrations in the hardback edition may have been cleared for your original edition only and you need to check whether you can grant rights on to the paperback publisher. The paperback publisher may have plans to use a completely different cover design (which may need author approval). If they wish, however, to use a variation on your jacket design they may need to clear this right with the original artist or designer.

Conflicting Sub-licences

You may have a wide range of subsidiary rights which you have exploited or intend to exploit on behalf of your author. You need to ensure that the granting of these does not conflict with your contract with a paperback publisher and vice versa. For example:

- A licence to a publisher of *large-print* editions of a work may grant them the right to publish in both hardback and paperback editions. This will conflict with a licence of paperback volume rights unless you specifically exclude large-print editions from your paperback licence.

- The licensing of rights to a publisher to produce an *educational edition* for schools (to include introductory material or notes on the work) may also include the right to publish such an edition in paperback. Again, you need to exclude these rights from a paperback licence if you have placed them elsewhere.

- There could also be a conflict if you have granted a *book club* the right to publish a paperback edition of the work. A book club contract hardback copies may also place restrictions on your paperback licence of the same title (**see Appendix C**).

- Finally, the publishers of *condensed books* publish paperback editions of their works. A subsequent paperback licence would have to exclude the right to publish or sub-license a paperback condensed book.

If you have granted any of these rights or wish to reserve the right to grant them separately in the future, then this needs to be fully understood by the paperback publisher at the time of negotiating a deal, and reflected in the contract.

Competition between Hardback and Paperback Editions

You need to consider the possible competition within a limited marketplace between your original hardback edition and the subsequent paperback edition.

Restrictions on the Paperback Edition

You may want to specify that the paperback publisher does not publish until around a year after your initial publication, as sales of your edition may come to a halt (and bookshops want to return copies) once the paperback edition is available, or even when the paperback edition is first announced to the trade, which could be as much as six months ahead of paperback publication.

A paperback publisher will want the right to publish earlier in non-exclusive open-market territories if there is a competing edition coming earlier from a US paperback publisher. They may also require you to inform them of the timing of a US paperback publication (if you were the licensor of the US rights) in order that they can match it. However, the early release of an open-market paperback edition could adversely affect your ability to sell translation rights in markets such as the Netherlands and Scandinavia where a English language cheap edition can diminish the market for a translation. The paperback publisher may also want assurance that you will not allow a publisher other than them or the US publisher to publish a paperback edition in the open market territories (**for further details on the open market, see Appendix A**).

You may also be pressed to allow earlier publication by the paperback publisher if there is a related film or television programme or other event with which they need to co-ordinate publication.

Restrictions on the Hardback Publisher

Conversely, the paperback publisher will want some reassurance that you will not cut the price of your edition or allow other cheap hardback editions onto the market that could compete with their paperback edition.

You may be asked not to remainder stock of your edition within a certain period of their paperback publication.

You may also be asked not to allow publication of any editions of a hardback edition at a substantially lower retail price. Obviously, you cannot control the price at which editions of your work are sold by bookshops, but a paperback publisher could reasonably take exception to a licensed cheaper 'own-brand' edition for a bookshop chain or other retailer, or a premium edition to be given away with a magazine or other product.

Specific Paperback Provisions

The paragraphs that follow list some of the terms and conditions that you may need to consider which relate specifically to the licensing of paperback or other reprint rights.

Length of Licence

It has been traditional to license paperback reprint rights for a limited period, often eight or ten years from the date of first publication of the paperback edition, with renewal by mutual agreement. Nowadays, a paperback publisher may be wary of taking a limited licence (rather than a licence for the full term of copyright) from a publishing house with its own paperback imprint. They may feel that there is a danger that the hardback publisher will take the rights back and publish in paperback themselves after the licensee has spent time and money developing a market for the work in paperback. The paperback publisher may be keen to include a clause granting them an option on the author's next work published by you, for the same reason.

Renewals

A renewal of a paperback licence is often for a shorter period (e.g., five years). Renewal negotiations may include the payment of a refresher advance by the paperback publisher, to reflect the expected royalty income over the next couple of years. If the licence is not to be renewed, the paperback publisher will want the right to sell off existing stock of their edition at the end of the licence period. You may not, however, want them to reprint within the last few months, to prevent the market from becoming flooded with copies of their edition. This is important if you do plan to publish your own paperback edition shortly afterwards.

Supply of Production Material

To create the paperback edition the paperback publisher may need material from you, for example, electronic files of the illustrations or of the final text, from which to print. You will need to negotiate payment for this material, and if the paperback publisher is using your original typesetting design, you can also charge an offset fee per page.

Revisions for the Paperback Edition

Publication of a paperback reprint is an opportunity to rectify any typographical mistakes or correct any factual errors that crept into the first hardback edition, so, when supplying copies of the book or files for production you should supply any required corrections to the paperback publisher.

The paperback publisher may wish to update their edition with new material. You need to be clear whether revisions are included within the licence, or whether they will need to pay a separate fee to the author for any additional work. You (and/or the author) may want approval over any revised material. Any more substantial amendments or abridgements (e.g., editions in an unusual format, compilations etc) should always be subject to approval.

Free Copies

The paperback publisher will probably require copies of your edition to use for sales, marketing and publicity ahead of their own publication. You need to agree how many copies you will provide free of charge and arrange payment, usually at a discount, for others.

Royalties

Paperback royalties are normally at a lower rate than those for hardbacks, though escalating rates are often built in. Obviously, the break points for rising royalties will be much higher than they would be for hardbacks as the sales expectations are normally substantially higher. Within general trade publishing, home royalties are commonly based upon the UK recommended retail price. A lower rate, also on UK retail price, for export has largely been superseded by a royalty rate similar to the home rate, but based on the price received. This is especially important when the publisher needs to compete with a US edition in the open market.

Returns

The level of returns tends to be higher on paperbacks than on hardbacks, so a paperback publisher will be keen to include a reserve against royalties for returns in the contract.

High Discount Royalties

There are many channels of distribution open to the publisher of mass-market paperbacks including book clubs, book fairs, supermarkets, display marketing (a variation on door-to-door sales), bind-ons onto magazines, own brands and promotional editions. To achieve these sales, which will be at very high discounts, the paperback publisher will want to pay a reduced royalty, often based on the price received rather than on the recommended retail price. You may wish to resist high discount provisions which give you lower rates on special promotions through the regular bookshop chains, though it is becoming difficult to secure sales in high quantity without agreeing very high discounts. You can ask for approval of such deals, but the paperback publishers will need to move quickly and the approval process may lose them time, and the deal.

Bonuses

One feature of paperback advances is the inventive use of ‘bonus’ payments, for example, an additional advance payable if a film of the work is released or an additional advance if the book reaches (or stays for a minimum period in) the top levels of the best-seller lists. Such provisions need careful wording: for a film bonus you may wish to define how broad the theatrical release of such a film needs to be, and decide whether a film based upon the book, but with a different title, will also trigger the payment; for bestseller lists you may need to decide whether such appearances have to be during consecutive weeks.

APPENDIX C

Book Clubs

Before the abolition of the Net Book Agreement in 1997, retail price maintenance meant that membership of a mail-order book club was one of the few ways of buying books at prices lower than those set by the books' publishers. Now bookshops, other high street retailers, supermarkets, workplace sales operations, mail-order catalogues and internet booksellers all sell books at a discount off the publisher's recommended retail price and clubs have lost this unique feature. This has led to a severe decline in sales through book clubs, as they struggle to remain a distinct sales channel.

The term 'book club' could include not only clubs with individual members who receive catalogues detailing the club's selections and order from the club, but also children's book clubs who distribute catalogues through schools, or organise school book fairs to reach children and their parents. There are other sales operations which send out catalogues and supply books direct to customers, yet do not define themselves as book clubs, and as all sales channels make increasing use of the internet to elicit orders for books, the distinctions between these different sales channels have become even more blurred. The main suppliers still regarded as book club operators are Book Club Associates (BCA), Readers Union and Scholastic. BCA were once part of the world-wide Bertelsmann-owned family of book clubs, and are now owned by a Munich-based industrial holding, Aurelius, and offer general fiction and non-fiction as well as running clubs specialising in children's books, science fiction and fantasy, history, military books and books on railways. Readers Union have wrapped their specialist book clubs in the areas of crafts and outdoor pursuits into a web-based bookselling operation, and Scholastic work primarily through schools who distribute catalogues to their pupils.

In the past, in order to qualify for the special discounts offered to them a book club had to sell books only to its members or prospective members. Members had to fulfil a membership commitment – either to buy a certain number of books from the club each year, or to react by rejecting a pre-selected book which the club would otherwise send them automatically at regular intervals. Some clubs still hold quite closely to membership requirements but do so for their own commercial reasons, as, to cover the cost of discounting and recruitment, they need to keep members loyally buying books for an extended period.

Clubs purchase copies of the publishers' edition of the work in either hardback or paperback, and these are supplied by the publishers on receipt of a purchase order from the club. The order specifies the quantity ordered, the agreed purchase price and the agreed delivery date. Publishers should consider whether their standard terms of sale (normally printed on the back of their invoice) are adequate to cover this type of sale, or whether they want further commitments from the club regarding timing, the sector of the book market to which they are selling, or the territories in which they may sell. Some publishers have agreed a master agreement with a club to apply to all future purchases and then receives purchase orders for each order of an individual title. On copies sold to the book club, the publisher would pay to the author a royalty which is often specified separately in the head contract and may be based on the price received by the publisher from the club rather than on the recommended retail price, or on the club's selling price to its members.

Occasionally, if a club believes it will sell in significant quantities, it might reprint a book for its members under licence from the publisher, paying an advance and royalties (based on the member price) and using production materials from the publisher to create its own edition. This edition might be in a different format (commonly a smaller format hardback edition with lower production values). The income from such a sub-licence would be divided with the author according to the terms of the head contract. Alternatively, a club might buy copies from the publisher's stock, but pay a price for the books which excludes the royalty element, paying a separate royalty and advance. Deals of this type are rare in the UK these days.

Book Club Contracts

Any deal which involves an arrangement more complex than supplying books, inclusive of royalty, against a purchase order, will need to be covered by a contract. The basic terms required in a contract to cover all three ways of operating are very similar, and involve the licensing of book-club rights to the club, granting rights and imposing responsibilities and restrictions on both parties.

Particular care needs to be taken in the negotiation of master agreements. It may be convenient (and cut down on paperwork) to set out the main contractual requirements between parties in one agreement, but it is important to remember that the rights granted may need to differ for each individual title. The territories, the length of licence and warranties and indemnities need to reflect the terms of the original head contract with the author and, if the rights that the publisher may grant differ from those reflected in the master agreement, this needs to be made clear to the club before agreeing to supply copies to them under the terms of the master agreement.

Among the issues that the publishers and the clubs will be keen to see covered in a contract are the following:

Publisher's Publication Details

The contract will specify the publisher's publication date and published price and it is very important for the clubs to know if there is any change in these details as they will be announcing details to their members.

Any change in the publisher's recommended retail price can cause problems for a book club. Club members are protected by the Consumer Protection Act which requires that when clubs advertise books at a discount, showing a price comparison with the full list price, this price has to be a price recommended by the publisher and for it to have validity as a recommended retail price there must be a core of retailers offering the book at that price. If the list price shown is inaccurate, or no copies are being sold at this price it could be argued that they are deceiving the public. Clubs which offer a discount also have member confidence to consider – they need to demonstrate that they are offering a true discount on all the books they are offering. The club will, therefore, require publishers to inform them in advance of any price change to the book, and may want to renegotiate the deal if the price has dropped.

Delivery of Copies

If the publisher is supplying books to the club, the timing of the delivery of the books is also crucial. The club will specify a delivery date to enable them to dispatch at the same time all books ordered by members from a particular seasonal offering. If books do not arrive in time, the club will incur additional costs if they have to send the books in a separate later mailing to members. The club may seek to recover this additional expense from the publishers.

Reproduction of Material

Prompt delivery of advance material to the clubs is also important. The club will need a copy of the jacket image to reproduce in its catalogue or on its website. This needs to be supplied early enough and to be of sufficiently high quality for reproduction. Use of the jacket image to advertise the book should not create any permission problems. However, adapted use of the jacket artwork for the cover of a book-club catalogue or as background for a web page, or use of any interior photos or illustrations from the book, may need to be cleared separately with the rights holder of that material.

If printing for themselves, the clubs will require production materials from the publisher – electronic files of the text, illustrations and jacket or cover. An appropriate fee to cover these materials, the right to offset and the right to use any artwork will have to be negotiated with the club.

If a club is printing its own edition , publishers may need to check that they are in a position to grant them use of the jacket artwork (or inside illustrations or other copyright material not belonging to the author) for their edition. This will depend on the rights cleared by the publisher when obtaining rights for its own edition. Printing of copies for the club by the publisher will normally be covered without a need for separate clearance, especially as it is now rare for clubs to request copies with a separate imprint which could be regarded as a separate edition.

Website Use

As the clubs are advertising books to members and recruiting new members through websites, they will need to use book jackets and extracts from the text of featured books on their websites. If permission to do this is not covered in the publisher's contractual arrangements with the author, illustrator or the owner of photographs or artwork derived from an outside source, permission may have to be cleared separately.

Remainders

Both the club and the publishers will need some agreement in the contract regarding remaindering of unsold stock. Book club orders are normally supplied as a firm sale without the option to return stock to the publisher. The clubs make inventive use of their overstocks, creating special offers and even mystery packages for members, but ultimately may need to dispose of remaining books. Publishers will want to ensure that this does not take place too soon after their own publication and may want first option to buy the stock back.

However, the clubs too will want reassurance that publishers will not dispose of surplus stock cheaply at a time when they are still investing money in promoting a title through the clubs, so they may require a time limit for remaindering by the publisher.

Cheap Editions and Premium Use

The clubs may also want assurance that publishers will not produce or license substantially cheaper editions which will compete with their club offers. They may require a time limit on publication of a subsequent paperback edition. As books can be discounted by any outlet, the publisher cannot control how cheaply their books are sold by retailers. However, the club would expect the publisher not to create special cheap editions, cheaper own-brand editions for chains, or premium editions to be given away, all of which could compete with the club editions.

The clubs also regard mail order, display marketing and door-to-door bookselling operations, all of which offer books at high discounts, as major competitors. Although such sales are not mentioned in the contracts, clubs may not be interested in ordering books that publishers have also sold or intend to sell in bulk to such operators.

Publishers may also want to limit recruitment use (also known as lead or premium use) by the club. These books are offered to the public at very low prices (often as loss-leaders) through advertisements, to recruit new members. It is common for publishers to allow such use by the club only after a few weeks or months from the date of first publication of the trade edition, if they feel that sales through the regular book trade would be adversely affected.

Publication Date

Publishers will want to specify from which date the club may offer the book to its members. Most clubs expect to be able to offer their editions simultaneously with the publisher's edition unless specifically agreed otherwise. In common with online booksellers, the clubs are also increasingly asking to allow pre-ordering of the books through their magazines or websites, so members can order books in advance which would then be supplied on publication.

Exclusivity

Some book clubs may demand exclusive book club rights for a particular title to which they are making a heavy financial commitment. Because of the lack of competing clubs nowadays this is normally only a problem for books – for example children's titles – that could work in more than one club.

APPENDIX D

Licensing permission rights

A Why and when is it Necessary to Seek Permission?

The only safe general rule is that quoted by one judge many years ago: 'If it's worth copying, it's *prima facie* worth protecting'. Users should also remember that previous publication on the internet of material they wish to reproduce does not mean that the material is not protected by copyright (although it may be subject to a Creative Commons Licence). The necessity for permission to reuse should always be considered for reproducing material sourced from the internet.

Under UK copyright law, permission should be sought from the rightsholder (usually via the publishers) to reproduce any substantial parts of any copyright work (for what is or is not a 'substantial part' see below). However, there are a number of exceptions, including what has become known as 'fair dealing' for the purposes of criticism or review (there are other exceptions relating to research and private study, and for educational and library purposes). It is, therefore, not necessary to seek permission for any reproduction which counts as fair dealing for criticism and review. However, a number of important issues need to be borne in mind:

- The use must first and foremost be 'fair dealing', which is a subjective test which may vary depending on the facts of each case. However, any commercial motive is very unlikely to count as fair dealing, as is any use which conflicts with normal exploitation of the work by the original author and publisher.

- There must be a significant element of actual criticism and review (i.e., substantial comment, as opposed to mere reproduction), although this is sometimes interpreted liberally.

- There must be 'a sufficient acknowledgement' in each case, crediting at least the title and the author.

What is or is not a 'substantial part' is also a subjective test, depending as much on the quality or significance of the extracts copied as the quantity of words or lines. In a 2001 case involving extracts from James Joyce's *Ulysses*, an extract of 250 words, constituting less than one thousandth of the entire text, was nevertheless held to be 'substantial', largely on the basis of their unique and distinctive quality (**see Note (8) to Clause 1 of Precedent One**).

All this needs to be borne in mind when considering previous industry rules of thumb, such as the 1980s trade practice cited in the 'Coles Notes' case (*Sillitoe Book Company Ltd v McGraw Hill* (1983 FSR 545)), which is probably now highly unreliable. That case set out the following guidelines for word and line limits:

Permission should be sensibly sought as follows:

From a copyright prose work

(a) for any extract of longer than 400 words;

(b) for a series of extracts totalling more than 800 words, of which any one extract is more than 300 words;

(c) for an extract or series of extracts comprising one-quarter of the work or more.

From a copyright work of poetry

(a) for an extract of more than 40 lines;

(b) for a series of extracts totalling more than 40 lines;

(c) for an extract comprising one-quarter or more of a complete poem;

(d) for a series of extracts comprising together one-quarter or more of a complete poem.

These are still often quoted yardsticks, but in view of the latest decisions on (relatively small) 'substantial parts', such as the James Joyce case cited above, they should now be treated with extreme caution.

It is worth mentioning here the permissions guidelines endorsed by a significant number of members of the International Association of Scientific, Technical and Medical Publishers (STM). The latest STM Permissions Guidelines and Signatories (2009) can be found at http://www.stm-assoc.org.

B Fees – An Overview of the Principles

This section looks at the motivations for setting specific fee scales, before looking in more detail at the practical calculation of fees for (1) prose/poetry/prayers and recipes and (2) photographs/illustrations and similar material.

General Practice

Permissions are always granted non-exclusively; they normally cover the English language in the available requested formats only – although sometimes this is further limited to a specific quantity of copies or period of time. It is standard practice to include the open market when giving permission.

When to Charge/Minimum Fee

There are many circumstances in which fees are paid for permission to reproduce copyright material. The fee will vary according to the use. At one extreme, a publisher may charge for a short extract used in a textbook; at the other, the fee may be for a photograph used in an advertisement. Finding a just balance between what is a proper return to author and publisher and what is a proper and liberal attitude to other authors and publishers is not at all easy, and individual commercial circumstances must always govern any fees charged.

One unavoidable overhead is the cost of handling small permission fees, which increases as staff and processing costs increase. Many publishers share the fee received with their author (often on a 50/50 basis) and need to compare the value of the fee against the cost of processing the permission. Consequently the rightsholder may feel that the minimum it can handle as a fee is e.g., as low as £20 or £50 or more. Any decision should always bear in mind how much of the fee the publisher is passing to the author; it is probable that the greater the share regularly paid out, the higher the minimum fee will be set.

Added to this, it should be obvious that the more people and processes (automated or not) involved, the less likely it is that a small fee will represent good value for money against the bottom line. Perhaps less obviously, that value will decrease if the permission requests handled include those where no fee can reasonably be charged: rights for the visually impaired attract no fees; the publisher may have a large repertoire of titles in which the rights have reverted: it may not have acquired (or may have licensed) US or foreign language rights. It could be argued, therefore, that the setting of a minimum scale is of less importance overall than setting a scale of fees that ensures that income actually received offsets the administration of the many requests which have to be administered but for which all the rightsholder can do is incur a cost. Subject to the use made of their material, publishers may therefore feel that their minimum fee policy means there will be no charge for requests for, e.g., prose of under 250–400 words (although some publishers, and literary estates, may feel that they should continue to charge for small extracts of particular value (see James Joyce case, above).

As yet no 'trade practice' – quite outside the realm of fair dealing – has yet developed 'setting' a modest level of reproduction of copyright work for which fees may in practice not be sought. The general rule remains that it is highly advisable to seek permission from the relevant rightsholder unless it is very clear (bearing all the above in mind) that reproduction would count as 'fair dealing' for the purposes of criticism or review. You may well need to seek legal advice from a lawyer in this field, in the event of any doubt. Actual permissions rates and any applicable discounts, though, are first and foremost a commercial issue for individual publishers to decide themselves.

Calculating Fees

The most obvious issues informing the licensor of the potential value of the material requested are:

(a) Which territory is being sought?

(b) Which format/s (e.g., print, audio, web, other electronic) will the material be used in?

(c) Which language/s will the material be used in?

(d) What is the extent/nature of the material being requested?

Additionally the potential licensor may wish to know how many copies of the end product are being issued and the retail price of that end product.

It is important to remember that some applicants for permissions may be publishers who are actively aiming to license rights in their publications (e.g. US rights, translation rights, low-price reprint rights etc) and for this reason they may seek at the start to clear a broader range of rights for third party copyright material than for use their own English language edition/s alone. Their requests may thus be for the non-exclusive use of a designated piece of material in all languages throughout the world, for use in their own English language edition/s of a specified work and for reuse by their sub-licensees of that work in licensed editions. It is of course a matter for the licensor to decide whether to grant this broader range of rights and to charge a correspondingly higher fee. As some licensors calculate on a per language basis, this could be prohibitively expensive given the total number of languages worldwide, but they may be open to a pragmatic approach for the project by quoting rates for up to, say, ten languages from a longer list of languages (e.g., from Europe and or the Far East) which the applicant feels are appropriate to the project. This is always subject to realising that if such rights are not granted, the applicant will face a situation where rights will have to be recleared separately for each individual sub-licence they may arrange; this can affect the overall prospects for sub-licensing, and in some cases a potential sub-licensee may wish to omit the material concerned altogether.

Most publishers will have established a minimum fee that they are prepared to handle and this, in turn, is likely to have led to establishing a value to all uses which the publisher feels justified in charging for. For *prose* this is likely to be a given fee for a given number of words/number of pages; for *poetry/ prayers* this may be established on a per line basis; for *recipes* it will be a fee for the whole of the recipe (it being unlikely that only part will be quoted!); for *illustrations* (see below). These rules of thumb can be applied whether the requested materials are published first in print form, online or otherwise. With this baseline and the information above having been supplied, the potential licensor will be equipped to calculate a preferred fee. A formula for doing so is set out below:

Step 1	
Prose fee calculation based on	£xxx for xxx number of words for world rights
Illustrations fee calculation based on	£xxx per illustration (plus extra for colour/prominent use?) for world rights
Poem/prayer fee calculation based on	£xxx for first x lines, £yyy next y lines, £zzz per line after for world rights
Step 2	
Territory calculation	BCN/USA = x% of world fee (often as much as 50%) Major territory = y% of world fee (often as much as 33%)
Step 3	
Individual calculation for e.g. prose:	territory x number of format x number of words x language

The above system can be applied to reproduction in all formats (e.g. using x words of printed material for reproduction in an electronic product or y words from a website in a book). Trade practice is that each format in which material is to be used has identical value to a traditional print only permission licence. The STM Permission Guidelines noted above also address the members' position in this regard.

There is the possibility that the licensor may feel able to offer a discount if one application addresses two or more formats. The logic for this is that only one set of paperwork and one administration process is necessary, whereas two individual applications means the same administration costs need to be absorbed on each occasion. The same may occur if more than one language per application is sought. Requestors should be wary of asking for 'all languages' as this could lead to a request for a very large fee given the multiplicity of languages worldwide.

Furthermore, there are a number of *additional issues* to reflect upon where the preferred fee may simply work against the material being utilised:

The rate per line/poem may need to be reduced if the poem appears in a literary or scholarly journal or an anthology which contains a large number of poems in copyright, or in a book with a small print run. When assessing the fee, it is worth remembering that for *new poets* very often their only other outlet is publication in such anthologies. Thus it may be felt appropriate to charge further fees at a significantly reduced rate for new poets. Established poets may well command full fees.

Where the *prose extract* is complete in itself (such as a chapter or a short story) some publishers charge an additional fee, depending on the size of the piece.

Use for educational purposes no longer appears to command a lower scale of fees. However, general practice remains for the charging of reduced fees for *critical or scholarly works with low print runs* where the extracts used are in excess of the normal limits of fair dealing.

Suggestions for Assessing Fees for Illustrations

The considerations in the immediately preceding section on calculating fees for prose etc apply, but in addition the licensor may wish to think about the following:

(i) How the illustration is to be used: for example, if someone wants to use an inside illustration from one book on the cover or jacket of another, it may be reasonable to charge a substantially higher fee.

(ii) If the illustration is to be used in another medium (e.g., a greetings card or poster) some special arrangement needs to be made – a royalty-based merchandising deal (**Precedent Seventeen** covers the latter). Likewise if several illustrations are to be used from a particular artist or a particular book an advance/royalty arrangement might be more appropriate.

(iii) If publishers are to charge an 'access' fee when supplying images for which permission to reproduce has already been obtained. For example, if an image is to be supplied as a high resolution file, a charge (often 10–15%) is added to the actual cost of supply to cover handling charges and overheads. Sometimes a lending fee is charged for unique materials (like original artwork) plus a penalty fee (like all fees this should be agreed and sometimes paid in advance) for every week the material is kept beyond a certain period. A written undertaking should be obtained from the borrowers that they will be responsible for and will make good any loss or damage incurred while the material is in transit or on loan to them.

(iv) Most good artists (and publishers) do not like stories equally famous for their illustrations to be re-illustrated, so it is as well to stipulate that, if the purchaser is not intending to use illustrations from the source book (for which normally a fee would be charged), he/she shall not re-illustrate the story without express written consent. It is not uncommon that the user be required to assign the copyright in the altered material to the original artist.

(v) Does it necessarily follow that a colour reproduction is worth more than a black and white reproduction? Equally, does the size of the original (or the reproduction) have any bearing on the level of fee? In copyright terms, both are works of equal merit and the size of the reproduction (e.g., full page as opposed to quarter page) does not actually affect the fact that the act is still one of reproduction of a complete copyright work. Trade practice amongst publishers does, however, continue to suggest that size of reproduction dictates size of fee and this appears to be universal if clearing rights from newspapers.

Suggestions for Assessing Fees for Performances

(i) When prose extracts or poetry from the work of an individual author form a substantial part of a programme before a paying audience (e.g., a special programme at the National Theatre) it is desirable to gear the fees to a percentage of box-office takings. If it is a shorter extract or extracts it might be sensible to work out something on a time basis (so much per minute – or half minute in the case of a poem).

(ii) For competition recitals, see Precedent One, Note to Clause 14(xvii).

(iii) For amateur performances of a full-length play the fee should consider the number of performances and the likely audience numbers (taking into account the ticket price). The scale for sketches or one-act plays works on identical terms but generally the fee is much reduced, depending on the eminence of the author.

C Specimen Letter for Seeking Permission to Reproduce Material

We are preparing a Work entitled AAAA, edited by BBB, which will be published in 2013. It will be first published as a hardback edition/paperback edition (with accompanying CD-ROM). The book is designed for (target market), will be approximately CCC pages, priced around £DDD and will have a limited print run of only EEE copies.

We would like to include the following material in our publication

Material to be used:

From your journal:	*ECONOMICS REVIEW Vol 3, issue 3 (ISSN xxx)*
Title of article:	*The Economics of Dumping Waste*
Authors:	*Michael Smith*
OR	
From your book:	*approx 1500 words from WASTED ECONOMICS (2008) (ISBN xxx)*
Authors:	*John Jones*

We are seeking non-exclusive rights to include the material in our Work in the English language/*in all languages/in the (list) languages* in print, electronic and audio format, in all editions and forms (including marketing material) for distributionby us/*by ourselves and by our licensees for the Work* throughout the world. If you do not hold all or any of the rights for this material, please let me know as soon as possible whom I should contact. If you require a special credit line or other conditions, please make these clear as soon as possible; otherwise we will include a simple credit to the material, its author and the publisher. If this material can only be reproduced for a small fee, we ask that you to consider the very limited print run as well as the educational nature of the book.

A 'Permission Granted' slip is included at the foot of this letter for your convenience.

Please let us know if you need further information. In the meantime, we look forward to your reply. A response by xxxx would be appreciated *(users should note that this does not mean that no response means that permission is given and it is dangerous to rely upon such wording).*

Yours

PERMISSION GRANTED

Signed____

D Specimen Form for Licensing Permission

Name and address of requestor

Permission Number

Title of our publication	[*This is e.g. the book or journal plus article name*]	('Our Work')
Author of Our Work	[*Book and contributor author name*]	('Our Author')
Publisher of Our Work		('the Licensor')
Extent of extract	[*Number of pages/words/name of article*]	('Our Extract')
Author and title of your publication		('Your Publication')
Publisher of Your Publication		
For use only in	[*SPECIFY FORMAT e.g. hardback book*]	
Other conditions	[*e.g. limited print run*]	

Conditions

The permission requested is granted free of charge only on the following conditions and your use of Our Extract will indicate your acceptance of these conditions.

1. This permission will be valid only if we receive a fee of *£ [ ]* [*if in UK: + £ Value Added Tax*] within 30 days of the date below. Payment of this fee indicates your acceptance of these conditions.

   The fee must be received at the following address, quoting the above reference number. [*Address/Bank details*]

2. This permission is for non-exclusive use of Our Extract in Your Publication once only in the English language.

3. The maximum extent of the territories in which this permission can be exercised is [*enter territory granted*].

4. This permission will be cancelled without further notice on the earliest of the following occurring: (a) if the fee specified has not been received by us within 30 days of the date below; (b) if Our Extract has not been used as permitted within 1 year of the date of this licence; or (c) when Your Publication is no longer available; or (d) 5 years after the date of this licence; or (e) should you fail to fulfil **any** of the other conditions of this licence. Cancellation of this licence due to your failure to fulfil any of the conditions will be without prejudice to monies due to us.

5. No alterations to Our Extract as published by the Licensor may be made without our prior written approval. Our Extract may not be used in any context or in any way which will distort or alter Our Author's original intention and meaning. If requested, you will supply a complete typescript of Your Publication so that Our Author (and/or we) may consider the context in which Our Extract is to be used. If the context is not approved we will notify you and in those circumstances you will not use Our Extract and this permission will be considered cancelled. Until approval is given you will not use Our Extract.

6. You will reproduce the following prominently with Our Extract:

   (i) acknowledgements to the title of Our Work and Our Author

   (ii) the copyright notice included in Our Work

   (iii) the words "Reproduced by permission of xxx".

7. Neither the title of Our Work nor Our Extract will be used as the title of Your Publication, nor will Our Author's name be given greater or lesser prominence than the name of any other copyright owner whose material is included in Your Publication (other than the author of Your Publication).

8. This permission does not include the use of copyright material by any party other than Our Author included in Our Extract. Consent to use such copyright matter must be sought by you from the copyright owner concerned.

9. If we ask you to do so, you will supply us without charge with one finished copy of Your Publication for Our Author (or if Our Author is more than one person, one for each person).

10. This permission **does not** cover any use beyond that specified in this licence (including the manufacture of copies beyond any stated limit). Please re-apply for permission for any further use.

11. This permission is granted to you only and is not transferable to any other person or organisation.

12. All rights not specifically granted to you under this licence are reserved to the Licensor.

PERMISSION TO USE OUR EXTRACT ABOVE IS GRANTED ONLY ON THE ABOVE CONDITIONS

If you cannot comply with one or more of these conditions this permission is invalid. However, please contact [*the Permissions Department*] with details; and we may be able to grant permission on an alternative basis.

For and on bchalf of

Your company name

....

Date

Items 2 and 11 of the above permission letter would need to be adjusted if the permission being granted is extended to include the sub-licensees of the applicant and languages in addition to the basic English language rights granted.

E Typographical Arrangement: A Publisher's Right

UK copyright law provides for a separate copyright in the typographical arrangement (i.e., in the design and arrangement of the typeface on the printed page) which belongs to the publisher. In other words, each book carries two distinct copyright elements (in the work itself, and in the typographical arrangement). If, for example, a paperback or reprint publisher wishes to use the originating publisher's typographical arrangement for his own edition of a book, normal practice is to charge that publisher an offset fee, which at the time of writing is in the region of £3.50 per page. This fee should never be confused with the cost of supplying the digital file which for an adult novel may be as low as £100.

Copyright in the typographical arrangement of a published edition of a work lasts for 25 years from the end of the year in which it was first published.

It is worth mentioning that only a few other countries have this right (e.g., Canada). Most notably US publishers have no similar right and while, under the Berne Convention to which both parties are now signatories, US publishers are afforded the same copyright protection for their typographical arrangement under UK law as British publishers, there is, unusually, no reciprocity for British publishers in the US, since there is no US typographic right. In practice, UK and US publishers tend to make individual bilateral arrangements and agree fees (sometimes only nominal) on a book-by-book or publisher-by-publisher basis (see also **Appendix A**).

Nowadays most requests for permission to photocopy or scan extracts from books are channelled through the CLA (Copyright Licensing Agency), which deals with both the authors' and the publishers' interests through their respective licensing bodies (**see Appendix E**).

F Fees for Published Texts Broadcast by the BBC within the UK

The following fees were revised by agreement between the BBC, the Publishers Association and The Society of Authors with effect from 1 August 2009 (the current rates at the time of writing; for current rates see the Publishers Association's website):

TELEVISION:

Prose (per minute)	£29.44
Poetry (per ½ minute)	£35.32

RADIO:

Core Service Radio	
Plays/Prose (per minute)	£17.10
Poetry (per ½ minute)	£17.10

Prose for Dramatisation (per minute)	£13.33
Prose Translation (per minute)	£11.40

World Service Radio (English)/BBC Digital Radio originations

Plays/Prose (per minute)	£8.55
Poetry (per ½ minute)	£8.55
Prose for Dramatisation (per minute)	£6.66
Prose translation (per min)	£5.70

Local Radio

Plays/Prose (per minute)	£4.27
Poetry (per ½ minute)	£4.27
Prose for Dramatisation (per minute)	£3.32
Prose Translation (per min)	£2.85

Since 2005 the BBC, the Publishers Association and The Society of Authors have had a recommended form of Licence Agreement for each of the following uses by the BBC: Use of an Extract on the Radio; Use of the whole Work on the Radio; and Use of an Extract on TV. These Licence Agreements include terms and conditions relating to all foreseeable methods of exploitation of their programmes by the BBC. By including all likely methods under the one Agreement and providing for a licence in all languages and territories for the copyright term, the three parties sought to reduce the amount of time spent by the rights owners and the BBC on processing a variety of licences worth comparatively small sums. However, (i) facility was built into each Agreement to allow a rightsholder to decline to licence the rights on this basis (e.g., they may not control all such rights) by notifying the BBC prior to signature, and (ii) the BBC accepted that various forms of material after, for example, five years should be subject to the then current recommended fee scale as opposed to the rate agreed at the time the licence was entered into. The Publishers Association and The Society of Authors were also very clear that they could only recommend adoption of these terms by their members, but it remained the prerogative of each rights owner to negotiate such provisions as they felt appropriate.

APPENDIX E

Collective Licensing of Reprographic Rights

1. Introduction

During the 1980s, organisations began to be set up around the world with the aim of meeting the growing needs of those who wanted to copy parts of copyright works (and who, with the improving technology of photocopiers, now could) and those who found the business models that protected their intellectual property at risk from multiple unauthorised copies of their works. These reproduction rights organisations, as they became known, were to be found first in Scandinavia, the UK, the United States, and other parts of Europe. They banded together in 1980 to form what became the International Federation of Reproduction Rights Organisations (IFRRO).

The origins of the British solution to collective licensing of reprographic rights lie in the findings of the Whitford Committee of 1977. This gave a clear call to rights owners to devise a voluntary scheme that would allow users (initially, in the education sector) to copy parts of copyright works beyond the narrow terms of fair dealing, but within reasonable limits and, by implication, in a way that would not threaten the legitimate interests of the rights owners – authors and publishers. Thus were the Authors' Copyright and Licensing Society (ALCS) and then the Publishers Licensing Society (PLS) born. Together they established the Copyright Licensing Agency (CLA) to license reprographic rights for books, journals, and magazines.

2. Background

The task of reconciling the interests of those who create copyright works – authors, artists, and their business partners, publishers – with those who use them through copying – students, teachers, researchers, people in business and in government – is still with us, and has intensified now that technology has made high-quality copying so easy.

Now that so much communication is done electronically, together with the exchange and transfer of information in digital form, the demand for licences that allow only photocopying has largely disappeared. Users now generally want to scan parts of works in printed form and, increasingly, they need to be able copy from publications that are already in some kind of e-format. Paper is no longer the vehicle for copying although printed copies are still needed. Within limitations users also need to be able to store and distribute parts of copied works, to share them with authorised colleagues, and to do so in a secure environment.

Initially, rights holders, especially publishers, were cautious about agreeing to extend the original photocopying licences to include scanning and the copying of works already in digital form, believing that they might lose control of those rights or that copying would undermine core sales of their products, in whatever form. Advances in technology had also allowed pirates – those who systematically reproduce multiple copies of whole works without authority or payment to rights owners – to flourish. At the same time, the Internet and the World Wide Web had made it easier for rights holders to spot misuse of their works, and to pursue cases of illicit copying.

Much of the revenue from collective licensing activities is based on photocopying, and this still makes up the lion's share of revenues earned for rights owners. Estimates of copying figures in schools and universities show that in Britain photocopies are still made on a very large scale – and that additional copying from print to digital and of digital originals is increasingly important to users.

Now it is clear that collective licensing is part of an orderly print plus digital marketplace, just as it was part of a managed print marketplace. It is also clear that Reproduction Rights Organisations (RROs) are a powerful voice in the fight against piracy, and can be well placed to detect and pursue infringements.

Since it was incorporated in 1981, PLS has distributed over £247 million to publishers, a huge testimony to the strength and success of collective licensing in partnership with authors and artists. It is also clear evidence for those who initially opposed collaboration and collective licensing, and who accused the pioneers of being in danger of 'spending pounds to chase pennies'.

3. Structure of ALCS and PLS

The two rights owner representative groups, ALCS and PLS, have similarities of structure and purpose. Each needs members to mandate their works to become part of the licensed repertoire. Both are controlled by broader representative bodies (elected authors ALCS, and the Association of Learned and Professional Society Publishers, Periodical Publishers Association, and Publishers Association for PLS). Each is responsible for making payments of copying fees to their constituency, and for consulting their constituencies about strategy and licence development.

3.1 ALCS

The Authors' Licensing and Collecting Society (ALCS) is the UK collecting society for writers of all genres of literary and dramatic copyright works, including fiction, journalism, plays, poetry, academic texts, TV and radio scripts and story-lines, dramatisations, translations, abridgements and adaptations. The organisation's aim is to ensure writers are fairly compensated through the licensed use of their works. Writers' primary rights are protected by contract, but it is the life of the work over the decades following publication that ALCS is keen to have properly monitored and fairly rewarded. Types of usage range from the limited photocopying and scanning of published works, to the lending of books in public libraries throughout Europe, and the broadcast retransmission or recording of audio-visual content.

ALCS is dedicated to protecting and promoting authors' rights:

- by encouraging the establishment of collective licensing schemes, where appropriate, and ensuring that fees resulting from such schemes are efficiently collected and distributed;
- by building an understanding of the value of the contribution writers make to society and the economy.

Established in 1977 and wholly owned and governed by the writers it represents (of whom there are currently over 78,000), ALCS is a not-for-profit, non-union organisation. The Society's governing body, the Board of Directors, is composed of elected writers. Since its foundation, ALCS has paid writers over £230 million in fees, and today it continues to identify and develop new sources of income for writers. In the last financial year ALCS paid out a total of £23.4 million to over 58,000 writers.

3.2 PLS

The Publishers Licensing Society was established in 1981 by trade associations to represent the interests of a wide range of publishers, from the multi-nationals to the single-title publisher. Its role is to:

- oversee a collective licensing scheme in the UK for book, journal, and magazine copying;
- stimulate innovation and good practice in rights management;
- clarify the relationship between traditional copyright management practices and those needed in the digital age.

PLS obtains non-exclusive mandates from publishers to grant licences for the making of copies of parts of copyright works. It also provides an indemnity to customers, via CLA, for limited copying of non-mandated works provided that the rights owner has not chosen to add these to a list of titles of specific works excluded from the scheme. The licences cover photocopying or other methods of duplicating, scanning of print material, and the right to authorise the copying of digital works on an opt-in basis by publishers.

In the year ending 31 March 2010, PLS distributed £28.4 million in revenue. Although education at both school, college and university level still accounts for the majority of revenues, the area of greatest growth has been government and business. Since it began, PLS has distributed a total of over £247 million to publishers.

4. Repertoire

As with all collective licensing, it was clear that licences would only prove attractive to users if as much of the repertoire of works as possible was available to copy. Conversely, there are some publications that depend on multiple sales for their economic viability, and should be excluded from any copying licence. A small number of excluded categories are thus a feature of collective licensing in the UK, the most important being workbooks (although this is currently under review), sheet music, maps, and newspapers.

Publishers and authors, as well as giving the authority to include their works in collective licences offered to users by means of a mandate, or non-exclusive licence, have the freedom to exclude certain works, as well as expressly withdrawing from any participation in giving mandates at all.

5. Organisational Structure of CLA

Together the ALCS and PLS established the Copyright Licensing Agency (CLA) to license reprographic rights for their repertoire of books, journals, and magazines.

A 'bipartite agreement' between ALCS and PLS establishes the basis of their partnership, and outlines the split of royalties between authors and publishers. Most of the licence revenue collected from book copying is shared equally. For journal copying, where authors have often assigned rights to the publisher, the share payable to publishers is larger. This agreement is renewed every five years, and was last signed in 2005. It was revised and extended on a rolling basis in 2009.

Together ALCS and PLS empower CLA through an 'authority to act' which is co-terminous with the bipartite agreement. The governance structure for CLA is stable with a Board that consists of 13 directors: six appointed by

ALCS, six appointed by PLS, and one jointly appointed by ALCS and PLS to represent artists' interests through DACS (Design and Artists Copyright Society). An independent Chairman acts on behalf of those diverse and sometimes competing (if not conflicting) interests.

6. CLA's mission

CLA has a dual-market responsibility, responding on the one hand to users' needs for licences that meet their legitimate requirements to copy parts of copyright works, yet taking full account of rights owners' concerns about how their works are accessed. Its stated mission is to:

- Act as a bridge between rightsholders and users, to facilitate the development of licences and licensing strategies which continue to meet the worldwide market demand for user-friendly, good-value services, providing ready access to the works of the creators and publishers whom they represent.
- Develop cost-effective collective management schemes which complement the core business activities of creators and publishers, and do not undermine or conflict with their business strategies.
- Distribute the maximum fee revenue to creators and publishers in respect of copying under CLA licences, using methods which set the global standard for cost effectiveness and accuracy in the collective licensing sector.
- Promote respect for copyright, and to discourage piracy and infringement, by establishing robust copyright promotion and compliance activities in the UK, and by co-operating with lead bodies and with CLA-like organisations worldwide in the establishment and enforcement of strong laws, and in the development of appropriate copyright licensing infrastructures.

CLA sees its principal licensing areas in the UK as being education, government and industry. Each of these broad categories has several subgroups, often with differing copying patterns and requirements.

Education	**Government**	**Business**
Primary schools	National government	SMEs
Secondary schools	Local government agencies and departments	Corporates
Further education	Public bodies	
Higher education		

7. Collective Licensing Revenue

CLA licences now broadly cover all UK schools (including private and language schools), as well as further and higher education establishments. Most government departments and many agencies are licensed, and over 50% of the business sector is in the fold – particularly those in banking, the law and legal services, and the pharmaceutical industry – and this number is steadily increasing.

CLA has made significant progress in extending the range and value of its licences. These licences normally comprise three elements: the right to photocopy, to scan print works and to copy digital products. Most sectors now offer these extended licences.

As the licences have been extended, a number of standard terms and conditions have become established. Some of these date back to the inception of CLA's first licences, such as the principle of copying the equivalent of only one chapter of a book, one article from a journal or 5% of the work. Others have evolved in the last few years:

- The user must own a lawful copy of the work.
- Copies are for internal use only, and cannot be delivered to third parties, or sold.
- Text and still images are covered by the licences. Audiovisual content and moving images are not.
- The licences do not allow systematic storage in a network.
- Publishers have the right to 'opt-in' to new or extended licences and may exclude works if they choose.

8. How are the Licences Administered?

Most of the licences available to users in the UK are blanket licences. The fees are calculated on the basis of the number of students (education), or professional employees (government and business). Users who want to copy take out a licence that allows them to copy a limited part (normally up to 5%, or one chapter) of a copyright work, and to produce as many copies as may be needed for internal purposes. Allocation of the licence fee is done retrospectively by means of interview, record keeping, and by surveys.

Since the Copyright Tribunal's decision in December 2001, individual transactional licences are limited to document delivery business. Here, publishers can stipulate a rate per page or article (as well as other limitations on numbers or copies taken, or on value).

9. How is the Money Distributed?

Money collected from licensees is allocated to titles on the basis of sample data collected by interview, record keeping, or surveys. This is only possible once a licence has been in place long enough for surveys to be conducted, and data gathered.

The data collected give hard evidence of only a fraction of the amount of actual copying being done, but the data collection methods strike a good balance between being representative and being cost-effective. More detailed data collection would add significantly to the costs of CLA, ALCS and PLS, which are top-sliced from licence revenue before being distributed to the relevant rights owners.

Rights owners whose works show up in the surveys will get an allocation of money that often appears to indicate a very high level of copying, but this may only be because a large amount of money is distributed on relatively small data samples. With small companies or societies, this used to mean that very large sums were distributed to them alternating with periods in which it appeared (deceptively) that none of their works was being copied. Because these variations occasionally troubled rights owners, CLA now maintains a data pool for three years to smooth out distributions.

Problems can also arise over the issue of company ownership, as the frequent changes that have taken place through mergers and acquisitions can make it difficult for PLS to maintain its records of who owns what.

Money from overseas RROs is of two kinds – those that are accompanied by data about what has been copied, and those with no title-specific data. For the non-title specific money, distributions are made on the basis of previous UK allocations.

10. Bilateral Agreements with Overseas RROs

The broader the repertoire an RRO can offer its licensees the better, and it is one of CLA's priorities to secure bilateral agreements with similar organisations overseas, particularly those in English-speaking countries where British books, journals and periodicals are being widely and extensively copied, and, equally, where much publishing in the English language takes place. CLA presently enjoys such agreements with RROs in a wide array of countries including Australia, Brazil, Canada, Denmark, France, Finland, Germany, Greece, Italy, Iceland, Ireland, Japan, Kenya, Malta, the Netherlands, New Zealand, Norway, South Africa, Spain, Sweden, Switzerland, the United States, and Zimbabwe.

11. Limits to Copying

A CLA licence is not a *carte blanche* to unrestricted copying. The conditions for photocopying are clearly set down and are required to be displayed alongside every machine within the control of the licensee. The wording varies slightly depending on the category of the licensee. CLA also produces various user guides for retention by licensees and there is a warning notice to be placed on the top of copying machines which acts as a reminder to users.

12. What Role for Collective Management in the Digital Age?

Photocopying revenues continued to grow through the early years of the twenty-first century. As more and more resources of all kinds become available electronically, we can anticipate that photocopying printed pages in order to distribute multiple copies will become increasingly unnecessary. While some copies may still end up being distributed on paper, the originals from which they are printed will be increasingly digital.

The role of collective management in the digital era is currently debated internationally by users, rights owners, collecting societies, and government. IFRRO has established some principles after consultation with stakeholders:

- business will change from print to predominantly digital in the future, with the rate of change varying by sector;
- there is consensus that RROs have a role to play in the digital future, provided that they operate under voluntary mandates, as some rightsholders will choose to go it alone;
- rightsholders must have the right to opt in or out, by scheme, by territory, and to fix transactional prices where appropriate;
- more granular reporting is anticipated;
- collective solutions must not conflict with primary sales/licensing but where possible enhance them;
- RROs must be prepared for changes in the way they operate, particularly with regard to cross-border licensing and bilateral agreements.

There are many calls for global rights management systems which are significantly more user-focused than those currently provided. Rights information is normally internal to each organisation, may be richly or poorly documented, and in general lacks a user-facing gateway. More work needs to be done to make explicit what may and may not be done with a particular work, under what terms, and to grant permission or redirect the request. Ideally this information should be easily discoverable when the user discovers or accesses the content they are interested in using.

The UK publishing industry actively engages in discussions about the way collective management of rights should be handled in the future. PLS's role will continue to include the collective licensing of photocopying and print digitisation.

PLS also engages in practical pathfinding initiatives; for example, it is a founding partner of the ARROW initiative to network together databases of rights information held within bibliographic data organisations, collective management bodies, and publishing houses. This will provide an online service, initially for libraries wishing to digitise items in their collection, designed to clarify the rights status of works and signpost from whom a licence can be obtained, if needed. PLS is also beginning to explore with publishers what role there might be for collective licensing agencies to issue multinational licences, either on a competitive or collaborative basis.

13. Conclusion

The activities of collecting societies and the negotiation and administration of reprographic rights is generally a subject that inspires interest and concern only when sums of money become significant, or where rights owners' interests are compromised. At other times, awareness of how the system works remains on a par with most authors' and publishers' knowledge of copyright law itself.

However, collective management is an issue increasingly on the minds of government regulators, and as an industry we must work to articulate the role that collective licensing bodies play in creating fully functional digital marketplaces. Now that collective licensing in the UK has passed the twenty-fifth anniversary of its establishment, it is a measure of its success that the author and publisher community so hugely values both the revenues it generates and the protective interest it takes on rights owners' behalf. Most companies continue to reaffirm the importance and value of this work and the vital importance of voluntary collective licensing over statutory exceptions, or government-imposed levies.

APPENDIX F

People with Print Disabilities

Introduction

Roughly 10% of people in the developed world, and 15% of people in developing countries, have a print disability. By a person with a print disability we mean any reader who is blind, whose vision cannot be improved sufficiently by the use of corrective lenses, who is unable to hold or manipulate a publication, who is unable to focus or move the eyes, or who is dyslexic. In addition there are a range of disabilities that can impact the way people access, navigate, read, and use electronic publications.

There are good commercial, ethical, and legal reasons for publishers to increase the accessibility of all their publications, whether print or digital.

The UK Legal Background

Under the UK Disability Discrimination Act 1995, it is illegal for 'service providers' to discriminate against disabled people. The legislation is mainly aimed at libraries, schools, shops, restaurants and hotels, but includes all those that provide goods or services to the public. It therefore applies to publishers of either print or digital materials.

Disability legislation in the UK applies to all those who have a substantial, continuing disability which means they cannot carry out normal day-to-day activities. In addition to the general protection under disability legislation, people who are blind or who have serious visual impairments can also benefit from a copyright exception under the Copyright (Visually Impaired Persons) Act 2002. This law defines a visually impaired person as someone who is blind, or a person who is partially sighted or whose sight cannot be adequately improved by the use of corrective lenses, or a person who is unable through physical disability to hold or manipulate books or to focus or move their eyes.

The Copyright (Visually Impaired Persons) Act 2002 is available online at http://www.opsi.gov.uk/acts/acts2002/ukpga_20020033_en_1 and provides two different exceptions with slightly different conditions. These apply to commercially published literary, dramatic, musical or artistic works (including typographical copyright), but it does not apply to recorded performances or databases.

1. A single copy for personal use – individuals may make, or they may ask others (such as teachers, librarians, parents, or carers) to make such copies for them free of charge and without asking permission from the rights holder(s), a single accessible copy in another format. This could, for example, mean a Braille format or a more accessible digital version of the work. It is necessary for the copies to be made from lawfully acquired originals, and these must not be adapted unnecessarily. The copies must also carry a statement that they are made under the Act, and carry an acknowledgment. Copies cannot be made when a commercially produced text in a suitable format is available.

2. Multiple copies for collective use – educational organisations and not-for-profit bodies such as the Royal National Institute for Blind People (RNIB) may make multiple copies of the same copyright work for their members without permission. However this exception cannot be applied when an accessible format is commercially available, or when a relevant licensing scheme exists. If the exception is used to create multiple copies then the copies must be made from lawfully acquired originals. The copies must also carry a statement that they are made under the Act, and carry an acknowledgment. The organisation making the copies must notify the rightsholder that the copies have been made. Where technological protection measures have been disabled in order to access the text, they must be reapplied before the copy is sent to the user.

Making works accessible in the UK

Discrimination can occur if people with disabilities are treated less favourably than other people, or if reasonable adjustments are not made for the disability concerned. If necessary, a publisher must therefore provide a reasonable alternative method of making its services available to disabled people where physical feature makes it impossible or unreasonably difficult for them to do so. Publishers who have well structured digital files for their books may be in a position to sell or supply accessible editions and may sell these through normal supply chain channels, other publishers may rely on licensing schemes to grant permission for accessible copies to be produced.

An individual person who is blind or visually impaired may make a single copy for personal use and does not need to ask permission at all provided the above conditions are complied with. However, if such an individual (or teacher, librarian, etc. acting on behalf of the person) does ask for permission, a publisher may wish to issue a free licence so that there is a record of the use. This need only be a very simple document confirming that the individual has the right to make a copy and listing the above conditions.

An industry collective licensing scheme (see **Appendix E**) is operated by the Copyright Licensing Agency (CLA) licence and effectively renders the second exception under the Copyright (Visually Impaired Persons) Act 2002 unnecessary. This licence is available to organisations supporting a wider array of disabilities than those in the Act itself, for example to those supporting people with dyslexia. In practice therefore organisations wishing to make multiple copies need to seek permission, ideally via the CLA licence, and should be referred to the CLA, Saffron House, 6-10 Kirby Street, London EC1N 8TS, http://www.cla.co.uk/.

The existence of this collective licensing scheme means that organisations supporting people with print disabilities have access to a much wider repertoire of works. The licence has also helped to create an atmosphere of cooperation and mutual understanding between rights holders and organisations helping print disabled people.

If you do receive a permissions request from a person with a disability, or a support organisation, do be sympathetic. Although the requester may already have the rights under exceptions to copyright law or CLA licence; however, it may save time if you are in a position to say yes. The following suggestions may be helpful:

- It is good practice to ask authors to transfer print-disabled rights non-exclusively to the publisher in order to ensure that it can deal expeditiously with such requests.

- Publishers must decide whether to charge or what to charge. Because the cost of producing special formats considerably exceeds any price charged, and where the formats have no commercial value beyond the specialist use being sought, a zero rate has been widely accepted.

- Some organisations will sometimes request an electronic file as the best source for transcription. Publishers may have difficulty providing a copy in a suitable electronic format. It is for the publisher to decide what the best copy that it can provide is or whether the organisation is best served in starting from a printed copy, as is sometimes the case.

- If licensing commercial rights to specialist large-print producers, do think carefully about making these agreements non-exclusive, or having the rights revert back to you if they are not used. Some producers only supply to the library market, for example, and this means that the existence of an accessible work will never be promoted through the normal book supply chain.

Making works accessible in Europe

Every European country has a copyright exception for people with print disabilities, but the precise definitions of beneficiaries and details of how the exception operates will differ from country to country. See http://www.wipo.int/meetings/en/doc_details.jsp?doc_id=75696 for a WIPO survey of such exceptions around the world in 2007. In 2009 a 'Stakeholders Dialogue' was convened by the European Commission, and brought together representatives from the European Blind Union and the Federation of European Publishers to find practical ways of enabling the cross-border transfer within Europe of accessible formats created by charities that support people with print disabilities. These accessible formats are often very expensive to create – for example a single Braille file can cost £2,000 to produce – and it was recognised as an expensive duplication of effort that the same file might be made into accessible formats more than once.

In June 2010 a Memorandum of Understanding was agreed between the parties. This is scheduled to be formally signed in September 2010 and will create a network of Trusted Intermediaries, or organisations that have the trust of both disabled persons and rightsholders and are authorised to transfer files across borders under the terms of the Memorandum. At the time we go to press it is anticipated that the existing CLA licence in the UK will satisfy the needs of this Memorandum of Understanding, and that the full text of the Memorandum will be available via the website of the Federation of European Publishers.

Making works accessible internationally

In 2008 the World Intellectual Property Organisation (WIPO) established a 'Stakeholders Platform' which brought together representatives from the International Publishers Association and the World Blind Union. This platform is progressing practical projects in parallel to discussions under the auspices of the WIPO Standing Committee on Copyright which is considering whether or not there is a case for a new international copyright treaty to enshrine minimum exceptions into international law.

To date the treaty discussions are not progressing quickly with four separate, and remarkably different, proposals put forward by different member states. Some of these are for recommendations and others are for formal binding treaties. Some are for people with print disabilities only and others are much broader and encompass a range of other interests including educational institutions and libraries. There is great divergence, and so far the WIPO process has not helped participating member states find common ground and it is therefore rather unlikely for this process to yield results quickly.

In happy contrast the work of the Stakeholders Platform is gaining momentum with two collaborative projects now launched. The first is a project to create an enabling technological framework to assist more publishers to produce accessible publications as a normal part of their production processes, and this will result in the creation of good practice guidelines and some open source production tools. EDItEUR is leading this work on behalf of the publishing industry. The second is a project to pilot the Trusted Intermediaries concept (first developed by the WIPO Stakeholders Platform) in an international context, including testing whether this model can efficiently extend to serve the needs of print disabled people and rights holders in the developing world.

For further information please refer to http://visionip.org/stakeholders/en/.

Further Guidance

A wealth of information is available to help publishers meet the needs of customers with print disabilities.

- Towards Accessible e-Book Platforms: Good Practice Guidance on Future Developments (http://www.techdis.ac.uk/resources/files/e-books%20leaflet%20final.pdf). See http://www.techdis.ac.uk/index.php?p=9_33_3 for an overview of the underpinning research.

- World Wide Web Consortium guidelines for web-based products: http://www.w3.org/WAI/guid-tech.html.

- EDItEUR is our industry's international standards body, and it has recently received a 3-year grant to develop good practice guidelines for publishers. Watch its website at http://www.editeur.org/ for developments.

- Publishers Association guide to meeting permissions requests from people with print disabilities: http://www.publishers.org.uk/index.php?option=com_docman&task=doc_download&gid=273&Itemid).

- Publisher Accessibility Newsletter: (http://publisherscontentforum.com/index.php?option=com_content&view=category&layout=blog&id=21&Itemid=17).

APPENDIX G

Reversionary Provisions of the Copyright Act 1911

Introduction

The proviso to the Copyright Act 1911, s 5(2) provided that, *where the author was the first owner of the copyright*, no assignment of the copyright or grant of any interest in it made by him/her (otherwise than by will), after the passing of that Act, should be valid beyond the expiration of 25 years from the death of the author. The interest in copyright was to be seen as part of the author's estate, and any agreement entered into by him/her attempting to dispose of the reversionary interest beyond the period of 25 years from his/her death should, with exceptions for collective works, be null and void.

It is thought that this limitation on an author's powers to contract was made in the interests of his/her family, but, whatever the reason, it has remained to this day, through transitional provisions of the 1956 Act, a complicated and dangerous trap which publishers need to understand at least in outline. The point is put well in paragraph 614 of the Whitford Committee Report:

> *'Despite the ending of the reversionary rights provision in respect of new assignments and licences, the importance of its effects in respect of old assignments and licences has recently become increasingly apparent. In fact it will take a very long time for these to disappear completely. Thus an author making an assignment in his twenties just before 1 July 1957 may not die until say 2020, in which case the life-plus-25-year period will not expire until the year 2045.'*

(a) The Copyright Act 1956 provided that the proviso should continue to apply to assignments and licences made before 1 July 1957, the operative date of the 1956 Act. *The proviso does not affect documents made after this date, nor does it apply if a further assignment or licence is made after this date.* In the absence of such a further assignment or licence, however, any assignments or licences made between 1 July 1912 and 1 July 1957, to which the proviso applies, will only operate until the end of the first 25-year period following the death of the author.

(b) *The proviso only applied in a case where the author was the first owner of the copyright.* It did not apply, therefore, in the case of an engraving, photograph or portrait 'commissioned' by some other person, or in the case of a work made by an author in the employment of some other person under a contract of service or apprenticeship. In such event the owner of the copyright was able to assign it for the full term.

(c) Since only the author him/herself was prohibited from assigning the copyright or an interest in it, the proviso does not apply to posthumous works.

The Copyright, Designs and Patents Act 1988 now governs the position through para 27 of Schedule 1 to the Act. In effect, the proviso to the 1911 Act, s 5(2) is re-enacted in respect of an assignment of copyright or a grant of interest in it made by the author, *being the first owner of copyright*, in the years between the coming into effect of the 1911 and the 1956 Acts. As stated above, therefore, the proviso does not affect documents made after 1 July 1957, but the Whitford Committee's warning, reproduced above, still stands.

This Appendix states a very general position. Any publisher or author who believes that their rights may be affected by the 1911 reversionary provisions should seek legal advice.

APPENDIX H

Moral Rights

The Copyright, Designs and Patents Act 1988, which came into effect on 1 August 1989, carried out the basic proposals of the 1986 White Paper and incorporated explicitly for the first time in UK law the concept of *droit moral*, which had long been a feature of legislation in continental Europe. It makes detailed provision for the two basic moral rights: the right of paternity (called in the Act 'right to be identified as author') and the right of integrity (called in the Act 'right to object to derogatory treatment of work'), both of which have the same period of duration, that is, now life plus 70 years, as copyright itself. This differs from the provision for moral rights in the legislation of the countries of continental Europe, where such rights are perpetual.

Right to be Identified as Author

Section 77 states that the author of a copyright literary, dramatic, musical or artistic work has the right to be identified as the author of the work whenever the work is published commercially. The right is not infringed unless it has been asserted in accordance with s 78. That section provides that the right may be asserted generally, or in relation to any specified act or description of acts, either:

(a) on an assignment of copyright in the work, by including in the instrument effecting the assignment a statement that the author asserts in relation to that work his right to be identified; or

(b) by instrument in writing signed by the author.

Legislation in the countries of continental Europe does not require the author to assert his or her moral rights; the UK has considered abandoning this requirement, although at the time of writing it seems likely to remain.

Right to Object to Derogatory Treatment of Work

Section 80 states that the author of a copyright literary, dramatic, musical or artistic work has the right not to have his work subjected to derogatory treatment when that work is published commercially. 'Treatment' means any addition to, deletion from or alteration or adaptation (other than a translation) of the work, and treatment is derogatory if it amounts to distortion or mutilation of the work, or is otherwise prejudicial to the honour or reputation of the author.

This incorporation of moral rights is sensibly qualified in three important ways:

(1) The moral right of paternity must, as set out above, be *asserted* by the author. This provision follows the sense of the Berne wording which refers to the right of the author to *claim* paternity.

(2) The moral rights are subject to *consent* (which may be oral) and to *waiver* (which must be in writing).

(3) Moral rights do not, in general, attach to employee works, to works published in a newspaper, magazine or similar periodical, or to collective works of reference. Both computer programs and computer-generated works are also exempt from moral rights.

There will, therefore, be some publishers, particularly STM (science, technical and medical) publishers who rely heavily on employee authors, or who publish largely within (a) the scope of 'a newspaper, magazine or similar periodical' and/or within (b) the scope of 'an encyclopaedia, dictionary or other collective work of reference', who will find that moral rights do not often apply in their field. For authors are excluded by the Act from moral rights protection wherever what they write constitutes a work 'made for the purposes of such publication [i.e., at (a) and/or (b)] or made available with the consent of the author for the purposes of such publication'.

Works of Joint Authorship

Under the Act a work of joint authorship means 'a work produced by the collaboration of two or more authors in which the contribution of each author is not distinct from that of the other author or authors' (s 10). Authors of such joint works as constitute collective works of *reference* are excluded from moral rights protection (see (3) above). All other joint authors, however, have severally the two moral rights. Each joint author, for example, must assert his/her right to be identified as a joint author, and the right to object to derogatory treatment is a right of each joint author. It follows that a waiver under s 87 of either or both moral rights by one joint author does not affect the rights of the other joint authors (s 88). Particular care will, obviously, be needed to ensure that *all* authors of works of joint authorship assert or waive, as the case may be.

False Attribution of Work

This is not a true moral right, since moral rights belong to authors. The right not to have one's name falsely used as the name of the author of a literary, dramatic, musical or artistic work belongs to anyone, whether he/she is an author or not. However, the right, which was also provided under the Copyright Act 1956, is placed in Chapter IV of the Act, entitled 'Moral Rights', and is therefore noted here. The right is infringed by the issue to the public of copies of a work in or on which there is a false attribution (i.e., a false statement, express or implied, as to who is the author). The right continues to subsist until 20 years after a person's death (which contrasts with the longer period of 70 years *post mortem auctoris* protection for the truly authorial moral rights of paternity and integrity).

Right to Privacy

Under the Copyright Act 1956, the commissioner of a photograph was the owner of copyright in the photograph. He was, therefore, in a strong position to prevent, if need be through the issue of an injunction, the subsequent publication, to the embarrassment of him and of his family, of the photograph. With the change in the Copyright, Designs and Patents Act 1988 of the status of a photograph to being simply a work of art, the photographer became the author of a work of art who owns copyright in the photographs he takes.

This change of status worried both the government and opposition as the Bill worked its way through Parliament, because of the danger of invasion of privacy through, for example, the sale of a wedding photograph to the tabloid press by a photographer, with the commissioner, the father of the bride perhaps, left with no remedy, since the UK then had no general law of privacy (although it increasingly now has – see below).

Section 85 of the 1988 Act, therefore, provides that a person who for private and domestic purposes commissions the taking of a photograph, or the making of a film, has the right not to have copies of the resulting copyright work issued to the public.

Since October 2000, when the Human Rights Act 1998 incorporated the European Convention on Human Rights into UK law, UK law has expressly contained the right for all citizens to respect for their private and family life (Article 8). An increasing number of celebrities including David and Victoria Beckham and Michael Douglas and Catherine Zeta-Jones, have tried to make use of the protection afforded by the Act, and have to a large extent been supported by the courts. However, courts have had to balance individual rights to privacy against the corresponding right to freedom of expression which Article 10 gives to the media, and it seems likely that the courts will be occupied with this balancing act for some time. Nevertheless, it does now seem certain that UK citizens are at last on the way to having a fully-fledged right to privacy. This is, of course, an independent statutory right, quite separate from their moral rights.

Transitional Provisions

These very important provisions are set out in Schedule 1 to the Act. They provide, inter alia, that:

(a) the rights of paternity and integrity do not apply to a work the author of which died before the commencement date of the Act, 1 August 1989;

(b) the rights of paternity and integrity do not apply to things done before the commencement of the Act;

(c) the rights of paternity and integrity do not apply in respect of 'existing works' – that is, works made and completed before the commencement date of 1 August 1989 – to anything which by virtue of an assignment of copyright or a licence granted before commencement may be done without infringing copyright.

The practical upshot of the transitional provisions is that in respect of works contracted for and completed in typescript before 1 August 1989, moral rights will not apply. For works, however, contracted before 1 August 1989 but not completed (i.e., not 'existing works') at that date, moral rights will apply.

Conclusion

Most publishers will by now surely have considered carefully their policy towards *droit moral*. In so far as the great majority of publishers give proper credit on title page and on jacket/binding (and on the menu pages of any website or online service) to the author of a book, and in so far, again, as the great majority of publishers do not (without lengthy prior consultation with, followed by consent of the author) go beyond routine copy-editing of what the author writes, neither of the two moral rights of paternity or of integrity should cause concern.

The following kinds of publishing issues may well arise in the context of moral rights:

(1) It is not so much the *author's* right of paternity which may cause trouble, as such a right alleged by a freelance editor/'ghost writer' who says that a work which he/she has substantially rewritten, or even partially written, is substantially therefore his/her work so that he/ she has a right of paternity and a right to be named on the cover, the

title page, etc. A waiver of moral rights may be appropriate in some circumstances.

(2) The borderland between normal copy editing and heavy, but in the publisher's judgment necessary, editing is obviously a grey area.

(3) In some works, for example, series of monographs, and in works of multi-authorship, especially medical texts for practitioners, the expert general editor may well have a 'right to edit' written into his/her agreements with both publisher and contributors. How far may this contractual right conflict with the moral right of integrity of individual specialist authors (up to and beyond 50 of them in such medical works)? **See also Precedent Three**.

(4) Publishers of art books may need to consider how far indifferent reproduction of a copyright work of art (poor colour quality, cheap and unsuitable paper) may fall foul of the artist's right of integrity.

(5) Photographers have expressed the view strongly that insensitive cropping may add up to invasion of a photographer's right of integrity.

(6) The representatives of artists and artists' estates, for example, the Design and Artistic Copyright Society (DACS) have made clear that the 'stamping' of the title or author of a work over their client's works of art may, again, add up, in their eyes, to invasion of the right of integrity.

Finally, it is important to bear in mind that moral rights in the UK do not apply to every case, and are subject to numerous exceptions under UK law. The realistic stance of the UK government should keep invocation of the right to the kind of wrongful treatment of an author which no trade association would care to defend.

It may be helpful for publishers to have for consideration possible forms of wording for the assertion of the moral right to be identified as author (attached as Schedules I and II to this Appendix).

There will certainly be occasions, most especially in dealings with freelance writers, re-writers and editors of all kinds, when neither the right of paternity nor the right of integrity may, for obvious reasons, be appropriate. In such dealings, publishers may wish to build in a 'waiver' clause, and a suggested form of wording for waiver, possibly as part of a letter, possibly as part of a short contract, is attached as Schedule III to this Appendix. Waiver is permitted under the terms of s 87(2) of the 1988 Act, by contrast with the provisions of legislation on moral rights in continental Europe.

Schedules

The author is well advised to make a written general assertion of his/her right to be identified as the author of his/her work. This might sensibly be attached to the typescript of the work, and a possible form of wording follows as Schedule I.

In the author/publisher contract, whether a contract for assignment of copyright from author to publisher or a contract for grant of an exclusive licence from author to publisher, a clause should be inserted on the lines suggested in Schedule II.

Schedule III sets out suggested wording for waiver of the author's moral rights to be identified as author of, and to object to derogatory treatment of, a work.

Schedule I

I, [*name to be inserted*], being the author of the work entitled [*title, or provisional title, of work to be inserted*], hereby assert generally my moral right to be identified as its author whenever it is commercially published in the United Kingdom.

Schedule II

The Author by this assignment/instrument in writing asserts his/her moral right to be identified as the Author of the work in relation to all such rights as are granted by the Author to the Publisher under the terms and conditions of this Agreement.

The Publisher hereby undertakes:

- to print on the verso title page of every copy of every edition of the work published by it in the United Kingdom the words 'the right of [*the author*] to be identified as author of this work has been asserted by him/her in accordance with the Copyright, Designs and Patents Act 1988';

- to make it a condition of contract with any licensee concerning any edition of the work to be published in the United Kingdom that a notice of assertion in the same terms as above shall be printed in every edition published by such licensee;
- to set the name of the author in its customary form with due prominence on the title page and on the binding, jacket and/or cover of every copy of the work published by it and to make it a condition of contract that a similar undertaking is made in respect of any editions of the work licensed by it.

Schedule III

The Author hereby waives, in accordance with the Copyright, Designs and Patents Act 1988, s 87, his/her moral rights (a) to be identified as author of and (b) to object to derogatory treatment of the work he/she is undertaking for the Publisher under the terms of this agreement with regard to such rights as are granted by the Author to the Publisher under the terms of this agreement.

APPENDIX I

Publishers Association Code of Practice on Author Contracts

Guidelines for Book Publishers

The Code of Practice, first issued by the UK Publishers Association in 1982 and most recently updated in 2010, is an important document and has represented a milestone on the road to an equitable framework for author-publisher contracts. There are, perhaps, two tasks which face those who support the Code. The first is to find forms and styles of informal dispute settlement which are appropriate to a trade rather then a professional association. The creation of the Publishers Association's Informal Disputes Settlement scheme has been a positive initiative, and referral to it has been built into the Precedents in this eighth edition. The second task is to reach out to creators of intellectual property rights and find ways of working with them to ensure that further milestones are passed in common purpose.

A constructive and co-operative relationship between book authors (and the agents and representatives acting for them) and their publishers is vital to successful publishing. Dissatisfaction may arise, however, perhaps because a title is not the success the author and publisher hoped for, or because of lack of clarity or misunderstandings of the publishing contract. In order to help eliminate the causes of such misunderstandings, this Code of Practice attempts to address some of the areas which may lead to avoidable conflict, and is recommended to PA members in their dealings with authors.

[Note: This Code of Practice applies only to agreements under which an author assigns or licenses an interest in the copyright of a work to a publisher, and does not apply to agreements whereby an author invests money in publication of a work.]

(1) The publishing contract must be clear, unambiguous and comprehensive, and must be honoured in both the letter and the spirit.

Matters which particularly need to be defined in the contract include:

(i) a title which identifies the work or (for incomplete works) the nature and agreed length and scope of the work;

(ii) the nature of the rights conferred, the ownership of the copyright (an assignment or an exclusive licence), whether all publication rights are included, whether electronic rights are included, and the formats, territories and languages covered;

(iii) the time scale for delivery of the manuscript and the time scale for publication (which may need to be held over for market reasons);

(iv) the payments, royalties and advances (if any) to be paid, what they are in respect of, and when they are due;

(v) the provisions for sub-licensing;

(vi) the responsibility for preparing the supporting materials (e.g. indexes, illustrations, content for accompanying websites or other ancillary material etc.), and for obtaining permissions and paying for the supporting materials in which the copyright is held by third parties;

(vii) the term of the contract if appropriate, and any termination and reversion provisions.

Should the parties subsequently agree changes to the contract, these should be recorded in a separate written memorandum or side letter, and a copy kept with the main contract.

(2) The contract should be clear about ownership of the copyright.

In some fields of publishing, such as trade publishing, an exclusive licence should be sufficient to enable the publisher to exploit and protect most works effectively. In other fields of publishing (e.g. encyclopaedic and reference works, certain types of academic works, publishers' compilations edited from many outside contributions, some translations and works particularly vulnerable to copyright infringement because of their extensive international sale) it may be appropriate for the copyright to be vested in the publisher, to make it easier for the publisher to protect the work as a whole.

(3) The publisher should be aware of the author's moral rights.

The author's moral rights are personal statutory rights in the UK and elsewhere in the EU, in particular the right to be credited as the author whenever the work is exploited commercially (the right of paternity), and the right to object to derogatory treatment of the work (the right of integrity). A publisher drafting a publishing contract should be aware of these rights. In addition, the right of paternity may require formal 'assertion' by the author, and this is usually most conveniently done by the publisher on the book or menu page itself, on the author's behalf.

However, the rights of paternity and integrity do not apply to certain works, including collective works such as encyclopaedias, dictionaries or year books, or works created in the course of employment. In addition, the 1988 Copyright Designs and Patents Act provides for the possibility of waiver of the author's moral rights in appropriate circumstances, and if and when such circumstances are likely to arise (e.g. in the case of a sale of film or TV rights) the publisher should have the right to ask for a formal signed waiver, either wholly or partially, depending on the position. Adequate time should be allowed in the publishing timetable to permit discussion of the need for any waiver, and if necessary commissioning of an alternative author or contributor.

(4) The publisher should be willing to explain the terms of the contract and the reasons for each provision, particularly to an author who is not professionally represented.

(5) Where appropriate the publisher must give the author a proper opportunity to share in the success of the work.

In general, the publishing contract should seek to achieve a fair balance of reward for author and publisher, although there are publishing circumstances (eg academic publishing), where publication may be its own justification, and royalties and fees may not be affordable or appropriate. On occasion it may be appropriate, when the publisher is taking an exceptional risk in publishing a work, or the origination costs are unusually high, for the author to assist the publication of the work by accepting initially a low royalty return. In such cases, it is also appropriate for the publisher to agree that the author should share in any eventual success by, for example, agreeing that royalty rates should increase, perhaps via a sliding scale, to reflect that success (although royalty accelerators may not be possible on e-editions, where one unit is not necessarily one sale).

If under the contract the author receives an outright or single payment, but retains ownership of the copyright, the publisher should be prepared to share with the author any income derived from a use of the work not within the reasonable contemplation of the parties at the time of the contract, e.g. by making terms for other distribution and licensing subject to mutual agreement in due course.

(6) The publisher must handle manuscripts promptly, and keep the author informed of progress.

All manuscripts and synopses received by the publisher, whether solicited or unsolicited, should be acknowledged promptly on receipt. (If the publisher does not acknowledge unsolicited materials, it should make that clear on its website.) The author may be told at that time when to expect to hear further, but in the absence of any such indication at least a progress report should be sent by the publisher to the author within six weeks of receipt. A longer time may be required in the case of certain works, e.g. those requiring a detailed assessment, particularly in cases where the opinion of specialist readers may not be readily available, and in planned co-editions, but the author should be informed of a likely date when a report may be expected.

It is important, however, for the publisher to know if the manuscript or synopsis is being simultaneously submitted to any other publisher.

(7) The publisher must not cancel a contract without good and proper reason.

It is not easy to define objectively what constitutes unsuitability for publication of a commissioned manuscript or proper cause for the cancellation of a contract, since these may depend on a variety of circumstances. In any such case, however, the publisher must give the author sufficiently detailed reasons for rejection. Some of the most common reasons are set out at (a)–(c) below.

When a publisher requires changes in a commissioned manuscript as a condition of publication, these should be clearly set out in writing.

(a) Time

If an author fails to deliver a completed manuscript according to the contract or within the contracted period, the publisher may be entitled (inter alia) to a refund of advances already paid on account. However, it is commonly accepted that (except where time is of the essence) advances are not reclaimable until the publisher has given proper notice of intent to cancel the contract within a reasonable period from the date of such notice. Where the advance is not reclaimed after the period of notice has expired, it is reasonable for the publisher to retain an option to publish the work.

(b) Standard and quality

If an author has produced the work in good faith and with proper care in reasonable accordance with the publishing proposal and brief, and the terms of the contract, but the publisher decides not to publish on grounds of quality, the publisher should not expect to reclaim on cancellation that part of any advance that has already been paid to the author. If, by contrast, the work has not been produced in good faith and with proper care, or the work does not conform to what has been commissioned in terms of content, level and style, the publisher may be able to reclaim the advance.

(c) Defamation or illegality

The publisher is under no obligation to publish a work that there is reason to believe is defamatory or otherwise illegal.

Compensation

Depending on the grounds for rejection,

[1] (if the grounds are not reasonable) the publisher may be liable for further advances due and an additional sum may be agreed to compensate the author, or

[2] (if the grounds *are* reasonable) the author may be liable to repay the advances received.

In the former case, the agreement for compensation may include an obligation on the author to return advances and compensation paid (or part of them) if the work is subsequently placed elsewhere.

Resolution of disputes

Ideally, terms will be agreed privately between the parties, but in cases of dispute the matter should be put to a mutually agreed informal procedure (such as that available under the PA's Informal Arbitration Procedure), or an equivalent scheme, or, if this cannot be agreed, to arbitration or normal legal procedures.

(8) The contract must set out the anticipated timetable for publication.

The formal contract must make clear the time scale within which the author undertakes to deliver the complete manuscript, and within which the publisher undertakes to publish it. It should be recognised that in particular cases there may be valid reasons for diverging from these stated times (such as a need to clear extra permissions, or legal problems such as libel), or for not determining strict time scales and each party should be willing to submit detailed reasons for the agreement of the other party, if these should occur.

(9) The publisher should be willing to share precautions against legal risks not arising from fault or carelessness by the author.

For example: libel. While it remains the primary responsibility of the author to ensure that the work is not libellous, the publisher may also be liable. Libel therefore demands the closest co-operation between authors and publishers, in particular in sharing the costs of reading for libel or of any insurance considered to be desirable by the parties. Other risks include contempt of court or breach of privacy.

(10) The publisher might consider assisting the author by funding additional costs involved in preparing the work for publication.

If under the contract the author is liable to pay for supporting materials, e.g. for permissions to use other copyright material, for the making and use of illustrations and maps, for costs of indexing, etc. the publisher may in certain circumstances, depending on the type of publication and on the nature of the compensation paid to the author, be willing to fund such expenses, to an agreed ceiling, that could reasonably be recovered against monies that may subsequently become due to the author.

(11) The publisher must ensure that the author receives a regular and clear account of sales made and monies due.

The period during which sales are to be accounted for should be defined in the contract and should be followed, after a period also to be laid down in the contract, by a royalty statement and a remittance of monies due. Publishers should always observe these dates and obligations scrupulously. Accounts should be rendered at least annually, although some are able to pay more frequently.

The publisher should be prepared, where appropriate and on request, to disclose details of the number of copies printed, on condition that the author (and the agent) agree not to disclose the information to any other party, apart from professional advisers if required.

Publishers should be prepared to give authors indications of sales to date, which must be realistic bearing in mind frequency of accounting, unsold stock which may be returned by booksellers or stock supplied on consignment.

(12) The publisher must ensure that the author can clearly ascertain how any payments due from sub-licensed agreements will be calculated.

Agreements under which the calculation of the author's share of any earnings is dependent on the publisher's allocation of direct costs and overheads can result in misunderstanding unless the system of accounting is clearly defined. Co-editions, where the publisher is investing in printing for licensees, should be distinguished from arms-length licences where the publisher would not normally allocate direct costs and overheads.

(13) The publisher should if possible keep the author informed of important design, promotion, marketing and sub-licensing decisions.

Under the contract, final responsibility for decisions on the design, promotion and marketing of a book is normally vested in the publisher. Nevertheless, the fullest reasonable consultation with the author on such matters is generally desirable, both as a courtesy and in the interests of the success of the book itself. In particular the author should, if interested and if willing to make themselves available, be consulted about the proposed jacket, jacket copy and major promotional and review activities, be informed in advance of the publication date, and receive advance copies by that date. When time permits, the publisher should advise the author about the disposition of major sub-leases, and let the author have a copy of such licence agreements on request, or (where confidential) supply disclosable details.

(14) The publisher should inform the author clearly about opportunities for amendment of the work in the course of production.

The economics of typesetting and printing can make the incorporation of authors' textual revisions after the book has been set extremely expensive, even where the author is supplying text on disc. Publishers should always make it clear to authors, before a manuscript is put in hand, whether proofs are to be provided or not, on whom the responsibility for reading them rests and what scale of author's revisions would be acceptable to the publisher. If proofs are not being provided, the author should have the right to make final corrections to the copy-edited typescript, and the publisher should take responsibility for accurately reproducing this corrected text in type.

(15) It is essential that both the publisher and the author have a clear common understanding of the significance attaching to the option clause in a publishing contract.

The option on an author's work can be of great importance to both parties. Options should be carefully negotiated, and the obligations that they impose should be reasonable, clearly stated and understood on both sides. Option clauses covering more than one work may be undesirable (and may be unenforceable), and should only be entered into with particular care.

(16) The publisher should recognise that the remaindering of stock may effectively end the author's expectation of earnings.

Before a title is remaindered, the publisher should inform the author and offer all or part of the stock to the author on the terms expected from the remainder dealer. Whether any royalty, related to the price received on such sales, should be paid is a matter to be determined by the publisher and the author at the time of the contract. In appropriate areas of publishing, the question of whether remaindering of stock should trigger a reversion or partial reversion of rights to the author may need careful thought, particularly if the title might subsequently be considered for inclusion in a print-on-demand programme

(17) The contract must set out reasonable and precise terms for the reversion of rights.

When a publisher has invested in the development of an author's work on the market, and the work is a contribution to the store of literature and knowledge, and the publisher expects to market the work actively for many years, it is reasonable to acquire publication rights for the full term of copyright, on condition that there are safeguards providing for reversion in appropriate circumstances.

The circumstances under which the grant of rights acquired by the publisher will revert to the author (e.g. fundamental breach of contract by the publisher, or when a title has been out of print or has not been available on the market for a stipulated time) should form a part of the formal contract. It should be noted that it is increasingly common for publishers to be able to maintain availability of titles via print-on-demand and e-book technology, thereby reducing the likelihood of books going out of print, although whether this interpretation is reasonable or not may depend on the circumstances. Reversion should not normally apply where the copyright has been purchased via a full assignment, or to multi-authored or edited works, particularly where these go through multiple editions.

(18) The publisher should endeavour to keep the author informed of changes in the ownership of the publishing rights and of any changes in the imprint under which a work appears.

Most publishers will expect to sign their contracts on behalf of their successors and assigns, just as authors will sign on behalf of their executors, administrators and assigns. But if changes in rights ownership or of publishing imprint subsequently occur, a publisher should certainly inform and, if at all possible, do what they reasonably can to ensure publishing continuity for an author in these new circumstances.

(19) The publisher should be willing to help the author and the author's estate in the administration of literary affairs.

For example, the publisher should agree to act as an expert witness in questions relating to the valuation of a literary estate.

(20) Above all, the publisher must recognise the importance of co-operation with the author in an enterprise in which both are essential.

This relationship can be fulfilled only in an atmosphere of confidence, in which authors get the fullest possible credit for their work and achievements.

APPENDIX J

Territories of the World

This Appendix continues to become more complex: first, because the English language is the dominant world language whose use becomes ever more widespread.

Secondly, the territories and nation states of the world continue to change.

Thirdly, it remains important to remember that an American Justice Department's anti-trust lawsuit in the mid-1970s against many major US publishers forced the British publishing industry to abandon the trade-wide British Traditional Market Agreement as such. Nothing in the Final Judgment of the District Court, however, restricts the power of US and UK publishers, acting as *individual* publishing houses, of (to quote the Final Judgment itself) 'acquiring, granting, or otherwise transferring exclusive or non-exclusive copyright rights, or from exercising or authorising the exercise of such rights under the copyright law of any country' (Final Judgment in *US v Addison-Wesley,* US District Court, Southern District of New York, filed 23 November 1976). The question of exactly which countries or territories are negotiated between US and UK publishers on an exclusive basis is a vital component of any publishing agreement between them.

Fourthly, the territorial exclusivity of copyright dealings which underpins the exclusivity of the UK home market in publishing contracts is in conflict with the 'single market' requirements of the amended Treaty of Rome, which demand that there should be no impediments to the free flow of goods across the national boundaries of states which are members of the European Economic Area. The consequence is that, in the words of Paul Scherer, a former President of the Publishers Association, 'if you want exclusivity in the UK, you must have exclusivity in Europe'. In 2006 there was renewed and heated debate on the question of territories to be controlled by UK and US publishers on an exclusive basis and on a non-exclusive basis in open-market territories and this debate has continued, particularly with the rise of eBooks as a more prominent platform and concerns about the ability to impose territorial restrictions in the digital environment. Europe has been the main focus of attention because of concerns over leakage of US editions into the UK home market, but some US publishers have recently been seeking to include India, Malaysia and Singapore as non-exclusive territories (**see Appendix A**).

This Appendix tackles the issues as follows:

(1) Schedule 1 sets out a list of the nations and territories of the world as they existed as this Eighth Edition went to press.

(2) Schedule 2 lists the territories which UK publishers have, in general and subject always to negotiation on individual territories, reasonably expected to be granted on an exclusive basis – primarily the countries of the British Commonwealth, but with a number of additional countries. However, in recent years UK publishers have come under increasing pressure from US publishers reluctant to agree to the inclusion on non-Commonwealth countries in the UK publishers' exclusive territories; countries of the Middle East are a frequent bone of contention. British publishers may wish to seek to retain exclusive rights in former Commonwealth member states such as Fiji and Zimbabwe on the grounds that their absence from membership may be temporary.

(3) Schedule 3 offers options for publishers to explore in deciding what 'Europe' might mean in the context of 'we need exclusivity in Europe'. The notes are updated to take account of the position at the time that this edition goes to press and we continue to cover the ongoing expansion of the European Single Market.

SCHEDULE 1

The Nations and Territories of the World by Continents and Regions

Africa
Algeria
Angola
Benin
Botswana
Burkina Faso
Burundi
Cameroon
Cape Verde Islands
Central African Republic
Chad
Comoros
Congo
Congo (Democratic Republic of, formerly Zaire)
Cote d'Ivoire (Ivory Coast)
Djibouti
Equatorial Guinea
Eritrea
Ethiopia
Gabon
Gambia, The
Ghana
Guinea
Guinea-Bissau
Kenya
Lesotho
Liberia
Libyan Arab Jamahiriya
Madagascar
Malawi
Mali
Mauritania
Mauritius and dependencies of Mauritius
Mayotte
Morocco
Mozambique
Namibia
Niger
Nigeria
Réunion
Rwanda
St Helena and dependencies of St Helena
São Tomé and Principé
Senegal
Seychelles
Sierra Leone
Somalia
South Africa
Spanish Presidios
  Ceuta
  Melilla
Sudan
Swaziland
Tanzania
Togo
Tunisia
Uganda
Zambia
Zimbabwe

Middle East
Bahrain
Egypt

Iran
Iraq
Israel
Jordan
Kuwait
Lebanon
Oman
Qatar
Saudi Arabia
Syria
United Arab Emirates
Yemen

North America
Canada
Greenland (Kalaallit Nunaat)
Mexico
St Pierre et Miquelon
United States and its territories and possessions

Central America and West Indies
Anguilla
Antigua and Barbuda
Aruba
Bahamas
Barbados
Belize
Bermuda
Cayman Islands
Costa Rica
Cuba
Dominica
Dominican Republic
Grenada
Guadeloupe
Guatemala
Haiti
Honduras
Jamaica
Martinique
Montserrat
Netherlands Antilles
Nicaragua
Panama
Puerto Rico
St Kitts and Nevis
St Lucia
St Vincent and the Grenadines
El Salvador
Trinidad and Tobago
Turks and Caicos Islands
Virgin Islands (British)
Virgin Islands (American)

South America
Argentina
Ascension Island
Bolivia
Brazil
Chile
Colombia
Ecuador
Falkland Islands
French Guiana
Guyana
Paraguay
Peru
South Georgia and South Sandwich Islands
Suriname
Uruguay
Venezuela

Asia
Afghanistan
Bangladesh
Bhutan
British Indian Ocean Territory
Brunei
Cambodia
China (People's Republic of)
East Timor
*Hong Kong
India
Indonesia
Japan
Kazakhstan
Korea, North
Korea, South
Kyrgyzstan
Laos
*Macao

* Special Administrative Regions of the People's Republic of China

Malaysia
Maldives, The
Mongolia
Myanmar (Burma)
Nepal
Pakistan
Philippine Islands
Singapore
Sri Lanka
Taiwan
Tajikistan
Thailand
Turkey
Turkmenistan
Uzbekistan
Vietnam

Oceania
American Samoa
Australia (including territories of Ashmore and Cartier Islands, Australian Antarctic Territory, Christmas Island, Cocos (Keeling) Islands, Coral Sea Islands Territory, Heard and MacDonald Islands and Norfolk Island)
Fiji
French Polynesia
Guam
Kiribati
Marshall Islands
Micronesia, Federated States of
Nauru
New Caledonia
New Zealand (including territories of Tokelau (Union Islands), the Ross Dependency and associated states of the Cook Islands and Niue)
Northern Mariana Islands
Palau
Papua New Guinea
Pitcairn Islands
Solomon Islands
Tonga
Tuvalu
Vanuatu
Wallis and Futuna Islands
Western Samoa

Europe
Albania
Andorra
Armenia
Austria
Azerbaijan
Belarus
Belgium
Bosnia and Herzegovina
Bulgaria
Croatia
Cyprus
Czech Republic
Denmark (including the Faroe Islands)
Estonia
Finland
France
Georgia
Germany
Gibraltar
Greece
Hungary
Iceland
Irish Republic
Italy
*Kosovo
Latvia
Liechtenstein
Lithuania
Luxembourg
Macedonia, Former Yugoslav Republic of
Malta
Moldova
Monaco
Montenegro
Netherlands
Norway (including territories of Jan Mayen Island, Norwegian Antarctic Territories and Svalbard)

*self-declared independent state now recognised by over 60 nations

Poland
Portugal (including Madeira and the Azores)
Romania
Russia (includes Russia in Asia)
San Marino
Serbia
Slovakia
Slovenia
Spain (including the Balearic Islands, the Canary Islands and the Spanish Overseas Territories)
Sweden
Switzerland
Ukraine
United Kingdom of Great Britain and Northern Ireland (including the Channel Islands, the Isle of Man and the Isles of Scilly)
Vatican City State

Antarctica

British Antarctic Territory

SCHEDULE 2

Territories Often Secured as Exclusive by British Publishers

Many name changes have occurred over the years. The names below are up to date as this edition goes to press; but older names may appear in earlier schedules. The previous names are, therefore, indicated below, for ease of reference. The list also indicates which territories are currently British Dependencies, etc, which are currently members of the Commonwealth of Nations and which are neither. The latter remain in the list because of their past connections with Great Britain as former colonies or protectorates, or for geographical reasons.

+ Anguilla
* Antigua and Barbuda
* Australia and territories administered by Australia [See Schedule 1]
* Bahamas
* Bangladesh (formerly East Pakistan)
* Barbados
* Belize (formerly British Honduras)
+ Bermuda
Bhutan
* Botswana (formerly Bechuanaland)
+ British Antarctic Territory
+ British Indian Ocean Territory
+ British Virgin Islands
* Brunei
* Cameroon (formerly the UN trusteeships of the British Southern Cameroons and the French Cameroons)
* Canada
+ Cayman Islands
* Cyprus
* Dominica
Egypt
+ Falkland Islands
Fiji
* Gambia, The
* Ghana (formerly the Gold Coast and British Togoland)
+ Gibraltar
* Grenada
* Guyana (formerly British Guiana)
Hong Kong [See Note (2)]
* India
Iraq
Irish Republic
Israel
* Jamaica
Jordan
* Kenya
* Kiribati (formerly the Gilbert Islands)
Kuwait

- * Lesotho (formerly Basutoland)
- * Malawi (formerly Nyasaland)
- * Malaysia (comprising Malaya, Sabah (formerly British North Borneo) and Sarawak)
- * Maldives, The
- * Malta and Gozo
- * Mauritius and dependencies of Mauritius (including Rodrigues)
- \+ Montserrat
- * Mozambique
- Myanmar (formerly Burma)
- * Namibia (formerly South West Africa)
- * Nauru
- * New Zealand and territories administered by New Zealand [See Schedule 1]
- * Nigeria (formerly Nigeria and the Cameroons)
- * Pakistan
- * Papua New Guinea
- \+ Pitcairn Islands
- * Rwanda
- * St Christopher [otherwise St Kitts] and Nevis
- \+ St Helena and dependencies of St Helena (Ascension and Tristan da Cunha)
- * St Lucia
- * St Vincent and the Grenadines
- * Samoa
- * Seychelles
- * Sierra Leone
- * Singapore
- * Solomon Islands (formerly British Solomon Islands)
- Somalia, Democratic Republic of (formerly British Somaliland)
- * South Africa
- \+ South Georgia and South Sandwich Islands (formerly administered by the Falkland Islands)
- * Sri Lanka (formerly Ceylon)
- Sudan
- * Swaziland
- * Tanzania (formerly Tanganyika and Zanzibar)
- * Tonga (or the Friendly Islands)
- * Trinidad and Tobago
- \+ Turks and Caicos Islands
- * Tuvalu (formerly the Ellice Islands)
- * Uganda
- * United Kingdom of Great Britain and Northern Ireland, including the Channel Islands, the Isle of Man and the Isles of Scilly
- * Vanuatu (formerly the New Hebrides)
- Yemen (formerly Aden and People's Democratic Republic of Yemen)
- * Zambia (formerly Northern Rhodesia)
- Zimbabwe (formerly Southern Rhodesia)

Notes

(1) + indicates British Dependent Territories, etc.

(2) Hong Kong became a Special Administrative Region of the People's Republic of China on 1 July 1997 and is no longer a member of the Commonwealth of Nations; it remains to be seen whether in practice it can remain exclusive to UK publishers.

(3) * indicates member of the Commonwealth of Nations (Zimbabwe was suspended from membership in 2002 and left in 2003; Fiji was suspended in 2006 following a *coup d'etat*).

(4) The following relate to territories which may be found on older schedules:

   (a) The Leeward Islands include the following Commonwealth members and Dependencies: Anguilla; Antigua and Barbuda; British Virgin Islands; Dominica; Montserrat; St Christopher (St Kitts) and Nevis.

   (b) The Windward Islands include the following Commonwealth members: Grenada, St Lucia; St Vincent and the Grenadines.

SCHEDULE 3

The European Single Market

The question 'What is Europe?' in the context of the European 'Single Market' is still complex. The formation of the European Economic Area took effect on 1 January 1994 and there are continuing plans for expansion.

While the free movement of goods requirements of the Treaty of Rome applied to members of the European Union (pre-1 November 1993 the European Community) and the European Free Trade Association, the same could not be said of the 'exhaustion of rights' doctrine (i.e., that copyright owners may not by virtue of exclusive national territorial rights seek to prevent the movement within the Single Market of copyright goods put on the market anywhere within the Single Market with the consent of the copyright owner). In 1982 the European Court of Justice, in the *Polydor Ltd and RSO Records Inc v Harlequin Record Shops and Simons Records* [1982] ECR 329, 1 CMLR 677 decision, held that the exhaustion of rights doctrine did not apply to goods put on to the market in EFTA member states so as to override exclusive rights in the EC. The formation of the EEA has simplified this position, since it is thought to supersede that ruling, subject to certain conditions relating to the origin of goods with respect to the EFTA states and without any doubt or conditions in the case of Austria, Finland and Sweden which have been members of the EU since 1 January 1995. The *Polydor* case continues to have force in respect of Switzerland which did not join the EEA. In summary, the formation of the EEA may have provided a finite Single Market (the original 15 members – now 27 – of the EU and three of EFTA) to which the rules on free movement of goods and the exhaustion doctrine apply; though those states' associations with other countries (and their various territories and dependencies) both present and potential do not equate to a finite situation in a practical sense.

A major expansion of the EU took place in May 2004 when a number of countries from central and eastern Europe (the three Baltic States of Estonia, Latvia and Lithuania, the Czech Republic, Hungary, Poland, Slovakia and Slovenia joined, together with Malta and Cyprus (both applicants since 1990, albeit with Cyprus membership relating to the Greek occupied territory). Bulgaria and Romania became members from 1 January 2007, so at the time of writing membership stands at 27. Croatia, Macedonia and

Turkey are official candidate countries in ongoing membership negotiations, but membership for Turkey (an applicant since 1987) remains controversial. Albania, Iceland, Serbia and Montenegro (independent from Serbia since 21 May 2006) have formally applied for membership but decisions are unlikely before the end of 2010. Bosnia and Herzogovina and Kosovo (under United Nations Security Council Resolution 244 of 10 June 1999 as it is a self-declared independent state) are also potential candidates but negotiations have been delayed for a number of reasons, including stabilisation and security issues. Armenia, Georgia, Moldova and Ukraine have all stated that they wish to seek membership but have not been finally accepted for candidacy.

While certain territories which are not members of the EU or EFTA, such as Andorra, San Marino, etc, either have special arrangements with the EU which effectively make them part of the Single Market or have been considered for practical convenience to be part of the Single Market, the possible expansion of the Single Market has normally been covered in more general terms by catch-all wording similar to that in Schedule 3C below. Though catch-all wording provides comfort, the ability to include it in contracts, especially those for the licence of rights, is not a foregone conclusion and its application could well be problematical.

Schedule 3A deals with the current position and with the addition of the catch-all wording it may be considered adequate and may serve its purpose for the time being – though in realistic terms the inclusion in a schedule defining Europe of those states which have applied for membership of the EU requires full consideration, irrespective of any catch-all wording. Certainly when a long-term view is a factor the inclusion of the states in Schedules 3A and 3B representing the Continent of Europe may be the simplest approach.

SCHEDULE 3A

Countries of the European Economic Area and Related States

- • Andorra
- * Austria
- * Belgium
- * Bulgaria
- * Cyprus (Greek territory)
- * Czech Republic
- * Denmark
- * Estonia
- * Finland
- * France (including the Overseas Departments of French Guiana, Guadeloupe, Martinique and Réunion)
- * Germany
- • Gibraltar
- * Greece
- * Hungary
- + Iceland
- * Irish Republic
- * Italy
- * Latvia
- + Liechtenstein
- * Lithuania
- * Luxembourg
- * Malta
- • Monaco
- * Netherlands
- + Norway (including Jan Mayen Island and Svalbard)
- * Poland
- * Portugal (including the Azores and Madeira)
- * Romania
- • San Marino
- * Slovakia
- * Slovenia
- * Spain (including the Balearic Islands and the Canary Islands)
- * Sweden
- ° Switzerland
- * United Kingdom of Great Britain and Northern Ireland, including the Channel Islands, the Isle of Man and the Isles of Scilly
- • Vatican City State

Notes

* European Union members of the European Economic Area.

\+ European Free Trade Association members of the European Economic Area.

° European Free Trade Association member not a member of the European Economic Area, though has applied for membership of the European Union; the reasons behind its failure to join the EEA may preclude EU membership.

• Regions or countries which have special arrangements with the European Union which make them, subject in some cases to certain exceptions, part of the European Economic Area.

Other territories included in this schedule are included for practical convenience due to their geographical position. Norway and Switzerland have both applied to join the European Union but their applications were frozen when voting in domestic referenda decided against membership.

NB The details with respect to the territories of France, Norway, Portugal and Spain, which are integral parts of the countries concerned and part of the European Economic Area, should be included for the avoidance of doubt; there are territories of each of these countries which are not necessarily part of the European Economic Area and are detailed in Schedule 3D.

SCHEDULE 3B

Territories with association agreements with the European Union (or seeking such agreements) and eligible (or may be recognised as eligible) for membership of the European Union in the future.

*	Albania	*	Macedonia
	Armenia		Moldova
	Azerbaijan	*	Montenegro
	Belarus	+	Russia
	Bosnia and Herzegovina	*	Serbia
*	Croatia	*	Turkey
	Georgia		Ukraine
*	Iceland		

Notes

* Territories with association agreements which have applied for membership of the European Union.

+ For practical reasons it is unlikely to be possible to divide exclusivity between the European and Asian republics and regions of Russia.

SCHEDULE 3C

The following examples of catch-all wording are not without some benefit though, as previously noted, their application with respect to a particular territory may prove difficult if not impossible. The first example does fix a date for its application (though it should be noted that first publication does not apply by edition) and while this gives only one shot at the definition of the Single Market with respect to the title concerned, it is likely to be found more acceptable particularly in agreements for the licence of rights.

> *'Any additional territory which shall become a member of the European Union or the European Free Trade Association or the European Economic Area prior to the date of first United Kingdom publication of the Work by the Publishers shall be deemed to be included in this Schedule from the date of such territory's commencement of membership.'*

> *'Any additional territory which shall become a member of the European Union or the European Free Trade Association or the European Economic Area during the term of this Agreement shall be deemed to be included in this Schedule from the date of such territory's commencement of membership.'*

SCHEDULE 3D

Territories with connections with the European Union or with member states of the European Economic Area but not thought to be territories to which the exhaustion of rights doctrine and the free movement of goods provisions apply.

Algeria
Denmark
    Faroe Islands
*   Greenland
France
*   Overseas territories: French Polynesia, French Southern and Antarctic Territories, New Caledonia and dependencies and Wallis and Futuna Islands
*   Territorial collectivities: Mayotte and St Pierre et Miquelon
Israel
Lomé Convention Countries

Netherlands
*   Aruba
*   Netherlands Antilles
Norway
    Norwegian Antarctic Territories
Portugal
    +   Macao (see Note 2)
Spain
    Spanish Presidios of Cueta and Melilla
United Kingdom
*   British Dependent Territories (see Schedule 2) other than Gibraltar

Notes

(1) Countries and territories which have special relations with European Union members. Member states apply to their trade with these countries and territories the same treatment as they accord other member states and each country and territory applies to its trade with member states (and the other countries and territories) the same treatment it applies to the member state with which it has special relations.

(2) + Once a Portuguese colony, Macao became a Special Administrative Region of the People's Republic of China on 20 December 1999, but still retains some links with Portugal.

APPENDIX K

Member States of International Copyright Conventions

Relatively few countries in the world now remain outside membership of one or more of the international copyright conventions. This Appendix lists current member states of the now three major conventions: the Berne Convention (established in 1886 and subject to the Paris Revisions of 1971), the Universal Copyright Convention (established in 1952 and subject to the Paris Revisions in 1991) and the much more recent World Intellectual Property Organisation Copyright Treaty (WCT). This resulted from a series of meetings of the Committee of Experts on the Berne Protocol and New Instrument in December 1996, but only came into force on 6 March 2002 following ratification by the required minimum of 30 member states. Eleven of the twelve most recent EU member states ratified the WCT relatively early; the original 15 member states were unable to do so until all had implemented into their domestic legislation the requirements of the 2001 EU Directive on the Harmonization of Certain Aspects of Copyright and Related Rights in the Information Society; they finally ratified the WCT on 14 March 2010, and Estonia did so on the same date.

The lists below indicate membership of a convention, but not the exact text ratified by each member state or any specific reservations made by a state at the time of ratification.

State	Berne	UCC	WCT
Albania	X	X	X
Algeria	X	X	
Andorra	X	X	
Antigua & Barbuda	X		
Argentina	X	X	X
Armenia	X	X	
Australia	X	X	X
Austria	X	X	X
Azerbaijan	X	X	X
Bahamas	X	X	
Bahrain	X		X
Bangladesh	X	X	
Barbados	X	X	
Belarus	X	X	X
Belgium	X	X	X
Belize	X	X	
Benin	X		X
Bhutan	X		
Bolivia	X	X	X
Bosnia-Herzogovina	X	X	X
Botswana	X		X
Brazil	X	X	
Brunei Darussalam	X		
Bulgaria	X	X	X
Burkina Faso	X		X
Cambodia		X	
Cameroon	X	X	
Canada	X	X	X
Cape Verde	X		
Central African Republic	X		
Chad	X		
Chile	X	X	X
China	X	X	X
Colombia	X	X	X
Comoros	X		
Congo	X		
Costa Rica	X	X	X
Cote d'Ivoire (Ivory Coast)	X		
Croatia	X	X	X
Cuba	X	X	
Cyprus	X	X	X
Czech Republic	X	X	X
Democratic People's Republic of Korea (N)	X		
Democratic Republic of Congo	X		
Denmark	X	X	X
Djibouti	X		

State	Berne	UCC	WCT
Dominica	X		
Dominican Republic	X	X	X
Ecuador	X	X	X
Egypt	X		
El Salvador	X	X	X
Equatorial Guinea	X		
Estonia	X		X
Fiji	X	X	
Finland	X	X	X
France	X	X	X
Gabon	X		X
Gambia, The	X		
Georgia	X		X
Germany	X	X	X
Ghana	X	X	X
Greece	X	X	X
Grenada	X		
Guatemala	X	X	X
Guinea	X	X	X
Guinea-Bissau	X		
Guyana	X		
Haiti	X	X	
Holy See	X	X	
Honduras	X		X
Hungary	X	X	X
Iceland	X	X	
India	X	X	
Indonesia	X		X
Irish Republic	X	X	X
Israel	X	X	X
Italy	X	X	X
Jamaica	X		X
Japan	X	X	X
Jordan	X		X
Kazakhstan	X	X	X
Kenya	X	X	X
Kyrgystan	X		X
Lao People's Democratic Republic		X	
Latvia	X		X
Lebanon	X	X	
Lesotho	X		
Liberia	X	X	
Libyan Arab Jamahiraya	X		
Liechtenstein	X	X	X
Lithuania	X		X
Luxembourg	X	X	X

State	Berne	UCC	WCT
Macedonia (former Yugoslav Republic of)	X	X	X
Madagascar	X		
Malawi	X	X	
Malaysia	X		
Mali	X		X
Malta	X	X	X
Mauritania	X		
Mauritius	X	X	
Mexico	X	X	X
Micronesia (Federated States of)	X		
Monaco	X	X	X
Mongolia	X		X
Montenegro	X	X	X
Morocco	X	X	
Namibia	X		X
Nepal	X		
Netherlands	X	X	X
New Zealand	X	X	
Nicaragua	X	X	X
Niger	X	X	
Nigeria	X	X	X
Norway	X	X	
Oman	X		X
Pakistan	X	X	
Panama	X	X	X
Paraguay	X	X	X
Peru	X	X	X
Philippines	X		X
Poland	X	X	X
Portugal	X	X	X
Qatar	X		X
Republic of Korea (S)	X	X	X
Republic of Moldova	X	X	X
Romania	X		X
Russian Federation	X	X	X
Rwanda	X	X	
St Kitts & Nevis	X		
St Lucia	X		X
St Vincent & the Grenadines	X	X	
Samoa	X		
Saudi Arabia	X	X	
Senegal	X	X	X
Serbia	X	X	X
Singapore	X		X
Slovakia	X	X	X
Slovenia	X	X	X

State	Berne	UCC	WCT
South Africa	X		X
Spain	X	X	X
Sri Lanka	X	X	
Sudan	X		
Suriname	X		
Swaziland	X		
Sweden	X	X	X
Switzerland	X	X	X
Syria	X		
Tajikistan	X	X	X
Thailand	X		
Togo	X	X	X
Tonga	X		
Trinidad & Tobago	X	X	X
Tunisia	X	X	
Turkey	X		X
Ukraine	X	X	X
United Arab Emirates	X		X
United Kingdom	X	X	X
United Republic of Tanzania	X		
United States of America	X	X	X
Uruguay	X	X	X
Uzbekhistan	X		
Venezuela	X	X	X
Vietnam	X		
Yemen	X		
Zambia	X	X	
Zimbabwe	X		

Index

[all references are to page number]